WITHDRAWN
NDSU

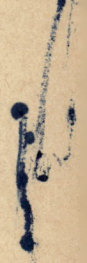

ALLYN AND BACON'S SERIES OF SCHOOL HISTORIES

MODERN HISTORY

EUROPE

FROM CHARLEMAGNE TO THE PRESENT TIME

BY

WILLIS MASON WEST

PROFESSOR OF HISTORY IN THE UNIVERSITY OF MINNESOTA

REVISED EDITION

ALLYN AND BACON

Boston and Chicago

ALLYN AND BACON'S SERIES OF
SCHOOL HISTORIES

12mo, half leather, numerous maps, plans, and illustrations

ANCIENT HISTORY. By Willis M. West of the University of Minnesota.

MODERN HISTORY. By Willis M. West.

HISTORY OF ENGLAND. By Charles M. Andrews of Yale University.

A SHORT HISTORY OF ENGLAND. By Charles M. Andrews.

HISTORY OF THE UNITED STATES. By Charles K. Adams. and William P. Trent of Columbia University.

THE ANCIENT WORLD. By Willis M. West.
    Also in two volumes : PART I : GREECE AND THE EAST.
                              PART II : ROME AND THE WEST.

COPYRIGHT, 1903 AND 1907,
BY WILLIS MASON WEST.

DDA

Norwood Press
J. S. Cushing Co. — Berwick & Smith Co.
Norwood, Mass., U.S.A.

PREFACE.

My *Ancient World* closed with the epoch of Charlemagne. The present volume traces the interaction and development of the various forces which the ancient world had brought together and which had been partially fused in the Empire of Charlemagne. The treatment covers eleven centuries;[1] but as much space is given to the last hundred years as to the preceding thousand, and, throughout, an unusual amount of attention is paid to the history of England. It seems fitting to offer a brief explanation for these two departures from custom.

(*a*) For American students some knowledge of English history is essential. Much of that history, however, is meaningless or misleading, apart from its setting in the history of the continent of Europe; and, whatever be ideally desirable, many secondary schools find it impossible to devote one year to modern Europe and another to England. Therefore I have tried to combine in some measure the advantages of the two separate subjects. If the result be satisfactory, vexing problems of time and arrangement are simplified.

On the other hand, as American history more and more is gaining an important place for itself in high school courses, that subject need be touched upon in a book of this kind only for illustration or where the connection of events requires it.

(*b*) Four years ago, when I was asked to write a Modern History for high schools, I agreed to do so provided I might give half my space to the period since the beginning of the French Revolution. There was then no text-book upon any such plan, but within a few months past two excellent books have

[1] This use of the term "Modern History" is discussed in § 4.

appeared with a somewhat similar distribution of space. This is good evidence of a wholesome trend in historical teaching. We can well afford to treat with brevity the more ephemeral phases of the Middle Ages, however quaint, if thereby can adequate space be won for the marvelous nineteenth century, and so for an intelligent introduction to the twentieth. When a choice must be made, we ought to sacrifice the past to the present.

In connection with this principle, the present volume is still peculiar in the large proportion of attention given to the most recent history. An author is strongly tempted to pass lightly over the generation since the Franco-Prussian War, and the difficulties of the opposite course are apparent. Yet only by surmounting them is one main end of our study attainable. To check the story at 1871 is to stop upon the brink of a vast and sudden change, and therefore to leave for the youth a chasm between past and present much wider than that represented ordinarily by a human lifetime. The high school course in history ought to put the student in touch with present movements in politics and society. To secure this result, the teacher must seize eagerly upon striking opportunities, as they arise, to connect current history with the closing narrative in the text. The latter part of the book affords such aid as it can in numerous suggestions for reports of this nature.

WILLIS MASON WEST.

UNIVERSITY OF MINNESOTA,
MINNEAPOLIS, January, 1904.

REVISED EDITION

THE changes in the face of the world during the past three years have made it necessary to revise and add to portions of this volume. To give this revision its due perspective and connection, I have been obliged to rewrite large parts of the closing fourth of the book.

W. M. W.

February, 1907.

CONTENTS.

	PAGE
LIST OF MAPS	ix
LIST OF ILLUSTRATIONS	x

SECTION
1–5. INTRODUCTION: THE ELEMENTS, THE FIELD, AND THE
  PERIODS 1

PART I.—LATIN CHRISTENDOM, FROM CHARLEMAGNE TO LUTHER.

CHAPTER I.—A NEW SERIES OF DARK AGES, 814–1100.

6–10.	I.	Disruption of the Empire of Charlemagne	9
11–17.	II.	The New Barbarian Attack	12
18–40.	III.	Feudalism	22
41–44.	IV.	France from Verdun to the Twelfth Century	51
45–51.	V.	Germany from Verdun to the Empire, 843–962	55
52–65.	VI.	The Holy Roman Empire of the German People, 962–1056	60
66–76.	VII.	Empire and Papacy, 1056–1122	74
77–86.	VIII.	Empire and Papacy, 1122–1273	85
87–88.	IX.	Results of the Struggle between Emperors and Popes	94

CHAPTER II.—THE AGE OF THE CRUSADES, 1100–1300.

89–91.	I.	Conditions in the East before the Crusades	98
92–105.	II.	The Crusades	103

CHAPTER III.—WESTERN EUROPE FROM THE BEGINNING OF THE CRUSADES TO THE REFORMATION, 1100–1520.

106–116.	I.	The Rise of the Towns	116
117.	II.	The Rise of Monarchic States	132

CONTENTS.

SECTION			PAGE
118–147.	III.	Europe by Separate States: England to 1500	133
148–154.	IV.	Europe by Separate States: France	163
155–156.	V.	Europe by Separate States: Spain	168
157.	VI.	Europe by Separate States: Scandinavia	170
158–160.	VII.	Europe by Separate States: Germany	171
161.	VIII.	Europe by Separate States: Switzerland	174
162.	IX.	Europe by Separate States: The Netherlands	177
163–167.	X.	The Papacy in the Fourteenth and Fifteenth Centuries	179
168–169.	XI.	New Perils from the East: Tartars and Turks	184
170–173.	XII.	The Political Situation at the Opening of the Reformation	187

CHAPTER IV. — THE TRANSITION TO A NEW AGE: THE RENAISSANCE, 1350–1550.

174–177.	I.	Nature of the Renaissance	191
178–186.	II.	Medieval Science and Philosophy	193
187–194.	III.	Literature and the Fine Arts	205
195–199.	IV.	The New Learning of the Renaissance	217

PART II. — THE PERIOD OF MONARCHIC STATES, 1520–1789.

CHAPTER I. — PRELIMINARY CONSIDERATIONS.

| 200. | I. | The Main Lines of Development | 225 |
| 201–204. | II. | Tables of Sovereigns | 225 |

CHAPTER II. — THE AGE OF THE PROTESTANT REFORMATION, 1520–1648.

| 205–218. | I. | The Rise of Protestantism | 228 |
| 219–232. | II. | A Century of Religious Wars | 240 |

CHAPTER III. — ENGLAND IN THE SEVENTEENTH CENTURY.

| 233–235. | I. | Preliminary: Survey of the Yorkist and Tudor Periods, 1485–1603 | 254 |
| 236–244. | II. | Religious and Political Conditions under the Early Stuarts | 259 |

CONTENTS.

SECTION			PAGE
245–248.	III.	The Great Rebellion and the Commonwealth	272
249–250.	IV.	The Restoration and the Revolution	276
251–254.	V.	Constitutional Gains	278

CHAPTER IV.—FROM THE PEACE OF WESTPHALIA TO THE FRENCH REVOLUTION.

255–257.	I.	General Characteristics	281
258–265.	II.	The Age of Louis XIV—French Leadership	282
266–269.	III.	The Rise of Russia	288
270–280.	IV.	The Rise of Prussia	291
281–284.	V.	The Expansion of England	299

PART III.—THE AGE OF NATION STATES.

CHAPTER I.—THE FRENCH REVOLUTION.

285–287.	I.	Fundamental Characteristics	303
288–312.	II.	Conditions before the Revolution	305
313–332.	III.	First Period, 1789–1792: Constitutional Monarchy	323
333–346.	IV.	Second Period, 1792–1795: the First French Republic under Revolutionary Government	341
347–355.	V.	Third Period, 1795–1799: the Republic under the Directory	356
356–375.	VI.	The Consulate and the Empire, 1799–1815	363

CHAPTER II.—THE PERIOD OF REACTION, 1814–1848.

376–380.	I.	The Congress of Vienna—Rearrangements	382
381–401.	II.	Attempts to maintain the System of 1815	388

CHAPTER III.—FRANCE SINCE 1815.

402–412.	I.	The "Divine Right" Monarchy, 1815–1830	406
413–418.	II.	The Constitutional Monarchy, 1830–1848	413
419–424.	III.	The Revolution of 1848 and the Second Republic, 1848–1852	417
425–432.	IV.	The Second Empire, 1852–1870	422
433–451.	V.	The Third Republic, to the Present Time	430

CHAPTER IV. — CENTRAL EUROPE SINCE 1848.

SECTION			PAGE
452–456.	I.	The Revolutions of 1848 and the Restorations	449
457–463.	II.	The Unification of Italy	457
464–471.	III.	The Unification of Germany	466
472–487.	IV.	The German Empire since 1871	478
488–490.	V.	Italy since 1870	494
491–493.	VI.	Austria-Hungary since 1848	498

CHAPTER V. — THE SMALL STATES OF WESTERN EUROPE.

495–504.	I.	The Iberian Peninsula, Spain and Portugal	504
505–511.	II.	Holland and Belgium	515
512–520.	III.	The Swiss Republic	519
521–526.	IV.	The Scandinavian Kingdoms	527

CHAPTER VI. — ENGLAND IN THE NINETEENTH CENTURY.

527–528.	I.	Conditions in 1815	533
529–540.	II.	Political Reform	542
541–548.	III.	Legislation for Social Reform, to 1884	558
549–552.	IV.	The Irish Question	569
553–555.	V.	English Politics in the Twentieth Century	574
556–564.	VI.	Colonies and Dependencies	576

CHAPTER VII. — SLAV EUROPE.

565–575.	I.	Russia	583
576–582.	II.	The Balkan States	597

CHAPTER VIII. — THE NEW AGE: A SUMMARY OF CONDITIONS AND PROBLEMS.

583–584.	I.	European Alliances	608
585–591.	II.	The Expansion of Europe into Africa and Asia	610
592–594.	III.	Moral and Scientific Movements, and the Outlook	618

BIBLIOGRAPHY 627

INDEX AND PRONOUNCING VOCABULARY . . . 637

MAPS.

All the maps, with two exceptions (Nos. 4 and 14), are full-page maps.
Nos. 15, 23, 31, 34, 37, and 39 are double-page maps.

		PAGE
1. The Carolingian Realms at the Division of Verdun, 843. Colored	*facing*	10
2. European Peoples about 900. Colored	*facing*	14
3. England about 900		17
4. The Empire of Knut the Great		20
5. Political Divisions of Europe about 900. Colored	*facing*	50
6. The Holy Roman Empire, 962–1000. Colored	*facing*	63
7. German Colonization on the East, 800–1400. Colored	*facing*	71
8. The Holy Roman Empire in the Eleventh Century, in the Time of Henry III. Colored	*facing*	73
9. Italy in the Time of the Hohenstaufen. Colored	*facing*	93
10. Germany and Italy during the Interregnum, 1254–1273. Colored	*facing*	96
11. The Eastern Empire in the Tenth and Eleventh Centuries		101
12. Europe and Other Mediterranean Lands by Religions, about 1100 (Time of the First Crusade). Colored	*facing*	102
13. The Crusading Latin States in Syria		108
14. The Latin Empire at Constantinople, 1204–1260, with Neighboring States		110
15. Dominions of the Hansa and of the Teutonic Order. Colored	*following*	130
16. England and France at Different Periods (a Series of Four Maps). Colored	*facing*	164
17. The Spanish Kingdoms of the Middle Ages. Colored	*facing*	169
18. Europe toward the Year 1400. Colored	*facing*	173
19. The Swiss Confederacy, 1291–1500		175
20. Southeastern Europe at the entrance of the Ottoman Turks. Colored	*facing*	185
21. The Ottoman Dominions at their Greatest Extent		186
22. Europe in the Time of Charles V. Colored	*facing*	189
23. Germany about 1550. Colored	*following*	233
24. The Netherlands at the Truce of 1609		243
25. Territorial Changes effected by the Thirty Years' War. Colored	*facing*	252

MAPS.

			PAGE
26.	Europe, 1740–1789. Colored	facing	284
27.	Prussia at the Death of Frederick the Great		297
28.	Europe in 1802. Colored	facing	364
29.	Europe in 1810. Colored	facing	378
30.	Europe in 1815. Colored	facing	388
31.	The Germanic Confederation from 1815 to 1867. Colored	following	393
32.	The Growth of Italian Unity		465
33.	Prussia, 1807–1871		473
34.	The German Empire since 1871. Colored	following	480
35.	Austria-Hungary, to show Race Distribution. Colored	facing	500
36.	The Balkan States after 1878–1881. Colored	facing	597
37.	Europe about 1900. Colored	following	604
38.	Africa in 1900. Colored	facing	611
39.	The World in 1900, to show the Possessions of the World Powers. Colored	following	614

ILLUSTRATIONS.

1.	Remains of the Viking Ship found at Gökstad	14
2.	Conway Castle (a typical feudal castle). From *Old England*	22
3.	Plan of a Medieval Castle of the Larger Sort, with Moat and Drawbridge. From Gautier's *La Chevalrie*	23
4.	Drawbridge and Portcullis. From Gautier's *La Chevalrie*	24
5.	Guy's Tower, Warwick Castle. From *Old England*	25
6.	Kenilworth Castle To-day	26
7.	Kenilworth Castle, as it appeared in 1620; after a fresco painting of that date. From *Old England*	27
8.	Stoke Castle. A modest manor house of the thirteenth century. From Turner's *Domestic Architecture*	28
9.	Interior of the Hall of Stoke Castle	29
10.	Dancers. As represented in an English manuscript of the thirteenth century. From Lacroix, *Mœurs, Usages*, etc.	35
11.	A Court Fool. After a medieval miniature in brilliant colors	36
12.	Ancient Manor House, Melichope, England; in its present condition. From Wright's *Homes of Other Days*	40
13.	Interior View of a Window in Melichope Manor House	41

ILLUSTRATIONS. xi

		PAGE
14.	One of the Open Fields of the Manor of Lower Heyford, Oxfordshire. From Andrew's *History of England*	42
15.	A Reaper's Cart. After Jusserand's *English Wayfaring Life*; from a fourteenth century manuscript	43
16.	Falconry. From a medieval manuscript reproduced by Lacroix	45
17.	Knight in Armor. From Lacroix, *Vie Militaire*	46
18.	Monks busy in Field Labor. From Lacroix; after a thirteenth century French manuscript	47
19.	The Temporal and the Spiritual Power; a mosaic of the tenth century in the Church of St. John, Rome. From Lacroix	68
20.	The Court of Lions, Alhambra	99
21.	Doorway to the Hall of the Ambassadors, Alhambra	100
22.	Church of the Holy Sepulcher at Jerusalem; present condition	104
23.	A Crusader's Effigy. Funeral slab in Salisbury Cathedral	111
24.	Old Street in Rouen; present condition	118
25.	Town Hall, Oudenarde, about 1525. From Lübke	120
26.	Ruins of a Rhine Castle, with a Modern Town below	123
27.	St. Mark's, Venice	128
28.	Windows of a House in Venice. Twelfth century. From Ruskin	129
29.	Windows of Venetian Palace. Thirteenth century. From Ruskin	130
30.	Interior of Hall of Merchant Princes at Dantzig. From Lübke	131
31.	Battle of Hastings. Bayeux Tapestry. From *Old England*	136
32.	William the Conqueror and the Pope's Consecrated Banner. From the Bayeux Tapestry	137
33.	A Norman Ship. From the Bayeux Tapestry	138
34.	Norman Doorway, St. Peter's, Northampton. From *Old England*	139
35.	Silver Penny of William I	140
36.	Silver Penny of Stephen	140
37.	Stephen. After an engraving based on a coin portrait	141
38.	Effigy of Henry II. From his tomb. From *Old England*	143
39.	Sections of Magna Carta in Facsimile	147
40.	A Fourteenth Century Bridge in Rural England, near Danby in Oxfordshire. From Jusserand's *English Wayfaring Life*	152
41.	Seals of Edward III; before and after the assumption of the arms of France	153
42.	An English Carriage of the Fourteenth Century. After Jusserand's *English Wayfaring Life*; from a fourteenth century psalter	154
43.	The Parliament of 1399, which deposed Richard II. From *Old England*, which follows a contemporary manuscript	159

ILLUSTRATIONS.

		PAGE
44.	Hall of the Cloth-makers' Guild at Ypres. From Lübke	178
45.	Monk teaching the Globe. After a thirteenth century manuscript. From Lacroix, *Science and Literature*	194
46.	Seal of the Faculty of Theology of Paris. Fourteenth century. From Lacroix, *Science and Literature*	197
47.	Seal of the Picardy Nation, University of Paris. Fourteenth century. From Lacroix	198
48.	Illustration from a Fifteenth Century Manuscript. From Lacroix, *Vie Militaire*	211
49.	Salisbury Cathedral, from the Southeast. Built 1200–1250. From *Cathedral Churches of England*	212
50.	Salisbury Cathedral. View from south to north transept	213
51.	The Cloisters, Salisbury Cathedral	214
52.	Cathedral of Rheims	215
53.	Church of Saint-Maclou at Rouen. Fifteenth century	216
54.	A Lower Corner of the Ducal Palace, Venice	217
55.	Charles I. After a painting by Van Dyck	273
56.	Cromwell. After the painting by Sir Peter Lely	275
57.	Louis XIV	287
58.	Church of St. Basil, Moscow	288
59.	Peter the Great. After a portrait by Kneller	289
60.	Frederick the Great. After a painting by Ramberg	293
61.	Voltaire	316
62.	Napoleon at Arcola. After the painting by Gros	360
63.	The Vendome Column, Paris	367
64.	Arch of Triumph, Paris	369
65.	Napoleon toward the Close of his Rule	379
66.	Napoleon III	424
67.	"France is Tranquil." A cartoon from *Harper's Magazine*, representing France under Napoleon III	426
68.	Mazzini	458
69.	Victor Emmanuel II	460
70.	Cavour	461
71.	Garibaldi	463
72.	Bismarck	475
73.	Proclamation of the German Empire	476
74.	William I of Prussia	477
75.	First Adhesive Penny Postage Stamp	564
76.	Sir Robert Peel	565
77.	Gladstone	568
78.	The First Railway Passenger Train	619

MODERN HISTORY.

INTRODUCTION.

THE ELEMENTS, THE FIELD, AND THE PERIODS.

The chief interest in history lies in the fact that it is not yet finished.
— ASHLEY.

1. A Summary of Earlier Progress.[1] — Seven thousand years ago the Nile and Euphrates valleys developed an imposing material civilization: men learned to practise many arts and crafts, to build roads and canals, and, with ships and caravans, to seek out the treasures of distant regions; while the accumulated wealth was spent by the rulers with gorgeous pomp and splendor. War and trade carried this culture slowly around the eastern coasts of the Mediterranean; and, before 1500 B.C., Phoenician colonists had scattered its seeds widely in many regions. A thousand years later, Persia saved the slow gains of ages from barbarian ravagers, and united and organized the civilized East under an improved political system. All this Oriental civilization, however, was marred by serious imperfections: its governments were despotic; its art was conventional and monstrous; its thought, extravagant and superstitious. At best, its benefits were for the few; it was uniform and passive; and it threatened to become stagnant. Among the Hebrews, it is true, there had grown up a pure religion whose truth and grandeur were to influence profoundly the future

---

[1] The story of this earlier progress has been told in a preceding volume of this series of histories, — West's *Ancient History*. Reference will be made to that volume simply as *Ancient History*.

world, but for centuries to come it was to remain an exclusive possession of one small people.[1]

But now appeared a new culture. A widely diffused European civilization had been rising slowly, through obscure periods of time. It borrowed from the East; but from the first it had its own peculiar traits: it was marked by diversity, freedom, and active energy, and intellectually by moderation and naturalness.[2] In the hands of the Greeks, about 500 B.C., this culture burst into sudden bloom. Then for nearly two hundred years it wrestled with Persia in war; and finally, through the genius of Alexander, it welded East and West into a Graeco-Oriental world.

In the end, however, the huge passive East would have absorbed the small Greek creative element, had not the latter found reënforcement from the second peninsula of Southern Europe. Rome, drawing largely from the Greek culture, gave a Latin civilization to the western Mediterranean coasts, and then combined the Latin West with the older Greek East into a Graeco-Roman world. The Roman Empire embraced the Mediterranean fringe of the three Old-World continents, — a broad belt stretching from the Euphrates to Britain, between the southern deserts and the northern waters of the Rhine, the Danube, and the Black Sea. In language and culture, the West remained Latin, and the East, Greek; but in politics and law and in patriotic sentiment, the fusion was complete.

For nearly four centuries after the birth of Christ this vast region rested in peace and prosperity, while, under the favorable conditions of this social unity, Christianity grew up and spread victoriously over the civilized world. Then, happily not until then, the Empire began to disintegrate, and there came upon the stage two new forces, the Teuton and the Slav, and soon after a third in Mohammedanism. In four frightful centuries of invasion and disorder, Asia and Africa became the prey of the Mohammedan and were wholly lost to our western civilization, while

---

[1] *Ancient History*, §§ 67, 78, 506.   [2] *Ancient History*, §§ 80, 81.

§ 2]   THE ELEMENTS, THE FIELD, THE PERIODS.   3

the two halves of Europe fell asunder, — Southeastern Europe becoming Slavic-Greek, and Western Europe Romano-Teutonic.

From this time, it is this Western Europe and its offshoots with which history is chiefly concerned. At first it seemed submerged in barbarism, but gradually two new organizing forces grew up, — the papacy and the kingdom of the Franks, — and the restoration of the Roman Empire by Charlemagne and the Pope, in the year 800, marks the successful fusion of the old and new elements in the West. This event, therefore, makes a convenient close for the great period of human development that we call Ancient History. In that period the various forces that were to make our western world of to-day had been brought together. The subsequent working of these forces is the theme of Modern History,[1] and will be treated in the present volume.

2. The Stage and the Actors in Modern History. — For nine hundred of its eleven hundred years since 800 A.D., human progress was made almost wholly within the limits of the Romano-Teutonic Empire of Charlemagne and in its fringes in the new Teutonic states of England and of the Scandinavian peninsulas. The scene of history had shifted to the west and had shrunken in size. Some Teutonic districts outside the old Roman world had been added; but vast areas of the Roman territory itself had been abandoned,[2] and the Mediterranean —

---

[1] The seven centuries from 800 to 1500 are sometimes classed, with the four centuries of disorder before Charlemagne, as the Middle Age. The three hundred years from 800 to 1100, in their gloom and disorder, do resemble the unhappy period from 400 to 800 ; and indeed, in accordance with recognized custom, this volume sometimes uses the term " medieval " to cover the thousand or eleven hundred years of fusion and reorganization that intervene between the progressive period of the ancient world and the progress of the modern world since 1500. However, in order to bring out more clearly the real value and meaning of these intermediate centuries, this volume prefers to regard the four hundred years before Charlemagne as the close of Ancient History, and the period after Charlemagne as the beginning of Modern History (cf. *Ancient History*, §§ 4 and 595, note 2).

[2] The Euphrates, the Nile, the eastern Mediterranean, all Asia with Eastern Europe to the Adriatic, and Africa with Western Europe to the Pyrenees, were gone.

the center of the old Roman world — had become an ill-defined moat between Christian Europe and Mohammedan Africa, while its place as the highway of civilization was taken over, as well as might be, by the Rhine and the North Sea.

In the later centuries of the modern era, it is true, especially in the last two hundred years, this little Europe was to expand marvelously over new continents and to replace the Roman Mediterranean and the Teutonic Rhine by the mightier highways of the Atlantic and Mississippi, by the passage round the Cape, and by the Indian Ocean. To-day, too, we are in the throes of a yet more wondrous growth; and all eyes center upon the Pacific, where ancient civilized peoples of the Far East, — unknown to either Alexander or to Rome, — are about to mingle their life with ours. But when Modern History began, all this growth was hidden in the distant future. For almost a thousand years, even the eastern half of Christian Europe was to count for little in our development: not until the nineteenth century, indeed, were the great Slav empire of the North and the new Slav and Greek nations of Southeastern Europe to be drawn into the current of our civilization. And with all the expansion of the stage in these later times, *the chief actors, so far, have been the Teutonic and the Latin peoples, and their descendants in the new regions of the world to which European culture has recently been transplanted.*

3. The Inheritance with which Modern History began. — Through Rome, the western peoples were also the heirs of Greek mind and Oriental hand,[1] but much of this inheritance was to be recovered only in later times. In 800 A.D., Europe was still sunk deep in the barbarism that followed the long anarchy of the invasions, and the brief revival of Charlemagne had not gone far toward restoring civilization. Schools and

---

[1] "There was a great heritage of manual skill and mechanical arts which had been slowly built up in Egypt, Phoenicia, Greece, and Carthage, and which was incorporated in the culture which the Romans diffused; and it may be doubted if any of the industrial arts known and practised by the Romans was wholly lost in the West." — CUNNINGHAM, *Western Civilization*, II, 6.

learning were almost extinct; commerce hardly existed; communication between district and district was almost impossible; money was so scarce that revenue had to be collected in produce; and manners and morals were alike deplorable. When we turn from the darker side to count the positive institutions with which Modern History began, we observe (1) the Christian church, with the papacy and monasticism; (2) the Empire; (3) the remains of municipal life in Southern Europe; (4) the serf organization of labor; (5) the new nobility, with the germs of the coming feudal system; (6) a new Romano-Teutonic kingship; and (7) popular assemblies of freemen.[1] There was also for all educated men a common language, the Latin, and, through it, a common culture.

4. The Course of Development after Charlemagne.[2]— Modern History at first sight seems a pathless maze, — many threads of development crossing each other in curious tangles. For our purpose, however, we may find a guide through the labyrinth by fixing our attention upon the successive ways in which European society has organized itself. (1) First we see a single *Latin Christendom*, bound together feebly by the church, but, for most political purposes, broken into innumerable fragments under aristocratic rulers. (2) Then, Christendom divided into two camps, but at the same time the small "feudal" units combined into *a few large states ruled by monarchs.* (3) Lastly, the peoples in these new units took the final control of the government into their own hands, and the monarchic states became *nation-states.* These three great forms of European society give us a basis for dividing Modern History.

a. For seven hundred years after the disappearance of Charlemagne's Empire, Western Europe found its chief bond of union in the Roman

---

[1] Such assemblies on a national scale were soon to die out, but local assemblies, especially in the English counties, were to have important influence on later political development. *Ancient History*, §§ 613, 614.

[2] This section may be *read* now by students; but they should not be obliged to reproduce it; and it will have more meaning as the stages of development are reached.

(Latin) church. Through this organization it formed one Latin Christendom. Nations were not yet made. Not Britain or Italy or France, but Christendom, was the true fatherland for men and the true object of patriotism. The period falls into two main subdivisions. (1) From 814 to about 1100, we have three centuries of "Dark Ages," caused by a new series of barbarian invasions and continued by the "feudal" violence of the local military organization that society adopted to ward off these invasions. (2) From 1100 to 1500, Europe was astir with new impulses to progress, — intellectual, commercial, and political.[1] Town life, universities, new religious movements in and out of the church, new principles of government, the rediscovery of Greek learning, new literature, new art, new inventions, greater material wealth and comfort, were making over society.

The first two centuries of this period, from 1100 to 1300, were the age of the crusades, which tremendously augmented all the impulses to change, and these two hundred years are sometimes treated as a distinct period. Some writers, indeed, close the first great age with the crusades, and make the two hundred years from 1300 to 1520 the beginning of the next age, — to which they certainly bear a strong likeness in many features. For our purpose, however, it is more convenient to follow the more general custom, and to class these two centuries with the preceding ones. It should be clearly seen, of course, that they contained the forces which were to bring that age to a close. They prepared the "Reformation," and formed the transition to the next great period, the second of the three into which we divide Modern History.

b. A number of remarkable events group themselves near the end of the fifteenth century: the invention of printing; the use of gunpowder, which destroyed the superiority of the knight in armor; the discovery of America (1492); the definite beginning of the Reformation (1520); and the consolidation of strong monarchic governments, in England under the Tudors, in France under Louis XI, and in Spain under Ferdinand and Isabella. These events, and the forces that grew out of them, revealed a new world of thought and feeling, as well as a new physical hemisphere, and Europe passed into a new age, with a new form of social organization. Latin Christendom was broken into two camps by the Protestant

---

[1] The church remained the central fact for Europe all through these centuries, although its importance is greatly obscured in the first sub-period by the disorder and violence in society, and in the closing part of the second sub-period by the rising intellectual revolt which was to disrupt it and by the rising monarchies which were soon to displace it as the type of European organization.

Reformation. The church, so far as it had represented the chief social organization, gave way to monarchic "states," which remained the form under which society progressed for the next three centuries, down to the French Revolution (1789). The intermarriages and treaty relations of the ruling families, and the policy of preserving the "balance of power," led to the beginning of modern international law, and in some measure preserved the unity of Europe.

The age was one of almost constant war: during the first half of the period, — to the Peace of Westphalia (1648), — the wars largely grew out of religious differences; in the second half, they grew out of the personal ambitions of the ruling monarchs, the commercial jealousies between the different countries, and the rivalry for the new worlds east and west.

c. The last century of the second age (the eighteenth century) showed a rising consciousness of the rights of the people.[1] All over Europe, governments took a new tone toward the subject masses, acknowledging the duty of governing *for* them, and despots undertook great paternal and beneficent reforms (§ 280). In France, in the last years of the eighteenth century, this movement was suddenly taken up by the people themselves; and after the French Revolution, monarchic states gave way rapidly to nation-states, — the form in which society organizes itself to-day.[2]

5. The Divisions of Modern History in this Volume. — Thus the progress in Modern History has been from *theocracy and feudal aristocracy* to *monarchy* and then to *democracy*. This volume will treat Modern History under the following great divisions: —

---

[1] In England, which at this time was far ahead of the rest of Europe politically, the king had already ceased to be the state; but even in England until well into the nineteenth century, no large part of the nation had really entered into political power.

[2] Louis XIV of France (1643–1715) could say with perfect truth, "I am the State." To-day in nearly all civilized countries the nations are the "states." Some thinkers urge that our nation-states are not the final or the ideal form of social organization, and that they are even now tending to give way to a higher form in greater race federations (Teutonic, Latin, Slav), or in that supreme "federation of the world" of which Tennyson wrote. The student of history will learn not to look upon any social form as unchangeable.

> "Our little systems have their day;
> They have their day and cease to be.
> They are but broken lights of Thee,
> And Thou, O God, art more than they."

PART I. **Latin Christendom,** from Charlemagne to Luther (seven centuries), 814–1520: *Europe a theocracy, modified by the disorder of local feudal aristocracy,* and, toward the close, by the development of monarchic states.

    1. A new series of "Dark Ages," from the Norse invasions to the crusades, or the *age of Feudalism* (three hundred years), 814–1100.

    2. Four hundred years of slow revival, 1100–1520, the first half known as the period of *the crusades* and the latter part as *the Renaissance.*

PART II. **Monarchic States:** *the disruption of Christendom and the rise of European monarchies,* 1520–1789.

    1. *The Reformation* and wars of religion, 1520–1648.

    2. Dynastic and commercial wars, 1648–1789: colonial expansion.

PART III. **Nation States:** *recent and contemporary Europe from the French Revolution to to-day,* 1789–1904: *rising democracy* in politics and in industry; *political federation; territorial expansion; marvelous growth* in wealth and population.[1]

---

[1] With reference to the proportion of space given to these periods in this book, see the Preface.

PART I.

LATIN CHRISTENDOM — FROM CHARLEMAGNE TO LUTHER.

CHAPTER I.

A NEW SERIES OF DARK AGES, 814-1100.

I. DISRUPTION OF THE EMPIRE OF CHARLEMAGNE.

6. The Failure of Charlemagne. — Charlemagne died in 814 A.D., and his Empire did not long survive him. His brilliant attempt to organize Western Europe was to carry mighty influences on into coming centuries,[1] but at the moment it seemed to have been only a glorious failure. There followed a long period of reaction toward barbarism, — an age of turmoil, ignorance, ferocity, and misery. Not until well toward the close of the eleventh century did civilization again reach so fair a promise. The decline and disruption of the Empire were due partly to internal conditions and partly to a new series of barbarian invasions (§§ 7-17).

7. Internal Causes of the Political Decline. — The only natural tie between the widespreading regions of the Empire of Charlemagne had been the common religion. The various sections differed in race,[2] in language, and in custom and law; and

---

[1] Cf. *Ancient History*, § 649. The Empire of Charlemagne is a point of light between the four centuries that precede and the two or three that follow.

[2] With wise moderation Charlemagne had refrained from adding territory outside of that in which the Teutons had in some degree established themselves (*Ancient History*, §§ 639, 640); but, of course, not to note minor distinctions, there were wide differences between the pure Germans of Saxony

these differences were already creating local and tribal feeling, which in some districts was to grow later into national patriotism. The different parts of the Empire, too, were fitted by nature to be the homes of distinct peoples; and the old Roman bonds of trade and travel had long gone to decay. Charlemagne's tremendous energy and broad tolerance held his dominions together during his life, but time was not given him to change these adverse conditions.

Moreover, Frankish feeling demanded that each son of a king should inherit part of his father's realm. It was only by accident that Charlemagne himself had succeeded to the undivided Frankish state, and only the death of his two elder sons enabled him to transmit the Empire unbroken[1] to his surviving heir, *Louis the Pious.* The reign of this weak prince made melancholy shipwreck amid the quarrels of his sons over their inheritance. Seven distinct plans of partition were tried in twenty-seven years (between 817 and 843), and most of them were accompanied by bloody civil war.

8. The New Map of Europe: the Treaty of Verdun. — The greatest of these struggles closed with the *Treaty of Verdun,* in 843. This treaty began the map of modern Europe. *Lothair,* the eldest grandson of Charlemagne, held the title of Emperor, and therefore wished to retain the two imperial capitals, Rome and Aachen. Accordingly, in this division, he kept Italy (that part of it which had belonged to the Empire) and a narrow strip of land from Italy to the North Sea. This northern strip lay in the valley of the Rhone and in the western valley of the Rhine, and so included Burgundy and old Austrasia. The rest of the Empire was made into two kingdoms — that of the East Franks and that of the West Franks — for Lothair's

---

and Bavaria, with their unmixed Teutonic speech, and the Latinized Lombards of Italy or the Romanized Gauls of Aquitaine, with their growing "Romance" languages (based on the old Latin, but modified by Teutonic influences). See *Ancient History,* §§ 590 and 616, and compare the map opposite this page with that facing page 14.

[1] Special report: Charlemagne's plan for partition in 806; see especially Emerton's *Medieval Europe,* 9–12.

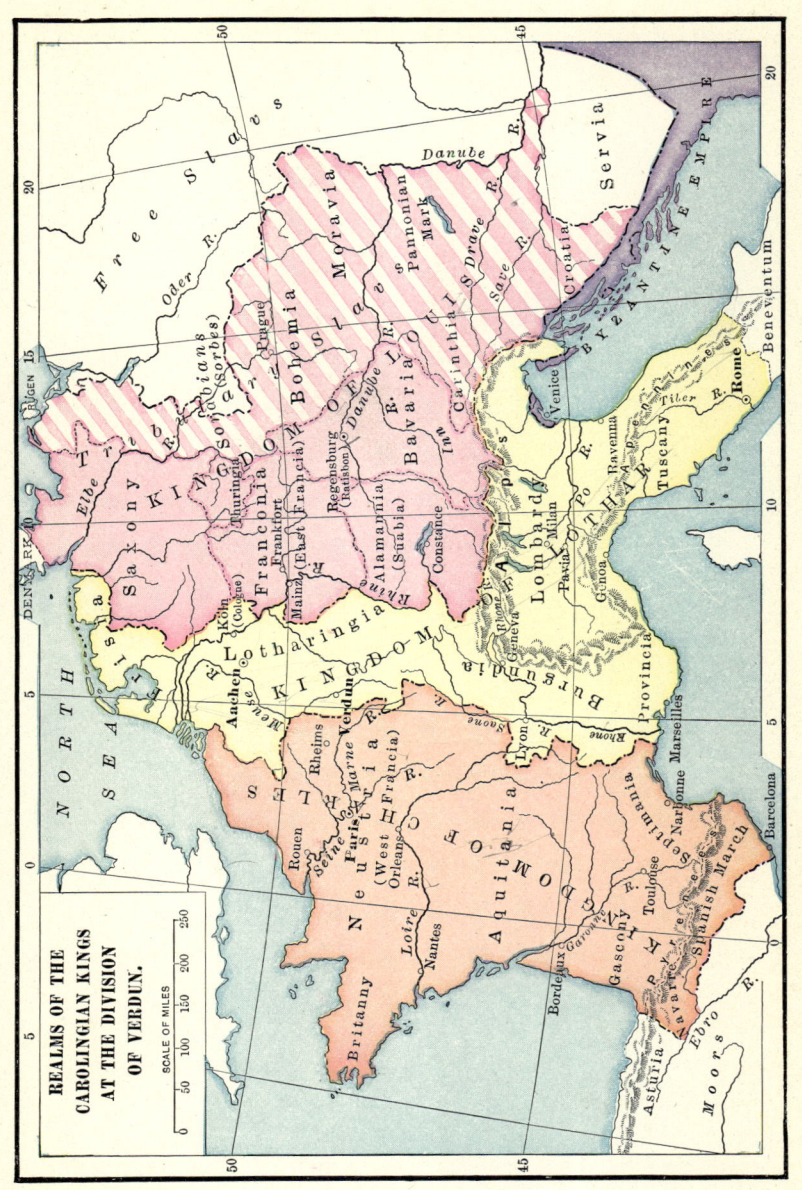

two brothers. Lothair's intermediate strip contained the districts where the Roman and Teutonic elements had most intermingled. Thus the eastern and western kingdoms were left sharply contrasted, while each in itself was fairly homogeneous in race and compact in territory, and so fitted for independent development. The eastern kingdom lay beyond the Rhine and was purely German: it was to grow into the Kingdom of the Germans. The western kingdom had more mixture of race; the Teutonic elements, however, were being absorbed rapidly, and it corresponded fairly with the extent of the new French language then just rising.[1] It was finally to take the name of France.

9. Continued Disruption of the Middle-land. — The Treaty of Verdun was followed by many more partitions between the degenerate Carolingians; but the lines it had laid down were in the main to prevail, and to it most of the present states of Western Europe can trace their origin.

Lothair's Middle Kingdom was to prove the weakest of the three great states created by the treaty. Its ruler was supposed to hold some vague suzerainty over the other two kings; but this unwieldy middle-land lacked unity, both in geography and in race. Italy almost at once fell away from the rest; and then the northern district, intermediate between France and Germany and drawn to both sides, crumbled into fragments doomed to absorption in their stronger neighbors. On the whole, the middle-land was more German than French, and most of it soon became attached to the eastern kingdom (§§ 48–64 *b.*). Some centuries later,

---

[1] The "Oath of Strasburg," between two of the brothers during the war, to confirm their alliance against the third, shows the growing difference between the languages spoken in the eastern and western parts of the Empire. Charles, the king of Neustria (the land of the West Franks), swore in the language of his brother's German army, and Lewis, king of Bavaria (East Franks), swore in the Neustrian tongue, so that each army might know what was promised by the other party. The double oath begins: —

"Pro Deo amur et pro christian poblo et nostro commun salva-
"In Godes minna ind in thes christianes folches ind unser bedhero gehalt-
ment dist di in avant in quant Deus savir," etc.
nissi fon thesemo dage frammordes so fram so mir God gewizci," etc.

These are the earliest records in the French and German tongues. The French is half way between Latin and modern French. See Emerton's *Medieval Europe*, 25–28, or Munro's *Middle Ages*, 19–20, for the story of the oaths, with the full text and the translation.

France began to seize parts of it, and, ever since, it has been a debatable land. From it came the many "Little Kingdoms" that were to confuse the map and the politics of Europe for centuries, — Savoy, Arles, Provence, Lotharingia (Lorraine), Franche Comté, and so on. Three of these small states survive, — in modern Holland, Belgium, and Switzerland. Another (Savoy, §§ 457, 463) was to grow into the modern kingdom of Italy; and others lie at the root of the Alsace-Lorraine trouble of to-day.

10. The Later Carolingians. — One cause of the decline of the age was the incapacity of the later Carolingians, as compared with the great founders of their house. For a century after Verdun, political history is little more than a tangle of ferocious and treacherous family quarrels. Early Carolingians had won such surnames as "the Hammer" and "the Great": their descendants were known as "the Bald," "the Simple," "the Fat," "the Stammerer," "the Child," "the Lazy." The numerous branches of the family died out, one by one; and in 911 in Germany and in 987 in France, and still earlier in some of the small states, the nobles elected native princes from among their own number, and so founded national dynasties.

EXERCISE. — Draw the Division of Verdun from memory, preferably upon "outline maps," with about the same degree of detail as that in the map facing page 10.

FOR FURTHER READING. — Students may profitably consult one or two of the following: Oman, *Dark Ages*, 383–445; Emerton, *Medieval Europe*, 14–35; Church, *Beginnings of the Middle Ages*, 140–156; Bémont and Monod, *Medieval Europe*, 211–228; Duruy, *Middle Ages*, 139–155. An excellent discussion of the period is given in Adams, *Civilization*, ch. viii.

II. THE NEW BARBARIAN ATTACK.

From the fury of the Northmen, O Lord, deliver us. — Prayer in church service of the tenth century.

11. Renewal of the Invasions. — The distracted Europe of the ninth century was endangered also by a new peril. Once more barbarian invasion threatened the civilized world. The Carolingian kings, instead of combining against the barbarians, only strove the more desperately to plunder one another, each one taking advantage of the others' misfortunes. Even within one kingdom, the people of different sections felt no common interest in repelling the attack, but selfishly allowed their neighbors to suffer, until the evil reached themselves. Moreover, there was no organized post to carry news, and the roads were so poor that troops could hardly be collected quickly enough to meet the scattered and swift attacks.

Thus Europe seemed at the mercy of the invaders. On the east, hordes of wild *Slavs* and of wilder *Hungarians* broke across the frontiers, ravaged Germany, and penetrated sometimes even to Rome or to Toulouse in southern France; the *Mohammedan Moors* from Africa attacked Italy, Sicily, and southern France, establishing themselves firmly in many districts and turning the Mediterranean into a Mohammedan lake; fierce *Norse* pirates harried every coast, and, swarming up the rivers, pierced the heart of the land.

The Slavs and Moors had appeared earlier in history;[1] but two of the invaders were fresh forces in European development (§§ 12, 13).

12. The Hungarians (Magyars) were a Turanian people. They resembled the Huns in customs and character, and, though not closely connected with them, they probably belonged to the same Tartar-Finnish stock. Advancing westward from their old homes in the Ural-Volga country, they reached the upper Danube in 889, and for the next sixty years they proved the most terrible scourge that Europe had ever known. They were small, active nomads, moving swiftly on scraggy ponies, — slaying, burning, carrying off captives and all movable plunder, and laying waste the land.

13. The Norsemen were a new branch of the Teutons, and the fiercest and wildest of that race.[2] They dwelt in the Scandi-

---

[1] *Ancient History*, §§ 569, 626, note, and 640.

[2] *Ancient History*, §§ 555-561. There is a fine description of the Northmen in Green's *Conquest of England*, 50-59. See also Boyesen's *Story of Norway*, Johnson's *Normans*, Mabie's *Norse Stories Retold*, Jiriczek's *Northern Hero Legends*, and the *Story of the Burnt-Njal*.

navian peninsulas, and were still heathen. They had taken no part in the earlier Teutonic invasions; but, in the ninth century, population was becoming too crowded for the scanty resources of their bleak lands, and they were driven to seek new homes. Moreover, at this time, leaders arose, — their imagination kindled, perhaps, by the achievement of Charlemagne, — to unite the independent and scattered tribes into kingdoms; and the more adventurous spirits among the conquered turned to the sea to preserve their independence. Some of them colonized distant Iceland, — pilgrims, in a fashion, for liberty's sake, — and set up there a free republic; but the greater number resorted to a life of warfare and plunder at the expense of richer countries.[1] The Swedes expanded to the east, conquering the Finns and Slavs, while the Danes and Norwegians turned toward the west.

REMAINS OF VIKING SHIP, found at Gökstad, Norway. It is of oak, unpainted; length over all, 79 feet 4 inches, from stem to stern; breadth of beam, 16½ feet; perpendicular depth, 6 feet in the middle, 8½ feet at the extremities.

The Norse ships were long, open boats, seventy-five feet by twelve or fifteen, carrying a single square sail, but driven for the most part by thirty or forty long oars. They could be beached on any but the rockiest coast, or they could be run far up the rivers. A boat bore perhaps eighty warriors; and each man was perfectly clad in ring mail and steel helmet, and armed with lance, knife, bow, and the terrible Danish axe. Daring, indeed, were the long voyages of the Northmen in their frail craft. Often they were tossed in ruin by the fierce storms of the northern seas; but the survivors, rallying again around the chief-

---

[1] Of course, before this time the Norsemen had spent their energies largely in plundering each other: the firmer government of the new king made this life less possible now at home, and they sought new fields.

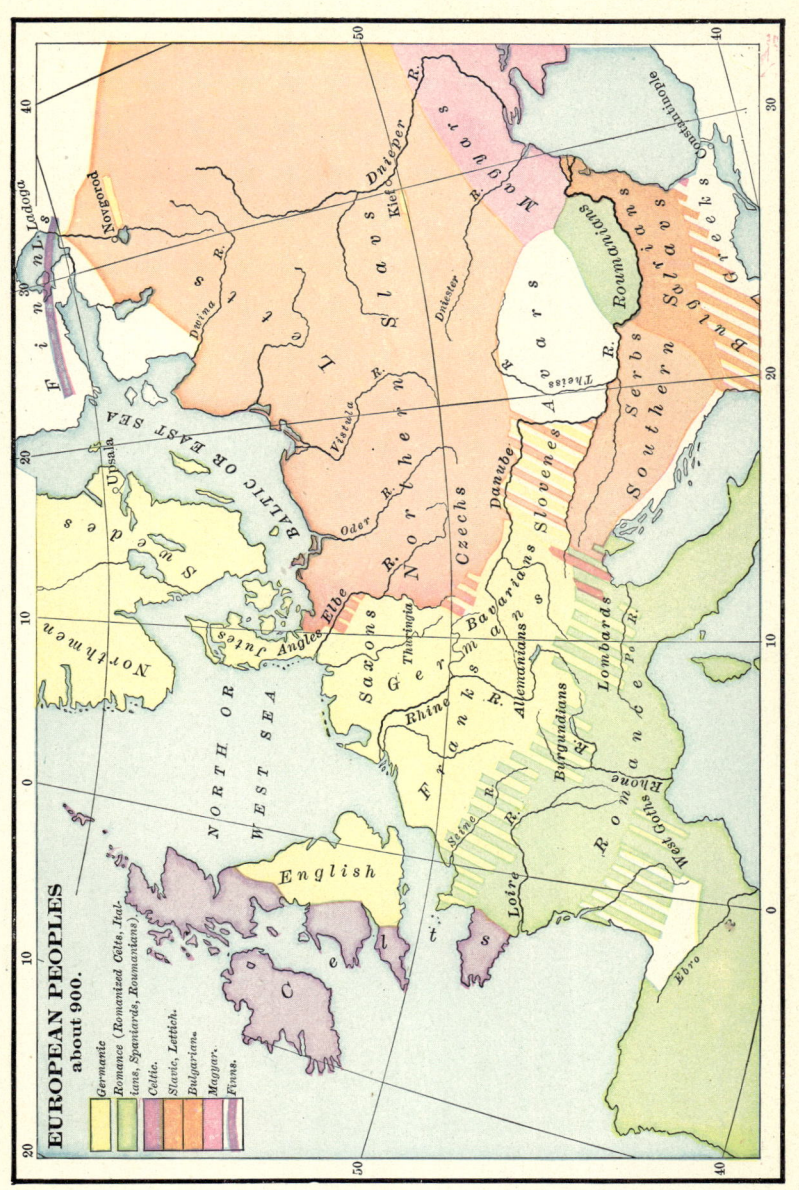

tain's vessel, laughed at winds and floods: "The blast," they sang, "aids our oars; the hurricane is our servant and drives us whither we wish to go."

14. The Norse Raids. — Fleets of these "Vikings," or "sons of the fiords," sometimes counting hundreds of boats, sometimes only two or three, set forth upon the "pathway of the swans" to plunder Western Europe, as their relatives, the Jutes and Saxons, had harassed Britain four hundred years earlier. There is a story that Charlemagne, from the coast of Gaul, once saw some Norse ships in the Mediterranean, and shed tears, predicting that after his death his kingdom would suffer unspeakable woes from those new foes. Certainly the great Emperor maintained fleets to prevent such pirate attacks; but in the quarrels of his weak successors the Norsemen found their opportunity. Every part of the Empire felt their raids. They not only plundered the open country, but they sacked cities like Hamburg, Rouen, Paris, Nantes, Bordeaux, Tours, Cologne. Within one period of a few years, they ravaged every town in old Austrasia, and finally stabled their horses in the cathedral of Aachen, about the tomb of Charlemagne. A characteristic sport of the raiders, according to popular stories, was to toss babes upon their spears, from point to point. Especially did they plunder and burn the churches and monasteries, against which their heathen rage and scoffing were particularly directed and wherein were collected the wealth and treasures of the day. Little wonder that when a band was defeated, the enraged people flayed captives alive and nailed their skins to the church doors.

After a time, of course, like their earlier kinsmen, the Norsemen ceased to be mere plunderers, and became conquerors. They settled the Orkneys, Shetlands, Hebrides, little patches on the north of Scotland, and the whole west of Ireland, and finally established themselves in the east of Britain and in the north of France. These two latter colonies were the last important infusions of Teutonic blood into the old Roman world (§§ 15–16).

15. Rolf the Dane : Settlement in Normandy. — In 911, Charles the Simple, King of France, finally stopped the Norse raids in his country by establishing some of the Norse bands on the northern coast to defend it. He gave his daughter in marriage to their leader, *Rolf* (Rollo), on condition that Rolf accept Christianity, with his people, and acknowledge Charles as his overlord[1] for his new dukedom.

Normandy, as this district came to be called from its new inhabitants, was, of course, really an independent state. Its dukes maintained stern order; and this security quickly peopled the land from the neighboring provinces, so that it became one of the most populous and prosperous parts of Europe. Churches and rich abbeys rose on every side; agriculture flourished; and the serfs grew into free peasants. *The Norsemen themselves, with peculiar adaptability, took on French customs and culture, adopted French language and French ideas, and as "Normans" became the foremost champions of this civilization, even extending it into new lands.* Indeed the most important results of the creation of Normandy were the subsequent Norman conquest of England (§§ 16, 123, 124) and of southern Italy (§ 67 *b.*), and the introduction of French civilization into those lands.

16. England and the Danes and Normans. — The conquest of Britain in the fifth and sixth centuries by the Angles and Saxons left the eastern half of the island divided into several petty German states,[2] with numerous unconquered Celtic districts in the west. The German states farthest east — the Kentmen, South Saxons, East Saxons, and East Angles — were soon shut off from contact with the Celtic territory and ceased to grow; but Wessex (the kingdom of the West Saxons) and Mercia and Northumbria (two of the kingdoms of the Angles) continued to expand at the expense of Celtic tribes. Plainly, leadership in the island was destined to fall to one of

---

[1] Special report: the story of Rolf's act of homage to Charles.
[2] For a brief account of the formation of these states, see *Ancient History*, §§ 591–594.

THE NEW BARBARIAN ATTACK.

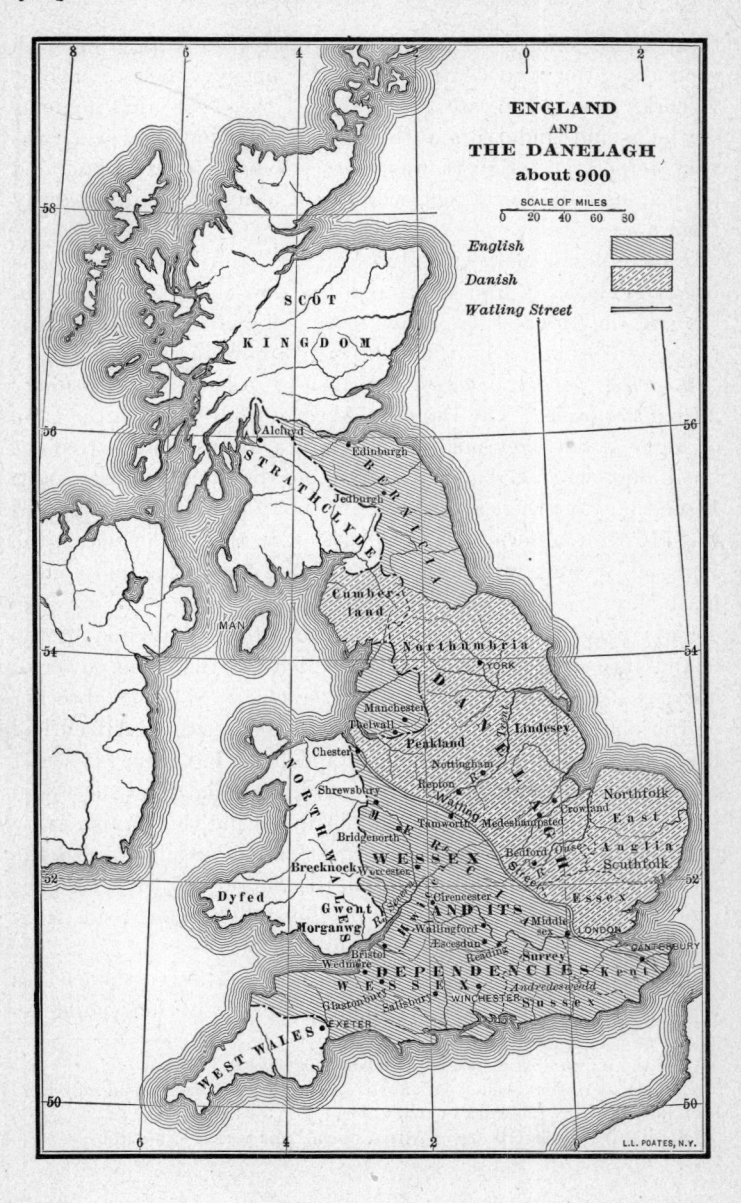

ENGLAND AND THE DANELAGH about 900

these three "mark" states.[1] They had been struggling with each other for two centuries for the mastery, when, in 827, Egbert,[2] King of Wessex, brought all the Teutonic kingdoms of the island under his authority. The union, however, was very imperfect. Egbert was simply a head king surrounded by jealous tributary kings, who might at any time break away from a weak ruler.

This was the political situation when the Danish invasions began. These at first shattered the new-made union, but in the end they helped it to grow more complete. The story fills two centuries and a half, and falls into four chapters.

a. First period: Danish settlements; division of the island; Alfred's reforms. The Danes had begun their raids in the time of Egbert, but they made no attempt at permanent settlement until 850, when a band wintered on the southeastern coast. From that time their attempts grew more and more eager, until in 871, after a series of great battles, in the last of which the King of Wessex was slain, they became for a time undisputed masters.

This period was to close, however, with a division of the island into a Saxon South and Danish North. The power of Wessex soon revived under *Alfred the Great* (871–901), brother of the slain king. Just after the Danish victory, Alfred had been driven into hiding in moors and fens; but from his secret retreats he made many a daring sally, and finally he succeeded in reorganizing the Saxons and in defeating the Danish army (878).[3] The Danes accepted Christianity, withdrew into the north, and, by the later *Treaty of Wedmore* (885), received for their own the territory north of the old Roman road from London to Chester (Watling Street).

The several kingdoms in the south now allowed themselves to be absorbed in Wessex, which plainly was their chief de-

---

[1] For the term *mark states*, see *Ancient History*, § 276, note.

[2] Egbert had spent some years at the court of Charlemagne, and may have been influenced by the work of that ruler.

[3] Special report: anecdotes of Alfred during this period of his life.

fense against the invaders; and Alfred's half of the island became one Saxon state. The rest of Alfred's life was given to strengthening his kingdom against the danger of future invasions and to removing the evil results of the desolating struggle. He reorganized the army, created an English navy, reformed many political and judicial institutions, and, in particular, ardently encouraged the spread of learning among his people. His own day knew him by the honorable name of "Alfred the Truthteller"; later generations looked back at him as ".England's Darling"; and few kings have so well deserved the title of "the Great."

b. Second period: reconquest of the Danelagh. The Danish king in the north of the island was supposed to render some vague obedience to the Saxon king; but in fact *the Danelagh,* or the land of the Danes' law, was an independent state, like Normandy in France. The second period of warfare (900-950) went to the reconquest of this Danelagh by the great successors of Alfred, — Edward the Unconquered, Athelstane the Glorious, and Edmund the Doer of Deeds. Of course this movement was welcome to the old English inhabitants of the northern districts; but, along the eastern coast especially, the country had become largely Danish in blood and very completely so in character. Indeed, all the ruling class were Danes; and, in spite of their nominal subjection to Wessex, these districts kept their hope of future independence. Still, under *Edgar the Peaceful* (957-975), the great-grandson of Alfred, the island rested in prosperity and order, and even the kings of the Celtic tribes in the far west and north came to Edgar's court to acknowledge his overlordship.

c. Third period: conquest by Denmark. After Edgar, however, there came a new era of civil strife, and under *Ethelred the Redeless* (Ethelred, the man "without counsel"), the island was conquered (1002-1016) by Swegn and *Knut,* kings of Denmark. Denmark had now become a united Christian kingdom, and this conquest in the eleventh century was not for *Danish settlement,* like that of the ninth century: it was for the purpose of making England a part of a great Scandinavian Empire.

d. The Norman Conquest. Knut the Great (1016–1035) proved a wise ruler and a true English king; but his sons were unworthy successors, and in 1042 the Witan[1] of the

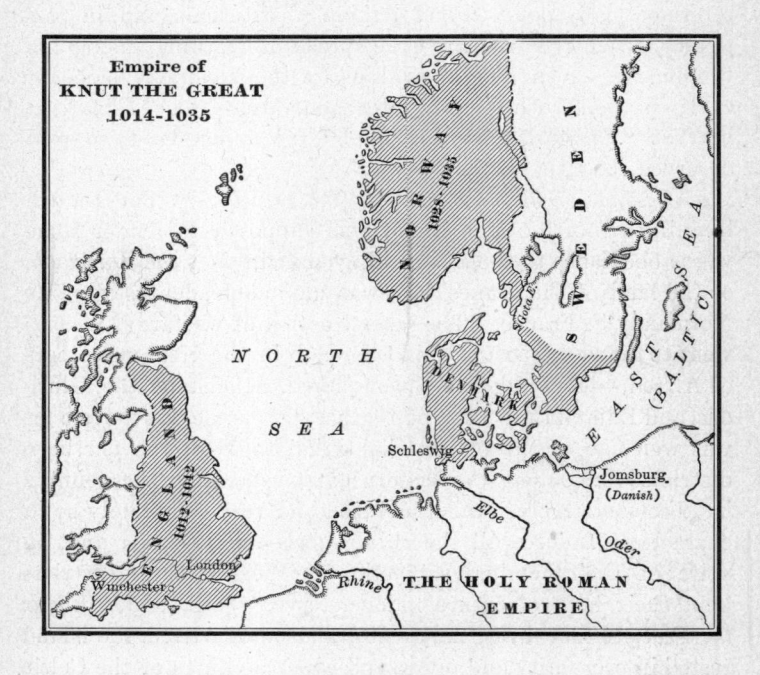

island restored the old Saxon line by electing for their king *Edward the Confessor,* son of Ethelred and of the Norman Emma. This reign was to result in a new Danish conquest, — a conquest this time, however, by *Danes who had become Frenchmen.* Edward was more monk than king. Half Norman by birth, he had lived long at the Norman court, and he

---

[1] Or Witenagemote; this was the meeting of the "wise" men, the National Assembly of great lords and ecclesiastics, which with the king ruled the land and promulgated laws, and which sometimes elected a king.

brought crowds of Norman favorites with him to England. At his death the English Witan chose the hero *Harold*, the most powerful Saxon noble, for their king; but *William, Duke of Normandy*, claimed the throne, — on the ground of a promise from Edward and of distant relationship, — and, aided by a new Danish invasion and by fatal jealousy between Danish England and Saxon England, he conquered the island in 1066, at the decisive battle of *Hastings*, or Senlac.[1]

17. Significance of the Ninth Century Invasion. — The conquests of England by Knut and by William the Conqueror have been told in the last section to save space, but plainly they do not resemble the invasions of the earlier period, with which we here are mainly concerned. In conclusion, it should be noted that the barbarian invasions of the ninth century, unlike those of the fifth, did not create a new society. When we look for their permanent results, beyond the misery they caused, we note (1) that they brought in some new Teutonic stock to invigorate northern France and eastern England; (2) that they helped along the political union of England; (3) that they hastened the breaking up of the Empire of Charlemagne; and (4), chiefly, that they forced Europe to take on a new social and military organization for defense. This organization we call *feudalism* (§§ 18 ff.).

FOR FURTHER READING. — On the invasions in general, Duruy, *Middle Ages*, 156–170; Oman, *Dark Ages*, ch. xxiv; or Bémont and Monod, 229–240. On the invaders, see § 13, note. A longer treatment may be found in Keary's *The Vikings in Western Christendom* or in Du Chaillu's *Viking Age*. A translation of the Norse *Heimskringla* should be accessible; or, if it is not, students should read the extracts given in the *Old South Leaflets*. On the Danes in England, advanced students may consult Green's *Conquest of England* or Freeman's *Norman Conquest*, I. For Alfred the Great, probably the most scholarly account is Plummer's *Alfred the Great* (1902); but students will enjoy the biographies by Hughes, Bowker, and Pauli. A biography by York-Powell is in preparation (1903). The period of the Norman Conquest is treated in historical

---

[1] The Saxon institutions and the results of the Norman Conquest are treated in §§ 118–124.

fiction, from different points of view, in Kingsley's *Hereward*, Bulwer's *Harold*, and Tennyson's *Harold* (drama).

SPECIAL REPORTS. — 1. Ruric and the Norse kingdom in Russia. 2. The Varangians at Constantinople. 3. The Norse in Ireland. 4. Norse voyages to "Vinland the Good" in America. 5. Alfred the Great's life and work. 6. The Battle of Hastings.

CONWAY CASTLE. — From *Old England*.

III. FEUDALISM.

A. ORIGIN: THE PRODUCT OF ANARCHY.

A protest of barbarism against barbarism. — HEGEL.

18. The Successor of the Empire of Charlemagne. — The ninth century, as we have noticed, saw the territorial beginnings of Germany, France, and Italy, and, outside the old realm of Charlemagne, of England, Norway, Denmark, and Sweden, as well as of various small kingdoms in the valleys of the Rhine and Rhone. But the nations to occupy these territories were not yet made, and the new royal governments proved unequal to the needs of the age (§ 11). A few centuries later, the monarchies in some of these countries were to become the chief agents in making new nations; meantime the church held Europe together in sentiment; but everywhere, so far as maintaining order was concerned, *the immediate successor of the Empire of Charlemagne was the feudal organization.* This new form of social and political government was to dominate Europe for four hundred years and to play a leading part in many countries up to the nineteenth century. Indeed, it has left important traces in the European institutions of to-day.

19. The Dissolution of the Old Society and the Emergence of a New Order. — The rise of feudalism shows strikingly how strong the instinct in society is to set up some government that will protect life and property. After Charlemagne, through the renewal of barbarian invasions from without and the collapse of government within, the ninth century became an age of indescribable horror and misery. The strong robbed the weak; brigands swept over the land, to kill, torture, and plunder at will; and society seemed on the point of universal dissolution. *But out of this anarchy there emerged a new social order resting on force.* Here and there, and finally in greater and greater numbers, some petty chief planted himself strongly on a small domain. Perhaps he had held it formerly as an officer of the king; perhaps he had seized it from another: in any case he kept it henceforth for himself, warding off all

MEDIEVAL CASTLE of the larger sort, with moat and drawbridge. — From Gautier's *La Chevalerie.*

attack. By so doing he became a protector of others. The benefactor in that age was the man who could fight. "The noble, in the language of the day, is the man of war, the soldier (*miles*), and it is he who lays anew the foundation for modern society."[1] His ancestry was of little consequence: he was himself to be the ancestor of the later European aristocracy. "He is perhaps a Carolingian count, or a beneficiary of the king,[2] or, in a few cases, the sturdy proprietor of a territory of his own. In one place he is a valiant abbot; in others he is a converted pagan, a retired bandit, a rude huntsman. In any event, the noble is the powerful man, who, at the head of his troop, instead of fleeing or paying ransom, offers his breast, stands firm, and protects a patch of soil with his sword." "In those days," says an old chronicle, "kings, nobles, and knights, to be always ready, kept their horses in the rooms in which they slept with their wives."

IMAGINATIVE PICTURE to show drawbridge (with chains to raise and lower it) and part of portcullis. — From Gautier's *La Chevalerie*.

Finally, through the growth of this military generation, each district was provided with its settled body of soldiers and with its circle of frowning castles; and then the invasions ceased.

---

[1] Taine, *Ancient Régime*, 6. Taine's fine passage, pp. 5-8, is largely quoted or adapted in this and the following section.

[2] One who held lands granted by the king.

20. Military Features: Castles and Mailed Horsemen. — *Feudalism was primarily the product of military necessity;* and its whole nature was typified in two military features, the castle and the mailed horseman. Castles rose at every ford and above each mountain pass and on every hill commanding a fertile plain. They were enormous buildings of massive stone, crowned by frowning battlements whence boiling pitch and masses of rock could be hurled down upon assailants. Usually the single narrow approach was across a moat, by a drawbridge, to a heavy iron gate and a portcullis which could be dropped from above, while the bridge was protected by flanking towers, from whose narrow slit-like windows bowmen could command the road. Sometimes the walls inclosed several acres, with a variety of buildings and with room to gather cattle and supplies; but in such cases there was always an inner "keep," or especially strong tower, with its own series of fortifications and, if possible, with its own well. Until the days of gunpowder, such strongholds were virtually impregnable to ordinary attack and could be captured only by surprise, by treachery, or by famine. Upon these walls the Norse invaders might spend their force in vain. In later times, secure of such retreat, a petty lord could sometimes defy even his own sovereign with impunity, and too often the castles became themselves the seats of robber-barons who oppressed the country around them. To-day their gray ruins all over Europe give a peculiar picturesqueness to the landscape, mocking, even in decay, the slighter structures of modern times.[1]

GUY'S TOWER, THE "KEEP" OF WARWICK CASTLE. — From *Old England*.

---

[1] The walls were often enormously thick, so that a man crawling out of a window would have to creep thrice his length.

The castles afforded a *refuge* for man and treasure. But during the invasions, the problem in *the field* had been to bring to bay the swiftly moving assailants, — the light horsemen of the Hungarians, or the Danes with their swift boats for refuge. The Frankish infantry[1] had proved altogether too slow. Feudalism met this need also. Each castle was always ready to pour forth its band of trained and faithful men-at-arms (horsemen in mail) under the command of the knight, either to gather

KENILWORTH CASTLE TO-DAY.

quickly with other bands into an army under a higher lord, or by themselves to cut off stragglers and hold the fords and passes. The raider's day was over; but meantime the old Teutonic foot-militia, in which every freeman had a place, had given way to an iron-clad cavalry, — the symbol and the resistless weapon of the new feudal aristocracy.

21. Feudal Classes and the Origin of Feudal Privileges. — While the disorders were at their worst, any man of courage

---

[1] The change to cavalry is sometimes ascribed to Martel before Tours (*Ancient History*, § 625), and something *was* then attempted; but the fighting force remained infantry among the East Franks (Germans) until after 900, and in "France" the horsemen were not important until some time after Charlemagne.

who could get together an armed force and fortify a dwelling, found the neighborhood ready to turn to him as its master. Other weaker landlords gladly surrendered to him their lands,[1] to receive them back as "fiefs" (§ 26); while they themselves became his "vassals," acknowledging him as their "lord" and, at call, fighting under his banner. In return, the lord promised these vassals protection in all just rights. The soldiery, so provided, afforded protection to other classes. The peas-

KENILWORTH CASTLE, as it appeared in 1620; after a fresco painting of that date. The walls of Kenilworth inclosed seven acres.

ants saw that they were no longer to be slain or driven captive by chance marauders. They ventured to plow and sow, to raise crops and to rear children. In case of danger they found asylum in the circle of palisades at the foot of the castle. In return for this security they cultivated the lord's crop, acknowledged him as their landlord, and paid him dues for house, for cattle, and for each sale or inheritance.[2] The village became his village; the inhabitants became his villeins ("villains").

---

[1] This practice was known as "*commendation*."
[2] This paragraph also is largely based upon Taine's graphic passage referred to above.

Besides these resident laborers, who had some claim to consideration, fugitive wretches gathered on the lord's lands, to receive such measure of mercy as he might choose to grant; and these sank into the class of "serfs,"[1] of whom already there were many on all large estates.

Both these last classes were largely at the lord's mercy, but they were necessarily gainers through their relation to him. One master, however tyrannical, could not be so great an evil as exposure to constant anarchy. Hence there grew up peculiar privileges of the lord, which in later times came to be unspeakably oppressive and obnoxious, but which in origin were usually connected with some benefit conferred by him. The lord's services did not stop with defense against robbers. He slew the wild beast, and so came finally to have the sole right to hunt, — with atrocious game laws to preserve animals, large and small, for his pleasure. He was also the sole organizer of labor: he built the mill, the oven, the ferry, the bridge, the highway, with the labor he protected: then he took toll for the use of all these conveniences; and later he demolished the mill that the villeins would have built for themselves. Moreover, he took the courts under his care, and rapidly assumed the power of a sovereign. *His territory became a little state.* The greater nobles coined money and made war and treaties, like very kings.[2] As a rule, at

---

[1] The terms "serf" and "villein" are explained in § 34. Of course the above statement does not pretend to give the origin of agricultural villeinage: that institution goes back to Roman times.

[2] It is estimated that in France in the tenth century, out of some seventy thousand nobles, about two hundred exercised these sovereign powers.

first when the lord did these things, it was best for his dependents that he should do them.

"Later the masters of these castles were the terror of the country, but they saved it first; and though feudalism was to become so oppressive in the latter part of its existence, it had its time of legitimacy and usefulness. *Power always establishes itself through service and perishes through abuse.*" — DURUY, *Middle Ages*, 201.

"Disastrous as were most of the effects of the system, it at least justified its existence by saving Christendom from the foe without. ... The price at which Christendom bought its safety was enormous: nevertheless no price was too high when the future of Europe was at stake. Any ransom was worth paying, if thereby Rome was saved from the Saracen, Mainz from the Magyar, Paris from the heathen of the North." — OMAN, *Dark Ages*, 512.

22. Decentralization: Feudalism a Multitude of Separate Local Organizations. The Growth of Feudal Attachment. — Under the new organization, each locality was to a great degree independent of every other district. The king had been expected to protect and care for every corner of his realm, and as a fact he had protected none; but each little chieftain proved able to care for his own small corner when he was left to himself. The king lost authority and the nobles usurped it. *In each country, feudalism meant the replacing one ineffective central authority by countless disconnected but effective local authorities.*

INTERIOR OF THE HALL OF STOKE CASTLE.

Politically this was an evil, but it answered its immediate purpose of military defense, and the evil, real though it was, had alleviations: gradually, within each feudal unit, habit and local patriotism bound together the different classes and made the fief, large or small, an object of love and devotion to its inhabitants. The lord was admired and almost worshiped by his people; and in return, however harsh himself, he permitted no one else to injure or insult one of his dependents. A rough paternalism ruled in society. Perhaps the system was more rough than paternal; but it was better than anarchy, and it nourished some virtues peculiar to its own day.[1]

23. Economic Causes that assisted the Rise of Feudalism: Lack of Money and of Roads. — Economically, as well as politically, each locality had been thrown upon its own resources and had been compelled to provide for its own needs. Commerce had almost ceased, and there was little money. The rich man's wealth was in land; but he could make land pay only by renting it for service or for produce. He rented part of it to smaller "nobles," who paid him by fighting for him, and part to workers, who raised and harvested his crops, and gave him part of their own: and of course the man who had no land was glad to exchange his services for the use of land in one way or the other. Moreover, the difficulty of communication between district and district tended to break up society into small units, each sufficient unto itself, economically as well as politically. These conditions, however, would not of themselves have made each of these properties a "state." They counted for less in producing the feudal system than did the political causes.

24. Essential Elements of Feudalism; the Preparation in Earlier History; the Real Causes. — It is quite possible to trace back some of the

---

[1] A passage from Joinville's *Memoir of St. Louis* illustrates this better side of the feudal relation. Joinville was a great French noble about to set out on a crusade; at Eastertide he summoned his vassals to his castle for a week of feasting and dancing in honor of his approaching departure. "And on the Friday I said to them: 'Sirs, I am going beyond sea and know not whether I shall ever return; so draw near to me. If I have ever done you any wrong, I will redress it to one after another, as is my practice with all who have anything to ask of me.' And I made amends to them according to the decisions of those dwelling on my lands; and that I might not influence them, I withdrew from their deliberations and carried out without dispute whatever they decided."

elements of feudalism to earlier Roman and Teutonic history. Thus, serfdom was undoubtedly connected with the Roman institution of coloni.[1] But serfdom was not an essential part of feudalism, and was not found long in some feudal countries. It is often said that the three essential elements of feudalism were (1) *fealty*, or the personal relation between lord and vassal, which took its peculiar form from the old Teutonic institution of "companions";[2] (2) *the beneficium*, or the piece of land granted by one man to another in return for service, a practice that had both Roman and Teutonic models; and (3) *jurisdiction*, or the possession of governing power by the owner of a piece of land over all those dwelling on it, a connection of political authority with landholding which dates in some degree, perhaps, from the early Teutonic conquest,[3] and which the Carolingian counts helped to develop[4] in the ninth century by seizing upon their governments for hereditary fiefs. Moreover, the feudal system grew through the practice of *commendation*[5] (p. 27, n. 1), for which again both Roman and Teutonic history afforded precedents.

These antecedents, however, were not the *causes* of feudal organization: they were *materials* out of which men built a new social structure when the old one had collapsed. No doubt they in some measure determined the character of the structure, and they made its construction more rapid, when it had once begun; but it began because of the ninth century conditions we have described. Feudalism was *caused*, on the political side, by the breakdown of all other authority, and on the economic side, by the absence of money and by the difficulty of communication.[6]

B. Feudalism as a Completed Growth.

25. Feudal Theory often opposed to Feudal Practice. — Feudalism lasted in its vigor over four hundred years, — almost as long a time as has elapsed since its decay. Thus it was one of the most enduring institutions that western civilization has known. Rising out of anarchy, it kept many anarchic

---

[1] *Ancient History*, § 549.
[2] *Ancient History*, §§ 560, 561.
[3] *Ancient History*, § 611.
[4] *Ancient History*, § 645.

[5] This practice became so general that nearly all pieces of land which had been held as freeholds were converted into fiefs.

[6] Such conditions have produced feudal systems in other times and in other lands, as in ancient Egypt and in modern Japan; and no doubt in Europe they would have produced some kind of a feudal system, more slowly, without these earlier institutions just noted.

traits, and naturally it was one of the most complicated systems the world ever saw. Some writers, indeed, refuse to call it a *system* at all. At first the relations of the various classes differed widely in different localities, and each district fixed its own customs and law. To a great degree this remained true as long as feudalism lived at all; but gradually the kings' lawyers built up a theory, of beautiful simplicity, to which facts in some measure came to conform. This theory helped to undermine feudal independence in favor of royal power, but it also preserved some feudal institutions for future times.

26. Land Tenure and Social Classes. — In the feudal theory, *the holder of any piece of land was only a tenant of some higher landlord;* and, besides the clergy, there were two main classes of society, — the fighters, who were "noble," and the workers, who were ignoble. The king belonged to the fighting class and was the supreme landlord. He let out most of the land of the kingdom, on terms of military service, to great vassals. Each of these parceled out most of what he received, on like terms, to smaller vassals; and so on, perhaps through six or seven steps, *until the smallest division was reached that could support a mailed horseman for the noble's life of fighting.* Every such grant — a dukedom or a few acres — was a "fief"; and the grant *carried also the power of government over those dwelling on the land.*

Each noble kept some of his land in his own hands, to live upon. The king and the great lords kept vast amounts, usually scattered in many pieces; the smallest nobles necessarily kept all of theirs. This land was "domain" land. Every village and rising town was part of the domain of some noble, and every domain included at least one village of agricultural laborers. Part of a domain went to make holdings for the serfs and villeins, from which they might raise their own subsistence, and the rest was tilled by them for the lord directly, under the management of his bailiff.[1] These workers

---

[1] The necessity of making use of the produce on the spot where it was raised, explains partly why kings and great lords in this age were always

had no power of government, but only the privilege of being governed.

Thus the theory suggests a symmetrical hierarchy, which might be diagrammed on a blackboard. In practice there was no such regularity. Many of the smallest vassals held their land directly of the king or of the greatest lords, — not of a lord just above them in importance, — and the holdings and obligations differed in all conceivable ways. Often, great lords held part of their lands from smaller ones, and even kings were vassals for part of their kingdoms, — perhaps to vassals of their own. Thus the various grades were interlocked.[1] There were many holders, even small ones, without a lord at all, until the convenient maxim of the lawyers — "no land without a lord" — finally reduced them to tenants of the king, at least; and as the king had all he could do to look after his great vassals, the small ones were still left pretty much to themselves.

Except for the smallest knights, all these landlords of the fighting class were "suzerains"; and, except perhaps the king, all were vassals. There was no great social distinction between the lord and his vassals: vassal and lord lived commonly on terms of familiarity and mutual respect. The vassal was always a "noble," and his service was always "honorable." It included other matters than fighting (§§ 28–30), but it must never be

---

moving from one of their castles to another during the year. It was easier for the court to go to the produce than to bring the produce to the court.

[1] See Robinson's *Western Europe*, 113–115, for a striking illustration of such complexity. The Count of Champagne in the thirteenth century was lord of twenty-six castles, each the center of a separate fief. Most of these fiefs the count held of the French king, but for others of them he was vassal to the Duke of Burgundy, to the Archbishop of Rheims, to the Archbishop of Sens, to four neighboring bishops, and to the abbot of the monastery of St. Dennis. Says Dr. Robinson: "To all these persons the count had pledged himself to be faithful and true, and when his various lords fell out with one another, it must have been difficult to see where his duty lay." The count had divided his land among some two thousand knights: many of his vassals, however, held lands also of other lords, — in some cases of some of the liege lords of the count himself. The student will find it interesting to read Dr. Robinson's full statement, and to note his valuable map and diagram.

confounded with the "ignoble" service paid by serfs and villeins, upon whom rested this society of feudal fighters.

In the ninth century, fiefs became hereditary. For three hundred years more, a man from the lower ranks sometimes received a fief as a reward for his services, and so became a noble; but in the twelfth century nobility became strictly hereditary. In order the more easily to secure the services due them, the lords objected to a vassal's dividing a fief among his sons: thus became established the practice of "primogeniture," or inheritance of landed property by the eldest son only. But on the continent all the sons of a noble kept their nobility, even if they were landless; and (unless they entered the clergy) it became their aim to win lands, by serving some great lord who might have fiefs to bestow.

In England, the term "noble" had a much narrower meaning: it applied only to the greatest lords, and to their eldest sons after them. *The whole "gentry" class in England would have been nobles on the continent.* (Cf. § 136.)

27. The Feudal Contract. — In theory the relations between lord and vassal were regulated *by bargain,* for mutual advantage. The receiving of a fief was accompanied by the solemn ceremony of *homage.* The future vassal, with head uncovered and sword ungirt, knelt before the lord, placing his folded hands between the lord's hands, and swore to be the lord's "man";[1] he took also an oath of *fealty,* and promised to perform many specific obligations. The lord raised the vassal from his knees, gave him the "kiss of peace," *invested* him with the fief, — usually by presenting him with a sword or a clod of earth as a symbol, — and promised to *defend* him in it.[2]

Very commonly the exact terms of the original contract were not preserved, and then the obligations had to be regulated by custom or by the decisions of other vassals in the lord's court (§ 29) or by appeal to the sword. Indeed, such quarrels were the chief cause of the incessant "private wars" of the period (§ 33).

---

[1] Latin, *homo;* whence the term homage.
[2] For forms and contemporary accounts, see *Pennsylvania Reprints*, IV, No. 3. Some of the contracts were exceedingly fantastic. Perhaps the most remarkable one on record is given in Robinson's *Western Europe*, 110, note.

The most important duties of the vassals may be classed under three heads, — military service, court service, and payment of financial aids (§§ 28–30).

28. Military Service of the Vassal.[1] — The vassal was to present himself, at the call of his lord, to serve in war. Perhaps he was to come alone or with a single squire, or perhaps he was to bring an army of knights and men-at-arms, — according to the size of his fief and the terms of his holding. For neighborhood service he might be required to call out even his serfs. He could be compelled to serve only a fixed time each year, — commonly forty days, — but for that time he was to maintain himself and his men. If he remained in the field longer, it was of his free consent, and the lord assumed the maintenance.

The short term of service made the feudal army of little use for distant expeditions; and indeed vassals were sometimes not under obligation to follow their lord out of the realm. The absence of general organization, too, and of all discipline except that of a lord over his immediate followers, made the feudal array an unwieldy and uncertain instrument for offensive warfare.

DANCERS, as represented in an English manuscript of the thirteenth century. — From Lacroix, *Moeurs, Usages*, etc.

29. Court Service of the Vassal. — The vassal was bound to serve also in the lord's "court," usually at three fixed periods each year. As judicial bodies, these courts gave judgment in legal disputes between vassals; and as councils, they advised the lords in all important matters. A vassal, accused even by his lord, could be condemned only by this judgment of his peers (*pares*), or equals. The lord was only the presiding officer, not the judge.

---

[1] For contemporary descriptions and for forms of summons, see *Pennsylvania Reprints*, IV, No. 3, and Jones, *Source Extracts*, 74–85.

The second office of the court, however, was even more important: the lord could not count upon support in any serious undertaking unless he had first secured the approval of his council: in feudal language, the council "advised and consented."[1]

Moreover, in deciding the force of local custom and in sanctioning new regulations, these bodies came nearer being legislatures than did any other institution in that age. Thus the "feudal court" had a share in all three functions of government, — administrative, legislative, and judicial.[2]

30. Financial Obligations of the Vassal. — The vassal was called upon also for financial assistance, but his contributions were made only upon special or unusual occasions, and were not looked upon as "taxes." Upon receiving a fief, either as a gift or as an inheritance, he paid the lord a sum of money.[3] In theory this was a present, in exchange for the more valuable present from the lord: it was called a *relief,* and commonly it amounted to a year's revenue. If the vassal wished to sell or to give his fief to another, he was obliged to pay a *fine upon alienation.* Upon other occasions he made payments known as *aids:* the three most common purposes were to ransom the lord, if a prisoner, and to help meet the expense of knighting the lord's eldest son and of the marriage of his eldest daughter. Similar to such payments, but more oppressive, was the obligation *to entertain the lord and all his following* upon a visit.

A Court Fool; after a medieval miniature in brilliant colors. Many great lords kept such jesters.

---

[1] This expression, through English practice, has come down into our constitution: our President is empowered to do certain things "with the advice and consent" of the senate.

[2] These functions were not at all clearly distinguished until much later.

[3] The payment of this sum by the son of a deceased vassal was a recognition of the fact that in theory the fief had been granted only for the life of the previous holder and that it had reverted to the higher lord.

These four — reliefs, alienation-fines, the various aids, and entertainment — cover the payments made by an actual vassal in possession; but the lord had other claims upon the fief, which under certain circumstances might produce revenue. (1) He assumed the *guardianship of a minor heir*, and took to himself the revenues of the fief at such times, on the ground that there was no holder to render the service for which it had been granted. (2) He claimed the right *to dispose of a female ward in marriage*, — so as to secure for her a husband who should be a satisfactory vassal, — and then commonly he sold to the woman the right to marry without interference. Sometimes to extort a huge sum he presented a hateful suitor.[1] (3) In the absence of heirs, the fief returned (*escheated*) to the lord; and (4) if the vassal's duties were not performed, it might come back to him by *forfeiture*. In general, however, all these latter rights — except the control over marriage — became so limited by custom that they were of little consequence.

31. Obligations of the Lord. — By way of obligation toward a vassal, the lord was bound to defend him against attack, to treat him justly, and to see that he obtained justice from the co-vassals. The lord could not withdraw a fief, so long as the vassal was true to his bargain; and the vassal could hold the lord to the performance of *his* duties, or at least could try to do so, by appealing to the court of the lord's lord.

32. Extension of Feudal Tenure beyond Land; the Church Feudalized. — Feudalism dominated all the relations of man with man; and other things than land were given and held as hereditary fiefs, — the great offices of the kingdom, the right to fish in a stream, or to cut wood in a forest. Even the church became feudalized. A monastery or a cathedral drew its revenues largely from its serfs and villeins and from the church lands cultivated by them; and it provided for its defense by giving other lands to nobles on terms of military service. Thus bishops and abbots became suzerains, and they were also always vassals of some other lord.

---

[1] The *Pennsylvania Reprints* (IV, No. 3) contains extracts like the following from the English royal accounts: "Hawissa, who was wife to William Fitz-Roberts, renders 130 marks and 4 palfreys, that she may have peace from Peter of Borough, to whom the king has given permission to marry her, and that she may not be compelled to marry."

33. Violence of the Feudal Age. — Feudal *theory* paid elaborate regard to *rights,* but feudal *practice* was mainly a matter of *force.* There was no adequate machinery for obtaining justice; it was not easy to enforce the decisions of the crude courts against any offender who might choose to resist; and the natural thing seemed to be for any one who felt himself injured to take the law into his own hands. The spirit of the times, too, regarded war as the most honorable and perhaps as the most religious way to settle disputes; and, for the slightest causes, great or petty lords went to war with each other. These "private wars" became a chief evil of the age. They hindered the growth of industry, and commonly they hurt neutral parties quite as much as the actual participants. In the eleventh century the church, unable to stop such strife, tried to regulate it by proclaiming the "Truce of God," which forbade private war between Wednesday evening and the following Monday morning of each week and during the church festivals[1]; but it was long before this truce was generally observed.

34. The Substratum of Workers.[2] — The "upper classes" comprised the clergy and the nobles, — the "praying class" and the "fighting class." *These made up feudal society proper;* but they were fed and clothed by an immensely larger number of workers. The workers, whether legally free or servile, did not count in politics and not much in war, and they are hardly referred to in the records of the time except as cattle might be mentioned. They had few rights and many duties. Labor was almost wholly agricultural, and was performed, mainly, by serfs and villeins.

The serf was bound to the soil by law: he could not leave it, but neither could he be sold apart from it. He had his own bit of ground to cultivate, at such times as the lord's bailiff did not call him to labor on the lord's land. To be sure, he had to

---

[1] See *Pennsylvania Reprints,* I, No. 2, for such a proclamation, by the Archbishop of Cologne in 1083.

[2] Cf. § 36, note. The best short treatments are Emerton's *Medieval Europe,* 509–520, and Adams' *Growth of the French Nation,* 64–68.

pay for the use of his land a large part of its produce, and he was compelled to pay a multitude of other dues and fines; but if he succeeded in saving anything above a bare subsistence, it was usually left to him: so that there were some serfs with property,[1] although in theory all that they had was their lord's.

A step above the serf was the villein.[2] The villein was free in person: he could leave his land and go from one lord to another, if he found it to his advantage to do so. As a matter of fact, such changes were not very common; and in any case the villein must have some master, *for the landless and masterless man was an outlaw, at the mercy of any lord*. Practically, the most important distinction between villein and serf was that the villein's land was subject only to *fixed and certain* charges, not to arbitrary exactions. These definite charges, however, were almost as oppressive as the uncertain charges upon the serf's land, because they were usually so fixed as to leave the villein only the bare necessities of life.[3]

35. The Better Side of Serfdom. — We are too likely to think of the feudal age as one which degraded the laboring class from a higher standard. This is not the whole truth. It is true, that, in the violence of the

---

[1] Somewhat as there were some slaves with property in our South, in the days of slavery.

[2] There were many grades of service and of rights, sometimes even on the same domain; and serfdom and villeinage ran into each other in a most confusing manner, so that the two are often referred to under either name: but the broad distinction noted in the text is a convenient one to keep in mind. A difficult matter for the student to comprehend is, that the distinction applied primarily to *land* rather than to *persons:* some land was serf-land, and all who held it were serfs, or in danger of becoming serfs; while other land was villein-land, and if a serf was given a piece of it he rose into the position of villein.

[3] Cf. §§ 21–23. See also an excellent brief account in Emerton's *Medieval Europe*, 517–518, and a longer one in Cheyney's *Industrial and Social History*, 39–44. "The obligations of the villein toward his lord were either rents in kind, as provisions, grain, cattle, or poultry, products of the land and farm; or labor or services of the body, the *corvées* in the fields and vineyards of the lord, the building of the castle or cleansing of the moat, the repair of roads, the making of furniture, utensils, horse-shoes, plowshares, carriages, etc." — DURUY, *Middle Ages*, 210.

times, many men who had been free were thrust down into serfdom; but all slaves soon *rose* into serfdom, and, on the whole, despite its miseries, that institution was a step onward from the slave organization of labor in ancient times toward the modern free organization.[1] Moreover, there were two special conditions which helped to make the position of the serfs tolerable. (1) Population was scanty, all through feudal times, and landlords felt the need of more laborers: therefore, to keep his servants from running off to another lord, a wise master gave them good treatment, as ideas of good treatment went at that time. (2) Custom made law; and if a master allowed a serf to pay the same service, and no other, year after year, finally he lost the right to call for other service, and the serf had insensibly become a villein, with service *fixed* by custom. In this and other ways, in many parts of Europe, the serfs rose out of serfdom during the later part of the Middle Ages.

36. Life in the Village.[2] — To picture even roughly the life of the non-noble classes is not easy. There were few towns until the twelfth century, and, aside from the retainers of the nobles in the castles, most of the population dwelt in agricultural villages. The farmhouses were not scattered, each in its own field: they were grouped in villages of twenty or fifty dwellings. Each village had its church and usually its manor house. The latter might be a castle, or it might be little better than the homes of the peasants and be used only by the lord's steward. The other dwellings — low, filthy, thatch

ANCIENT MANOR HOUSE, Melichope, England; in its present condition. — From Wright's *Homes of Other Days*.

---

[1] *Ancient History*, § 549.

[2] The most graphic treatments of peasant life are in Jessopp's *Friars*, 87–112; Jenks' *Edward Plantagenet*, 46–52; and in Cheyney's *Industrial and Social History*, 31–52. Of the last, read especially 31–40 and 50–52. There is also a good treatment in Ashley's *Economic History*, I, 10–43. Special report: a comparison of a medieval village in Western Europe with a Russian "Mir"

or sod-roofed, one-room hovels, without chimney or window — straggled along either side of an irregular lane, where poultry and children played in the dirt. Attached to each house was its patch of vegetable garden, and its low stable and barn, — these last often under the same roof as the living-room. Each village had its smithy, and somewhere near, on a convenient stream, was the lord's mill. About the village lay its tracts of land, reaching away until bounded by the lands of other villages or by the waste.[1]

A rude rotation of crops was practised. The plowland was divided into three great "fields": one of these was sown to wheat (in the fall), one to barley (in the spring), while the other lay fallow to recuperate. Each field was divided into a great number of narrow strips, each as nearly as possible a "furrow-long," and one, two, or four rods wide; so that each contained from a quarter of an acre to an acre. Usually the strips were separated by "balks," or ridges of turf. A peasant's holding was about thirty acres, ten acres in each "field"; and his share in each lay not in one piece, but in fifteen or thirty scattered strips. The lord's land, probably half the whole, lay in strips like the rest, and was managed by his steward.

Of course this kind of holding compelled a common cultivation: each man must sow what his neighbor sowed; and as a rule, each could sow, till, and harvest only when his neighbors did. Agriculture was extremely crude. Only six or eight bushels of wheat or rye were expected from an acre. Walter

INTERIOR VIEW OF THE UPPER WINDOW SHOWN IN MELICHOPE MANOR HOUSE. This view shows the depth of the wall, — into which, indeed, the stairway is cut.

(village) of to-day, as described in Wallace's *Russia*, or in Leroy-Beaulieu's *Tsars and Russians*.

[1] Cf. Gibbins' *Industrial History of England*, 21, for a suggestive diagram of such a village and its lands.

of Henley, a thirteenth century writer on agriculture, says that threefold the seed was an average harvest, and that often a man was lucky to get back his seed corn and as much again. The breed of all farm animals was small. The plow required eight oxen. Carts were few and cumbrous. The distance to the outlying parts of the fields added to the labor of the villagers. There was little or no cultivation of root foods:

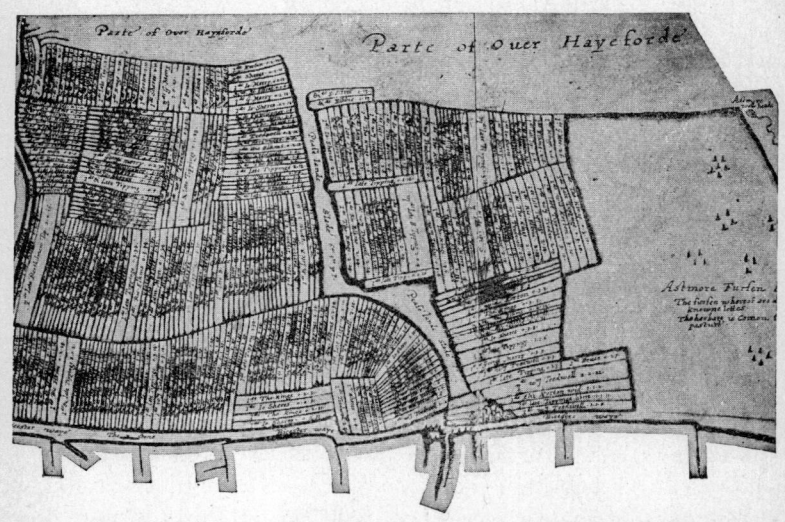

ONE OF THE OPEN FIELDS OF THE MANOR OF LOWER HEYFORD, OXFORDSHIRE. This manor now belongs to Corpus Christi College, Oxford. — From Andrews' *History of England*.

potatoes, of course, were unknown; sometimes a few turnips and cabbages and carrots, rather uneatable varieties probably, were grown in garden plots behind the houses. In the "fields," wheat and rye were raised as breadstuffs, barley for the brewing of beer, and sometimes peas and beans, commonly for fodder.

The most important crop was the wild hay, upon which the cattle had to be fed during the winter. Meadowland was twice as valuable as plowland. The meadow was fenced for the hay harvest, but was afterward thrown open for pasture; and usually there was other extensive pasture and wood land, where lord and villagers fattened their cattle and swine. It was difficult to carry enough animals through the winter for the necessary farm work and breeding; those to be used for food were killed in the fall and salted down. The large use of salt meat (the only meat for half the year) and the little variety in food were in part the causes of loathsome diseases among

A REAPER'S CART GOING UPHILL. — After Jusserand's *English Wayfaring Life*; from a fourteenth century manuscript. Note the force of men and horses necessary. The steepness of the hill is, of course, exaggerated, so as to fit the picture to the space in the manuscript.

the people. The chief luxury of the poor was honey; and well-to-do peasants often had a hive of bees in their garden plot.

Each village was a world by itself. Several villages might belong to one lord, but they had little more intercourse with each other on that account. The lord's bailiff secured from some distant market the three outside products needed, — salt, millstones, and iron for the plowshares and for other tools. Except for this, a village carried on its primitive system of industry in complete isolation, — unless a war desolated it, or a royal procession chanced to pass through it. Commonly in the ninth century it had not even a shop. The women of each household wove rough cloth for the single garment that covered them; and the men prepared leather for their own heavier clothing.

This shut-in life was unwholesome and stupefying and morally degrading. Measured by our standards, it was often indescribably ferocious, indecent, and cheerless. Certainly it was worse than anything the worst slums of our modern cities can show; but probably it was a great step up from the average condition of the laboring (slave) population of earlier ages.

37. Life in the Castle: Chivalry.[1] — Many stories give us some picture of the life of the noble classes. We know that they dwelt in gloomy fortresses over dark dungeons where prisoners rotted, and that they had fighting for business, and hunting with hound and hawk and playing at fighting for pleasures. We can see the ladies busied over tapestries and embroideries, in the chambers; gay pages flit through the halls, or play at chess in the deep windows; and in the courtyard lounge gruff men-at-arms, ready with blind obedience to follow the lord of the castle on any foray or even in an attack upon their king.

This grim life had its romantic and gentle side, indicated to us by the name *chivalry*. The term at first meant the nobles on horseback (from the French *cheval*, horse), but it came to stand for the whole institution of "knighthood," with all its ideals. Chivalry has been called the "flower of feudalism." It did not reach formal development until the twelfth century, but it can best be treated here.

Each feudal lord of consequence was surrounded by a social court (not to be confused with the legal "court," or council, § 29), where his leading vassals often attended. In this court, as in a school, the sons of his vassals were brought up and trained, under the lord's eye, in all the duties of a fearless and blameless knight. This education had two stages. Until about fourteen the boy was known as a *page;* and, aside from the train-

---

[1] Good treatments are given in Henderson's *Short History of Germany*, I, 112–121, or in Stillé's *Studies*, 346–352. Longer accounts may be found in Cutts' *Scenes and Characters of the Middle Ages*, 311–460, and in the histories of Chivalry by James, Mills, and Cornish.

ing in the use of light arms, his attendance was paid mainly to the mistress of the castle, by whom he was taught obedience and courtesy and a knight's duty to religion and to the ladies. Later, the page became a *squire* to the lord, serving about his person, arming him for the field, and accompanying him to battle, with special care for his safety.

FALCONRY. — From a medieval manuscript reproduced in Lacroix, *Moeurs, Usages*, etc.

After five or six years of such service, the squire was ready to become a *knight*. Admission to this order was a matter of imposing and symbolic ceremonial. The youth fasted and confessed his sins, and then spent a night in the chapel in prayer and vigil over his arms. The next day, after listening to a sermon upon the duties of knighthood, he appeared before his lord, and, kneeling, took the vows to be a brave and gentle knight, to defend the church, to protect the ladies, to be faithful to his fellows, and to succor the distressed, especially widows and orphans. The ladies of the castle then buckled on the golden spurs, and the lord struck him lightly over the shoulder with the flat of his sword, pronouncing a formula, such as "In the name of God, of St. Michael, and of St. George, I make you knight."

Thus chivalry was the result of the church's trying to take possession of feudal society: it was an imperfect attempt to fuse the ideals of the Teutonic warrior and of the Christian. Its faults were twofold. (1) It was exclusive: its spirit was altogether a class spirit; it recognized no obligations except to nobles; even the vow to protect women did not apply to any women but those of gentle birth. (2) It carried some of its virtues (bravery and devotion to ladies) to such extremes as to make them fantastic, if not vicious. The ideals, too, were not always reached; and a perfect knight may have been no more common than is a perfect gentleman to-day. But chivalry did help to soften manners and to humanize society. Along with other feudal institutions, it developed a high sense of personal honor and of personal independence, and, at the same time, of personal loyalty to a lord; it elevated women; and it had much to do with creating the modern home and our ideal of a gentleman.[1]

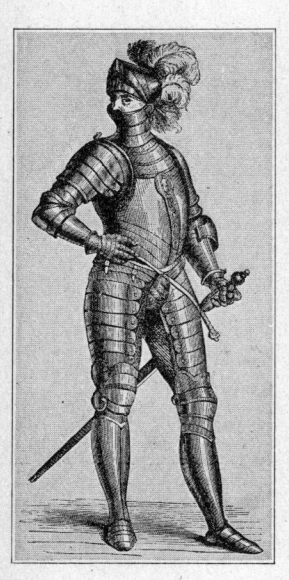

KNIGHT IN ARMOR, visor up. — From Lacroix, *Vie Militaire*.

---

[1] Toward the year 1400, when chivalry was decaying, Chaucer gives this picture of his typical knight: —

> "A knight there was, and that a worthy man,
> That fro the time that he first began
> To riden out, he lovéd chivalry,
> Truth and honor, freedom and courtesy. . . .

38. The Men of Religion in the Feudal Age. — The two contradictory ideals of the feudal age were those of the knight and of the monk. The village priest was a peasant in origin, and usually remained essentially a peasant in his life, marrying in the village (until the eleventh century) and oftentimes working in the fields with his neighbors. He was a peasant with a somewhat better income than his fellows, with a little learning and a revered position, and with great power for good.[1] In corresponding manner, the great ecclesiastics — bishops and archbishops — were essentially of the noble class, both in origin and in manner of life, fitting in all respects into the feudal framework. But the monks[2] were a distinct

MONKS BUSY IN FIELD LABOR. — From Lacroix, after a thirteenth century French manuscript.

> And tho that he was worthy, he was wise,
> And of his port as meek as is a maid.
> And never yet no villainy he said
> In all his life, unto no manner wight.
> He was a very perfect, gentle knight."

About seventy years later, in Malory's *King Arthur*, another beautiful ideal is pictured. When Sir Ector found Sir Lancelot dead, — " He fell down in a swoon . . . and when he waked it were hard for any tongue to tell the dolefull complaints that he made. 'Ah, Lancelot,' he said, . . . 'thou wert the courteoust knight that ever bore shield; and thou wert the truest friend to thy lover that ever bestrode horse; and thou wert the truest lover among sinful men that ever loved woman; and thou wert the kindest man that ever struck with sword; and thou wert the goodliest person that ever came among the press of knights; and thou wert the meekest man and the gentlest that ever ate in hall among ladies; and thou wert the sternest knight to thy mortel foe that ever put spear in rest.' "

[1] Cf. § 72 for a fuller statement regarding the non-monastic clergy. The best treatment of the priest is Cutts' *Parish Priests and their People*.

[2] Monasteries are treated briefly in the *Ancient History*, §§ 602-605. For monastic life, cf. Jessop's *Coming of the Friars*, ch. iii.

class. They sought to escape the anarchy and the violence of the world about them, and in their quiet retreat they lived religious lives of industry and prayer. To other men in those evil days, their temperance, abstinence, and self-sacrifice seemed more than human; and their saintly reputation long defended them, even when corruption for a time had crept in among them. For centuries they deserved this reverence. The thousands of monasteries that dotted Europe were the chief centers of industry, peace, and religion, and the sole refuge of learning.[1] From them came most of the great religious revivals of the Middle Ages.[2]

39. Cautions for the Student. — To avoid common misconceptions regarding feudalism, it is well to fix in mind the following points: —
  (1) The kings kept their old authority *in theory*, and therefore were always something more than great feudal lords, though the difference was vague.
  (2) "Vassal" never means serf: a vassal was free and noble, though he was, by bargain, the "man" of some "lord."
  (3) Strictly speaking, feudal society contained *only* suzerains and vassals, though these classes made up but a small part of the population.
  (4) Serfs and villeins were not part of the feudal system: that is, their relations to their masters were not feudal relations, in strict language. But some such classes were necessary to the existence of the feudal classes above them.
  (5) Feudalism did not create serfs, to begin with, but it did thrust down into the position of serfs and villeins many men who had formerly been free.
  (6) In feudal times, society was always more complex and less symmetrical than would seem from any single account.

40. Extracts from Joinville's Memoir of St. Louis, to show the Moral Ideas of the Best Lay Society about 1300.

[The book was dedicated to the son of the ruling king, a great grandson of St. Louis.] "And because I see no one who ought to have it

---

[1] Special report: the monasteries and learning (see especially Putnam's *Books and their Makers in the Middle Ages*, ch. i.). Munro's *Middle Ages*, 127, gives a map of monasteries in France, which the student should see.
[2] Cf. §§ 59, 66, 72 close, and footnote 2.

so rightly as you who are his heir, I send it to you, that you and your brothers and others who may hear it read, may take good example from it and put these examples in practice, that God may be pleased with you. ... The memory of the great king is a great honor to all his lineage who would resemble him in doing good and who seek to imitate him, but great dishonor to those of his blood who elect to do evil; for the people will point the finger at them and say that the sainted king from whom they are descended would never have consented to such evil actions. ... The saint [Louis was canonized about thirty years after his death] loved truth to such a degree that even with the Saracens he would not draw back from what he had promised. As to his palate he was so indifferent that never did I hear him ask for any particular dish, as many men do, but he ate contentedly of whatever was served up to him. He was measured in his speech. Never in my life did I hear him speak ill of any one; nor did I ever hear him name the Devil, — a name widely spread in this realm; and it is a great disgrace to the kingdom of France, and to the king when he suffers it, that one can hardly speak without saying 'the Devil take it' and it is a great sin to devote to the Devil a man given to God from the moment that he is baptized. In the Joinville household, whoso utters such a word receives a box on the ears or a slap on the mouth, and bad language is almost wholly suppressed. ... He asked me once whether I wished to be honored and enter Paradise through death? Keep yourself then from doing or saying aught which, if all the world knew, you could not avow and say, 'I did this,' 'I said that.' He told me to refrain from contradicting anything said in my presence, providing there was no sin in remaining silent, because hard words engender strife. ... He used to say that a man should so equip his person that the grey-beards of the day should not be able to say that it was over done; nor the young men that there was anything wanting. After the king's return from over the sea, he lived so devoutly that he never wore furs of different colors, or scarlet cloth, or gilt stirups or spurs. I was reminded of this by the father of the king who now reigns [Philip the Hardy] alluding once to the embroidered coats of arms fashionable now-a-days. I made answer to him that never in the voyage over the sea did I see embroidered coats ... and that he would have done better to have given the money to the poor and to have worn plain clothes as his father used to do."

[Joinville gives also this extract from Louis' deathbed testament to his son.] "Fair son, the first thing that I teach thee is to mould thy heart to love God. If God send thee adversity, accept it patiently, and render thanks, and know that thou hast deserved it. If he send thee prosperity, thank him humbly, that thou be not worse through pride. Bear thyself so that thy confessor and friends may venture to reprove thee for thy misdeeds. Attend devoutly to the service of Holy Church both with mouth and mind. Let thy heart be gentle and compassionate toward the poor and the afflicted, and comfort them so far as in thee lies. Help the right and uphold the poor man until the truth be made manifest [*i.e.* while the case is undecided]. Bestow the benefices of the church upon men of unspotted lives. Wage no war with any Christian prince, except it be necessary after grave deliberation. Be careful to have good provosts and bailiffs, and make frequent inquiries about them, and about all thy servants as to how they conduct themselves, and whether they are guilty of overmuch greed and deceit. . . . Fair dear son, I bestow upon thee all the benediction a good father can give a good son. And may the blessed Trinity preserve and defend thee from all evil, and give thee grace to do the will of God."

FOR FURTHER READING. — Excellent "source" material will be found in *Pennsylvania Reprints*, IV, No. 3, and in Jones' *Source Extracts*, both of which have been referred to in the notes. These volumes should be used exhaustively for feudalism. The student should also know Froissart (fourteenth century), — at least in Lanier's charming volume, *The Boys' Froissart*, — and Joinville's *Memoir of St. Louis* (thirteenth century). For modern accounts, the best statements are those in Adams' *Civilization* and his *Growth of the French Nation*, and in Emerton's *Medieval Europe*. Advanced students will find an admirable treatment in Seignobos' *Feudal Régime*. There is a vast literature on the subject of feudalism; but the older accounts, such as those of Hallam, Robertson, and Guizot, are more or less untrustworthy, especially regarding the rise of the institution. For special features, — chivalry, village life, etc. — see footnote references to §§ 21, 36–38. Historical fiction upon the feudal period is particularly valuable: Scott's novels, of course, must not be overlooked, although they give a false glamor to the age, and perhaps they should be corrected by "Mark Twain's" scathing treatment in his *Connecticut Yankee in King Arthur's Court*. Other excellent portraits are given in Robert Louis Stevenson's *Black Arrow* and Conan Doyle's *White Company*. Charlotte Yonge's *Little Duke* and Stockton's *Story of Viteau* are good for younger students and will be enjoyed by older ones. Martineau's *Prince and Peasant* pictures the abuses of feudalism at a later period.

SPECIAL REPORTS. — 1. The revolt of the Norman peasants in 997, and the way it was regarded by feudal society. (See a medieval account in Jones' *Source Extracts*, 87–88. This may well be made a class exercise instead of an individual topic.) 2. Tournaments. 3. The amuse-

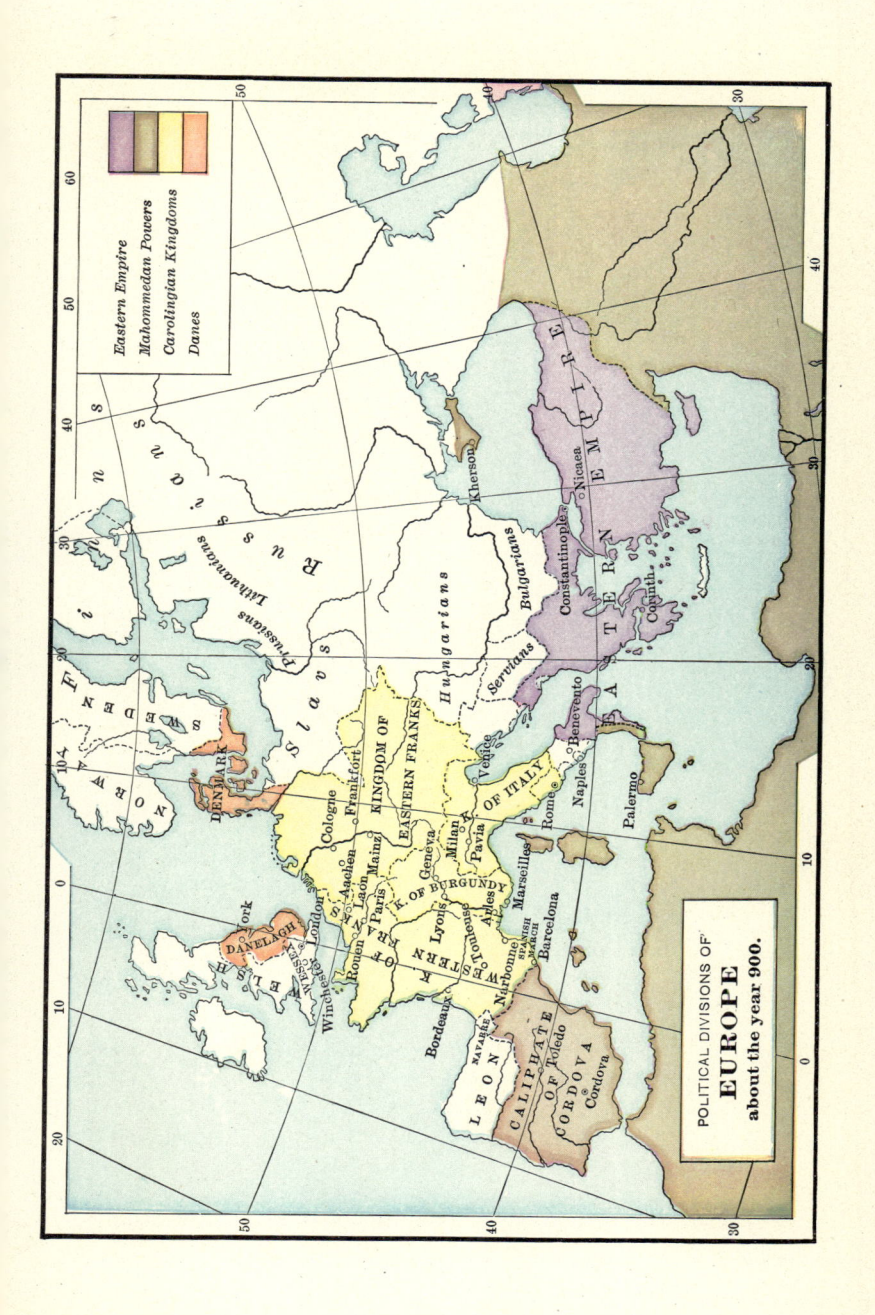

POLITICAL DIVISIONS OF
EUROPE
about the year 900.

ment of hunting in feudal times. 4. Life in a feudal castle. 5. Heraldry. 6. Armor. 7. Life in a monastery.

For the second, third, and fourth topics, material should be sought in the better historical novels dealing with the period. Students may also be called upon to find incidents in such literature illustrating the various paragraphs in the preceding treatment. For topic 7, see especially Jessopp's *Coming of the Friars*.

SUGGESTIONS FOR REVIEW UPON DIVISIONS I-III.

1. Let the class prepare review questions, each member five or ten. Criticise the questions, showing which ones help to bring out important facts and contrasts and likenesses, and which are merely trivial and curious.
2. Make lists of important names or terms for rapid drill, requiring brief but clear explanation of each term. The following terms are suitable: *suzerain* (liege), *vassal, serf, villein, Lotharingia, Romance language, Oath of Strasburg, Magyars, Rolf the Dane, feudal aids*. This number may be increased threefold. Let the class preserve such lists for future reviews.

IV. FRANCE FROM VERDUN TO THE TWELFTH CENTURY.

A. RISE OF A NATIVE DYNASTY.

41. The Last Carolingians and the Dukes of France. — By the Treaty of Verdun (§ 8), Charles the Bald, a grandson of Charlemagne, became King of the West Franks (843–877). His reign—the longest of any of his race after Charlemagne — was concerned only with wars against his brothers, nephews, and grand-nephews, in the kingdoms about him, and with the ravages of the Norse pirates. Three feeble successors [1] held the throne for seven disastrous years. Then the nobles of France passed over the only survivor of this branch of the Carolingians, a boy of five years, to be known later as Charles the Simple,[2] and offered the crown to *Charles the Fat*, of the German branch. By the death of all competitors, Charles had already become Emperor and ruler of Germany and of most of the old Middle Kingdom; and so now for a moment nearly all of the Empire of Charlemagne was reunited. Charles, however, was a sluggish coward, incapable of decision or action, on account of disease and corpulence. In 887,

---

[1] Louis the Stammerer (877–879) and his two sons, joint rulers, Louis III (879–882) and Carlman (879–884).

[2] A third son of Louis the Stammerer.

he was deposed by a general revolt, and the dominions of the Carolingians fell apart upon the old lines of the Division of Verdun. *France was never again to be joined to the Empire.*

Then for a hundred years (887–987), the crown passed back and forth between the Carolingians and a new family who were finally to establish themselves firmly upon the throne.[1] In the universal despair of the preceding fifty years, the only successful leadership in the north of France against the Norse inroads had come from a hero of humble birth who became known as Robert the Strong.[2] Robert saved Paris from destruction, and extended his lands until they reached from the Seine to Orleans on the banks of the Loire. Somewhat later, this territory was known as the *Dukedom of Francia.* After Robert's death in battle against the Norsemen, his son *Odo* continued his policy. Odo became the most powerful nobleman in France, and was practically an independent sovereign.

By this time there had grown up similar great lordships all over the kingdom, — Flanders, Brittany, Poitou, Anjou, Gascony, Aquitaine, Toulouse, Burgundy, Champagne, Blois, — each ruled by its hereditary count or duke. On the deposition of Charles the Fat, the great nobles chose Odo king. *Odo was the first French*[3] *king of France.* His reign went to struggles with jealous rivals and to beating off the Northmen. At his death he named as his successor *Charles the Simple* (§ 41), the heir of the Carolingians. After more changes back and forth, the direct Carolingian line ran out (987), and *Hugh Capet*,[4] a grand-nephew of Odo, was chosen king by a council of nobles and clergy.

---

[1] The alternations were as follows: —

Old line: Charles the Fat, 884–887 ; deposed.
New line: Odo, 887–898.
Old line: Charles the Simple, 898–922 ; died in prison, 929.
New line: Robert, 922–923 ; (Rudolph of Burgundy, 923–936).
Old line: Louis IV, 936–954 ; Lothair, 954–986; Louis V, 986–987.
New line: Hugh Capet, elected in 987.

[2] According to one story, he was descended from a Parisian butcher; a more probable account makes him a descendant of one of the Saxons whom Charlemagne had removed from their homes to the heart of Gaul.

[3] The Carolingians had been Germans (*Ancient History*, § 636, note). The line ruling in Gaul had, however, become partly French, and perhaps the chief importance in the change of dynasty lay in getting rid, in France, of the Carolingian imperial *tradition.*

[4] Hugh's surname came from his custom of wearing an abbot's cope, or cape: he was a "lay abbot."

B. Conditions confronting the Early Capetians

42. The "Feudal Kingship" of the First Capetians.[1] — Hugh Capet was crowned, not as "King of France," but as "King of the Gauls, Bretons, Danes, Normans, Aquitanians, Goths, Spaniards, and Gascons." This title shows something of the composite nature, at that date, of the realm we call France. In later times, French kingship was to become the type of absolute and centralized government (§ 264), and it is this kind of kingship that comes naturally before our minds when we speak of even the early French kings; so it is hard for us to get a clear idea of the difficulties before the first Capetians. The election of Hugh did not increase his actual power. It did increase his duties and his claims to power; but his resources for performing those duties and enforcing those claims rested almost solely at first on his old possessions as Duke of Francia. Several of the great princes ruling over the rest of France were each quite as powerful as the king. Hugh was now in theory their sovereign: but so far as they obeyed him at all, they obeyed him not as sovereign, but as suzerain; and this tie between the great vassals and the feudal king was precisely the least real of all the links in the whole chain of lords and vassals. France had no national machinery for government. In particular, there were three wants.

a. There was no system of French law, and there were no national courts. Each great fief was building up its own local law from its own customs; and the king's "court" was little more than a court for his vassals only, just as each vassal had a court for his own subjects (§ 29).

b. There was no national revenue, no general system of taxation. The king's income came from his own domain land (§ 26) and from the irregular feudal aids (§ 30).

c. There was no national militia. When the king needed an army, his forces came (1) from his own immediate feudal

---

[1] Read the admirable treatment in Adams' *Growth of the French Nation*, 55-59, from which this and the two following sections are condensed.

followers in his hereditary duchy, and (2) from such of his great vassals elsewhere as friendship might bring to his aid. Not till much later was the king able to compel the attendance of these princes: at first he was obliged to accept any excuse for staying away that they deigned to make.[1]

43. The Work before the Capetian Kings and Some Elements of Their Success. — The proper task for the Capetian kings was to make, from these composite, decentralized feudal fragments of a kingdom, a new French nation with a common language, common customs, and common patriotism. This work, after some centuries of constant effort, they were to accomplish. The chief forces and conditions that made for their success may be classed under four heads: —

a. The hereditary possessions, or private fortunes, of the dukes of Francia (§ 41).

b. The support of the church. That organization felt the need of a strong king to protect both itself and society at large against the violence of the greedy nobles; and in that age, when bishops and abbots were themselves feudal lords, the church could give not only moral support, but also important material aid.

c. The Roman idea of government. The Capetians refused to accept the theory of a merely feudal kingship: they used that theory when it suited their purposes, but, from the first, with elastic policy, they claimed also the rights of a centralized monarchy. This theory was based upon Roman ideas,[2] and it found ready support from the lawyers, when that class rose to importance in the eleventh and twelfth centuries.

d. The undisputed succession to the throne for many generations. The Capetians were to rule France for more than eight hundred years, or as long as France was to have kings at all. For a century the crown had been elective in practice, and no

---

[1] In all these respects, however, the Capetians were better off than the Carolingians had been, since the latter had had almost no feudal resources of their own.

[2] *Ancient History*, § 613.

doubt the Teutonic theory of an elective kingship had always survived. In Germany, election was soon to become the regular practice; but the election of Hugh Capet was the last such incident in French history. For three centuries each king left a son old enough, or nearly old enough, to assume the government; and in the absence of contending claims, the succession became strictly hereditary. The long line of able rulers held resolutely to one royal policy, and so the unbroken succession itself became a factor in their final victory.

44. The Early Reigns, to the Twelfth Century.[1] — The Capetian success, however, did not begin in earnest in the period treated in this chapter. The first three kings of the new dynasty, surrounded with difficulties as they were, hardly held their own. The fourth king, Philip I, ruled nearly fifty years, and prepared for the later advance by increasing the private domain of his house. In the early part of his reign occurred the conquest of England (§ 16) by the Duke of Normandy, a vassal of the French king; and in the latter part, the crusades began (§§ 92 ff.). These events were both to have a mighty influence upon the development of the French monarchy, but their results were not to show until a later period, when the consolidation of France had already made some progress (§§ 150-152).

V. GERMANY FROM VERDUN TO THE RESTORATION OF THE EMPIRE, 843-962.[2]

A. GERMANY AT THE CLOSE OF THE CAROLINGIAN PERIOD.

45. The Great "Stem Duchies." — With the break-up of the Carolingian state, the Germans, more plainly than before, appear divided into four great "stems," — Saxons, Franks, Suabians (Alemanni), and Bavarians.[3] Besides these the Lotharingians must be counted as a fifth German people,

---

[1] The reigns for this preliminary period were as follows: Hugh, 987-996; Robert, 996-1031; Henry I, 1031-1060; Philip I, 1060-1108. For earlier reigns, see §§ 6, 7, 41, note; for later reigns, see table, § 148.

[2] For the remaining century and a half of the period treated in Part I, Germany is a part of the Holy Roman Empire; see Divisions VI, VII, and VIII.

[3] Cf. map, facing page 63. Advanced students will find an excellent treatment of the "stems" in Fisher's *Medieval Empire*, I, 48-93.

though that duchy was for a while connected with the realm of France. Each of the five divisions rallied around a native duke, and, at times, seemed likely to become a distinct nation. The two most important stems were the German Franks (Franconians) and the Saxons. Since the time of Clovis, the Franks had been the dominant people; but now the more vigorous Saxons were to gain the leadership. Of all the German races the Saxons were the least touched by Roman culture and Roman ideas. The old paganism still lingered among the wild moors of their northern frontiers, and as a people they kept many primitive Teutonic customs.

46. The Proper Work of the German Kings, and some Hindrances to Success. — For many years after the Carolingians, Germany was to be a federation of great duchies, the duke of the strongest nation ranking over the others as king. The two proper tasks for the king were to unite these five German peoples and to beat off the heathen invaders.

In marked contrast with the Capetian line in France, the German royal families were all to die out after two or three generations; so that Germany, frequently compelled to choose a new line of rulers, preserved the old principle of election, which was so soon to disappear in France. This condition weakened the monarchy at critical periods. Moreover, a strong ruler was always tempted to try to secure also the fragments of the old Middle Kingdom and of Italy, on the west and south, and to revive the imperial dignity of Charlemagne. In these attempts, German kings were to dissipate energy needed for Germany itself.

B. Rise of Native Dynasties :[1] Historical Outline to 962.

47. The Change from Carolingian to Native Rulers: Conrad the Franconian. — On the deposition of Charles the Fat (§ 41), *Arnulf*, a German Carolingian, secured the throne; but in 911

---

[1] The Carolingian rulers of Germany from Verdun to the election of a new line were as follows: Lewis II (Lewis the German), 843-876 ; Lewis III

his line died out with his son, *Lewis the Child*. The German nobles then had at least enough national feeling to prevent them from turning to the French Carolingian, Charles the Simple (§ 41). Instead they elected *Conrad*, the Duke of Franconia. Conrad (911–919) tried in vain to crush the other dukes. Finally he came to see that his family was not powerful enough to unite Germany; and at his death, with true patriotism, he recommended for his successor the mightiest of his rivals, *Henry of Saxony*.

48. Henry I, 919–936 (the Saxon House). — Henry reversed Conrad's policy towards the dukes. He recognized them as necessary centers of power; he bound them to himself as friends and ruled through them, so that he sometimes appeared master of all Germany. He also added finally to his kingdom the fifth duchy, Lotharingia.

But the most important part of Henry's work was his successful defense of the realm against the Hungarians (§ 12). He first bought an interval for preparation, a nine years' truce, by payment of annual tribute, and he used the time to organize his military resources. At many important points near the frontier, he built strongholds.[1] A militia also was organized in the exposed districts, so that one man of nine might always be on guard in these forts, while the other eight tilled the land of their absent brother. Such fortified places not only afforded refuge for the countrymen when invasion came; they also made any invasion difficult. To reduce them was almost impossible, and for the invader to pass on, leaving them in his rear, was extremely hazardous. When his preparations were complete,

---

(the Young), 876–882; Charles the Fat, 882–887; Arnulf, 887–899; Lewis IV (the Child), 899–911.

[1] Henry ordered that all markets and festivals should be held within walled places, so as to make them centers of social life; and in later times many of these strongholds grew into great cities, giving to the King his most honorable surname, "the Builder of Cities." He was also called "Henry the Fowler," because the messenger from Conrad's brother with the news of the election to the throne had found him, falcon on wrist, at his favorite sport of hunting in the Harz mountains.

Henry refused to pay further tribute, and a new invasion by the Hungarians was decisively repulsed.

In 936, Henry was succeeded by his son Otto.

49. Otto I, 936-973: the Dukedoms united; the Barbarians conquered. — *Otto the Great* carried his father's work to completion in both its phases. At his coronation he required the four great dukes to serve him as marshal, steward, cup-bearer, and chamberlain; and the first years of his reign were spent in forcing upon these reluctant princes a real recognition of the royal authority. In this work, Otto turned to the clerical lords for help. The bishops and abbots, on their part, as in France (§ 43 *b*), favored a strong government and gladly threw their mighty influence on the royal side, while in return the king augmented their power and their lands. By 950, Otto had won. All the dukes had been reduced to obedience; indeed, for a time, they seemed no longer hereditary local rulers, but mere appointees of the king. Under Conrad, the dukes had been rivals and enemies; under Henry, friendly supporters, but still possible rivals; under Otto, they had become servants, and, at one time, after years of anxious conflict, all the great dukedoms were united in the King's own family.[1]

In protecting Germany from invasion, Otto was even more successful. While he had been busy with internal quarrels, the Hungarians had renewed their raids, and in 955 they poured into the country in greater force than ever before, — according to the chroniclers, numbering a hundred thousand horsemen. Augsburg, on the Lech river, detained them by holding out under its hero-bishop through a terrible siege, and Otto advanced hastily to the relief of the imperiled city. He set out with a small body of followers; but contingents from all Germany loyally joined him on the march, and Saxons, Franconians, Suabians, Bavarians, all took part in the deliverance of Germany, in the decisive *Battle of Lechfeld*. No quarter was

---

[1] The royal victory, however, was far less complete than at first seemed the case; and, for many generations the dukes proved centers of resistance to royal authority.

given in the long and terrible pursuit across the border. The Hungarians never again attacked Christendom: they settled in the valleys of the Theiss and Danube (where they still live) and soon adopted Christianity and entered the family of European nations (§§ 64 c, 65 a).

50. German Expansion to the East. — Otto followed up his success firmly and wisely. Year by year, the Slavs were forced farther back, and "*marches,*" or "marks," were established along the whole eastern frontier, under watchful commanders, to ward off attack.[1] The heathen barbarians were compelled to receive missionaries and to permit the building of monasteries that were to Christianize and civilize them. Private enterprise saw an opportunity; and German nobles, eager for land, began a great colonizing movement, which was soon to extend Germany on the east from the Elbe to the Oder and to carry German civilization and swarms of German colonists among the Slavs of the Baltic coasts. Otto pointed out the direction in which Germany should expand, and indeed began the movement which was finally to double the size of his country and to civilize even wider areas.[2] The prestige of Germany was firmly established among neighboring peoples: the warlike dukes of Bohemia and Poland and even the famous Harold Blue-Tooth, King of Denmark, recognized Otto as overlord. Best of all, the various peoples of Germany seemed for a time to have learned that safety and honor lay in national union under a strong king.

51. A New Course of Political Development for Germany: Otto and the Empire. — Thus, before 960, Otto had succeeded apparently (1) in consolidating Germany into the most powerful and best united state in Europe, (2) in warding off all

---

[1] At the extreme southeast was the East Mark (against the Hungarians), which was to grow into Austria; another of these marks was the beginning of the later Prussia. Cf. *Ancient History*, § 276 c and note, and see in this volume §§ 270 ff.

[2] Read Lavisse, *Political History of Europe*, 45-48. Cf. also in this volume §§ 64 c, 65 a, and maps following pages 70 and 130.

attack from without, and (3) in starting his countrymen upon a course of national expansion toward the barbarous east. He now felt strong enough to interfere in Italy and to restore the Empire. Two military expeditions across the Alps accomplished his design (§ 53) and opened a new chapter of history for both Germany and Italy.

For Further Reading. — Emerton, 90–114, or Tout, *Empire and Papacy*, 12–27.

VI. THE HOLY ROMAN EMPIRE OF THE GERMAN PEOPLE.

The Empire at its Height, Otto I to Henry III, 962–1056.

The history of the Empire is the key to the whole history of medieval Europe. — Freeman.

By a strange freak of fortune, the title and traditions of the Caesars pass to the latest barbarian arrival within the circle of the civilized nations of the west. — Herbert Fisher.

To men of that time, living amid the perpetual strife of small principalities, the vision of one universal Empire of law and right shone with an alluring brightness, which we, accustomed to a system of national governments and international relations, can hardly understand. — Freeman.[1]

A. Restoration and Character.

52. Otto's Motives for restoring the Empire. — For the sixty-three years between Arnulf's death and Otto's invasion of Italy, the Empire in the West had lapsed.[2] The idea, however, was still a vital force in Europe. Otto's father, the cool and practical Henry, is said to have dreamed grandly of its realization, and Otto's own more ardent spirit had long been fired by the vision of wider sway and of taking up again the imperial work of Charlemagne.

This aspiration was not mere vulgar ambition. In that age a ruler strong enough for the work could not but feel it his supreme duty to restore the Roman Empire, the symbol of univer-

---

[1] Cf. Freeman's "Holy Roman Empire" in the *First Series of Essays*, especially pages 126, 127, and 133.

[2] Except for the name Emperor, assumed from time to time by petty Italian princes.

sal order and peace. Otto, moreover, had another motive sternly practical: the Pope, he believed, had been trying to interfere with his control over the ecclesiastical lords of Germany, upon whose support the throne rested; and he thought it needful to be able to control that potentate.

53. The Occasion and the Restoration (962): Otto in Italy. — The condition of Italy furnished an excuse for German intervention. Like other states of the period, Italy was broken into fragments, and the disintegration there was so complete that no local dynasty could set up even the form of a national kingship. Colonies of Saracens had established themselves on the southern coasts, dividing that part of the peninsula with the Lombards and the Byzantine Empire; and central Italy was devastated by invasion, turbulence, and famine. Finally, in the incessant struggles between petty principalities, an imprisoned princess called for help to Otto, the hero of the North. Otto seized the opportunity. In a first expedition, he was crowned King of Italy, at Pavia, and he married the beautiful suppliant, Adelheid, whose adventures had shed romance on even the dark pages of Italian history in that age. In a second expedition, *in 962, Otto was consecrated Emperor by the Pope at Rome.*

Most of Otto's remaining years were spent in restoring order in Italy (§ 60). Ten years after the imperial coronation, his son was married to a Byzantine princess, and the glorious pomp and splendid ceremonial that celebrated this union of the two Christian empires gave the world a new sense of the power of the German state.

54. The Restoration Disastrous in the Future, but Natural and Beneficial at the Time. — The connection with Italy first really lifted Germany from its ancient barbarism and brought to it the culture and art of the older world. Modern German writers, however, sometimes blame Otto bitterly, claiming that his ambition caused needless woe to his country in future times. And it is true that Otto was the first of a long line of German kings, who, for three centuries, at intervals of a few years, led splendid German armies across the Alps, to melt away beneath the Italian sun, and that his policy influenced future German rulers often to neglect true German interests. For the whole duration of the Empire, German strength and German enterprise were frittered away in foreign squabbles, while the opportunity to make a permanent German state and to develop German national feeling was lost. Quite as serious were the results to Italy. A German king, however much he was "Roman emperor," could hardly enter Italy without a German army at his back, and the southern land became in practice a conquered province, ruled by foreigners whom the natives looked upon as uncouth northern barbarians.

It should be remembered, however, that what Otto did, any great and good king in his place would have tried to do. The action was natural, if not inevitable, and it was applauded at the time by the best men of both Germany and Italy. The very chaos of the age disposed men to dwell reverently upon the idea of universal peace and justice under the wise providence of a supreme ruler elevated above all temptation; and for centuries to come, many of the greatest and most generous spirits longed passionately for the realization of this idea in a universal empire. For this faith, four hundred years after Otto, Dante (§ 188) suffered life-long exile from his beloved Florence; and Petrarch, even later (§ 189), believed one imperial government for all the world as plain a necessity as is one head for the human body.[1] Nor was this feeling restricted to lonely thinkers: it permeated the masses also; and, before Otto's fateful journey into Italy, while he stood victor amidst the carnage of Lechfeld's glorious day, his conquering host with common impulse had hailed him "Emperor of the Romans."

Moreover, despite the evils of the distant future and some serious drawbacks from the beginning, the new policy was productive of much good. Whether the good balanced the evil, it is perhaps even now impossible to say. The restored Empire was to last more than eight hundred years, into the nineteenth century (§ 370). During the latter part of this long period, it was little more than a mockery; but for the first three hundred years it was a mighty agent in keeping down feudal anarchy, in helping to reform the church, in civilizing Germany, in extending the sway of Christian civilization over the barbarous Slavs, and in holding together Central Europe, — when very possibly no other power could have done these things so well.

---

[1] With reference to the breaking up of Christendom into separate states, Petrarch speaks of "the hideous portent of a creature of many heads biting and snapping at each other"; see a lengthy extract from Petrarch's *Letter to the Romans* in Bryce's *Holy Roman Empire*, 256. Dante wrote his *De Monarchia* to establish this same view of the necessity of one imperial rule. Cf. also the third theme sentence at the head of Division VI, page 60.

THE HOLY ROMAN EMPIRE
962 to 1000

55. The Nature of the Restored Empire. — After its restoration the Empire is known as "the Holy Roman Empire of the German People." Two new terms in this title are significant.

a. The new Empire was *Holy:*[1] it partook of the nature of the church, and its most serious problems — indeed, the question of its success — were to turn upon the relations between popes and emperors.

"The theory of the Medieval Empire is that of a universal Christian monarchy. The Roman Empire and the Catholic Church are two aspects of one society, a society ordained by the Divine Will to spread itself over the whole world. At the head of this society in its temporal character, as an empire, stands the temporal chief of Christendom, the Roman Caesar. At its head in its spiritual character, as a church, stands the spiritual chief of Christendom, the Roman Pontiff. Caesar and Pontiff, alike, rule by divine right, each as God's immediate vicar within his own sphere. *Each is bound to the other by the closest ties. . . . And each of these lofty offices is open to every baptized man;* each alike is purely elective. . . . Here is a conception as magnificent as it was impractical."[2]

b. The new Empire was *German.*[3] (1) It was less universal than the Carolingian Empire[4] had been. Charlemagne had been ruler over practically all Latin Christendom. The restored Empire never included the French part of Charlemagne's territories, while, outside the old imperial bounds, new states were now growing up, north, west, and east, — in England, in the Scandinavian lands, in Spain, in Poland, and in Hungary, — all for the most part beyond any real imperial control. (2) The fact that France was not included made the

---

[1] The term "Holy" does not appear in the official title until the time of Frederick I (§ 79); but the new character appears from Otto's time, and it is customary to use this name for the whole period after 962.

[2] Freeman, "Holy Roman Empire," in *First Series of Essays*, 136, 137; the student should read at least the context of this quotation. The best statement upon the subject, probably, is the chapter entitled, "Theory of the Medieval Empire" in Bryce's classic work, *The Holy Roman Empire*. All students should read at least pages 104–112 of that chapter.

[3] Cf. the second theme sentence at the head of Division VI.

[4] It would be profitable at this point to review the relation of Charlemagne to the older Roman Empire. See *Ancient History*, §§ 517, 518.

new Empire more German, and less Roman, than the old. Otto had attached the imperial dignity finally to the German kingship, preventing forever its becoming attached to the kingship of France or Italy or Burgundy; and in so doing, he had really created a new empire, — one with its elements mingled in new proportions. *Roman tradition* still furnished the *theory* of the world state, but the *German people* furnished all the *physical support* upon which the actual imperial structure rested.

56. The German and the Roman Crowns. — For three hundred years, each holder of the imperial throne was crowned thrice:[1] once at Aachen, as King of Germany; once at Milan or Pavia, as King of Italy; and finally at Rome, as Emperor. In theory the imperial throne was to be filled by free election at Rome, and any free man in Christendom might be chosen; but in practice no one was eligible for the imperial election until he had become King of Germany, and every king of Germany who could march to Rome was at once saluted Emperor.[2] A candidate cared for success in the first election — to the throne of Germany — mainly in order to make sure of the third — to the imperial throne. And so, after a time, the first election changed its form: the very title "King of Germany" ceased; and, instead, at Aachen men chose a "King of the Romans" — a new title, indicating the nature of the election as a mere step to the higher imperial dignity.

B. THE CHURCH AT THE RESTORATION OF THE EMPIRE.

57. The Church the Strongest Bond of Union for Medieval Europe. — The hardest thing to understand about the centuries we are now studying is the way the church pervaded all the life of the time. Christianity was not only a religion: it was a government. In a sense, Christendom was a political state. Especially was this true while the Empire was in abeyance, and afterwards when at times the popes had made themselves superior to the emperors (§§ 69, 82–84). Later, there arose other agencies to do much of the work that in this early period fell to the church. Thus in no Christian land to-day

---

[1] Often he was crowned a fourth time as King of Burgundy (§ 64 *b*).
[2] Read Freeman, *First Series of Essays*, 266.

does any church fill so large a place, or hold so great authority, as the Catholic church did throughout Western Europe from the eighth to the fifteenth centuries.

During all this time, in fact and in theory, the church included all inhabitants of Christendom, except Jews. Indeed, it was as impossible then to think of a man in Christian Europe as outside the church, as it is now to think of a Frenchman in France outside the French nation. When the Carolingian Empire had been shattered into feudal fragments, the units that we call national states, in which to-day our political life centers, had not yet developed: men still felt themselves citizens of a vaster fatherland, and gave to Christendom something of the loyalty that we to-day give to our country. The unity of this universal church was preserved and its authority was exercised by its organized official body, the clergy, or "the church" in a narrower sense. The church had gained great power by rendering inestimable services. Upon it, over large areas, depended not only private morals but also public order. With its spiritual thunders and the threat of its curse, it many times protected the widow and the orphan from the brutal baron who would have regarded no earthly power.

The church building [1] of each parish, too, was the social center for the people. In it took place the most solemn events in each life, — the christening, confirmation, marriage, and burial. Near it, on the Sunday holiday, between the sacred services, occurred sports and games; and from its steps, the priest gave the people most of the news they received about the outside world.

58. Decline of the Church in the Ninth and Tenth Centuries. — Even the church, however, could not escape the decay that was going on everywhere in the ninth century. Both learning and morals declined, in the violence of the times; and, after feudalism had put an end to barbarian invasion, the ferocity

---

[1] Observe that "church" is used in this section in three senses. The first two are easily confused. The student will have constant occasion to discriminate between them in his reading.

and greed of that institution tended to infect religion. The church was growing worldly. To its great offices were attached revenues, lands, and political and even military duties. Bishops and abbots came to pay more attention to these financial and civil matters than to their spiritual duties. They bought their places from the kings with money and with promises of support; and then sold the lower offices, which were under their jurisdiction, on like terms, for their own aggrandizement. This evil of *simony*,[1] or the purchase of ecclesiastical office, permeated all ranks of the clergy. The rule of St. Benedict,[2] too, had fallen to decay, and often even the monasteries were no longer centers of moral earnestness.

The papacy also suffered sadly.[3] In the early part of the tenth century, it had lost all vital authority over Europe at large, and the popes had sunk again to mere bishops of Rome. In Rome itself, the papacy lost public reverence and became the tool of the nobles in their private quarrels, until popes were set up and deposed by corrupt rings of Roman lords. In nine years, from 896 to 904, there were nine popes, — the changes being connected with furious struggles within the city. One pope caused the body of his predecessor, of a different faction, to be dug up, mutilated, and flung into the Tiber. For half a century, infamous women by their intrigues raised their lovers and their sons in swift succession to the throne of St. Peter. Christendom was left without a head, and the evil results called loudly for reform. This reform was to come from two sources, — the great emperors (§§ 60, 63, 65), and a remarkable religious revival within the church itself (§ 59).

---

[1] This name was suggested by the story of the offensive offer of the magician Simon, related in the Acts of the Apostles.

[2] *Ancient History*, §§ 603, 604.

[3] See *Ancient History*, §§ 627-635, for a brief account of the rise of the papacy; for the decline, see Alzog, II, 292-298, and Adams, *Civilization*, 227-238.

59. Cluny and Reform.[1] — In 910, a pious duke founded a new monastery at *Cluny* in Burgundy, and here began one of the greatest and most fruitful revivals in history. The abbot restored the rules of St. Benedict with such success that soon good men everywhere, as they struggled against evil, turned to Cluny for advice and leadership. The Benedictine rules, however, had left each monastery a separate unit; now a more effective organization was adopted. New monasteries, and old ones as they were reformed under the influence of Cluniac missionaries, were joined as daughter societies to the mother monastery of Cluny. The abbot of Cluny appointed the heads of the daughter institutions and retained control over them, and from time to time there were held assemblies of delegates from all the monasteries of the order. This centralized government produced rapid and wholesome results. Everywhere, in that brutal age, the widespread brotherhood lived holy, self-denying lives, and built up influence for good about them. Their power grew for two centuries, and they came to dominate the church.

Besides the reform of individual lives, the leaders of the Cluniac movement had two main objects: they sought to reform the machinery of the church *by doing away with simony and with the marriage of the clergy;* and, in order to accomplish the first purpose, they strove to *elevate and purify the papacy.*

a. To prevent simony, they insisted that every bishop and abbot should be elected by the clergy of the ecclesiastical unit concerned, instead of being appointed by the civil power. This was a natural demand. For many students to-day it is not so easy to understand why the reformers objected to the marriage of the clergy. However, men have always had a tendency to think of holiness as connected with celibacy; and from almost the beginning of Christianity attempts were made to keep the clergy from marrying. Outside of the monasteries these attempts seem to have broken down in the ninth century, and over most of Europe the clergy were husbands and fathers (§ 38); indeed, there had appeared a

---

[1] Read Tout, *Empire and Papacy*, 97–101; Emerton, 195–198; or Adams, *Civilization*, 239–244. Henderson's *Documents*, 239, gives the "Foundation of Cluny."

tendency to make their offices hereditary. But the men of Cluny believed ardently that the clergy could not do their proper work unless they were set off from all concern regarding family, so that they might devote their lives without reservation to the service of religion. After some two centuries of bitter struggle the reformers were successful, and the rule that the clergy must not marry became universal in the Latin church.

b. The results of the attempt to exalt the papal power can be considered best in connection with the story of the relations between popes and emperors (§§ 60 ff.). The great emperors of the tenth and eleventh centuries began the reformation, which the Cluniac religious revival was finally to complete.

60. Otto I and the Beginning of the Reform of the Papacy. — Otto I had tried to fix the relation of the popes to the Empire. He confirmed the ancient "donations" of Pippin and Charlemagne,[1] but he also decreed that in the future no pope should be consecrated until he had taken an oath of allegiance to the emperor. Roman patriotism and the papal party resented this attempt to make the pope a vassal of the Empire. Pope John XII (a dissolute criminal, as it happened) plotted to drive the Germans out of Italy. Otto deposed him and set up another pope in his place. Soon after, the Romans drove out Otto's pope and elected another, — a worthy and noble man. Otto besieged the city, captured it, banished the rival pope, and restored his own candidate.

THE TEMPORAL AND THE SPIRITUAL POWER: a mosaic of the tenth century in the Church of St. John, Rome, representing God giving the keys to St. Peter and the banner to Constantine. — From Lacroix, *Vie Militaire.*

---

[1] *Ancient History*, §§ 634, 635, 638.

THE EMPIRE—OTTO I TO HENRY III.

Otto's purpose was mainly political, and he had begun a struggle between popes and emperors, which was to endure three hundred years; but incidentally he had also begun a reform of the papacy which was to lift it to a pinnacle of glory.

61. Three Theories of the Relations of Popes and Emperors.—This struggle soon forced men to define their ideas about the relations of pope and emperor, and three theories appeared: (1) that the pope and emperor were equal and independent heads of Christendom,—one of the spiritual power, the other of the physical power,—bound, however, to act in close agreement and harmony; (2) that the pope was independent in purely spiritual concerns, but that in political matters, as a ruling prince of the Empire, he was a vassal of the emperor; and (3) the Cluny idea that the pope as the more direct representative of God was the superior of the emperor and able to command his obedience. The first theory was no doubt the most nearly in accord with the fundamental idea of a "Holy" Empire (cf. § 55 a), and for a long time it seems to have received general acknowledgment, at least in words; but, when disputes arose, it could not be worked, and in practice men had to choose between the other two theories.

C. OUTLINE OF POLITICAL HISTORY FROM OTTO I TO THE DEATH OF HENRY III, 973–1056.

62. Reference Table of German Kings,—from the close of the Carolingians to the "Great Interregnum," 911–1254.[1]

a. Conrad I (Franconian), 911–918.

b. **The Saxon Dynasty:** Henry *I*, 919–936; Otto *I*, 936–973 (Emperor, 962–973); Otto II, 973–983; *Otto III*, 983–1002; Henry II, 1002–1024.

c. **The Franconian Dynasty:** Conrad II, 1024–1039; *Henry III*, 1039–1056; *Henry IV*, 1056–1106; (Rudolph, Hermann, Conrad, set up as claimants against Henry, from 1077 to 1093); Henry V, 1106–1125.

d. Lothair II (Saxon), 1125–1137.

e. **Hohenstaufen (Suabian) Dynasty:** Conrad III, 1138–1152; (Henry of Saxony, opponent) *Frederick I*, 1152–1190; Henry VI, 1190–1197; (*Welf Dynasty*, Otto IV, 1198–1218, during minority of Frederick II; opposed by Frederick's uncle, Philip, until 1208); *Frederick II*, 1218–1250; Conrad IV, 1250–1254.

---

[1] The earlier German kings are named in § 47, note. The kings in the present table, after Otto I, were also all Roman Emperors; but they usually began

63. Otto II and Otto III. — The ten years of Otto II were spent mainly upon Italian interests: the danger to Germany from the imperial dignity of her king was already appearing. It became plainer in the next reign. Otto III (983–1002) was only three years old at his father's death. The first Otto had been German in feeling, as in blood. His grandson, this third Otto, was more Roman, and even more Greek, than he was German. He had been educated under the influence of his Greek mother and his Italian grandmother (§ 53). His learning won him the title "Wonder of the World," but it had also imbued him with notions ill-suited to a German king. He grew to manhood, devoted to religion and enthusiastic for church reform, but with absurdly exalted ideas of his imperial position. He was unselfish, ardent, noble, but visionary, mystical, unpractical.

Otto assumed the government in 996, while a boy sixteen years old, and the remaining six years of his short life were spent in Italy. His first concern was to elevate the papacy, and he at once appointed to that dignity his cousin and intimate friend, Bruno, who took the name of Gregory V.[1] Says Emerton (*Medieval Europe*, 135): —

For a moment it seemed as if Empire and papacy, in the hands of these two enthusiastic youths united by ties of blood and by the closest sympathy, might be about to realize the ideal of the medieval world, — each standing for the highest expression of authority in the Christian community, and yet each aiding the other to carry out his peculiar aims.

---

to rule as emperors somewhat later than the dates when their kingly rule began. To secure the succession to his family, the emperor usually secured the election of his son to the kingship in his own lifetime, — sometimes while the boy was a mere babe. The theory of election was maintained, and at the extinction of a dynasty, the election was real. The elections were conducted by the great nobles — for a long time without any settled procedure. Toward the close of the period, however, a regular "electoral college" began to emerge, — one of the most peculiar institutions of the Middle Ages (§ 159).

[1] Gregory was the first pope from without Italy, and his appointment marks an era in the development of the papacy into a world power. Plainly, if the bishop of Rome was to be the spiritual head of Christendom, it was needful that at his election the choice should not be restricted to Italians.

GERMAN COLONIZATION ON THE EAST AT THE EXPENSE OF SLAVS, LETTS, AND MAGYARS, 800-1400.

On Gregory's death, soon after his appointment, Otto appointed a Frenchman, Gerbert.[1] Gerbert sympathized with Otto in his imperial ideas, and the young prince now passed rapidly to more and more impractical designs. He began to construct a great palace on the Aventine for the imperial residence; and he planned to make Rome the real as well as the nominal head of the Empire, so as to rule Germany from that center. He introduced Oriental ceremonial and pomp into his court, and he dreamed of conquering the Byzantine Empire and uniting Greek and Latin Christendoms. But suddenly both Germany and Italy flamed into revolt, and in the midst of defeat Otto died of fever. A German chronicler of the time exclaims: —

The sin of this king was that he would not look upon the land of his nativity, delightful Germany, — so great was his love of dwelling in Italy, where savage destruction runs armed with a thousand languors and a thousand deaths. . . . *He designed a great and impossible task*, for he tried to raise the Roman Empire to its power under the ancient kings.

64. The Empire in the First Third of the Eleventh Century. — The two immediate successors of Otto III gave their energies to Germany. While they were so busied, the papacy sank into shame and impotence; but they did restore the strength of the German kingship. In the half century between Otto I and the close of these reigns, four great changes with important bearing upon the power of the Empire took place in Western Europe.

a. On the north, the great Danish state (§ 16), which had promised for a time to be a formidable rival, went to pieces rapidly after the death of Knut the Great (1035); and in this connection, it is to be remembered that England was still in the period of weakness before the Norman conquest, and that France was distracted with feudal anarchy.

---

[1] Gerbert had been an ally of the Capetians in their struggle with the expiring Carolingian line (§ 41), and, while in exile during the reign of the last Carolingian, he had been the tutor of the youthful Otto. His unusual learning, derived in part from the Spanish Saracens, had made him suspected of sorcery by the ignorant.

b. On the west, through the relationship of the ruling families, the kingdom of Burgundy, or Arles, was added to the Empire, without serious warfare.

c. On the eastern frontier, the Christian Empire extended its military rule over a wide stretch of "marches"; and, by its missionaries, its colonists, and its example, it pushed back even farther the borders of heathendom. By the year 1000, Poles, Hungarians, and Bohemians had not only accepted Christianity, but had also become real states with settled governments. This organization saved these lands from being Germanized in blood by gradual conquest and settlement, as the lands between them and the Elbe had been: they kept their Magyar and Slav speech and nationalities; but their civilization was to be German in source and character, and from time to time they all recognized some vague overlordship in the Empire.

d. Within Germany, by the steady policy of the great kings, the former duchies were beginning to break up into smaller units, each depending directly on the king. The extension of Germany to the east had added other such states, also; so that now, instead of being composed of four or five large governments, the realm was made up of many feudal units, — counties, marks, and new duchies, — of varying size. The future was to show that under a weak ruler this condition would lead to all the more serious anarchy; but for the moment it was easier for a strong king to control the many smaller, scattered units, than it had been to regulate the five powerful duchies.

65. Henry III (1039-1056) came to the throne under more promising auspices than any earlier German king. The promise was well fulfilled. Henry was a good man and a great ruler, and he raised the German kingship to the highest point it was ever to reach. His reign had three important phases.

a. Germany was extended, and strengthened against attacks from without. By a series of remarkable victories, Henry

THE EMPIRE
IN THE ELEVENTH CENTURY
(Time of Henry III)

reduced the Magyar kingdom of Hungary and the Slav dukedoms of Poland and Bohemia to fiefs of the Empire. The relation was wholly different from the uncertain suzerainty the Empire had possessed before. Hungary, it is true, broke away again in Henry's own reign, and with Poland the connection was not to be permanent; but Bohemia was to remain always part of the Empire and was soon to become one of its leading states (§ 159).

b. Within Germany, both church and state were reformed. (1) Henry enforced the "Truce of God" (§ 33), which had not before been introduced into Germany, and even tried to widen it into the "Peace of the Land," by exacting oaths from all German nobles to give up private war and to submit all differences to public courts. At the same time he encouraged the growing towns by new and wider grants of trading privileges. (2) He allied himself closely to the party of Cluny, and in particular he put down simony. To be sure, he kept the appointment of the higher clergy strictly in his own hands, but only for the public good: he never sold such offices for money or personal advantage.

c. The papacy was again reformed. A boy pope, ten years old, — a depraved little wretch, according to the accounts of the time, — had given way to three rivals, all claiming the throne of St. Peter at once. Under Henry's control, two church councils deposed all three claimants and gave power of appointment to the Emperor. Henry filled the papal chair four times, each time with a German. Perfect harmony existed between the Emperor and these popes, and Henry even left his infant son under the Pope's guardianship. The rule of that son, the future Henry IV, was spent in fierce conflict with the papacy (§ 74).

For Further Reading. — Emerton, 135–209; Bryce, *Holy Roman Empire*, 103–158; Tout, *Empire and Papacy*, 27–64; Stephens, *Hildebrand*, 10–37; Henderson, *Short History of Germany*, I, 49–57.

The references upon Subdivision *B* (the church) will be given in connection with the following Division; see pages 84, 85.

VII. EMPIRE AND PAPACY, 1056-1122.

Human pride invented the power of kings; divine pity established that of bishops.... He [the pope] *may depose emperors.... He may absolve subjects from their allegiance to wicked men.... He himself may be judged by no one.* — GREGORY VII.[1]

A. HILDEBRAND, POPE GREGORY VII.

66. The Youth of Hildebrand. — The central figure in the great struggle between Empire and papacy was the son of a Tuscan peasant. His name was *Hildebrand,* and he was brought up at Rome in a rich monastery, where his uncle was abbot.[2] Here the young monk became imbued with the ideas of the Cluny reformers, and later he lived for a year in the Cluny monastery. His body was frail and his voice weak, but he had a fiery soul, indomitable energy, and great practical sagacity. His ability soon attracted attention, and in 1045, at the age of twenty-one, he became chaplain to the pope. Then, for many years, under successive popes, he seems to have been the power behind the throne, shaping a growing and consistent papal policy.

67. The Work of Hildebrand as Counsellor. — Three important steps in the development of the papacy were taken in this period, through Hildebrand's statesmanship.

a. A close alliance was formed with a popular reform party that had appeared in Lombardy. This party was made up largely of the lower classes, and was led by popular agitators. Its opponents styled it the "Pataria," or the party of the ragamuffins. Its purposes were social, religious, and patriotic: it opposed the wealth and corruption of the higher clergy, the

---

[1] The entire statement of Gregory is found in Emerton's *Medieval Europe,* 244, 245, and in Henderson's *Documents,* 366, 367. Students should read it in connection with § 68.

[2] This is one illustration of the democratic nature of the church. Long after the gulf between nobles and non-nobles in lay society became impassable (§ 26 note), men of humble, and even of servile, birth could rise in the church to the highest dignities, and so become the masters of lords and kings.

dependence of the church upon lay lords, and the dominance of Germans in Italy.

b. In the south of the peninsula, other allies were found. Early in the eleventh century, bands of Norman adventurers had established themselves in Apulia, and finally their leader, *Robert Guiscard* (Wiscard, or the crafty), had built up a powerful Norman state, which in the next century was to be known as the Kingdom of Sicily.[1] At first, these strangers seized territory, not only from Saracen and Greek, but even from the Pope; but, in 1059, Hildebrand negotiated a treaty with them which secured for the papacy their powerful aid. The Pope conferred upon Robert the title of Duke of Apulia and Calabria; and in return, Robert became a vassal of the papacy for these fiefs.

c. A church council was persuaded to adopt a decree regulating the method of electing popes (1059). Thereafter the election was to be made, not by a gathering summoned and controlled by the emperors or by some noble just then in power in Rome, but by a fixed and independent body of churchmen. This body was to consist of the seven "cardinal bishops" of Rome and its vicinity; but their choice was to require confirmation by the other clergy and the people of Rome, — while vague clauses in the decree referred also to some meaningless authority in the emperor.[2]

68. Hildebrand becomes Gregory VII: Theories and Policy. — Hildebrand might have been made pope on more than one occasion before he finally accepted the place. At last, in 1073, an enthusiastic popular uprising, confirmed by the cardinals, forced the election upon him. He took the name of

---

[1] Special report: the growth of the Norman state; see Johnson's *Normans* or Freeman's *Story of Sicily*.

[2] Read Emerton, 217, 218, or Stephens, *Hildebrand*, 46, 47, or Alzog, II, 344-348; and see Henderson's *Documents*, 361-365, for the two versions of the decree. This decree is the origin of the "College of Cardinals," which still elects the popes; the "college" now numbers seventy, representing all the important lands in which the Catholic church is found, and no confirmation of their choice is required.

Gregory VII, and began to work with fresh vigor to make real his dream of a universal Roman monarchy, with the pope, not the emperor, for its supreme ruler. At first, to be sure, he aimed mainly to complete the moral reform of the church and to bring it absolutely under papal control; but the opposition he encountered from temporal rulers forced him on to the further aim of raising the papacy above all other powers in the world. The Empire was to be subject to the papacy, as the body to the soul. The pope, as the immediate representative of God, was to be the final arbiter between kings.[1]

Gregory's life proved that his convictions were sincere and unselfish. They were shared, too, by the purest and ablest churchmen of the age. Nor was there anything new in them. The new thing was for a man to be found with the noble daring to try to live up to these ideas when they brought him into conflict with the sovereigns of the earth.

The church itself, however, in the hands of a resolute man, was a tremendous power, and it had been taking on an organization that was to help in enforcing its claims against temporal rulers. Four points in that organization should be noted (§§ 69–72), — ecclesiastical courts, power of excommunication and interdict, revenues, and the hierarchic organization with the system of councils and legates.

B. The Church in the Age of Hildebrand.[2]

69. Ecclesiastical Courts and Canon Law. — The church had its own system of courts, — archdeacons', bishops', archbishops', and papal, — altogether independent of the public courts in the different lands of Christendom; and there had been developed also a complex system of church law, known as "canon" law.[3]

---

[1] See various letters of Gregory's in Henderson's *Documents*, 365–405. Cf. Stephens' *Hildebrand*, 153–157.

[2] Much of the following account holds good for the earlier centuries also. Cf. §§ 5, 57. The best treatments in elementary text-books are in Robinson's *Western Europe*, 201–215, and Munro's *Middle Ages*, 169–183.

[3] Read Emerton, 582–585, on the canon law; and Jessopp's *Friars*, 81 ff., on the exemption of "clerks" from civil jurisdiction.

The clergy claimed the privilege of trial in these courts, no matter what the question or the charge against them; and cases against laymen might also be tried there when religious or moral questions were involved; for instance, cases depending upon laws of marriage and inheritance, commercial morality, taking of interest, and all matters connected with church revenues.

The right of the clergy to be tried in clerical courts was known as "benefit of clergy." The practice had its good side. Ordinary courts and ordinary law partook of the violent and ferocious life of the age. Trials were rude; and ghastly or repulsive punishments were inflicted for trivial offenses, — often, no doubt, upon the innocent. It was a gain when the peaceful and moral part of society secured the right to trial in more intelligent courts and by more civilized codes.[1]

But the church law was too mild to deal with serious crimes. It did not use force in its punishments, but only required the offender to punish himself by penances of various kinds or by fines, or payments to the church.[2] Unfortunately this mildness was seriously abused. Its advantages tempted men to "take Holy Orders," until, besides the preaching clergy and the monks, the land swarmed with "clerics" who were really only lawyers, secretaries, scholars, teachers, or mere adventurers. Some of these, by their crimes, brought disgrace upon the church and danger to the state, and made it necessary for the civil power, as fast as it grew strong enough, to reclaim jurisdiction. On this issue there arose a long strife between church and state in many lands.

70. Penalties. — Despite its gentleness, the church had two mighty weapons to compel obedience to its commands, —

---

[1] Moreover, in the Middle Ages, all corporations, even trade gilds, very commonly had courts with considerable power of jurisdiction over their own members. The demand of the church was not out of keeping with the ideas and practice of the age, as such a claim would be now. (Cf. §§ 112, 113, 180.)

[2] For the worst crimes, it is true, a clerk might be degraded from his order, and then for a second offense he might be tried in an ordinary court.

excommunication and *interdict*. A bishop could declare any man in his diocese excommunicated, and a pope could decree excommunication against any man in Christendom. In modern language, excommunication was a universal boycott for all religious and social and business relations. If it was obeyed by the community, it cut a man off absolutely from all communication with his fellows, and practically made him an outlaw. No one might speak to him or give him food or shelter, under danger of similar penalty, and his very presence was shunned like the pestilence.

What excommunication was to the individual, the interdict was to a district or a nation. Churches were closed, and no religious ceremonies were permitted, except the rites of baptism and of extreme unction. No marriage could be performed, and there could be no burial in consecrated ground.[1] "The dead were left unburied, the living were unblessed."

71. Revenues: Peter's Pence. — All churches and ecclesiastical lords had their revenues, of course, from rents and landed properties; and there were also many dues and fees paid to the clergy. But besides all this, — which corresponded fairly well to the income of the lay lords of the time, — there was also a papal system of taxation extending over all Christendom, long before any king had so effective a revenue system for his particular country. The most famous element in this taxation was *Peter's Pence*, or a penny for each hearth each year, collected over Western Europe by an organized body of papal officers; much more important, however, were the many enormous payments made by the clergy.

72. Political Organization. — In political organization, too, the church was ahead of the civil states of Europe. In

---

[1] In this extreme form, the interdict was rarely proclaimed; and, of course, a decree of excommunication against a king was always disregarded by many of his followers. But, on the other hand, few kings or peoples could hold out against the mere threat of these terrors in an age when religious practices were so interwoven with the fiber of daily life. The *Pennsylvania Reprints*, IV, No. 4, gives several decrees of interdict. Notice especially the reply to one by the Doge of Venice in 1606.

England or in France, a "Convocation" of clergy, under an archbishop, provided for the church a better machinery for unity of action than the civil state had yet attained in its rude gatherings of nobles; while there was no civil organization for Europe at large to correspond with the Councils of Christendom summoned by the popes.

In general, the government of the church was monarchic. No decree of a Council was valid without the assent of the pope, and all the lower clergy were subject to removal by him. Next to the pope stood the archbishops, each with a vague supervision over the other bishops of his province, and with a court for appeals from the bishops' courts. Each bishop was the head of a diocese and was charged with the ordination and the oversight of the lower clergy in that district. His church was the cathedral, and it had its force of canons and other clergy to assist in the work of the bishop's court and in the services of religion. Only the bishop could administer confirmation or consecrate churches. In each parish, the village priest was charged with the care of souls. He heard confession of sins, imposed penances, and granted to sincere penitents the absolution without which they did not hope for God's forgiveness. To the dying he administered extreme unction, and daily he worked for his parishioners the miracle of the Mass.[1] Besides all this hierarchy of secular clergy, there were, of course, the numerous bodies of monks in their separate communities.[2]

At Rome, about the papal court, there were large numbers of clergy to act as clerks and to assist in preparing and transacting the business of this vast centralized government. Moreover, largely by Gregory VII, there was created a system of papal "legates" to act in all the lands of Europe as ears, eyes, and hands for the pope, somewhat as the Missi Dominici three centuries before had done for Charlemagne in his Em-

---

[1] Roman Catholics, of course, believed then as now that the sacramental bread and wine are changed into the very body and blood of Christ. This is the doctrine of *transubstantiation*.

[2] Many new orders of monks arose in this and the next century, — created by the same religious revival of which mention has just been made. Withdrawn from the world, as they were, still some of them by their holy lives and strong characters came to exercise mighty influence upon society. Perhaps the most powerful man in Europe between Pope Gregory VII and Pope Innocent III (§ 82) was Bernard of Clairvaux, a simple monk. Munro's *Middle Ages*, 126-131, has an admirable brief account of several of the new monastic orders and of Bernard's work. Special reports : Bernard of Clairvaux; Cistercian monks; Carthusian monks.

pire.[1] These papal representatives could revoke the decisions of bishops' courts, or depose the bishops themselves; and with curt haughtiness[2] they claimed the obedience of the mightiest kings of Europe.

C. The Investiture Strife between Emperors and Popes.

73. An Irrepressible Conflict. — The strife between the rising civil states and the claims of the church came to a head upon the question of "investitures." The struggle was fiercest in the Empire, — where it lasted almost fifty years, from 1075 to 1122, — and it can best be studied there; but students of France and England will find that it played its part there also.

The emperor appointed and "invested"[3] all bishops and abbots. This practice was not always connected with simony, but it made that evil much more common, and naturally the church tended to regard the two things as practically the same. The great conflict was unavoidable. The real cause of the strife was the twofold nature of bishops and abbots: they were spiritual officers, and, as such, it was not fit that they should be appointed by lay rulers; but they were at the same time temporal lords, and, as such, the emperors needed to keep control over them. In Germany, nearly half the land and resources of the realm were in the hands of these great ecclesiastics. Plainly no civil ruler could consent to yield their appointment to any power but himself. Just as plainly, no great and good pope, with the interests of religion at heart, could willingly see these clerical officers appointed by any lay power, with the frequent disregard of spiritual interests that would surely follow.[4]

---

[1] *Ancient History*, § 645.

[2] Notice Shakspere's portraiture of the legate and the kings, in *King John*, Act III, Scene I.

[3] Cf. § 27, for the meaning of the term.

[4] Toward the close of the struggle, Henry V (§ 75) and Pope Paschal II came to a formal agreement to do away with the cause of the trouble by separating church and state: the clerical princes were to give up their fiefs, and the emperor then would leave their appointment wholly to the church (Emerton, 267, 268). But the plan was too far in advance of the age, and it was given up on both sides without serious attempts to put it in force.

74. Progress of the Struggle, to the Deaths of Gregory and of Henry IV.

In 1075, Gregory threatened to excommunicate all bishops and abbots who should thereafter receive their investiture from a lay ruler, and, likewise, every lay ruler who should venture to invest an ecclesiastic with his office. This was a declaration of war.

Gregory's great opponent was to be the young emperor, *Henry IV.* During the minority of this sovereign (§ 65, close, and § 62), Germany had fallen back toward anarchy, and the conditions were serious indeed, when, at fifteen, Henry assumed the management of the kingdom (1065). Henry was an able, strong-willed ruler, and had it not been for a faulty training throughout his youth, he might have become a great and noble king. Unhappily, he seems to have been licentious in morals, and he was certainly headstrong and violent. He proved a generous master to the lower classes and he favored the rising towns, but he was to be engaged in a life-long, deadly contest with the two great forces of his age, feudalism and the church. Soon after his accession, the Saxon nobles revolted, and for some years the young King was busied in a desperate effort to keep his crown at all. He had just come out victorious, for a time, from this contest, when the decree of Gregory regarding investitures summoned him to a mightier conflict.

The opening of the strife was sharp and rude. Henry continued to invest clerical lords and also to show favor to some whom Gregory had condemned for simony. Gregory summoned him to Rome, and threatened excommunication unless he gave up this policy and also reformed the vices of his private life. Henry replied, with a council of German bishops, by declaring Gregory guilty of infamous crimes and by pronouncing his deposition. News of this action was sent to Rome, with agents to secure the election of another pope; and the messenger delivered his notice roughly, while Gregory was conducting a sacred service. Gregory's response was to declare the German bishops excommunicated, and Henry deposed.

Henry's letter to Gregory had been addressed, "Hildebrand, not pope but false monk"; and it had closed, "Descend and surrender the apostolic chair, which thou hast usurped. . . . I, Henry, king by the grace of God, together with all my bishops, do call to thee, 'Get thee down, get down to everlasting damnation.'" Gregory's reply ran : "O St. Peter, chief of the apostles, . . . for the honor and security of thy church, in the name of Almighty God, Father, Son, and Holy Ghost, I withdraw, through thy power and authority, from Henry, the king, who has risen against thy church with unheard of insolence, the rule over the whole kingdom of the Germans and over Italy. And I absolve all Christians from the bonds of the oaths which they have taken and shall take to him; and I forbid any one to serve him as king." [1]

Encouraged by this action of the Pope, Henry's enemies in Germany again took arms. The clergy fell away, — unable to stand before the terrors of the papal bull, — and in a few months Henry was helpless. A council of nobles was called, over which the Pope was to preside, to decide the question of Henry's deposition. By swift submission, Henry saved his crown. He hurried into Italy and met the Pope, already on his way across the Alps, at *Canossa*. The stern Gregory refused to see the suppliant, who stood barefoot, in a penitent's garb, through three days of extreme cold, amid the snow and rocks before the castle gate. Admitted finally to the Pope's presence, after promising abject submission to his will, whatever it might be, Henry threw himself in tears at the feet of his conqueror, crying, "Spare me, Holy Father, spare me!" Gregory also was moved to tears. He raised Henry to his feet, gave him the kiss of peace, and promised him absolution.

But the Pope had pushed his victory too far, or else not far enough. The foes of Henry in Germany felt that the Pope had deserted them, and the mass of the nation were angered by the humiliation of their King.[2] The hostile nobles did try

---

[1] See the documents in full, in Henderson's *Documents*.

[2] Germany has never altogether ceased to resent the disgrace. In 1872, in a conflict between the new German empire and the papal party, Bismarck rallied the national feeling to the side of the government by his exclamation, "Be sure we shall not go to Canossa!" (§ 482). This sentence is engraved upon Bismarck's monument at Harzburg.

to set up another king; but German patriotism rallied around Henry, and he easily kept the upper hand. After some delay, since there was no change in the matter of royal investitures, Gregory issued another decree of deposition against Henry; but the opportunity was gone. The German bishops, returning to Henry's side, again declared Gregory deposed, and went through the form of electing another pope in his place. There followed a distressing tangle of wars. Finally, Gregory was driven from Rome, and soon after he died in the south of Italy (1085), exclaiming sadly, "I have loved righteousness and hated iniquity; therefore I die in exile."[1]

The quarrel was soon renewed with the new Pope, Urban II. Henry's sons were stirred up to rebel against their father, wars were waged incessantly, and in his old age the Emperor met many reverses. For years he was a prisoner, and he died in 1106, broken-hearted, in the midst of defeat and shame. For five years his body lay in unconsecrated ground, before the church would remove the curse from his ashes.

75. The Concordat of Worms. — Henry V, the son of Henry IV, had been an ally of the popes against his father, but as emperor he was obliged to resist their claims as his father had done. Finally, at the city of Worms (1122), the long quarrel was settled by a reasonable compromise. Bishops were to be elected by the clergy and consecrated by the pope; but the emperor was to have a possible veto upon any election, inasmuch as the candidate was to receive from him the investiture of the episcopal lands, which were to be held as by a faithful vassal.[2]

The struggle between Empire and papacy was not over, by any means, with the Concordat of Worms; but one chapter was closed, and it is well to see what had been accomplished. Henry IV had outlived Gregory by a score of years, and, though conquered and humiliated, he had prevented

---

[1] Still, Gregory was in large part victorious. He lives in history as one of the world's greatest men, — one who built an empire, not by sword and cannon, but by intellect and moral earnestness.

[2] This compromise seems to have been modeled upon one made just before in England between Henry I (§ 125) and Anselm. The English contest is a good subject for a special report.

the complete victory of Gregory's ideas. His son, the papal ally, had become the papacy's foe, and had forced that power to a compromise. Still, no emperor could ever again make and unmake popes as the Ottos and Henry III had done; while the popes did retain a powerful influence in making emperors,[1] and their right even to depose temporal rulers had been powerfully asserted. To all men the papacy had become the final court of appeal and the chief source of justice, righteousness, and mercy.

76. Political Results of the Struggle: Feudal Anarchy; Civic Independence. — During the fifty years of incessant conflict between emperors and popes, and in the long absence of the emperors from Germany, the German nobles had been growing more and more independent of royal authority. The popes, of course, had fostered the tendency, as their best weapon against the emperors; and the feudal lords had been able to satisfy their rebellious instincts under the guise of a pious alliance. As a result the strong German kingship of the eleventh century was dissolving in feudal anarchy, and the most that the great successors of the Henrys succeeded in doing was for a time to arrest the deplorable tendency.

One other political result of the contest was wholly unexpected. The pope turned to the city democracies of Italy for help against the emperor and the Italian nobles; and the emperor called upon the German cities for aid against the pope and the German nobles. Emperor and pope each strove for the monarchic principle, but out of their conflict came strength to the beginnings of popular liberty.

FOR FURTHER READING. — Henderson's *Select Documents*, 351-409, gives much of the source material for the platform of the two parties. There are brief accounts in Henderson, *Short History of Germany*, 58-75; Emerton, 212-268; Tout, *Empire and Papacy*, 110-150; Bryce, *Holy Roman Empire*, 103-163. Roman Catholic views are presented admirably

---

[1] A contemporary artist painted a famous picture of the Emperor Lothair II (§ 62) kneeling before Innocent II for coronation. This painting was preserved in the great audience hall of the papal palace, and beneath it was inscribed: "The King comes before the gates, first swearing due honor to the city. He is then made the vassal of the Pope, and takes the crown which the latter *bestows*." The second emperor after Lothair, Frederick Barbarossa, in a quarrel with Pope Adrian, objected vehemently to this inscription, and finally secured the removal of the picture and a partial disclaimer of the theory of papal suzerainty, but the claim was frequently revived. Indeed, it was soon revived by Adrian himself: "What were the Franks," he wrote to the Emperor, "till [Pope] Zacharias welcomed Pippin? What is the German king now till consecrated at Rome by Holy Hands? The chair of Peter has given and can withdraw its gifts."

by Alzog, *Church History*, and by Barry, *The Papal Monarchy*. Storrs, *Bernard of Clairvaux*, lecture ii, gives an illuminating survey of the situation and the problems. Other treatments may be consulted in Stillé, *Studies;* Stephens, *Hildebrand;* Vincent, *Age of Hildebrand*; Bowden, *Gregory VII;* Lea, *Sacerdotal Celibacy* (ch. xiv on Gregory's reforms); Milman, *Latin Christianity;* and in other church histories.

VIII. EMPIRE AND PAPACY, 1122-1273.[1]

A. CONDITIONS UNDER THE HOHENSTAUFEN EMPERORS.

77. Parties: "Ghibelline" and "Guelf." — The Franconian line expired with Henry V, but it was soon followed[2] by a dynasty yet more brilliant, though possessed of less real power. The Hohenstaufen took their name from their ancestral castle, perched upon a crag in the Alps. Near this first seat of the family lay the village of *Waiblingen*, where Conrad III, the first emperor of the line, was born. This village also gave a name to the family. The chief rivals of Conrad for the throne had been Henry the Proud, and afterward his son Henry the Lion, of the *Welf*[3] family, which held great possessions in Bavaria and Saxony. In a siege during the civil war between Conrad and Henry, these family names, Waibling and Welf, are said to have been used as war cries; certainly they finally became party names. The Welfs of course were allied with the popes against the Hohenstaufen emperors; and soon in Italy the two names — in softened form, Ghibelline and Guelf — stood respectively for the imperial and the papal party.[4]

78. The Controversy between Emperors and Popes renewed: the Real Point at Issue. — Under the Hohenstaufen, the old strife between emperors and popes opened again, — upon new questions. At bottom, as before, it was a contest to decide which

---

[1] The period treated in this Division (VIII) belongs chronologically under Chapter III, "The Age of the Crusades"; but it will prove simpler to continue the story of the Empire at this point, since the central interest for the Empire is the same as in the epoch we have been studying.

[2] After one intervening reign; cf. § 62 *d*.

[3] The English monarchs since George I have been Welfs.

[4] The names continued to be used between the two factions in Italian towns after they had lost all significance except that of family or local interest or ambition, so that we have a byeword, — "as meaningless as the squabbles of Guelfs and Ghibellines." In general, the democratic factions were Guelfs, while the aristocratic party took the name Ghibelline.

power should be the world-sovereign; but the immediate occasion of most of the outbreaks in the twelfth and thirteenth centuries was a conflict of policies regarding Italy. The emperors were bent upon consolidating the peninsula into a single state, with a strong central government. The popes dreaded this, and believed that it would put an end to their independence, even as spiritual rulers. Accordingly, they gave their energies to stirring up enemies against the emperors.

B. FREDERICK BARBAROSSA AND THE LOMBARD LEAGUE.

79. Frederick I (1152–1190): Character and Program. — The second Hohenstaufen was *Frederick Barbarossa*, or Red Beard. Mr. Tout calls him "the noblest embodiment of medieval kingship, the most imposing, the most heroic, and the most brilliant of the long line of German princes who strove to realize the impracticable but glorious political ideal of the Middle Ages."[1] Frederick was a distinguished man and general before he became king. Almost alone among the leaders of the miserable Second Crusade (§ 96), he had returned with some glory. As sovereign, he was first a German king, and he spent much of his life in establishing peace and order in his northern realm. This was the most successful part of his work; but he was also a Roman emperor, and he brought to the throne strong and clear convictions[2] about the imperial authority. He has been fitly called an imperialist Hildebrand, and he strove with energy and insight to restore the waning glory of the Empire.[3]

80. The Struggle with the Lombard League: Legnano; Peace of Constance. — These views and plans brought the King into

---

[1] *Empire and Papacy*, 247. See also *ib.*, 272, for an excellent estimate of Frederick's character and ability.

[2] He was influenced by the revival of Roman law, with its teaching that "what a king pleases has the force of law." This phase of Roman law was a chief reason for Frederick's favor to the rising University of Bologna, where that subject was taught (§ 130 *b*).

[3] Special reports: the city of Rome in the time of Frederick I, especially under Arnold of Brescia; Alexander III and Frederick.

conflict with the rising towns of northern Italy, and the struggle that followed is to us the most important matter in Frederick's reign. To the Lombard cities (which had been growing in wealth and independence during the long struggle over investitures) the imperialistic ideas of the new King meant tyranny. To Frederick, the incessant and remorseless private wars of town with town, and the bloody faction-fights within the leading cities, together with their new republican theories, seemed anarchy; and he determined to reduce these turbulent communities to order, and to rule them through imperial lieutenants stationed in each city. Time after time, German armies crossed the Alps to subdue the Lombard towns. Milan, the greatest city in the Po valley, was razed to the ground, and its inhabitants were scattered in unwalled villages and oppressed by crushing taxation. Some years afterward, however, while Frederick was at Rome, a sudden pestilence of the Italian summer swept away his army; twenty-five thousand men perished in a week, "slain by the angel of the Lord," like the host of Sennacherib before Jerusalem, said the papal party. The cities seized their chance and flew to arms. They had organized in the Lombard League,[1] and allied themselves with the Pope; and at the *battle of Legnano, 1176*, the Emperor was completely defeated, barely escaping with life.

Legnano is one of a very few battles in almost four hundred years of incessant fighting that deserve commemoration. In two respects, it stands for the victory of a new age. (1) It was won by a citizen infantry against the feudal horsemen who had so long been irresistible in the field, and so it prophesied a new era in warfare and consequently in social organization. (2) It secured, immediately, the recognition of the freedom of the Lombard towns.

A great Peace Convention was held at Venice, a new kind of meeting in history, whither came representatives of all the inter-

---

[1] Emerton, 302, 303. This was the first important federation since Greek days. Special report: comparison with the Achaean League.

ested parties. To draw the papal party from the side of his other foes, Frederick cast himself at the feet of Pope Alexander III, imploring forgiveness (cf. § 74); but the Peace of Constance, signed soon after, was substantially dictated by the free cities. The towns recognized the imperial overlordship in words, and bound themselves to pay certain tribute; but they secured the recognition of their rights to fortify themselves, to raise their own troops, to wage war on their own account, even against each other, to coin money, and to regulate all their internal concerns. *Practically, they had become free republics.*

81. Frederick's Place in History. — Despite the defeat of Legnano, Frederick remained the greatest and most honored monarch in Europe. His court was one of pomp and splendor. He looked upon France and England as fiefs of the Empire, and the sovereigns of those lands regarded the Emperor with profound respect, if not quite as their overlord. When an old man, Frederick set out upon the Third Crusade (§ 97), and had he lived longer, that expedition would probably have had a far different ending; but he was drowned while bathing, after a hot day's march, in a little stream in Asia Minor.

Of all the German kings, Barbarossa, even more than Charlemagne, is the popular hero with the German people; and legends long told how he was not dead, but sleeping a magic sleep, upright upon a golden throne in the heart of the Kyffhäuser Mountain, crown on head and scepter in hand, waiting for the appointed time, when, in his country's need, he should come again to bring the reign of peace and justice.

C. THE PAPACY AT ITS HEIGHT.

82. Innocent III[1] **(1198–1216).** — Barbarossa's son, Henry VI (1190–1197), married the heiress of the Norman kingdom of Sicily, and so brought South Italy into union with the Empire. At Henry's death, his son, afterward Frederick II, was a child of three years; and for a score of years Ghibelline and Guelf claimants warred for the imperial crown, with the Pope holding the balance of power. During this period, more

---

[1] Upon Innocent, read Alzog, II, 573–586, or Tout's *Empire and Papacy*, 313–335. Further accounts may be found in Barry's *The Papal Monarchy* and in Balzani's *Popes and Hohenstaufen*.

plainly than ever before, the sovereign power in Europe was the papacy, under the stern morality, tremendous energy, imperious character, and able administration of *Innocent III.*

Innocent set forth the papal claim to the lordship of the world in language more glowing and forceful [1] even than that of Gregory VII, and he enforced his claims with far more striking success. Never was the general reverence for the papacy so profound and so widespread. Within the Empire, Innocent was favored by the political situation. He became feudal overlord and protector of the Tuscan towns, and he was guardian of Frederick, the child-king of Sicily; thus he was safe from attack by Italy, north or south. At the same time, the conditions in Germany enabled him to make and unmake emperors. In France and England, it is true, there now ruled mightier kings than any previous pope had had to deal with outside the Empire; but even these sovereigns were forced to obey the commands of Innocent's legates (§ 72 and note). Philip Augustus, the haughty and successful sovereign of France, was compelled to take back an innocent wife whom he had just put away for another; and John of England even surrendered his kingdom and received it back as a fief of the Holy See, promising annual tribute to Rome. The kings of Portugal and Aragon, rising Christian states [2] in the Spanish peninsula, were Innocent's vassals, and he interfered at will in the government of the other kingdoms there, — Navarre, Castile, and Leon, — as well as in the new Slavonic kingdoms on the eastern frontier of Europe.

Innocent was also a moral reformer, and he led a successful movement for a revival within the church.[3] He adopted the Friar reform (§ 84), which asked for recognition, and he crushed the Albigensian [4] movement, which rejected the church (§ 83).

---

[1] See extracts in Tout, *Empire and Papacy*, 314, 315.

[2] These states were being formed by warfare against the Moors in Spain. See § 155 and the map there.

[3] Special report: the Lateran Council of 1215.

[4] The name came from Albi, or Albiga, a town in southern France, where the sect had many adherents.

83. The Crushing of the Albigenses. — The Albigenses were the most formidable of several heretical sects produced in the twelfth century by a general social and religious discontent. All these movements seem to have drawn strength chiefly from popular feeling against the wealth and corruption of the higher clergy; and most of them quickly subsided when the church roused and reformed itself. But the Albigenses rejected important doctrines of the church, and soon came to rebel against its government. They had their home in Languedoc, or southeastern France, and in that region the dislike for the clergy became so intense that the old byword, "I had rather be a Jew," was exchanged for "I had rather be a priest." Popes and church councils made various ineffectual attempts to reclaim the heretics, and finally Innocent III proclaimed a holy war against them as "more wicked than Saracens." For a hundred years, popes had been preaching a war of the cross against the Mohammedans in Palestine (§ 93): now a crusade was preached against a sect of Christian heretics. Raymond, the mighty Count of Toulouse, tried to protect his subjects; but the feudal nobles of northern France rallied to the Pope's call. Besides the religious motive, these lords hated the rising democracy of southern city-France, and hungered for its rich plunder. A twenty-years' struggle, marked by ferocious massacres, exterminated the heretics and the rising prosperity of Languedoc.

84. The Begging Brotherhoods (Mendicant Friars).[1] — The growing towns of the eleventh and twelfth centuries did not at first fit into the older organization of the church. Neither the rural parish priests nor the monks furnished the machinery to care for the religious needs of the crowded populations. The poorer inhabitants were miserable in body, too, beyond all words, — fever and plague stricken, dying slowly of want and filth and wretchedness such as no modern city knows. Early in the thirteenth century, these conditions, together with the

---

[1] The best brief accounts are given in Jessopp's *Coming of the Friars*, 1-52, and in Lea's *History of the Inquisition*, ch. i.

spread of heretical movements, called forth a general religious revival, with the rise of two new orders of religious workers, — the Franciscan and the Dominican brotherhoods.

The Franciscans (1209) took their name from their founder, *Francis of Assisi*. "Saint Francis," says Dr. Jessopp, "was the John Wesley of the thirteenth century, whom the church did *not* cast out."[1] He was moved by a passionate pity for the ignorant, dying, despairing dregs of the population in the medieval Italian towns about him. A little group of eleven youths caught the inspiration of his noble enthusiasm and self-renunciation. Francis walked to Rome and secured sanction for his plans from Innocent III, and at once the little band of "brothers" (*friars*) began their mission. They went forth, two and two, to the poor and the outcasts, living from day to day in the midst of noisome wretchedness, to act as healers and preachers. They nursed lepers, ministered to the poor, and, with short, homely, fervent speech, preached to all the love of Christ for men and the call to turn from sin. They gave themselves utterly to serve their suffering fellows. Money they would not touch. Literally they were barefooted beggars, with one garment, living from day to day upon chance alms.[2] *They were not monks.* The monk lived in a quiet cloister, and, however beneficial his services were to the world, his first care was for his own soul. The friar sought instead to save the souls and heal the bodies of others, and he went out into the world wherever he could find most suffering and sin.

The Dominicans (1215) grew out of the zeal of *St. Dominic* to convert the Albigenses from their heresy. Dominic was a powerful and fiery preacher, learned in all the theology of the age. Thus, while the Franciscans in origin were missionaries

---

[1] Wesley was the leader of the great Methodist revival in England in the eighteenth century, and Dr. Jessopp's church (the Church of England) "cast out" Wesley's followers. Renan, *New Studies in Religious History*, 305-329, has a good study of St. Francis, as has also Jessop, *Coming of the Friars*, 9-19. The best long account in English is Sabatier's *St. Francis*.

[2] Cf. the precept of Christ to his disciples, *Matthew* x, 9, 10. The Franciscan "rule" is translated in Henderson's *Documents*, 344.

to the poor to alleviate suffering, the Dominicans were preachers to the better classes to combat intellectual error. Naturally the Franciscans (Grey Friars) were of gentler, the Dominicans (Black Friars) of sterner, character.

Before long, however, these differences in character and purpose disappeared, and the two orders became almost identical. They formed a disciplined, omnipresent, devoted soldiery for the church and for the papacy, vastly more effective than the secluded monks, filling for three centuries the place afterward taken by the Jesuits (§ 215).[1] At first they had no central homes of any kind; but as their numbers grew day by day, some fixed abode became necessary. Before long, too, wealth was showered upon them. At first, they had renounced property, not only as individuals, like the monks, but even as orders; but afterward they began to accept it in trust for the poor, and finally for their own use, until they became among the richest orders in Europe.

D. FREDERICK II.

The most gifted of the sons of men, . . . a wonderful man in a wonderful age. — FREEMAN.

85. Character. — Frederick II has been called the last of the great medieval emperors and the first of the great modern kings. Unlike his grandfather, Barbarossa, he was an Italian by birth and nature. In person, he was slight, bald, near-sighted. A Mohammedan historian wrote that as a slave he would not have brought a hundred drachmas. He was an enthusiastic patron of literature, a founder of one of the early universities (§ 180 *a*), and himself a scholar and an author, of no mean ability, in prose and in verse. He wrote charming songs, not in Latin, but in the new Italian tongue of every-day life; and Dante (§ 189) afterward regarded him as the father of Italian poetry. He was deeply interested in the science of

---

[1] As early as 1221 the Dominicans reached England, passing at once to London, Oxford, York, and other towns.

ITALY
IN THE TIME OF
THE HOHENSTAUFEN
(about 1200)
SCALE OF MILES
0 50 100 150 200
FRANCE
KINGDOM OF ARLES
SAVOY
MONT FERRAT
SALUZZO
LOMBARDY
RHETIA
TRENT
FRIULI
CARINTHIA
MARCH OF VERONA
VENETIAN REPUBLIC
KINGDOM OF HUNGARY
SERVIA
EASTERN EMPIRE
ROMAGNA
TUSCANY
ANCONA
MARCH OF CAMERINO
SPOLETO
ST. PETERS PATRIMONY
ABRUZZO
CHIETI
ITALY
KINGDOM OF NAPLES AND SICILY
CALABRIA
CORSICA
SARDINIA
ELBA
Ligurian Sea
ADRIATIC SEA
Arles
Nice
Milan
Pavia
Mantua
Padua
Venice
Trieste
Fiume
Pola
Alessandria
Parma
Po R.
Genoa
Reggio
Bologna
Ravenna
Florence
Pisa
Ancona
Civita Vecchia
Rome
Tiber R.
Ajaccio
Cagliari
Naples
Capua
Salerno
Brindisi
Otranto
Palermo
Reggio
Syracuse
2
6
10
14
18
20
44
40

the Arabs; he ridiculed trial by ordeal and other medieval superstitions; and his own codes of law were far in advance of the barbarous customs and ideas of the age. He was a modern, rather than a medieval man, in his habit of thought and feeling: a many-sided man, warrior, statesman, law-giver, scholar, poet. At the same time, in his private life he was immoral, and sometimes in his public policy cruel and unscrupulous, so that Dante puts him, alone of all the emperors, in hell; and, with all his wonderful genius, he gave his life's energies to buttressing a hopelessly outgrown and tottering system, so that he left no positive result behind him and was only "the most dazzling of a long line of imperial failures."

86. Frederick and the Popes: the Fall of the Hohenstaufen. — The death of Innocent III, in 1216, left the field clear for the moment for the young Emperor, who was just coming to manhood. Politically, there was an irreconcilable opposition of interest between Frederick and the papacy. As Emperor, Frederick was master of North Italy; and as King of Sicily, he was master of the South. Thus he seemed about to bring to success the cherished policy of his house and to establish a consolidated Italy. The chief obstacle to this success was the existence of the Papal States, stretching across Italy from sea to sea. It was almost inevitable that Frederick should wish to join the two parts of his realm. It was certainly inevitable that the popes should fear lest their temporal principality should be crushed between the two arms of the Hohenstaufen power, and that the danger should make them Frederick's relentless foes.

During much of his reign, the Emperor was under sentence of excommunication and deposition. On one occasion during the struggle, when the papal throne became vacant, it was filled by the election of a man who had always been favorable to the imperial side. But Frederick did not deceive himself with false hopes: when he was congratulated, he replied, "I have only lost a friend; no pope can be a Ghibelline." Innocent IV, the new pope, proved, indeed, one of the most formidable opponents any emperor had encountered. Frederick maintained the war during his life, but towards the close with lessening chances of success. He spent his last years like a lion at bay, amid the fierce onslaughts of open enemies and the cruel treacheries of trusted friends; and his death (1250) was followed by quick, complete, and final ruin for his plans, and by the extinction of his family in the relentless strife waged against them by the papal party.

In 1254, the death of Frederick's oldest son, Conrad IV, ushered in a long interregnum for the Empire, and marked the separation of Germany from Italy. To crush another of Frederick's sons, Manfred, in Sicily, the Pope called in *Charles of Anjou*, brother of Louis IX of France (§ 149), and gave him the Sicilian crown.[1]

FOR FURTHER READING. — Emerton, 271–356; Tout, 245–273, 304–335, 358–392; Henderson, *Short History of Germany*, ch. iv; Bryce, *Holy Roman Empire*, chs. xi and xiii. Longer treatments may be consulted in Barry, *The Papal Monarchy;* Freeman, "Frederick King of Italy" and "Frederick II," in *First Series of Essays;* Milman, *Latin Christianity;* Balzani, *Popes and Hohenstaufen;* Alzog, *Church History;* Lea, *History of the Inquisition* (opening chapters); and A. L. Smith, *Frederick II, the Wonder of the World.*

IX. RESULTS OF THE STRIFE BETWEEN EMPERORS AND POPES.

87. Results to the Papacy and to Italy. — The popes had won. They had prevented Italian unity; they had preserved their own predominance as princes in central Italy; and they had excluded the Germans. It is true they had not saved Italy from foreign domination. They had only called in one foreigner against another;[2] and as a result of their policy, Italy,

---

[1] Brief special reports: the tragic story of Conrad IV; of Enzio; of Manfred; of Conradin.

[2] The calling in of the Angevines (house of Anjou) against the Hohenstaufen will remind the student of the calling in of the Franks five centuries before against the Lombards (*Ancient History*, §§ 634, 638).

for centuries to come (§§ 171, 173), was to be the battle ground of France, Spain, and Germany. Incidentally, however, they had assisted the rising Italian towns in the revolt against imperial despotism, and so had helped to prepare for the rich civic life of northern Italy in the next two centuries.

Apparently, the papacy emerged from the two hundred years' contest the unchallenged head of Christendom, and for a time some of the wearers of the papal crown took a loftier tone toward worldly monarchs than even Gregory or Innocent had done. But the victory was short-lived. The growing monarchies in France and England were about to rebel against papal domination in temporal affairs (§ 163), and, in less than fifty years after the death of Frederick II, the papacy entered upon the long "Babylonian Captivity" (§ 165).

88. Results to the Empire and to Germany. — The emperors had failed utterly. Two hundred years later, an English chronicler wrote of the period following the death of Frederick II, "*The Empire in a manner ceased here.*" Certainly the character of the Empire changed radically: (1) Italy was lost, as France had been four centuries earlier; and (2) even in theory the union between the spiritual and temporal headship of Christendom was dissolved. The Empire in character was no longer either "Holy" or "Roman"; it remained only "German."[1]

This was not all. In Germany also there was a striking change. The idea that had made the soul of the Empire was gone; but so, too, was the physical embodiment of it in the German kingdom (§§ 55 *b* and 56). The title King of Germany had long since disappeared in the scramble for the higher dignity of the imperial title (§ 56); or, as Freeman puts it, the

---

[1] From the thirteenth century the Empire is often spoken of as the "German Empire." The term is good as a description, — just as we speak of the "Greek Empire" at Constantinople, — but it is not a proper title in a strict sense. The only empire in history with the title "German Empire," is the one created by Bismarck and King William in 1871.

kingly crown of Germany had been "crushed beneath the loftier imperial diadem." But now more than crown and title had vanished. Says Mr. Bryce, in a sentence of profound meaning, "The kingdom of Germany broke down beneath the weight of the Roman Empire." For the greater part of three hundred years, Germany had been the strongest state in Europe — far in advance of England or France. That leadership was now lost. The emperors had squandered the strength of their northern kingdom in the vain attempt to build up a kingdom in Italy. For twenty years after the last Hohenstaufen (1254–1273), there was no emperor in Germany [1] and no king. These years were the "Great Interregnum," the period of "*Fist-law.*" During this time there was no pretense of central government. The old kingdom had dissolved into a mass of petty fragments, some three hundred in number, — free cities, duchies, marks, counties, — each virtually an independent monarchy or city-republic. The chance to make a united German nation was postponed six hundred years. In 1273, the name of Emperor was revived by the election of *Count Rudolph of Hapsburg:* but little more than the name remained (§§ 158 ff.).

REVIEW EXERCISES.

1. Fact drills (cf. *Ancient History*, 245, 246, for suggestions).
    a. *Dates:* 843, 962, 987, 1066; (class fill in the events). 1075–1254 (struggle between Empire and papacy), 1122 (Concordat of Worms, which divides struggle of Empire and papacy into two chapters), 1176 (Legnano).
    b. *Fix other events in connection with the dates given above;* such as Lechfeld, Lombard League, Peace of Constance.
    c. *Extend list of terms* for brief explanation (see page 51): *Hugh Capet, Guelf, benefit of clergy, Pataria, Peter's Pence, Canossa, mark states,* etc.

---

[1] Two emperors were elected during this period, — a Spaniard and an Englishman (the brother of Henry III), — but neither of them actually appeared in Germany to enter upon the government.

GERMANY AND ITALY
During the Interregnum
1254-1273

SCALE OF MILES
0   50   100   200

2. Make a syllabus of the work so far. This may be done readily from the headings of paragraphs, upon the plan of the Analytical Table of Contents in the *Ancient History*.
3. Review questions by the class (cf. page 51). For example: give the two divisions of the struggle between Empire and papacy, characterizing each, and naming leaders and chief events.
4. Catch-word reviews (cf. *Ancient History*, 153).
    a. Germany from Charles the Fat to 962.
    b. The Holy Roman Empire, to 1273.
5. Map review. Compare the four maps on the Empire (including the one on the Partition of Verdun) for varying boundaries and for increase in number of political divisions.

CHAPTER II.

THE AGE OF THE CRUSADES, 1100-1300.

I. CONDITIONS IN THE EAST BEFORE THE CRUSADES.

89. The Mohammedan World[1] before the Coming of the Turk. — From 800 to 1100, Western Europe had stood to Asia much as Asia now stands to Europe. It was far below both the Greek and the Mohammedan world in civilization. The Mohammedans still ruled from the Pyrenees to the Ganges and the Jaxartes. This wide dominion, it is true, was broken up into many states, but the civilization of the Saracens had not yet begun to decline. They had utilized the old culture of Persia and of Greece. Their governments were as good as the Oriental world had ever known. Their roads and canals encouraged commerce and bound together distant regions. Their magnificent cities were built with a peculiar and beautiful architecture.[2] Their manufactures were the finest in the world, both for beautiful design and for delicate workmanship. Their glass and pottery and metal work, their dye-stuffs, their paper, their preparations of leather, all represented industries almost or wholly unknown to the West. We still speak of "Toledo" blades and "Morocco" leather. Their agriculture was scientific, with the use of irrigation and fertilizers; and by grafting they had produced many new varieties of fruit and flowers.

In intellectual lines their superiority was no less marked. While Europe had only a few monastic schools to light its

---

[1] On early Mohammedanism, see *Ancient History*, §§ 620-626 and 648.
[2] Saracenic architecture was characterized by the horse-shoe arch, the dome, the turret, the graceful minaret, and a rich ornament of "arabesque."

"Dark Ages," the Arabs had great universities, with libraries containing hundreds of thousands of manuscripts. Philosophy, theology, law, rhetoric, were subjects for special study; much progress had been made in astronomy; chemistry had been begun; algebra had been greatly developed; spherical trigonometry had been created; and while Europe still treated

THE COURT OF LIONS, ALHAMBRA.

disease from the point of view of an Indian "Medicine Man," the Saracens had established, on Greek foundations, a real science of medicine.

90. The Byzantine Empire. — Midway in character, as in geographical position, between Latin Europe and Mohammedan Asia, lay the Greek Empire, living on for centuries its quiet, orderly life. In material prosperity it was unexcelled anywhere in the world, and in intellectual activity it was surpassed only by the Saracens. Until recently, writers have been accustomed to refer to the Greek Empire as altogether mean and uninteresting. The opinion of later scholars is indicated in the following brief characterizations.[1]

"A government which with all its faults, for many centuries discharged its functions better than any contemporary government in the world. . . . Wise legislators, able administrators, valiant generals, profound scholars, acute theologians were the natural product of the soil, century after century."— FREEMAN, "Byzantine Empire," in the *Third Series of Essays*.

"The Empire of the East maintained its existence like an agitated flame, sending forth great gleams of light, which vanished only to reappear with renewed brightness. During more than six centuries [after Charlemagne's Empire fell] it defended itself against the darkness that finally overtook it."— LAVISSE, *Political History of Europe*, 30.

DOORWAY TO THE HALL OF THE AMBASSADORS, ALHAMBRA.

The Empire was a civilized state, standing on the defensive against barbarian attack, and waging its wars mainly by means of Norse mercenaries. Its emperors were often devoted scholars and able authors, as well as great rulers. Constantinople in magnificence and extent was unapproached by the rude towns of France and Germany; and its wealth, splendor,

---

[1] There are good statements in Tout's *Empire and Papacy*, 151, 152; and see, for detail, 152–175. Students may consult also Oman's *Byzantine Empire*, and Finlay's *History of Greece*.

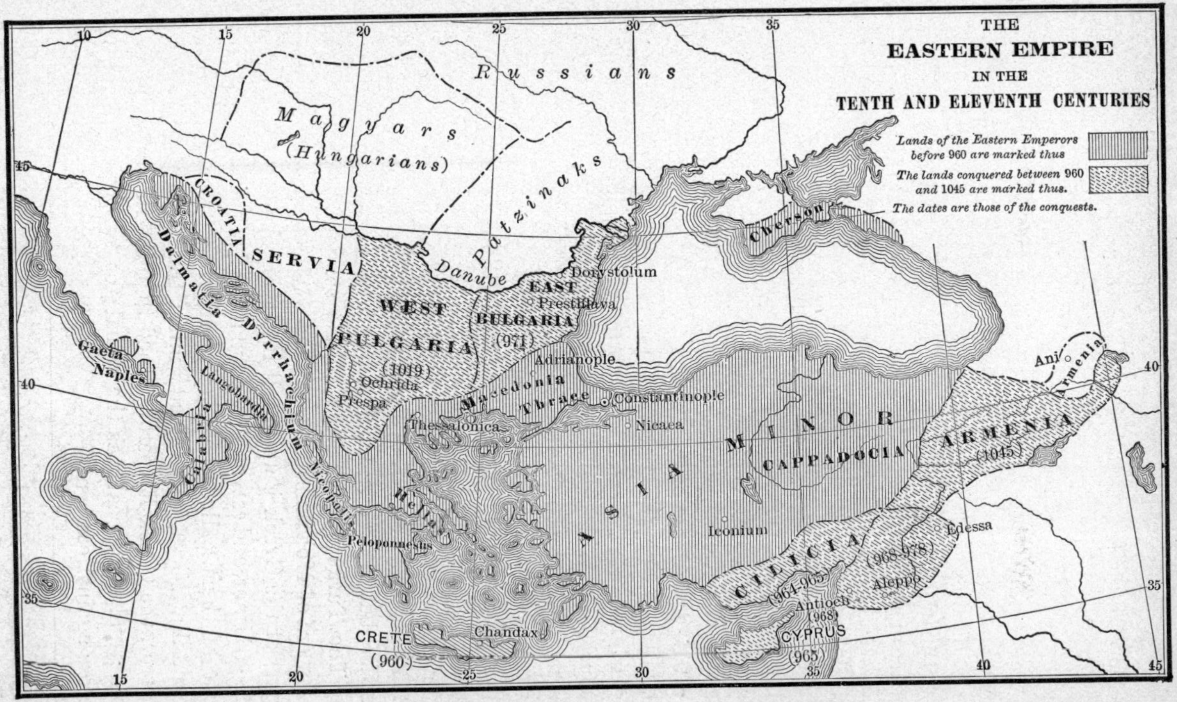
THE
EASTERN EMPIRE
IN THE
TENTH AND ELEVENTH CENTURIES
Lands of the Eastern Emperors before 960 are marked thus
The lands conquered between 960 and 1045 are marked thus.
The dates are those of the conquests.
Russians
Magyars (Hungarians)
Patzinaks
CROATIA
SERVIA
Danube
Dorystolum
EAST BULGARIA (971)
Prestlava
WEST BULGARIA (1019)
Ochrida
Prespa
Adrianople
Macedonia
Thrace
Constantinople
Nicaea
Thessalonica
Dalmatia
Dyrrhachium
Nicopolis
Gaeta
Naples
Langobardia
Calabria
Hellas
Peloponnesus
CRETE (960)
Chandax
ASIA MINOR
CAPPADOCIA
ARMENIA (1045)
Ani
Armenia
Cherson
Iconium
CILICIA (964-965)
Antioch (968)
CYPRUS (965)
Aleppo
(968-978)
Edessa

and comforts, — its paved and lighted streets, its schools and theaters, its orderly police system, its hospitals and parks, — were all new features to the few visitors from the West. Such trade as Western Europe possessed, was mainly in Greek hands; and the "Byzant," the coin of Constantinople, was the standard of coinage over Europe.

During most of its history, the Empire comprised the greater part of Asia Minor, many islands, and at least the coast regions of the Balkan peninsula in Europe. The more distant parts of that peninsula were divided between two Slav peoples, the Servians and the Bulgarians.[1] These peoples were sometimes tributaries, sometimes foes, of Constantinople, but from that source, they, like the Russians, had drawn their Christianity and civilization.

91. Appearance of the Turks. — In the eleventh century, the civilization of the Saracens received a fatal blow, and the existence of the Greek Empire was endangered. Political supremacy in the Mohammedan world fell to the *Seljuk Turks*, a new Tartar people from beyond the Jaxartes. The Turks were to play somewhat the same part in the Saracenic world that the Teutons had played in the old Roman world, — with this tremendous difference, that even to the present day they have not assimilated civilization. The Saracenic culture survived long enough to be transplanted into Europe during the crusades, but in its own home it was doomed to swift decay.

The Turks were at least mighty soldiers, and they began a new era of Mohammedan conquest. Almost at once the greater part of the Greek Empire fell into their hands. They overran Asia Minor, and established a number of principalities there, — one of them, called the Empire of "Roum" (Rome), with its capital at Nicea, only seventy miles from Constantinople. In terror, the Greek Emperor turned to Western Christendom for aid; and his appeal was the signal for two centuries of war, cross against crescent.

---

[1] *Ancient History*, §§ 581, 624.

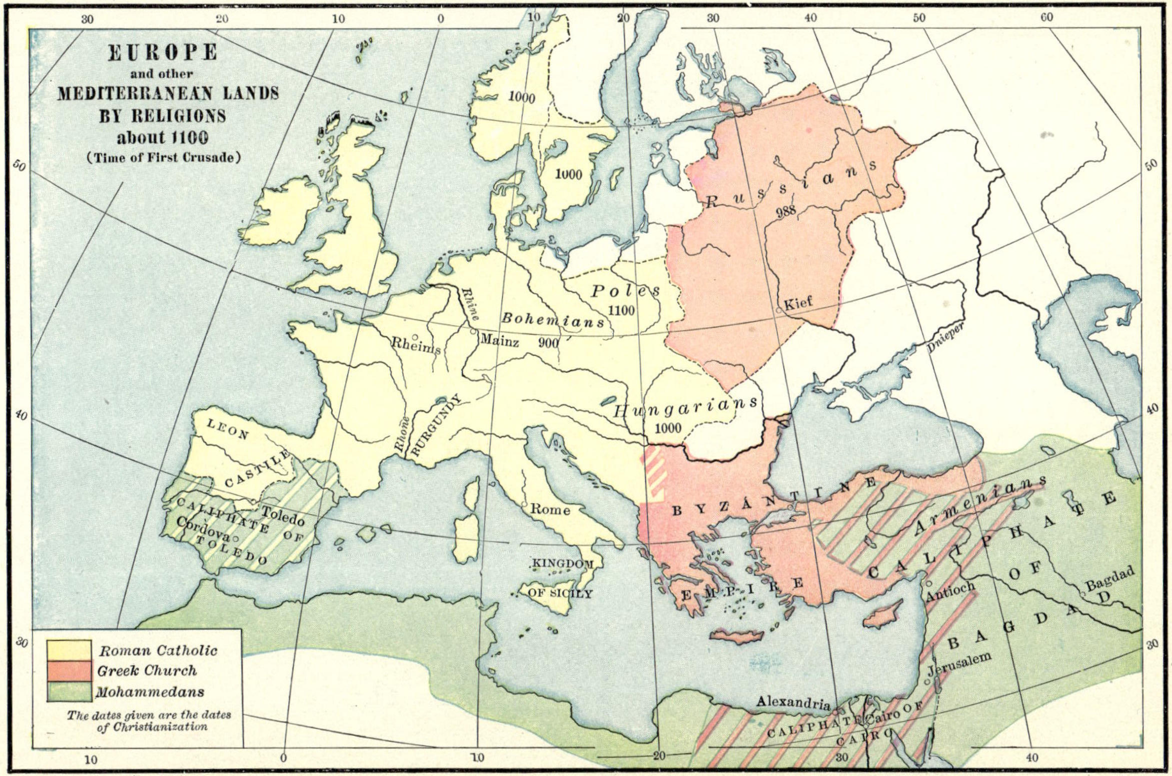
EUROPE
and other
MEDITERRANEAN LANDS
BY RELIGIONS
about 1100
(Time of First Crusade)
Roman Catholic
Greek Church
Mohammedans
The dates given are the dates of Christianization
1000
1000
Russians
988
Kief
Dnieper
Poles
1100
Bohemians
900
Rhine
Mainz
Rheims
BURGUNDY
Rhone
Hungarians
1000
LEON
CASTILE
CALIPHATE OF TOLEDO
Toledo
Cordova
Rome
KINGDOM OF SICILY
BYZANTINE EMPIRE
Armenians
CALIPHATE OF BAGDAD
Bagdad
Antioch
Jerusalem
Alexandria
Cairo
CALIPHATE OF CAIRO

II. THE CRUSADES.

THE WEST TAKES THE OFFENSIVE AGAINST THE EAST.

The point upon which the Middle Ages turned from the darkness and disorder of the earlier times to the greater light and order of modern times. — GEORGE BURTON ADAMS.

A lamentable tale of divided counsels, of incredible ignorance, of heroic bravery, and of frightful sacrifice. — EMERTON.

A. CHARACTER AND CAUSES.

92. Place in History. — In the ninth century, Europe for a while had seemed defenseless against plundering bands of Norse or Saracen raiders, but now — so strong had it grown under the military system of feudalism — for two hundred years it poured a ceaseless stream of mailed knights into Asia. From about 1100 to about 1300, there was fighting between Christian and Mohammedan in the East, and during all this time bands of nobles from various parts of Europe kept going off to join the war. At times, it is true, there were particularly impressive movements of mighty armies into Asia, and these are commonly known as the eight crusades; but this numbering of a few great expeditions must not blind us to the more important fact that the conflict was practically continuous.

To a broad view, the crusades were one more chapter in the age-long struggle between East and West,[1] in which Marathon, Zama, Arbela, and Tours had been earlier episodes. But it is also true that the appearance of the Turk gave a new aspect to the strife. It was no longer a conflict between two types of civilization. It was thenceforth for centuries a conflict between the only possible civilization and a brutal and destructive barbarism, — as before had been the case only at brief moments of time, in the old Scythian invasions or in the attack of Attila's Huns.[2]

---

[1] Cf. *Ancient History*, §§ 153, 176, 240, 358, 625.

[2] *Ancient History*, § 570. True, in 1100 the Europeans were excelled in culture by the lands which had just fallen to the Turk; but there was no hope for those lands after the Turkish conquest.

93. Causes of the Crusades: the Greek Appeal and the Abuse of Pilgrims by the Turks. Urban at Clermont. — The Greek call for aid against the infidel, the common foe of all Christians, was the immediate occasion for the crusades; but that call would probably have produced little effect if Western Europe had not had deep grievances of its own against the Turk.

The key to the understanding of the crusades is found in the fact that *they were simply a new form of pilgrimage, and the only kind any longer possible.* Pilgrimages to holy shrines were a leading feature of medieval life: good men made them to satisfy religious enthusiasm; evil men, to secure forgiveness for crime; sick men, to heal bodily ills. A pilgrimage was an act of worship, and it was regarded as meritorious in itself. Chief of all pilgrimages, of course, was that to the land where Christ had lived and to the tomb where His body had been laid. In particular, after the religious revival early in the eleventh century (§ 59), a steady stream of pilgrims from Europe visited Palestine, sometimes in bands of hundreds. In 1064, the archbishop of Mainz led one company of seven thousand to the Holy Land.

CHURCH OF THE HOLY SEPULCHER AT JERUSALEM; present condition. This church was built by Constantine about the year 325 and was restored by the Crusaders in 1099. It is supposed to contain the place of the burial of Christ.

The Saracens had permitted these pilgrimages, and had even encouraged them as a means of revenue; but in 1076 the Turks captured Jerusalem from the Arabs, and at once began to persecute all Christians there. Tales of suffering and of wrongs, told by returned pilgrims, filled Europe with shame and wrath, and prepared Latin Christendom to respond to the Greek Emperor's appeal for aid. Each crusader marched to avenge pilgrims and at the same time to make a pilgrimage himself. He was "*an armed pilgrim*" to the holiest of shrines.

The messengers from Constantinople came to *Pope Urban,* as the head of Christendom, in 1095. Twenty years before, Gregory VII had wished to put himself at the head of an army to relieve the Eastern Empire from a threatened Turkish advance, but had been prevented by the strife with Henry IV. Now Urban at once assumed the leadership, and at a great council of French nobles at *Clermont,* preached a war of the Cross against the infidel. His eloquence [1] thrilled the multitude to a frenzy of enthusiasm, and they caught up his cry, "God wills it! God wills it!" A great expedition was arranged for the following spring, and all over Europe men were called upon to "take the cross," — that is, to pledge themselves to the expedition by fastening a red cross on the breast.[2] The political motive, to relieve the Greek Empire, sank almost out of mind. The crusaders seemed to think only of recovering the Holy Sepulcher.

There were, however, other motives, less noble, and less prominent in records, but hardly less potent. *Multitudes of nobles were influenced largely by greedy hopes of winning new principalities in Asia.* Indeed, the Greek Emperor, in his letters to western leaders, laid chief emphasis on this inducement, and even Pope Urban did not neglect it in his address at Clermont. "Wrest the land from that wicked race," said he, "and

---

[1] See *Pennsylvania Reprints,* I, No. 2.

[2] Special report: the preaching of Peter the Hermit, its real value, and the old error regarding its importance as a cause of the crusades. See, especially, *Pennsylvania Reprints,* I, No. 2.

possess it for yourselves." [1] Many men, too, were moved in great measure *by military ardor and by the mere spirit of adventure*, — the desire to see the world ; while others found in the crusades a chance *to escape punishment for crime*.[2]

None the less, the real cause of the crusades was religious zeal: the war was truly a " war of the cross," and all these grosser motives only helped to rally recruits about a banner which a high enthusiasm had set up.

B. The Story.

94. The First Crusade and Preliminary Movements. — The crusades opened with a pathetic and absurd movement which shows both the sincere enthusiasm and the ignorant credulity of the age.[3] Great hordes of peasantry, impatient of delay, without waiting for the army of nobles, set off to rescue the Holy Land, under a preaching monk and a beggar knight, *Peter the Hermit* and *Walter the Penniless*. These multitudes — ignorant, unorganized, almost unarmed, and altogether without supplies — expected divine guidance and aid. Most of them perished miserably in the terrible journey through the Danube valley, either by starvation and disease, or by the attacks of the Christian natives, whose lands they were pillaging for food; and the remnants, as soon as they reached Asia, were annihilated by the Turks.

In the spring of 1096, swarms of the real crusaders began to make their way through Europe to Constantinople, the

---

[1] Closely related to this consideration was the need of some outlet for the increasing population of France. That country had just sent the Normans into England and Italy, and other bands of adventurers into Portugal. In like manner, she now poured her swarming military population into the East. The crusading armies were so dominantly French that the Greeks and Mohammedans came to use the names "Frank" and "Latin" interchangeably, and to apply either term to any inhabitant of Western Europe.

[2] Urban dwelt upon this inducement also, and urged those "who have been robbers" to "become soldiers of Christ." From the moment a man took the cross, the church promised him forgiveness for all past sins, and forbade all attacks, even by the law, upon his person or his property. For some curious documents illustrating these points, see *Pennsylvania Reprints*, I, No. 2.

[3] Special report, to show a like lesson : the Children's Crusade.

appointed place of meeting. There they gathered, some three hundred thousand strong, according to the chroniclers, — one hundred thousand of them mailed horsemen, — the most formidable army Europe has ever sent against Asia. The Greek Emperor, fearful lest these fierce allies might turn upon his own realm, hastened their departure into Asia. There they endured terrible suffering and loss, in march, skirmish, battle, and siege, while the leaders quarreled savagely among themselves; but fortunately the Mohammedans at this time were even more broken up into hostile camps, and in July, 1099, the Christians stormed Jerusalem, amid hideous butchery and wild transports of religious enthusiasm.

95. The Latin States in Syria, and the Military Orders. — The First Crusade is said to have cost Europe a million lives, — counting the reënforcements that poured into Asia each year while the struggle had been going on, — but no doubt the figures are greatly exaggerated. Two important political results were accomplished. (1) The Greek Empire recovered much of Asia Minor. (2) The greater nobles among the crusaders divided the conquered Syrian districts among themselves and set up there four "Latin states," of which the chief was the "Kingdom of Jerusalem." Each ruler divided his realm in feudal fashion among his retainers, and, on the soil of Asia, a complete feudal society sprang up, to continue the war against the crescent.

These Latin states found the core of their fighting force in a new institution, which combined in a remarkable fashion the two opposite ideals of the age, — that of the monk and that of the knight. Three orders of *fighting monks* arose.[1] The *Knights of St. John*, or of the Hospital, grew out of an organization to care for the sick and wounded: soon the nurses became themselves warriors and knights; they took the monk's threefold vow of poverty, chastity, and obedience, and added a fourth,

---

[1] Brief accounts are given in Emerton, 372–374, and in Tout, *Empire and Papacy*, 189–191. The Teutonic Order is treated in Henderson's *Short History of Germany*, 173–181.

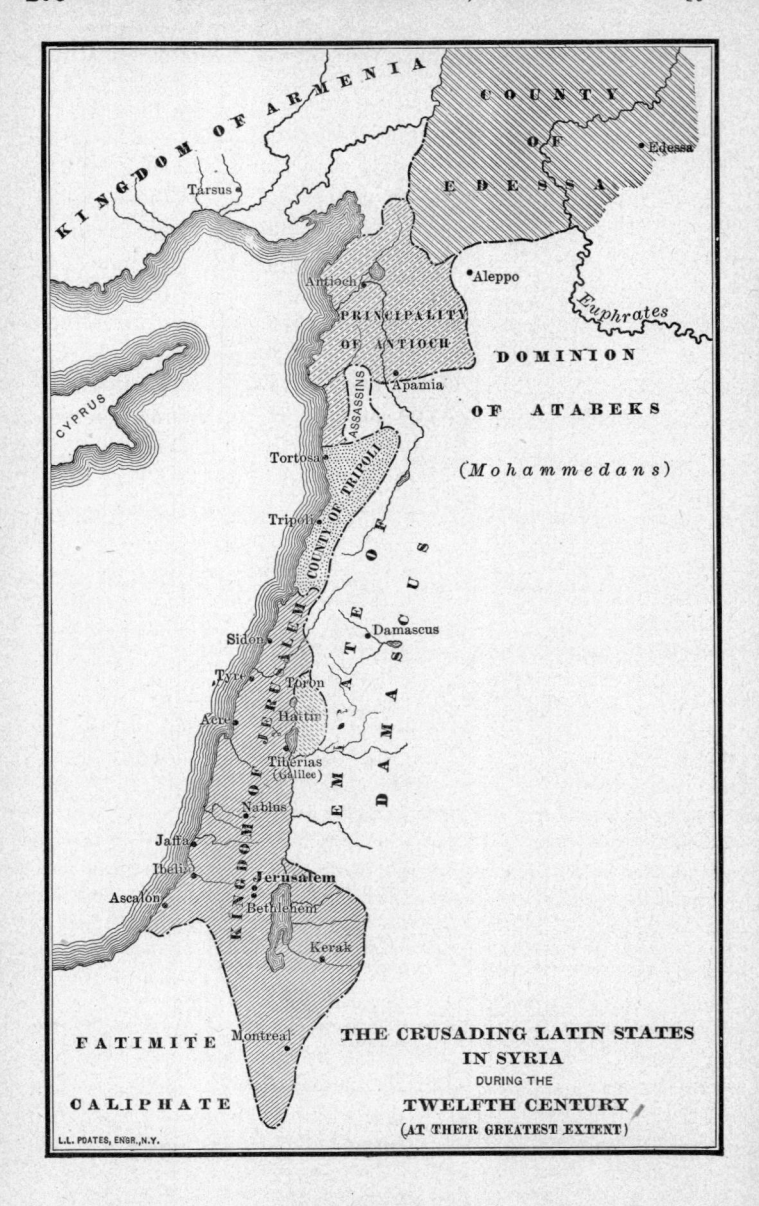

THE CRUSADING LATIN STATES IN SYRIA DURING THE TWELFTH CENTURY (AT THEIR GREATEST EXTENT)

binding themselves to perpetual warfare against the infidel. The *Templars* arose in like manner out of a society to succor distressed pilgrims, and the name came from the fact that the eight or nine knights who originally composed the organization dwelt in a house near Solomon's Temple. The *Teutonic Order* grew out of the hospitality of a German merchant toward his needy countrymen in Jerusalem. All three orders played important parts in later history.

96. The Second Crusade. — For nearly fifty years the new Latin states, reënforced by the annual streams of pilgrim-crusaders, kept the Mohammedan from the Holy Land. Finally, however, the enemy began to gain ground again, and in 1147, Europe was alarmed by the fall of Edessa, the foremost outpost of the Christian power in Syria. St. Bernard (§ 72, note) at once preached another great crusade. This time, Emperor Conrad III and King Louis VII of France were persuaded to lead the expedition. The enterprise failed miserably, from bad generalship and ignorance; but the numbers of crusaders left by it in Palestine enabled the Christian states there to make head, for a time, against the enemy.

97. The Third Crusade. — Each new generation was ready for its new crusade; and forty years after Conrad's failure, the capture of Jerusalem by Saladin[1] called Europe again to arms. The Christian states in Palestine had been reduced to a mere strip of coast, but now the great sovereigns of Western Europe — *Frederick Barbarossa* of Germany, *Philip II* of France, and *Richard* of England — united in a mighty effort for the recovery of the Holy Land. The Third Crusade is the best known and the most romantic of the whole series; but it failed to produce important results, because of the death of Barbarossa (§ 81) and the jealousies between the French and English kings.

98. Fourth Crusade: the Latin Empire at Constantinople. — The true crusading era closed with the Third Crusade. The failure of that movement, it is true, at once called forth another effort, but the Fourth Crusade was diverted from its purpose as a religious war against the infidel into a commercial war upon a Christian state. Venice furnished the ships for the expedition; and her rulers, jealous of Constantinople's monopoly of the eastern trade, persuaded the crusaders to attack the Greek Empire. For a time that venerable empire disappeared, and the crusaders shared the booty among themselves. Venice took some three-eighths of the old imperial territory, mostly islands and coast regions;

---

[1] Special report: character and work of Saladin.

various petty fragments were made into Frankish principalities, like the "Duchy of Athens";[1] and a "Latin Empire" was set up at Constantinople (1204). Long wars followed between this Frank, or "Latin," state and the remnants of the Greek power;[2] and fifty years later, in 1261, the Greek Empire at Constantinople was restored. It was to endure two centuries more, but it never recovered its former vigor. The Fourth Crusade, in its greedy attack upon this ancient champion of Christendom in the East, was a crime against the cause of the crusades.

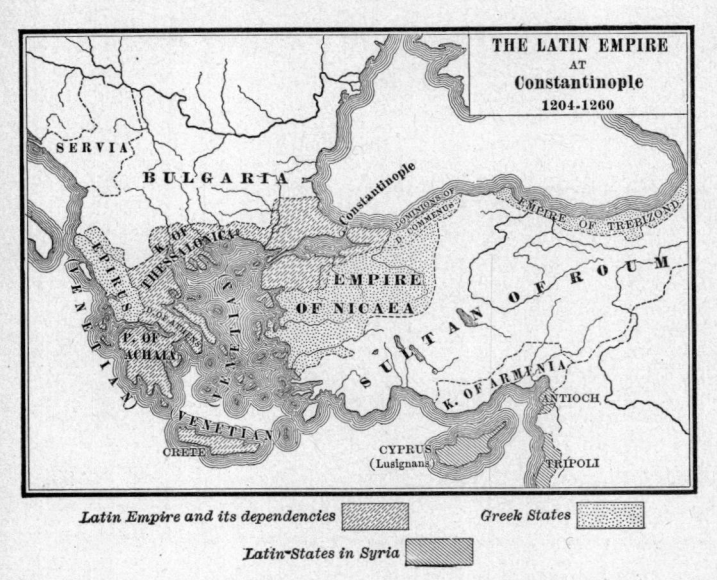

99. The Later Crusades are of minor consequence. Their actual military operations were carried on largely in Egypt, which had become a chief center of Mohammedan power. After a terrible loss of life in the Fifth and Sixth Crusades, the Emperor Frederick II (§§ 85, 86) recovered Jerusalem by peaceful negotiation (1230): but it was soon lost again to the

---

[1] Advanced students may like to read Finlay's account of the Dukes of Athens, *History of Greece*, IV, 132–173. It was the brilliant court of these medieval "dukes" that Chaucer and Shakspere had in mind in their references to *ancient* Athenian history; cf. "Duke Theseus," in *A Midsummer Night's Dream*.

[2] This of course still called itself "Roman," — so that we read for a time of the wars of the "Latins" against the "Romans."

Turks. Then, in 1249, Louis IX of France organized the Seventh Crusade. This attempt came to nothing; and the crusading spirit expired with another expedition, twenty years later, in which Louis died at Tunis.

Before 1300, the last territory of the Latins in Syria had fallen finally to the Turks; and thereafter, men who still wished to fight for the cross went to aid the Christian princes in Spain against the Moors, or warred against the heathen on the northeast of Europe. The Teutonic order removed to Germany and took up the conquest and settlement of heathen Prussia, so laying the foundation for the greatness of a future German state.[1] The Knights of St. John withdrew to Rhodes, where in constant warfare, for two hundred years more, they formed the outpost of Christendom against Mohammedanism.

100. Why the Crusades ceased.—The crusades ceased because they had themselves produced a new age and a new spirit. Men had found interests and duties nearer home. This is well shown in a story told by Joinville in his life of St. Louis (cf. § 40). Joinville, one of the greatest nobles of France, came of a family of famous crusaders; he had accompanied Louis IX on the Seventh Crusade, and had persisted in continuing it after all the other counsellors of the King had advised return; but when Louis made his second expedition, Joinville stoutly refused to go at all. The King had summoned his nobles to a great assembly. Joinville, suspecting the purpose, tried to excuse himself from attending; and, when he arrived, he found the other nobles in consternation. "Never believe me," said one knight of the royal council, "if the King is not going to take the cross." Whereupon another replied, "If he does, it will be one of the saddest days that ever befell France. And if we do not take the cross we shall lose the King's affection; and if we do take it, we shall lose God's favor, because it will not be on His account that we take it." Joinville was pressed by the King to join,—"Whereto I replied that while I was serving God and the King beyond sea before, the officers

EFFIGY FROM A FUNERAL SLAB in Salisbury Cathedral, 1250. The crossing of the legs indicates a crusader.

---

[1] See maps following pages 70 and 130.

of the King had ruined myself and impoverished my people; and that if I wished now to please God I should remain here to defend my people; for if I risked myself for the cross when I saw clearly that it would be for the damage of my people, I should bring down upon me the wrath of God, who gave his life to save His people. . . . And I considered that those committed a deadly sin who advised him to that voyage, because France was then at peace with itself and all its neighbors, and after his departure, its condition has never ceased to grow worse and worse."

C. Results upon Western Europe.

101. Importance. — During the crusading centuries, Europe made great progress in culture. Sometimes this advance is ascribed wholly to the crusades. These movements themselves, however, would not have been possible, if an advance from the condition of the ninth century had not already begun. But, though the crusades did not begin the advance, they did increase and modify it. They failed of their avowed object; but they retarded Mohammedan advance for some centuries, and their indirect results upon Europe were vastly more important to the world than the recovery of Palestine would have been.

102. Intellectual Results. — In their effect upon the intellect, the crusades stand to medieval Europe somewhat as the Persian wars to Greece, or the Punic wars to Rome: they brought new energies into play and opened up new worlds of thought. They gave at once some new possessions in science, art, medical knowledge, and architecture. They furnished heroic figures and a romantic setting for the poet's use, so that literary activity was stimulated and numerous histories of the crusades were written. The horizon was widened: men had gained acquaintance with new lands, new peoples, new standards of life and conduct. Best of all, Europeans had learned that there was more to learn and that the despised infidel could teach them much. Even among the Arabs they had found men brave, just, honorable, and religious. There was a new stir in the intellectual atmosphere, and the way was prepared for the intellectual uprising of the Renaissance (§§ 179–189).

103. Commercial Results. — As long as the Latin states in Syria lasted (nearly two hundred years), they were practically military colonies, dependent upon Europe for weapons, horses, and supplies of food. From the first, such supplies had to be transported by sea, and, after the Second Crusade, the crusaders themselves always journeyed by ship. This stimulated shipbuilding, and led to an increased production in Europe of many commodities for these new markets.

Even more important was the reappearance in the West of long-forgotten Oriental products.[1] Europeans now learned to use sugar-cane, spices, dates, buckwheat, sesame, saffron, apricots, melons, oils, perfumes, and various drugs and dyes, and, among new objects of manufacture, cottons, silks, rugs, calicoes, muslins (from Mosul), damasks (from Damascus), satins, velvets, delicate glassware, the cross-bow, the windmill. Many of these things became almost necessaries of life; some of them were soon grown or manufactured in Europe; others, like spices,[2] could not be produced there. In consequence, commerce with Asia augmented enormously. For a time, Venice and Genoa, assisted by their favorable positions, monopolized much of the new carrying-trade, but all the ports of Western Europe were more or less affected.[3]

104. Money replaces Barter.[4] — All these commercial transactions, as well as the fitting out of the crusades themselves, called for *money*. The system of barter and of exchange of services, by which Europe had lived for some centuries, was outgrown, and a new economic system was born. Bankers now appeared,[5] and coinage received a marvelous impetus.

---

[1] On the older trade with the East, see *Ancient History*, § 478.

[2] In the absence of fresh meat in winter and of our modern root-foods, spices became of immense importance for the table.

[3] This commercial activity called for quicker methods of reckoning; and at this time Europe adopted the Arabic numerals (*Ancient History*, § 2 note).

[4] Cunningham, *Western Civilization*, II, 74–77; Adams, *Civilization*, 297.

[5] Until this time the Jews had been the only money-lenders. Christians had regarded all lending for interest (usury) as sinful. An excellent topic for a report by an advanced student is the treatment of the Jews in Western Europe during the Middle Ages.

105. Political and Social Results of the Crusades. — The crusades undermined feudalism and encouraged new social forces. The introduction of money did away with the economic basis of feudalism (§ 23): the relations between tenant and landlord no longer needed to rest upon exchange of services for land. The presence of money, too, enabled the kings to collect national revenues, and so to maintain disciplined and regular standing armies, more efficient than the old feudal array (§ 28). But the crusades struck more direct blows than these at feudalism. They swept away multitudes of the feudal lords themselves. Hundreds of thousands of barons and knights squandered their possessions in preparing for the expedition, and then left their bones in Palestine; so that in Europe the ground was cleared for a new society and for a new system of government.

And the crusades helped new social and political systems to grow up, to take the place vacated by the dying feudalism. To get money wherewith to equip their followers for the crusades, the great barons mortgaged their possessions to the kings, and sometimes the smaller barons sold theirs outright; while both classes sold charters of rights to the rising towns. Thus the kings consolidated their dominions and got rid of dangerous rivals; and at the same time the towns rose to political power. Until the twelfth century there had been only two "estates," or political classes, in European society, — clergy and nobles. Now the townsmen appeared as a "third estate."[1] This "third estate" wanted order, and the kings could help to secure it; while the kings wanted money, and the third estate could supply it. So these two elements allied themselves still further against the weakened remnants of the feudal system, and soon feudalism was little more than a form. It was succeeded, as a political system, by the free cities

---

[1] The peasantry did not yet count politically, but even they were benefited by the new conditions: the fact that they might be tempted to run away to the towns (which were always glad to afford them refuge) helped to secure them better treatment from their lords.

(§§ 106 ff.) and by the "new monarchies" (§§ 147 ff.). The members of a new nobility which soon appeared, with the title and honors of the old, were dependent on the monarch, instead of being his rivals.

FOR FURTHER READING. — Three contemporary accounts are printed in the volume, *Chronicles of the Crusades;* Joinville's account in his *St. Louis* — one of the three narratives in that volume — is especially excellent. Further source material will be found in *Pennsylvania Reprints,* I and II, and Archer's *Crusade of Richard I* in the series, "English History by Contemporary Writers."

Modern accounts: Archer and Kingsford, *The Crusades* (probably the best account in English; especially good for the "Kingdom of Jerusalem"); Tout, *Empire and Papacy,* 175–197, 295–304; Cox, *The Crusades;* Gray, *The Children's Crusade;* Gilman, *The Saracens;* Emerton, *Medieval Europe,* ch. xi; Adams, *Civilization,* ch. xi; Pears, *Fall of Constantinople;* Oman, *Byzantine Empire,* and *The Art of War;* Cutts, *Scenes and Characters of the Middle Ages,* 157–194; Lane-Poole, *Saladin;* Perry, *St. Louis.* See also references in footnotes.

In fiction: Scott's *Talisman.*

SPECIAL REPORTS. — 1. Impressions that a student gets from the letters of crusaders given in *Pennsylvania Reprints,* I, No. 4.   2. The Third Crusade.   3. The Latin Kingdom of Jerusalem.   4. The warfare of the crusaders (see Oman's *History of the Art of War*).

EXERCISE. — Catchword review of the crusades.

CHAPTER III.

WESTERN EUROPE FROM THE BEGINNING OF THE CRUSADES TO THE REFORMATION, 1100-1520.

I. THE RISE OF THE TOWNS.

A. SIGNIFICANCE.

106. Society ceases to be exclusively Rural: a Fourth Type added to the Three of Earlier Centuries. — Ancient civilization had been a city civilization. Thus, though Gaul was civilized late, yet in the last century of Roman rule it contained over a hundred flourishing cities with municipal institutions.[1] But in the fifth century A.D., through the barbarian invasions, city life in Western Europe gave way to a less organized country life. This was one of the most striking and far-reaching results of that terrible period. *European society remained essentially rural for over five hundred years, and, after the development of feudalism, the three typical figures in that society were the tonsured priest, the mailed horseman, and the field laborer bent with toil and hard fare.* Then, in the eleventh century, cities again appeared; and alongside the priest, the knight, and the peasant, there stood forth another figure, — *the townsman,* or burgher.

Feudalism was to remain dominant for a while, but the rising towns stood for forces hostile to its life; and the men of the town — traders and artisans — were finally to replace the knights as the decisive force in society. *Feudalism had arisen out of war, and it was militant in purpose and nature. The towns grew out of trade ;* and, though they could and did fight valiantly, *they were essentially industrial.* When they fought they

---

[1] *Ancient History,* §§ 478, 479.

did so, not as a business, but in order that they might have a chance to carry on their real business of peaceful industry.

107. Material Well-being. — It is difficult for us to realize how much this appearance of the burgher meant to European society. The twelfth and thirteenth centuries saw one of the greatest social and economic changes in the world's history. Labor ceased to be wholly agricultural: the new towns were workshops and trading factories. New wants, new comforts, new occupations appeared. Rude country barter and "payment in kind" were replaced by money transactions and by bills of exchange. Peasant villages were transformed into walled towns of three thousand or three hundred thousand inhabitants.[1] Thatched hovels, with dirt floors, gave way to comfortable and even stately burghers' homes. Universal misery and squalor among the industrial classes were replaced, for a large part of the population, by happy luxury; and there followed a lavish expenditure for town halls and cathedrals and for civic feasts and shows.

Still, even on the material side, the medieval European city fell far behind the ancient Greek or Roman city or the contemporary Arabian city. There were no street lights at night, no city water supply, no sewerage, no street-cleaning, no paving. Dead animals rotted in the streets and narrow lanes; and the story is told that on one occasion in the fifteenth century a German emperor, warmly welcomed in a loyal city, was almost swallowed up, horse and rider, in the bottomless filth, as he entered the city-gate. Frankfort, in 1387, found it necessary to forbid the building of pig-sties in the public streets, and Ulm a little later was troubled by swine running loose. Within doors, too, the material prosperity was not for all. Says Dr. Jessop, " The sediment of the town population was a dense

---

[1] Milan, in Italy (§ 80), counted some three hundred thousand inhabitants and some of the largest German cities numbered perhaps fifty thousand; but in general the towns were small, — from three thousand to six thousand people. Up to the year 1500, England had only three cities with over twelve thousand inhabitants.

OLD STREET IN ROUEN, present condition. The Cathedral is visible at the opening of the street into the square. Probably the appearance of the street has changed little since the fourteenth century.

slough of stagnant misery, squalor, famine, loathsome disease, and dull despair." There was no adequate police system, and street fights were constant. At night, no well-to-do citizen stirred abroad without his armor and a guard of stout apprentice lads, and he was always compelled to fortify and guard his house.

108. The Political Change. — The change was political also. The townsmen became the "third estate" (§ 105). The importance of the political change, however, great as it was, is easily overstated. The townsmen were not the "people" of a nation, in the modern sense. They were only one more "class" risen from the unreckoned mass, to stand beside the two smaller but higher classes previously recognized. Society continued for centuries to be organized in classes, not as one people; and the new "third estate" looked down upon the great mass of unskilled workmen and of agricultural laborers with the same bigoted and haughty contempt with which it was itself regarded by the nobles.[1] So far as the burghers fought for popular liberty, they did so unconsciously: they thought only of their own liberties and of those of their class; and their spirit was as narrow and jealous as that of any feudal lord. Even within a city, political rights, like material comforts, were only for a part of the inhabitants, — the traders and the skilled artisans. These were organized in gilds, or unions (§ 112), and monopolized the government of the city. Unskilled laborers had no political rights. Moreover, the merchants and the artisans were mutually jealous; and for two centuries (1200-1400), in city after city, the aristocratic merchant gild struggled in ferocious civil war to shut out the more democratic craft gilds from the city government.[2]

For a time in the thirteenth century it must have seemed possible that all Europe might give up the feudal for the city life, and become an enlarged copy of ancient Greece. The Lombard League had defeated the great Barbarossa. The Con-

---

[1] For an excellent statement, see Adams' *Civilization*, 305-307.
[2] At Magdeburg in 1302 the democratic party, securing the upper hand, burned ten aristocratic aldermen at the stake at one time.

federacy of the Rhine (§ 116) claimed equality with the princes of the Empire. In southern France the cities predominated over feudalism. In the rising Christian states in Spain, the towns were among the freest in Europe, and were bound together in a Holy League to resist feudal encroachment. Even in England, an early beginning of such a league was to be seen in the alliance of the Cinque Ports (§ 113). In distant Russia, great cities, like Novgorod, Vladimir, Kief, and Moscow, had grown up, where the ringing of the town bell called thousands of citizens to arms, to prescribe terms to princes. And the germs of the future Hanseatic League (§ 116) were beginning to dominate the coasts and waters of the northern seas.

TOWN HALL, OUDENARDE: about 1525.
From Lübke.

Most of these unions, however, were short-lived. The cities were to remain important factors in European life; indeed they were to grow more and more important: but it was soon apparent that there was no danger of their becoming the controlling political force. Like the ancient city, the medieval town lacked permanence and stable order, and could not of itself provide a safe basis for popular liberty. No doubt this was well. It was a good thing that Europe did not pass too rapidly into the city stage, but moved instead toward that larger *national* life which the cities of ancient Greece never reached.[1]

---

[1] *Ancient History*, § 93.

At the same time, when the cities fought feudalism, however selfishly, they fought on the side of human welfare. The townsmen of France or Germany were not "the people" of these lands, and they did not care for national life; but still they helped, more than any other agency, to make peoples and nations. They aimed only at their own good, but they wrought the good of mankind.

B. Origin of the Towns, and their Revolt.

109. Roman Influences in Old Towns. — The origin of the towns is obscure. The crusades increased trade, and trade built cities; but we do not know clearly what materials it found to build with, nor what the exact procedure was. In Italy, and perhaps in southern France, the Roman towns had lived on; but their population had shrunken terribly, their old institutions had been altered or altogether lost, and, politically, each one had become subject to some bishop or neighboring lord. Before 1100, however, Italy and southern France were dotted again with prosperous, self-governing cities. It is impossible to say just how far their new institutions were based upon their ancient life: but certainly they had some relation to the old Roman world; and, by example and suggestion, they must have had something to do with the form of town life in more northern countries, when it developed there a little later.

110. The Origin of the New Towns. — Over northern France and along the Rhine, the Roman towns for the most part had disappeared, and the medieval cities of these regions and of England and Germany were essentially new growths. They arose in various ways.[1] Sometimes they grew out of agricultural villages, favorably situated for trade and protected by the castle of a powerful noble or by the residence of a bishop, or around monasteries, out of the groups of artisans and peasants attracted by the employment and security there. Sometimes they grew up in the "burghs," or fortified places, established by Henry the Builder and other kings to check the invasions (§ 48). Sometimes a "grant of a market" caused a village, or even a place previously uninhabited, to develop into a city.

---

[1] For outline of different theories, see Ashley's *Surveys*, 167-212.

A Grant of a Market was essentially the grant of a stricter law to secure the peace of the market-place, with the establishment of a court to enforce that law and to regulate questions of trade. Such grants were made sometimes to nobles, who then profited by the market-tolls and fines; but the German kings, from the time of Henry and Otto the Great, granted these privileges to groups of traders, especially within certain of their fortified places or at a meeting of trade routes. The privileges of a market drew settlers; and sometimes a permanent town grew up, while the market-law became the core of a city-constitution.

The Right of Asylum was another curious element in town growth. This seems to have grown out of the protection anciently afforded fugitives by temples and churches. Even an escaped serf could not be reclaimed by his master, after he had lived unmolested a year and a day within the city walls.

111. Two Centuries of Revolt against the Lords. — At first the towns must have seemed merely overgrown villages of peasants, with some admixture of traders and artisans. No doubt, in northern Europe anyway, each inhabitant remained for a while the direct dependant of the feudal lord upon whose domain the town grew up. The first great advance lay in changing the *individual dependence of the citizens* into a *collective dependence of the city*. The town, as a corporation, took upon itself all the relations of its separate inhabitants toward the lord. It was an immense gain when the corporation, through its elected officers, negotiated regarding the dues and services to be paid by the citizens in a body, instead of each helpless individual being left to settle for himself, at the lord's mercy.[1] Probably the change began in a small way, and grew into custom in some districts through the compliance of certain lords; but by 1100 the towns generally had begun to contend for the express recognition of such conditions in "charters."

They secured their end, by war and by purchase, through the twelfth and thirteenth centuries. Some towns rose in

---

[1] The gain was somewhat like that which the trade-union of to-day enjoys, compared with the position of single workmen bargaining with a great employer.

arms five or six, or even a dozen, times, at intervals of years, and suffered terrible punishment before final success,[1] and some were never successful. Nor did one victory end the

RUINS OF A RHINE CASTLE, with a modern town below.

contest. The first charter won from a lord was usually brief and vague, and became the occasion for many later struggles

---

[1] Mrs. Green's *Town Life*, I, 313–316, gives an interesting story of the struggle of Bristol with the Lords of Berkeley, about the year 1300. In England, however, the conflict was exceedingly mild, compared to that on the continent. In particular, in France and Germany, the small noble was fiercely bitter toward the towns. In Germany, in the anarchy that followed the Hohenstaufen failure and in the long weakness of the central government in the next century, the "robber-knights," shut out from the towns by the walls, were still wont to descend from their castle-crags upon any unwary townsman, and even upon armed caravans of traders, to plunder and to carry off for ransom. Such unhappy prisoners were left in damp dungeons until perhaps their limbs rotted off, — so that to "rot a peasant" became a

for more precise grants. As a rule, each town had a number of these documents, sacredly guarded in its iron-bound town chest.

The great lords felt less jealousy toward the towns than the small nobles did, and some of them gave charters willingly, to encourage the growth of cities upon their domains and so to secure increased revenue. In the struggle between emperors and popes, the emperors sold liberties lavishly to German towns, to secure means wherewith to try vainly to crush the liberties of Italian towns; while the popes, in turn, favored the towns in Italy. During the crusades, too, great numbers of lords sold charters recklessly; and of course, all over Europe, the towns found their advantage in the destruction of noble families by the crusades.

112. Organization in Gilds. — The inhabitants of a town, except the unskilled laborers, were grouped into *gilds*. These gilds were as old apparently as town life itself in Western Europe. The principle underlying the gild organization was, that, in a given district, all men occupied in the same kind of work ought to be united to help each other and to arrange matters of common interest. Each medieval town had its *merchant gild* and its several *craft gilds*. The latter were unions of artisans, — weavers, shoe-makers, glovers, bow-makers, drapers, tanners, and so on. York, a small English city, had fifty such gilds; Cologne had eighty; some towns had even a larger number.

German byword. This horror seems incredible at first, but the physical fact is easily understood, if one comprehends the nature of the damp, filthy, fetid, cramped dungeons, together with the effect of the rusty irons upon the limbs. Even in England as sad a fate might befall a vagrant, through the ordinary delays of justice. The Rolls of Henry III (§ 133) contain the following entry: "Assizes held at Ludinglond. The jury present that William Le Sawage took two men, aliens, and one woman, and imprisoned them at Thorlestan, and detained them in prison until one of them died and the other lost a foot, and the woman lost either foot by putrefaction. Afterward he took them to the court of Ludinglond to try them. And when the court saw them, it was loath to try them, because they were not attached for any robbery or misdeed. And so *they were permitted to depart.*"

Each craft gild contained three classes of members, — masters, journeymen, and apprentices. The master owned a shop, — probably part of the house where his family lived, — and employed one or more journeymen, besides a band of apprentices. Strictly, apprentices were not members of the gild, except in prospect, but they were governed by its rules. They were boys or youths bound out by their parents for a term of years to learn the trade. They lived in the master's house, ate at his table, and he furnished their clothing and taught them "all he knew." On the expiration of the term of service (three, seven, or ten years), the apprentice became a free journeyman, working for wages. For the next few years he traveled from place to place, practising his trade in various cities, to see the world and to perfect himself in his "mystery," as the secrets of the trade were called. If he could save the small amount of money needed, he finally set up a shop of his own and became a master. As a master, he continued to work with his own hands, living among his dependents with a more or less paternal care over them.

The modern separation between capital and labor had not yet begun, so far as the skilled trades were concerned. The gild was not organized, as the modern trade-union is, to regulate the relations of workmen to employers. It was a *brotherhood*, containing both workmen and employers. Its purposes were (1) to prevent competition (and so all who practised the trade were forced to enter the gild and abide by its rules) ; (2) to prevent monopoly of materials or opportunity by any of its members (and so each "brother" had a right to share in any purchase by another, and no one could sell except at appointed times and places) ; (3) to keep up the price (which was fixed by the gild) ; and (4) to maintain a high standard of goods (and so the gild punished severely all adulterations, the mixing of poor wool with good, and the giving short weight). *Thus the gild aimed to protect both producer and consumer.*

The gild was also a fraternal insurance society : it provided assistance for a needy member, attended to the burial of a deceased member, and, if he died poor, paid pensions to his wife and children and the dowry for his daughter's marriage. Moreover, the gild had social features. Indeed, many a gild originated as a social club for men engaged in the same trade ; and throughout the Middle Ages the gild feasts were the chief social events in the lives of the members of the union. In connection with this social character, the gilds had many rules minutely regulating the conduct of the brethren toward one another.[1]

C. POLITICAL FATE OF THE TOWNS IN DIFFERENT LANDS.

113. Towns in England. — The degree of actual independence possessed by the towns varied, in different lands, with the strength of the royal government. Everywhere out of England, for a time at least, they waged private wars, like feudal nobles,[2] and exercised the other powers of the greatest lords. In England the towns did not grow up till later than on the continent. They found the royal authority more firmly established; and so, like the English nobles, they never possessed the extreme feudal independence common elsewhere in Europe. The powers they did possess, however, astound a modern student. Each town was an isolated unit. It built its walls and armed and trained its citizen-militia to defend them. It elected its own officers and prescribed their powers. Even the royal officers could not enter its gates without permission from the town authorities, and they could exercise no direct control within its walls. The townsfolk paid a tax to the government, regarding which they or their representatives had been consulted, and they furnished troops, upon occasion; but both tax and troops they levied in their own way and by their own officers. Offenses committed within the town were tried in the mayor's court, and were punished by ducking in the pond, by fines, flogging, mutilation, beheading, or by hanging in chains on the town gallows at the city gate.[3] The town passed

---

[1] Special report: what further can be learned regarding the relations of the gild members to each other, from the collection of gild regulations published in Guernsey Jones' *Civilization in the Middle Ages*, and in the *Pennsylvania Reprints*, II, No. 1.

[2] Sometimes the towns became "feudal persons" and took on the *forms* of feudalism: a town became the vassal of a lord, or of the king or emperor, and also perhaps a suzerain over nobles or even over vassal towns.

[3] On the continent the city authorities sometimes exposed criminals in iron cages, pulled away the flesh of blasphemers with red-hot tongs, and boiled

ordinances upon many matters now regulated by the state or the nation. They did not fix their own weights and measures and coinage, as the continental towns commonly did; but each town determined its own tariffs on goods brought through its gates, and discriminated in favor of its own citizens, even against other Englishmen. The Cinque Ports, a league of five ports on the English Channel, waged war on their own account with French and Flemish towns, while their respective countries were at peace; and it was customary for a town to make its own treaties with other English towns regarding trading privileges.[1] The magistrates supervised all industries and in particular they looked after the making and sale of food-stuffs, — bread, corn, ale, wine, meat, and fish, — fixing the quality, price, and time and place of sale. An important duty of the authorities was to provide against a season of scarcity by collecting grain in the town granaries.[2]

Gradually the English towns lost the more extreme of their separate liberties, but not until they had received full compensation for them in the share they secured in Parliament (§§ 134–136).

114. Towns in Italy. — Italy shows the greatest degree of town authority. The remoteness of imperial power favored city independence at an early period (§ 76), and, in this land, medieval town life reached its most vigorous development. Indeed, the nobles were compelled to come into the towns and become citizens, instead of remaining rural landlords in their isolated castles, as they did elsewhere in Europe. The Lombard League, in the Po valley, numbered sixteen independent

---

forgers in oil, pouring in cold water from time to time, that death might not come too quickly.

[1] Cheyney states (*Industrial and Social History of England*, 89) that Southampton had formal agreements with seventy towns, and that, in a period of twenty years, the London authorities sent three hundred letters on such matters to the officials of some ninety towns.

[2] This custom prevailed also on the continent. Emperor Charles V (§ 172) in 1540, at Nuremberg, was given bread to taste made from wheat that was said to have been kept in the town granary one hundred and eighteen years.

cities in its little territory, and each of these bustling communities possessed an intense and fervid life.[1] They gave birth to a new art and a new literature, and were soon to be the homes of a brilliant and splendid culture (§§ 189 ff.); they waged the bitterest, most destructive wars among themselves, regarding trading privileges and boundary disputes; and they passed through rapid and frequent revolutions in government, with cruel class-struggles in each city (§ 77, note).

ST. MARK'S, VENICE. — From a photograph.

Before 1300, most of the Italian cities had sunk under the rule of "tyrants," who found their opportunity in this civic strife. Some of these despots were of ancient noble families, others were mere military adventurers; some were enlightened rulers, others were among the vilest wretches and most inhuman monsters the world has ever seen. *Florence*, with her strong democracy, retained her freedom until after 1400; indeed, she

---

[1] Compare with the old Greek cities (*Ancient History*, § 198).

kept the forms of freedom, under her *Medici*[1] rulers, for nearly a century more. *Venice*, under her remarkable oligarchic government, built up a mighty maritime empire, like that of Carthage or of Athens, and stood forth as one of the chief Powers in Europe until after 1500. By that time the Turks had seized much of her former territory; but the city retained its separate existence and its name as a Republic until the wars that followed the French Revolution (§§ 351, 352).

115. Towns in France. — In France the southern towns were for a time almost as independent as those in Italy, and many of those in the north secured greater liberties than were known in England. However, when the French kings were finally victorious over feudalism (§ 153), they proceeded to perfect the consolidation of the realm by bringing the towns completely under their authority. Thus, before 1400, after a shorter life than elsewhere in Europe, the early liberties of the towns had wholly disappeared, and they were ruled by royal officers.

WINDOWS OF A MODEST HOUSE IN VENICE, twelfth century. — From Ruskin. (The beauty of design is fully equal to that of the fine window in the illustration on page 130.)

116. Towns in Germany: Confederation of the Rhine; the Hansa. — In Germany after 1250 many towns became known as "free cities of the Empire." Like the German principalities, they were virtually sovereign states, with only nominal allegiance to a shadowy emperor (§§ 88, 160). Most of them belonged to one of two great leagues: —

---

[1] Special reports: the Medici rule in Florence; famous Florentines from 1250 to 1500; Venice from 1000 to 1500. (For material, see page 132.)

a. The Confederacy of the Rhine numbered some fifty of the leading towns of southern Germany. It was organized for defense against the nobles, and for a time it seemed likely to secure a position, in the Diet of the Empire, equal to that of the great princes. This brilliant promise was ruined by a victory of the princes over the League at the battle of Döffingen (1388), but many of the separate towns retained their independence into the nineteenth century.

b. The Hanseatic League ("Hansa," — an old German word for "union") was composed of eighty northern German towns. It grew up about 1300, out of earlier unions of small groups of cities; and it was organized, not for political purposes, like the Lombard and the Rhine Leagues, but to protect trade against pirates and robbers, and to secure greater advantages in foreign countries than single cities could secure for themselves. It came to monopolize and control the trade of the North and Baltic Seas and much of the overland trade from Italy. It established colonies, or "factories," in foreign cities, as in London,[1] Novgorod, Bergen, Bruges, and Wisby; and by war, or threats of war, it won trading privileges from the kings of England and other northern countries. In 1370 Waldemar of Denmark was compelled after long strife to sign the *Peace of*

WINDOWS OF A VENETIAN PALACE, thirteenth century. — From Ruskin.

---

[1] See map. The Hanseatic settlement in London was known as the *Steelyard*. Each such colony had its own government and its own soldiery, independent of those of the other parts of the city in which it was embedded. The importance of the Hansa in English trade is indicated by the fact that the coin (pound) of the "Easterlings" (from the East, or Baltic, Sea), became the "pound sterling" in English currency; and the trustworthy character of their wares is shown by the meaning of the word "sterling" in our language.

DOMINIONS OF THE HANSA AND OF THE TEUTONIC ORDER AT THEIR GREATEST EXTENT.
(About 1400.)

Hansa towns are shown thus:- Groningen
Foreign Factories of the League thus:- •Bruges
Cities in which the League, or some of its members, possessed trading privileges thus:- Yarmouth

TERRITORY OF THE TEUTONIC ORDER.

- 1309.
- Added up to 1410.

Gulf of Finland
Abo
Neva R.
Reval
Esthland
1346
Novgorod
Stockholm
DAGO
ÖSEL
Dorpat
Pernau
Livland
1237
Pskof
Wetten
Wisby
Wenden
Windau
Riga
Kurland
Mitau
Dvina
Dünaburg
Kalmar
Polotsk
Vitebsk
1384
Memel
BALTIC SEA
Niemen
Kovno
BORNHOLM
Konigsberg
Rudau
Oliva
Braunsberg
Rügenwalde
Stolp
Danzig
Elbing
Kolberg
Marienburg
Pomerania
1310
Dirschau
Prussia
Grodno
Kammin
Gollnow
Löbau
Kulm
Kulmerland
Stargard
Neumark
1402
Thorn
1328-43
Bug R.
Pripet R.
Vistula
Frankfort
Oder
Kalisz
Breslau
Krakow

Stralsund, which provided that future Danish kings must have the sanction of the League before they mounted the throne. For a century the League was one of the Great Powers of Europe. The Hansa flag floated over nearly every merchant ship of the northern seas and over every counting house from London to Novgorod. The League owned fisheries and mines; and in their trading posts there met for exchange the furs and

INTERIOR OF HALL OF MERCHANT PRINCES AT DANTZIG. Originally a Hall of the Teutonic Knights (about 1300).— From Lübke.

hides from Russia, the grain from Poland, the amber from the Baltic coasts, the metals of Saxony, the wines of the Rhine, the wool and tin of England, the cloths of Holland, and the more distant products of the South and East.

As the other northern countries developed, the Hansa lost its preëminence and its special privileges. Many of its cities were ruined in the religious wars of the sixteenth and seventeenth centuries. Some of them, however, remained sovereign states until late in the nineteenth century; and three of them — Hamburg, Bremen, and Lübeck — entered the present

German Empire, when it was formed in 1871, on a footing of equality with the other confederating states (§ 472).[1]

FOR FURTHER READING. — Source material: town charters and gild rules are given in *Pennsylvania Reprints*, II, No. 1, and by Guernsey Jones in his *Civilization during the Middle Ages*, 121-149.

Modern accounts: brief statements of great value are to be found in Adams, *Civilization*, 290-310; Cheyney, *Industrial and Social History of England*, 57-95; Munro, *Middle Ages*, ch. xiv; Robinson, *Western Europe*, ch. xviii; Green, *English People*, I, 206-225; Cunningham, *English Industry and Commerce*, I, 197-214; Henderson, *Short History of Germany*, I, 181-202; Zimmern, *The Hansa Towns;* Lodge, *Close of the Middle Ages*, 419-450 (for the Hansa); Emerton, *Medieval Europe*, 520-540; Symonds, *Short History of the Renaissance in Italy*, 13-51; Duffy, *Tuscan Republics;* Gibbins, *Industrial History of England.* Advanced students may use the excellent treatments of Ashley, *Economic History*, I, 67-123, and II, 3-189. All students with time for reading such extended works will enjoy Mrs. Green's *Town Life in the Fifteenth Century;* Hazlitt's *Venetian Republic;* Mrs. Oliphant's *Makers of Venice* and *Makers of Florence;* Villari's *Florence;* Neil's *Venice;* Brown's *Venetian Republic;* and the various volumes of the Medieval Town Series, especially *Rouen, Moscow, Toledo, Florence, Nuremberg, Bruges, Verona,* and *Prague.*

SPECIAL REPORTS. — 1. Mystery plays as presented by the gilds. 2. The Hansa and the herring fishery. 3. Fairs in the Middle Ages (see Cheyney's *Industrial and Social History*, 75-79).

II. RISE OF MONARCHIC STATES.

117. The "New Monarchies" and their Task. — Before 1300, Europe had tried various principles of organization. *Feudal aristocracy* and *town democracy* had both been found wanting in order and permanence. The ideal of a *universal monarchy* had been shattered by the quarrel between popes and emperors. The *papacy* (theocratic rule) had seemed to come out of that struggle triumphant, but almost at once it was to fall before a new form of organization, — the separate *monarchic states*, into which Europe had been growing. Says Lavisse, "From the wreck of the two universal powers [papacy and empire], the various nationalities emerged. Just as Christendom had succeeded the Roman Empire, so 'Europe' succeeded 'Christendom.'"

---

[1] For the towns of Flanders, see § 162.

This rise of "New Monarchies,"[1] each with a definite territory, is the political change that characterized the close of the Middle Ages. Each such territory had contained several distinct, mutually jealous classes, — nobles, burgesses, artisans, clergy, peasantry, — and for centuries, French nobility and German nobility had had more in common with each other than either had with the townsmen of their own country. So of the other classes. Social unity and sympathies had not been *national*, German or English: they had followed the lines of *class-cleavage* across Europe. The monarchies were to change all this. They were to weld these classes, within each of their respective territories, into one nation with a common patriotism. Probably no king put this end before him clearly as his task; but the result followed naturally from the thing the king did strive for, — namely, to consolidate the numerous petty feudal states within his realm into one state with a uniform administration centering in his will.

While this was being accomplished, some old liberties were lost and the monarchs became despots: but the liberties were of a kind that had proved to be intertwined with anarchy, and the seeming loss was only for a time. A few centuries later there was to grow up a freer, broader, more secure freedom than had ever before been possible.

In Germany and Italy the destructive conflict between papacy and Empire ruined all chance for progress toward national monarchies for hundreds of years. Until 1250, these countries had been the centers of interest; then leadership passed to England, France, and Spain, — the lands in which the new monarchic movement was best developed.

III. EUROPE BY SEPARATE STATES: ENGLAND TO 1500.[2]

A. WHAT THE NORMANS FOUND.[3]

118. Importance of Saxon Local Institutions. — At the time of the Norman conquest (§ 16), the Saxons in England had developed certain institutions which were to have a lasting

---

[1] This term "New Monarchy" has come to be used for the despotic, centralized monarchies that appeared in France, Spain, and, in some degree, in England, about 1500; they were new, as compared with the old Teutonic and the feudal kingship.

[2] For England in 1066, review § 16.

[3] Cf. a good brief treatment of Saxon institutions in Andrews' *History of England*, 40-52. Very few books give the recent views upon this topic in a form usable by young students.

value. Those that pertained to the court and the king's government were to be replaced, under the conquerors, by somewhat different Norman institutions; and the Normans, also, drew tighter the loose bonds which previously had held the local units together: but the local divisions themselves survived, as did also for the most part the old Saxon machinery for justice and government within each unit.

These local divisions were of three orders,— shires, hundreds, and townships (§§ 119-121).

119. Shire and Shire Court. — As Wessex had extended her sway over the island (§ 16), the former tribal kingdoms sank into *shires*,[1] and in the end all England came to be divided into about forty units of this name. The shire — or county, as the Normans called it — was adopted also by the church as a bishop's diocese. Its three important officers were the *ealdorman, the sheriff, and the bishop*. In form, the ealdorman was appointed by the king and Witan. Oftentimes, however, he was the descendant of the ancient tribal chief, and the king felt constrained to appoint him; in any case, he was one of the most powerful nobles of the district, with local interests and sympathies, and his office was almost sure to pass on to his son. The sheriff was at first merely the king's reeve, or bailiff, for the shire, to look after the king's lands there and to collect the king's revenues; and until the Norman period he was much inferior in power to the ealdorman.

Ealdorman and bishop together presided over the *shire court*, or shire-moot. This was a survival of the old folk-moot of the tribal kingdom.[2] It was made up of the landlords of the shire and apparently of some of the most important men from each hundred and village. In this court the actual government of the shire was carried on, and some judicial cases were tried.

---

[1] The first shires originated in this way. But in most of the old Danelagh the ancient tribal divisions seem to have been wiped out by Danish rule; and there the successors of Alfred divided the land arbitrarily into shires.

[2] *Ancient History*, §§ 559, 612.

120. Hundred and Hundred Court. — Before the tribal kingdoms sank into shires, they had local divisions of their own, under various names. These divisions, or others framed in imitation of them, remained as subdivisions of the shire, and were known as hundreds. Each hundred had its court, made up much like the shire court; and this busy body was the chief unit for the administration of justice.

121. Townships and Boroughs. — Within the hundred were townships, or villages, and perhaps one or more boroughs. A few boroughs, like London or Winchester, were important cities and capitals; but most of them at this time were merely large and especially protected villages. The township does not seem to have had any important powers of self-government. So far as we can see, such political powers as its inhabitants possessed they must have exercised in the popular courts of the shire and hundred.

122. Anglo-Saxon Feudalism. — The local units had fallen to a great degree under the influence of local nobles. Sometimes a great lord had secured from the king the right to hold a private court alongside the popular court of the hundred.[1] There was a serious lack of effective machinery to secure uniformity in the different shires and to compel obedience to the laws of the king and Witan. Moreover, the freemen of the villages were sinking somewhat in condition. After Alfred's time, it was necessary for each free villager to attach himself to some lord. This did not make him unfree in his own eyes or in the eyes of the law: it was rather a device to make surer of his obedience to the law; for the lord was made responsible for him. But in return the villager made one or more of a great variety of payments to the lord, and, in some cases at least, his land had begun to pass into the condition of villein land on the continent (§ 34, note).

---

[1] Such grants seem to have been not really grants of jurisdiction, but rather grants of fines to be levied in the courts, in return for seeing that the proper procedure was carried on. All our knowledge, however, of Anglo-Saxon feudalism is vague and unsatisfactory.

B. The Norman Period,[1] 1066-1154.

123. General Effect of the Norman Conquest (1066). — The Norman Conquest took place in the early part of the reign of

BATTLE OF HASTINGS [§ 16], from the Bayeux Tapestry.[2] — From *Old England*.

Henry IV of Germany, when the Capetian monarchy in France was about eighty years old. The strong German kingship was just beginning to decline: the French kingship had hardly

---

[1] It is desirable, of course, that students should read more extensively on English history than on that of other single countries. Source material will be found in Lee's *Source Book*, Colby's *Sources*, Adams and Stephens' *Documents*, Henderson's *Documents;* but probably Hill's *Liberty Documents* contains enough for high schools, and it contains also valuable collections of critical comments upon important documents.

Of modern accounts, Green's *English People* remains the most attractive general history, though it gives undue value to early Saxon institutions and ascribes to the Saxons a certain degree of representative government which they did not possess. Either Andrews', Terry's, or Gardiner's *History of England* makes a good one-volume text. Advanced students may use Stubbs' *Constitutional History*, and all will find the treatment of Taswell-Langmead clear and readable. The volumes that represent the most critical scholarship (such as Round's and Pollock and Maitland's) can hardly be used by high school students, nor, unhappily, can Medley's shorter and scholarly work. Montague's *Elements* is an excellent manual. Freeman's *Norman Conquest* is the great authority for the narrative to William Rufus, and the same author's *William the Conqueror* is an excellent brief study. The opening pages of Stubbs' *Early Plantagenets*, and of Jenks' *Edward I* contain admirable summaries of the Norman period. Traill's *Social England* may be used to good advantage.

[2] The Bayeux Tapestry is a linen band 230 feet long and 20 inches wide, embroidered in colors, with seventy-two scenes illustrating the Norman Conquest and the customs of the time. It was a contemporary work.

begun to grow. Until this time, England had counted for little in the life of Europe. Its church had become almost independent of Rome, and in politics its foreign relations had been mainly with the Scandinavian countries of the north (§ 16). At home, from the time of Alfred the Great, the two chief dangers had been the growth of feudal anarchy (§ 122) and the splitting apart of Danish England and Saxon England (§ 16).

The Norman Conquest changed all these conditions. It brought the church again into dependence on Rome,[1] and drew England into the thick of European politics.[2] Within the island, it crushed together north and south, so that the two parts never again dreamed of separation, and it built up a strong central government. The kings were strong enough to keep down feudal tyrants, but not quite strong enough to become royal tyrants themselves. Through dread of royal power, nobles and people were drawn

WILLIAM THE CONQUEROR AND THE CONSECRATED BANNER SENT BY THE POPE (see footnote 1 below). — From the Bayeux Tapestry.

---

[1] The ecclesiastical condition was a factor in the conquest. The Pope blessed the enterprise and sent Duke William a consecrated banner. Afterward, Gregory VII demanded that William do homage to him for his realm. William haughtily refused (see his letter to Gregory in Lee, *Source Book*, No. 50). He filled the high places in the church with Normans in sympathy with Rome and with the Cluniac reform, and he developed separate ecclesiastical courts (§ 69), which had not existed before in England; but he guarded jealously against papal interference in his government. He forbade the clergy to place any of his knights under excommunication without consulting him; he declared any one an outlaw who should carry an appeal to Rome without royal permission; and no papal letter could be received in England without his sanction.

[2] For some generations the rulers of England were also Dukes of Normandy, and so great vassals of the French crown.

together[1] and became fused into an English nation, which in centuries of slow, quiet, determined progress, won constitutional liberty. *To the old spirit of Saxon freedom, the Normans added a new genius for organization.* The local institutions to a considerable degree remained Saxon, but the central government was to owe its efficiency to Norman influences. England was the first country in the world to work out for a large territory *the union of a strong central government and of free institutions.*

The conquest also brought in new blood, a higher culture, and new elements in language. Norman lords and clergy, and likewise Norman merchants and artisans, flocked into England. All these people spoke their own Norman-French tongue, and for a time only the lowest classes spoke English. Gradually, however, the English was to gain its place as the language of the whole people; and meantime it was to lose its more complicated grammatical forms and to be enriched by a multitude of Norman words.

A NORMAN SHIP, from the Bayeux Tapestry.— From *Old England*. (Cf. with the remains of the Norse boat, page 14.)

124. English Feudalism. — Feudalism had developed much more slowly in England than on the continent, and William the Conqueror was able decisively to influence its subsequent character. He confiscated the land of England, with legal formalities, on the ground that the holders had been traitors; then he granted much of it back to the old holders on payment of fines, and the rest he gave

---

[1] The sharp distinction between the Norman and the Saxon had disappeared before the close of the Norman reigns (§ 125). Scott's *Ivanhoe* pictures a state of affairs in this respect which had passed away at least two generations before the time dealt with in the story.

to his own followers. In all cases he introduced feudal tenure: that is, the land was to be held of the king on condition of feudal service.[1] But with the grants of land the king did *not* grant authority to the lord over his vassals to the extent that was customary on the continent. Feudalism was systematized, so far as land tenure went, and during the next two centuries the peasantry sank into villeinage; but the worst political evils of continental feudalism were avoided.

Many checks were introduced to keep the lords from usurping feudal independence. (1) No one lord was permitted to accumulate such vast possessions as were often held by single barons in France and Germany; and properties that the great lords did hold were

NORMAN DOORWAY, St. Peters, Northampton.— From *Old England*. (Note the massive round arch and the simple but effective ornament.)

scattered in different counties, so that each piece really became a surety for the lord's fidelity.[2] (2) The chief authority in a shire was now exercised, not by an hereditary ealdorman, but by the king's sheriff. (3) All freemen were required to swear fidelity directly to the king, so that they owed him allegiance

---

[1] Round (*Feudal England*, 292) shows that probably there were not more than five thousand knights in the whole of William's feudal army. An old legend, believed until recently, said sixty thousand.

[2] This fortunate arrangement came about probably not so much from design as from the fact that William really became master of the country only by degrees, and so had to reward his followers a little at a time.

even against their immediate over-lords. (4) The old national militia was preserved, and was put under the command of the royal sheriffs, so that the king was not wholly dependent upon a feudal army.

SILVER PENNY OF WILLIAM I.

125. The Four "Norman" Kings. — *William the Conqueror* (1066-1087) was king by right of the sword; but he went through the form of an election by an English assembly, and thereafter he ruled, as far as a conqueror could, with respect for English customs.[1]

William, by will, left Normandy to his eldest son Robert, and England to his second son *William Rufus* (the Red). This prince, to strengthen his claim, procured an election from an English assembly, after the old English fashion; but he proved unscrupulous, though able, and is remembered as a tyrant (1087-1100). He was succeeded by his brother, *Henry I*, the youngest son of the conqueror. Henry (1100-1135) had been born in England and he married an English princess. He, also, secured the form of an election, and in return he granted to the people of England a Charter of Liberties,[2] which a hundred years later was to become the model for a more important grant. Henry also began many important reforms in the government, but his work was undone in the anarchy of the next reign and had to be reconstructed by his grandson.

SILVER PENNY OF STEPHEN.

---

[1] Among the wise acts of King William was the taking of a great census of the kingdom, to determine its resources and the dues payable to the king. The results were recorded in the *Domesday Book*, and are still preserved, so that we have more exact knowledge about England at this time than about any other country. There seems to have been a population of about twelve hundred thousand people. One tenth of them, perhaps, were "burgesses," though at least half of these dwelt in what we should call mere villages.

[2] See charter and comments in Hill's *Liberty Documents*, 1-8. The charter is given also in Lee, Colby, and *Pennsylvania Reprints*, I.

The English nobles promised Henry to make his daughter Matilda his successor; but, after his death, his nephew Stephen secured an election. *Stephen* (1135-1154) was weak by nature, and his rule was distracted by civil war with the supporters of Matilda. His reign is the darkest period in English history after the Conquest. Feudal anarchy seemed at last to have seized upon the land. The contemporary chroniclers exclaim upon the misery of the age with bitter phrases: —

"Every powerful man made his castles, and when they were built they filled them with devils and evil men; they put men in their dungeons for their gold and silver, and tortured them with pains unspeakable... until men said that Christ and his saints slept.... In those days, if three or four men came riding towards a township, all the township fled hastily, believing them to be robbers.... That lasted the nineteen winters Stephen was king."

STEPHEN. From an engraving based probably on the coin portraits of his reign. — From Andrews' *History of England*.

EXERCISE. — The four Norman reigns may be summed up briefly, thus: William I, conquest, consolidation, provision against feudal disintegration; William II, tyranny; Henry I, the charter, and beginnings of judicial organization; Stephen, anarchy and civil war.

Observe that *the three successors of William I all had rivals for the throne, and so were kept in some measure in dependence upon the nation.*

SPECIAL REPORTS. — The Danegeld; Domesday Book; a fuller story of the Norman Conquest, with the harrying of the North; the making of the New Forest; character of William I; further matters of importance to be learned for this period from the reading of the *Anglo-Saxon Chronicle*.

C. THE EARLY PLANTAGENETS,[1] HENRY II TO EDWARD II, 1154-1341.

(TO THE HUNDRED YEARS' WAR.)

126. Henry II, 1154-1189. — Matilda had married Geoffrey Plantagenet, Count of Anjou. The son of this marriage, Henry, succeeded Stephen, and was the first of a long line of Plantagenet kings. The evils of Stephen's time had not lasted long enough to fix themselves upon England, and Henry quickly restored peace and good order. His reign is further notable for new territorial relations and for new administrative and judicial organization (§§ 127-130).

127. The Territories of the Plantagenets. — Through his mother, Henry was duke of Normandy and Maine, and he held also an old and shadowy claim upon Brittany, which he was soon able to convert into real lordship. Through his father, he was count of Anjou and Touraine. By marriage with the princess Eleanor, divorced wife of Louis VII of France (§ 149), he obtained Aquitaine, which then included Poitou and Gascony. Thus, besides his insular possessions, Henry ruled more than half of all France, — six or seven times as much territory on the continent as was held directly by the French king.[2] By imperfect conquest, Henry was also "King of Ireland."[3] For a time, too, he seemed to hold Scotland in subjection; and the reduction of Wales was going on slowly through every strong English reign.

Probably Henry II was the most powerful ruler in Europe. He was not strictly an English ruler, and his continental pos-

---

[1] For source material, see references in note on page 136. The "English History by Contemporary Writers" series (edited by York-Powell) contains several valuable volumes, especially, *The Misrule of Henry III* and *Simon de Montfort*. (The entire series should be in every high school library.) For modern accounts, see also page 136. In addition, for special periods: Stubbs' *Early Plantagenets*; Mrs. Green's *Henry II*; Kate Norgate's *John Lackland*; Jenks' *Edward I*; and Tout's *Edward I*. Jessop's *Coming of the Friars*, Jusserand's *English Wayfaring Life*, and Cheyney's *Industrial and Social History* are admirable for their special phases of development.

[2] See map facing page 165.

[3] Special reports: the conquest of Ireland; the English "Pale" and its government.

sessions are not to be regarded as English acquisitions. Henry thought of himself as a French prince with some important possessions in England and Ireland. None the less, he proved one of the greatest and most beneficent of English kings.

128. The Basis of English "Common Law": Itinerant Courts. — The most important of Henry's many reforms concerned the courts.[1] Until Henry's time the king's court was chiefly for causes in which the king or his immediate vassals were concerned. The great body of men sought justice in the decaying courts of the hundred and county or in the feudal courts that were growing out of these older popular courts.

If this condition had been allowed to continue, each district in England would have developed its own local customs (§ 29); and the only escape from the ensuing confusion would have come through the later introduction of Roman Law, with its tendency toward absolute monarchy (§ 79). This was the order of events in continental countries. That England followed a different course and gave us her "Common Law," we owe largely to the policy of Henry II. His "court" widened its functions, and opened its doors to all.[2] At the

EFFIGY OF HENRY II, from his tomb.— From *Old England.*

---

[1] Special report: Henry's quarrel with *Becket* over lay and ecclesiastical courts; the Constitutions of Clarendon. Cf. § 69.

[2] For one instance, — Henry announced that any free-holder, whose title to his land was attacked, should have his case heard in the royal courts. This weakened not only the feudal courts, but also the whole basis of feudal feeling. Henry weakened feudalism still further by encouraging the sub-tenants, or vassals of his tenants-in-chief, to pay *scutage*, or shield money, instead of serving personally in war. With the money so collected, the king could raise armies superior to the short-termed, undisciplined, feudal levies. But it is of more importance to see that the knights were put into the way of ceasing to be fighters: they gradually became more interested in managing their estates and in political life, and before long we speak of them in this new sense, as "knights of the shire."

same time, judges of the court were sent out, *as itinerant justices,* to sit in each community at fixed and regular intervals, as though the king were present in person. Thus the "customs" of the king's court became *common* law for all England. The nation was benefited, and the feudal courts were controlled and finally starved out. This bringing impartial justice to every man's door was a gift beyond price in the twelfth century, and it produced a reverence for the law and for the courts that was to become an instinct in the English mind.

129. Excursus : **Administration of Royal Justice in the Middle Ages.** — In theory the king could always do justice between contending claims; but the difficulty was for the man who suffered from injustice to get at the king. The kings of France and Germany depended more upon their personal efforts, and less upon organization, than was the case in England. They were marvels of energy, and they worked harder than any other men of their time; but they worked at a well-nigh impossible task. When Conrad II of Germany (§ 62) was passing in the royal procession to his coronation, three low-born persons — a peasant, a widow, and a child — pressed through the crowd and called to him for justice. Conrad kept the procession waiting while he heard their troubles and righted their wrongs, saying to the bishop who wished him to pass on, "Since I have been chosen as a ruler, it is better to do my duty at once; you have often said to me that it was not the hearer, but the doer of the law that was blessed." A moment later another man stopped the procession with his cries for justice, and was heard upon the spot. This was the way the German and French kings administered justice. Herbert Fisher (*Medieval Empire*, 168) says of the German king, "Instead of *organizing labor* on the great highway that was to lead from chaos to order, he *takes up the pick* and works devotedly, with face to the ground." Royal justice was simply what justice the king in person, with the assistance of the nobles about him, could get through with in the day, with all the interruptions of war, travel, and other business. There was *no fixed court*, and there were *no regular sessions at different places.* To render justice was a hard task for the king, and to secure it was impossible for most of his subjects.[1]

---

[1] This condition made possible the growth of irregular secret tribunals, with some of the characteristics of the modern frontier "vigilance committee." The most famous of such medieval institutions was the *Holy Vehme,* which appears in Scott's *Anne of Geierstein.* There is a good account in Henderson's *Short History of Germany,* I, 169–170.

A like truth held good for France, in large measure, even as late as the great Louis IX (about 1250). Joinville's Memoir (cf. § 40) gives many illustrations. Louis was a justice-loving king, and Joinville delights to dwell upon the stories of his judgments and the regulation of his primitive courts. "Sometimes I have seen him, in order to administer justice to his people, come into the garden of Paris dressed in a green coat, a surcoat of woolen stuff without sleeves, his hair well combed, and a hat, with white peacock feathers, on his head; carpets were spread, and all people who had business to be disposed of stood before him. . . . Certain nobles heard every day all pleadings at the gateway of the castle, and after mass the king heard all appeals from these decisions in person, seated on his bed.[1] . . . Many a time it happened in summer that he would go sit in the wood of Vincennes with his back to an oak, and make us take our seats around him. And all who had complaints to make came to him without hindrance of ushers. Then he would call a certain noble and say, 'Dispose of this case for me'; and when he saw anything to amend in the words of those who spoke he would correct it with his own lips." Elsewhere, Louis recommends his people 'to put up with any bearable injustice; and, with unconscious pathos, he admits his inability to secure justice for his subjects, even from his own officers, except in extreme cases.

130. Trial by Jury. — Trial by jury has been looked upon for centuries as a chief element in English freedom. This institution, also, comes first into notice in the reign of Henry II. The jury developed from foreign germs, but its value is due to its English growth. It seems to have arisen out of a custom of the early Frankish kings. When a dispute occurred as to their rights in a given district, they called together a number of the oldest and most reliable men to give witness in the matter. This form of inquiry, or "inquest," was brought by the Normans to England. The Conqueror's officers used it in each county and district in compiling the Domesday survey (§ 125, note); and the ignorance of the Norman rulers regarding the customs of the land gave frequent occasion for employing it.

So far, the sworn body of witnesses, or "jury," had been used only to determine matters in which the king was interested. Henry II extended the same method to some questions about

---

[1] This custom gave rise to the expression "bed of justice."

property where private individuals were concerned. That is, he created a trial jury for civil cases, to replace the old method of judicial combat. Under Henry, also, a jury was called in each county, at intervals, to "present" suspected criminals for trial. This was the origin of our *grand jury*, or jury of presentment.

For some time longer, those suspected criminals who were "presented" by the "jury of inquest" were tried by "ordeal" or by "combat";[1] but in 1215 the Lateran Council (§ 82, note) condemned the "ordeal," and after that time it became the custom in England to summon another, smaller jury (petit jury) to try the man whom the larger jury had accused.[2]

131. Richard I (1189-1199); John (1199-1216). — Henry II was followed by two sons in succession, Richard "the Lion Hearted" and John. Both were bad and tyrannical rulers. Richard spent only seven months of his reign in England, and those months solely for the purpose of getting money for his foreign wars. Fortunately he was as careless as he was tyrannical; and so in his desire for money he sold valuable charters to many rising towns. He is remembered as the leader of the Third Crusade (§ 97). England suffered little evil from his neglect, because the old officers of his father for the most part remained in charge and continued the old system. John was an abler man than his brother, but a more despicable character. Three events mark his reign. (1) Abroad he lost Normandy and all northern France to the French king. (2) After a long contest with Pope Innocent III, he was forced to surrender his crown, to receive it back again as a papal fief. (3) His oppression finally brought all classes of the nation to combine against him, and, *in 1215*, a general rising forced him to sign *Magna Carta*.[3]

---

[1] *Ancient History*, § 608.

[2] The accused still had the right to claim trial by combat. The noble classes commonly did so, for some generations; and the practice was not legally abolished until 1819, shortly after an attempt had been made to take advantage of the obsolete right. Cf. Taswell-Langmead, *English Constitutional History*, 5th edition, 103-105. For a long time the trial jury were witnesses as well as judges of the testimony. They were allowed, however, to call in other witnesses; and gradually a line was drawn between them and these others, until finally it became the rule that the "jurymen" should come without any knowledge of their own regarding the case, so as to hear and judge impartially the evidence submitted by the witnesses.

[3] Special reports: the story of the rising; Stephen Langton and his part in securing Magna Carta.

Nullus liber homo capiatur, vel imprisonetur, aut dissaisiatur, aut utlagetur,
No free man shall be taken, or imprisoned, or dispossessed, or outlawed,

aut exuletur, aut aliquo modo destruatur, nec super eum ibimus nec super
or banished, or in any way destroyed, nor will we go upon him nor upon

eum mittemus, nisi per legale judicium parium suorum vel per legem terrae.
him send, except by the legal judgment of his peers or by the law of the land.

Nulli vendemus, nulli negabimus, aut differemus, rectum aut justiciam.
To no one will we sell, to no one will we deny, or delay, right or justice.

SECTIONS 39 AND 40 OF MAGNA CARTA. The bars are facsimiles of the writing in the charter, in Latin, of course, with the curious abbreviations of the medieval Latin. Below each line is given the Latin in full with a translation. — From Andrews' *History of England*.

132. Magna Carta is the "first great document in the Bible of English Liberties." It was not unusual in the Middle Ages for the nobles to secure charters of liberties for themselves from their kings. In England, too, the great barons led this movement; but the peculiarity of the Great Charter is (1) that in it the barons promised toward their dependents the same rights they demanded for themselves from the king; and (2) that place was found for special provisions in the interest of the townsmen and even of villeins. The Charter became at once the standard of freedom, and in the next two centuries, English kings were called upon to confirm it no less than thirty-eight times;[1] while, as new needs arose, new meanings were read into it (cf. § 134, note 3).

133. Henry III, 1217-1272. — The long reign of John's son, Henry III, saw much disorder and tyranny, and much constitutional progress for

---

[1] Exercise: a study of Magna Carta. It is printed in all collections of documents upon English history (see bibliography, page 136), but it can be consulted best, with a collection of comments, in Hill's *Liberty Documents*, 9-32. Five-cent copies can be obtained in the Old South Leaflets.

which the King deserves no credit. Henry was a pious, frivolous, extravagant, weak tyrant. In the second half of the reign, the popular party found an able champion in the great *Simon de Montfort*, Earl of Leicester, the most powerful of the English nobles. The struggle[1] became open war, and Simon conquered at the *Battle of Lewes* (1264). For a year he was really master of England, until his defeat and death at *Evesham*[2] in 1265. That year is notable in the history of English freedom (§ 134).

134. The Beginning of Parliament. — After the Conquest, the Saxon Witan had given way to the "Great Council" of the Norman kings. In theory, the king ruled with the "advice and consent" of this body. In practice, the Council was the mere servant of a powerful king. All those who held land directly of the king ("tenants-in-chief") had a right to be present in this court; but in fact only the great lords attended. Magna Carta had provided that no new "tax"[3] should be imposed without the consent of the Great Council, and had prescribed the method of calling the Council: the great barons were to be summoned by letter, individually; the lesser barons, by a general notice read by the sheriffs in the county courts. These smaller barons, however, did not attend; and in the troubles of the reign of Henry III, on two or three occasions, notably *in 1254*, the sheriffs had been directed to see that each county sent knights to the gathering.[4] *Thus a representative element had been introduced into the Great Council.* So far, however, only the landholding aristocracy had been concerned. But after the Battle of Lewes, Earl Simon seized upon this system of representation and extended it. The writs for the famous "Parliament"[5] of 1265, issued by

---

[1] Special report: the Provisions of Oxford, of 1258.

[2] Special report upon this battle; see Green's *English People*, I, 303-304.

[3] The charter did not say "tax." Taxation proper had hardly begun. The document provided that no feudal aid or scutage (a kind of war tax) should be imposed without the consent of the Council. Later, when taxation developed, the nation read the idea of taxes into the document, in place of the feudal aids really referred to.

[4] Once, indeed, in John's reign, four knights from each shire had been summoned; but the Assembly seems never to have met.

[5] This name for the national assembly had come into use shortly before.

Simon's direction while the King was in his power, called for the attendance of two knights from each shire *and also of two burgesses from each borough,* to sit with the lords and clergy. Simon had taken a great step toward changing the *Great Council of royal vassals* into a *"Parliament" representing the people of England.*

135. The Model Parliament, 1295. — In the years that immediately followed the great deed of Simon, several national assemblies met, wherein towns and counties had some representation; but the exact form varied from time to time, and the powers of the representatives were slight and indefinite. In the *"Model Parliament"* of 1295, however, *Edward I,* the son of Henry III, adopted Simon's plan of thirty years before: each shire and each borough was called upon to send its two representatives, — since, as Edward's writ read, "that which touches all should be approved by all."[1] From that time, the regular representation of counties and boroughs became a fixed principle in the English national assembly. For the first time in the world's history, representative government was put upon a good working basis.

136. Lords and Commons. — After a half-century or so, Parliament began to sit in two "houses." The nature of this division was not the result of any deliberate plan, but it was of immense importance. Edward summoned to his Parliament the "three estates," — the clergy, the nobles, and the burgesses. The greater nobles and the greater clergy had personal summons: the other classes were to be represented by delegates, — the smaller landholders by the elected "knights of the shire," the towns by their chosen burgesses, and the lower clergy by elected representatives, one for each district. At first, all probably sat together. Had this continued, the townsmen would never have secured much voice: they would have been frightened and overawed by the nobles. The result would have been about as bad if the three estates had come to

---

[1] Hill's *Liberty Documents* gives the *Summons* and modern critical comment.

sit separately, as they did in France and Spain: with so many distinct orders, an able king could easily have played off one against the other. England again followed a course of its own. The inferior clergy, very happily, refused to attend Parliament, insisting instead upon their right to act in "Convocation," a purely ecclesiastical assembly. Thus they threw away a chance to secure political power. The great spiritual lords, with personal summons, were not numerous enough by themselves to make an "estate," and so they preferred to sit with the great lay lords, not as clergy, but as temporal barons. Thus, when the different orders began to sit apart, the great peers, lay and spiritual, who were summoned by individual letters, made a "House of Lords," while the representative elements — knights of the shire and burgesses — came together as the "House of Commons."[1]

The three estates had faded into two, and even these two were not distinct. For in England, unlike the case upon the continent, only the oldest son of a lord succeeded to his father's title and nobility and to the right to a personal summons to the House of Lords: the younger sons — and even the oldest son during his father's life — belonged in the gentry (gentleman) class, and at most were "knights of the shire." As such, oftentimes, the son or the brother of an earl sat for his county in the House of Commons beside the shopkeeper from the town. *The gentry in the Commons formed a link to bind Lords and Commons together,* and to preserve good understanding between them, so that the two houses upon occasion could act in unison in behalf of English liberty. The House of Commons, from the first, was much more than an "estate," and it was to widen into the representative of the nation.

137. The First Two Edwards. — Edward I (1272–1307) was the greatest of the Plantagenet kings. Apart from his development of Parlia-

---

[1] The knights were drawn to the lords by social ties; but they had been in the habit of acting with the burgesses in local matters, and, happily, now joined with them in the national assembly.

ment, his great legal reforms[1] have earned him the title, "the English Justinian." His weak son, Edward II (1307-1327), was controlled by unworthy favorites, and was finally *deposed by Parliament*.[2]

D. Period of the "Hundred Years' War," 1338-1453.[3]

138. Reference Table of Reigns.

a. The Plantagenets, from Edward III to the Lancastrian Branch.

Edward III, 1327-1377: son of Edward II; opening of the long war with France; the Black Death; growth of the Commons.
Richard II, 1377-1399: grandson of Edward III; *the peasant revolt of 1381;* attempt at personal rule; *deposition.*

b. The Lancastrians.

Henry IV, 1399-1413: Duke of Lancaster and cousin of Richard II; elected king by Parliament, after a brief civil war; recognized dependence on Parliament; remarkable growth of the Commons.
Henry V, 1413-1422: renewed Hundred Years' War, and conquered France.
Henry VI, 1422-1461: loss of France; throne of England claimed by the Duke of York, another descendant of Edward III; civil war; Henry deposed by his Yorkist conquerors.

139. The Hundred Years' War.

Ever since the greatest French vassal became king of England, it had been a matter of settled policy with the French kings, to undermine the power of the English rulers. John and Henry III had lost their French possessions north of the Loire, and Poitou to the south of that river: England kept only southwest Aquitaine. While the English Edwards were trying desperately to conquer Scotland, France continued her policy, by aiding that northern

---

[1] These reforms are too complicated to treat in this volume, but it may be stated that among other results they continued the weakening of feudalism.

[2] In the early Saxon period, the Witan had sometimes deposed a king, but this deposition of Edward II was the first instance of the kind after the Norman Conquest. There were to be other striking cases in English history (§§ 143, 242, 250).

[3] See references on pages 136 and 142. *Pennsylvania Reprints,* II, No. 5, deals with the time of Wyclif, and the Paston Letters give graphic views of the fifteenth century. See also notes on pages 155 and 157.

kingdom. Therefore, in 1338, Edward III declared open war upon France. This was the beginning of the "Hundred Years' War," which was to last, with brief truces, until 1453. Edward's purpose was largely commercial: he wished to preserve the trade with Gascony and to secure that of Flanders. To strengthen his position, especially with the Flemish vassals of France, Edward set up a somewhat fanciful claim to the

A FOURTEENTH CENTURY BRIDGE IN RURAL ENGLAND, near Danby in Oxfordshire. — From Jusserand's *English Wayfaring Life*.

French crown (§ 148, note), and each English king called himself also "King of France" from that time until 1802.

The English gained brilliant victories, overran France repeatedly, and brought home much plunder. England was prosperous, too, because of her growing commerce. Her people felt none of the direct ravages of war, except for the raids of French pirates on the coast; and for a time they bore cheerfully the cost of the French campaigns. The two important battles in Edward's reign were those of *Crécy* and *Poitiers*. At Crécy,

§ 139] ENGLAND — THE HUNDRED YEARS' WAR. 153

in 1346, a small English army, some sixteen thousand strong, defeated a French host three times its number. The significance of the battle lay in the fact that in the main it was won over the gallantest chivalry in Europe by the peasant bowmen who made the bulk of the English force, and that even the English horsemen had dismounted and fought on foot as pikemen.[1] The invincibility of the feudal horseman[2] was passing

SEALS OF EDWARD III before and after the assumption of the arms of France. On the seal to the right may be noticed the royal fleur-de-lis of France.

away. The like phenomenon was repeated a few years later at *Poitiers* (1356), where the numbers were seven to one (and quite as strikingly, three generations later, at *Agincourt*).

These victories bore little fruit. Neither castles nor towns opened their gates because of them; and before the end of Edward's reign, by cautious campaigning, the French had

[1] According to one old chronicler, gunpowder was used in this battle: the English are said to have had several small "bombards," "which, with fire and noise like God's thunder, threw little balls of iron *to frighten the horses*"!

[2] The term "infantry" had been to this time a contemptuous expression, from the same word as "infant," applied to the undisciplined mob of boys and men who followed the army of horsemen. The English had learned the value of infantry just before Crécy, in their defeat by the Scots at *Bannockburn*. Cf. the earlier example at Legnano, § 80. Special report upon Bannockburn.

recovered all their territory except a few cities on the coast. This was best for the interests of both France and England; but in 1415, after many years of truce, Henry V again invaded France, at a moment when the country was distracted by internal quarrels, and made himself master of the kingdom. His son, Henry VI, a child of nine months, was crowned in Paris as "King of France"; but again the French recovered themselves, and by the middle of the fifteenth century, just before the

AN ENGLISH CARRIAGE OF THE FOURTEENTH CENTURY. — After Jusserand's *English Wayfaring Life;* from a fourteenth century psalter. This carriage is represented as drawn by five horses tandem, driven by two postilions. Such a carriage was a princely luxury, equaling in value a herd of from four hundred to sixteen hundred oxen.

beginning of the civil war in England (§ 145), the English lost all France except Calais on the Channel.

140. The Black Death.[1] — The happy prosperity in England during the early part of the reign of Edward III, received a great shock from the *Black Death*. This was the most famous of all the great plagues of history. It had been devastating the East for some years; and in 1348, the year after Crécy, it reached England. Almost at a blow, it reduced the population of the island at least one-third.[2]

---

[1] For documents and contemporary accounts, see Lee, Colby, and *Pennsylvania Reprints*, II, No. 5. The best modern account is Gasquet's *The Great Pestilence.* See also Jessopp's *Coming of the Friars.*

[2] The results were not less terrible upon the continent. Some authorities estimate that the disease swept away half the population of Western Europe.

This terrible loss fell most heavily upon the working classes, but in the final result it helped along a great social change for their betterment. The lack of laborers was so great that wages doubled, and a new and higher standard of living was introduced. Parliament, it is true, in the interest of the landlords, tried, by foolish and cruel laws,[1] to keep the laborers upon the old footing; but individual landlords were so anxious to harvest their standing crops, that they did not venture to take advantage of such laws. Instead, they made more and more favorable terms with their old serfs, to keep them from running off to other districts, and gradually allowed them to exchange their labor services for fixed money rents. This amounted to a change from serfdom to freedom.

141. Social Discontent: Desire of the Peasantry for more Rapid Improvement; Wyclif and the Lollard Movement.[2] — The change was under way even before the coming of the Black Death, and it was practically complete before the middle of the fifteenth century. That is, the process was spread over a century. Rapid as this seems to the student of history, it was terribly slow to the laboring population of the time. The improvement that had taken place made them doubly impatient with the burdens that remained. No doubt, too, there were individual cases of bitter hardship, where a lord by legal tricks, or by reviving old and almost forgotten claims, or by downright violence, reduced his half-freed villeins to serfdom again.

There were also other causes, political and religious, for popular discontent. In particular the growing wealth and worldliness of the church began to attract attention. *Chaucer*, the great English poet of the age, indulged in gentle raillery[3] toward these features of the religious establishment; but more serious men could not dismiss them so lightly. The great

---

[1] See *Pennsylvania Reprints*, II, No. 5, for documents.

[2] Cf. Trevelyan's *England in the Age of Wycliffe*; Poole's *Wycliffe and Movements for Reform*; and Sergeant's *Wiclif*.

[3] Cf. the Prologue to the *Canterbury Tales*, for the descriptions of the monk, the prioress, the friar, and the pardoner.

John Wyclif at Oxford preached strenuously against such evils, and his most earnest disciples traveled from place to place spreading his doctrines through the land.[1]

These "poor preachers" were called "Lollards" (babblers) by their enemies. Some of them exaggerated into pure communism their master's teachings against wealth, and called for the abolition of all rank and property. John Ball, one of the "mad preachers," wrote words that rang through England from shore to shore, —

> "When Adam delved and Eve span,
> Who was then the gentleman?"

"This priest," says Froissart, a contemporary chronicler, "used oftentimes to go and preach when the people in the villages were coming out from mass; and he would make them gather about him, and would say thus: 'Good people, things go not well in England, nor will, till everything be in common and there no more be villeins and gentlemen. By what right are they whom we call lords greater folk than we? We be all come from one father and one mother, Adam and Eve, . . . but they are clothed in velvet and are warm in their furs, while we shiver in rags; they have wine, and spices, and fair bread; and we, oat cake and straw, and water to drink; they dwell in fair houses, and we have the pain and travail, the rain and the wind in the fields. Yet from our labor they keep their estate.' And so the people would murmur one with the other in the fields, and in the ways as they met together, affirming that John Ball spoke truth."

---

[1] Wyclif passed on from attacking the abuses in the church to attacking its doctrines, and finally took much the position occupied by Luther a century and a half later. Indeed, Wyclif has been called the "Morning Star of the Reformation." With his associates, he made the first complete translation of the Bible into English; and many copies made by his "poor preachers" were distributed through the land. Recently, an eminent Roman Catholic scholar, Father Gasquet, has advanced the theory that the so-called Wyclif's Bible was really an old, authorized Catholic translation; but this view has not met with general acceptance. There is no doubt, however, that, nearly a century earlier than Wyclif, friends of Roger Bacon began a critical translation from Greek into Latin (cf. *Cambridge Modern History*, I, 585 ff.).

Wyclif was protected, for political reasons, by the Duke of Lancaster, one of the sons of Edward III; and all attempts to persecute him failed. Some years after his death, however, the Council of Constance (§ 167) condemned his doctrines, and his ashes were then disinterred and cast into the river Swift. The Lancastrian kings, Henry IV and Henry V, persecuted the Lollards, and the sect soon disappeared from sight, but it may have had considerable influence upon the later English Protestant movement.

142. The Peasant Rising of 1381:[1] Disappearance of Villeinage.

— Thus the material was ready for a conflagration. While things were in this state, Parliament passed a heavy poll tax, bearing with unfair weight on the poor of the realm. With amazing suddenness and unanimity, the peasantry rose in arms. From all sides they marched upon London, and in a few days the kingdom was virtually in their hands. Their special demand was that all labor rents should be exchanged for fixed money rents; and they offered a fair rent, as prices then were. The strangest thing about the rising was the self-restraint shown by the peasants. The various bands sacked some buildings of the gentry class, — destroying especially the "manor rolls," or the written evidence of services due from villeins on an estate, — and they put to death a few lawyers and nobles. But women and children were not injured, and there was no attempt at general pillage and murder, such as usually mark servile insurrections and such as characterized the frightful risings of the peasantry in France in the same century. The French "Jacquerie"[2] was an outburst of blind, brute rage, upon the part of hopeless creatures, goaded past all endurance, seeking only to glut their vengeance. The English peasants stood upon a higher plane of comfort and of civilization, and their revolt was marked relatively by the moderation of men who had a definite program for social reform.

Unfortunately, the peasants lacked the organization needful to secure the results of their temporary success. Their leader, *Wat the Tyler*, was murdered treacherously in a conference, and his followers were persuaded to go home under written guarantee from the King that all their demands should be granted, together with free pardon for the revolt. When they had

---

[1] Ashley's *Edward III and His Wars*; Powell's *Peasant Rising*; Kriehn's "*Studies in the Sources of the Social Revolt*" (*American Historical Review*, VII, Nos. 2 and 3); and Trevelyan's *Age of Wycliffe*.

[2] "Jacques" is the general French name for a peasant. A vivid picture of a local rising in France is given in Conan Doyle's *White Company*.

dispersed, the property classes rallied and exacted a bloody and treacherous vengeance.[1]

In a short time, however, the movement toward emancipation began again with renewed force. We cannot be sure whether the revolt hastened or hindered the change.[2] Probably it did not very much affect the movement, except for a brief time; and it is best regarded as an unwise but very natural attempt to secure at a stroke the good results which were coming more surely by slow, peaceful development. In any event, except for isolated cases *villeinage had passed away from England before the Wars of the Roses* (§ 145).

143. The Growth of Parliament. — The French war made it necessary for Edward III and his successors to ask Parliament for frequent grants of money. The towns were growing wealthy and were able to supply the money: indeed the English success was due to this middle-class wealth as much, perhaps, as to the long-bow of the yeomanry. But Parliament took advantage of the needs of the King to secure gradual extensions of power. (1) It became an established principle that "redress of grievances" must precede a "grant of supply." (2) In the closing years of Edward III, the *Good Parliament* (1376) "impeached" the King's ministers, using the same method that has ever since been used for such purposes in English-speaking countries. (3) When Richard II[3] attempted a "personal" rule, without regard to Parliament, he was deposed (1399), and a

---

[1] Parliament refused to keep any of the pledges that the King had made, and told him he could not grant away the services due them, — their property, — without their consent.

[2] The older view was that the Peasant Revolt came because the landlords were trying to make the condition of the peasants worse than before; but the new view, presented in the text, is now clearly established. The discussions are generally too technical for high school students. An excellent statement of the present view is given in Cheyney's *Industrial and Social History*, 103-133; and page 120 gives a copy of the royal charters which were carried home by the peasantry to every village and which were afterward so cruelly disregarded.

[3] Edward's oldest son, the Black Prince, had died before his father; so Edward was succeeded by his grandson Richard.

§ 143] ENGLAND—GROWTH OF PARLIAMENT. 159

cousin was elected king in his place. (4) This sovereign, Henry IV (Henry of Lancaster), frankly recognized his dependence on Parliament. Under him the lower house made good its claims that all money bills must originate with it[1] and that it should audit the expenditures (1407); (5) it secured the right to judge of the election of its own members.

PARLIAMENT OF 1399, WHICH DEPOSED RICHARD II. — From *Old England*, which follows a contemporary manuscript. (The faces seem to be portraits.)

and (6) it compelled the King to dismiss his ministers and appoint new ones satisfactory to Parliament; (7) freedom of speech in Parliament and freedom from arrest, except by the order of Parliament itself, became recognized privileges of all members; (8) on three different occasions during Henry's reign, Parliament passed acts fixing the succession to the throne. (9) Under the next sovereign, Henry V, the older form of petitions to the king to make laws was changed, so that Parliament passed "bills," which the king had to accept or reject, and the wording of which he could not change without reference back to Parliament (1414).

---

[1] This has been the practice in English-speaking legislatures ever since.

144. The "Liberties of Englishmen." — Thus under the Lancastrians there was established in the breasts of Englishmen a proud consciousness of English Liberty as a most precious inheritance. With right they believed it superior to that possessed by any other people of the time. As Duruy remarks (*Middle Ages*, 436), "In the middle of the fifteenth century, the English people had in Magna Carta a declaration of their rights, in the jury a guarantee for their safety as individuals, and in Parliament a guarantee for national liberty." No man could be arrested except by order of a magistrate (not simply on the king's order); when arrested, he was entitled to speedy trial; and he could be condemned only by twelve men of his own neighborhood. Parliament voted taxes and superintended their expenditure, settled the succession to the throne, impeached offensive officers, and, upon occasion, deposed a king; and no law could be made or changed without its consent.

Sir John Fortescue, Chief Justice under Henry VI, wrote a book, *In Praise of the Laws of England*, for the instruction of Henry's son. The volume explains the English kingship in these words: —

"A king of England at his pleasure can not make any alteration in the laws of the land without the consent of his subjects, nor burden them against their wills with strange impositions. . . . Rejoice therefore, my good Prince, that such is the law of the kingdom you are to inherit, because it will afford both to you and to your subjects the greatest security and satisfaction. . . . [The King] is appointed to protect his subjects in their lives, properties, and laws; for this end *he has the delegation of power from the people*, and he has no just claims to any other power but this."

Some of the privileges of Parliament were soon lost (§ 147), it is true; and it must be understood, too, that the courts remained dependent upon the crown and often proved shamefully subservient to its will. Still, the liberties won in the Lancastrian period were of mighty importance both in their own day and in their influence upon future times. An ideal of free government had been established, toward which, centuries later, men were to struggle (§§ 237 ff.).

E. THE WARS OF THE ROSES AND THE YORKIST KINGS,[1] 1454–1485.

145. The Civil War. — In 1422, Henry VI became king, while less than a year old. The long minority gave time for factions to grow among the nobles; and when Henry assumed the government, he proved too weak and gentle to restore order. The misrule of the great lords caused widespread discontent, especially among the rising towns,[2] whose industries called for settled government; and, encouraged by this discontent, the Duke of York came forward to claim the crown.

Thus began the Wars of the Roses,[3] to last from 1454 to 1471. York was descended from a son of Edward III older than the one through whom the Lancastrians derived their claim to the throne; and the war, the most ruthless and bloody in English history since Danish times, was largely a selfish contest between great nobles. At the same time the chief significance of the struggle is in the fact that the Lancastrian strength lay in the feudal nobility of the north of England, while York was supported by the new middle class of the towns in the south.

Finally, York and the cause of the towns conquered. The Lancastrian family, with most of the great nobles of both parties, had been exterminated in battle or by assassination. The townsmen, however, could not dream of grasping political power; they wanted only protection. The political fruits of the victory fell to the new monarchy (§ 146).

---

[1] Gairdner's *Lancaster and York* is the best brief volume on this period. See also references on pages 136 and 142. Stubbs' great history just goes through the period. Stevenson's *Black Arrow* is an admirable story for a boy, and Bulwer's *Last of the Barons* is the most famous novel dealing with the age.

[2] Special topic: Cade's Rebellion. (The student must get the view of recent scholars and not be content with the slanders of the old writers.)

[3] The Yorkists assumed a white rose as their badge; the Lancastrians, a red rose. Students may be asked to find the scene in which Shakspere represents the choice of these symbols.

146. Reference Table of the Yorkist Reigns.

Edward IV, 1461-1483: neglected Parliament.
Edward V, 1483: a child; never crowned; son of Edward IV; murdered by his uncle, the regent, who became king.
Richard III, 1483-1485: a cruel tyrant, soon overthrown by a popular rising led by Henry Tudor, a connection of the Lancastrian line, who became king as Henry VII.

147. Results of the Civil War: Decline of Parliament; a "New Monarchy."
— The losses in the war had fallen in the main on the feudal classes. The old nobility was almost swept away, and the following Yorkist and Tudor kings set to work skillfully to crush whatever feudal independence remained. A new nobility was created, but it was dependent upon the king. The towns continued to grow in importance, but this did not mean a growth in political freedom. Without nobles for leaders, the towns and country gentlemen were still too weak to challenge the royal power.

Parliament lost authority and sank to insignificance. During the long war it had not been possible to hold true Parliaments. When the wars were over, the kings were so enriched by confiscations, that in ordinary times they could rule without new taxes, and so could get along for long periods without calling a Parliament. This policy was deliberately adopted, except when the king was confident that he could easily use Parliament as his tool. England entered the sixteenth century under the Tudor monarchs, Henry VII and his son Henry VIII, with a "New Monarchy," — a strong government, absolute in practice, though still following old constitutional forms. The occasional meetings of Parliament preserved these forms; but not for two hundred years was Parliament to play as large a part in the government as it had done in the century before the civil war. After all, however, the New Monarchy, in crushing the feudal forces, was preparing the way for a future parliamentary government infinitely more valuable than men had dreamed of in earlier times.

IV. EUROPE BY SEPARATE STATES: FRANCE.

There is no other modern nation which owes so heavy a debt of gratitude to its ancient line of kings as the French. France, as it exists to-day, and has existed through all modern history, with all its glorious achievements, is their creation and that of no one else. — GEORGE BURTON ADAMS.

148. Reference Table: Capetian Kings to 1547, with Accession Dates.

Hugh Capet	987	Philip V	1316
Robert II	996	Charles IV	1322
Henry I	1031	Philip VI (Valois)[1]	1328
Philip I	1060	John	1350
Louis VI	1108	*Charles V* (the Wise)	1364
Louis VII	1137	Charles VI	1380
Philip II (Augustus)	1180	Charles VII	1422
Louis VIII	1223	*Louis XI*	1461
Louis IX (the Saint)	1226	Charles VIII	1483
Philip III	1270	Louis XII	1498
Philip IV (the Fair)	1285	Francis I	1515-1547
Louis X	1314		

149. The Most Important Reigns.[2]—The real growth of France begins with the fifth Capetian, *Louis VI*. This King consolidated the hereditary Capetian duchy, the "Isle of France," by bringing his vassals into closer dependence upon himself, and so forged the weapon with which his successors were to consolidate all France. The "Isle of France" lay in the north-central part of the kingdom, remote from the sea, and comprised about a twelfth of French territory. The other parts were ruled by ten or twelve

---

[1] The first fourteen of these rulers came to the throne in the "direct line." Until Philip IV, the succession was always from father to oldest son. The last three of the fourteen were all sons of Philip IV, and all three died without male heirs. The crown then passed to their oldest cousin, a grandson of Philip III. This prince (Philip VI) had been Count of Valois, and his successors are known as the House of Valois. The death of the sons of Philip IV without a male heir was the occasion for the claim advanced by Edward III of England (§ 139): Edward's mother was a younger sister of these three kings. French law, however, did not recognize inheritance of the crown through females; and, if it had, Edward's claim would have been worthless, since the oldest son of Philip IV had left a daughter who had a male heir, and this claim would have preceded that of Edward's mother.

[2] At this point the student should re-read carefully §§ 42-44, for the nature and aims of the early Capetian monarchy.

great princes, who were vassals of the Capetians only in name. Louis VI did not add any of these territories permanently to the crown; but he prepared the way for their gradual acquisition.[1]

In the next four centuries, the five kings who had most to do in this great task were *Philip Augustus, Saint Louis, Philip the Fair, Charles the Wise, and Louis XI.* Before the death of the third of these five, — about 1300, when the four centuries were half gone, — the greater part of France had been united and the king had become stronger than all the other forces in the state. While the German kings were wasting their earlier strength in pursuit of impossible universal sovereignty, and while the English kings were beginning to share with Parliament the absolute power they had for a time possessed from conquest, the French kings were adding domain to domain and authority to authority, until they became the most absolute and powerful sovereigns in Europe.

150. Territorial Growth. — The making of France, territorially, consisted in adding the great feudal fiefs (§ 41) directly to the royal domain. In the eleventh century a duke of Normandy or of Aquitaine was as powerful as the king of France. But if the king himself could step into the place of such a duke, then the minor lords in Normandy or Aquitaine became his direct vassals and added to his power, instead of possibly adding to the weight of a rival. By marriage, by forfeiture, by war, the kings did themselves replace, one by one, the feudal princes. The striking advances came in connection (1) with the crusades (§ 105), (2) with the wars against the English kings, (3) with the crushing of the Albigenses, and (4) with the seizure of the dukedom of Burgundy (§§ 151, 152).

151. Acquisition of the French Domains of the Plantagenets. — Duke William of Normandy, even before he became William the Conqueror of England, was the chief rival of his liege,

---

[1] Louis VI did arrange a marriage for his son with Eleanor, heiress of Aquitaine, the largest of the French principalities; but the impolitic Louis VII, offended by Eleanor's conduct, secured a divorce. Eleanor at once married Henry Plantagenet (§ 126), and Aquitaine passed into English hands.

ENGLAND AND FRANCE, 1154–1453.

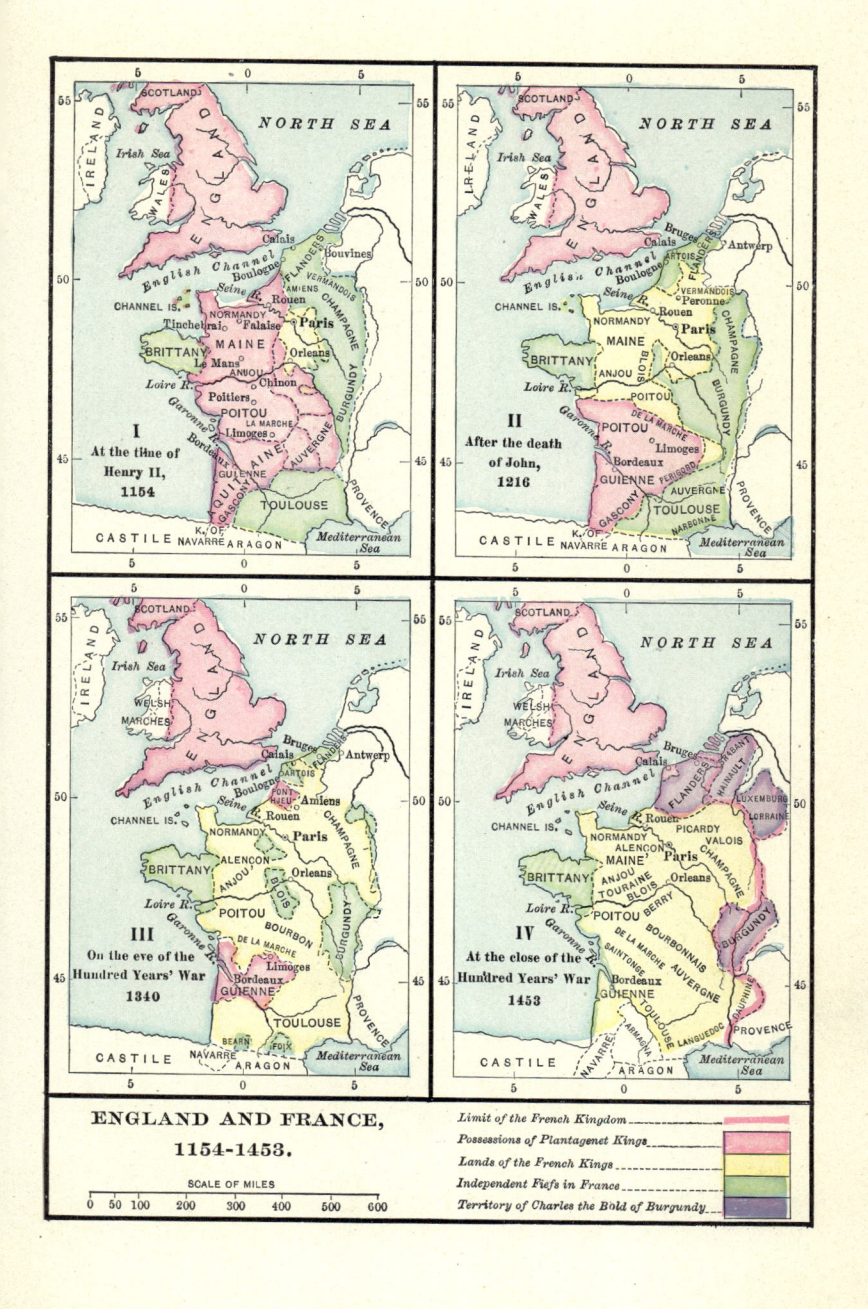

SCALE OF MILES
0 50 100 200   300   400   500   600

Limit of the French Kingdom
Possessions of Plantagenet Kings
Lands of the French Kings
Independent Fiefs in France
Territory of Charles the Bold of Burgundy

I. At the time of Henry II, 1154
II. After the death of John, 1216
III. On the eve of the Hundred Years' War, 1340
IV. At the close of the Hundred Years' War, 1453

§ 151]   FRANCE — CONSOLIDATION OF TERRITORY.   165

the king of France. Henry II of England ruled directly six or seven times as much territory in France as did Philip Augustus at the opening of his reign; and as late as this date (1180) "France" proper was still without a seaport. Under such conditions it was natural that the French kings should strive ceaselessly to stir up enemies for these great rival vassals and should seize every pretext to weaken them by war.[1] Through the folly and crimes of John of England (§ 131), Philip Augustus was able to declare John's fiefs in France forfeited and to enforce the forfeiture of a great part of them,— *the northwest quarter of France.* In this way, Normandy, Maine, Anjou, Touraine, and Poitou were added to the French crown, quadrupling the direct domain of the king, and giving him ports on both the Channel and the Atlantic. A century later, the persistent policy of the French kings brought on the Hundred Years' War with England (§ 139). That war falls into two great chapters. The first lasts until the time of Richard II in England. In the beginning, the English seemed completely victorious; but Charles the Wise taught the French to avoid pitched battles and to conquer by slow campaigns, and before 1400 the invaders were driven from all but a few ports on the coast. *Southwestern France had now been added to the royal domain,* and the realm had been again nearly doubled. To be sure, in a later period of the war, Henry V conquered the insane French king, Charles VI, and secured a treaty under which the English babe, Henry VI, was crowned at Paris as King of France; but the triumph was brief. French national feeling had come into being, as a result of the long struggle with the foreigner; and soon the devotion of an heroic peasant girl, *Joan of Arc,* freed her country.[2]

---

[1] Until the time of the unprovoked attack upon France by Henry V (§ 139), all the struggles with the English kings were really begun by France. Such war was not defensive war, but at least it was waged in the interest of national consolidation and order. Lasting peace was not possible while the realm was so fantastically cut up into opposing states.

[2] Special report: life and work of Joan of Arc. Read Oliphant's *Jeanne d'Arc* and Clemens' *Personal Reminiscences of Joan of Arc* (a novel).

Joan saw visions and believed that divine voices called her to her mission. That mission was, in truth, to give voice to the new national consciousness. Her enthusiasm was the prelude to a national uprising, before which the few invaders were swept away like chaff. Says Lavisse (*General View*, 64), French patriotism "blossomed in Joan of Arc and sanctified itself with the perfume of a miracle."

France emerged from the struggle after tremendous economic loss, and after long periods of terrible suffering and desolation,[1] but with consolidated territory, with a new popular patriotism, and with a strengthened government.

152. Acquisition of the Southeast and the Northeast. — About 1200, shortly before England's loss of French territory began, came the movement that paved the way for the acquisition of the principality of Toulouse; and, soon after the Hundred Years' War closed, Burgundy became French.

a. The Crusades against the Albigenses (§ 83) broke the power of the count of Toulouse, and left the way open for the kings to seize upon this corner of the French realm, piece by piece. From the days of Clovis until these crusades, southeastern Roman Gaul had really been independent of northern Teutonic Gaul.[2] Now the feudal North conquered the city South; but the monarchy reaped the benefit of the victory. At last the Capetians had won their way to the Mediterranean.

b. The duchy of Burgundy had been separated from the kingdom of Burgundy since the Treaty of Verdun (§ 8). It was in name a French province, but its rulers had aided England in the Hundred Years' War, in order to weaken the French kings and so better to preserve their own independence. Little by little, a series of able dukes had built up a composite state of wealthy provinces, — some of them fiefs of the Empire, some of France.[3] During the Wars of the Roses in England, Charles the Bold, Duke of Burgundy, was working zealously to weld his group of provinces into a kingdom and to persuade the Emperor to change the ducal title to the name of "king."

---

[1] The first period of the war was the time of the *Jacquerie* (§ 142).
[2] *Ancient History*, §§ 590, 616, 618, 619.   [3] See map following page 172.

Success would have restored the old Middle Kingdom of Carolingian days. For a time Charles seemed about to achieve his aim, despite the crafty intrigues of Louis XI of France; but in 1477 he was defeated and slain by the Swiss, whom he was trying to force into his growing state. He left no male heir, and the unscrupulous Louis at once seized Burgundy. The rich Flemish towns, it is true, escaped the French grasp, though they had been part of Burgundy (§ 162); but Louis found compensation by securing Provence, which Charles had hoped to add to his dukedom.

153. Administrative Development. — As the kings acquired the soil of France, step by step, the realm outgrew the simple feudal government. The kings then had to create new administrative machinery. *Philip Augustus* (about 1200) made a beginning by dividing the growing domain into districts and putting each under a royal officer. *Louis IX* (about 1250) greatly reduced the power of the feudal barons, by insisting rigidly on all the ancient rights of the crown. *Philip the Fair* (about 1300) introduced various new checks upon feudal rights and established a modern system of national taxation. At various times the feudal nobility made desperate attempts to regain their waning independence. They had risen in arms in formidable leagues at the openings of the reigns of Louis VIII and Louis IX, and they made another desperate attempt when *Louis XI* came to the throne. The young King fought valiantly in the field, but really won his victories by cunning and unscrupulous diplomacy. Afterward he chose his chief ministers from men of low birth, who necessarily remained wholly dependent upon royal favor, and before his death the feudal lords were reduced to complete dependence.

154. The Estates General. — Philip the Fair had completed his reforms by adding representatives of the towns to the nobles and clergy in the Great Council of France. This brought together all three "estates"; and the gathering was called the *Estates General,* to distinguish it from smaller gatherings in the separate provinces. The first meeting in this form was held in *1302*, only a few years after the "Model Parliament" in England (§ 135). Philip used the Estates General as a convenient taxing-machine. It never became a governing body, as the English Parliament did. The kings assembled it only when they chose, and easily controlled it. When they no longer needed it, the meetings grew rarer, and finally ceased.

FOR FURTHER READING. — Source material: Froissart's *Chronicles;* Commines' *Memoirs* (1464-1498).

Modern accounts: Adams' *Growth of the French Nation* is the best brief account, and quite as full as can be used with profit at this point. The same author has a shorter survey in his *Civilization*, ch. xiii. Lodge's *Close of the Middle Ages*, ch. xvi, is particularly good. Excellent treatments are given in Hutton's *Philip Augustus*, Smith's *The Troubadours*, and Lodge's *Charles the Bold*.

Fiction: Scott's *Anne of Geierstein* and *Quentin Durward* both treat of the time of Louis XI and Charles the Bold. Hale's *In His Name* is a story of the Albigenses, no doubt idealizing that sect. Conan Doyle's *White Company* (referred to on page 157) is deserving of mention under the head of France also; and Charles Reade's *Cloister and Hearth* has great value.

SPECIAL REPORTS. — 1. The Battle of Crécy.   2. The Battle of Poitiers.   3. The English long-bow and the art of war (Oman, *Art of War*, chs. vii, viii).   4. The Battle of Bouvines (1214), and its effects upon France, England, and Germany.

V. EUROPE BY SEPARATE STATES: SPAIN.

155. Territorial Growth. — Until the Moorish conquest in 711, the fate of Spain for some centuries had been not unlike that of Gaul or Italy, and certainly not less promising. The Mohammedan invasion, however, separated the course of development in Spain from that of the rest of Europe; and for centuries afterward "Africa began at the Pyrenees."

The wave of Moorish invasion had left unconquered a few resolute Christian chiefs in the remote fastnesses of the northwestern mountains, and Charlemagne recovered part, also, of the northeast. In these districts (*Asturia* and the *Spanish*

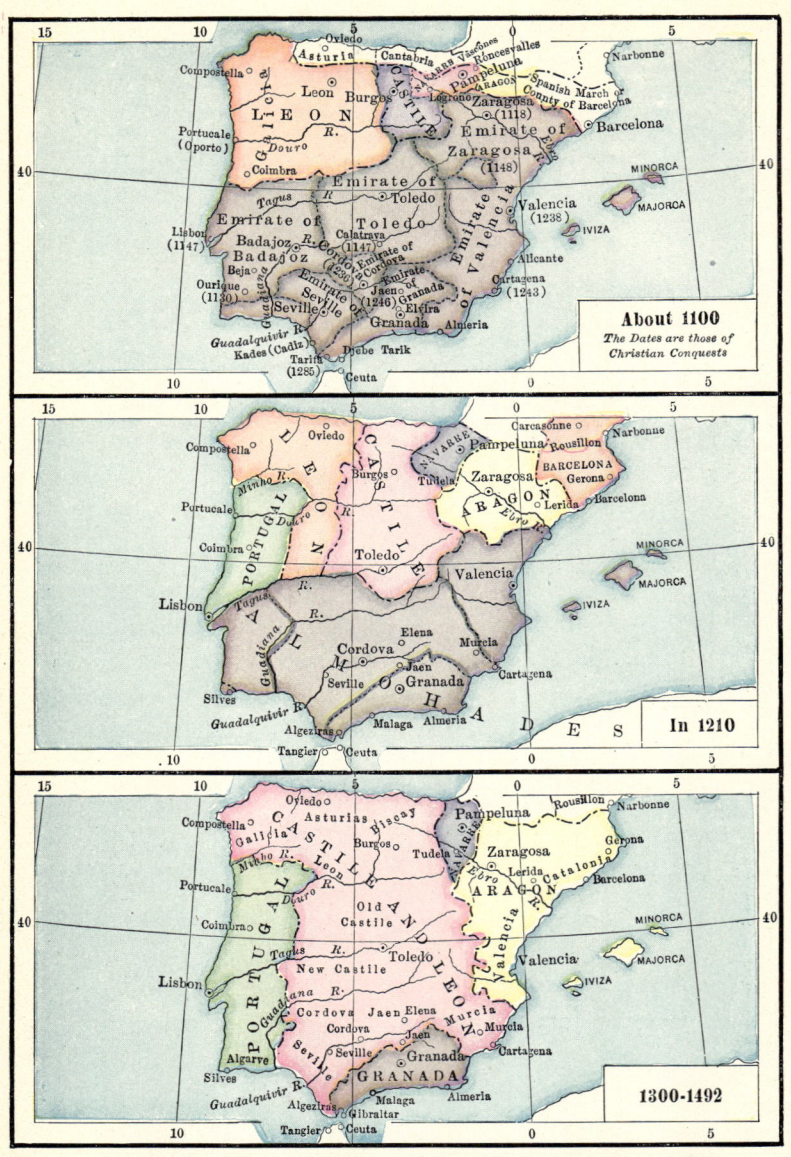

SPANISH KINGDOMS IN THE MIDDLE AGES

March), several little Christian principalities arose, to begin the long task of winning back their land, crag by crag and stream by stream. This they accomplished in eight hundred years of war, — a war at once patriotic and religious, Spaniard against African, and Christian against Infidel. The long struggle left the Spanish race proud, brave, warlike, unfitted for industrial civilization, intensely patriotic, and blindly devoted to the church.

During the eight centuries of conflict, the Christian states spread gradually to the south and east, — waxing, fusing, splitting up into new states, uniting in kaleidoscopic combinations by marriage and war, — until, before 1400, they had combined into three countries, Portugal, Aragon, and Castile. Nearly a century later, two of these were united by the marriage of Isabella of Castile with Ferdinand of Aragon; and in 1492 their combined power captured Granada, the last Moorish stronghold. Thus, in the year that Columbus discovered America under Spanish auspices, Spain at home had achieved national union and national independence, and she soon took her place (with her new-world dependencies) as the most powerful European state.

156. Growth of Monarchic Government. — The feudal lords of the many Spanish kingdoms had been the most turbulent and uncontrollable in Europe. In each petty state they elected their king and took the oath to obey him, in forms like this: "We, who are each of us as good as thou, and who together are far more powerful than thou, swear to obey thee if thou dost obey our laws, and if not, not." The towns of Spain, too, had possessed charters of liberties of the most extreme character, and in various kingdoms they had sent representatives to the national assembly of Estates, or the "Cortes," for more than a century before a like practice began in England. But Ferdinand of Aragon began to abridge all these privileges, and in the next two reigns (§§ 170, 209 ff.) the process was carried so far that Spain became the most absolute monarchy in Europe.

MAP EXERCISE. — "Castile" was at first merely a line of "castles." It was a "mark state" (cf. *Ancient History*, § 276, and note): it shut off Aragon on one side and Leon on the other from any effective contact with the Moors, as Barcelona, Navarre, and Asturia had been shut off still earlier. After this was accomplished, Castile was the state most likely to grow to supremacy. Cf. Wessex in Britain; § 16.

FOR FURTHER READING. — Tout, *Empire and Papacy*, ch. xx; Lodge, *Middle Ages*, ch. xx; Watts, *Christian Recovery of Spain*.

SPECIAL REPORT. — The Cid; see Clarke, *The Cid*.

VI. EUROPE BY SEPARATE STATES: SCANDINAVIA.

157. Soon after the year 800, Norse adventurers began to found small states, almost at will, on the fringes of Western Europe (§§ 14 ff.), and before the close of the century the Scandinavian lands themselves entered the political map of Europe as crude kingdoms. After that time, however, except for the brief empire of Knut (§§ 17, 64), they hardly touched the life of the rest of Europe until the seventeenth century. Within the peninsulas, feudalism was gradually introduced, though its hold upon Norway was never firm. The story of these northern lands is romantic: the very names of the Norse kings make a portrait gallery, — Eric Broadax, Hakon the Good, Hakon the Old, Olaf the Thickset, Olaf the Saint.[1] But after all, the history for the most part is only a record of meaningless wars, until, in 1397, the three kingdoms were united under Queen Margaret of Denmark, by the *Union of Calmar*.

This treaty had the form of a brief written constitution, signed by the principal men of the three nations. It provided that each country should keep its own laws and its internal administration, but that for foreign affairs the three should be joined in "perpetual union" under one hereditary sovereign. In practice, the "Union" made the states of the northern peninsula into dependencies of Denmark. Sweden soon rebelled, and finally, under her heroic *Gustavus Vasa*, established

---

[1] High school students will enjoy Carlyle's *Kings of Norway*.

her independence (1537). Norway became a mere province of Denmark, to remain so, with occasional rebellions, until 1814.

VII. EUROPE BY SEPARATE STATES: GERMANY.

"From the middle of the thirteenth century, Germany was merely an anarchical federation of principalities and republics. There was no longer any collective national life, no national army, finance, or judiciary. Everywhere war prevailed, and there was no longer any law save that of the fist. . . .

"Over this disorder a monarch presided who still called himself Emperor. But, under the trappings of his title, he was only a petty German prince, exploiting his high office to make the fortune of his house. Thus the Luxemburgs, poor squires of the county of Ardennes, and the Hapsburgs, small seigneurs of the county of Argovia, secured a family domain." — LAVISSE, *Political History of Europe,* 40.

158. Rudolph of Hapsburg, 1273-1291. — The Holy Roman Empire never recovered from the failure of the Hohenstaufen princes (§ 88). During the twenty years of interregnum (1254-1273), "robber barons" had harassed the land, and in many parts of the country each lord of a single tower had become practically a sovereign prince. Says Bryce, "These petty tyrants, whose boast was that they owed fealty only to God and the Emperor, showed themselves in practice equally regardless of both powers."

This anarchy was only slightly checked in 1273 by the election of *Rudolph of Hapsburg* as Emperor. Rudolph was a petty count of a rude district near the Alps, and no doubt the princes chose him because they did not fear his power. One of them, the King of Bohemia, refused to acknowledge him. Rudolph attacked Bohemia, and seized from it the duchy of Austria, which has ever since been the chief seat of the Hapsburgs. He completely abandoned the Italian policy of the earlier emperors; and throughout his reign he displayed much zeal in widening the boundaries of his personal domain. "Sit firm on Thy throne, O Lord," once prayed the Bishop of Basel, "or the Count of Hapsburg will shove Thee off." Rudolph gave much energy also to the restoration of order, so far as that task lay within his power. Along the Rhine alone, he demolished over one hundred and forty robber castles, and he once hung twenty-nine robbers at one execution.

159. The Electoral College and the Golden Bull. — At Rudolph's death the Electors refused to give the imperial crown to his son, though that prince was thoroughly capable; and the next fifty-five years saw five rulers *each of a different house from his predecessor*. The method of electing an emperor had varied greatly at different periods. On some occasions, a gathering of great nobles had made the choice in a fairly popular way, while at other times a few princes had settled the matter by private negotiation (§ 62, note). Before the end of the Hohenstaufen period, the right of election had fallen to a ring of seven princes. These "Electors" now passed the crown from family to family, and, at each new election, enriched themselves through extortionate demands upon the candidates.

To prevent such scandals and the dangerous disputes over membership in the electoral college, a Bohemian Emperor, Charles IV, with the consent of a Diet,[1] issued the Golden Bull (1356).[2] This document remained the fundamental law of the Empire through the rest of its history. It defined exactly the powers and procedure of the "college of Electors" and defined the members as the three Archbishops of Mainz, Cologne, and Trier, the King of Bohemia, the Duke of Saxony,

---

[1] The Great Council of German lords was known as a "Diet." To this gathering, representatives of the free cities were admitted in the fourteenth century (as had been the case earlier in the French Estates General, the English Parliament, and the Spanish Cortes). The Diet came to consist of three houses, — the Chamber of Electors, the Chamber of Princes (the greater nobles of the second rank), and the Chamber of City Representatives. The Diet could do nothing but pass resolutions, which nobody obeyed unless he chose to do so. The knights were not admitted, either in person or by representatives.

[2] So called from its gold seal, or *bulla*. (This word explains the term "bull" applied to papal documents.) For a brief special report on the Golden Bull, see Henderson, *Short History of Germany*, I, 159-162, or Bryce, *Holy Roman Empire*, 225-237.

EUROPE ABOUT THE Year 1400

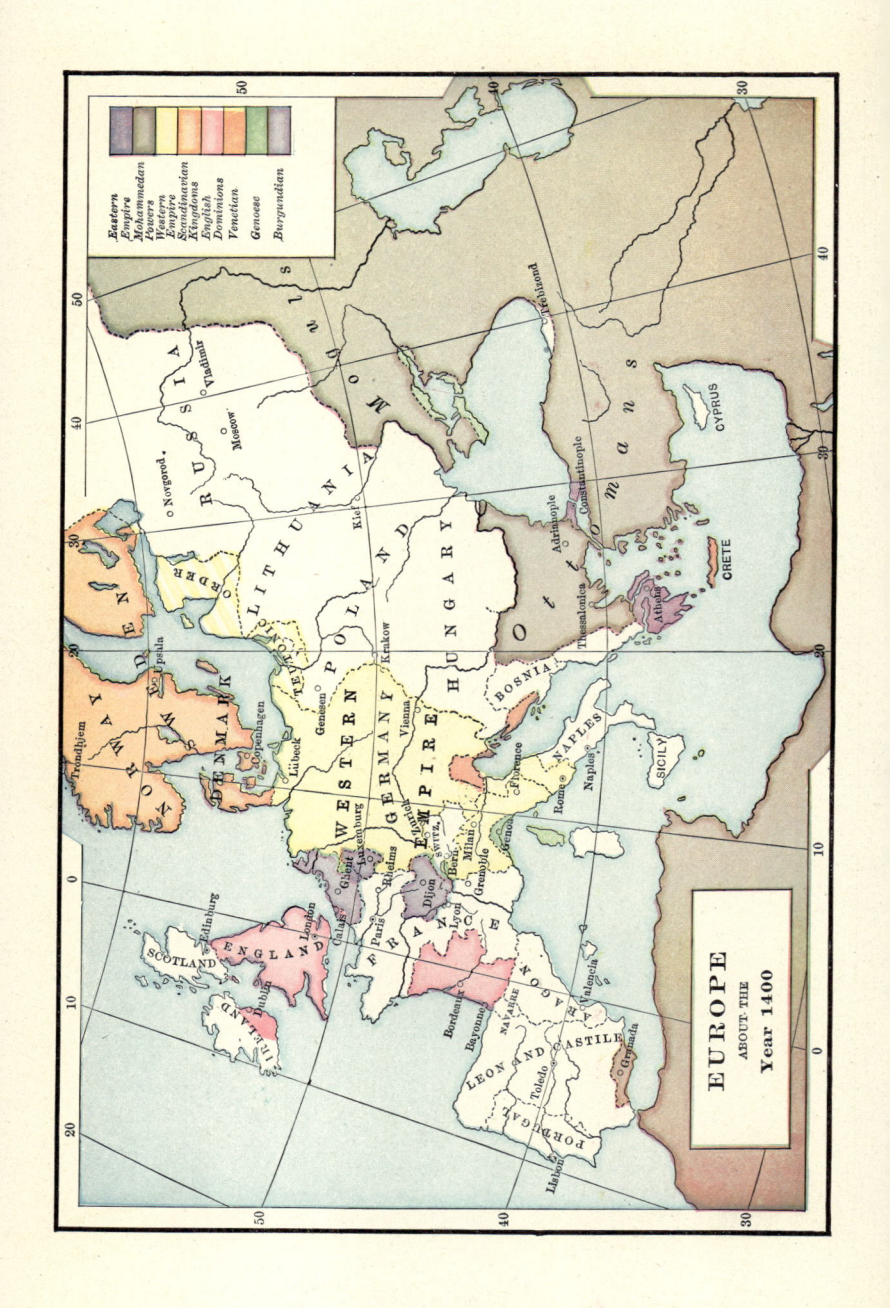

the Margrave of Brandenburg, and the Count Palatine of the Rhine.

160. The "Hapsburg" Empire. — Finally, in 1438, after a long line of Bohemian emperors, the imperial title came back to the Hapsburgs by the election of Albert, Duke of Austria. From this time to its disappearance in 1806, the title was to belong to the house of Austria, practically as an hereditary possession. The form of an election was always gone through, but the choice invariably fell upon the Hapsburg heir.[1]

The Empire after 1438 is sometimes called the "Austrian Empire" (cf. § 55). The phrase is not strictly correct, but it is significant. The emperor was little more than the honorary president of a loose confederacy made up of a multitude of petty sovereignties; and Austria did furnish such physical support as the imperial dignity possessed. From this time until the French Revolution, with rare exceptions (like Maximilian), the emperors spent their entire reigns within their Austrian domains, busying themselves exclusively with Austrian interests.

Albert was followed by the long but uninteresting reign of Frederick III (1440-1493), and then the crown passed to *Maximilian I* (1493-1519), the romantic hero of the Hapsburg race. Maximilian made a noble effort to reconstruct the Empire in the interest of order and good government, and so to bring Germany abreast of England, France, and Spain; but in the end he failed utterly, because of the selfishness of the nobles and the local jealousies between the provinces, and, it must be added, because of his own dreamy nature and haughty willfulness.

In the person of Maximilian's grandson, *Charles V*, the houses of Austria and Spain were united (§ 172), so introducing a new chapter in the history of Europe.

FOR FURTHER READING. — Bryce, *Holy Roman Empire*, 211-238, 303-320; Henderson, *Short History of Germany*, I, 122-240; Lodge, *Close of the Middle Ages*, 1-19, 98-123, and 394-418.

---

[1] Except in one case (1747), when the Hapsburgs had no direct male heir. The crown was then given to Francis I, the husband of the Hapsburg princess, Maria Theresa (§ 274), after a brief rule by a Bavarian rival.

VIII. EUROPE BY SEPARATE STATES: SWITZERLAND.

161. Switzerland began to grow into a political state just before the year 1300. The brave and sturdy peasantry, in the isolation of their mountain fastnesses, had preserved many old Teutonic customs and much of the old Teutonic independence.[1] Some small districts (cantons) in the German Alps had belonged to the Hapsburg counts. When Rudolph of Hapsburg became duke of distant Austria (§ 158), these older possessions were left to the administration of subordinate officers. The extortions practised by such agents prepared the mountaineers for revolt; and, in 1291, seventeen days after the death of Rudolph, the three "Forest Cantons" — *Uri, Schwyz,* and *Unterwalden* — formed a "perpetual league" for mutual defense against tyranny.

The league was not designed, at first, for independence.[2] The confederates pledged themselves to receive no "judge" who should have purchased his office, and none who should not be an inhabitant of the district, and they declared their purpose to establish quiet and peace, — "*yet in such manner, that every man according to his rank, shall obey and serve his overlord as it behooves him.*" The original Latin document of confederation is still preserved in the archives of Schwyz.

For two centuries, from time to time, the Hapsburgs invaded Switzerland with powerful armies, in order to reduce the mountaineers to complete subjection; and very soon the league against oppression by the lord's agents became a league for independence, against the lord himself. Freedom was practically established by two great victories, — *Morgarten* (1315) and *Sempach* (1386).[3] Between the two battles,

---

[1] Read the account of a modern Swiss "folkmoot," in the opening pages of Freeman's *Growth of the English Constitution.*

[2] Two of the cantons — Uri and Schwyz — are said to have had an older league, and to have secured recognition as free states from Frederick II in 1241.

[3] The myth of *William Tell* belongs to the period of Morgarten, and the myth of *Arnold Winkelried* to that of Sempach. These two stories are good subjects for special reports. Advanced students may be asked to present the modern criticism of the legends.

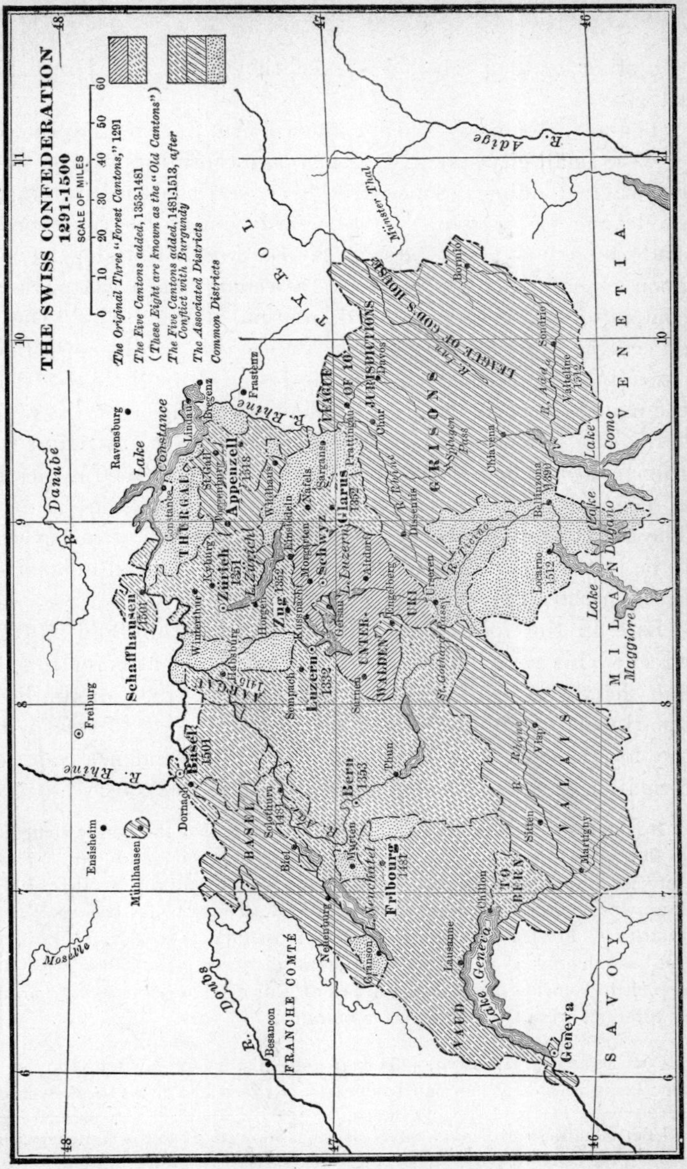
THE SWISS CONFEDERATION
1291-1500
SCALE OF MILES
0 10 20 30 40 50 60
The Original Three "Forest Cantons," 1291
The Five Cantons added, 1353-1481
(These Eight are known as the "Old Cantons")
The Five Cantons added, 1481-1513, after Conflict with Burgundy
The Associated Districts
Common Districts
R. Danube
Lake Constance
R. Rhine
TYROL
R. Adige
Münster Thal
VENETIA
MILAN
SAVOY
FRANCHE COMTÉ
Moselle
R. Doubs
Besançon
Ensisheim
Mühlhausen
Freiburg
Ravensburg
Lindau
Bregenz
Frastenz
Schaffhausen 1501
Basel 1501
Dornach
Solothurn 1481
Biel
BASEL
Bern 1353
Thun
Murten
Fribourg 1481
Neuenburg
L. Neuchatel
Granson
Lausanne
Chillon
TO BERN
VAUD
Lake Geneva
Geneva
Sitten
Martigny
Visp
R. Rhone
VALAIS
Luzern 1332
Sempach
Sarnen
UNTER-WALDEN
Engelberg
Habsburg
Winterthur
Kyburg
Zürich 1351
L. Zürich
Horgen
Zug 1352
Küssnacht
Morgarten
Einsiedeln
Schwyz
L. Luzern
Gersau
Altdorf
URI
Urseren
St. Gothard Pass
R. Ticino
Locarno 1512
Bellinzona 1390
Lake Maggiore
Lake Lugano
Lake Como
Constance
THURGAU
St. Gall
Toggenburg
Appenzell 1513
Wildhaus
Näfels
Glarus 1352
Sargans
Prattigau
LEAGUE OF 10 JURISDICTIONS
Chur
Davos
Disentis
R. Inn
LEAGUE OF GOD'S HOUSE
GRISONS
Splügen Pass
Chiavenna
Bormio
Sondrio
R. Adda
Valtelline 1512

five other cantons rebelled against their lords and joined the alliance.

The new members — among them Bern, Zurich, and Luzern — were small city-states, wealthier and more aristocratic than the original union. Soon after Sempach, the constitution of the league was revised. In the new document, the confederate cantons claimed to be states of the Empire, but all dependence upon feudal lords was expressly rejected. Each canton kept complete control over its own internal affairs. The "Diet," or central congress of representatives, was hardly more than a meeting of ambassadors, and was designed for little else than the management of foreign war and the division of the plunder. The union preserved this loose character until after the French Revolution (1798), and the history after 1500 is mostly a record of miserable petty quarrels between the cantons. The growth into the remarkable federal republic of to-day was to be in the main a matter of French and American influences, in the nineteenth century.

Late in the fourteenth century, Charles the Bold (§ 152) wrecked his reviving Middle Kingdom in an attempt to subdue the Swiss; and a few years later, in 1499, Maximilian, the Hapsburg emperor, was defeated and forced to treat with the League as a sovereign state.[1] Its independence was not formally recognized, however, until 1648 (§ 232).

It is notable, as in the case of Spain (§ 155), that the heroic struggles of the Swiss produced disastrous results upon their character. Their victories developed a passion for plunder and for fighting; so that, when there were no wars at home, great numbers of Swiss youth became "mercenaries." For centuries they were the most famous soldiery of Europe, and, strangely enough, when the great democratic movements of the French Revolution began, the thrones of European despots were guarded by hirelings from the free Swiss mountains.

FOR FURTHER READING. — The federal history of Switzerland is of peculiar interest to American students, but the reading can be done more

---

[1] Between these two conflicts, five cantons were added to the confederation, making the thirteen that formed the union till the French Revolution.

profitably in connection with the later history (§§ 512 ff.). Lodge's *Close of the Middle Ages* gives an excellent brief account. Scott's *Anne of Geierstein* pictures Swiss life about 1475.

IX. EUROPE BY SEPARATE STATES: THE NETHERLANDS.

162. The Netherlands (Low Countries) did not form an independent state in the Middle Ages, but they deserve a special treatment. They were made up of a group of provinces, part of them fiefs of the Empire, part of them French fiefs. The southern portion has become modern Belgium; the northern part, modern Holland. The land is a low, level tract, and in the Middle Ages it was more densely packed with teeming cities than any other part of Europe. Built, as many of them were, on land wrested from the sea,[1] these cities took naturally to commerce. It was here that the merchants from Italy and the south of Europe met and exchanged wares with the Hansa merchants. But as long as the Hansa controlled the northern trade, these Netherland towns were workshops even more than they were trading rooms: "Nothing reached their shores," says one historian, "but received a more perfect finish; what was coarse and almost worthless, became transmuted into something beautiful and valuable." Matthew Paris, a thirteenth century English chronicler, exclaimed that "the whole world was clothed in English wool *manufactured in Flanders.*"

The inhabitants were a sturdy, independent, slow, industrious, persistent people. Ghent claimed eighty thousand citizens able to bear arms, while Ypres is said to have employed two hundred thousand people in the weaving of cloth. No doubt these numbers are exaggerations; but wealth so abounded that the "counts" of this little district excelled most of the kings of Europe in magnificence. Early in the crusading age the cities had won or bought their liberties. Each province had its Diet, where sat nobles and city representatives.

---

[1] Amsterdam, Rotterdam, and many other cities to the north were built upon dams, or dykes.

The central fact in Netherland history through the thirteenth and fourteenth centuries was the trade with England for raw wool. The need of this commodity for the Flemish looms made Flanders the ally of England in the long struggle between that country and France (§§ 139, 151). During this period the dukes of Burgundy became masters of Flanders, and, after many revolts and cruel suppressions, the ancient liberties of the towns were somewhat abridged. When Charles the Bold of Burgundy lost his life in trying to extend his dukedom into a kingdom (§ 152), and when Louis XI of France then seized most of his possessions, the Flemish towns wisely chose to remain faithful to Mary, the daughter of Charles. In return for their fidelity, an Estates General of all the provinces secured from that princess a grant of *The Great Privilege*, the "Magna Carta of the Netherlands" (1478). This document promised that the provinces might hold Diets at will; that no new tax should be imposed but by the Estates General; that no war should be declared but by the consent of that body; that offices should be filled by natives only; and that Dutch should be the official language.

HALL OF THE CLOTH-MAKERS' GILD AT YPRES: begun in 1200; finished in 1364. Now the Town Hall. — From Lübke.

Mary married the young Maximilian of Hapsburg, soon to

become emperor (§ 160), and five years later she died, leaving an infant son Philip. Maximilian claimed the regency, and, after conquering the cities in war, he revoked The Great Privilege. His son Philip, however, assuming the government in 1494, restored the "ancient privileges" of the provinces; and The Great Privilege, though not expressly confirmed, remained the standard of rights in the hearts of the people.

Philip married Joanna of Spain (daughter of Ferdinand and Isabella), and a son, Charles, born in 1500, became the greatest ruler in Europe (§§ 172, 209 ff.). When his realms were divided, the Netherlands passed with Spain to his son Philip II, in whose reign began the terrible but glorious struggle that made this little spot of sea-rescued land a "holy land" to all who love liberty (§§ 221 ff.).

For Further Reading. — Rogers' *Holland*, and Griffis' *Brave Little Holland*, or the opening pages of *The Student's Motley*.

X. THE PAPACY IN THE FOURTEENTH AND FIFTEENTH CENTURIES.

163. The Revolt of France and England. — The thirteenth century conflict between popes and emperors had left the popes victorious; but at once new foes appeared to challenge their overlordship. In France and England the people were coming to have a new sense of national unity, and had already begun to rebel against papal authority in temporal matters [1] and to demand that the government of the land should be independent of all papal supervision. To this feeling, the Emperor Frederick II had tried to appeal in letters to the kings: "My house is on fire. Hurry, bring water, lest the fire spread to your house too!" And, soon after his fall, France and England did take up in earnest the struggle against papal claims.

---

[1] An early instance is afforded by the "Constitutions of Clarendon" in England, under Henry II (§ 128, note). Advanced students may be asked to report upon the situation during the reign of Henry III. Neither people nor kings, of course, had any intention of questioning the authority of the pope in spiritual matters. Their attitude in many respects was like that of the people and government of Italy toward the pope since 1870 (§ 490).

The conflict was hastened by the long wars between the French and English kings. Both needed money, and both were trying to introduce systems of national taxation in the place of the old feudal revenues. The clergy had been exempt from feudal services; but they owned so much of the wealth of the two countries, that the kings were not willing to leave them exempt from the new taxes. *Pope Boniface VIII issued a bull forbidding any prince to impose taxes on the clergy without papal consent, and threatening excommunication against all clergy who paid.* Thus the struggle began.

164. Edward I, Philip IV, and Boniface VIII. — When the English clergy, trusting in this papal decree, refused to pay taxes, Edward I outlawed[1] them; and it at once appeared that, in comparison with this practical "excommunication" by the state, the old clerical excommunication was mere stage thunder. The clergy generally paid, until, a little later, a compromise was effected whereby they were permitted to tax themselves.

France, however, was the scene of a sharper contest. As it progressed, Boniface set forth the old claims of papal supremacy over princes;[2] but Philip IV treated these claims with haughty contempt, and the Estates General (1302), even the clerical Estate, denied the Pope any control over the state and pledged their lives to defend the "ancient liberties of the French nation." Philip forbade the payment of any revenues from his realm to the Pope, and arrested the papal legate. Boniface threatened to depose the King. A few days later, a

---

[1] To outlaw a man was to put him outside the protection of the law: he could not bring suit to recover property or damages, and offenses against him were not "crimes."

[2] "The spiritual power has to establish the princely power. [The reference is to the consecration of kings at their coronation by ecclesiastics.] Therefore if the earthly power err, it shall be judged by the spiritual power. . . . A spiritual man judgeth all things, but he himself is judged by no one. . . . Whoever resists this power . . . resists the ordination of God. . . . Indeed we declare . . . that it is altogether necessary to salvation for every human creature to be subject to the Roman pontiff." The bull from which these sentences are taken, as well as the one regarding taxation, are given in Henderson's *Documents*, 432–437.

company of French soldiers, with an anti-papal clique of Roman nobles, besieged and captured Boniface; and the chagrin of the old man at the indignities and insults heaped upon him probably hastened his death (1303).

165. The "Babylonian Captivity." — Soon after the death of Boniface, Philip secured the election of a French pope, together with the removal of the papal capital to Avignon, a papal city in Provence, on the French frontier, controlled by French influence. Here the popes remained for seventy years (1309-1377), in "the Babylonian Captivity of the church."

Of course the papacy lost public respect. It was no longer an impartial umpire, even in appearance. Politically it had sunk into a mere tool of the French kings, and the enemies of France could not be expected to show it reverence. The English Parliaments of Edward III passed the great statutes of *Provisors* and of *Praemunire*, to limit papal control over church appointments in England and to prevent appeals from English ecclesiastical courts to the papal court. Even Germany, distracted as it was, had too much national feeling to allow to a "French pope" any voice in determining its emperor; and in 1338, the German Electors and a German Diet formally denied that the popes had any part in the choice of their ruler. In Italy the Papal States themselves fell into anarchy and revolution, so that there was imminent danger that the popes might lose their principality altogether.[1]

166. The Great Schism. The Hussite Heresy. — In 1377, to save the papal territory in Italy, Gregory XI returned to Rome; but this act was only the signal for a greater disaster than the exile itself. The next year saw two popes, one at Rome and one at Avignon, each hurling anathemas at the other. England and Germany supported the pope at Rome; France and Sicily the one at Avignon. It had become purely a question of politi-

---

[1] This was the period of the enthusiast *Rienzi*, the popular dictator of the city of Rome. Rienzi dreamed of making a renovated Rome the head of Italy and of the world. Special report: Rienzi's life and work. Students will enjoy Bulwer's novel, *Rienzi, the Last of the Tribunes*.

cal advantage whether a nation recognized the one or the other. The papacy was never to recover altogether from its loss of dignity and power during the century of exile and schism.

The church itself began to be threatened, as well as the papacy. The Wyclif movement (§ 141) took place toward the close of the exile. The Lancastrian monarchs, it is true, with the hearty approval of Parliament, repressed the Lollards savagely, and England seemed saved to Catholicism; but meantime the seeds of the Lollard heresy had been scattered in a distant part of Europe. Richard II of England had married a princess of Bohemia. Some of her followers had carried the teachings of Wyclif from the University of Oxford back to the Bohemian University of Prague; and about 1400 *John Huss,* a professor at Prague, became the leader in a radical reform movement along the lines that Wyclif had followed.

167. Unity restored: the Great Church Councils. — Under these ominous conditions, there arose a widespread demand within the church for a General Council, representing all Christendom, to restore unity of government and doctrine. This plan implied a power in the church higher than that of the pope, and it was opposed vehemently both by Rome and Avignon. Finally the cardinals called the *Council of Pisa* (1409). This body declared both popes deposed, and chose a new one. The result was three popes; for the Council was not really universal in character, and, acting with unwise haste, it failed to secure obedience.

Soon after, however, the new Pope, under pressure from the Emperor, called the *Council of Constance* (1414). Five thousand delegates attended, and all Latin Europe was represented. The Council put down heresy sternly. John Huss had come to the assembly under a "safe conduct" from the Emperor. This was shamefully disregarded.[1] Huss was imprisoned, tried, condemned, and burned at the stake; and

---

[1] The Emperor was assured by the great churchmen that no promise to a heretic was binding.

when his followers rose in arms, a crusade was preached against them.[1] The following year (1415), one of his associates, Jerome of Prague, was burned. (Cf. § 141, close.)

Though so bitter toward heresy, the Council acted in matters of church government with caution and wisdom. One pope was brought to resign; the others were deposed; and unity was established under a new pope, Martin V. The Council had designed other reforms, but Martin dissolved it before it could act further. It had already made provision for Councils at regular intervals of ten years, but this provision also the popes were to render valueless.[2] For the following century, down to the time of Luther, the history of the popes and of the church contains no striking developments.[3] Thus, alone of all the old institutions of Europe, the church passed out of the Middle Ages essentially unchanged in character.

FOR FURTHER READING. — Original material for this period is to be found in Henderson's *Documents*, 432–440, and in *Pennsylvania Reprints*, III, No. 6. (The latter treats of the Council of Constance.)

Modern accounts: concise treatments are given by Adams, *Civilization*, 392–415, and by Lodge, *Close of the Middle Ages*, chs. ii, ix–xi. A scholarly Catholic view may be found in Alzog's *Church History*, II and III, and in Pastor's *History of the Popes*, I. There is a good account by Creighton in his *History of the Papacy during the Period of the Reformation*, I and II. (These three works are all too diffuse for young students.) Poole's *Wycliffe and Movements for Reform* treats the Hussite movement.

---

[1] A war of fifteen or twenty years desolated Bohemia and crushed the more radical party among the Hussites. The moderate wing of the reform secured some recognition of their rights. Henderson's *Short History of Germany*, I, 215–220, gives a brief survey of the struggle.

[2] If the plan could have been adopted in good faith, it would have limited the papacy somewhat as Parliament limited the English kingship, and no doubt it would have made the subsequent history of Europe very different from its actual course.

[3] The most interesting episode in this period is the career and martyrdom of Savonarola, the Florentine reformer. This is a good subject for a special report by an advanced student. Savonarola appears prominently in George Eliot's *Romola*.

XI. NEW PERILS FROM THE EAST: TARTARS AND TURKS.

168. The Tartar Invasions of the Thirteenth Century.—During the later part of the crusading age, Europe was menaced suddenly by a peril which for a time seemed greater than that of the Turks. Shortly after 1200, a great military leader had appeared among the Tartars of the Asiatic steppes. Assuming the title *Genghis Khan*, or Lord of Lords, he organized the scattered nomad tribes into a terrible fighting machine, and set about the devastation and conquest of the world. The ancient Scythian and Hunnish invasions[1] were repeated upon a larger scale and with greater horrors. Fertile countries were turned into silent, dismal deserts. Populous districts became tombs, marked only by enormous pyramids of blackened corpses. Genghis himself conquered China, northern India, and Persia, while his son invaded Europe. In 1223, the rising Christian state of Russia was crushed by these heathen barbarians,[2] and southern Russia became a Tartar province. The Mongol Empire reached from Pekin and the Indus to Crimea and the Dnieper. The death of the Great Khan (1227) recalled his son to Asia and gave Europe a brief respite; but, ten years later, the assault was renewed. Moscow was burned, and northern Russia became a tributary province; Poland and Hungary were ravaged and conquered: half of Europe was Tartar, and these new Huns even crossed the Danube. In vain did Emperor Frederick II appeal for aid to the rest of Christendom. A German army under Frederick's son inflicted a slight check upon the invaders, but again Western Europe was saved only by the death of a Mongol emperor. Soon afterward the vast Tartar realm fell into fragments, and the pressing danger passed away.

The conquerors took on civilization, too, in China and India, from the subject races; but parts of Asia have hardly yet recovered from the ravages of the conquest. The whole subsequent development of Russia has felt its baleful influence; and for three centuries a Tartar state, The Golden Horde, maintained itself in southern Russia. The escape of Western Europe, through no great merit of its own, is one of the supremely fortunate events in history.[3]

---

[1] *Ancient History*, §§ 72, 569–571.

[2] These Mongols were not Mohammedans like their relatives the Turks (§§ 91, 169), but were heathen like the old Huns.

[3] Special report: the career of *Tamerlane*, another great Tartar conqueror, in the fourteenth century, who for a time checked the Turks (§ 169). The beneficial effect of the Mongol Empire upon geographical knowledge in Europe will be noted in § 197.

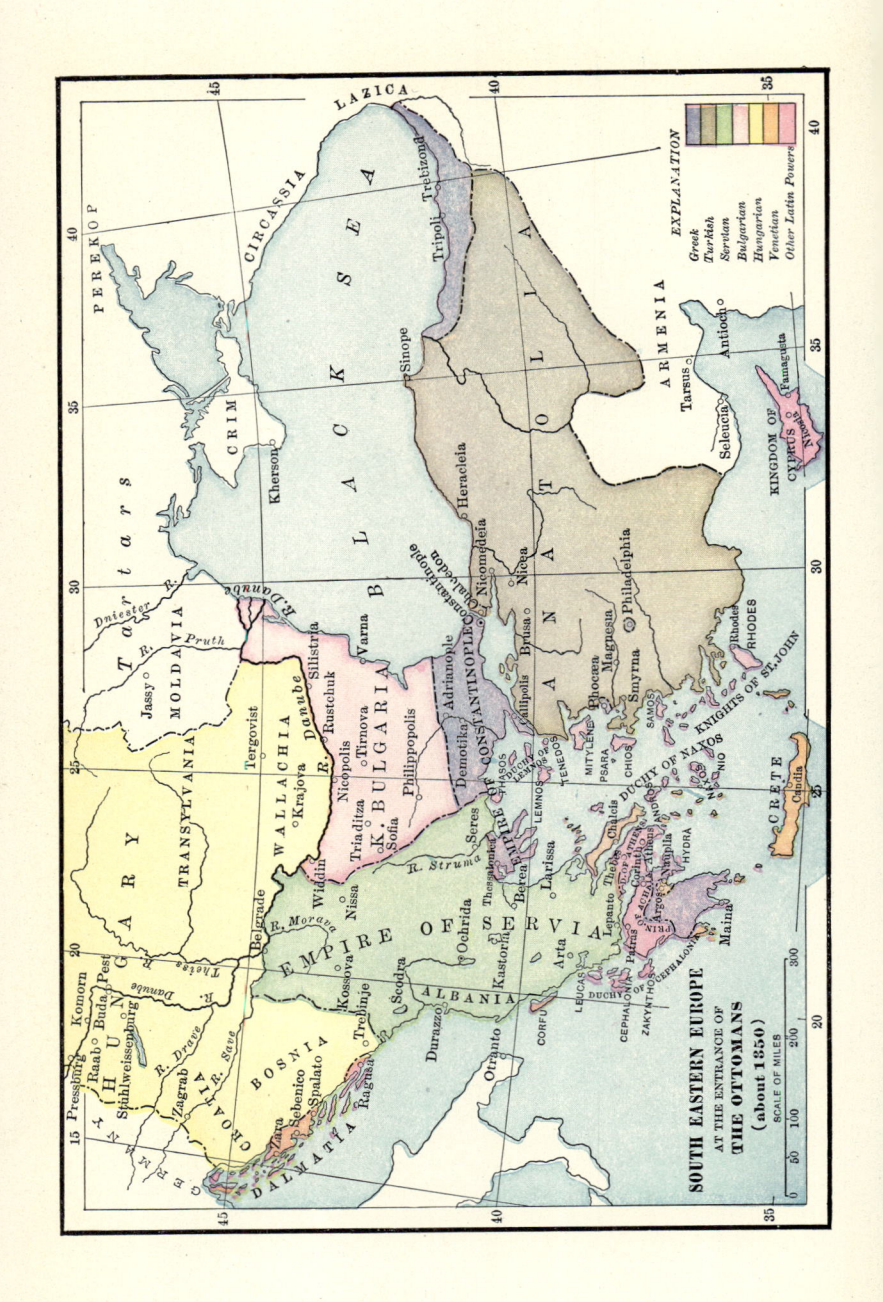

SOUTH EASTERN EUROPE
AT THE ENTRANCE OF
THE OTTOMANS
(about 1350)

169. Southeastern Europe and the Ottoman Turks (Mohammedans). — The Greek Empire never recovered fully from its overthrow in the Fourth Crusade. In the fourteenth century, the Servians (Slavs) built up a great state under their "emperor," *Stephen Dushan*, but both Greek and Slav were soon to fall before a new foe.

The *Ottoman Turks* first came to notice about 1240, when small bands of them from the distant Jaxartes appeared in Asia Minor, in the service of their kinsmen, the Seljuk Turks (§ 91). The newcomers soon became the ruling race, and in 1346, a century after their first appearance, they established themselves also on the European side of the straits, — though Constantinople held out for a century more, a Christian island encompassed by seas of Mohammedanism. At the *battle of Kassova* (1389), the Turks completed the overthrow of the Servians and other Slav peoples of the Balkan regions; and a few years later a crushing defeat was inflicted upon the Hungarians and Poles. About 1400, Tamerlane (§ 168, note) seemed for a moment to have shattered the Turkish power, but Mahomet I reconstructed the Empire, and in 1453 his son, Mahomet the Conqueror, entered Constantinople through the breach where the heroic *Constantine Palæologus*, last of the Greek emperors, had died sword in hand.

Constantinople has remained the capital of the Turkish Empire from that day to the present time. That empire continued to expand for over a century more (until about 1550): and for a time it seemed as though nothing could save Western Europe. Not until well into the nineteenth century did either Slav or Greek in the Balkan regions begin to find relief from Mohammedan oppression (§§ 576 ff.).[1]

The Turks were incapable of civilization, in the European sense, and they have always remained a hostile army encamped among subject Christian populations, whom their rule has blighted. A chief factor in

---

[1] The critical position of Hungary, and her heroic services against the Turk, may be made a topic for special report. The great defeats of the Turks at Lepanto (1571) and before Vienna (1683) will be noted in §§ 224, 257.

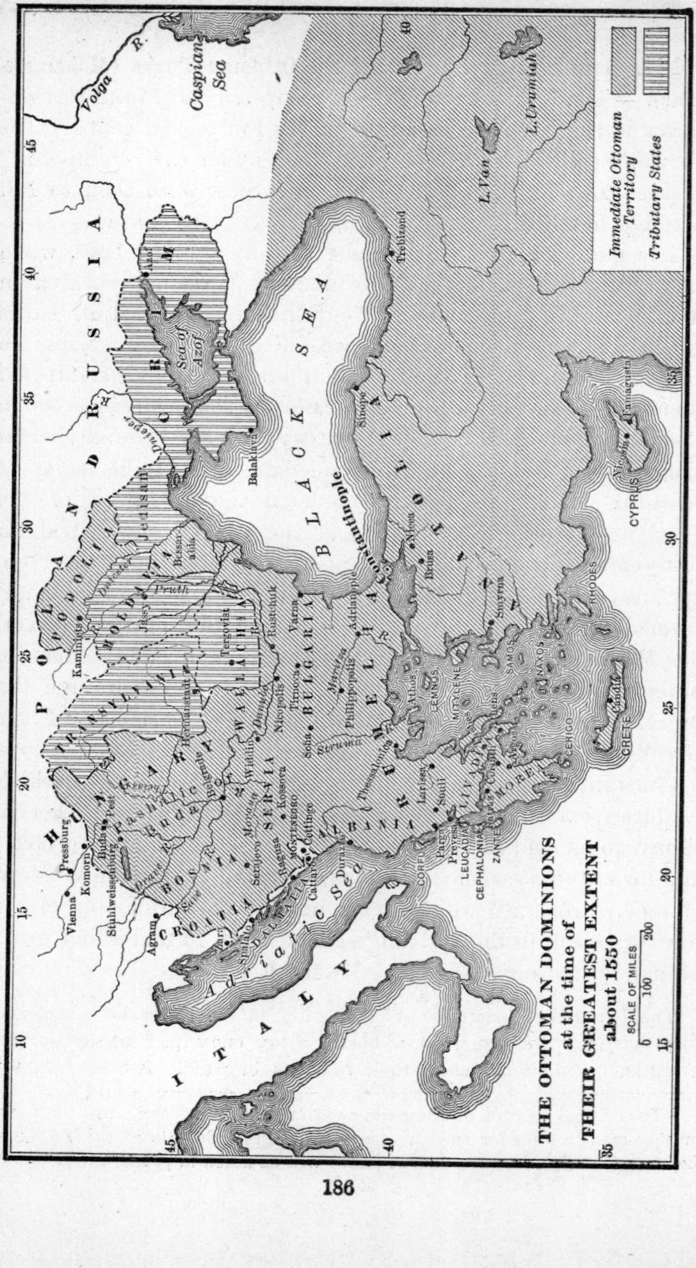
THE OTTOMAN DOMINIONS
at the time of
THEIR GREATEST EXTENT
about 1550
SCALE OF MILES
0 100 200
Immediate Ottoman Territory
Tributary States
POLAND
RUSSIA
HUNGARY
Pashalic of Buda
TRANSYLVANIA
MOLDAVIA
WALLACHIA
PODOLIA
Jedisan
Bessarabia
CRIM
CROATIA
BOSNIA
DALMATIA
SERVIA
MONTENEGRO
ALBANIA
BULGARIA
RUMELIA
LIVADIA
MOREA
ANATOLIA
ITALY
BLACK SEA
Adriatic Sea
Sea of Azof
Caspian Sea
Volga R.
Dnieper R.
Dniester
Pruth
Danube R.
Drave R.
Save
Maritza
Struma
L. Van
L. Urumiah
Vienna
Pressburg
Komorn
Buda
Pest
Stuhlweissenburg
Agram
Belgrade
Hermanstadt
Kaminiets
Jassy
Tergovist
Widdin
Nicopolis
Rustchuk
Tirnova
Varna
Sofia
Philippopolis
Adrianople
Constantinople
Balaklava
Azof
Sinope
Trebizond
Nicaea
Brusa
Smyrna
Thessalonica
Athos
Larissa
Souli
Parga
Preveza
Corinth
Athens
Ragusa
Cattaro
Cettinje
Durazzo
Serajevo
Kossova
Spalato
Zara
CORFU
LEUCADIA
CEPHALONIA
ZANTE
CERIGO
LEMNOS
MITYLENE
SAMOS
NAXOS
RHODES
CRETE
Candia
CYPRUS
Nicosia
Famagusta
10
15
20
25
30
35
40
45

their early success was the "tribute of children," organized into the famous fighting force of *Janissaries*. Says Freeman: "A fixed proportion of the strongest and most promising boys among the conquered Christian nations were carried off for the service of the Ottoman princes. They were brought up in the Mohammedan faith and were employed in civil and military functions. ... Out of them was formed the famous force of the Janissaries, the new soldiers who for three centuries — as long as they were levied in this way — formed the strength of the Ottoman armies. ... *In this way the strength of the conquered nations was turned against themselves.* They could not throw off the yoke, because those among them who were their natural leaders were pressed into the service of their enemies."

FOR FURTHER READING. — Mijatovich's *Constantine, the Last Emperor of the Greeks;* Oman's *Byzantine Empire*, chs. xxv, xxvi; Poole's *Story of Turkey*, chs. i–vii; Creasy's *Ottoman Turks*, chs. i–vi; Lodge's *Close of the Middle Ages*, 494–514; Freeman's *Ottoman Power*, 1–135.

XII. THE POLITICAL SITUATION JUST AFTER 1500, AT THE OPENING OF THE REFORMATION.

170. A Political Summary. — In the ninth and tenth centuries, three imposing figures seem to fill the stage of European history, — the Emperor of the East, the Emperor of the West, and the Pope. By 1500, the first had forever vanished, the second had shrunk into a petty prince, and the third, politically, had retired far into the background. In the tenth century, other western lands had been but a fringe to the mighty Holy Roman Empire (Germany and Italy). In 1500, Germany and Italy, weak and divided, were about to become the battle ground and the prey of new powers. On the north and west, England, Denmark, France, and Spain had grown into strong and unified monarchies; on the southeast, the Mohammedan power, which had just been driven from the west of Europe, had advanced to the Danube and was threatening Austria itself with conquest. The Empire had lost not only organization, but considerable territory: all claims upon Poland and Hungary were gone, and the northern Slavs and Swedes were seizing upon the lands once held by the Teutonic Knights; Switzerland was practically independent, and Holland soon was to be so (§§ 221-226); half the kingdom of Burgundy had already fallen to France, and the failure of Charles the Bold to reëstablish the "Middle Kingdom" had brought that same aggressive French realm into touch with the Rhine provinces of Germany, many of which it was soon to seize (§§ 212, 232, 259 ff.).

Farther east, there loomed a reviving Russian state at Moscow. *Ivan the Great* (1462-1505) threw off the Tartar yoke; and his grandson, *Ivan the Terrible*, extended Russian sway to the Caspian. However, Russia was still an inland state, shut off from the Black Sea by the Tartars, from the Baltic by the Swedes, and from any contact with Germany by the Poles; not until about 1700 was it to count in western politics.

171. New International Relations; the Conflict for Italy. — The breaking up of Christendom into clearly defined monarchic states introduced a new period. The leading states became intensely jealous of each other. France and Spain were at first the great rivals, and Italy was the first field of conflict.

In Italy, as in France and Spain, there had been some movement toward unity. The thirteenth century had seen the land broken up into a multitude of petty states; but by 1450 almost all of these had been brought under one or another of the five "Great States" — the kingdom of Sicily in the south, the Papal States in the center, and in the north the duchy of Milan and the so-called republics of Venice and Florence. During most of the second half of the fifteenth century Italy enjoyed comparative peace, but the movement toward consolidation had not gone far enough to afford security, now that other countries were united at home and were free to turn their attention to a defenseless neighbor. In 1494, Charles VIII of France crossed the Alps with a large army to assert his claim as King of Sicily.[1] Charles was animated by wild dreams of conquest. He marched victoriously from end to end of the peninsula, virtually its master, regulating matters at will, not only in his southern kingdom, but in the northern

---

[1] A claim which he derived from the House of Anjou (§ 86).

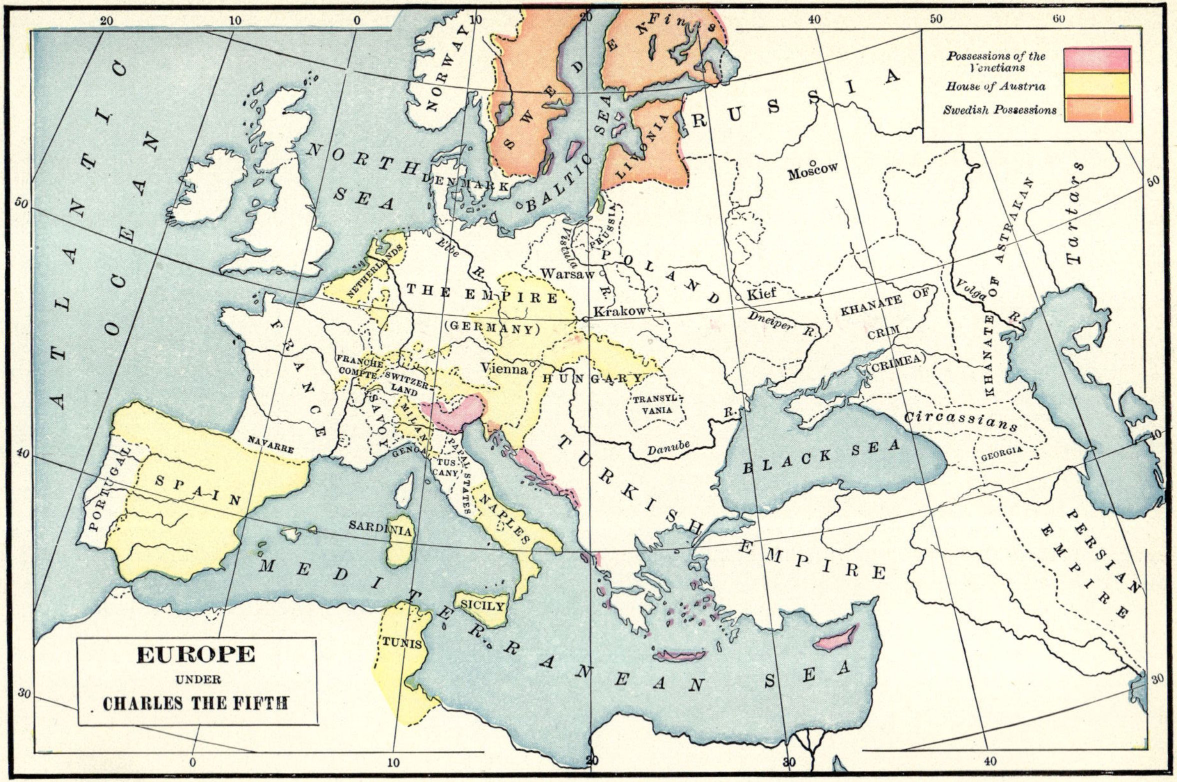

EUROPE
UNDER
CHARLES THE FIFTH

states as well. However, enemies quickly gathered behind him: Ferdinand of Aragon, also, claimed the kingdom of Sicily; Venice and some other states joined the anti-French party; and Charles secured his retreat into France only by a desperate battle. *Spain was left in possession of Sicily and Naples,* and the French dominion vanished as quickly as it had risen; but the expedition of Charles heralded three centuries of conflict between the European powers for the rich and beautiful peninsula.[1]

172. The Hapsburg Power: Dominions of Charles V. — While France was beginning to seize foreign territory, Ferdinand of Aragon was building up family alliances to strengthen the power of Spain. One daughter he married to the young English prince, soon to become King Henry VIII, and another to Philip of Hapsburg, son of the Emperor Maximilian (§§ 160, 162). From this last marriage in 1500, was born a child, Charles, who was almost to restore a universal empire.

The early death of his father left the boy Charles ruler of the rich provinces of the Netherlands, and in 1516 he succeeded his grandfather Ferdinand as king of Spain and of Sicily. In the same year, Francis I ascended the French throne.[2] These two ambitious princes were to be the chief political forces in Western Europe for a generation. In 1519, on the death of Maximilian, the two young kings, with Henry VIII of England, became candidates for the imperial title. Through the wealth of his Flemish merchants, Charles was successful; and his other widespread realms[3] gave a physical support to the position of Emperor, such as it had not possessed since Hohenstaufen days.

---

[1] Cf. *Ancient History*, § 273.

[2] Six years earlier, Henry VIII had become King of England, and five years later, Solyman the Magnificent became Sultan of the Turks.

[3] On his mother's side, Charles had inherited Spain and southern Italy and the gold-producing lands of America which the discovery of Columbus had just made Spain's. From his father and paternal grandfather he inherited the Netherlands, Austria, and other Hapsburg possessions. By election, he was Emperor of the rest of Germany and of northern Italy.

173. Charles and Francis in Italy. — Francis I had already been engaged in asserting a French claim on Milan in northern Italy, and the two great rivals now came into conflict. Compact France was probably nearly equal in power to all the scattered Hapsburg realms, and Francis found mighty reënforcement from an event which occurred just at this moment in Germany. In 1520 Martin Luther publicly burned a papal bull (§ 207) and started the Protestant Reformation, which was to split Germany at once into opposing camps and to render for ever impossible the restoration of the old imperial unity of Christendom, of which Charles perhaps had dreamed.

REVIEW EXERCISES.

1. Fact drills.
    a. Dates. Add to previous lists the following: —

1100–1300, Crusades.	1381, Peasant Rising.
1215, Magna Carta.	1414, Council of Constance.
1254–1273, Great Interregnum.	1453, Fall of Constantinople.
1295, Model Parliament.	1492, Columbus. Capture of Granada.

    b. Fix other events in connection with the above; such as the Swiss Confederacy (after the death of Rudolph, who becomes emperor 1273, at close of Interregnum), Innocent III, Albigensian heresy, Tartar invasions, the first Estates General (soon after the Model Parliament), etc.
    c. Extend list of terms for brief explanation (cf. pages 51, 96): "take the cross," Dukes of Athens, Teutonic Order, Janissaries, etc. (The list should be a long one for this period.)
2. Make a syllabus (cf. page 96).
3. Review and note force of all introductory "theme" sentences (in italics, at head of Chapters or Divisions, as on pages 1, 22, and 60).
4. Review questions presented by class (cf. page 51).
5. Map reviews and comparisons.
6. General topics : (*a*) parliamentary assemblies of Europe, — Diets, Estates, Cortes, etc.; (*b*) movements for religious reforms within the church ; (*c*) movements for religious reforms that threatened, at least, to act outside the church ; (*d*) history of the medieval church.

CHAPTER IV.

THE TRANSITION TO A NEW AGE: THE RENAISSANCE, 1350–1550.

I. NATURE OF THE RENAISSANCE.

174. Classicism and the Renaissance. — About 1350 there began in Italy a new movement, which we call the *Renaissance*. It is hard to date the period for all Europe, because it differed for different countries. It was well over in Italy by 1550, while in England it had hardly begun before 1500 and was to last through Shakspere's age, — to about 1600.[1] It was a period of tremendous change. Europe transformed its whole habit of thought and way of feeling. The name Renaissance is a fit one, because the change consisted largely in a "rebirth" into the world of an old, long-forgotten way of looking at life. This older way had expressed itself in the ancient classical art and literature; and naturally the men of the new age were passionately enthusiastic over all remains of the classical period. The term Renaissance is sometimes used as though it applied chiefly to this admiration for classical antiquity. The real characteristic of the period, however, was not its devotion to the past, *but its joyous and self-reliant attitude in the present*. The men of the Renaissance cared for the ancient culture of Greece and of Rome, because they found it in sympathy with what they themselves thought and felt in their own day.

175. Characteristics of the Middle Ages. — Between the classical and the renaissance ages there had intervened several centuries of very different life and thought. These centuries were the Middle Ages. Three characteristics had been especially

---

[1] This chapter runs over into the next era, as is natural in dealing with a transition age. At this point the student should reread §§ 4 and 5.

prominent. (1) Ignorance was the general rule; and even the learned followed slavishly in the footsteps of some intellectual master. (2) Man as an individual counted for little. In all his activities he was part of some gild or order or corporation. (3) The dominant intellectual forces were the ecclesiastical ideals. Beauty in nature was little regarded, or regarded as almost a temptation of the Evil One. Men not only felt it wrong to take delight in the world, but thought they ought always to think of the terrors of a world to come. The pagan's disregard for his shadowy future world [1] had been succeeded by so intense an interest in the future as to lead to neglect of the present life. Thus, during the Middle Ages, thousands upon thousands of the best minds withdrew from the world, giving up all natural pleasures and duties, to prepare for the world to come, by fastings and scourgings in monks' cells. Even princes and kings surrendered their pomp and power for this purpose.

176. Characteristics of the Renaissance. — The Renaissance changed all this. For the medieval instinct of blind obedience to authority and tradition, it substituted the free inquiring way in which the Ancients had looked at things.[2] It awoke to delight in flower and sky and mountain, in the beauty of the human body, in all the pleasures of the natural world, and also of the world of thought and imagination. A new self-reliance and self-confidence marked the individual, and a fresh and lively originality appeared in every form of thought.

The transformation from the medieval to the renaissance age is one of the two or three most wonderful changes in all history. It manifested itself first in art and literature, then in scientific study and in religion, and finally, long after, in politics. The change began in Italy. There it had its chief manifestation in the revival of art, but it produced also a revival of learning. This second phase of the Italian Renaissance was the first to travel into northern lands. It concerned itself with religion and the Early Church; and, together with the moral earnestness

---

[1] *Ancient History*, § 143. [2] *Ancient History*, § 83, close.

of the northern races and with the new confidence in individual judgment, it produced the Protestant Reformation. Sometimes it is said that the Renaissance was mainly artistic in the south of Europe and intellectual and moral in the north. Such a statement is convenient, but it should not blind us to the important part which Italy played in the early intellectual movement (§§ 189, 195).

177. Method of Treatment in this Chapter. — Thus the Renaissance was a revolt against the medieval spirit in all its forms. The causes were mainly intellectual. Accordingly, as an introduction, we must outline the intellectual side of European life during the Middle Ages, which has been omitted so far in this volume. The student should realize, too, that the changes about to be noted in various lines of thought and feeling (Divisions II–V) were intimately interrelated, although we can trace them best one by one.

II. MEDIEVAL SCIENCE AND PHILOSOPHY.

A. UNIVERSITIES.

178. Intellectual Studies in the " Dark Ages." — Intellectually, Western Europe lay in torpor through the early Middle Ages. Except for the brief gleam of Charlemagne's time, this unwholesome sleep was not broken until about the year 1100. For several centuries before that date, studying and teaching were confined to the schools connected with the monasteries and cathedrals; and in these, almost the whole aim was to prepare the clergy for their duties. Even this all-important task, through the eighth, ninth, and tenth centuries, was poorly performed. King Alfred in England lamented that hardly a priest south of the Thames could read the services he repeated by rote,[1] and like complaints were not uncommon

---

[1] " So clean was learning fallen away among the English that there were very few on this side of the Humber who knew how to render their daily prayers in English, or so much as to translate an epistle out of Latin into English. I ween that there were not so many beyond the Humber. They were so few that I can not think of a single one south of the Thames when I took the kingdom." — From Alfred's Preface to his Translation of Gregory's *Pastoral Care.*

on the continent. Some cathedral schools preserved faint traditions of the old learning, in their courses in "arts"; but in the best of them the studies were only a shrunken survival of the *trivium* and *quadrivium* of Roman times.[1] The work consisted in committing to memory dry epitomes of knowledge, and the teacher's task lay in dictating such abstracts, word by word, in Latin, for the students to copy. There was no inquiry, no investigation, no criticism; there was of course no study of nature, and there were almost no books. Such schools could not advance learning, but they did help to preserve, through the "Dark Ages," the spirit of scholarship and a little of the older knowledge, and so made it possible for Europe to advance again when more favorable conditions had been provided.

MONK TEACHING THE GLOBE; after a thirteenth century manuscript now in the National Library at Paris. — From Lacroix, *Science and Literature*.

179. **The Rise of Medieval Universities.** — Better conditions appeared about the beginning of the twelfth century. From that time, Europe was ever more and more astir with intellectual life. The rising towns established lay schools to train for business pursuits;[2] medical and legal services, which had been performed before

---

[1] The ancient trivium comprised language, rhetoric, and logic; the quadrivium included music, arithmetic, geometry, and astronomy. The student would do well at this point to review the *Ancient History*, §§ 258, 259, 483, 484, 539-542, and 647. The remarkable Irish and English Schools, just before and after Charlemagne, to some degree form an exception to the statement in the text. They might be made the subject of a special report. See Zimmern's *Irish Culture*.

[2] Such schools used the vernacular, instead of Latin; and, besides reading and writing, they taught a little arithmetic and geography.

by the clergy, were now prepared for by special study; some of the old cathedral schools began to feel the influence of Arabian culture from the Universities of Cordova and Alexandria; Constantinople, through Venice, began to introduce Greek learning into Italy; and all these impulses were intensified, of course, by the crusades.

The result of these forces was the medieval university. The early institutions of this character grew up as voluntary associations of teachers [1] and students. Usually they appeared alongside some cathedral school, but they were lay schools, not ecclesiastical schools; and, like many medieval associations, they took on the gild form.[2] The earliest universities did not come into existence at any precise moment. Most of them finally received papal bulls or royal patents, confirming their privileges; but these documents simply recognized and sanctioned institutions which had slowly formed themselves. At a later time, however, popes and kings became the founders of many universities. The term "university" did not at first imply instruction in all forms of knowledge:[3] a university always comprised a course in "arts," and, for the graduates of this course, one or more professional courses, — law, medicine, or theology.[4] The "arts" course continued to be based upon the ancient trivium and quadrivium, and the great majority of university students never went beyond it.

180. Typical Early Universities. — The three universities usually selected as types of the early period are Salerno, Bologna, and Paris.

---

[1] It was commonly the personality of some great teacher which determined that a university should grow at one place rather than at another; see § 180.

[2] The students working for the first degree corresponded to the apprentices of the trade gilds; the bachelors of arts, to the journeymen; and the "masters" and "doctors" to the trade "masters." Even the forms of public examinations and graduation, some of which still survive, were modeled upon trade gild customs.

[3] Indeed the word "university," as used in the early charters, meant only "all of you," and was sometimes applied to organizations which had nothing to do with teaching, — even to trade gilds.

[4] Theology included philosophy.

Curiously enough, each of the three grew out of a different specialty, — Salerno from the study of medicine, Bologna from that of Roman law, and Paris from that of theology.[1]

a. Near Salerno was a great Benedictine monastery, which even through the Dark Ages had been noted for its excellence in medical instruction. Probably the science of the Arabs in southern Italy had some effect upon it in this respect. Somewhat before 1100, according to a rather legendary story, *Constantine the African*, a Carthaginian Greek who had studied in the most famous Arabian schools, came to Salerno and gave a wide reputation to a school of medicine there, distinct from the monastery school. Certainly before 1100 there was such a lay school, with important privileges conferred by Robert Guiscard (§ 67 *b*). This "University of Salerno," then, was the first "university." The medical course of five years required a preparatory course of three years in "arts."

Salerno, however, had no courses in law or theology. Before 1200 these latter subjects had become famous at Bologna and Paris; and then the Emperor Frederick II, in 1224, established a University of Naples, to combine all the branches of instruction, "in order that those who hunger for knowledge may find *within the kingdom* the food for which they yearn, and may not be forced to go into exile to beg the bread of learning in strange lands." The medical college at Salerno was incorporated in this new institution. This University of Naples was the first university *created* by royal charter.[2]

b. At Bologna, about 1100, *Irnerius*, a teacher in an "arts" school, became deeply interested in Roman Law.[3] There are various legends that try to account for this interest. The certain fact is that because of it Irnerius practically rediscovered Roman Law for Western Europe. He began to teach it to all who would study, and Bologna was soon thronged with the students who gathered around him. In 1158, Frederick Barba-

---

[1] "It was the needs of the human body which originated Salerno; it was the needs of men as related to each other in a civil organism which originated Bologna; it was the eternal needs of the human spirit in its relation to the Unseen that originated Paris." — LAURIE, *Rise of Universities*, 109–110.

[2] It was distinctly a "state" university. The state appointed the professors, endowed chairs, and issued licenses (or degrees) to students in the different professions. The professors were free from taxes and military service, and possessed a variety of other privileges. Like privileges were accorded to the teachers in other medieval universities. Cf. *Ancient History*, § 483.

[3] Roman law had never died out in Italy, and indeed it had always been studied in some Italian schools; but, after the work of Irnerius, its study and use spread rapidly over the West.

§ 180] PRECEDING MOVEMENTS — UNIVERSITIES.   197

rossa confirmed by charter various rights which the "University" had come to enjoy.[1]

The government of the University was vested in the body of students, not in the city or state or even in the teaching body. This community of scholars not only managed its own internal affairs, deciding what studies should be pursued and how long the lecture hour should last, but it also judged its own members in all cases, both civil and criminal, in which they were connected with outsiders. As the University grew, there occurred much disorder and crime and many serious conflicts between students and citizens. These were the first "town and gown" combats. The city authorities wished to assume jurisdiction over the students, in criminal cases at least; but the Pope, in 1254, confirmed the "ancient rights" of the University. Like other early universities, the institution had almost no buildings, or fixed plant, and the ease with which it could migrate to a neighboring town made the city content to put up with much inconvenience rather than risk losing so large a population and so famous a school.[2]

c. The University of Paris grew directly out of an "arts" school connected with the Cathedral of Notre Dame. In the eleventh century, a learned monk, William of Champeaux, as head master, had made that school one of the three or four most famous in France and had given new prominence to the study of theology there. But the impulse to a real university dates from the work of *Abelard* as head of the school, about 1115. Abelard[3] did not remain long at Paris,

SEAL OF THE FACULTY OF THEOLOGY OF PARIS; fourteenth century. — From Lacroix, *Science and Literature*.

---

[1] "We owe," says the charter, "protection to all our subjects, but especially to those whose knowledge enlightens the world." Bologna was soon known as the "Mother of Laws."

[2] The great University of Padua did grow out of a secession from Bologna, and a secession from Paris to Oxford first made the last named city a real university town.

[3] Abelard is one of the saddest and most romantic figures of the Middle Ages. An advanced student might prepare a special report upon his life.

and thousands of students followed him from that school to different places and even into the desert, when he retired for a time to a hermitage; but his brilliant intellect had given to the study of theology and philosophy an impulse which his remaining students at Paris carried on, until to the old "arts" school there was soon added a new and distinct body of teachers in theology and philosophy. A new faculty in arts grew up also. Several hundred masters of arts and of theology gave instruction, each in his own dwelling, to all who came as students.[1]

Gradually the masters organized, especially to confer degrees; and by 1140 there seems to have been a definite "University of Paris." From time to time the French kings and the popes confirmed its privileges or gave it new ones. At Paris, unlike democratic Bologna, the controlling power was really vested in the masters,[2] not in the students. The latter, however, had some voice. As at other universities of note, the students came from all parts of Europe.[3] Naturally, those from one country grouped themselves together for mutual assistance, and such a group was known as a "nation."[4]

SEAL OF THE PICARDY NATION OF THE UNIVERSITY OF PARIS; fourteenth century. — From Lacroix.

---

[1] In this way arose the "Latin Quarter" of Paris. The district known by that name is still inhabited largely by students.

[2] This aristocratic organization was finally to become the dominant one in European universities.

[3] There was a surprising fluidity in medieval life. Merchants, soldiers of fortune, friars, journeymen, were always on the move; but the poor wandering scholar was the typical traveler of them all. He shared in some degree the clerical privileges, and begged his way from place to place. Young men thought nothing of passing from Oxford to Paris or Bologna and back again, to sit at the feet of this or that famous teacher and to see the world by the way. Indeed, we are told that public stage coaches in Europe originated mainly in the needs of travel which gradually developed in connection with the universities.

[4] A "nation" might include the students from several adjoining countries. The "English nation" at Paris contained men from all the north of Europe

At Paris, before 1200, there were four of these "nations," each with various subdivisions; and the nations and subdivisions chose from their masters certain deans and proctors to look after matters of discipline. A university, even of the aristocratic type, was truly a "Republic of Letters."[1]

181. Value of the Medieval University. — University life and training grew more and more popular: the fourteenth century saw fifteen new universities founded; the fifteenth century saw twenty-nine. Moreover, the number of students at the old foundations increased rapidly, and, according to contemporary authorities, from twelve to twenty thousand was not an uncommon attendance at a single institution.[2] The work in the main was a slavish study of texts, and Latin continued to be the sole learned language.[3] However, the mere bringing together so many youthful minds, glowing with desire for knowledge, tended to produce an intellectual tumultuousness; and in theology, where the reason was sometimes allowed to speculate a little, university men were more ready than the rest of Europe to receive new ideas.[4] But in other lines of study, the method of instruction tended to produce an overwhelming respect for tradition and authority. The movement which produced the universities was a kind of prelude to the true Renaissance of two centuries later: at the time the old habits of thought were too strong, and there was too little knowledge, for a successful intellectual revolution. Thus the universities were captured by the medieval spirit and *became one of the most striking characteristics of "medievalism." They do not belong to the true Renaissance.* They became the strongholds of the "Schoolmen" (§§ 182-185). The new impulses of the fifteenth century, which were to carry Europe on into a broader intellectual life, did not arise within their walls and found admission at all only after stern struggles.

---

[1] Read Laurie, 167-170 and 195-199.

[2] No doubt, these figures are merely loose estimates and very great exaggerations, like most other medieval statements of numbers.

[3] This fact encouraged the practice of traveling from one university to another. Students who went from Paris to study at Bologna did not need a new language.

[4] Wyclif, Huss, and Luther were all connected with university teaching.

B. Scholasticism.

182. The "Scholastic Method." — The twelfth and thirteenth centuries, with their intellectual revival, developed a new and peculiar intellectual method. This became known as *scholasticism*, or the method of the schools. Its one weapon was the "formal logic" of Aristotle,[1] which had never been quite forgotten in Europe. This logic consisted in throwing knowledge into the form of "syllogisms." There are several kinds of syllogisms, but each contains three statements, of which the third, the "conclusion," follows irresistibly from the two "premises": thus, —

> All A is part of B;
> C is part of A;
> therefore C is part of B.

The intellectual effort in scholasticism lay in the *selection* and *arrangement* of suitable premises, and in *stringing one syllogism to another*, so as to build up into one system all the fragments of knowledge that the age possessed. These fragments were few and insignificant; and the method of scholasticism could not discover new knowledge. At best it was suited only to test and to arrange, not to discover.[2] And so, lacking other material, the Schoolmen turned in upon their own minds, and constructed huge systems of speculative philosophy, highly organized, but, apart from the mental gymnastics involved in constructing them, utterly barren for purposes of practical life. Scholasticism ignored the whole world of nature and

---

[1] *Ancient History*, § 207.

[2] This holds good, unless we call the development of geometrical truths out of a few axioms a discovery. Geometry is the kind of study for which the method of the Schoolmen is perfectly fitted. The trouble with them was that they tried to apply that method to other kinds of study for which it was not fitted at all, or else they ignored those other studies. This drawing of conclusions from premises is *deduction*. Modern science employs this method, of course, but its first task is to establish the truth of its premises, and to collect great masses of them, by *inductive* methods (observation and experiment).

of men; and it knew nothing of observation and experiment as means of study.

About the year 1600, Francis Bacon (§ 199) very properly said: it was a "degenerate learning" that "did reign among the Schoolmen, ... who did out of a great quantity of matter and infinite agitation of wit, spin out unto us those laborious webs. ... For if the wit, and mind of men ... work upon itself, as the spider worketh his web, then it is endless and bringeth forth indeed cobwebs of learning, admirable for the fineness of thread and work, but of no substance or profit." — *Advancement of Learning.*

With all its faults, however, scholasticism was the first effort of the awakening mind of Europe. Men had turned to seek knowledge in an unfortunate direction; but they displayed amazing eagerness. The disputations of the Schoolmen developed power in making precise definitions and subtle distinctions;[1] and it is difficult for us to comprehend the intellectual stir and enthusiasm that agitated Europe as a result of their speculations. Still, scholasticism is memorable as a striving, not as a product. Indeed, it not only could not of itself make progress, but in two ways it was actually to retard progress. It constructed so complete a *speculative* system that it had no room for *new facts;* and its system was so connected with theology that finally to question a philosophic theory was to incur the condemnation of the church. In character, as well as in time, *scholasticism belongs to medievalism, not to the Renaissance.*

183. Scholasticism and Theology. — The Schoolmen set to work to put the church doctrines into a logical system. The first great Schoolman in this sense was the Italian *Anselm*, whose life was spent mainly as prior and teacher at the Norman monastery of Bec, and afterward as Archbishop of Canterbury under William II and Henry I of England. Anselm

---

[1] It is easy to fling cheap witticisms at the Schoolmen for their disputes as to how many spirits could stand on the point of a needle. Criticism of this kind, however, shows ignorance of the real problem the Schoolmen had in hand, — in this case, the nature of space.

felt that the highest exercise of the human reason was to fashion clear statements about the divine truths previously accepted by faith. Man was not to question whether a given doctrine was true, but he might use his reason to learn why it was true. This Anselm said explicitly: —

> Whether that is true which the universal Church believes' with the heart and confesses with the mouth, no Christian can be permitted to question; but, while holding fast to it without doubting, and loving and living for this faith, he may and should search in humility for the grounds of this truth. If he is able to add to his faith, intelligence, let him thank God; if not, let him not turn against his faith, but bow his head and worship.

This came to be the general position of the Schoolmen, but not until after an interesting attempt to exalt human reason to a higher place. *Abelard*, the second great Schoolman, was a Frenchman of bold, restless intellect. He tried to use reason to test the truth of theological doctrines. He does not seem himself to have doubted the teachings of the church, but his appeals from all authority to reason as a sufficient guide, aroused the more devout and far-seeing churchmen. St. Bernard (§ 72, note) declared that not reason, but love and faith, enabled man to understand the ways of God. Abelard was condemned by church councils, and he recanted and burned his works. The earlier attitude of Anselm prevailed.[1]

184. Scholasticism and Science. — By the thirteenth century Europe had recovered other works of Aristotle besides his Logic, and the Schoolmen exercised themselves upon these writings also, but without in the least learning Aristotle's

---

[1] Another great division among the early Schoolmen was that into *Nominalists* and *Realists*. One party urged, somewhat as Plato had done, that our general names, such as "virtue" and "tree," stand for *real* existences: the general, or universal, tree, these *Realists* held, exists in the divine mind, and all individual trees are merely manifestations of it; virtue is an essence in itself, independent of all virtuous deeds and thoughts. The *Nominalists* held, on the other hand, that such terms are mere *names* for the qualities we mentally abstract from concrete deeds and trees: there are individual trees, but no general tree; there are virtuous persons, but no virtuous essence, independent of persons.

method of scientific observation. Some little science did creep into Europe from the Arabs, especially astronomy and chemistry. But the astronomy was mainly astrology, a system of fortune telling by the stars; and the chemistry was largely a deluded search for the "philosopher's stone," which should transmute metals into gold, or for the elixir of life, a drink that should confer immortality. Men who dealt in either science, honestly or as quacks, were generally held to be wizards, who had sold their souls to the devil in return for forbidden knowledge.

185. The Great Schoolmen of the Thirteenth Century. — The Schoolmen, with their barren method, continued almost undisputed masters of the intellectual field through the thirteenth century. The three great names of the century are those of *Albert the Great*, *Thomas of Aquino*, and *Duns the Scot*. Albert (Albertus Magnus, died 1280) was a German Dominican friar who had studied at Bologna and at Paris. He mingled with his studies enough of curious speculation upon the properties of stones, plants, and animals to be accused of the "black art." Thomas Aquinas (died 1274) was an Italian Dominican, and a pupil of Albertus Magnus. He studied at Naples and Paris, and afterward lectured at Paris to immense audiences. His great work summing up Christian theology is the most complete of all such published systems and is still looked upon as a standard authority. Duns Scotus (died 1308) was among the last of the great Schoolmen. He was so popular that an able disputant was proud to be called "a Duns." When a better intellectual method arose, after the revival of Greek learning, the term became one of opprobrium. It survives in "dunce."

186. Roger Bacon: a Forerunner of the Scientific Method. — The thirteenth century saw one memorable attempt to study nature in a scientific way. *Friar Bacon*[1] (Englishman, died 1294) is sometimes called a Schoolman, but he spent his life in pointing out the lacks of the scholastic method and in trying to make clear the principles of scientific study. His "Great Work" was a cyclopedia of thirteenth century knowledge in geog-

---

[1] Roger Bacon, the thirteenth century friar, must not be confused with Francis Bacon, his more famous but no more deserving countryman, of three centuries later (§ 199).

raphy, mathematics, music, and physics. Bacon wins more and more recognition from scholars now, but in his own day he was listened to only to be persecuted. He was a devoted student, working under difficulties incredible and incomprehensible to us. Fourteen years he spent in prison. More than once he sought all over Europe for years for a copy of a book, when a modern scholar under like wants would need only to send a note to the nearest bookseller. He learned of the ocean east of China, and speculated convincingly upon the feasibility of reaching Asia by sailing west into the Atlantic (§ 197). He knew much about chemical explosives, and is believed to have invented gunpowder. He is thought also to have used a combination of lenses as a telescope. Probably he foresaw the possibility of steam: certainly, he prophesied that in time wagons and ships would move swiftly without the help of horses or sails. In 1258, Brunetto Latini, the tutor of Dante, visited Roger Bacon and wrote as follows to a friend in Italy: —

Among other things he showed me a black, ugly stone called a magnet, which has the surprising quality of drawing iron to it; and if a needle be rubbed upon it and afterward fastened to a straw, so that it will swim upon water, it will instantly turn to the pole star. . . . Therefore, be the night never so dark, neither moon nor stars visible, yet shall the sailor by help of this needle be able to steer his vessel aright. This discovery so useful to all who travel by sea, must remain concealed until other times, because no master mariner dare use it, lest he fall under imputation of being a magician, nor would sailors put to sea with one who carried an instrument so evidently constructed by the devil. A time may come when these prejudices, such hindrances to researches into the secrets of nature, will be overcome; and then mankind will reap benefits from the labor of such men as Friar Bacon, who now meet only with obloquy and reproach.

Bacon's work deserved to introduce a new scientific era; but he found no followers. He lived at least a century too soon to influence the world about him. Scholasticism was to fall, not before his demonstration of its weakness, but through new popular needs and through the recovery of more of the knowledge of the Greeks than the scholastic system could hold.

FOR FURTHER READING. — (1) *On Universities:* Sources: *Pennsylvania Reprints*, II, No. 3, contains much valuable information concerning "the Medieval Student"; Henderson's *Documents*, 262–266, gives the foundation charter of the University of Heidelberg. Modern accounts: Laurie's *Rise of Universities;* Compayré's *Abelard;* Jessopp's *Friars* (ch. vi, "The Building up of a University"); Mullinger's *Cambridge* (chs. i–iii); Brodrick's *Oxford;* and Rashdall's *Universities in the Middle Ages* (for advanced students only).

(2) *On Scholasticism:* Rashdall and Compayré, as above; Stille's *Studies* (ch. xiii); Poole's *Medieval Thought;* Church's *Anselm;* Morison's *Bernard;* and Storrs' *Bernard.*

III. LITERATURE AND THE FINE ARTS.

A. LITERATURE: HUMANISM.

187. From 800 to 1300: Latin Chronicles. — From the eighth century to the thirteenth, practically all writing in Western Europe was in Latin, and was therefore the possession of a small class.[1] Various spoken dialects had arisen from the mixture of Roman and Teutonic elements, but these were not yet the vehicle of literature. The Latin, too, was a crude and barbarous jargon, very unlike the polished diction of Cicero. The only writers were monks, and the writings consisted almost exclusively of the *Lives* of saints and of barren chronicles concerned mostly with narrow local interests.

These monkish chronicles form a large part of the material upon which the historian has to draw for his knowledge of several centuries, but their use is made exceedingly difficult by several characteristics.

a. The chroniclers usually lacked all sense of historical proportion. They cared more about the acquisition of the wonder-working bones of some saint by a monastery, or the election of a new abbot, than about a great war or the coronation of a new monarch; while the deeper forces in a people's life they seem not to have thought of at all.[2]

---

[1] For some centuries, knowledge belonged so exclusively to the clergy that a man had only to show an ability to read, in order to establish his right to "benefit of clergy" (§ 69).

[2] The *Anglo Saxon Chronicle* has this entry for the important year of 1066 in England: "In this year King Edward died, and Earl Harold succeeded to

b. They were incredibly credulous. What are intended for sober historical narratives are interfused, in perfect good faith, with the wildest stories of miracles. Indeed, the more marvelous a story, the more eagerly the writer seized upon it and the less likely he was to question its truth.

c. They seem not to have distinguished clearly between the purposes of history and fiction. Most of the historical narratives partook of the nature of our "historical fiction." Even the contemporary accounts of the crusades, though earnest histories in form, were intended not so much to state exact truth as to amuse noble patrons by fable or by lively invention or by flattery.

d. They were oftentimes quite ready to forge a history or a charter for a pious purpose. A considerable portion of the official documents and charters preserved through the Middle Ages have been proved to be more or less clumsy forgeries.[1]

188. Rise of Vernacular Literatures in the Thirteenth Century. — Even after the thirteenth century, Latin continued to be the chief language of science and philosophy. But poets and story-tellers needed to use the speech of the common people. This had been done all along by the minstrels, who, as wandering adventurers or as retainers of some lord, formed a characteristic part of medieval life; and after 1200 there arose in various lands a popular poetry that began to deserve the name of literature. *Spanish ballad poets* chanted the Song of the Cid (commemorating the national hero in the conflict with the Moors). In the language of northern France, the *trouveurs* celebrated the adventures of Charlemagne and Roland or of King Arthur and his Table Round. In the softer language of the south of France (Languedoc) the *troubadours* sang of love, as did a like class of poets, the *minnesingers*, in Germany. Similar songs were written in the dialect of southern Italy at the Sicilian court of Frederick II (§ 85).[2] In the north of Europe

---

the kingdom and held it forty weeks and one day. And in this year William came and won England. And in this year Christ Church was burned. And in this year a comet appeared."

[1] Cf. *Ancient History,* § 635, with reference to the "Donation of Constantine," the most famous forgery of the age.

[2] But in the next generation, Dante's *Divine Comedy* made his Tuscan dialect the literary language for the whole of Italy.

the *Scandinavian poets* wove the ancient Norse ballads and legends into a mighty mythic epic, the *Heimskringla*, — as the Germans also had done with their early legends, in the *Nibelungen Lied*. England was more backward, because of the new language imposed for a while by her Norman conquerors. The *Anglo Saxon Chronicle*, it is true, did not quite die out until the close of Stephen's reign, and soon afterward rude popular songs celebrated the deeds of Earl Simon; but not until the fourteenth century did popular poetry of a high order awaken in that island. Finally, toward the close of the century, in the *Canterbury Tales*, Chaucer, "the Father of English Poetry," accomplished the fusion of the Saxon and the Norman French into a literary English, while at almost the same time Wyclif translated the Bible into the common tongue.

Like the thirteenth century university and the Schoolmen, *the troubadours and minnesingers were characteristically medieval.* But this rise of native literary languages was a necessary prelude to any wide-spread knowledge or to any true national movements. Now that each country had in its own language a fit means for scholars to use, it was possible to attack the medieval system in science and theology with a chance of popular support.

189. The Literary Renaissance. — The Renaissance began in Italy, and began in literature even sooner than in painting. Italy was the natural home for such a movement. Italy's Vergil had been read by a few scholars all through the Middle Ages, and had dominated literary ideals almost as completely as Aristotle's Logic had dominated philosophy. The Italian language was nearer the Latin, too, than was that of any other country, and probably more of the manuscripts of the ancient Roman writers survived in Italy than elsewhere.

Three names are commonly associated with the Italian literary Renaissance, — Dante (1265–1321), Petrarch (1304–1374), and Boccaccio (1313–1375), — all citizens of Florence. The greatest of the three was *Dante* (§ 188); but, after all, Dante's thought belonged to the Middle Ages: it is only in his independence and self-reliance that he prophesied a new era. *Petrarch*, in the next generation, was the conscious champion of a new age. In feeling and aspiration he belonged wholly to the Renaissance, — which he did much to bring to pass. His graceful sonnets are a famous part of Italian literature, but his chief influence upon the world lay in his work as a tireless critic of the medieval system and as an ardent advocate of classical ideals. He attacked vehemently the superstitions and the false science of the day; he ridiculed the mighty tomes of the Schoolmen as "heaps of worthless rubbish"; the universities themselves he laughed at as "nests of gloomy ignorance"; and he ventured daringly even to challenge the infallibility of Aristotle, — who, he said, was after all "only a man."

But Petrarch did more than merely to destroy. It was desirable that the world should recover what the Ancients had possessed of art and knowledge, that it might take up progress again where they had left off. Petrarch began an enthusiastic search for classical manuscripts, and his disciples soon made this zeal fashionable throughout Italy.

Among these disciples the most famous was *Boccaccio*, nine years Petrarch's junior. He is widely famed as the writer of the *Decameron*, a collection of a hundred tales, which made him the father of Italian prose, as Dante was of Italian poetry; but, as in the case of Petrarch, Boccaccio's real worth to the world lay mainly in the impulse he added to the revival of classical learning.

After Boccaccio, Italian literature declined suddenly for almost two centuries, probably because enthusiasm was directed rather to painting and sculpture. Not until the close of the Renaissance did Italy again produce great authors, — in the poets *Tasso* and *Ariosto*. But meantime, as we shall see (§ 195), scientific study began in this southern land; and it should be added that the Florentine *Machiavelli*, in his famous work *The Prince* (about 1513), began the modern study of politics.

The new enthusiasm for the classics became known as *humanism* (Latin *humanitas*, culture). Within seventy years of Petrarch's death, or before 1450, the Humanists had recovered practically all the literary remains we now have of the Latin authors and a large part of the surviving Greek manuscripts. Oftentimes the neglected manuscripts were found decaying in moldy vaults. Many had been mutilated, or had been erased in order that the parchment might receive some monastic legend.[1] Much had been wholly lost; and if the humanistic revival had been a little longer delayed, a great deal that we now possess would never have been recovered.

190. Recovery of the Greek Language. — With all their zeal for Greek manuscripts and Latin translations of them, the early Humanists were ignorant of the Greek language; but after about the year 1400, the knowledge of that tongue grew rapidly. Greek scholars were invited to the Italian cities and were given professorships in the universities. The increasing danger in the Greek Empire from the Turk made such invitations acceptable, and the high prices paid by princely Italian collectors drew more and more of the literary treasures of Constantinople to the Italian cities. Many a fugitive scholar from the East found the possession of some precious manuscript the key to fortune and favor in Italy.[2]

191. The Place of Humanism in the History of Education. — At first, humanism had been stoutly resisted by the universities, especially outside Italy, but it finally captured them and established a "new education." The earlier "liberal education" had contained no Greek and had given little acquaintance with the Latin authors. The courses in "arts" were now broadened so as to furnish a true classical training. Monkish Latin was replaced by the refined style of Cicero, and the barren and often misleading "compendiums" in earlier use were supplanted by a fuller knowledge of the great works of classical antiquity at first hand. From that time to the present day the classics have held a prominent place in educational systems, — until recently, almost an exclusive place.

The value of this recovery of the past cannot be overstated. Greek thought and knowledge and the grand and beautiful conceptions of Greek and Latin literature have been gradually absorbed into our modern thought and literature, which they still color. But merely as concerned the system of education, the change was less revolutionary than at first appeared. The spirit of the Schoolmen survived in the schools strongly

---

[1] In some cases this later writing has since been carefully removed, and the original writing restored faintly, through chemical processes.

[2] The value of such a manuscript furnishes an essential element in the plot of George Eliot's *Romola*.

enough to conquer the conquerors. The originality and independence of the early Humanists was soon exchanged in the universities for servile imitation and dependence upon authority. Cicero became almost as great an intellectual tyrant as Aristotle had been. The study of the classics took on an unwholesome formalism, from which it had to be rescued much later by a new scientific movement.

B. THE FINE ARTS.

192. Medieval Painting and Architecture. — Classical art had been as completely lost through the early Middle Ages as classical learning. Medieval art existed only as the handmaid of religion. Monks "illuminated" missals and other religious books, — painting with tiny brushes in brilliant colors on parchment, — and they designed gay page-borders and initial letters, sometimes with beauty and delicacy. On a larger scale, the only paintings were rude altar pieces, representing stiff Madonnas and saints, in conventional and unnatural colors. The painters knew little of either anatomy or perspective; and even the flowing draperies which they used freely could not hide their ignorance of how to draw the human body.

Architecture, too, until the twelfth century, was relatively poor and rude. The style was the *Romanesque*, based upon old Roman remains and characterized by the round arch. The only buildings of any pretension, aside from the massive feudal castles, were churches, and the general plan for these was furnished by the old basilica.[1] But in the twelfth and thirteenth centuries, the Romanesque gave way to a new French style, called *Gothic;* and architecture, especially in churches and cathedrals, reached one of its greatest periods. The older elements were all used, but with marvelous transformations and with important additions. Gothic architecture modified the round arch into the lighter *pointed arch,* and it used the old Greek column with a new freedom and variety, adding *lofty, curiously vaulted ceilings.* It substituted the *tower* for the dome, and

---

[1] *Ancient History,* § 488.

§ 192]   PRECEDING MEDIEVAL ART.   211

ILLUSTRATION FROM A LATE MEDIEVAL MANUSCRIPT (fifteenth century), showing in the foreground Maximilian of Austria, Mary of Burgundy, and their son Philip. — After Lacroix, *Vie Militaire*.

added, perhaps from the Saracens, heaven-pointing *spires*. By the use of the new *flying buttress*, strength was gained, so that it became safe to pierce the walls with row upon row of tall windows, giving the effect of lightness and complexity. New opportunities for ornament were found in the *tracery*, or open-

SALISBURY CATHEDRAL, from the southeast; built, 1200–1250. The spire rises 404 feet from the ground. — From *Cathedral Churches of England*.

ings in the stonework about doors and windows, in the *moldings* of the window frames, and in the use of *stained glass*.[1]

The total result was a new architecture, so different from

---

[1] Sculptured figures were used, also, to fill the niches about the portals, but they were the robed forms of saints carved rudely in stone, not the marble-sculptured bodies of athletes in which ancient art had delighted.

§ 192] PRECEDING ART—GOTHIC ARCHITECTURE. 213

the older styles as to permit little comparison. Gothic architecture indeed is *the most perfect product of the Middle Ages*,

SALISBURY CATHEDRAL. View from south to north transept.—From
Cathedral Churches of England.

and a Gothic cathedral is one of the wonders of the world to-day. Such structures could have been reared only in an age of intense faith and spiritual longing, and they form the finest expression of the highest life of the time. They are religious aspirations in stone.

193. Renaissance Art. — Architecture was the one beautiful thing that suffered at the Renaissance, when the noble Gothic was replaced by imitations of the older Roman and Greek styles. In painting and sculpture, on the contrary, there was great gain. These arts were reborn into the world, with the rebirth of a delight in life; and painting, at least, reached a perfection never before known.

This was particularly true in Italy. In that land, with so many remains of ancient art still preserved, or buried in the soil and now eagerly sought for, the new movement became preëminently artistic. Art dominated the whole people, not merely a select few. Great popular processions did honor to single paintings, and famous works were produced in an abundance almost inconceivable.

THE CLOISTERS, SALISBURY CATHEDRAL.

The new artistic impulse is usually dated from the work of *Giotto*, early in the fourteenth century, but Italian painting culminated in the eighty years from 1470 to 1550. Between these dates came the work of *Perugino, the Bellini, Fra Bartolommeo, Michael Angelo, Raphael, Giorgione, Correggio, Titian, Andrea del Sarto, Leonardo da Vinci,* and *Tintoretto.* Each town had its able artists, but nearly all the greatest masters, like most of those just named, belonged to Florence or to Venice. Many of these men practised more than one art. Thus Michael Angelo was great as architect and sculptor as well as painter, and he was not without fame as a poet.

Until about 1450, the paintings were mainly frescoes, or paintings upon plastered ceilings, in churches or palaces. But one of the *Van Eyck* brothers in Holland, about the middle of the fifteenth century, invented new methods of preparing oil paints, so that painting upon canvas became possible. About the same time, engraving of copper plates and the use

CATHEDRAL OF RHEIMS.

of woodcuts came into use, — to do for works of art something of what the invention of printing was about to do for books.

The great period of Dutch art was to come a little later, between 1600 and 1660, with *Rubens, Van Dyck,* and *Rembrandt.* In the same century came the great Spanish painters, *Velasquez* (1599–1660) and *Murillo* (1618–1682). The other great painters of the renaissance age outside of Italy were the Germans *Albert Dürer* (1471–1528) and *Holbein* (1498–1543). Neither England nor France produced much in this direction during these centuries. France did have her *Poussin* (1594–1655); and some of the great Italians — Andrea del Sarto and Leonardo — found their chief patronage in Paris from Francis I, just as a century later the English sovereigns entertained Holbein, Rubens, and Van Dyck.

194. The Pagan Side of the Italian Renaissance. — There was an evil side to the Renaissance. The men of the new movement, having cast off old restraints and beliefs, fell often into gross and shallow skepticism and into shameless self-indulgence and sensuality. Religious faith and private morals both declined, and for a time Italian society sank lower than the old Pagan world.

CHURCH OF SAINT-MACLOU AT ROUEN; fifteenth century.

The north of Europe was saved, in the main, from this phase of the Renaissance by a greater moral earnestness and by the fact that in the north the movement was more purely intellectual and less artistic and sensuous than in Italy.

IV. THE NEW LEARNING.

195. A Scientific Study of "Sources" for a Knowledge of Early Christianity. — The purely intellectual side of the Renaissance manifested itself first in a new historical attitude — in a desire *to get at the real sources* of the knowledge of past centuries, and in *a critical treatment of corrupted or forged documents.* Plainly, this new historical criticism was akin to the enthusiasm of the Humanists for the recovery of faithful copies of classical writings; but it was also related to a fervent religious desire to remove abuses in the church and to get back to the spirit and practices of primitive Christianity. Like other renaissance movements, historical criticism had its birth in Italy; but it was to find its more abiding home north of the Alps.

A CORNER OF THE DUCAL PALACE, VENICE. Venetian Gothic (fourteenth century), influenced by Byzantine art.

The first modern scholar with the critical scientific spirit was *Laurentius Valla*[1] (died 1457), private secretary to Pope Nicholas V. Among other works, Valla edited the New Testament carefully in Greek, and he proved the falsity of the "Donation of Constantine."[2]

---

[1] If we except Roger Bacon (§ 186). Petrarch was rather a man of letters than a scholar, though he, too, showed much of this scientific spirit in dealing with old manuscripts. It is notable that Roger Bacon called attention to the need of recovery and translation of the documents of early Christianity. See *Cambridge Modern History*, I, 585-592.

[2] *Ancient History*, § 635.

Valla's work was taken up by *John Colet*, the Englishman, and by *Erasmus*, the Hollander. Colet studied in Italy, and, upon his return to England, lectured at Oxford upon the New Testament, treating it as an historical presentation of early Christianity. He influenced a considerable group of enthusiastic followers. The most important of them was Erasmus, whose influence was not confined to any one country, but was European in extent. In 1516, Erasmus published the New Testament in Greek and in Latin, with the text carefully revised and with critical notes. Afterward he edited the writings of many of the early Christian Fathers. In another class of works, — *The Colloquies* and *The Praise of Folly*, — with unsurpassed wit and graceful ridicule he lashed the false methods and the folly of the monks and the Schoolmen, and so prepared society to turn to the serious constructive side of the "New Learning."

Erasmus has been called "the Scholar of the Reformation," and he did furnish Luther with much material ready for use; but he was not himself a revolutionist. Like Valla and Colet, he worked only for reform within the church.

196. Inventions. — The new intellectual movement was marked by a number of new inventions or by the first practical applications of them. Four demand special attention.

a. Gunpowder had been known for over a century, but its first serious use was in the wars between Charles V and Francis I, about 1521. This invention gave the final blow to the already dying feudalism.

b. Printing was to do more to advance the new order than gunpowder could do to destroy the old. The invention of printing from movable type came at a happy moment, just when the Humanists had fairly completed their recovery of ancient manuscripts. The invention is claimed for different people and places; but the first effective process seems to have been that practised by *John Gutenberg* at Mainz in Germany, about 1450.[1]

---

[1] Special report: ancient "printing" from seals and blocks, especially in China, and the development in Germany of movable type of one size (cf. Whitcomb's *Modern Europe*, 28, 29, for an admirable brief statement).

In less than twenty-five years, printing presses were at work in every country in Southwestern Europe, and, before 1500, Venice alone had sent out over three thousand editions of famous books. No previous invention had spread its influence so rapidly. The new process seems to have reduced the price of books by four-fifths at once, and so, of course, it enormously increased their circulation. It preserved the precious works recovered by the Humanists, and spread broadcast the new thought of the Reformation (§§ 205 ff.).

c. *The telescope* (§ 198) gave knowledge of other worlds.

d. *The mariner's compass* more than doubled the area of the known globe, and shifted the stage of historical action.

197. Geographical Discoveries.[1] — The Ancients had played with the notion of sailing around the earth. Aristotle speaks of "persons" who held that it might be possible; Eratosthenes[2] feared that the great expanse of ocean could not be traversed; and Strabo[3] suggested that one or more continents might lie in the Atlantic between Europe and Asia.

During the Roman period, however, no great motive had impelled men to make trial of these guesses, and during the Middle Ages a different geographical theory had gained control. Men had come to believe that the known habitable earth was bounded on all sides by an uninhabitable and untraversable world, — on the north by snow and ice, on the south by a fiery zone, on the west by watery wastes stretching down an inclined plane, up which men might not return, and on the east by a dim land of fog and fen, the abode of strange and terrible monsters.[4] The Indian Ocean, too, was thought to be a lake encompassed by the shores of Asia and Africa.

The first step in the discovery of America and in the other marvelous explorations of the fifteenth century lay in the correction of these views. This was accomplished in part by a

---

[1] See Fiske's *Discovery of America* or Payne's *History of the New World*.
[2] *Ancient History*, § 259. [3] *Ancient History*, § 491.
[4] For some of these ideas, see the curious and interesting *Travels* of Sir John Mandeville (thirteenth century).

better geographical knowledge of Asia, which was acquired in the thirteenth and fourteenth centuries. Louis IX of France sent Friar Rubruquis as ambassador to the court of the Tartar Khan in central Asia; and the friar on his return reported that he had heard of a *navigable ocean east of Cathay* (China), with a marvelously wealthy island, Zipango (Japan). This rumor of a navigable ocean to the east made a leap in men's thought. Friar Bacon in England (§ 186) at once raised the question whether it might not be the same ocean as the one that washed Europe on the west and whether men might not reach Asia by sailing west into the Atlantic. Indeed, Bacon wrote a book to support these conjectures, adding many opinions of the Ancients; and extensive extracts from this volume were copied into a later book, which was to become a favorite of Columbus'.[1]

Moreover, the Mongol emperors (§ 168) helped indirectly to give Europe true geographical ideas. They opened China to western strangers to a degree altogether new for that land, and, while their dominion lasted, many strangers and merchants visited the East. Among these were three Venetians, the *Polos*, who on their return sailed from Pekin through the straits into the Indian Ocean and up the Persian Gulf. *This proved true the rumor of Rubruquis regarding an eastern ocean, and proved also that the Indian Ocean was not landlocked.*[2]

From this time it was possible to think seriously of reaching India by sailing west; and soon afterward commercial condi-

---

[1] Such speculation implies that scholars understood the sphericity of the earth. See *Ancient History*, §§ 259, 540, for the origin of this knowledge and for its temporary loss to Christendom. Saracenic schools, however, preserved the truth, and some European thinkers had been familiar with it, even in the "Dark Ages."

[2] Travelers in that age did not often write descriptions of their travels. One of these Polos, however, being captured, soon after his return, in a sea fight between Venice and Genoa, remained a prisoner in Genoa for some years; and the stories that he told of his adventures were written down by one of his fellow captives. Thus was made "The Book of Ser Marco Polo," one of the most widely read books of the later Middle Ages.

tions changed so as to impel men earnestly to the attempt. The crusades had given a new impulse to trade with the Orient, until many eastern products were become almost necessities of daily life to Europe (§ 103); but in the fifteenth century, the progress of the Ottoman Turks threatened the old trade-routes. Constantinople, the emporium for the route by the Black Sea, finally fell into their hands, and each year their power crept further along the coast of Asia Minor and Palestine, endangering the remaining route by the Red Sea. Under these circumstances the question was forced home to Europe whether or not a new route could be found; and the speculations of Bacon and the discoveries of the Polos pointed to an answer.

The Portuguese, under Prince Henry the Navigator, had already been engaged in building up a Portuguese empire in Africa and in the islands of the Atlantic (Azores, Canary, and Verde[1]); and about 1470 they began to attempt the circumnavigation of Africa. In 1486, a Portuguese captain, *Bartholomew Diaz*, while engaged in this attempt, was carried far to the south in a storm, and on his return to the coast he found it *on his left hand* as he moved toward the north. He followed it several hundred miles, well into the Indian Ocean, when his sailors compelled him to turn back to Portugal. India was not actually reached until the expedition of Vasco da Gama in 1498, after more memorable voyages in another direction.

One of the sailors with Diaz in 1486, when in this way he rounded the Cape of "Good Hope," was a Bartholomew Columbus, whose brother *Christopher* had also sailed on several of the Portuguese voyages, but now for some years had devoted himself to the more daring theory that India could be reached by sailing west into the open Atlantic. Portugal, well content with her monopoly of African exploration, refused to assist Columbus to try his plan, and Henry VII of England declined to furnish him ships; but finally Isabella of Castile,

---

[1] The name "Cape Verde" indicates the surprise of the discoverers (1450) at verdure so far south.

while the siege of Granada was in progress, fitted out his small fleet, and in 1492 Columbus added America to the possessions of Spain.

The marvels of the new regions of the earth, so disclosed, added mightily to the intellectual stir of the times. For a century or two, however, the immediate material gain was confined to the two countries which had begun the explorations. The Mediterranean trade decayed and the Italian cities lost their commercial importance; but Portugal built up a great and wealthy empire in the Indian Ocean and in the adjoining islands of the Pacific, while Spain acquired the wealth of Mexico and Peru, and poured forth multitudes of adventurers to create a new Spain in America.

198. Physical Science. — The new scientific methods which Valla and Erasmus had applied to history and theology, were applied a little later to the natural sciences. The first great representative of this movement was the Polish astronomer *Copernicus*. The universally accepted system of astronomy was that of Ptolemy.[1] The earth was believed to be the center of the universe, and all the apparent movements of the sun and stars were explained by complex theories as to their rotation about the earth. Copernicus proved that the earth was only one member of a solar system which had the sun for its center. This discovery not only revolutionized the particular science of astronomy: it also helped to revolutionize thought about man and the world, by opening up such immensities of worlds and such possibilities of other forms of life as had never before been dreamed of.

When the work of Copernicus was printed (1543),[2] the long series of devastating wars between Catholic and Protestant Europe was just beginning (§ 211). These wars were to have Germany for their especial battle ground, and for a long time they destroyed all chance of scientific or literary development

---

[1] *Ancient History*, § 492.

[2] Copernicus, from fear of persecution, delayed the publication of his discovery many years, until just before his death.

in that country. In another way the great struggle repressed scientific thought, even more completely, in the Catholic countries. At the opening of the Renaissance, the popes had been among the most active patrons of the new movement; but now the reaction against Protestant revolt threw control into conservative hands, and the church used its tremendous power to stifle the teachings of the new science.

Still, much was accomplished. In Italy, *Galileo* (1564–1642) discovered the laws of the pendulum and of falling bodies, invented the thermometer, and, using a hint from a Holland plaything, constructed the first real telescope. He had already adopted the Copernican theory of the universe, and with his telescope he was able to demonstrate its truth by showing the "phases" of Venus in her revolution about the sun. His teachings, however, were considered dangerous and unsupported by scripture. He was summoned to Rome, imprisoned, and forced publicly to abjure his teaching that the earth moved around the sun.[1] Galileo's contemporary, the German *Kepler*, making use of the observations of the Danish astronomer, Tycho Brahe, established the exact laws of the motions of the planets; and in England, a little later, *Sir Isaac Newton* stated the law of gravitation.

199. England and the Renaissance. — England was a relatively poor and barbarous country, and had lagged behind in the early movements of the Renaissance. But about 1600, in the reign of Elizabeth, that land began to take a leading place both in science and in literature. Shortly after 1600 *Harvey* laid the basis for a true study of medicine by the discovery of the way in which the blood circulates,[2] and *Napier* widened the

---

[1] The story is told that as Galileo rose from his knees after making his recantation, he whispered to a friend, "But it does move, nevertheless."

[2] The history of this discovery illustrates strikingly the slow progress of new ideas in past times, as compared with the ready welcome given them in our own day. In earlier centuries it had been believed that the bright blood of the arteries and the dark blood of the veins were two distinct systems, one coming from the heart, and the other from the liver. Half a century before

application of mathematics by the invention of logarithms. At about the same time, *Francis Bacon*, statesman and philosopher, in his essays and especially in his *Novum Organum*, called the attention of the world to the necessity of true scientific methods of observation and experiment and induction. However, the real glory of the Elizabethan age was the English drama, with *Shakspere* for its foremost representative, among such other great authors as Marlowe, Greene, Beaumont, Fletcher, and Ben Jonson.[1] Another form of English poetry in the same age is represented by Spenser's *Fairy Queen*.

FOR FURTHER READING. — For Division II, see page 205. For Divisions I, III, and IV, the following works may be used, particularly by advanced students : Adams' *Civilization*, 364–391 ; Lodge's *Close of the Middle Ages*, 515–523 ; Pearson's *Symond's Short History of the Renaissance;* Robinson and Rolf's *Petrarch;* Emerton's *Erasmus;* Froude's *Erasmus;* Poole's *Illustrations of Medieval Thought;* Beazley's *Prince Henry;* Winsor's *Columbus; The Cambridge Modern History*, I. Saintsbury's *Flourishing of Romance* is a delightful treatment of medieval literature. Lübke's *History of Art* is particularly good for the medieval period; and Moore's *Gothic Architecture* is excellent. In fiction, Reade's *Cloister and Hearth* and George Eliot's *Romóla* picture renaissance movements.

Harvey's time, the identity of the two systems had been discovered, together with the purification of the dark blood in the lungs, and with a full understanding of the functions of the heart. The discoverer was Servetus, a young Spanish physician. But Servetus, who held opinions regarding the Trinity somewhat like those of modern Unitarians, was put to death for heresy (§ 217). It chanced that he had announced his medical discovery about the blood in the book in which he published his heretical opinions in theology; and his persecutors sought out the copies of this book, to burn them, so zealously that only two copies have survived. Thus the great discovery seems to have received no attention, until it was made again, independently, by Harvey, fifty years later. Even then it was not at once accepted, though its truth could be so easily demonstrated. A fierce controversy raged over it, inasmuch as it had not been taught by the Ancients; and, as late as 1700, it was solemnly questioned at Harvard College.

[1] No attempt is made to treat this topic of Elizabethan literature, because high school students will probably give much more attention to it in other classes than is possible here.

PART II.

THE PERIOD OF MONARCHIC STATES, 1520–1789.

CHAPTER I.

PRELIMINARY CONSIDERATIONS.

I. THE MAIN LINES OF DEVELOPMENT.

200. As we enter upon the later centuries of modern history, the story grows more and more complex. There is a confusing multitude of actors, and important events crowd upon one another in a bewildering maze. To secure a clear view we must fix our attention upon a few great movements and characteristics. Those most demanding notice in the three centuries between the Renaissance and the French Revolution are:—

1. The Protestant Reformation (the religious revolution), 1520–1648.
2. The struggle in England between Parliament and the Stuart despotism, 1603–1688.
3. The predominance of France under the absolutism of Louis XIV, 1643–1715.
4. The changes in the political map of Europe in the first half of the eighteenth century: rise of Russia and Prussia (Peter the Great and Frederick the Great) and decline of Sweden and Poland.
5. Reform by benevolent despots in the second half of the eighteenth century.
6. The changes in the world-map: the eighteenth century struggle for world-empire between England and France, 1690–1783.

II. TABLE OF SOVEREIGNS OF LEADING STATES.

201. Spain.

Charles I, 1516–1556 (Emperor Charles V, 1519–1556): the Reformation in Germany and the rivalry of France prevents the conquest of Europe; abdicated in favor of his son.

Philip II, 1556–1598: revolt of the Netherlands; "Invincible Armada."
Philip III, 1598–1621: expulsion of the Moriscoes.
Philip IV, 1621–1665.
Charles II, 1665–1700: last of the Spanish Hapsburgs.
Philip V, 1700–1746: first Spanish Bourbon (§ 261).
Ferdinand VI, 1746–1759.
Charles III, 1759–1788, brother of Ferdinand.
Charles IV, 1788–1808: seizure of Spain by Napoleon (§ 367).[1]

202. Emperors of the Holy Roman Empire and Archdukes of Austria.

Charles V, 1519–1556 (Charles I of Spain).
Ferdinand I, brother of Charles, 1556–1564: added Bohemia to the Hapsburg realms by marriage with Anne of Bohemia.
Maximilian II, 1564–1576.
Rudolph II, 1576–1612.
Mathias, 1612–1619, brother of Rudolph.
Ferdinand II, 1619–1637, cousin of Rudolph.
Ferdinand III, 1637–1657.
Leopold I, 1658–1705.
Joseph I, 1705–1711.
Charles VI, 1711–1740: brother of Joseph I; died without male heir.
Charles VII, of Bavaria, 1742–1745: a fugitive much of his short reign; war with Maria Theresa.
Francis I (of Lorraine), 1745–1765: husband of *Maria Theresa* (daughter of Charles VI and Archduchess of Austria).
Joseph II, 1765–1790: son of Maria Theresa; restoration of the Hapsburg line.
Leopold II, 1790–1792 (brother of Joseph).
Francis II, 1792–1806: Empire ends; "Emperor of Austria," 1804–1835.
Ferdinand I (the "First" because "Emperor of Austria"), 1835–1848.
Francis Joseph I: nephew of Ferdinand; became emperor, 1848.

203. France.

Francis I, 1515–1547.
Henry II, 1547–1559: followed by his three weak sons;
Francis II (1559–1560),
Charles IX (1560–1574),
Henry III (1574–1589):
these four reigns a period of religious civil war; *Catherine of Medici*, the Queen-mother, the evil genius of the last three reigns.

---

[1] Charles died in France before the overthrow of Napoleon. The subsequent rulers of Spain are named in §§ 495–499.

Henry IV, 1589–1610 : cousin of the preceding kings and the *first Bourbon king; Edict of Nantes.*
Louis XIII, 1610–1643 : rule of *Richelieu.*
Louis XIV, 1643–1715 : rule of *Mazarin* during the King's minority ; wars and foreign conquests ; supremacy of France in Europe; *revocation of Edict of Nantes.*
Louis XV, 1715–1774, great-grandson of Louis XIV.
Louis XVI, 1774–1792 : grandson of Louis XV ; the Revolution.[1]

204. England.

a. Tudors.

Henry VIII, 1509–1547 : son of the first Tudor king, Henry VII (§ 147) ; separates Church of England from Rome; followed in succession by his three children.
Edward VI, 1547–1553.
Mary, 1553–1558 ; Catholic reaction.
Elizabeth, 1558–1603.

b. Stuarts.

James I, 1603–1625.
Charles I, 1625–1649: civil war ; *execution.*
(*The Commonwealth and Protectorate*, 1649–1660.)
Charles II, 1660–1685.
James II, 1685–1688.
The "Glorious Revolution" of 1688.

c. House of Orange.

William III and Mary, 1689–1702 (Mary died in 1694).

d. The Last Stuart.

Anne, second daughter of James II, 1702–1714.

e. Hanoverians (Welfs : House of Brunswick).

George I, 1714–1727.
George II, 1727–1760.
George III, 1760–1820 (grandson of George II).
George IV, 1820–1830.
William IV, 1830–1837 (brother of George IV).
Victoria, 1837–1901 (niece of William) : *parliamentary government.*
Edward VII, 1901–.

---

[1] A table of the rulers and governments of France after 1792 may easily be made by the student from §§ 338–377 and 402–444.

CHAPTER II.

THE AGE OF THE PROTESTANT REFORMATION.
1520-1648.

I. THE RISE OF PROTESTANTISM.

A. LUTHER AND GERMANY.

205. Martin Luther and the Abuse of "Indulgences." — The abuses within the church which called forth efforts for reform from Colet and Erasmus drove more impetuous spirits into complete revolt. This revolt was to divide Western Christendom into opposing camps for centuries. We call the movement the Protestant Reformation. Its leader was *Martin Luther* (1483-1546), son of a Thuringian peasant. Luther was a straightforward, forceful man, with a blunt, homely manner that went straight to the heart. Erasmus addressed scholars; Luther spoke to the people. He had become an Augustinian friar and a professor in the University of Wittenberg in Saxony. He was a born fighter, and, in 1517, at the age of thirty-four, he entered upon a struggle with Rome.[1]

Luther's revolt grew out of his opposition to the sale of "Indulgences." The theory of the church was, that the pope, as the representative of St. Peter, might, in reward for some pious act, remit the punishment in purgatory to a sinner who had truly repented and who had so far as possible atoned for his sins. The ignorant multitude, however, unable to read the Latin documents, thought that the "Letters of Indulgence" promised unconditional pardon; and this unwarranted belief

---

[1] When it became plain that Luther's movement was to break up the unity of Christendom, Erasmus and nearly all the other Humanists were violently repelled by it. Such disruption seemed to them a greater evil than the faults it sought to cure. Cf. § 195, close.

seems to have been encouraged grossly by some professional "pardoners," who peddled such "letters" for money.[1]

Criticism of these evils was not new. Over a hundred years before Luther, Chaucer had devoted the only bitter lines in the *Canterbury Tales* to the Pardoner, with his wallet "bretful of pardons, come from Rome all hot." In the time of Luther the evil had grown in dimensions: Erasmus had written scathing words against it, and earnest and radical spirits were ready for an outbreak. Luther had criticised it in earlier writings; and in 1517 a visit to Wittenberg by Tetzel, a Dominican friar, with a batch of these papal letters, called forth a more vehement protest from him.

206. Luther posts his Theses. — In accordance with a University custom, Luther expressed his protest in the form of a paper posted on the Wittenberg church door, containing ninety-five propositions,[2] upon which he challenged all comers to public debate. The theses were in Latin, and they admitted the old church doctrine of papal indulgences; but their protest against the abuse of the practice met with so ready a popular response that in a few days they were known and discussed in German all over the land.

---

[1] It had long been common to grant "Indulgences" in return for gifts of money for pious purposes; and in a period of ignorance and moral decline, this practice slipped easily into what was practically an almost undisguised selling of indulgence for sin. The church, aroused to reform by the Protestant secession, recognized this danger. The *Council of Trent*, which sat at intervals from 1545 to 1563, to expiate heresies and reform morals, reaffirmed emphatically the need of three acts in the penitent to secure the entire remission of sins, — "to wit, contrition, confession, and atonement." The Council then condemns "those who assert that indulgences are useless, or who deny the power of the church to grant them. . . . In granting them, however, the Council desires that . . . moderation be observed. . . . And, being desirous of mending the abuses which have crept in, by occasion of which the honorable name of indulgences is blasphemed by heretics, the Council ordains . . . that all evil gains for the obtaining thereof be abolished." In later times the practice of granting indulgences in return for money has been discontinued. A translation of a Letter of Indulgence is given in *Scribner's Monthly*, XII, 80. See also *Pennsylvania Reprints*, II, No. 6.

[2] *Pennsylvania Reprints*, II, No. 6.

Luther was honestly amazed at this result. He seems at first to have had no thought of denying papal authority. He dedicated to Pope Leo X certain writings in defense of his position, and in a letter to Leo he says: —

By what unlucky chance it is that these particular propositions of mine, more than all others, should go forth into nearly all the earth, I am at a loss to know. They were set forth here for our use alone, and how they should come to everybody's knowledge is incredible to me. . . . But what shall I do? Recall them I cannot; and yet I see that their notoriety bringeth upon me great odium. In order then to soften my adversaries, and to gratify my friends, I send forth these trifles [proofs, etc.] to explain my theses. For greater safety, I let them go forth, most blessed Father, under your name and under the shadow of your protection. Here all who will may see how basely I am reproached and belied by my enemies. . . . Save or slay, call or recall, approve or disapprove, as it shall best please you, I shall acknowledge your voice as the voice of Christ presiding and speaking in you.

However, Luther found himself unable to defend this original position against the skillful logic of his critics; and by degrees he was driven into open rebellion against all papal authority. Soon he denied the infallibility of the pope and of church councils, and appealed to the Bible as the rule of conduct and of faith. This meant, of course, Luther's judgment of the Bible. So Protestantism unintentionally was to come to stand for the right and duty of individual judgment in matters of religion.

207. Burning of the Papal Bull: Luther at Worms. — Finally, after trying to convert the rebel by legates, Pope Leo X issued a bull threatening Luther with excommunication if he did not within two months abandon his position. This bull Luther burned before the town gates in December, 1520 The open conflict between the German friar and the Catholic church had begun.

The next year Charles V summoned a Diet of the Empire at Worms, to settle affairs in Germany. Luther attended, under a safe conduct, and fearlessly reaffirmed his position

His friends had tried to dissuade him from attending the Diet, pointing to the fate of Huss a century before; but Luther persisted, saying characteristically, "I would go on if there were as many devils in Worms as there are tiles on the housetops." Before the Diet he showed no faltering, though the power of the Empire and of the church were arrayed in scornful contempt against him; and he closed his statement with the heroic words, "Here I stand. As God is my help, I can no otherwise."

The Diet pronounced the ban of the Empire against him and ordered his writings burned. Luther was carried off into hiding by his friends, and he spent a year at the Wartburg castle translating the New Testament into German. Meantime his teachings spread rapidly over North Germany.

208. The Peasant War. — The German peasants were in a more deplorable condition than those of France or England. The new religious doctrines spread among them in somewhat distorted form, accompanied by new ideas of property rights. In 1525, the peasants rose in arms, avenging centuries of suffering by terrible cruelties toward their masters. Luther seems to have sympathized with their earlier demands,[1] but evidently he came to fear that his reform would be associated with anarchy, and he called loudly upon the Protestant princes to put down the rebels with the sword. The rising was finally stamped out, and apparently the peasantry won no improvement from it.

B. CHARLES V AND THE REFORMATION.

209. A Respite for the Reformers. — The ban of the Empire would have been enforced and Lutheranism would have been crushed at its birth, if the young and zealous Catholic Emperor, Charles V, had had his hands free. Happily for Protestantism, his reign was spent in incessant wars.[2] While

---

[1] See *Pennsylvania Reprints*, II, No. 6, pages 25–30, for the peasants' statement of their program. Some of these radical Protestants were called *Anabaptists*, because of their doctrines about baptism. Ten thousand of them are said to have been put to death in the cruel vengeance of the victorious lords.

[2] Cf. §§ 170–173. It is a peculiar fact that the two countries destitute of settled government gave Europe the Renaissance and the Reformation. The intense civic vigor of the small Italian states was a condition favorable to the intellectual activity and independence of the Renaissance, and the absence of an effective central government was the condition which permitted Protestantism so long to grow unchecked in Germany.

the Diet of Worms was condemning **Luther, the Spanish** towns were rising in revolt and Francis I of France was seizing Italian territory. The rebellion was put down promptly and the ancient liberties of the Spanish towns were extinguished; but the wars against France and against the Turk, with only brief truces, filled the next twenty-three years (1521–1544); and so for a generation the new faith was left to grow strong.[1]

210. "Protestants"; the Augsburg Confession; League of Smalkald. — The first important interruption in the French wars came in 1529. Charles at once summoned a Diet at Speier, which reaffirmed the decree of Worms. Against this decision the Lutheran princes presented a protest. This act gave the name *Protestant* to their party. The following year, in a Diet at Augsburg, the Lutherans put forward a written statement of their beliefs.[2] Charles, however, autocratically demanded from the princes the execution of the decrees of Worms and Speier, and prepared to enforce them by arms. In defense, the Protestant nobles organized the *League of Smalkald;* but an open clash was once more postponed, because of an attack upon Germany by Solyman, the Turkish Sultan.

211. Opening of the Religious Strife in Germany: Peace of Augsburg. — Before Charles was again at liberty to give his attention to his Protestant subjects, Lutheranism had become the religion of most of Germany and of all Scandinavia, while the English church had cut itself off from Rome as an independent Episcopal Church, and a new Presbyterian heresy had begun to spread rapidly in France and even in Germany (§§ 216 ff.). Try as he might, Charles did not find himself free

---

[1] The striking incidents connected with these wars were (1) the Battle of Pavia (1525) and the capture of Francis; (2) the capture and sack of Rome by the army of Charles (made up largely of German Lutherans), when the Pope for a time had sided with France; (3) the alliance between Francis and the Turkish Sultan, Solyman the Magnificent, and Solyman's invasion of Germany; (4) the ravages of Turkish pirates along the Mediterranean coasts. These topics may be assigned students for special reports.

[2] This "Augsburg Confession" is still the platform of the Lutheran Church.

GERMANY
ABOUT 1550

SCALE OF MILES
0 10 20 40 60 80 100

REFERENCE
- *Boundary of Empire*
- *Hapsburg Territories*
- *Ecclesiastical Territories*
- *Imperial Cities*

10
12
14
16
Bishopric
Duchy of Schwerin
Duchy of Mecklenburg
Lauenburg
Stettin
Pomerania
Lüneburg
Lauenburg
Duchy of Brunswick
Priegnitz
County Ruppin
Uckermark
Stendal
Neumark
Netze
R.
KINGDOM
Elbe
Margraviate of Brandenburg
Oder
Wartha
Obornik
Brunswick
Lüneburg
Altmark
Havel
Küstrin
Posen
OF
Celle
Berlin
Köln
Spree
Storkow
Frankfort
Schwiebus
Sievershausen
Brunswick
Brandenburg
Arch. of Magdeburg
Mittlemark
Bishopric
Wolfenbüttel
Hildesheim
Magdeburg
Halberstadt
Zerbst
Margr. Lower Lusatia
52
POLAND
Wolfenbüttel
Halberstadt
Goslar
Wittenberg
Lübben
Guben
Fraustadt
Bruns.
Grubenhagen
Anhalt
Dessau
Kottbus
Glogau
Mansfeld
Duchy of Sagan
Nordhausen
Mansfeld
Halle
Mulde
Torgau
Duchy of
Göttingen
Eisleben
Elbe
Mühlberg
Bober R.
Prin. of Liegnitz
Richsfeld
Frankenhausen
Merseburg
(To Mainz)
Leipzig
Upper Lusatia
Oder R.
Mühlhausen
Naumburg
Merseburg
Lobau
Görlitz
Silesia
Electorate of Saxony
Prin. of Brieg
Gotha
Erfurt
Weimar
Zeitz
Dresden
Wartburg
Jena
Duchy of
(To Mainz)
Saale
Chemnitz
Zittau
Schmalkalden
Zwickau
Elbe R.
County of Glatz
Glatz
Cy. Henneberg
Cy. Reuss
Plauen
Adorf
Eger R.
Saxony
KINGDOM
Bishopric of Königsberg
Kulmbach
Bayreuth
Eger
Prague
50
Bishopric of Bamberg
March R.
Würzburg
Bayreuth
OF
Bamberg
Peraun
Pilsen
Sazawa R.
Upper
Moldau
Margraviate
(To Bayreuth)
BOHEMIA
Tabor
of
Brünn
Windsheim
Nuremberg
Altdorf
Rothenburg
Moravia
Schwabach
Palatinate
Ansbach
Naab R.
Ansbach
Altmühl R.
Ratisbon
Budweis
Thaya R.
Bishopric
Eichstädt
Bishopric of Passau
Nördlingen
Landau
Arch. of
Donauworth
Ingolstadt
Neuburg
Duchy of
Altdorf
Passau
March R.
Ulm
Augsburg
Landshut
Danube
Linz
Pressburg
Burgau
Bavaria
Mölk
Vienna
Lech R.
Enns
R. Austria
48
Bishopric of
Steyer
Augsburg
Munich
Isar R.
Inn R.
Salzach
Neustadt
Salzburg
Berchtesgaden
KINGDOM OF HUNGARY
Kempten
Enns R.
Lindau
Arch of
Leoben
Bruck
Vorarlberg
Ehrenberger Pass
Hall
Pinzgau R.
Salzburg
Duchy of Styria
Raab
Innsbruck
Gastein
Graz
Brenner
County of Tyrol
Duchy
(To Salzburg)
Engandin
Mur R.
(To Bamberg)
of
Tyrol
Brixen (Bishopric)
(To Görz)
Klagenfurt
Radkersburg
10
Etsch R.
12
VENICE
Carinthia
Bleiburg
16

to strike in Germany until 1546, the year of Luther's death. Then two brief struggles settled the contest for the time. In the first, Charles seemed completely victorious over the Smalkald League; but almost at once the defeated princes rallied again, drove Charles in hurried flight from their domains, and forced him to accept the *Peace of Augsburg* (1555). According to this treaty, each ruling prince of the Empire was free to choose between Lutheranism and Catholicism for himself and for all his subjects,[1] except that if an ecclesiastical ruler became a Protestant, he was to surrender his lands to the church, from whom they came.

212. Abdication of Charles. — The Protestants in their last rising had sought aid from Henry II, the new French king; and France for her reward had seized some German districts, including the city of Metz. Charles proved unable to recover the territory. Chagrined at the loss and disheartened by the split within the Empire, he abdicated his many crowns in 1556. His brother *Ferdinand* succeeded him in the Austrian possessions, and soon after as emperor, while his son Philip II received the Netherlands, Spain, Naples, and Spanish America.

C. The Counter-Reformation.

213. Protestantism in the South of Europe, and its Check. — For a time it seemed as though Protestantism would overrun the south of Europe also, but the Romance lands and South Germany were finally saved to the old church. France was to remain Catholic, partly as the result of religious wars (§§ 227 ff.). The same may be said of much of South Germany and of modern Belgium (§§ 231, 222); and the final victory of Catholicism elsewhere was due partly to the terrible repression of the new faith by the Inquisition. More important than this element of violence, however, was the purifying of the old faith by the movement known as the *Counter-Reformation*.

---

[1] Observe that this peace secured toleration only for rulers, not for the people, and that it disregarded all Protestant sects except the Lutherans.

214. The Inquisition, or Holy Office, had been organized in a comparatively mild form for the suppression of the Albigensian heresy (§ 83). After open resistance in Languedoc had been crushed, the Pope appointed a special court to hunt out and try heretics there. This court soon became a regular part of the machinery of the church. A little before 1500, it was introduced into Spain to deal with Jews and Moors who had adopted Christianity but who afterward returned to their old faiths; and after the appearance of Lutheranism, the authorities of the church turned to it to deal with this more alarming heresy. The court was reorganized and enlarged; and in this final form it is generally known as the "*Spanish Inquisition.*" It held sway in Portugal and in Italy, as well as in all the wide-lying Spanish possessions, but France and Germany never admitted it in any considerable degree.

The methods of the Inquisition were atrocious, and its story is one of the darkest that blot the pages of history. The Inquisitor encouraged and commanded children to betray their parents, and parents their children. Upon secret accusation by spies, a victim disappeared, without warning, to underground dungeons. The trial that followed was a gross farce. The court did not confront the accused with his accuser, nor allow him witnesses of his choosing; and it extorted confession by cruel and ingenious tortures, carried to a point beyond which human courage could not endure. Acquittals were rare. The property of the convicted went to enrich the church, and the heretic himself was handed over to the government for death by fire.

Persecution of unbelievers was characteristic of the age and disgraced every sect, Protestant as well as Catholic, but no Protestant land possessed a device so admirably calculated to accomplish its evil purpose as this Spanish Inquisition. Unquestionably it sifted out for destruction thousands upon thousands of the stoutest hearts and best brains of Spain, and no doubt it played a great part in the intellectual blight that soon fell upon that people (§ 224).

215. Reform within the Church: the Council of Trent; the Jesuits. — A pleasanter form of the reaction against Protestantism lay in the great reform within the Catholic church. This movement was organized by the *Council of Trent* (1545–1563). Catholic forms were not changed; but some doctrines were more exactly defined, abuses were pruned away, and a greater moral energy was infused into the church.[1]

The new religious enthusiasm gave birth to several new religious Orders. The most important of these was that of the *Jesuits*. This "Order of Jesus" was founded in 1534 by *Ignatius Loyola,* a gallant Spanish gentleman of deep religious convictions. Loyola had designed his society for missionary work among the Mohammedans; but an accident prevented his setting out, and he soon adopted wider projects. The Jesuits stood to the friars somewhat as the friars stood to the older monks (§ 84): holding fast like both these Orders to an intensely religious private life, they represented a further advance into the world of public affairs. Their members mingled with men in all capacities. Especially did they distinguish themselves as statesmen and as teachers. Their schools were the best in Europe, and many a Protestant youth was won back by them to Catholicism. In like manner, as individual counsellors, they converted many a Protestant prince — especially in Germany, where the religion of the prince determined that of his people (§ 211).

Much of the success of the Jesuits was due to their perfect obedience to their superiors, and to their rigid military organization. They became the chief soldiers of the pope in checking the advance of Protestantism in Europe, and their many devoted missionaries among the heathen in the New Worlds won vast regions to Christianity and Catholicism.

---

[1] This beneficent effect upon the Catholic world from the Protestant secession corresponds to the moral awakening in the Church of England, two hundred years later, caused by the great Methodist secession. In some part, no doubt, the reform resulted from forces within the church, independent of the Protestant revolt. The work of Erasmus was one of these forces.

D. Protestant Sects.

216. Division into Sects the Natural Result of Protestantism. — The right of private judgment, which lay at the basis of Protestantism (§ 206) and which was thoroughly in accord with the spirit of the Renaissance, resulted in a multitude of sects. These sects were scandalously hostile to each other; and, in Germany in particular, the mutual hatred of Lutherans and Calvinists seriously weakened the cause of the Reformation.[1] Undoubtedly, on the other hand, the variety of thought and the rivalry between the sects contributed to intellectual and moral activity. The two most important Protestant movements after the growth of Lutheranism have already been referred to (§ 211), but now demand fuller treatment.

217. Calvinism. — The Father of the Presbyterian church and of Puritan theology was *John Calvin*, a Frenchman. Calvin had promptly adopted Luther's teachings against the papacy, but he added new ideas of his own regarding church government and religious doctrine. The city of Geneva afforded him an opportunity to put his system into practice. Geneva was a French town in the Swiss Alps. It was not a member of the Swiss confederation; but it had just established itself as a free city-republic by rebellion against an ecclesiastical lord; and the bitter struggle left the people disposed to Protestantism. Here Calvin, a fugitive from France, took up his abode in 1536, and soon he was the absolute dictator of the little state. Geneva became a Puritan "theocracy," and furnished many hints for the future American Puritan commonwealths.

Calvin's writings influenced profoundly his own and future times. The more ardent reformers from all Europe flocked to Geneva to imbibe his teachings, and then returned to spread Calvinism in their own lands. From Geneva came the seeds

---

[1] Catholics pointed to these divisions as proofs of the necessity of relying upon the collective wisdom of the church, rather than upon the individual judgment.

of Scotch Presbyterianism, of the great Puritan movement within the English Church, of the leading Protestant movement among the Dutch, and of the Huguenot church in France.

Calvin's government repressed amusements and tyrannized over the private lives of citizens, but it made Geneva a sober and industrious commonwealth. One terrible deed stains Calvin's fame. *Servetus,* a learned physician, who denied the doctrine of the Trinity and who had had literary controversies with Calvin, ventured to visit Geneva. He was promptly arrested, tried for heresy, and burned at the stake.[1]

The Calvinistic doctrine in its original form seems to nearly all men of the present time too sober and merciless. It was, however, sternly logical. It made strong men, and it appealed to strong spirits. Fortunately, in the course of historical movements, it became the ally of political freedom in Holland, England, and America.

218. The Church of England and English Puritanism. — In England, separation from Rome was at first the act of the monarchs, rather than of the people, and the motives were personal and political, rather than religious. *King Henry VIII* had shown himself zealous against Luther, and had even written a book to controvert him. A little later, however, Henry desired a divorce from his wife, the unfortunate Catherine of Aragon, aunt of Charles V (§ 172). Catherine's only child was a girl (Mary), and Henry was anxious for a male heir, in order to maintain public peace and tranquillity. Moreover, he desired to marry Anne Boleyn, a lady of the court for whom he had begun to feel a guilty passion. After long negotiation, the Pope refused to grant the divorce. Thereupon Henry put himself in the place of the Pope so far as his island was concerned, and secured the divorce from his own courts.

The secession of the English church was accomplished in the years 1532–1534, by two simple but far-reaching measures of Henry's servile Parliament. (1) The clergy and people were

[1] See § 199, note. In the year 1903, Calvinist subscriptions from all over the world erected at Geneva a noble "expiatory statue" to Servetus.

forbidden to make further payments to "the Bishop of Rome"; and (2) the "Act of Supremacy" declared Henry the "only supreme head on earth of the Church of England."

Parliament was ready to follow the king in all matters, in the reign of the despot Henry; but in this case, no doubt, its willingness was partly due to the old English feeling for independence of papal control (§ 164), and partly, perhaps, to some sympathy for the Lutheran movement.

Henry wished no further change; but his chief advisers and agents — his minister, Thomas Cromwell, and the Archbishop of Canterbury, Cranmer — had secret leanings toward the Reformation, and they secured from him some additional measures. The English Bible was introduced into the church service, and the doctrine of purgatory was declared false. At Henry's wish, too, Parliament dissolved the hundreds of monasteries in England. Some of the wealth of these institutions went to found schools and hospitals, but Henry seized most of the lands for himself, parceling part of them out to the gentry and to a new nobility, who were thus attached to the new movement.[1]

This was as far as Henry could be persuaded to go; and to the close of his reign he continued to behead the "traitors" who recognized the papal headship and to burn the "heretics" who denied the leading papal doctrines.[2] During the short reign of Henry's successor, the boy Edward VI, England was ruled by a clique of great Protestant lords, who tried to carry the English church into the full tide of Protestantism. Priests were allowed to marry; and the use of the old litany, of incense, tapers, holy water, and the surplice, was forbidden. The English Prayer Book and the "Thirty-nine Articles" of the English church date from this period.

---

[1] Forty thousand families are said to have been enriched by such gifts. Of course this created a mighty influence hostile to reconciliation with Rome.

[2] Henry's most famous victim was *Sir Thomas More*, a Catholic gentleman, and one of the noblest Englishmen of any age. More was beheaded for refusing to declare the marriage with Catherine illegal. One Protestant sufferer was Anne Askew, a gentlewoman of good position, who was burnt for saying "The bread [of the communion] cannot be God." Cf. § 72, note.

But though the nation had felt no great opposition to Henry's casting off papal supremacy, it was still overwhelmingly Catholic in doctrine and feeling; and Edward's half-sister Mary, on her accession to the throne, had no difficulty in doing away with the Protestant innovations of her brother's time. Mary, however, desired to undo also her father's work; and Parliament readily voted the repeal of the anti-Catholic laws, except that it stubbornly refused to restore the church lands. Finally the Pope wisely waived this matter, and the nation was solemnly absolved and received back into the old church. Then Mary proceeded to destroy her work by a bloody persecution of the Protestants, which roused popular fear and detestation and so prepared for another change.

Over two hundred and seventy martyrs perished at the stake, — about half the entire number that suffered death for conscience' sake in all English history. The most famous executions were those of Bishops Ridley and Latimer[1] and Archbishop Cranmer.

A few Catholics had been burned by Edward's Protestant government, and even Latimer had preached in commendation of the torture of the Catholic Father Forest, roasted in a swinging iron cradle over a slow fire; but the number of these Catholic victims had not been enough to arouse popular feeling in a people like the English of that day. So, too, in the long reign of forty-five years that followed, — nine times as long as Mary's, — there were nearly as many Catholics put to death as there had been Protestant executions under Mary; but there was no sudden piling up of executions, and moreover, nominally, death was inflicted in most cases not for religious faith but for treason against Queen Elizabeth.[2]

Mary's brief and troubled reign was followed by the long and glorious rule of her half-sister, *Elizabeth*. The new Queen desired probably to return to the ecclesiastical system of her father: certainly she had little sympathy with extreme

---

[1] As Latimer and Ridley approached the stake the former called out courageously to his friend, "Play the man, Master Ridley; we shall this day by God's grace light such a candle in England as I trust shall never be put out." The words were well justified by the result.

[2] Elizabeth's ministers used the rack and other instruments of torture upon their Catholic victims; but such deeds were secret in the Tower, and the executions took place, not at the stake, but on the more familiar scaffold.

Protestantism. However, she was the daughter of Anne Boleyn, whose marriage with Henry was not recognized by the papal party. Accordingly, that party denied Elizabeth's claim to the throne; and in self-defense the Queen was forced to rely upon the Protestants. Throughout her reign, England was threatened by the Catholic Powers, and only Elizabeth's shrewd statesmanship saved her country from its incessant perils. Finally Philip II, with the blessing of the Pope, sent a mighty Spanish armament, the "Invincible Armada," for the conquest of England (§ 223). The heroic English navy, aided by a great storm in the North Sea, beat off the invasion (1588); and for the rising generation the gallant struggle identified patriotism with Protestantism. Thus, before Elizabeth's death (1603), England was Protestant in religion; and even the Puritan doctrines from Geneva had begun to spread widely among the people (§ 233).

FOR FURTHER READING. — Source material in *Pennsylvania Reprints*, II, No. 6, and III, No. 3.

Modern accounts: Johnson, *Europe in the Sixteenth Century*, especially on the Counter-Reformation and Calvinism, 261–276; Adams, *Civilization*, 416–442; Köstlin, *Luther*; Beard, *Luther*; Häusser, *Reformation*; Seebohm, *Protestant Reformation*; Alzog, *Church History*; Pastor, *History of the Popes*; Creighton, *Papacy*; Walker, *Reformation* (especially good); Fisher, *Reformation*; Perry, *Reformation in England*; Ward, *Counter-Reformation*; Creighton, *Age of Elizabeth*; Creighton, *Queen Elizabeth*; Beesly, *Elizabeth*.

SPECIAL REPORTS. — 1. Mary, Queen of Scots. 2. The Armada. 3. Sir Francis Drake. 4. Sir Walter Raleigh. 5. John Knox.

II. A CENTURY OF RELIGIOUS WARS.

219. General Survey. — The Peace of Augsburg (§ 211), which closed the first religious wars in Germany, proved unsatisfactory to both parties; and soon each was charging the other with infringing the terms of the treaty. There seems little doubt but that the Protestant Powers did systematically disregard the provisions intended to preserve church lands to the Catholic church. But though there were incessant bickerings,

Germany had no further civil war for over sixty years. Just this interval was filled, however, with terrible religious strife in the Netherlands and in France; and then the age closed, as it began, with a civil war in Germany, — the most destructive in history. From the opening of the Smalkald war to the end of the Thirty Years' War (1546-1648) is a century of almost continuous religious strife. The close of the period is marked by the rapid decay of Spain, by the further disruption of Germany, by the rise of France, of the Dutch Republic, and of England, and by the development of political liberty in England.

A. SPAIN AND THE NETHERLANDS.

220. The Power of Spain under Philip II. — Philip II succeeded his father (§ 212) as the most powerful and most absolute monarch in Europe. The Spanish infantry were the finest soldiery in the world. The Spanish navy was the unquestioned mistress of the ocean. Each year the great "gold fleet" filled Philip's coffers from the apparently exhaustless wealth of the Americas. In 1580, Portugal and her East India empire fell to Spain,[1] and the Spanish boast that the sun never set upon Spanish Dominions became literal fact.

221. The Netherland Revolt. — Charles V had seriously infringed the old liberties of the Netherlands and had set up the Inquisition in that country, with frightful consequences;[2] but the great majority of the people had been attached to him, as their native sovereign, and had felt a warm loyalty to his government. Philip continued all his father's abuses, without possessing any of his redeeming qualities, in Dutch eyes. He seemed a foreign master, and he ruled from a distance through

---

[1] The ruling line of Portugal ran out; and Philip II, closely related to the extinct family, claimed the throne. The Portuguese were unwilling to be annexed to Spain, but Philip easily seized upon the country. It remained Spanish until 1640, when its independence was established by a successful revolt. Meantime most of its colonial empire, except Brazil, had passed from Spain to Holland (§ 225).

[2] Protestant writers used to claim that from fifty thousand to one hundred thousand men and women were burned, strangled, or buried alive, within the Netherlands during Charles' reign. These numbers appear to be mere guesses and serious exaggerations, but it is plain that the actual facts were horrible.

foreign officers. Finally, Protestant and Catholic nobles joined in a demand for reform. These demands were mainly political; but just at this time the Protestant mobs in the cities rose in fury to sack the churches and cathedrals (1566), and so gave a look of religious strife to the beginning of the movement against Spain.

Philip's reply was to send the stern Spanish general, Alva, with a veteran army, to enforce submission. Alva's council is known as the *Council of Blood*. It declared almost the whole population guilty of rebellion, and so deserving of death, with confiscation of goods. With disgraceful disregard for even the forms of law, the Council proceeded to enforce the atrocious sentence upon great numbers, — especially upon the wealthy classes, — and in 1568 a revolt began.

The struggle between the small disunited provinces and the world-empire was to last over forty years. In the beginning, it was essentially a conflict for political liberty, but it soon became a religious struggle. It was waged on both sides with an exasperated and relentless fury that made it a byword for ferocity, even in that brutal age. The worst excesses were chargeable to the Spaniards, because they made war upon women and children, as well as upon men. City after city was given up to indiscriminate rapine and massacre, with deeds of horror indescribable.

Over against this dark side, stands the stubborn heroism of the Dutch people, unsurpassed and hardly matched in all history, — a heroism which saved not themselves only, but also the cause of Protestantism and of political liberty for the world.

222. William the Silent. The Dutch Republic. — The central figure on the side of freedom was *William of Orange*, the leading noble of the land, known in history as William the Silent. He is not unfitly called the Dutch Washington. The persistent, courageous statesmanship of this hero over and again snatched a new chance from crushing defeat, and finally made his countrymen a nation. The seven northern provinces,

THE NETHERLANDS
at the Truce of 1609
SCALE OF MILES
0 10 20 30 40 50 60 70 80
The Seven United Provinces
The Provinces still Retained by Spain
NORTH SEA
EAST FRIESLAND
Embden
Jemmingen
GRONINGEN
Groningen
WEST FRIESLAND
Heiligerlee
OVERYSSEL
R. Ems
Enkhuisen
Alkmaar
Zuyder Zee
Haarlem
Amsterdam
HOLLAND
Deventer
Naarden
Leyden
Utrecht
The Hague
Zutphen
Delft
R. Rhine
Doesburg
Brill
Rotterdam
R. Waal
Nimwegen
SCHOUWEN
Dort
Grave
Mook
D. OF CLEVE
I. OF WALCHEREN
Ziericksee
Gertruydenberg
Middleburg
Goes
Breda
Flushing
Sluys
Scheldt
Hulst
Turnhout
Venloo
Ostende
Bruges
Antwerp
Ghent
Neuss
Dunkirk
Dendermonde
Mechlin
Gravelines
Ingelmunster
Alost
Cologne
FLANDERS
Brussels
Maastricht
Ypres
St. Trond
Waterloo
Ramillies
Liege
St. Omer
Lille
Gembloux
Namur
Orchies
Mons
NAMUR
ARTOIS
Valenciennes
Arras
Douai
HAINAULT
Cambray
Cateau Cambresis
LIMBURG
R. Meuse
WESTPHALIA
ARCHBISHOPRIC OF COLOGNE
DUCHY OF JULICH
PICARDY
LUXEMBURG
Luxemburg
ARCHBISHOPRIC OF TREVES
R. Oise
R. Aisne
R. Meuse
CHAMPANGE
BISHOPRIC OF VERDUN
BISHOPRIC OF METZ
R. Marne
LORRAINE
Paris

Dutch in blood and Protestant in religion, became independent, as "The United Provinces."[1]

The turning point of the war was the *relief of Leyden* (1574). For many months the city had been closely besieged, and the people were dying grimly of starvation. Fifteen miles away, on the North Sea, rode a Dutch fleet with supplies; but all attempts to relieve the suffering town had failed. Then William the Silent cut the dykes and let in the ocean on the land. Over wide districts the prosperity of years was engulfed in ruin; but upon the invading sea the relieving ships rode to the city gates, and Dutch liberty was saved.[2]

223. English Aid. Spain's "Invincible Armada" attacks England. — In 1584, William was assassinated by a fanatic, at the instigation of Philip II; but now at last Elizabeth of England was ready to render tardy aid. For many years, individual English adventurers had joined the Dutch army, or, like Drake, had attacked the Spaniards in half-piratical fashion in the New World. It was clear that only the successful resistance of the Dutch had kept Philip from long since attacking England; and finally, in 1585, Elizabeth sent a small English army to the Netherlands.[3]

Philip then turned upon England. His preparations for invading the island were delayed by a gallant exploit of Drake, who sailed into the harbor where the expedition was preparing

---

[1] This new state is often called the Dutch Republic, or the Netherlands. Its government was vested in a States General, representing the different provinces, and in a Stadtholder. The most important of the seven provinces was Holland, which has given its name, in popular usage, to all seven. The ten southern provinces of the old Netherlands soon gave up the struggle and returned to Spanish allegiance. They were largely French in race and Catholic in religion. Protestantism was of course completely stamped out in them. After this time, they are known as the Spanish Netherlands, and then as the Austrian Netherlands again, and finally as modern Belgium (§ 505).

[2] In memory of its heroic resistance, William offered Leyden exemption from taxes or the establishment of a university. The citizens finely chose the latter; and the University of Leyden, ever since one of the most famous universities in Europe, arose to commemorate the city's deed.

[3] Anecdote of the dying Sir Philip Sidney and the drink of water.

and burned the Spanish fleet, "singeing the beard of the Spanish king," as the old sea-rover described it; but in 1588 the "Invincible Armada" at last set sail for England (§ 218, close). English ships of all sorts — mostly little merchant vessels hastily transformed into a war navy — gathered in the Channel; and, to the amazement of the world, the small but swift and better handled English vessels completely outfought the great Spanish navy in a splendid nine-days' sea fight. As the shattered Spaniards fled around the north of Scotland, a mighty storm completed their overthrow. England was saved, and the prospect for Dutch success was greatly improved. Spain never recovered her supremacy on the sea, and the way was prepared for the English colonization of America.

224. The Decay of Spain. Her final Service to Christendom at Lepanto. — The war between Spain and Holland dragged on twenty years more, but in 1609 a truce was concluded which virtually established the independence of the Dutch Republic. From this time, Spain sank rapidly into a second-rate power. The narrow bigot, Philip III, drove into exile the Christianized Moors, or Moriscoes. These were the descendants of the old Mohammedan rulers of the land, who had been left behind when the Moorish political power had been driven out, in the preceding centuries. They numbered over half a million, — perhaps a twentieth of the entire population, — and they were the foremost agriculturalists and almost the sole skilled artisans and manufacturers in the peninsula. Their pitiless expulsion inflicted a deadly blow upon the prosperity of Spain. For a time the wealth she drew from America disguised her fall, and she continued to furnish financial resources for the Catholic Powers through the Thirty Years' War (§ 231). But after the Armada she never played a great part in Europe, and, relying upon the plunder of the New World for riches, she failed to develop the industrial life which alone could furnish a true national prosperity.

One great service Spain had rendered Christendom, just before England and Holland broke her naval power. For a generation, Turkish fleets, almost unchecked, had ravaged the Christian coasts of the Mediterranean, even burning villages far inland and sweeping off the peasants into captivity. Cyprus had fallen before their attack, and Malta had been saved only by the heroic efforts of the Knights of St. John.[1] Finally Spain,

---

[1] Special report: the siege of Malta; read Prescott's account in his *Philip II*, if available.

Venice, and the Pope joined their naval strength, and in 1571 the combined Christian fleet annihilated the great Turkish navy at *Lepanto*, on the Greek coast. Lepanto was the greatest naval battle since Carthaginian days. Over six hundred ships engaged. The Turks lost thirty thousand men, and twelve thousand Christian rowers were freed from their horrible slavery at the oar. The Turks never recovered their former naval importance; and indeed the turning point of their power is often dated from this defeat.

225. The Prosperity of the Dutch Republic. — The most marvelous feature of the struggle between the little Dutch state and Spain was that Holland actually grew wealthy during the contest, although the stage of a desolating war. This strange result was due to the fact that the Dutch were a maritime people, drawing their riches not from the wasted land, but from the sea, and that during the war they plundered the possessions of Spain in the East Indies. The little republic built up a great colonial empire, and, especially after Spain's naval supremacy had been engulfed with the Armada, the Dutch held almost a monopoly of the Asiatic trade for all Europe. One hundred thousand of their three million people lived constantly upon the sea.

Moreover, success in so heroic a war stimulated the people to a wonderful intellectual and industrial activity. They taught to all Europe scientific agriculture and horticulture, as well as the science of navigation. In the seventeenth century the presses of Holland are said to have put forth more books than all the rest of Europe. Motley sums up this wonderful career of Holland briefly: —

The splendid empire of Charles V was erected upon the grave of liberty. . . . But from the hand-breadth of territory called Holland rises a power which wages eighty years' warfare [1] with the most potent empire upon earth, and which, during the struggle, becomes itself a mighty state, and, binding about its slender form a zone of the richest possessions of the earth, from pole to tropic, finally dictates its decrees to the empire of Charles.

---

[1] Motley includes in this number the Thirty Years' War, § 230.

B. WARS OF THE FRENCH HUGUENOTS.

226. Conditions in France. — The French Protestants were Calvinists, and are known as Huguenots. By 1560, they counted one man out of twenty in the population, and, because of the logical appeal of Calvin to the intellect, their numbers were made up almost wholly from the nobles and the wealthy middle class. Francis I and Henry II persecuted the new faith, but not continuously enough to crush it. Henry was followed by his three sons, — Francis II, Charles IX, and Henry III, — all weak in body and in mind. During their reigns (1559-1589), power was disputed between two groups of great lords. Each was closely related to the failing royal family, and each hoped to place a successor upon the throne. One of these groups was the Catholic *Guise* family; the other was the Protestant *Bourbons*, who counted as their leaders the King of Navarre and the Prince of Condé. In the background was the chief figure of all, the crafty, cruel, and utterly unscrupulous Queen-mother, *Catherine of Medici*, who played off one party against the other in whatever way might best promote her own control over her feeble sons. These were the conditions that bred civil war in France.

227. Period of Strife; St. Bartholomew. — War between the two factions opened in 1562 and lasted, with brief truces, to 1598. More than the other struggles of the period, it was marked by assassinations and treacheries, which struck down almost every leader on either side. The most horrible event of this character was the *Massacre of St. Bartholomew* (August 24, 1572). An honest attempt had just been made to establish a lasting peace, and a marriage had been arranged between the Huguenot leader, the young Henry of Navarre, and the sister of King Charles IX. The grandest character of the age, the Protestant *Coligny*, became one of Charles' chief counsellors, and soon won remarkable influence over him. Catherine of Medici had favored the arrangement at first; but she had not expected to see her own power over her son so superseded, and she passed over secretly to the Guises again. One attempt to assassinate Coligny failed, and the King threatened vengeance for the attack. Then the conspirators, as a desperate resort, played upon his religious fears and bigotry with a new plot to cleanse France from heresy at one blow; and his consent was finally won for a general massacre of the Huguenots. Large numbers of that sect were assembled in Paris to witness the marriage of their chief. The secret was kept perfectly, to the appointed moment; and then the mob of Paris bathed in Huguenot blood. Ten thousand victims fell in France. Nothing else so well shows the terrible ferocity of the religious struggle in Europe as the reception of this news. The Protestant world shuddered with horror and fear; but great and good men among the Catholics, believing that the stroke had barely averted a treacherous uprising by the Huguenots, loudly expressed their joy and offered special services of praise to God.

228. Henry IV; the Edict of Nantes. — Henry III, who showed himself too moderate for the Catholic League, and who, in order to secure greater freedom of action, had had the Duke of Guise murdered, was himself struck down by a Catholic assassin. Henry of Navarre was the nearest heir to the throne, and he became king as *Henry IV*, but only after four years more of civil war with the Catholic League. Finally, to secure Paris, which he had long besieged, Henry accepted Catholicism, declaring lightly that so fair a city was "well worth a mass." His purpose, of course, was not only to secure the capital, but also to give stable peace to his distracted country. In this he was thoroughly successful. The thirty years of conflict closed; and in 1598 the *Edict of Nantes* established toleration for the Huguenots. They were granted full equality before the law; they were to have perfect liberty of conscience, and to enjoy the privilege of public worship, except in the cathedral cities; while certain towns were handed over to them, to hold with their own garrisons, as a security for their rights.[1]

---

[1] This last measure was no doubt needful, but it carried with it a political danger: it set up a state within a state, and hindered the unity of France.

Henry IV proved one of the greatest of French Kings, and he was one of the most loved. With his sagacious minister, the Protestant *Duke of Sully*, he set himself to restore prosperity to desolated France.[1] Roads and canals were built, new trades were fostered, and under the blessings of a firm government, the industry of the French people with marvelous rapidity removed the evil results of the long strife. Before his death, Henry had begun to think himself ready to enlarge France again by foreign conquest at the expense of the Hapsburgs; but in 1610 he was assassinated by a half-insane Catholic fanatic.

229. Richelieu: Separate Political Power of the Huguenots crushed; German Protestants aided. — At the death of Henry IV, his son Louis XIII was a boy of nine years. During the long regency of the weak Queen-mother, anarchy again raised its head; but France was saved by the commanding genius of *Cardinal Richelieu*. Richelieu became the chief minister of the young King in 1624, and he remained the controlling power in France until his death (1642). He was a sincere French patriot, and, though an earnest Catholic, his statesmanship was guided always by political, not by religious, motives. He crushed the great nobles mercilessly, and he waged war upon the Huguenots to deprive them of La Rochelle and their other garrisoned towns, which menaced the unity of France. But when he had captured their cities and held the Huguenots at his mercy, he kept toward them in full all the other pledges of the Edict of Nantes. As a statesman, he wished to use Catholic and Protestant together for the upbuilding of the nation; and he carried out his purpose by aiding the German Protestants in the religious war that was going on in Germany against the Catholic Emperor, — so securing a chance to seize imperial territory for France. To make the king supreme in France, he waged war upon the

---

[1] One of Henry's treasured sayings was, that, if he lived, the poorest peasant should have a fowl in the pot on a Sunday.

Protestants within the nation; to make France supreme in Europe, he aided in war the Protestants of Germany.

After Francis I, France had given up Italy and had begun to work for a frontier to the Rhine. Henry II had made a beginning (§ 212), and Richelieu laid the foundation for the rapid additions that were to come in the reign of Louis XIV (§§ 263, 264). At first this policy was not mere greed: it was partly a policy of self-preservation. With the Austrian and Spanish Hapsburgs united or in alliance, France was for a time in serious danger of being crushed between them. The failure of Spain against Holland and the policy of Richelieu against Austria did away with that danger.

C. The Thirty Years' War in Germany.

230. The Parties and Leaders. — Fortunately for German Protestants, the two immediate successors of Charles V on the imperial throne were liberal in temper, — disinclined either to persecution or to religious war. So for sixty years more, the new faith gained ground rapidly, until it spread over much of South Germany and held almost exclusive possession of Bohemia, the home of the ancient Hussite reform and now a Hapsburg province.[1] Strife was incessantly threatening, however. The Hapsburgs strove to restrict Protestantism in their hereditary dominions, while the Protestants vigorously endeavored to secure even the ecclesiastical lands there. These conditions led to the last of the great religious wars. It began just a century after Luther posted his theses at Wittenberg, and it is known as the *Thirty Years' War* (1618–1648). Beyond doubt, it was the most destructive and terrible war in all history. The divided Protestant princes showed themselves timid and incapable, and, had the war been left to Germany, a Catholic victory would soon have been assured. But first Denmark (1625–1629) and then Sweden (1630) entered the field in behalf of the Protestant cause, and, at the last, Catholic France under Richelieu (1635–1648) threw its weight against the Emperor.

---

[1] Ferdinand, brother of Charles V, had secured this realm for his house, by marriage with Anne, heiress of Bohemia.

The war was marked by the career of four great generals, — Tilly and Wallenstein on the imperial side, and Gustavus Adolphus, King of Sweden, "the Lion of the North," and Mansfeld on the side of the Protestants. Gustavus was at once great and admirable; but he fell at the *battle of Lützen* (1632), in the moment of victory; and thereafter the struggle was as dreary as it was terrible. Mansfeld and Wallenstein from the first deliberately adopted the policy of making the war pay by supporting their armies everywhere upon the country. The excessive horrors of the great struggle must be charged in large measure to these men. At the close of his career, Wallenstein seems to have been planning to betray the Emperor to the Swedes; but he was arrested and murdered by imperial messengers (1634).

231. Effect upon Germany. — The calamities the war brought upon a whole people were so monstrous and indescribable that it seems weak to dwell upon brilliant characters or striking events. It was a huge, blasting ruin, from which Germany had not fully recovered in the middle of the nineteenth century. Season by season, for a generation of human life, armies of ruthless freebooters harried the land with fire and sword. The peasant, who found that he toiled only to feed robbers and to draw them to outrage and torture his family, ceased to labor and became himself robber or camp-follower. Half the population and two-thirds the movable property of Germany were swept away. In many large districts, the facts were worse than this average. The Duchy of Wurtemberg had fifty thousand people left out of five hundred thousand. Populous cities had become hamlets; and for miles upon miles former hamlets were the lairs of wolfpacks. Not until 1850 did some sections of Germany again contain as many homesteads and cattle as in 1618.

Even more destructive was the result upon industry and character. Whole trades, with all their long-inherited skill, had passed from the memory of men.[1] Land tilled for centuries became wilderness, and men became savages. The

---

[1] An instance of this is the wonderful old German wood-carving. A genuine old piece of German cabinet-work is easily placed before 1618, because the war simply wiped out the skill and the industry.

generation that survived the war had come to manhood without schools or churches or law or orderly industry. The low position of the German peasantry, morally and mentally, well into the nineteenth century, was a direct result of the Thirty Years' War.

232. The Peace of Westphalia, 1648. — The war was closed by the Peace of Westphalia. This treaty was drawn up by a congress of ambassadors from nearly every European Power. It contains three distinct classes of stipulations, — the provisions for religious peace in Germany, the territorial rewards for France and Sweden, and the political provisions to secure the independence of the German princes as against the Empire.

a. The principle of the Peace of Augsburg was reaffirmed and extended. Each sovereign prince was to choose Catholicism, Lutheranism, or Calvinism; and his subjects were to have three years to conform to his choice, or to withdraw from his realm.[1]

b. Sweden, which was in that day a great Baltic power, extending around both the east and west shores of that sea, secured also most of the south coast. Pomerania — with the mouths of the Oder, Elbe, and Weser — was the payment she received for her part in the war. This gave Sweden control over German commerce. France annexed most of Alsace, with some fortresses on the German bank of the Rhine. The independence of Switzerland (§ 161) and of the Dutch Provinces (§ 225) was expressly recognized.

c. Besides this loss of imperial territory, there were various political rearrangements within Germany, which made clear the lack of unity in the Empire. The states were expressly

---

[1] The practice of toleration had gained ground so far that the Catholics in the North German Protestant states were rarely molested. Many of the South German Protestants, however, were driven into exile. Indeed, this was the first cause of the coming to America of the "Pennsylvania Dutch"; most of the German immigration to America before the Revolution was connected with this expulsion or with the devastation of the Rhine provinces a little later by Louis XIV (§ 265).

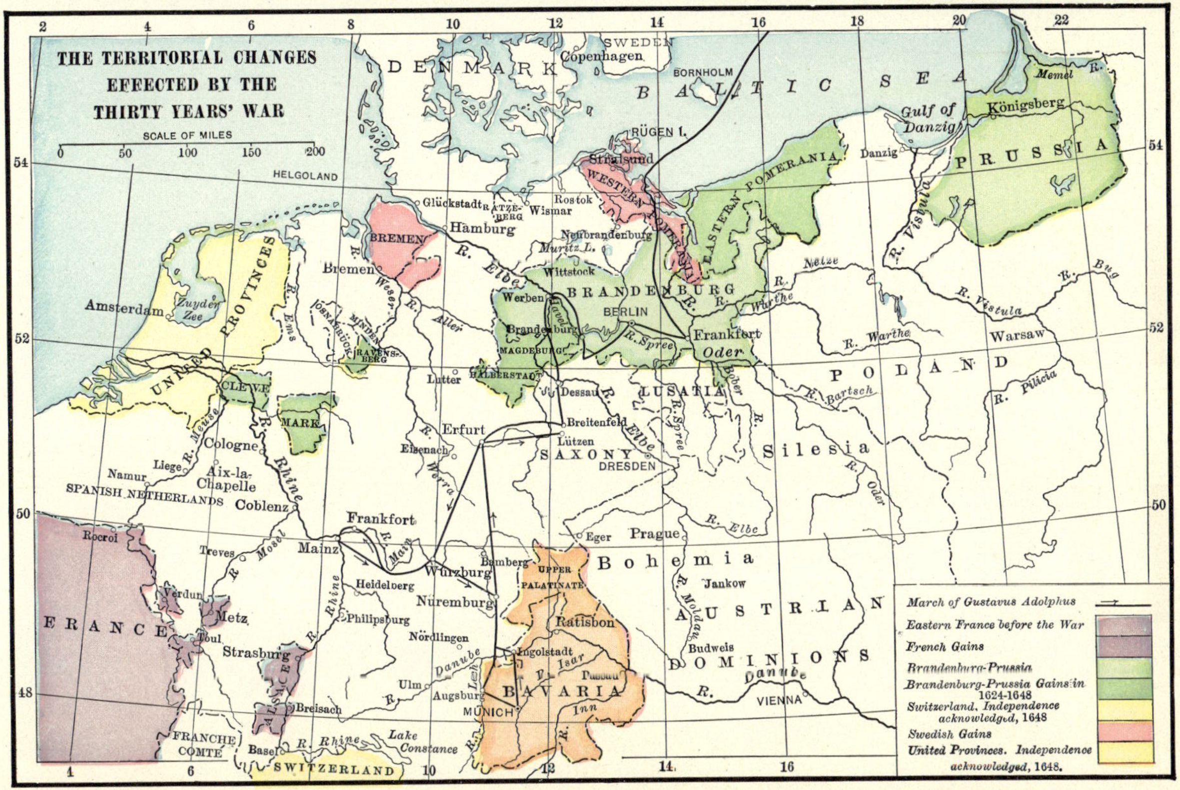
THE TERRITORIAL CHANGES
EFFECTED BY THE
THIRTY YEARS' WAR
SCALE OF MILES
0 50 100 150 200
March of Gustavus Adolphus
Eastern France before the War
French Gains
Brandenburg-Prussia
Brandenburg-Prussia Gains in 1624-1648
Switzerland, Independence acknowledged, 1648
Swedish Gains
United Provinces. Independence acknowledged, 1648.
DENMARK
SWEDEN
Copenhagen
BORNHOLM
BALTIC SEA
Gulf of Danzig
Memel
Königsberg
PRUSSIA
Danzig
RÜGEN I.
Stralsund
WESTERN POMERANIA
EASTERN POMERANIA
HELGOLAND
Glückstadt
RATZEBERG
Wismar
Rostok
Hamburg
BREMEN
Bremen
Neubrandenburg
Muritz L.
Wittstock
BRANDENBURG
Werben
BERLIN
Brandenburg
MAGDEBURG
HALBERSTADT
Frankfort
Oder
Amsterdam
Zuyder Zee
UNITED PROVINCES
OSNABRÜCK
MINDEN
RAVENSBERG
CLEVE
MARK
Lutter
Dessau
LUSATIA
Breitenfeld
Lützen
SAXONY
DRESDEN
Erfurt
Eisenach
Silesia
Cologne
Liege
Aix-la-Chapelle
Namur
SPANISH NETHERLANDS
Coblenz
Frankfort
Mainz
Treves
Rocroi
Verdun
Metz
Toul
FRANCE
Strasburg
ALSACE
Breisach
Basel
FRANCHE COMTE
SWITZERLAND
Lake Constance
Heidelberg
Philipsburg
Würzburg
Bamberg
Nuremburg
Nördlingen
Ulm
Augsburg
MUNICH
Ingolstadt
Ratisbon
Passau
UPPER PALATINATE
BAVARIA
Eger
Prague
Bohemia
Jankow
Budweis
AUSTRIAN DOMINIONS
VIENNA
POLAND
Warsaw
R. Elbe
R. Weser
R. Ems
R. Aller
R. Rhine
R. Meuse
R. Mosel
R. Main
R. Werra
R. Danube
R. Lech
R. Isar
R. Inn
R. Spree
R. Havel
R. Oder
R. Bober
R. Moldau
R. Warthe
R. Netze
R. Vistula
R. Bug
R. Pilicia
R. Bartsch
2 4 6 8 10 12 14 16 18 20 22
54 52 50 48

granted the right of forming alliances with each other or with foreign powers; and all possibility of important action by the imperial Diet was taken away, by a provision that in votes which concerned religion no state of the Empire should be bound, except by its own consent.

FOR FURTHER READING. — Motley's *Dutch Republic* and *United Netherlands;* Häusser's *Reformation;* Johnson's *Europe in the Sixteenth Century* and Wakeman's *Ascendancy of France*, to page 105; Creighton's *Elizabeth;* Green's *English People;* Baird's *Huguenots;* Willert's *Henry of Navarre;* Gardiner's *Thirty Years' War;* Henderson's *Short History of Germany;* Fletcher's *Gustavus Adolphus;* Dodge's *Gustavus Adolphus;* Perkins' *Richelieu;* Putnam's *William the Silent.*

In fiction: Kingsley's *Westward, Ho!* (for England and the Armada); Schiller's *Wallenstein;* Bulwer's *Richelieu.*

EXERCISES. — 1. A catchword review of the Reformation in Germany, through the whole period.   2. Contrast the character of the Reformation in Germany with that of the movement in England.

CHAPTER III.

ENGLAND IN THE SEVENTEENTH CENTURY.

(RISE OF POLITICAL LIBERTY, 1603–1688.)

I. PRELIMINARY: SURVEY OF THE YORKIST AND TUDOR PERIODS, 1485–1603.[1]

233. An Era of Change, 1450–1600. — The century and a half from 1450 to 1600, — the age of the Wars of the Roses and of the Tudors, — had been a period of tremendous changes in English life, intellectual, religious, political, and economic. (1) The Renaissance (originating in Italian influence) had created a new intellectual life (§ 199), with the abounding spontaneous energy and the enthusiastic self-reliance that we associate with the names of Shakspere and Elizabeth and Raleigh. (2) The Reformation (due to German influence, to the general renaissance movement, and to the personal desires of monarchs) had introduced new religious organization and feeling (§§ 218, 223). (3) On the ruins of the two chief political forces of earlier times, — feudalism and the church, — the sovereigns had built up a new political system.[2] (4) Lastly, a transformation took place in the economic organization of society (upon which had rested both the old feudalism and the old church): the rural organization was revolutionized, and

---

[1] It has been convenient to trace some phases of English history in the sixteenth century by themselves in §§ 218, 223; but before taking up the great struggle between Parliament and kings, in the seventeenth century, it is desirable to give fuller attention to the preceding hundred years.

[2] Edward IV and Henry VIII, it has been noted, carried further the work of the Wars of the Roses in crushing the old nobility, and Henry VIII and Elizabeth did away with the independence of the church.

towns grew into new prominence. Thus the last change has to be studied from the two view-points of country and of town (§§ 234, 235).

The first three changes have been treated in some detail in the previous chapters. The fourth is more difficult to grasp. In a sense, it underlies the others. The discontent of the towns brought about the victory of the Yorkists over the feudal party of the Lancastrians in the Wars of the Roses (§ 145). The towns, too, were the strongholds of the Reformation movement against the Catholic rural districts and especially against the Catholic North. And in the towns developed the new intellectual life of the renaissance age.

234. The Economic Change in the Country: Inclosures. — By 1450, after a century of progress, villeinage had disappeared (§§ 141, 142). The small farmer was living in rude abundance; and comfort surrounded even the farm laborer, — with his cow, sheep, or geese, on the common, his four-acre patch of garden about his cabin, and good wages for his labor on the landlord's fields. From about 1425 to about 1500 was a golden age for these lower rural classes.

Sir John Fortescue (§ 144) boasts of their prosperity, as compared with that of the French peasantry: "They drink no water, unless at times by way of penance. They are fed in great abundance with all kinds of flesh and fish. They are clothed throughout in good woolens. . . . Every one, according to his rank, hath all things needful to make life easy and happy."

The large landlords had been relatively less prosperous. Since the rise of their old laborers out of villeinage, their land was no longer a source of wealth. Indeed, they were "land-poor." They paid high wages, while, under the wasteful common-field system, crops were small (§ 36).

But by 1450 a change had begun which was to create a new prosperity for the large holders and cruelly to depress the smaller holders. This change is connected with the process of "inclosures" for sheep-raising. There was a steady demand for wool at good prices, to supply the Flemish markets (§ 162), and enterprising landlords began to raise sheep instead of grain. Large flocks could be cared for by a few hands, so that the high wages mattered less; and profits proved so enticing that soon there was a mad rush into the new industry. But sheep-raising called for large tracts of land. It was possible only for the large landholders; and even these were obliged to hedge in their share of the common "fields." Therefore, as far as possible, they turned out the small tenants, whose holdings interfered with such "inclosures," and often they inclosed also the woodlands and meadows, in disregard of ancient rights of common pasture.

Some small tenants were protected by the courts, on the ground that they had a right to their holdings as long as they paid the customary rents, shown in the copyroll of the manor. This class were known as "copyholders." They ranked next to the freeholders in dignity, and probably exceeded them in number. Below them came various classes of "leaseholders," who could be turned off whenever their leases ran out, and also a class of "tenants at will," who could be evicted at any time. Even the copyholders seem to have found the courts a poor defense against the greed of the wealthy classes, and the freeholders themselves often found it best to sell, however much they wished to keep their holdings.

Sir Thomas More, for a time chief minister of Henry VIII, lamented these conditions bitterly: "A careless and unsatiable cormorant may compass about and inclose many thousand acres within one pale, and the husbandmen be thrust out of their own; or else by fraud, or violent oppression, or by wrongs and injuries, they be so worried that they be compelled to sell. . . . They [the landlords] throw down houses; they pluck down towns [villages], and leave nothing standing but only the church, to be made a sheep-house." [1]

Statesmen bewailed that sheep should take the place of the yeomanry who had won Crécy and Poitiers, and who, Bacon said, were also "the backbone of the revenue"; and from 1488 to 1600 the government made many attempts by laws to check

---

[1] Cf. *Ancient History*, §§ 397, 398. More's *Utopia* may be assigned for a special report. See also page 238, Note 2, for Sir Thomas More.

inclosures.[1] But all such legislation was ineffective. Neither did popular riots and insurrections avail anything.[2] The confiscation of the monastery lands and their transfer into the hands of a new landlord class gave fresh impetus to the inclosure movement; and it went on until the profits of sheep-raising and grain-raising found a level.

This had come to pass by 1600, when grain had risen in value, because of the rapid growth of population in the towns. But meantime multitudes of villages had been swept away and half of all those in England had been injured.[3] Multitudes of the evicted peasantry became "sturdy beggars," or tramps,[4] to terrorize the rural districts; and the laborers who were not evicted found that prices for their food and clothing rose twice as fast as their wages did.

Through these changes, however, the prosperity of the larger landowners was restored, and a new landed gentry arose, to take the lead in society and politics.

---

[1] Special report upon these attempts.

[2] There were a series of these risings in the reigns of Henry VIII and Edward VI. They were usually connected with dissatisfaction at the religious changes made by the government; but it is plain that the fundamental cause was the discontent caused by inclosures. Advanced students may be assigned these risings, or, at least, Kett's rising, for a special report.

[3] This was one reason why so many honest Englishmen were so ready to try their fortunes in colonizing America. John Winthrop, the great Puritan leader, declared that England "grows weary of her inhabitants, so as man who is the most precious of God's creatures, is here more vile and base than the earth we tread upon and of less prize among us than a horse or an ox."

[4] Of these the justices often hung large batches without trial. It is estimated that in the century of Elizabeth and Shakspere seventy thousand "beggars" were executed in fifty years. Cf. Sir Thomas More's piteous picture: "By one means or another, either by hook or by crook, they must needs depart, poor wretched souls — men, women, husbands, wives, fatherless children, widows, woful mothers with young babes. . . . All their household stuff, which is very little worth, though it might well abide the sale, yet being suddenly thrust out, they be constrained to sell it for a thing of nought. And when they have wandered till that be spent, what can they then else do but steal, and then justly, pardy, be hanged, or else go about begging? And yet then also they be cast into prison as vagabonds, because they go about and work not, — whom no man will set to work though they never so willingly proffer themselves thereto."

After 1550, the inclosures were less rapid, and from 1550 to 1640 the movement changed its character. It ceased to be a landlord movement for sheep-farming. It became an arrangement among the small holders whereby, in place of his thirty or so scattered acre strips, each received three or four compact holdings, which he might fence in and *till in his own way.* In the end, this was to lead to improved methods of farming, and, no doubt, it helped at once to develop more individuality and self-reliance than the system of common cultivation could have done, and so to produce the yeomen, who, when imbued with the stern teachings of Calvinism, were to make Cromwell's Ironsides (§ 245).

235. The Economic Change in the Towns. — Meantime, so far as the national welfare was concerned, the sufferings of the agricultural population had been more than offset by the growth of the towns, with a new prosperity resting upon home manufactures and foreign trade. From the time of Edward IV, the kings had made it their especial care to favor the towns and their industries. Skilled workmen, driven from the Netherlands by the Spanish wars and from France by the persecution of the Huguenots, were welcomed gladly and given many favors. Thus manufactures had grown up. In Elizabeth's day, English wool was no longer sold to Flanders. It was worked up at home, the manufacture giving employment to great numbers of workmen;[1] and then the finished product was sold, with other commodities, in foreign markets, by English merchants.[2] These "merchants" had so increased in number and wealth that practically they made a new class in English society. About 1350 a royal inquiry could find a list of only 169 important merchants in England. In 1601 more than twenty times that number were engaged in the Holland trade alone. By purchase of land and by royal gifts from the confiscated church property, the members of this class rose into a

---

[1] The introduction of such new industries finally absorbed the classes evicted from the land by inclosures.

[2] A "merchant" was a trader who sent goods to a foreign country. Companies were formed to trade to Russia, or India, or other distant parts of the world; and sometimes a single merchant owned a considerable fleet of ships for such trade (cf. Shakspere's Antonio, in *The Merchant of Venice*).

new gentry, whose capital and energy helped to restore prosperity to the land.

Two features of the new town life call for attention. (1) The gild system was rapidly breaking down and was being replaced by the "domestic system" of manufactures. The work was carried on, as before, by masters, journeymen, and apprentices; but the gap between masters and journeymen was growing, and in the absence of the strict gild supervision, there was greater freedom as to methods.[1] Indeed the old towns, where the gild regulations to some degree remained in force, began to be replaced as manufacturing centers by new towns without such checks on individual capitalists.

(2) The king's authority was extended. Trade and manufacture, formerly regulated by single towns and their gilds, had now become matters of national concern and were regulated, so far as they were controlled at all, with paternal interest and anxiety by the king or Parliament. Royal proclamations fixed the number of pence for which a fat goose might be sold at Christmas or in midsummer, established a certain standard for foods, and tried to prescribe the best methods of manufacture. It is interesting to see that in general men felt it proper and natural for the government to attend to such matters.

II. RELIGIOUS AND POLITICAL CONDITIONS UNDER THE EARLY STUARTS.

At every moment some one country more than any other represents the future and the welfare of mankind. — EMERSON.

236. The Religious Situation at the Accession of James I. — English politics in the seventeenth century were concerned largely with questions of religion. The Church of England contained a large Puritan element, which for a time seemed about to get control of the organization. This "Low Church" wing did not wish to separate church and state, but only to carry the church farther from the forms of Catholicism and to secure a more serious morality. There was also a Presbyterian element, which wished to change the organization, but which did not count for much in England until the Civil War (§ 245),

---

[1] The change corresponds in some measure to the change in agriculture from common to individual tillage.

though in Scotland it had already won control, under its great preacher, John Knox. Moreover, in Elizabeth's day, there had appeared in England a few small bands of Independents, or "Separatists," so called because they believed that each church should be a *separate* religious community, ruling itself *independently* of the state and of other churches. These Independents were the Puritans of the Puritans. They were the germs of later Congregationalism. Elizabeth persecuted them savagely, and her successor continued that policy. Some of the Independent churches fled to Holland; and one of them, from Scrooby in northern England, after staying several years at Leyden, founded Plymouth in America (1620).

237. The Political Situation at the Accession of James I. — Constitutional liberty in England had fallen low under the Tudors;[1] but, after all, Henry VIII and Elizabeth had ruled absolutely, only because they made use of constitutional forms and because they possessed a shrewd tact which taught them just where to stop. Moreover, toward the close of Elizabeth's long reign, when foreign perils were past, the tone of Parliament began to rise again. Men spoke boldly of the popular checks upon the royal power. Parliament asserted its right to discuss matters of government, and Parliament and the courts forced the great Queen to give up the practice of granting monopolies.[2] It was plain to keen observers that only the reverence for Elizabeth's age and sex, and the gratitude due her for her great services to the kingdom, held off an open clash between the sovereign and Parliament. Upon her death, the clash began, — to last through eighty-five years.

---

[1] No measure proposed by the crown could become law without consent of Parliament, and that body controlled all new grants of money. But the monarch (or his ministers) prepared nearly all measures that came before Parliament; he could veto any act of Parliament; and, after a law had been made, he could virtually nullify it by special proclamations. Moreover, the monarch could, upon occasion, resort to violence against individuals, and so it was extremely hazardous for any one persistently to oppose him. See an excellent statement in Andrews' *England*, 308-310.

[2] Special report upon the dispute over monopolies.

Elizabeth was succeeded by her relative James I (James Stuart), already King of Scotland. James was learned, pedantic, and conceited, — "the wisest fool in Christendom," as Henry IV of France called him. He sincerely believed in the "divine right" of kings: that is, he believed that the king, as God's anointed, was the source of law and could not himself be controlled by law. James and his son not only practised absolutism, but they also preached it on every occasion. They were despots on principle, and cared for the forms, as well as the reality, of absolutism. Naturally, the nation which had been growing restive under the beneficent, elastic tyranny of the great Tudors, soon rose in fierce opposition against the noisy, uncompromising, needless tyranny of the weak Stuarts.

From 1603, when the first James mounted the throne, until 1688, when his grandson, the second James, ignominiously ran away from it, England was constantly engaged in strife between this "divine right" of kings and the right of the people. Through all that seventeenth century, too, this little patch of land was the last remaining battle ground for political liberty. In all other important states, — in Spain, in France, in Austria, in the Scandinavian lands, in the petty principalities of Germany and Italy, — despotism was supreme. In England both sides recognized the fact. Said the second Stuart king, Charles I, in a crisis of his reign, "I am ashamed that my cousins of France and Spain should have completed what I have scarce begun"; and at the same time a patriot exclaimed in fervent exhortation to his party, "England is the last country which retains her ancient liberties; let them not perish now."

238. The Issue defined, and the Parties. — The issue was soon stated. In the first few weeks of his new sovereignty, James gave several practical proofs of his disregard for law and of his arbitrary temper;[1] and then in a famous utterance, on a

---

[1] On his royal entry from Scotland, James ordered a thief to be hung without trial; and when he summoned his first Parliament he ordered that contested elections should be settled, not by Parliament, but by his courts. Liberal Englishmen resented these things fiercely.

solemn occasion, he summed up his theory: "As it is atheism and blasphemy in a creature to dispute what God can do, so it is presumption and high contempt in a subject to question what a king can do." This became the tone of the court party. About this time Dr. Cowell of Cambridge University published a Law Dictionary, *The Interpreter*, in which under the title "King" it was stated, "He is above the law by his absolute power, and though he do admit the estates into counsel, it is only by his benignity." [1]

When Parliament assembled, it took the first chance to answer these new claims. The Speaker of the Commons, replying to the King's opening address, in place of the usual formal expression of grateful thanks to his majesty, reminded James sharply of his limited powers. "New laws," said the Speaker, "cannot be instituted, nor imperfect laws reformed . . . by any other power than this high court of Parliament." Parliament continued in this tone. It gave money grudgingly, and it soon addressed to the King an "Apology," stating the parliamentary doctrine. After declaring that the King must have been misled by misinformed persons, or he could not have held such views of the English government as he had expressed, the statement continues, "that the privileges and liberties of Parliament are their right and inheritance, no less than their lands and goods; that to withhold them is to wrong the whole realm; that in this session the privileges of this house have been more universally impugned than ever before since the beginning of Parliaments."

The struggle so declared, continued for forty years before it became war. This period of constitutional wrangling falls into four broad divisions, — the reign of James I (1603–1625), the first three Parliaments of Charles I (1625–1629), the period of "No Parliament" (1629–1640), and the early period (1640–1642) of the Long Parliament (§§ 239–244).

There were, as yet, no organized political parties. But there was a "court party," devoted to the royal power, consisting of most of the

---

[1] Soon afterward Parliament showed a determination to take stern action against Cowell, and so the copies of the work were called in and destroyed.

nobles and of the "High Church" clergy, and an opposition "country party," consisting of the mass of country gentry, some Puritan nobles, and the Puritan element generally.

239. Constitutional Wrangling during the Reign of James I. — Throughout James' reign Parliaments met but rarely, and would have met still less often, had it not been that the wasteful extravagance of the court kept the King in need of money.[1] Every session of Parliament was marked by some clash between the King and that body. James succeeded in turning the law courts into his tools, by making it plain that he would dismiss every judge who would not act and think as he wished (an interference with the courts wholly new in English history); but Parliament on the whole held its own. It insisted stubbornly on its control of taxation, on freedom of speech, and on its right to impeach the King's ministers. James became exceedingly unpopular toward the close of his reign, because he failed to support his son-in-law, the Elector Palatine in Germany, the Protestant leader in the opening of the Thirty Years' War (§ 230), and because he wished his son Charles to marry a Spanish princess.[2] However, Charles was personally insulted by the Spanish court, and in the last year of James'

---

[1] The economic revolution noted in § 234 had decreased the wealth of the kings (whose property was in land), while the rise in prices and the increasing duties of the government called for a larger expenditure. Thus Elizabeth and James were really poor. This fact is the key to much of the history of the time.

[2] In James' third Parliament (1621), the Commons had begun to express dissatisfaction with the marriage that James had planned. James sharply forbade such discussion. "Let us resort to our prayers," said one of the members, "and then consider this great business." The outcome of the consideration was a resolution, "that the liberties, privileges, and jurisdictions of Parliament are the ancient and undoubted birthright of the subjects of England, and that the arduous and urgent affairs concerning the King, the state, the church, the defense of the realm, the making and maintenance of laws, and the redress of grievances, which happen daily within this realm, are proper subjects for debate in Parliament; and that in the handling and proceeding of those businesses, every member of the Commons . . . has freedom of speech . . . to bring to conclusion the same." James tore out this page of the records and dissolved Parliament.

life, the Prince succeeded in forcing him into war with Spain, to the great joy of the nation.

240. The Early Parliaments of Charles I. — In March, 1625, in the midst of shame and disgrace because of mismanagement of the war, James died. In May, Charles I met his first Parliament. He quarreled with it at once, dissolved it, and turned to an eager prosecution of the war, trusting to win the nation to his side by glorious victory over the hereditary enemy. Ignominious failure, instead, forced him to meet his second Parliament in 1626.

It is now that Sir John Eliot stands forward as a leader of the patriots. Eliot is the "first great commoner." In her earlier struggles with her kings, England had depended upon her nobles for leaders. The Wars of the Roses had annihilated the old nobility, and the new nobles could never assume the old leadership. The gentry, however, had been rising in importance, and the Tudor monarchs had begun to use them as ministers of the crown. Now one of this class was to lead the opposition to the crown. Eliot was a Cornish gentleman, thirty-three years of age, courtly in manner, ardent and poetic in temper. His mind was enriched by all the culture of the time, and afterward in weary years of imprisonment he could find consolation in his Tacitus, Livy, Epictetus, and Seneca. He was an athlete and a courtier, and at the same time a deeply religious Puritan; but his mind was never tinged with the somber feeling of the later Puritanism.[1]

Eliot stood for the control of the King's ministers by Parliament. Everything else, he saw, was likely to prove worthless, if the executive could not be held responsible. The king's person could not be so held, except by revolution and deposition; but his ministers might be impeached and punished; and, under fear of this, they might be held in control. In

---

[1] This passage, and much of the following account of Eliot's work, is condensed from Green's treatment of Eliot in his *History of the English People*. Students who can read further will find Forster's *Life of Eliot* an intensely interesting book.

pursuance of this principle, Eliot persuaded the Commons to impeach the Duke of Buckingham, the King's favorite and the instrument of much past tyranny. Charles stopped the proceedings by casting Eliot into prison and dissolving Parliament.

241. Charles' Attempts at Benevolences and Forced Loans. — The King fell back upon "benevolences," or the begging of "free gifts," to raise a revenue. These benevolences had been asked occasionally from individual men of wealth ever since the Wars of the Roses, but now they were asked of all tax payers, through the county courts. County after county refused to give a penny, often with cheers for Parliament. Some sheriffs refused to ask for the "free gift." The County of Cornwall, Sir John Eliot's county, answered "that if they had but two kine, they would sell one to supply his majesty, — *in a parliamentary way.*" Charles passed to a "forced loan," — virtually a tax levied by the usual tax machinery, — a tax thinly disguised by the false promise of repayment. Force and persuasion were both used. Some of the pulpits, manned now by the anti-Puritan party, rang with the cry of "passive obedience" and the doctrine that to resist the king was eternal damnation. As a patriot of the time put it, this section of the clergy "improved the highwayman's formula into Your money or your life eternal." More immediate penalties, however, were resorted to. Poor freeholders who refused to pay were "pressed" into the navy, or a turbulent soldiery was quartered in their defenseless homes; and two hundred English gentlemen were confined in disgraceful prisons, to subdue their obstinacy. Among these gentlemen was a young squire who had based his refusal upon a clause in Magna Carta and who was rewarded with so close an imprisonment, that, his kinsman tells us, "he never did look the same man after." This was *John Hampden's* introduction into the company of patriots. Equal heroism was shown by hundreds of poorer unknown men. George Radcliffe wrote from his prison to his "right dear and loving wife," who was eager to have him submit in time to have Christmas with her, "Shall it be thought I prejudice the public cause by beginning to conform, which none yet hath done of all that have been committed, save only two poor men, a butcher and another, and they hooted at like owls among their neighbors?"

Thus the forced loan raised little revenue; and with an armament poorly fitted out, Buckingham sailed against France, with which England was now at war. For the third time in four years an English army was wasted to no purpose; and, sunk in debt and shame, Charles met his third Parliament in 1628.

242. The "Petition of Right": Eliot's Final Struggle. — The imprisoned country gentlemen were released before the elections, and some seventy of them (all who appeared as candidates) sat in the new Parliament, in spite of the royal efforts to prevent their election.

Before Parliament met, a caucus of the country leaders decided, against Eliot's desire, not to press the action against Buckingham, but to try to obtain some guarantee for their personal liberties, which had just been so seriously threatened. For two months the Commons debated the recent infringements of English liberties and some way to provide security. The King offered to give his word that such things should not occur again, but was told that his oath had already been given at his coronation. Finally the house passed the *Petition of Right*, a document that ranks almost with Magna Carta in the history of English liberty. This great law first recited the ancient English statutes, from Magna Carta down, against arbitrary imprisonment, arbitrary taxation, quartering of soldiery upon the people in time of peace, and against forced loans and benevolences; then it named the frequent violation of right in these respects in recent years; and finally it declared all such infringements illegal. The Lords tried to save the King's dignity by adding an evasive clause to the effect that it was not intended to interfere with "that sovereign power wherewith your majesty is entrusted." But the Commons rejected the amendment after a striking debate. "Sovereign power," said one, "would mean power above condition;

they could not leave the King that, for he had never had it."[1] "The King's person I will call sovereign," said another, "but not his power"; and a third added, "Magna Carta is such a fellow that he will have no sovereign." Finally, the Lords, too, passed the Petition, and Charles, after evasive delays, felt compelled to sign it.

In form, the document was a petition: in fact, when passed and assented to by the King, it became a revision of the constitution down to date, so far as the personal rights of Englishmen were concerned.[2] Almost at once, however, in recess of Parliament, Charles broke the provisions of the Petition;[3] and he also made it clear that through his appointees, the bishops, he intended to introduce such changes as he wished into the church, in favor of the "High Church" party. Parliament reassembled in bitter humor. Heedless of the King's pleading for money, it affirmed its own control over religion to be supreme in England,[4] and then turned to punish the officers who had acted as the King's agents in the recent infringements of the Petition of Right. Proceedings were stopped by the Speaker's announcing that he had the King's command to adjourn the House. Men knew that it would not be permitted to meet again, and there followed a striking scene. The Speaker was thrust back into his chair and held there by two of the patriots; the doors were locked against the King's messenger; and Eliot in a ringing speech moved a series of resolutions, which were to form the platform of the liberal party in the dark years to come. Tumult gathered. Royalist members

---

[1] Mr. Gardiner questions the correctness of this reading; but it is at least in perfect harmony with the spirit of the rest of the debate.

[2] For the document and critical comments, see Hill's *Liberty Documents*.

[3] Especially by levying customs at the ports, by royal order merely.

[4] This was the occasion for Eliot's daring speech: "There is a custom in the Eastern churches of standing at the repetition of the creed, to testify their purpose to maintain it, — not only with the body upright, but with the sword drawn. *Give me leave to call that custom very commendable.*" And the Commons voted Eliot's resolution, — that they would resist all innovation in religion, if need be, with their lives, — by a standing vote, leaning upon their loosened swords.

cried, Traitor! Traitor! Swords were drawn. The usher pounded at the door with the royal message of dissolution. But the bulk of the members sternly voted the resolutions, declaring traitors to England any one who should bring in innovations in religion without the consent of Parliament, any minister who should advise the illegal levy of taxes, any officer who should aid in their collection, and every citizen who should voluntarily pay them. And in the moment's hush, when the great deed was done, Eliot's voice was heard once more, and for the last time, in that hall: "For myself, I further protest, as I am a gentleman, if my fortune be ever again to meet in this honorable assembly, where I now leave off, I will begin again." Then the doors swung open, and the angry crowd surged out. Eliot passed to the Tower, to die there a prisoner four years later. But Eliot's friends remembered his words: when another Parliament did meet, where he had left off, they began again.

Eliot could have had his liberty if he had bent to acknowledge himself wrong. His wife died; friends fell away; consumption attacked him, and his enemies knew that he must yield or die. His son petitioned for his release, on the ground that doctors had certified that without it he could not live. The King refused. "Though Sir John be brought low in body, yet is he as high and lofty in mind as ever." A month later, Eliot was dead. His son presented another petition, that he might have his father's body for burial. The request was refused, and there was inscribed on the paper, — a mean act of a mean king, — "Let Sir John's body be buried in the church of that parish where he died." So Eliot's body rests in the Tower, and the spot is not marked.

243. Eleven Years of "No Parliament." — On the dissolution of the third Parliament of Charles, England entered a gloomy period. The King adopted a policy of ruling by royal edicts, and no Parliament met for eleven years, 1629–1640. During this period, in many ways, the government sought the welfare of the nation, and in particular it gave attention to the needs of the poor; but its methods were thoroughly despotic and bad.

To avoid the necessity of calling Parliaments, Charles practised rigid economy. Additional financial resources were invented, and an ancient demand upon seacoast counties to furnish ships for the national navy in time of invasion, was stretched into a precedent for a "ship-money tax" for all England in time of peace. *John Hampden* refused to pay the twenty shillings assessed upon his lands, and the famous "ship-money case" went to the courts (1637). The slavish judges decided for the King, as had been expected, and the King's friends were jubilant, seeing in the new tax "an everlasting supply on all occasions"; but Hampden's purpose was achieved. He had won a moral victory. The twelve-day argument of the lawyers attracted wide attention, and the court in its decision was compelled to state the theory of despotism in its naked hideousness, declaring that there was no power to check the king's authority over his subjects, — their persons or their money, — " For," said the Chief Justice, "*no act of Parliament makes any difference.*" The theory of the Stuart rule was made clear to all men. It remained to see how long England would endure it.

The chief servants of the crown during this period were *Archbishop Laud* and *Thomas Wentworth*. Wentworth had been a member of the country group and had been one of the leaders in securing the Petition of Right; but soon afterward he passed over to the side of the King and later he was rewarded by the earldom of Strafford. His old associates regarded him as an apostate from the cause of liberty; but it is possible that he sincerely expected to secure the good of England through upholding the royal power. Certainly he was a political genius. He reduced turbulent Ireland to order, and ruled there with an iron hand, — drilling an army against the day of reckoning he foresaw. Laud was an extreme High Churchman and a conscientious bigot. He reformed the discipline of the church and ennobled the ritual; but he persecuted[1] the Puritan clergy cruelly, with imprisonment and even with

---

[1] As a result of this and of the political discouragement, that sect founded the colony of Massachusetts Bay. Practically all the immigration this colony received came in the ten years, 1630–1640, while Charles ruled without Parliament.

mutilation, and in 1638 he tried to force Episcopacy upon Presbyterian Scotland.[1] The Scots rose, signed a "covenant" to defend their religion, and marched to the border. Charles' system of absolutism fell at a breath, like a house of cards. Wentworth's Irish troops proved unreliable. England would give no help without a Parliament. Charles summoned a Parliament, and quarreled with it. The Scots advanced into England, and the King called a new Parliament (November, 1640), to be known in history as the *Long Parliament.*

244. The Long Parliament, to the Civil War. — The great leaders of the Long Parliament were the commoners *Pym, Hampden, Sir Harry Vane,*[2] *St. John, Holles,* and, somewhat later, *Cromwell.* Pym succeeded to the place of Eliot, and at an early date indicated that the Commons were the real rulers of England. When the Lords showed inclination to delay reform, he brought them to time by his veiled threat: he "should be sorry," he said, "if the House of Commons had to save England *alone.*"

The Scots remained encamped in England, — virtually allies of the Parliament. Thus the King had no resource but to assent to Parliament's bills. Parliament secured itself by a law that it could be dissolved only by its own vote, and then took up its serious program. Its purpose was first to punish past tyranny, and secondly to prevent its recurrence. For the first purpose, it began where Eliot had left off, and sternly put into action the principles of his last resolutions. Laud, who had "brought in innovations in religion," and Wentworth, who had advised and helped carry out the King's policy, were condemned to death as traitors; the lawyers who had advised ship-money and the judges who had declared it legal were cast into prison or driven into banishment; and forty committees were

---

[1] Scotland had been joined to England when her King James had become King of England, but each country had its own Parliament, laws, and church: the union was "personal," and consisted in the fact that the two countries had the same king. This remained the theory until 1707 (§ 281 *a*).

[2] Vane had spent some time in Massachusetts and had been governor there.

appointed, one for each county, to secure the punishment of the lesser officers concerned in the illegal acts of the government. The martyrs whom the tyranny of Charles and Laud had imprisoned were freed from their dungeons and welcomed to London by rejoicing multitudes, who strewed flowers beneath the feet of their advancing horses. Parliament's second purpose was to some degree attained by abolishing the courts of the *Star Chamber* and the *High Commission*, extraordinary judicial bodies, through which Charles and Laud had worked.[1]

These measures filled the first year,[2] and so far Parliament had been almost a unit. But now a split began. A Presbyterian and an Independent party (the "Root and Branch" men, with Vane and Cromwell for leaders) began to attack Episcopacy itself; and other radical leaders, like Pym and Hampden, felt it necessary to secure further political safeguards against the King, since they could not trust his promises. On the other hand, a moderate party who dreaded anarchy, and a church party who feared for Episcopacy, drew toward the King. These elements were led by Falkland and Hyde, two of the noblest of English patriots. Meantime Charles was suspected, justly, of plotting with the Irish and the army; and terrible news of a massacre of English Puritans in Ireland, by a native rising, brought about decisive action in Parliament. Pym introduced a *Grand Remonstrance*, a series of resolutions appealing to the country for further support against the King and the High Church party, and proposing two definite measures: (1) a synod of clergy to reform the church, and (2) parliamentary approval of the King's choice of ministers. After an all-day and almost all-night bitter debate, the Commons adopted the Remonstrance (November 22, 1641) by the narrow majority of eleven votes, amid a scene of wild confusion.

---

[1] These peculiar courts dated from Tudor times, and had been designed, the first to control the great nobles, and the second to carry through the separation from Rome; but Charles had used them for general political tyranny against the nation. They had no juries, and the Star Chamber corresponded in many ways to the French administrative courts (§ 448).

[2] The trial of Laud came later; but he was already a prisoner.

Then the moderate party passed over unreservedly to the King's side, and a little later Charles tried to reverse the small majority against him in the House, and to intimidate the Radicals, by seizing five radical leaders on a charge of treason.[1] The attempt failed and the opposition was tremendously strengthened. London rose in arms to protect Parliament. Parliament demanded control of the militia and of the education of the royal princes. Charles withdrew from the city and raised the standard of civil war (1642).

III. THE GREAT REBELLION AND THE COMMONWEALTH.

245. The Civil War. — Many who had gone with Parliament in all its earlier reform, now chose the King's side rather than rebellion and the danger of anarchy. The majority of the gentry sided with the King, while in general the trading and manufacturing classes and the yeomanry fought for Parliament. At the same time it must be remembered that the struggle was a true "civil war," dividing families and old friends.[2]

At first Charles was successful. The shop-boys of the city trainbands could not stand before the chivalry of the "Cavaliers,"[3] and the Puritan nobles, who led the parliamentary armies, were afraid to conquer their king too completely. Both conditions were soon changed. *Cromwell*, a colonel in the parliamentary army, had raised a troop known as *Ironsides*. He had seen that the only force Parliament could oppose to the traditional bravery of the English gentleman was the religious enthusiasm of the extreme Puritans. Accordingly, he had drawn his recruits from the Independents of the east of

---

[1] Special report: the story of the attempt.

[2] An instructive contrast may be drawn between the civilized nature of this war and the character of the Thirty Years' War in Germany, which was going on at the same time. In England, non-combatants were rarely molested, and as a rule property rights were respected.

[3] The King's party took the name, "Cavaliers," from the court nobles; while the Parliamentarians were called "Round Heads," in derision, from the cropped hair of the London 'prentice lads. The portrait of Cromwell (page 275) shows, however, that Puritan gentlemen did not crop their hair.

England, — mostly yeomen farmers. They were men of godly lives, free from all the usual license of a camp. They prayed before battle, and then charged, with the old Hebrew battle psalms upon their lips. Mainly by these troops the great battle of *Marston Moor* was won. Then Cromwell was put in chief command, and he reorganized the whole army upon this "*New Model.*" Soon after, the victory of *Naseby* virtually closed the war (1645).

Says John Fiske: "If we consider merely its territorial area or the number of men slain, the war of the English Parliament against Charles I seems a trivial affair, contrasted with the gigantic but comparatively insignificant work of barbarians like Genghis Khan or Tamerlane; but if we consider the moral and political issues involved, and the influence of the struggle on the future welfare of mankind, we soon come to see that there never was a conflict of more world-wide significance than that from which Oliver Cromwell came out victorious. . . . To speak of Naseby and Marston Moor as merely English victories, would be as absurd as to restrict the significance of Gettysburg to the state of Pennsylvania. If ever there were men who laid down their lives in the cause of all mankind, it was those grim old Ironsides, whose watchwords were texts from Holy Writ, and whose battle-cries were hymns of praise."

CHARLES I. — After a famous painting by Van Dyck.

246. Parliament and the Army: Pride's Purge. — When the war began, the Episcopalian party in Parliament had withdrawn to join the King, and the Presbyterians were left in control. Then, to buy the aid of the Scots, Parliament made the English church Presbyterian, and it wished to enforce unity of belief and worship along Presbyterian lines. Dissensions at once broke out, upon this issue, between Parliament and the Independents of the army. Charles, now a prisoner, sought to play off each party against the other, — intending, as he wrote to his wife, to keep promises to neither.[1] The result was a series of risings, Presbyterian and Royalist, and a "Second Civil War." The New Model army quickly stamped out the risings, and *purged Parliament by military force*,[2] leaving only a "Rump" of Independents (December, 1648).

247. England a Republic. — The remnant of the Commons abolished monarchy and the House of Lords, and set up a Republic under the name of *the Commonwealth* (1649). "The people," they declared, in a famous statement of principle, "are, under God, the original of all just power; and the Commons of England in Parliament assembled, being chosen by the people, have the supreme power in this nation."

Under the "Commonwealth," the Long Parliament continued to form the government, without reëlection. Early in the year it had brought the deposed King to trial for treason, and Charles had been executed January 30, dying with better grace than he had lived. The Scots, unprepared for this extreme action and angered at the overthrow of Presbyterianism, crowned the son of the dead king as Charles II, and invaded England to place him on the throne. Cromwell crushed them at *Worcester*, and the young "King of the Scots" escaped to the continent.

248. The Protectorate. — Cromwell was now anxious for a new Parliament and a settlement of the constitution. The Rump refused to dissolve, and finally Cromwell dispersed it with his troopers (1653). He then made some further sincere

---

[1] "Be quite easy," Charles wrote, with shameless and characteristic duplicity, "as to the concessions I may grant. When the time comes I shall know very well how to treat these rogues, and, instead of a silken garter, I will fit them with a hempen halter."

[2] This military expulsion of the Presbyterian majority from Parliament is known as *Pride's Purge*, from the name of the officer who carried out the order. Vane was the leader of Parliament after this event. Pym and Hampden were already dead.

efforts to secure a new constitution through a national convention; but the body chosen proved unwise and dilatory, and at last Cromwell and the army officers impatiently took the construction of the machinery of government into their own hands. The real difficulty was that the Independents represented only a small minority of the nation. They were unwilling to surrender the results of their victory in war, and so they maintained themselves in despotic power by the discipline of the New Model. Cromwell assumed the title of *Lord Protector* (1654), and continued to rule as virtual dictator. In practice, his authority exceeded that of any recent sovereign. His rule was stained by cruelties in Ireland (as were also his military campaigns in that island),[1] but it was in other respects wise and firm. He made England once more a Great Power, peaceful at home and respected abroad.

CROMWELL. — After an engraving from the portrait painted by Sir Peter Lely.

At the best, however, his rule was the rule of the sword, not that of law. The great experiment of a Republic[2] had failed miserably in the hands of its friends; and on Cromwell's death, the nation, with wild rejoicings (1660), welcomed back Charles II.

---

[1] Special reports: Cromwell in Ireland; the "Instrument of Government," or the constitution of the protectorate.

[2] There were several interesting constitutional experiments and proposals by the Republican party during this period, which might be assigned to advanced students for special reports. See especially the "Agreement of the People," of 1647. Cf. Hill, *Liberty Documents*, 78–113.

IV. THE RESTORATION AND THE REVOLUTION.

249. The Later Stuarts. — With the restoration of the Stuarts, the great age of Puritanism was over. At the court and among the young cavaliers, the stern and somber morality of the Independents gave way to unbridled excesses and shameful licentiousness, with the King to set the fashion. Literature became indescribably indecent and corrupt.[1] To a great degree this became the tone of English society for many years, although of course the middle classes continued to include large numbers of God-fearing homes. The established church became again Episcopalian; and dissenters — Protestant and Catholic — were cruelly persecuted. The *Cavalier Parliament*, chosen in the fervor of the welcome to the returned monarch, was enthusiastic for church and king, and Charles shrewdly kept this assembly through most of his reign (until 1679). Still, the great constitutional principles for which the Puritans had contended were victorious and were adopted by their old enemies. Even the Cavalier Parliament insisted strenuously on Parliament's sole right to impose taxes, to regulate the church, and to control foreign policy; and Charles' second Parliament secured Englishmen against arbitrary imprisonment, by the *Habeas Corpus Act*.[2]

Charles said lightly that he had no mind to go on his travels again, and at any cost he avoided a clash with Parliament. He was slowly building up a standing army, however, and he sold himself to Louis XIV, King of France, in return for subsidies.

---

[1] This statement applies to the court literature of the Restoration, — a considerable body of English drama. However, it should be noted that defeated Puritanism uttered itself nobly in just this age of political overthrow. *Milton*, the great pamphleteer of the Commonwealth, who for many years had abandoned poetry for political writings, now, as a blind and disappointed old man, gave the world his famous work, *Paradise Lost;* and *John Bunyan*, a dissenting preacher, lying in jail under the persecuting statutes of the Cavalier Parliament, composed his *Pilgrim's Progress*.

[2] The principle of this Act is older than Magna Carta, but the Act of Charles' time first provided adequate machinery, much as we have it to-day, to enforce the principle.

There is reason to think that beneath his merry, careless exterior, Charles nursed plans of absolutism more dangerous than his father's; but, if so, his death came in 1685, before he was ready to act.

His brother *James II* was a thorough despot, and less pliable. James was a Catholic, and, in the interest of his oppressed co-religionists, he interfered with the laws and the courts in high-handed fashion, while he rapidly increased the standing army. This conduct created a wide-spread belief that he intended to make the English church Catholic, and so it brought on *"the Glorious Revolution" of 1688*. James' opponents invited over *William of Orange*, the Stadtholder of Holland, husband of James' daughter Mary. When William landed with a small army, James found himself utterly deserted, even by his troops, and he fled to France.

250. The "Glorious Revolution." — The story of the Revolution is not a noble one. Selfishness, duplicity, and treachery mark every step; and, except William of Orange, all the chief actors on both sides fail of our sympathy. There is no longer a patriot Eliot or Pym or Hampden, or a royalist Hyde or Falkland. As Macaulay says, it was "an age of great measures and little men"; and the term "glorious," which English historians have applied to the Revolution, must be taken to belong to results rather than to methods.

Those results were of mighty import. A Convention-Parliament declared the throne vacant, drew up the great Declaration of Rights, the "third great document in the Bible of English Liberties,"[1] and elected William and Mary joint sovereigns, on condition of their assenting to the Declaration. Thus the supremacy of Parliament over the king was once more firmly established. The new sovereigns, like the old Lancastrians, had only a parliamentary title to the throne.[2]

---

[1] The next regular Parliament turned this document into the "Bill of Rights." Cf. Hill's *Liberty Documents*.

[2] Special report: the story of the struggle between England and France, 1690 to 1695, especially the "Battle of La Hogue."

V. CONSTITUTIONAL GAINS.

251. Parliamentary Control of Purse and Sword: Annual Meetings. — William III ranks among England's greatest kings; but he was unpopular, because a foreigner, and his reign was spent in wars against the threatening power of Louis XIV of France, who undertook to restore James. England entered upon a century in which the chief interest was foreign expansion (§ 283). During the first few years, however, some striking progress was made in the machinery of free government.

The judges were made independent of royal removal, and a *triennial bill* provided for a renewal of Parliament by fresh election once in three years.[1] Parliament hit also upon a simple device to prevent the king's abusing his power of dissolving the assembly: it resolved to pass *revenue bills,* no longer for the life of the sovereign, but only for one year, and to defer their passage until other business had been attended to. In like manner, *the Mutiny Act,* giving officers of the army authority over their troops, was passed only for a year. That is, *power of purse and sword was delegated only for a year at a time.* Thus it became absolutely necessary for the government to assemble Parliament each year, and thenceforward Parliament has virtually fixed its own adjournments. So simply and indirectly was solved the constitutional puzzle of four centuries.

252. Ministerial Government. — Almost equally simple, though not so quickly perceived, was the method of solving the remaining political problem of parliamentary government, — how to control effectively the appointment of the king's ministers. Parliament could remove and punish ministers, as it had done at intervals since the time of the Edwards, and recently in the case of Strafford and Laud; but such action could be secured only against notorious offenders, and it amounted almost to a revolution in itself. Some machinery was wanted, by which ministers acceptable to Parliament could be secured peaceably.

---

[1] In 1716 this was changed to the present seven years' term.

The desired result was accomplished *indirectly*, and the first step was made in the reign of William III. Political parties — Whigs and Tories — had appeared in England in the latter part of the reign of Charles II.[1] Since that time, they have never ceased to be an important element in the government, although they were not for a long time to acquire the importance that political parties now have. There was no exact statement of principles, but the Whigs wished to limit the royal authority on every occasion, while the Tories preferred to sustain it and wished to prevent all further liberalizing of the constitution. At first William had tried to balance the two parties by keeping leaders from each among his ministers. But Parliament showed great jealousy of all the measures of the government, and there was danger of a deadlock. Then a shrewd political schemer suggested to the King that he appoint all his ministers from the Whigs, who made the majority in the Commons: such men would have the confidence of the House, and that body would have to support some positive measures, instead of blocking all proposals. William showed his political capacity by accepting this suggestion; and a little later, when the Tories secured a majority in the House, he carried out the principle by replacing his ministers with Tories. In the next century, this *government by the ministry* became an established part of the English constitution.

The ministers, at first, were not a compact " ministry " controlled by one leader, as at present, nor were they then ministers of the Commons, but really " ministers of the king," as they are still in name. The king

---

[1] The Radicals had introduced a bill to exclude from the throne the Duke of York, the King's brother and heir. The supporters of the bill were known as Exclusionists, and great petitions were sent up from the country to support their program. The Catholics and the conservative political factions sent up counter-petitions expressing horror at such a proposal. Thus the friends and opponents of the measure became known as Petitioners and Abhorrers. The first were called Whigs (Whey-eaters) by their enemies, after a term applied to the extreme Scotch Calvinists ; and the second party were called Tories (bog-trotters), after the Irish rebels who supported the Catholic and royal policy. The division was really between the supporters of royal and the supporters of parliamentary sovereignty.

had great influence in determining the majority in the Commons, both in the elections, and afterward by buying support with his favor and with appointments and money ; and oftentimes his ministry created a majority in the Commons instead of the elected majority creating the ministry. This remained true until the nineteenth century. None the less, the change just outlined was momentous, even at the time ; and in the middle of the next century, under the stupid and indifferent Georges I and II, the Commons really ruled England through the great minister *Robert Walpole*. Thus a system devised to enable the king more smoothly to rule the Commons, became the means whereby the Commons rule the king.

253. Act of Settlement: Royal Title dependent upon Parliament. — On the death of William without an heir (Mary died some years before), the crown passed to Anne, Mary's younger sister, in accordance with a previous Act of Parliament. This "Act of Settlement" further provided that if Anne died without offspring, the throne should pass to the German house of Brunswick, the nearest Protestant heirs. The Act passed over the son of James II, and expressly excluded Catholics from the throne. In pursuance of the Act of Settlement, on Anne's death, George I became king, and his successors have followed in accordance with the same law. The title of the present king is based strictly on Act of Parliament.

254. Limitations upon Progress. — Thus the seventeenth century seemed to have made England a free country. The victory was not complete, however. Parliament was supreme over the king; but Parliament itself was largely the possession of the aristocracy. Owing to changes in wealth, this became even more marked in the next century. The real government of England became a landed oligarchy, and it took the great parliamentary reform of the nineteenth century to establish popular control (§§ 531-537).

For Further Reading. — For general works covering this period, see footnote 1 on page 136. Gardiner's *First Two Stuarts* and his *Cromwell* are brief works by the greatest authority on the period. Firth's *Cromwell* is an admirable work by a scholar whose name ranks only second to that of Gardiner. Morley's *Cromwell* and Hale's *Fall of the Stuarts, 1678-1697*, are very good treatments of the later period. Jenks' *Constitutional Experiments of the Commonwealth* and Borgeaud's *Rise of Democracy* are readable and suggestive. There is good fiction for the seventeenth century, especially George MacDonald's *St. George and St. Michael*, Blackmore's *Lorna Doone*, and Scott's *Woodstock*.

CHAPTER IV.

FROM THE PEACE OF WESTPHALIA TO THE FRENCH REVOLUTION.[1]

I. GENERAL CHARACTERISTICS.

255. Wars to maintain the Balance of Power in Europe, and to secure Colonial Empire. — The century of wars about religion was closed by the Peace of Westphalia. There followed a century of selfish and dynastic wars. The last period of the Thirty Years' War had revealed new principles of action. Catholic France aided Protestant North Germany, in order to break the power of the Hapsburgs, which had so long ringed her about. The Peace of Westphalia removed Spain from the leadership of Europe and put France in that place. It also introduced a new period of international politics. The chief object of most statesmen, through the next age, was to keep any one country from becoming too strong for the safety of its neighbors. This was called maintaining the Balance of Power. For many years France was the country that threatened that balance, and so league after league of other countries was organized against her. International morality was low and selfish, however, and commonly the nations were willing to let a strong Power rob a weaker neighbor, if they could find "compensation," and so maintain the "balance," by themselves robbing some other weak state. The theory of the balance of power came to mean not that an unscrupulous monarch should be prevented from plundering a defenseless one, but that he must be compelled to share his booty with the other strong ones.

Before 1700 the area and the objects of strife widened beyond Europe, and the various wars merged into a titanic struggle between France and England for world-empire, — with the result, toward the close of the period, of making England the sole great colonial power and of establishing the new American Republic.

---

[1] This century and a half has strongly marked characteristics (§§ 255-257). The period is a difficult one, however, for young students, and perhaps this chapter should be read and discussed with open books, without formal recitations. At this point, the student should reread carefully §§ 4 and 5.

256. Absolutism within; Dynastic Interests abroad. — Louis XIV of France (§ 264) is reported by legend to have once said, "I am the state." In his day the words might have been used truthfully by almost any monarch outside England. A few great rulers dominated the period. Indeed, the stage is almost filled by three monarchs, — Louis XIV of France (1643-1715), Peter the Great of Russia (1689-1725), and Frederick the Great of Prussia (1740-1786). The main influence of Peter was spent directly upon his own country, but Louis and Frederick belonged to all Europe, and the period divides itself into the Age of Louis XIV and the Age of Frederick II.

Absurd as it seems to us, the personal characteristics of monarchs became, even more than before, mighty factors in the histories of whole peoples. The wars of this age were *dynastic*, or family, wars; and the personal likings or hatreds of the princes, as well as their family interests, sometimes interfered curiously with devotion to the theory of a balance of power.

257. Readjustment of the Map of Northern and Eastern Europe. — About 1700 the map of northern Europe underwent a striking transformation. For a long time the two most powerful states there had been Sweden and Poland. Sweden had saved Protestantism in North Germany in the Thirty Years' War; and, a generation later, *John Sobieski*, King of Poland, saved South Germany from the Turks by driving back the Mohammedan army from Vienna (1683). Notwithstanding such mighty services, it was still true that neither of these two Powers had ordinarily played a very important part in European affairs. And now Sweden was to shrink up, and Poland was to disappear, before two new Powers, Russia and Prussia, which ever since have been leading factors upon the European stage.

II. THE AGE OF LOUIS XIV — FRENCH LEADERSHIP.

258. Mazarin and the Fronde. Early Years of Louis XIV. — During the long minority of Louis XIV, affairs were managed by *Cardinal Mazarin*, who continued the policy of Richelieu (§ 229). The most important event of the period was the crushing of the *Fronde*, the last rising of the French nobles against the royal power (cf. § 152).

Louis himself assumed control in 1661. At first it seemed as though he would continue the wise policy of Henry IV. With his great minister *Colbert*, he introduced order and economy into the finances, encouraged new manufactures, and, with ardent zeal, watched over the welfare of the New France growing up in America (§ 282). But in 1667 Louis turned to a career of foreign aggression, and a series of wars filled the remaining forty years of his life.

259. First Period of Wars, 1667-1678. — Louis had married the daughter of Philip IV of Spain, but had expressly renounced any future claim upon the Spanish throne. On Philip's death, however, Louis claimed the Spanish Netherlands for his wife, and marched into the Provinces with overwhelming force. The neighboring Dutch Republic saw its own danger, and resisted his progress. Through its efforts the *Triple Alliance* against Louis was formed between Holland, Sweden, and England. Louis yielded, keeping only a line of Netherland fortresses; but he yielded in order better to prepare to crush presumptuous Holland. Sweden and England he detached from the Alliance. Then he turned to attack the little Dutch Republic. His rapid successes alarmed the Dutch, and, by an internal revolution, they called to power *William of Orange*,[1] the great-grandson of William the Silent. William was not a supreme genius like that ancestor, but he was able, faithful, heroic, and more than any other man he foiled the French designs through the years to come. When it was urged upon him that conflict with France was hopeless, and that he would only see his country lost, he replied quietly, "There is one way never to see it lost, — and that is to die on the last dyke." With such grim determination, he finally cut the dykes, and the waves of the North Sea drove out the French army. Meantime he toiled ceaselessly in building up against France the *Grand Alliance*, comprising Spain, Austria, and Brandenburg. Louis was forced to accept peace, keeping, however, Franche Comté (which had been a detached Spanish province) and a strip more of the Spanish Netherlands.

260. "Reunions." Revocation of the Edict of Nantes. — These wars had lasted twelve years. During the next ten years of peace two significant movements occurred.

a. The "Reunions." A French court of inquiry, set up by Louis, declared that about a hundred little bits of territory along the Rhine frontier belonged to France, because of some previous connection with the realms recently acquired; and on this flimsy pretext Louis seized them, one after another.

---

[1] Ten years after this war, he became William III of England (§ 250).

The most important territory so gained was the great city of *Strasburg.*

b. Revocation of the Edict of Nantes. Louis was an ardent Catholic and hated heresy. In 1685 he decided to revoke the Edict of Nantes and to compel the Huguenots to accept Catholicism. Bodies of dragoons were quartered in the Huguenot districts, and terrible persecutions followed. Protestantism did disappear from French soil; but, despite the prohibition against emigration, the Protestants themselves by tens of thousands (perhaps three hundred thousand in all) escaped to England, Prussia, Holland, and America.

The effect upon France corresponded in a measure to the effect upon Spain from the expulsion of the Moriscoes. The Huguenots had been the most enterprising merchants and the most skillful artisans of France, and their flight dealt a crushing blow to the prosperity of that country, — coming, too, as it did, just when France was exhausted by wars. The remainder of Louis' reign was to be a period of failure and humiliation, and of preparation for the French Revolution a century later.

261. Second Series of Wars, 1689-1713. — The accession of Louis' enemy, William of Orange, to the throne of England (§ 250) was the signal for a new war. This time Louis meant to secure the Palatinate, a German province on the Rhine. As before, the French armies were victorious in the field; but, as before too, William checked Louis by a general European alliance. *France gained no territory*, and indeed surrendered some of the "reunions" of the preceding period. This war is known in American history as "King William's War." It was the beginning of a new Hundred Years' War (1689-1815) between France and England, for world-empire, — though it cannot be said that either country was conscious at first of the importance of the struggle outside Europe.

Louis hoped to make good his disappointment by arranging a partition of Spain. Charles II, the last Spanish Hapsburg, was dying. The crown would go naturally either to the Austrian Hapsburgs or to the children of Louis XIV, who were nephews of Charles. This time Louis seemed to prefer negotiation to war, and he arranged a partition treaty with William of Orange, in accordance with which the Spanish realms were to be divided among the Powers of Europe. But the proud Spanish people,

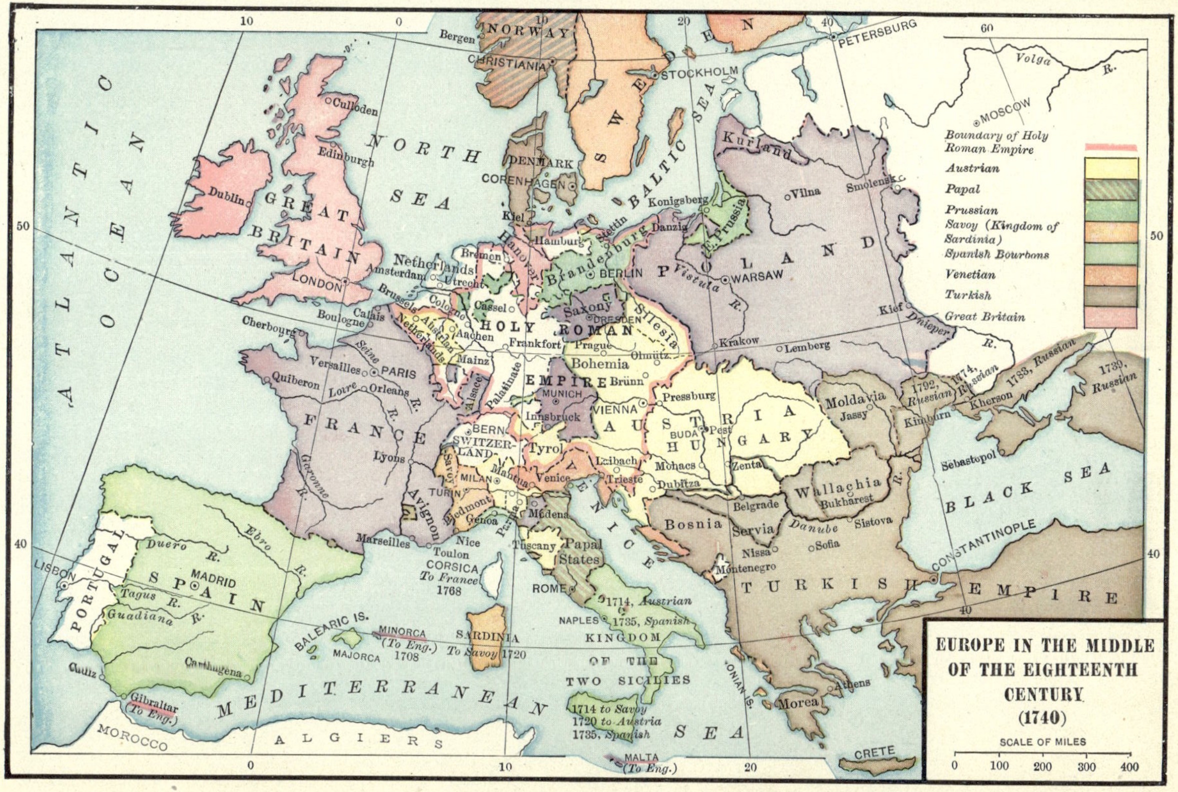
EUROPE IN THE MIDDLE OF THE EIGHTEENTH CENTURY (1740)
SCALE OF MILES
0 100 200 300 400
Boundary of Holy Roman Empire
Austrian
Papal
Prussian
Savoy (Kingdom of Sardinia)
Spanish Bourbons
Venetian
Turkish
Great Britain
ATLANTIC OCEAN
NORTH SEA
BALTIC SEA
MEDITERRANEAN SEA
BLACK SEA
GREAT BRITAIN
FRANCE
SPAIN
PORTUGAL
HOLY ROMAN EMPIRE
AUSTRIA
HUNGARY
POLAND
SWEDEN
NORWAY
DENMARK
TURKISH EMPIRE
KINGDOM OF THE TWO SICILIES
VENICE
ALGIERS
MOROCCO
CORSICA To France 1768
SARDINIA To Savoy 1720
MINORCA (To Eng.) 1708
MALTA (To Eng.)
Gibraltar (To Eng.)
1714 to Savoy
1720 to Austria
1735, Spanish
1714, Austrian
1735, Spanish

who had not been consulted, had no mind for such an assassination of their empire. They preferred instead the accession of Louis' younger grandson, as Philip V; and Charles II so arranged in his will. When this became known, on the death of Charles in 1700, Louis abandoned the partition plan and snatched at the whole prize. Said he exultantly, "The Pyrenees no longer exist." Then Europe united against France and Spain in the "War of the Spanish Succession,"—known in American history as "Queen Anne's War." In this struggle, for the first time, success in the field lay with the Allies. The English *Marlborough* and the Hapsburg *Prince Eugene* were two of the greatest generals of history, and they won splendid victories over the hitherto invincible armies of France, at *Blenheim, Ramillies, Oudenarde,* and *Malplaquet.*

The allies were supporting an Austrian Hapsburg for the Spanish throne; but unexpectedly this prince became Emperor Charles VI. After that event, to make him also King of Spain would have been to return to the days of Charles V, with the world-wide dominions of the Hapsburgs reunited. Accordingly, England and Holland withdrew from the alliance, and the *Peace of Utrecht* (1713) left Philip V King of Spain (with a renunciation of any claim upon the French throne). France had gained no territory in Europe, and in America she had lost Newfoundland and Nova Scotia to England. England also had acquired command of the Mediterranean, by securing from Spain the fortress of *Gibraltar* and the island of *Minorca.* Spain lost all her European possessions outside her own peninsula. To Austria fell the Netherlands, Milan, Naples, and Sicily.[1] To the Duke of Savoy fell Sardinia, with the title of a kingdom for his enlarged state.

262. Change in Austrian Policy. — Austria still furnished the emperor of the "Holy Roman Empire" at each election, but her rulers were turning their attention more and more away from the Rhine and toward the Danube. For almost three centuries, Austria had been one of the chief bulwarks of Christendom against the Turk. In 1683, Vienna had stood its last great siege at a critical moment, and had been relieved by a Polish army. Thereafter, Austria assumed the offensive, won back Hungary, and gradually extended her dominions down the Danube valley and the Illyrian coast. In the later part of the age of Louis XIV, the

---

[1] These arrangements as to Sicily and Sardinia were not completed at the Peace of Utrecht, but were partly arranged afterward between Savoy and Austria. The union of Savoy and Sardinia marks the beginning of the growth of the kingdom which a century and a half later was to consolidate Italy. Shortly before, in 1701 (§ 273), Brandenburg in North Germany had become the kingdom of Prussia; and this state, a century and a half later, was to consolidate Germany.

significance of this policy lay in the diversion of Austria's attention from the great European wars. Austria's general, Prince Eugene, won most of his famous victories over the Turks, not over the French. A century later, just before the French Revolution, Russia was to replace Austria as the chief enemy of the Turk, and to begin to acquire Turkish territory along the Black Sea, toward the Danube. Thus, as Turkey declined, Russia and Austria were to become rivals for the inheritance.

263. The Decline of Holland. — The Danubian policy of Austria had helped to give Louis XIV a free hand on the Rhine, and one of the results was the decline of Holland. In 1640, Dutch vessels carried the greater part of the commerce of the world. England, under the Commonwealth (1651 and 1652), had attacked Holland's carrying trade, first by "Navigation Acts"[1] and then by open war; and, after the Restoration in England, the government of Charles II on the whole had continued this policy. But finally Holland was driven by fear of French conquest to ally herself to her commercial rival, and after 1689, she followed the lead of England in politics, while that country drew to herself the old Dutch supremacy in commerce.

264. Estimate of Louis XIV. — Louis XIV dazzled the men of his age, and won the title of the Great King (*Grand Monarque*); but we can now see that his aims were mistaken, even from a purely selfish view, and that his failure was profound. From the time of Francis I to the time of Richelieu, France had been in real danger of being crushed in the hostile embrace of the Hapsburgs, whose realms encircled her. But after 1648, that danger had passed away; and Louis' wars against the Hapsburgs lacked whatever excuse had belonged to the policy of his predecessors. They, to some degree, fought for security; Louis fought only to enlarge his borders.

In this aim he was partially successful; but his wars exhausted France and left the nation burdened with debt through the next century. At the close of his reign, the industry of France was declining, under a crushing taxation of which more than half went merely to pay the interest on the debt he

---

[1] The Navigation Acts required all ships carrying goods between English colonies and English ports to be built and owned by Englishmen, — citizens of England or of the colonies. These Acts injured Holland and built up the New England merchant-marine and shipbuilding industries.

had created. Moreover, in his unjust attacks upon petty properties of his neighbors in Europe, he had wasted strength and opportunities that might have intrenched France as mistress in Asia and America (§§ 282, 284).

265. French Intellectual Leadership. — The Treaty of Utrecht marks the exhaustion of France and her decline from political leadership. But French intellectual supremacy survived through the next century. The court of Louis XIV remained the model on which every court in Europe sought to form itself. French thought, French fashions, the French language, spread over Europe and became the common property of all polite society.

This admiration for France was due partly to the outburst of French poetry at this time. It was the first great age in French literature. The leading authors were the dramatists, Corneille, Racine, and Molière.[1] At the same time, this literature was brilliant and sparkling, rather than great. Says George Burton Adams (*French Nation*, 230, 231): —

LOUIS XIV.

It was distinctly an age of quantity and finish in literature, rather than of quality. . . . The work is not constructive, but imitative. It is not free and strong, but careful and studied. It is, as it has been called, the most literary of literatures. Its theme is . . . the somewhat artificial man of society.

---

[1] A striking illustration of the influence of French literature is that a great English school of writers modeled themselves upon it. This is the body of 'correct poets,' of whom *Pope* perhaps is the most famous member.

III. THE RISE OF RUSSIA.

266. Russia as Peter the Great found Her. — As a "Great Power," Russia is the creation of *Peter the Great*. This unique ruler became master of Russia in 1689, at the age of seventeen. The Russians belonged to the Greek church, but they had no other tie with European life. In manners and thought they were Asiatic. They were Asiatic also in geographical relations. They held a vast area — the great eastern plain of Europe, reaching over into Siberia — but they had no seacoast except on the Arctic. Practically, Russia was an inland state, shut off from contact with Western Europe by hostile Sweden, Poland, and Turkey.

CHURCH OF ST. BASIL, MOSCOW; built about 1575, in the reign of Ivan the Terrible (§ 170). The building was painted brilliantly, in all the colors of the rainbow.

267. Peter's Character and Aims. — Peter was a barbaric genius of tremendous energy, clear intellect, and ruthless will. He admired the material results of western civilization, and he determined to Europeanize his people. As steps toward this, he meant to get the Baltic coast from Sweden and the Black Sea from the Turks, so as to have "windows to look out upon Europe."

After two campaigns against the Turks, the young Tsar decided to learn more about the western world he had admired at a distance. In Holland he studied shipbuilding, as a workman in the navy yards. He visited most of the countries of the West, impressing all who met him with his insatiable voracity for information. He inspected cutleries, museums, manufactories, arsenals, departments of government, military organizations. He collected instruments and models, and gathered naval and military stores. He engaged choice artists, gold beaters, architects, workmen, officers, and engineers, to return with him to Russia, with promises, not well kept, of great pay.

268. Russia veneered with European Culture. — With these workmen Peter sought to introduce western civilization into Russia. The manners of his people he reformed by edict. He himself cut off the Asiatic beards of his courtiers and clipped the bottoms of their long robes. Women were ordered to put aside their veils and to come out of their Oriental seclusion. It has been well said that Peter "tried to Europeanize by Asiatic methods." He "civilized by the cudgel."

PETER THE GREAT; after a portrait by Kneller.

The upper classes did take on a European veneer. The masses remained Russian and Oriental. The gap has never closed.

269. Growth of Russian Territory under Peter and Catherine II. — Peter also started Russia on her march toward the European seas. On the south, he himself made no permanent advance, despite a series of wars with Turkey; but he bequeathed his policy to his successors, and, ever since his day, Constantinople has been the goal of Russian ambition in this direction. The Baltic "window" Peter himself secured, by victory over Charles XII of Sweden, "the Glorious Madman of the North." Sweden was a thinly populated country with no great natural resources. For a century, a line of great kings and the disciplined bravery of her soldiery had made her a leading power in Europe; but such leadership could hardly be permanent. Sweden had grown at the expense of Russia, Poland, Denmark, and Brandenburg-Prussia; and when Charles XII came to the Swedish throne (1697) as a mere boy of fifteen, these states leagued against him.

Charles proved a military genius, and for a long time seemed victorious against this overwhelming coalition. But he wore out his resources in winning victories that did not destroy his huge antagonists, and he was as incapable a ruler as he was great in battle. Early in the struggle he defeated Peter the Great at *Narva*, with an army not more than an eighth as large as the Russian force; but while Charles was busied in Poland and Germany, Russia recovered herself, and in 1709 Peter crushed Charles at *Pultava*. As Peter had foreseen, the Swedes had taught him how to beat them. Sweden never recovered her military supremacy. Russia secured the Swedish provinces on the east coast of the Baltic as far north as the Gulf of Finland. These districts had been colonized, three centuries before, by the Teutonic Knights (§§ 95, 99), and German civilization was strongly implanted there. Thus the acquisition not only gave Russia a door into Europe, but actually brought part of Europe inside Russia. It was in this new territory that Peter founded St. Petersburg.[1]

The next important acquisition of territory was under the *Empress Elizabeth*,[2] who seized the southern half of Finland from helpless Sweden. Toward the close of the century, under Catherine II, Russia made great progress along the coast of the Black Sea. Under the same ruler occurred the partition of Poland (§ 278) and the acquisition by Russia of the eastern part of that kingdom, along with the rest of the southeastern Baltic shore. These last changes, however, can be understood only in connection with the rise of Prussia (§§ 270 ff.).

---

[1] Special report: anecdotes of the founding of St. Petersburg.
[2] Daughter of Peter; Empress from 1741 to 1762.

IV. THE RISE OF PRUSSIA.

A Rise of Prussia, to the Age of Frederick the Great.

270. Growth of a Mark into an Electorate. — Brandenburg was one of the "marks" established in the tenth century as bulwarks against the Slavs (§ 50). This mark was the germ of modern Prussia. Under a great race of fighting Margraves it grew from century to century, and during the Hohenstaufen period, its ruler became one of the Electors of the Empire.

271. Accession of the Hohenzollerns. — In 1415, the line of Brandenburg Electors ran out, and Frederick of Hohenzollern, a petty count in the Alps (like the Hapsburgs a century and a half before), bought Brandenburg from the Emperor. The new family was to play a part in North Germany comparable to that of the Hapsburgs in the South. Next to Saxony, Brandenburg was the most important of the German Protestant states in the wars of the Reformation.

272. New Territory: Cleves and Prussia. — Shortly after 1600 came the next important acquisition of territory. By family inheritance, the Elector of Brandenburg fell heir to two considerable principalities, — the duchy of Cleves on the extreme west of Germany, and the duchy of Prussia outside the Empire on the extreme east.[1] Thereafter the Hohenzollern Electors ruled three widely separated provinces, — on the Rhine, the Elbe, and the Vistula. The object of their politics was to unite these regions, by securing intermediate lands. To do this an army was necessary; and the army of the little Prussian state was soon among the largest and best in Europe.

273. The "Great Elector" and the First King of Prussia. — Toward the close of the Thirty Years' War, Frederick William, the "Great Elector," came to the throne of Brandenburg. He

---

[1] Prussia was the name given to a district which the Teutonic Knights had conquered in the fourteenth century from the heathen Slavs, and which had been partly colonized by Germans. In the fifteenth century, Poland had seized West Prussia. East Prussia afterward became a duchy in the hands of a branch of the Hohenzollern family, and in 1618 it passed to the Elector of Brandenburg.

at once took a leading part in the struggle; and, as his reward, at the Peace of Westphalia he secured eastern Pomerania. This brought Brandenburg to the sea. The chief services of the long reign of the Great Elector, however, were rendered not in war but in peace. He built roads and canals, drained marshes, encouraged agriculture, and welcomed the Huguenot fugitives from France after the revocation of the Edict of Nantes (§ 260).

Frederick, son and successor of the Great Elector, in return for aid against Louis XIV, secured the Emperor's consent to his changing the title "Elector of Brandenburg" for the more stately one of "King in Prussia" (1701); and Prussia soon came to be the name used for all the Hohenzollern dominions.

B. FREDERICK THE GREAT IN EUROPE; AND ENGLAND IN THE NEW WORLDS.

274. Wars of the Austrian Succession. — The second king of Prussia, Frederick William I, was a rude "drill sergeant," memorable only as the stupid father of Frederick the Great[1] and as the builder of the magnificent army which his son was to use so magnificently. Frederick II (the Great), ascended the Prussian throne in 1740. In the same year the Hapsburg Emperor, Charles VI, died without a male heir, and Frederick began his long reign by an unjust but profitable war.

By long negotiations Charles had secured the approval of all the European governments to the *Pragmatic Sanction*, — a royal decree whereby he appointed his daughter, Maria Theresa, his successor in the hereditary realms of the Hapsburg family. Frederick, however, disregarded Prussia's pledge, and unscrupulously took advantage of the supposed weakness of the new Archduchess of Austria. With his perfectly prepared army, he seized Silesia, an Austrian province upon which Prussia had some shadowy claim. This high-handed act was the signal for a general onslaught to divide the Austrian realms. Spain, France, Savoy, Bavaria, each hurried to snatch some morsel of the booty. But Maria Theresa displayed great courage and ability; her subjects, especially the gallant

---

[1] Special reports: anecdotes of Frederick's youth and of his father's court.

Hungarian nobles, rallied loyally to her support; and the wolves found the expected carcass very much alive. A little later, England and Holland added their strength to the Austrian side.

This *War of the Austrian Succession* was closed in 1748 by the *Peace of Aix la Chapelle*. Maria Theresa's husband, Francis of Lorraine, had been elected Emperor, and the Archduchess herself was now acknowledged as ruler of Austria. Frederick II kept Silesia, but Austria lost no other territory. Frederick had shown himself the greatest general of the age; he had added a large territory to his kingdom, which now reached down into the heart of Germany; and he had made Prussia the one great rival of Austria in Germany.

275. **The Contest outside Europe.** — Much more important, though less striking, was the contest outside Europe. England and Spain had already begun a colonial war in 1739, before Frederick started the general European war; and France in any case would soon have joined Spain. France, however, gave her energies chiefly to the European struggle, while England's activity was spent to a great degree in America. When the war began, the French had the advantage of position in America, holding the mouths of the St. Lawrence and the Mississippi, with the connecting water-ways; while the English colonists were stretched along a narrow fringe of coast in scattered patches, shut off from the interior by the Appalachians. The English Americans were more numerous, however, than the French; and the most important event of the war in America was the capture of the French fortress of Louisburg by a New England expedition. In India, the French leader, *Dupleix*, saw the chance to secure an Asiatic empire for his country, and,

FREDERICK THE GREAT; after an engraving from a painting by Ramberg.

though greatly thwarted by home indifference and jealousy, he did capture the English stations in that country.

The treaty of peace restored matters to their former position, both in America and Asia, but the war marks the growth of a consciousness in England and France that the two countries were rivals for vast realms outside Europe. The tremendous significance of the struggle they did not yet realize. Of course we can see now that whether Prussia or Austria were to possess Silesia, whether France or Austria were to hold the Netherlands, were questions wholly insignificant in comparison with the mightier question as to what race and what political ideas should hold the New Worlds.[1]

276. The "Seven Years' War" in Europe. — The War of 1740-1748 had resulted from Frederick's greedy attack upon Austria. In 1756, Austria began a war of revenge. Maria Theresa had secured the alliance of Russia, Sweden, and even of her old enemy France. Four great armies invaded Prussia from different directions, and Frederick's throne seemed to totter. His swift action and his supreme military genius saved his country, in the victories of *Rossbach* and *Leuthen*. The next year England entered the struggle as his ally. England and France had remained practically at war in America and India through the brief interval between the two European wars;[2] and now that France had changed to Austria's side, England had no choice but to support Prussia.

277. Victory of England in America and Asia. — In America the Seven Years' War is known as the "Great French War," or the "French and Indian War." The struggle was literally world-wide. Red men scalped each other by the Great Lakes of North America, and black men fought in Senegal in Africa; while Frenchmen and Englishmen grappled in India as well as in Germany, and their fleets engaged on every sea. The most tremendous and showy battles took place in Germany;

---

[1] The American English felt bitterly chagrined at the return of Louisburg to the French; but it was much more important for the British Empire to regain its hold upon India than to keep one French fortress in America.

[2] Braddock's campaign in America (1754) took place during this interval, before any formal declaration of war between France and England.

and, though the real importance of the struggle lay outside Europe, still the European conflict in the main decided the wider results. *William Pitt*, the English minister, who was working to build up a great British empire, declared that in Germany he would conquer America from France. He did so. England furnished the funds and her navy swept the seas. Frederick and Prussia, supported by English subsidies, furnished the troops and the generalship for the European battles. The striking figures of the struggle are (1) Pitt, the great English imperialist, the directing genius of the war; (2) Frederick of Prussia, the military genius, who won Pitt's victories in Germany; (3) Wolfe, who won French America from the great Montcalm; and (4) Clive in India.

The story of the struggle in America is too familiar to need repetition. The story of the conquest of India calls for a brief outline. Dupleix had been recalled by the shortsighted French government, and no French commander was left in India able to cope with the English leaders. *Clive* was an unknown English clerk at Madras. The Nabob of Bengal treacherously seized the English post at Calcutta, induced the garrison to surrender on the promise of good treatment, and then suffocated them horribly by packing the one hundred and forty-six Europeans in a close dungeon [1] through the hot tropical night. The young Clive was moved to vengeance. He organized a small expedition of a thousand Englishmen and two thousand faithful native troops, and at *Plassey* (1757) he overthrew the Nabob's Oriental army of sixty thousand men. Soon after, English supremacy was thoroughly established.

The treaty of peace left Europe without change. In India. the French retained only a few unfortified trading posts. In America, England received Florida from Spain, and Canada and the eastern half of the Mississippi Valley from France. France ceded to Spain the western half of the Mississippi Valley, in compensation for the losses Spain had incurred as her ally, and, except for her West Indian islands, she herself ceased to be an American power.

---

[1] This was the Black Hole of Calcutta, famous in literature.

278. The Partitions of Poland.—The anarchy of Poland gave its growing neighbors excuse to plunder it. The population consisted of about twelve million degraded serfs, and one hundred thousand selfish, oligarchic nobles. The latter constituted the government. They met in occasional Diets, and, when the throne became vacant, they elected the figure-head king. Unanimous consent was required for any vote in the Diet, — each noble possessing the right of veto. Under such conditions, the other Powers of Europe had begun to play with Poland at will. *Catherine II* of Russia determined to seize a large part of the country. Frederick II persuaded Austria to join him in compelling Catherine to share the booty. The "First Partition" in 1772, pared off a rind about the heart. The Second and Third Partitions, which completed the work and "assassinated the kingdom," had not even the pretext of misgovernment in Poland. The Poles had undertaken sweeping reforms; but Catherine did not mean that her prey should so escape, and a Russian army suddenly crossed the border (1793). Frederick II was dead and the new king of Prussia had approved the reformed Polish constitution; but now he sent his army to join the Russians. Austria was busied with a war against the French Revolutionists (§ 331), and so the Second Partition enlarged only the two other robbers. The Poles made an heroic defense, under their hero-leader *Kosciusko*, but this only led to the Third Partition, in which Austria again had a share. This partition wiped Poland off the map (1795).

Russia had gained far the greatest part of the territory, and she now bordered Germany on the east, as France did on the west. Plainly the true policy of the Germans, early and late, would have been the honest one of supporting the "buffer states"—Poland and Charles the Bold's Burgundy—against the greed of Russia and France. Failure to do so has left Germany exposed to immediate attack by powerful enemies and has compelled her to build up artificial frontiers of fortresses and bayonets.

279. The True Greatness of Frederick.—Frederick II had shown himself unscrupulous in diplomacy and a genius in war; but there was another side to his life, which, more properly than either war or diplomacy, earns him his title of "the Great." Most of his forty-six years' reign was passed in peace, and he proved a father to his people. All the beneficent work of the Great Elector (§ 273) was taken up and carried forward vigorously. Prussia was transformed. Wealth and comfort increased by great leaps. The condition of the peasantry was improved, and the administration in all its branches was made

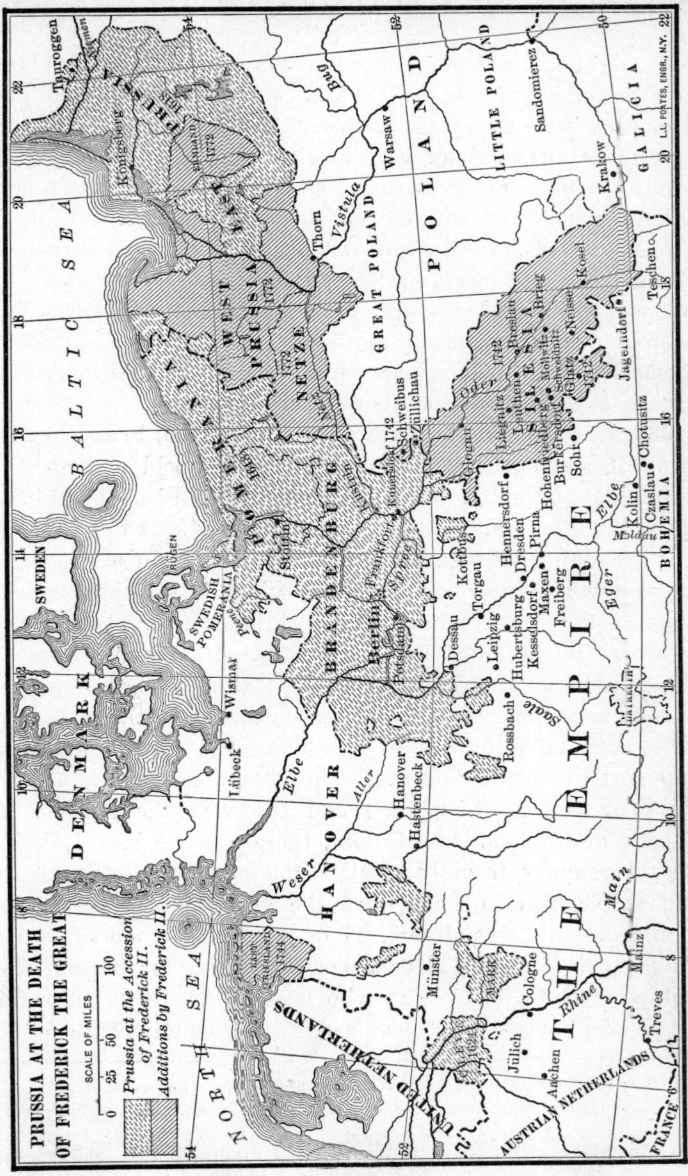
PRUSSIA AT THE DEATH OF FREDERICK THE GREAT
SCALE OF MILES
0 25 50 100
Prussia at the Accession of Frederick II.
Additions by Frederick II.
BALTIC SEA
NORTH SEA
DENMARK
SWEDEN
RÜGEN
SWEDISH POMERANIA
EAST PRUSSIA
WEST PRUSSIA 1772
ERMLAND 1772
NETZE 1772
POMERANIA
BRANDENBURG
HANOVER
SILESIA 1742
GREAT POLAND
LITTLE POLAND
POLAND
GALICIA
BOHEMIA
THE EMPIRE
UNITED NETHERLANDS
AUSTRIAN NETHERLANDS
FRANCE
EAST FRIESLAND 1744
MARK
Königsberg
Tauroggen
Thorn
Warsaw
Sandomierez
Krakow
Teschen
Kosel
Brieg
Neisse
Breslau
Jagerndorf
Glatz
Liegnitz
Leuthen
Mollwitz
Schweidnitz
Burkersdorf
Hohenfriedberg
Soor
Glogau
Züllichau
Schweibus
Kunersdorf
Küstrin
Frankfort
Stettin
Berlin
Potsdam
Kottbus
Torgau
Dessau
Leipzig
Hubertsburg
Kesselsdorf
Dresden
Pirna
Maxen
Freiberg
Hennersdorf
Rossbach
Kolin
Czaslau
Chotusitz
Wismar
Lübeck
Hanover
Hastenbeck
Münster
Cologne
Jülich
Aachen
Treves
Mainz
Vistula
Bug
Oder
Elbe
Spree
Weser
Aller
Saale
Eger
Moldau
Main
Rhine
Niemen
L.L. POOLE, ENGR., N.Y.

economical and efficient. Frederick was also an author and a patron of literature; and he is a type of the "crowned philosophers," or "beneficent despots," who sat upon the thrones of Europe in the latter half of the eighteenth century, just before the French Revolution. Under the influence of a new enlightened sentiment, created by a remarkable school of French writers (§ 302), government underwent a marvelous change. It was just as aristocratic as before, — no more *by* the people than before, — but despots did try to govern *for* the people, not for themselves. Sovereigns began to speak of themselves, not as privileged proprietors, but, in Frederick's phrase, as "the first servants of their states."[1]

280. The "Benevolent Despots." — Frederick of Prussia, Catherine of Russia, Charles III of Spain, Leopold of Tuscany, Ferdinand of Naples, Joseph II of Austria, all belonged to the class of philosophic, liberal-minded, "benevolent despots" of this age. In Sweden and Portugal, two great ministers sought to impose a like policy upon the kings. All these rulers planned far-reaching reforms, — amelioration or abolition of serfdom, the building up of public education, and reform of the church. Frederick's genius and tireless energy accomplished something for a time; but on the whole the monarchs made lamentable failures. One man proved powerless to lift the inert weight of a nation. The clergy and nobles, jealous for their privileges, opposed and thwarted the royal will. Except in England and France, there was no large middle class to supply friendly officials and sympathy. The most remarkable, and in some ways the greatest, of these philosophic despots, was Joseph II of Austria, the son of Maria Theresa; and he died disheartened, dictating for himself the epitaph, "Here lies a king who designed many benefits for his people, but who was unable to accomplish any of them."[2]

---

[1] Even Frederick's worst wars were designed to benefit Prussia.

[2] The kings had failed to bring about sufficient reform; and now, in France, *the people were to try for themselves* (§§ 285 ff.). Before entering upon that story, we will sum up one more phase of the eighteenth century (§§ 281-284).

V. THE EXPANSION OF ENGLAND.

281. Expansion of England, to the Opening of the Struggle with France. — In the reign of Elizabeth, England meant a state of fifty-eight thousand square miles, — about the size of Georgia. It did not include Scotland nor all of Ireland. The population was about four millions. The decisive steps in the great change into the vast empire of to-day belong to the eighteenth century, and much of the real progress was to take place in the nineteenth century; but some earlier beginnings call for notice.

a. The first Stuart king, James I (1603), joined Scotland and England under one crown. A little more than a century later, under Anne, the last Stuart sovereign, this "personal union" (§ 243, note) was made a real consolidation (1707). By the parliamentary "Act of Union," assented to by Scotland, the northern state gave up her separate legislature, received representation in the English Parliament, and became a part of the "United Kingdom."

b. Between the first and last Stuart reigns, Ireland was made English by conquest and colonization; and, during the Commonwealth, by sweeping acts of confiscation, English landlords were put in possession of the soil, so that the Irish peasantry became outcasts in their own land. No other part of England's empire was so unjustly acquired, and no other part has given her so much trouble.

c. During the Stuart period, too, the English colonies in America were founded. That story needs no telling here.

282. The French Colonial System. — When English expansion began, France had already begun to build up her colonial empire in Canada; and a little later, in the time of Louis XIV, La Salle secured the mouth of the Mississippi.

But the French colonies were petted and over-governed. They were hampered by well-meant but foolish restrictions and encouragements. Every new enterprise was fostered by aid from the government at home, — and fell into hopeless languor when the support was withdrawn. Moreover, no shadow of political life was permitted. The governors were sent out from France, and there was no sign of a colonial legislature or of popular county and town governments, all of which were found in the English colonies. The rulers did everything; the people did nothing.

The rulers were oftentimes farsighted, noble men; but the system was fundamentally weak, when compared with that of the English colonies growing up in neglect along the Atlantic coast. The French were better woodsmen and Indian fighters, man for man, than the English colonists; but they could not build a state; and when England had once conquered them, they submitted easily, — as the English colonists would never have done under French despotism. Louis XIV lost his last real chance for American empire when he refused to let the Huguenots settle in French America. They would have come in numbers, with families, and would have made farmers and artisans. The French who did come did not bring wives, and turned eagerly to hunting and fur-trading, rather than to agriculture. Thus, despite their early start and their better location and the much larger population at home, the French colonists did not grow in numbers as fast as did the English. In 1754, when the decisive struggle began, with Braddock's campaign, France had only about a fortieth as many colonists in America as England had, though her home population was four times as large as England's.

283. The Second "Hundred Years' War." — At the end of the seventeenth century began the long contest for empire between France and England. This struggle lasted with brief intervals for a hundred and twenty-six years, from 1689 to Waterloo in 1815. It falls into three chapters, 1689–1763, 1775–1783, and 1792–1815. The story of the first struggle has been told in outline in §§ 261, 275–279, in connection with the story of European wars. At the expiration of the period, England had dispossessed France in America and in Asia; Spain still held South America and half North America, but her power was evidently decaying, day by day; and Holland, too, with wide-spread colonial empire, was plainly in decline. *England stood forth as the leading world-power.*

This result was to be intensified by the third period of the struggle, whose story will be told in connection with the Wars of the Revolution and of Napoleon. The second period, that of the American Revolution, needs only brief reference (§ 284).

284. The American Revolution. — At the time, France and Spain saw in the American Revolution a chance to revenge themselves upon England by helping the best part of her empire to break away. To-day we see more justly that its real importance, even to Europe, lay in the establishment of an independent American nation and in teaching England to improve her system of colonial government. From the strictly American point of view, the war came because the English government unwisely insisted upon managing American affairs after the Americans were quite able to take care of themselves. England came out of the war with gains as well as losses, and with glory little tarnished. She had been fighting, not America alone, but France, Spain, Holland, and America.

Theodore Roosevelt has put finely the result and character of this wider struggle (*Gouverneur Morris*, 116) : " England, hemmed in by the ring of her foes, fronted them with a grand courage. In her veins the Berserker blood was up, and she hailed each new enemy with grim delight, exerting to the full her warlike strength. Single-handed, she kept them all at bay, and repaid with crippling blows, the injuries they had done her. In America, alone, the tide ran too strong to be turned. But Holland was stripped of all her colonies ; in the East, Sir Eyre Coote beat down Hyder Ali, and taught Moslem and Hindoo alike that they could not shake off the grasp of the iron hands that held India ; Rodney won back for his country the supremacy of the ocean in that great sea-fight where he shattered the splendid French navy ; and the long siege of Gibraltar was closed with the crushing overthrow of the assailants. So, with bloody honor, England ended the most disastrous war she had ever waged."

The secession of the American colonies did not injure England, as her friends and foes had expected it to do. The commerce of the United States continued to be carried on mainly through England, and, very soon, the new nation, with its growing wealth, was buying more English goods than the old colonies had been able to pay for. For her territorial loss, England found compensation, too, to some degree, in the acquisition of Australia.

FURTHER READING upon the subject of this chapter may profitably be confined to the expansion of Europe into the New Worlds. On this topic the best brief treatments are Woodward's *Expansion of the British Empire* (pp. 1–263) and Seeley's *Expansion of England*. Seeley's *Growth of British Policy* is good for advanced students. George Burton Adams' essay, "Anglo Saxon Expansion," in the *Atlantic Monthly* for April, 1897, is excellent reading. Caldecott's *English Colonization and Empire* contains an admirable treatment. For the great struggle in America, the student should read Parkman's Works, especially his *Montcalm and Wolfe* and his *Half Century of Conflict*. The following biographies, too, are good: Wilson's *Clive*, Malleson's *Dupleix* and *Lord Clive*, and Bradley's *Wolfe*. Mahan's *Influence of the Sea Power upon History, 1660–1783*, should not be omitted by the advanced student.

For Europe, the best general reference is the volume of the "Periods" series, — Wakeman's *Europe, 1589–1715*. Hassall's *Louis XIV* is an admirable treatment. Henderson's *Short History of Germany* may be used for Germany and for Frederick II.

REVIEW EXERCISES.

1. Fact drills.
    a. *Dates:* add the following with their significance: 1520, 1571, 1588, 1628–1629, 1648, 1640–1649, 1660, 1688, 1713, 1740, 1763, 1783.
    b. *Extend list of terms* for drill.
    c. *List twenty important battles* between 843 and 1789.
2. Continue the syllabus (page 190).
3. Review by countries, with "catch-words," from 843.
4. Review the introductory chapter of the book, and observe its application to the narrative up to 1789.
5. Make a brief paragraph statement for the period 1648–1787, to include the changes in territory and in the relative power of the different European states.

PART III.

THE AGE OF NATION STATES.

CHAPTER I.

THE FRENCH REVOLUTION.

Every aristocracy has three ages: it is founded in its age of violence; it degenerates into its age of privilege; and in its age of vanity it is extinguished. — CHÂTEAUBRIAND.

There are only two events in history, — the Siege of Troy and the French Revolution. — DISRAELI.

. . . An evidence of vitality, not of decay; the outcome of national convalescence; the result of a universal conviction of injustice and of a universal determination to install justice. — Adapted from SHAILER MATHEWS.

The nineteenth century is precisely the history of the work the French Revolution did leave. The Revolution was a creating force even more than a destroying one; it was an inexhaustible source of fertile influences; it not only cleared the ground of the old society, but it manifested all the elements of the new society. — FREDERIC HARRISON.

I. FUNDAMENTAL CHARACTERISTICS.

285. A True "Revolution." — Italy had given the world an intellectual revolution; Germany, a religious revolution; and now France was to give the political and social revolution. The three movements, — the Renaissance, the Reformation, and the French Revolution, — are the most important events since the Teutonic invasions. Preëminently, among the so-called "revolutions" in history, the French Revolution deserves the name. The English Revolution of 1688 only swept away a temporary interference with the old lines of development in English politics: it was a "conservative revolution," restoring the nation to an old groove. The like is true, to a great degree, of the American Revolution: that great movement divided the British Empire and made a new nation, but it did not itself materially change the character of American society or politics; like the English Revolution, it was a protest against new abuses. But the French Revolution overturned and swept away a society and institutions that had been growing up for centuries. It cut loose from the past, and started France upon new lines of growth.

286. The Revolution Constructive as well as Destructive. — The Revolution was a vast and fruitful reform. The work of destruction, with which it began, was accompanied by much horror and bloodshed, and often receives undue attention. But if the Revolution destroyed the old, it also built up the new: and this constructive side is far the more important. The Revolution did inflict much terrible agony upon a large class, and it took the lives of thousands of individuals, most of them, perhaps, innocent and worthy. But the really significant thing is not the temporary mob-rule with its horrors: the significant thing is the great national awakening which swept away an absurd society, founded by ancient violence and warped by time, to replace it with a simpler social system based more nearly on equal rights.

And even as to the destructive side, we must guard against prevalent exaggerations. Literature is full of hysterics and sentimentality on this matter. It is right that we should shudder at the violence and agony: but there is no danger that we shall not shudder sufficiently; for, as Carlyle says, those who suffered in the excesses of the Revolution were the few who could shriek and so create sympathy for their woes. The danger is, that we forget the relief to the dumb multitudes, who had been enduring worse tortures for ages, but whose inarticulate moanings hardly attract the attention of history. Carlyle touches a sad truth when he adds that not within ten centuries had there been any equal period with so little suffering, over France as a whole, as just those months of bloody revolution.

287. The Revolution directed against Social Inequality even more than against Absolute Government. — The Revolutionists were to take for their watchword the famous phrase, *Liberty, Fraternity, Equality.* But in practice they cared for liberty not so much in itself as because it was a means toward equality. "Fraternity" and "Equality" meant to them much the same thing; and they put the emphasis on this two-thirds of the motto. In other words, the Revolution was *social* even more than *political*.[1] The Revolution *came to be* a revolt against the monarchy, but *primarily* it was a revolt against the unjust privileges of the aristocracy. Had the monarch been willing and resolute to reduce those privileges himself, his own power probably would not have been attacked. The assault upon the monarchy was a means to an end.

II. CONDITIONS BEFORE THE REVOLUTION.

A. Social Classes.

288. The Privileged Drones. — In 1789, France had a population of about twenty-five millions. At the top were a quarter of a million of nobles and clergy. These were the two privileged orders. They were about equally divided in numbers and wealth. Together they owned half the soil of France, with all the fine buildings; and they took besides from the peasant, in church dues and feudal payments, over a fourth of his income. Moreover, they received in pensions and sinecure[2] salaries a large part of the taxes paid by the nation, while they themselves were nearly exempt from taxation.

---

[1] This is hard for American students to grasp, because in America our democracy in politics has grown out of democracy in society. But it is true that in France, political democracy was sought chiefly as a means of securing social and economic equality.

[2] A sinecure is an office to which no duties are attached.

Nor were financial advantages the only privileges of these orders. For instance, no man in the army could become an officer unless he could show that his ancestors on both sides had been nobles back to his great-great-grandfathers. Other privileges will be noticed in connection with the oppression of the peasantry (§§ 293-294). Arthur Young, an English gentleman traveling in France just before the Revolution, was indignant at the reckless driving of young French nobles in the crowded and narrow Paris streets, and declared that if English nobles were to drive so in London they would be soundly thrashed and rolled in the gutter.

These privileged nobles rendered little service to society. They had been useful in earlier times: but the monarchy had taken away their political power, giving all administrative offices to low-born clerks, and the nobles themselves had abdicated their other proper functions, as captains of local industry, by becoming mere courtiers.

Many of the poorer nobles, it is true, remained upon their shrunken estates, because they could not afford life at court: but even this class saw their highest ambition in a pension or an office which should enable them to exchange their "dull banishment" for the gayety of Paris, and so they failed to fill the proper place in country life. The wealthy nobles were absentee landlords; and to keep up luxuriant establishments in town they drove their bailiffs for money, while the bailiffs in turn harassed the cultivators. The nobles of this class had for their sole industry to amuse themselves and each other, — to dress gracefully, to phrase a jest wittily or a compliment acceptably, to win a pension, and to dine sumptuously. They had become a burdensome excrescence upon the nation.

289. Higher and Lower Clergy. — Of the hundred and thirty thousand clergy, half were monks and nuns. Of the rest, one out of six belonged to the "higher clergy." With insignificant exceptions, these were all of noble birth. From their immense revenues they paid paltry sums to subordinates, who performed for them their spiritual offices, while they themselves lived at court in idle luxury or in vice. The bishops and abbots enjoyed over five-sixths of the church revenues, while the forty thousand village priests and the other lower clergy lived on bare pittances. These priests numbered many devoted religious men; but they were of non-noble birth, and high offices were as hopelessly barred against the non-noble in the church as in the army. In consequence, the opening of the Revolution found the village priests (curés) on the side of the third estate.

290. The Burdened Workers. — The privileged drones were supported by some twenty-three millions of unprivileged and overburdened workers, — nearly a hundred to each aristocrat. Of these workers, great masses dragged out a haggard existence in hideous wretchedness. A century before the Revolution a French gentleman wrote, with somewhat cynical sympathy: —

> "Certain wild-looking beings, male and female, are seen in the country, — black-livid, sunburned, slaves of the soil, which they dig and grub with invincible stubbornness. They seem just capable of speech, and when they stand erect, they display the lineaments of men. They *are* men. At night they retire to their dens, where they devour black bread with roots and water. They spare other human beings the trouble of sowing, plowing, and reaping, and thus should not themselves lack bread."

A hundred years later, on the eve of the Revolution, Arthur Young (§ 288) speaks, with less rhetoric but with greater earnestness, of the misery of this class. Pitiful is his typical story of the peasant woman whom he overtook upon the road and whom he supposed to be seventy years old, but who proved to be only twenty-seven. Toil, want, and hard fare robbed the workers of youth and life. Famine was chronic in the fertile land of France in the eighteenth century, as it has been in Russia in the nineteenth. Taxation and feudal extortion discouraged agriculture. A fourth of the land lay waste. Of the rest, the tillage was poor, and the yield per acre was a third less than in England. If a poor season produced a crop failure in a single province, starvation followed, although neighboring provinces might possess abundance. Poor roads, and high tolls, and poverty, and the government's carelessness or inefficiency made it impossible for one district to draw relief from another. So the records are full of local famines and desperate revolts. At other times, when things were not quite so bad, great numbers of the peasants lived on a coarse bread made of bran and bark and acorns, — because of which, says an official report, "the children very commonly die."

The laborers in the towns were little or no better off. They were pallid, haggard, diminutive, — "sullen masses of rags and misery," — huddled in garrets and cellars. The regulations of the gilds shut out the masses of the town population from profitable trades and left them no chance to rise.

At the same time, it must be understood that this dark picture was not without relief. The condition of the peasantry varied greatly in the different districts; and in some places they lived a merry, prosperous life. In any case, the cause of the Revolution did not lie in their misery so much as in the progress they had made toward getting out of it (§ 292). To some extent, however, the justification of the Revolution does lie in that ancient misery.[1]

291. The Bourgeoisie. — Between the two social extremes came a small, but important, middle class, composed of bankers, lawyers, physicians, men of letters, merchants, and shopkeepers. This class is known by the French name of *bourgeoisie*. It was wealthy and proud, and its members possessed many economic privileges, which were bitterly grievous to the masses; but it was destitute of political power and of social privilege.

The middle class was less numerous than in England, but far more numerous and much more important than in Germany, Italy, or Spain. It was this class who made the Revolution possible. They began it, and for the first two years, on the whole, they controlled it. Then it slipped for a while from their hands, and, indeed, was directed against their class, in the interests of the masses; but with one or two exceptions, the bourgeoisie continued to furnish the leaders of the movement to the close.

---

[1] On the peasantry, see Taine's *Ancient Régime*, 329–345. For a more favorable view, cf. Lowell's *Eve of the French Revolution*, chs. xiii and xiv.

B. Feudal Burdens.

The misery of the peasant came from (1) the feudal burdens, (2) the extortionate taxation by the state, and (3) the absence of suitable provision for spiritual and intellectual needs. The first two of these factors will now be treated more in detail.

292. Peasant Landowners.[1] — Despite the evils mentioned above, and others yet to be noted, the French peasantry had been slowly improving in condition during the eighteenth century. They were behind the peasantry of England, but far in advance of that class in Germany or Spain. They played a part in the Revolution *because they had already progressed far enough to feel the possibility of further progress.* A million and a half were still serfs, but these were nearly all in Alsace or Lorraine, the regions lately seized from Germany. Elsewhere the twenty-two millions or more had become free in person, and many of them had become landowners. Perhaps a fourth of the soil belonged to the peasants; but most of it was held in lots so small that a family must eke out its existence by labor on other land belonging to a neighboring lord. The greater part of the peasants lived altogether by cultivating the land of great proprietors.

293. The Land Servile. — Even when the free peasant owned land, he owned it subject to many feudal obligations. Sometimes the dues were heavy, one or more days' work out of each week; sometimes they were merely trifling and vexatious, perhaps a pair of chickens a year. So long as he made the payments, a peasant-owner could not be dispossessed. He was subject, however, to many incidental burdens. He could not sell his land without paying the lord a part of the price. He could not sell produce except in the lord's market, and only after the lord had had first chance to sell his own; and then the peasant paid toll on each sale. The grain that he kept for his children he could grind only at the lord's mill, leaving there

---

[1] Read Tocqueville's *France before the Revolution*, bk. ii, ch. i.

one sixteenth the flour, and he could bake only in the lord's oven, leaving one loaf out of a certain number.[1]

294. The Game Laws. — Most grievous of all the feudal burdens were the nobles' rights, and sole rights, to hunt. Wild animals were protected by brutal game-laws such as had vanished in England more than four hundred years before. The peasant must not under any circumstances injure the rabbits or pigeons or deer that devoured his crop; but the nobles at will might ride over the crops to chase the game. The peasant might not own a dog, except by special permit; and if he did, he must keep it chained to a log. On penalty of death, the peasant might not carry a gun, even to kill the wolves. He could not fence his land without a special permit, and then he must leave wide gaps for the huntsmen's horses. He could not even enter his own field, to till it, between certain dates, when the pheasants were hatching or the rabbits were young. Year after year the crops were trampled by huntsmen or devoured by game. In some districts the peasants watched all night from May to October, armed with tin pans and kettles to make a hullabaloo. Arthur Young tells us how the peasant had come to identify the noble with the wild beast: at sight of a herd of deer his guide exclaimed, "There go the nobility, who devour us."[2]

C. Taxation.[3]

295. Unequal Distribution. — The irresponsible monarchy spent money extravagantly, wastefully, wickedly. The wars of Louis XIV left France burdened with a great debt. The dissolute, cynical Louis XV spent as much in vice as his

---

[1] Probably these burdens never all fell upon any one free peasant: they varied from district to district and from man to man.

[2] See Arthur Young's *Travels*, 82, 316, 317 (Bohn edition), and Tocqueville's *Correspondence*, I, 102. Striking summaries are given by Taine, *Ancient Régime*, 55–59. When the government broke down, in the summer of 1789 (§ 317), the peasantry attacked the game with a wholesale slaughter and with peculiar animosity. Cf. Young, 256.

[3] For a remarkable treatment, see Taine, *Ancient Régime*, 349–373 and 412.

predecessor had spent in war. The royal revenue was mismanaged, given away in pensions to unworthy favorites and needy nobles, and plundered by corrupt officials.

The treasury, emptied in these shameful ways, was filled in a manner equally shameful. Through devices and favors too numerous to mention, the privileged orders practically escaped taxation. The most grievous taxes they were free from altogether, and for the others they assessed themselves and paid a ridiculously small part in proportion to their wealth. Large numbers of the wealthier bourgeoisie, also, escaped, by purchasing exemption in the form of sinecure offices connected in name with the royal household. Thus payment was made only by those too poor to escape and least able to pay. The actual amount raised by the monarchy was not greater than France could have afforded. The evils were (1) that the revenue was wasted without any proper benefit to the nation; (2) that the wealthy classes did not pay; and (3) that various clumsy devices made the collection needlessly burdensome and offensive.

296. The Direct Taxes. — Of the many direct taxes, perhaps the most burdensome were the *taille* and the *corvée*.

a. The taille was originally a tax on the peasant's land; but over much of France it had become an arbitrary seizure of any part of his visible income. Each year the government decided how much a given district must pay. If a village showed signs of prosperity, its share was promptly increased. On one occasion a royal officer wrote, "The people of this village are stouter, and there are chicken feathers before the doors; the taxes here should be greatly increased next year."

Within the village, what one peasant did not or could not pay, his richer or less favored neighbor had to pay. The apportionment in these small units was left wholly to the appointed collector. He could favor one neighbor, or gratify a petty grudge by ruining another. But for each individual, too, in the long run, just as for the community, any evidence of well-being meant heavier taxation. So the peasants concealed their comforts jealously, if they had any, and by preference left their cottages unrepaired.

b. The corvée was the forced labor upon roads or upon other public works. For such purposes, the peasant might be called from his own crop at any time, even at the most critical moment, by the arbitrary order of an official.

It has been estimated that on the average a peasant paid over half his income in direct taxes to the government, and that the feudal dues and church tithes raised the amount to over four-fifths his income, while, from the remaining one-fifth, he had not only to support his family but also to pay various indirect taxes (§ 297).[1]

297. Indirect Taxes: the Gabelle. — The government placed a tax upon the sale of a great many articles.[2] The most famous of these indirect taxes in France was that upon salt. This was called the *gabelle*.[3] It raised the price of salt many times its first value. No salt could be bought except from the government agents, and every household was compelled by law to purchase from these agents at least seven pounds a year for every inmate over seven years of age. This amount, too, was for the table only. If a pig were to be salted down, the peasant must buy an additional supply for that purpose, and get a certificate that such a purchase had been made.

This tax was "farmed" to collectors, who paid the government a certain amount down, and then secured what they could get above that amount for their own profit. Only one-fifth the amount collected reached the treasury, and thousands of persons every year were hung or sent to the galleys for trying to evade the tax. Many other indirect taxes — on candles, fuel, grain, and flour — were farmed out in similar fashion.

Another class of vexatious indirect taxes were the tolls and tariffs on goods. These payments were required not only at the frontier of France, but again and again, at the border of

---

[1] Cf. Taine's *Ancient Régime*, 412, 413. It seems as though these figures must contain serious exaggeration, but they are the work of an industrious and earnest scholar, and they are usually quoted as conveying the essential truth. Perhaps they held good for some districts, and at least they establish beyond doubt the fact of terrible general oppression.

[2] Such a tax is usually called an indirect tax, because, directly, it is paid to the government by the dealers, and only indirectly by the actual consumers, in the added price they pay.

[3] Cf. Arthur Young's *Travels*, 315, 316 (Bohn edition). The gabelle varied in amount in different districts, and some provinces were wholly free from it.

each province and even at the gate of each town, as the goods traveled through the country. Workmen who crossed a river from their homes in one district to their day's work in another, had to pay a tariff on the luncheon in their pockets; and fish, on their way to Paris from the coast, paid thirteen times their first cost in such tolls.

D. THE GOVERNMENT.[1]

298. The Centralized Machinery. — Directly about the king was a *Council of State*, which formed the center of the administration. Subject to the king's approval, it fixed the taxes and the levy for the army, drew up edicts, and indeed ruled France. Its members were appointed by the king and held office only at his pleasure. France was made up of about thirty districts, which corresponded roughly to the old feudal provinces. At the head of each such province was an *Intendant* appointed by the king, from men of the third estate with legal training. Subject to the royal power, the Intendant was an unchecked despot, with tremendous power for good or evil. In the parish, the local officer — mayor, consul, or syndic — was sometimes chosen by the people, sometimes appointed by the Intendant, who could remove him at will. The parish assembly could not meet without the Intendant's permission; and it could not take any action without the government's approval. Had the wind damaged the parish steeple? The parish might petition for permission to repair it, — at their own expense, of course. The Intendant would send the petition, with his recommendation, to the Council of State at Paris, and a reply might be expected in a year or two.[2]

299. Tyranny over Individuals: Letters of the Seal. — A special convenience of the government was its practice of con-

---

[1] A clear and detailed account is given in Wilson's *The State*, 207-213.

[2] Tocqueville declares (*France before the Revolution*, 92) that in the musty archives he found many cases of this kind where the original sum needed for repair would not have exceeded five dollars.

signing individuals, high or low, to prison without trial, merely by a letter with the royal seal. Such letters were not only used to remove political offenders, down to the man who spoke jestingly of the king's mistress, but they were often secured also by private individuals of influence to remove rivals, and by parents to discipline unruly sons. Usually the imprisonments were for a few months; but sometimes the wretch was virtually forgotten and left to die in prison, perhaps without ever learning the cause of his arrest.[1] One minister is said to have signed one hundred and fifty thousand of these "lettres de cachet," besides sending out others, *signed in blank*, to his Intendants. Very properly did Blackstone, the English law writer, class France with Turkey as countries where "personal liberty" was "wholly at the mercy of the ruler."

300. Complications from Survivals of Old Local Governments and from Class Feeling. — This centralized machinery was likely to be clumsy, from the amount of detail it had to attend to. Moreover, it was complicated by many factors that did not show on the surface. It is important to understand that France was still a patchwork of territories which had been seized piece by piece by the kings. Each province had its own laws and customs, its own privileges and exemptions; and the Intendant, absolute as he was, had to respect these checks. Even the taxes varied widely; and salt, for instance, cost in one province ten or twelve times as much as it did in another just alongside. This absence of uniformity was a serious obstacle to efficient government. Moreover, tyrannical as the monarchy might be toward individuals, it never dared offend the nobles as a body, or the church; and ordinarily it showed respect to multitudes of local interests. France was covered with shadows of old local governments, which had lost their power for action but which remained powerful to delay and obstruct. Two classes of such survivals need attention, — the Provincial Assemblies of certain districts, and the Parlement of Paris.

a. Anciently, each province had had its Assembly of three estates. In the thirteenth century, the French kings began to abolish these assemblies; but several large provinces kept them until the Revolution.

---

[1] Arthur Young, *Travels*, 313 (Bohn edition), tells of an Englishman who had been kept in a French prison thirty years, although not even the government held a record of the reason.

These *Pays d'État* (Provinces with Estates), like Brittany, Languedoc, and Champagne, were all on the frontier. They had been acquired late, and had preserved their "Estates" by treaty. The Provincial Estates exercised considerable control over local improvements and local taxation, and their mere existence was a check upon royal absolutism.

b. The Parlement of Paris was a law court, like several others in France, but more important than any other. Membership was originally purchased from the king, but it had become a property right, and the seats were virtually hereditary, though a holder might sell his place. When the king issued a new edict, it was not considered in force until it had been "registered," or put on record, by this Parlement. This constituted a slight check upon the king's power of making laws. The Parlement could send back an objectionable edict with a remonstrance (though such action was most unusual), and so might possibly secure a reconsideration by the monarch. Of course, in such a case, the Parlement would explain that it felt sure the king had not meant quite what the words of the edict seemed to say; and of course, too, if the king was in earnest, he had only to summon the Parlement before him and in person order it to register.[1]

Toward the close of the reign of Louis XV, however, the Parlement had claimed the right of absolute veto and had refused to register, even when so ordered. Whereupon Louis had banished or imprisoned the members; but his successor had brought them back, to play a part in setting in motion the coming Revolution (§ 310).

301. The Government summarized. — Thus the government of France was a centralized despotism, anxious to keep the good opinion of the privileged classes and hindered in its work by the complex survivals of ancient local institutions. To run such a machine called for a Napoleon or a Bismarck; but hereditary monarchy in the eighteenth century had ceased to furnish great rulers.[2] Louis XIV had been a tireless worker. His successor, the selfish, keen-sighted Louis XV, was wont to say, with his mistress, "Let the good machine run itself; it will last our time; after us, the deluge;" or, as the same shameless king said about his coming successor, "I should like very much to see how Berry will pull through with it."

---

[1] This proceeding was known as holding a "bed of justice." Cf. § 129, note.

[2] Jefferson, with some exaggeration, wrote from Paris in 1787 to Monroe that there was not a crowned head in Europe with abilities to fit its possessor to act as a Virginia vestryman.

Under this "Berry" (Louis XVI), a benevolent idler, of infirm will and mediocre talent, the "machine" was to go to pieces and the "deluge" was to come.

E. The Men of Letters.[1]

302. Voltaire, Rousseau, and their Fellows. — A revolution, it has been said, requires not only abuses but also ideas. The combustibles were ready; now came the men of ideas to apply the igniting match. About 1750, there began a period of dazzling brilliancy in French literature. Never before in the history of the world had any country seen so numerous and so eminent a group of men of letters. *Voltaire*, the greatest of the illustrious company, had already won the fame he was to enjoy nearly thirty years more; *Diderot* and his associates began the great "Encyclopedia" in 1751; and two years later appeared the first work of *Rousseau*. Beside these men stood scores of others only less eminent. Most of the writing, except Rousseau's, was critical and destructive. With biting satire and keen mockery and powerful logic, these authors daringly attacked the superstitions and scandals of the church and the absurdities and evils of society. Most of them, it is true, confused the corruptions of the church with religion itself, and sometimes they are remembered chiefly for their

VOLTAIRE.

---

[1] On this topic see Mathews, 52–72, or Mallet, 28–45.

attack upon Christianity; but of course, "their glory lies not in their contempt for things holy but in their scorn for things unjust." They railed at absentee bishops of licentious lives; they questioned the privileges of the nobles; and they pitilessly exposed the absurdity and iniquity of the gabelle and of the "letters of the seal." Voltaire's powerful plea for religious tolerance and his life-long exposure of the folly and wrong of religious persecution had much to do with creating the free atmosphere in which we live to-day.[1]

303. Rousseau and Political Democracy. — Some of these authors had learned to admire English liberty and the English constitutional monarchy;[2] but most of them, like Voltaire, looked rather for reform by some enlightened, philosophic despot. One alone of all their number stood for democracy. This was Rousseau. He taught much that was absurd, as to an ideal "state of nature" "before governments were formed by men"; but he also taught the final and absolute sovereignty of the people. His most famous book (*The Social Contract*, 1762) opens with the words, "Man was born free, but he is now everywhere in chains"; and the volume argues passionately man's right and duty to recover freedom. Rousseau's moral earnestness and enthusiasm made his doctrine not a mere intellectual speculation, but a popular religion. He was preëminently the prophet of the political side of the coming Revolution.[3]

---

[1] J. R. Lowell says, "We owe half our liberty to that leering old mocker"; and Professor Jowett of Oxford, an English Churchman, declares that Voltaire "did more good than all the Fathers of the Church together." John Morley has well said that Voltaire's life, with its long challenge of all existing institutions, was of itself equivalent to a revolution. Voltaire is often incorrectly called an atheist. Though not a Christian, he was a deist, — a firm believer in a God revealed in nature and in the human soul.

[2] Buckle, *History of Civilization*, opening of ch. xii, has a marvelous ten pages of proof of English influence.

[3] Some years before the French Revolution, these phrases and ideas of Rousseau were to have a powerful influence in America. They did not create the American Revolution, but they may have determined to some degree how that great movement should justify itself in words. The passages about

304. Philosophic Liberalism becomes Fashionable. — When the French writers began to attack hoary abuses, they ran extreme personal risks and played an heroic part. The same movement, however, that produced these men of letters was at work in all social circles. The writers intensified the movement; and, before long, criticism of social arrangements became general. Even the privileged orders began to talk about their own uselessness. When the great noble in a popular play was asked what he had done to deserve all his privileges, and when it was answered for him, "Your Excellency took the trouble to be born," the audience of nobles in the boxes laughed and applauded. Part of this new attitude was only sentimentality; but there was also a real change. In the fifteen years just before the Revolution, society did become less artificial and less corrupt, and some of the nobles did try zealously to resume long-abandoned duties.

Upon the whole, however, this new pity for the poor proved helpless to relieve them. The mass of the privileged classes remained selfish and scornful. The chief influence of the new philosophy was in its effect upon the unprivileged masses. The third estate was imbued with a new consciousness of its wrongs and of its power, and with a determination to secure its rights. Said a famous pamphlet of *Siéyès* (§ 314) on the eve of the Revolution, "What really is the third estate? Everything. What has it been so far in the state? Nothing. What does it ask? To be something."

F. Attempted Reforms, from the Accession of Louis XVI to the Meeting of the States General, 1774–1789.

305. Character of the Sovereign. — In 1774, the dissolute but able Louis XV was succeeded by the well-disposed but irresolute Louis XVI. This Prince had a vague notion of what was right and a general desire to do it, but he lacked moral courage and will power. His weakness was as harmful to France as his predecessor's wickedness. He abandoned the wisest policy and the best ministers, rather than face the sour looks of the courtiers and the pouts of the Queen.

---

natural equality and freedom in the Declaration of Independence and in many of the original state constitutions are popularly supposed to be due to American admiration for Rousseau. Rousseau, however, drew these ideas to a great extent from John Locke and other English writers of the seventeenth century; and we cannot always tell whether an American document is affected directly by Rousseau or by the older but less impressive English literature.

The Queen was Marie Antoinette, daughter of the great Maria Theresa of Austria. She was young, high-spirited, and lovely; but she had come to the vile court of Louis XV as a child-bride, and had grown up under its evil influence. Historians differ regarding her character, but, at the best, she was ignorant, frivolous, and selfishly bent upon her own pleasures, without the slightest comprehension of her real duties. The King was greatly influenced by her, and, in matters of government, almost always for evil.

306. National Bankruptcy.—When Louis XVI came to the throne, the national debt was some five hundred million dollars, *and it was increasing each year by ten million dollars more*. This condition stirred the government to spasmodic attempts at reform. To the view of the court, the danger to France lay, not in the social injustice or in the misery of the masses, but merely in the empty treasury. Says Carlyle, with bitter scorn, "It is spiritual bankruptcy, long tolerated, now verging toward economic bankruptcy and become intolerable."

307. Turgot.— Louis XVI at once called to his aid *Turgot*, a man of letters, a reformer, and an experienced administrator. Turgot had been an Intendant for many years, and had made remarkable improvements in his district. Now he set about conferring still greater benefits on all France. He abolished the corvée, the internal tariffs on grain, and the outgrown gilds, with their restrictions on the right to labor. The frivolous expenses of the court were cut down, and the absurd pension list was curtailed remorselessly. Turgot planned other vast and far-reaching reforms, — to recast the whole system of taxation, to equalize burdens, to abolish feudal dues, and to introduce a system of public education: "a whole *pacific* French Revolution in that head," says Carlyle. But the Queen hated the reformer, who interfered with her pleasures; and Louis, who had promised unfailing support, wavered, grew cold, and, after only twenty months, dismissed the man who might perhaps have saved France from a revolution of violence.

Turgot rejected impatiently all ideas of reform by the people. He wished no States General. He belonged to the autocratic reformers of the day, and he expected to refashion France through the despotic power of the monarch. At the same time he tried to secure the support of public opinion. He recommended his reforms to the public, and explained his purposes, in prefaces to the royal edicts. In abolishing the corvée, a proclamation said, "The roads are made by the forced labor of those who are least interested in roads." The edict abolishing restrictions on trade declared, "The right to work is the most sacred of possessions; every law by which it is infringed violates the natural rights of man, and is null and void of itself. . . . The existing corporations are grotesque and tyrannical monopolies, — results of the selfish avarice and violence of their privileged members, and of the fiscal avidity of the crown."

Such language in royal documents was significant, and somewhat awkward when the crown soon afterward restored these "tyrannical monopolies"; but the striking fact was that the government should think it necessary to give its reasons at all. Soon it would be compelled to do so.

308. Necker. — Turgot's reforms were swiftly undone; but after a little, in 1776, *Necker*, another reformer, was called to the helm. Necker was not a great statesman, but he was a good business man with liberal sentiments; and he might have accomplished something for the national finances, if his difficulties had not been tremendously augmented in an unforeseen manner. In 1778, France joined America in the war against England. The new "loans"[1] to support the expense of the war greatly increased the national debt, and made it more impossible to pay the annual interest.[2] Necker secured a number of minor reforms, and he enforced a strict economy,

---

[1] When a nation sells bonds to raise money, the proceeding is called a loan.
[2] The American Revolution directly helped to bring on the French Revolution by sinking the French monarchy more hopelessly into bankruptcy. In other important but more indirect ways the American movement contributed to that in France. Lafayette and other young nobles who had served in America came home with liberal ideas strengthened; and the French regiments that had fought side by side with the American yeomanry had imbibed democratic ideas and were soon to declare themselves "the army of the nation," not of the king. Said Arthur Young in 1789, "The American Revolution has laid the foundation for another one in France;" and again, "A strong leaven of independence has been increasing here every hour since the American Revolution."

which angered the courtiers; but finally he found himself forced to more radical measures. He laid before the King a plan for comprehensive reform, much along Turgot's lines; but the universal outcry of the privileged classes caused Louis to dismiss him from office (1781). Just before that event, Necker published to the nation a detailed statement of the government's finances. This was a step farther than Turgot had gone in consulting the public. The statement showed in figures the miserable injustice of the existing system; and the minister retired, hated by the privileged orders, but the idol of the people.

309. Calonne and the Notables. — Once more, all the old abuses were restored. Then a new minister of finance, the courtly Calonne, adopted the policy of an unscrupulous bankrupt and tried to create credit by lavish extravagance. For a time this was successful; but in 1786 the annual deficit had risen to twenty-five million dollars, and even adroit Calonne could borrow no more money to pay expenses or interest. Under these conditions, the minister persuaded Louis to call together the Notables of France.

The Notables were not an elected body. They were composed of such leading nobles and clergy as the king pleased to summon. Still, this assembly, nearly a hundred and fifty strong, was in an imperfect way a representation of France. At least it represented the privileged orders. To the amazed Notables, Calonne suggested that the privileged orders give up their exemption from taxation. But all cried out against him, — the few Liberals for what he had done in the past, the many Conservatives for what he now proposed to do.

310. The Parlement of Paris and the States General. — Calonne gave way to a new minister, a favorite of the Queen, who found himself at once driven to the same plan. In fact it had become necessary to get more money, and that could be done only by taxing those who had something wherewith to pay. As the Notables were still stubborn, they were dismissed, and the King tried to force the plan upon the nobles by royal edict

The Parlement of Paris, representing the privileged orders, refused to register the edict, and cloaked their dislike to reform under the excuse that *the only power in France which could properly impose a new tax was the States General.* Louis summoned resolution to banish the Parlement, but it had given a rallying cry to the nation.

The *States General* (§ 154) had not met since 1614. Suggestions for assembling it had been made from time to time, ever since Louis XVI became king. At the session of the Notables, Lafayette had called for it. Now, after the action of the Parlement, the demand became universal and imperious. Finally, August, 1788, the King yielded, restored the Parlement, recalled Necker, and promised that the States General should be assembled.

G. Summary.

The States General were soon to inaugurate the Revolution. Before we take up that story, it is worth while to summarize the conditions and causes of the coming change.

311. The Chief Institutions of France were: (1) *a monarchy*, centralized, despotic, and irresponsible, but incumbered, ineffective, and in weak hands; (2) *an aristocracy*, wealthy, privileged, corrupt, skeptical; and (3) *an established church*, wealthy and often corrupt. Below these spread *the masses*, as a necessary but ugly substructure.

Like conditions existed also over the continent of Europe. In France, as compared with the other large countries, the nobles had fewer duties, the peasantry had risen somewhat, and more of a middle class had grown up. That is, *feudal society was more decayed and the industrial state was more advanced* in France than in other continental countries. This explains why the Revolution came in France. Revolutions break through in the weakest spots.

312. The Causes of the Revolution classified. — First among the causes of the Revolution, we must put the *unjust privileges* of the small upper class and the *crushing burdens* borne by the great non-privileged mass. These evils, however, were no greater than for centuries before. *But the consciousness of them was greater than ever before.* Not only was the system bad, but men knew that it was bad. The masses were beginning to demand reform; and the privileged classes and the government had begun to distrust their rights, and were to find their power of resistance weakened by such doubts. This new intellectual condition was due primarily to *the new school of French men of letters*, whose influence was strengthened by England and America. Then, the *financial bankruptcy of the national treasury* opened the way for other forces to act, and started the government itself upon the path of reform ; and *the inefficiency and indecision of the government* led the people finally to seize upon the reform movement themselves, — a result greatly hastened by the political doctrines made popular just before by Rousseau.

For Further Reading. — Source material may be found in the *Pennsylvania Reprints*, IV, No 5 (examples of cahiers); V, No. 2 (Protest of the *Cour des Aides*); and VI, No. 1 (short extracts from French writers of the time). Stephens' *Life and Writings of Turgot* gives translations of the writings of the great reformer. Arthur Young's *Travels in France in 1787-1789* is the best contemporary description.

Modern accounts : Lowell's *Eve of the French Revolution* is perhaps the best one-volume survey, for popular purposes, though the work is based only on secondary authorities, and the view of the Old Régime is perhaps too cheerful. Maclehose's *Last Days of the French Monarchy*, Grant's *Fall of the French Monarchy*, Dabney's *Causes of the French Revolution*, and Kingsley's *Ancient Régime* are also good. Tocqueville's *France before the Revolution* (especially book ii, chs. i, vi, ix, and xii) and Taine's *Ancient Régime* (especially on classes of society, 13-85, and 329-402) are among the greatest studies ever made of this period. John Morley's *Lives* of Voltaire, Rousseau, and Diderot, and his essays in his *Miscellanies*, upon "France in the Eighteenth Century" (Vol. III) and "Turgot" (Vol. II), are admirable and interesting. Say's *Turgot* is excellent. Lecky's *England in the Eighteenth Century*, V, ch. xx, and Buckle's *History of Civilization*, chs. viii-xiv, may be consulted by advanced students. The opening pages of most of the histories of the Revolution listed on page 343 have brief treatments of the conditions before 1789, — especially Shailer Mathews (pages 1-110), Mallet (5-50), and Gardiner (1-32).

III. FIRST PERIOD OF THE REVOLUTION, MAY, 1789– AUGUST, 1792: CONSTITUTIONAL MONARCHY.

A. The First Three Months: the Constituent Assembly at Versailles.

313. Election of the States General. — France had lost even the tradition of how to elect a States General. The government asked for suggestions, and learned societies showered down pamphlets of advice. Finally the country was divided into districts; the nobility and clergy of each district came together to choose their delegates; and the delegates of the third estate were elected by a complex system of electoral colleges. In choosing these colleges, all tax payers had a voice. When finally chosen, the States General consisted of about six hundred members of the third estate, three hundred nobles, and three hundred clergy. Of this last order, two-thirds were curés. The delegates possessed almost no political experience; but the bulk of the third estate were lawyers, and, as a whole, the gathering was scholarly and cultured. It contained no representatives from the "lower classes."

314. The States General becomes the National Assembly. — May 5, 1789, the King opened the States General at Versailles.[1] Before the elections, the Liberals had demanded (1) *double representation* for the third estate (or as many representatives as the other two orders together), and (2) *vote by member*, instead of by three separate orders. The double representation had been granted, but the other half of the question had been left to settle itself. The nobles and the clergy proceeded to organize as separate chambers, after the ancient fashion. This would have given the privileged orders two votes, to one for the third estate, and would have blocked all vital reforms. The third estate insisted that all three orders should organize in a single chamber, where its double membership could outvote the other orders combined. With wise generalship, it refused to "usurp the right to organize" until it should have been joined by the other "delegates of the nation"; and there followed a deadlock for five weeks.

But delay was serious. The preceding harvest had been a

---

[1] In the royal address, some reforms were suggested; but it was plain that the King hoped mainly for more taxes, and enthusiastic Liberals were sadly disappointed. Even Necker's three-hour address, which followed the King's, dwelt almost exclusively upon the need of prompt action to relieve the financial straits of the government. Read Carlyle's account of the procession.

failure, and famine was abroad in the land. In Paris every bakeshop had its "tail" of men and women, standing through the night for a chance to buy bread. Such conditions called for speedy action, especially as the ignorant masses had got it into their heads that the marvelous States General would in some way make food plenty. Finally (June 17), on motion of Siéyès (§ 304), an ex-priest, the third estate declared that by itself it represented ninety-six per cent of the nation, and that, with or without the other orders, it would organize as a *National Assembly*.[1] *This was a revolution. It changed a gathering of feudal Estates into an assembly representing the nation as one whole. Nothing of this kind had ever been seen before on the continent of Europe.*

315. The Tennis Court Oath: the National Assembly becomes the Constituent Assembly. — Two days later, the National Assembly was joined by half the clergy (mainly curés) and by a few liberal nobles. But the next morning the Assembly found sentries at the doors of their hall and carpenters within putting up staging, to prepare for a "royal session." Plainly the King was about to interfere. The gathering adjourned to a tennis court near by, and there unanimously took a memorable oath[2] *never to separate until they had established the constitution on a firm foundation* (June 20).

This Tennis Court Oath marks an era. The idea of a written constitution came from America. Six years earlier, Franklin, our minister to France, had published French translations of the constitutions adopted by the new American States. The pamphlet had been widely read, and had called forth much discussion. The instructions[3] of delegates to the Assembly had very commonly called, among other matters, for

---

[1] See Anderson's *Constitutions and Documents*, No. 1, for the decree.

[2] See the text in Anderson's *Constitutions and Documents*, No. 2.

[3] Nearly every gathering for choosing delegates to the Assembly, or even to the electoral colleges, had drawn up a statement of grievances and had suggested reforms, for the guidance of its representatives. These *cahiers* (kä-yā′) are the most valuable source of our knowledge of France before the Revolution. See *Pennsylvania Reprints*, IV, No. 5, for examples.

a constitution, but, so far, the idea had lain rather in the background. After the Tennis Court Oath, however, to make a constitution became the chief purpose of the Assembly; and that body soon became known as the *Constituent Assembly*.

On June 23, Louis summoned the three estates to meet him, and told them that they were to organize as separate bodies and to carry out certain specified reforms: if they failed to comply with the royal wishes, the King would himself "secure the happiness of his people." When the King left, the nobles and higher clergy followed. The new "National Assembly" kept their seats. There was a moment of uncertainty. It was a serious matter for those quiet citizens to brave the wrath of the ancient monarchy. Mirabeau, soon to be known as the greatest man in France, — a noble who had abandoned his order, — rose to remind the delegates of their great oath. The Marquis de Brézé, master of ceremonies, reëntering, asked if they had not heard the King's command to disperse. "Yes," broke in Mirabeau's thunder; "but go tell your master that we are here by the power of the people, and that nothing but the power of bayonets shall drive us away." Then, upon Mirabeau's motion, the Assembly decreed the inviolability of its members: "Infamous and guilty of capital crime is any person or court that shall dare pursue or arrest any of them, *on whose part soever the same be commanded.*"[1]

The King's weakness prevented conflict, and perhaps it was as well for him; for Paris was rising, and the French Guards, the main body of troops then in the capital, when ordered to fire on the mob, rang their musket butts sullenly on the pavement. The next day, forty-seven nobles joined the National Assembly, and in less than a week the King ordered the rest to enter.

316. Paris saves the Assembly; Fall of the Bastille. — However, the court planned a counter-revolution. A camp of several thousand veterans was collected near Paris, — largely

---

[1] The royal declaration and this decree are in Anderson, No. 3.

German or Swiss regiments who could be depended upon. Probably it was intended to imprison leading liberal deputies: certainly the Assembly was to be overawed or dissolved. July 9, Mirabeau boldly declared to the Assembly that such was the royal policy, and he secured an address from the Assembly to the King, solemnly requesting the immediate withdrawal of the troops. The King's answer was to banish Necker, who, as minister, had opposed the new royal policy. This was on the evening of July 11. About noon the next day, the news was whispered on the streets. Camille Desmoulins, a young journalist, pistol in hand, leaped upon a table in one of the public gardens, exclaiming, "Necker is dismissed. It is a signal for a St. Bartholomew of patriots. To arms! To arms!" By night the streets bristled with barricades against the charge of the King's cavalry, and the crowds were sacking bakeshops for bread and gunshops for arms. Three regiments of the French Guards joined the rebels. Various street conflicts took place. Some rude organization was introduced during the next day; and, on the day following, the revolutionary forces attacked the Bastille.

The Bastille was the great "state prison," like the Tower in England. In it had been confined political offenders and victims of "letters of the seal." It was a symbol of the Old Régime and an object of detestation to the Liberals. It had been used as an arsenal, and the rebels went to it at first only to demand arms. Refused admission and fired upon, they made a frantic attack. The fortress was virtually impregnable; but after some hours of wild onslaught, it surrendered to an almost unarmed force, — "taken," as Carlyle says, "like Jericho, by miraculous sound." The hangers-on of the attacking force massacred the garrison, and paraded their heads on pikes through the streets. Out at Versailles, Louis, who had spent the day hunting and had retired early, was awakened to hear the news. "What! a riot, then?" said he. "No, Sire," replied the messenger; "a revolution." Soon after, the Bastille was razed to the ground, and the anniversary of its destruction

(July 14) is still celebrated in France as the birthday of political liberty.[1]

The rising of Paris had saved the Assembly. The most hated of the courtiers fled from France. The King visited Paris, sanctioned all that had been done, sent away the troops, accepted the tricolor, the badge of the Revolution, as the national colors, and recalled Necker.

317. Anarchy; and Reorganization on the Part of the Bourgeoisie: Municipal Councils and Guards. — The fall of the Bastille gave the signal for a brief mob-rule all over France. In towns, the mobs demolished local fortresses. In the country, the lower peasantry and bands of vagabonds plundered and demolished castles, seeking especially to destroy the court rolls, with the records of servile dues. Each district had its carnival of plunder, with outrage and bloodshed.

More instructive than this anarchy, however, is the new order that evolved out of it. The King could not enforce the law: the machinery of the old royal government had simply collapsed. The Assembly did not dare interfere vigorously, because it might need the mob again for its own protection.[2] But everywhere the middle class organized locally against anarchy. In Paris, during the disorder of July 13, the electoral college of the city met at the Hotel de Ville, and assumed the authority to act as the Municipal Council. In other municipalities the like was done;[3] and in a few weeks, France was covered with new local governments composed of the bour-

---

[1] Read Carlyle's account of the celebration of the first anniversary.

[2] Six days after the fall of the Bastille, the moderate Liberals proposed to issue a proclamation denouncing popular violence. From an obscure seat on the Extreme-Left, Robespierre, then an unknown deputy, protested vehemently: "Revolt? This revolt is liberty. To-morrow the shameful plots against us may be renewed, and who will then repulse them if we declare rebels the men who have rushed to our protection!"

[3] This was the easier, because in many cases the electoral colleges, instead of breaking up after the election, had continued to hold occasional meetings during the two months since, in order to correspond with their delegates in the National Assembly. Cf. Stephens, I, 192 ff.

geoisie. The first act of the Paris provisional Council had been to order that in each of the sixty "sections" (wards) of the city, two hundred men should patrol the streets, to maintain order. This, or something like this, was done in all the districts of France. The new militia became permanent. It took the name *National Guards*, and in Paris Lafayette became the commander. Like the new municipal councils, the Guards were made up from the middle class; and before the middle of August, these new forces had restored order.[1]

318. Abolition of "Privilege." — Meantime, on the evening of August 4, the discussions of the Assembly were interrupted by the report of a committee on the disorders throughout the country. The account stirred the Assembly deeply. One of the young nobles who had served in America declared that these evils were all due to the continuance of feudal burdens, and, with impassioned oratory, he moved their instant abolition. One after another, in eager emulation, the liberal nobles followed, each moving some sacrifice for his order, — game laws, dovecotes, tithes, exclusive right to military office, and a mass of sinecures and pensions.[2] In like manner, representatives of the towns moved the surrender of ancient and exclusive rights possessed by their cities. Every proposal was ratified with applause. Our American minister, Gouverneur Morris, was disgusted with the haste, and even Mirabeau called the scene "an orgy of sacrifice." One night accomplished what might well have taken a year's calm debate, and no doubt much confusion and hardship resulted; but, on the whole, the work was necessary and noble, and it has never been undone. *The night of August 4 saw the end of feudalism and of legal inequalities in France.*[3]

---

[1] Taine gives the darkest picture of the disorders; see *French Revolution*, book iii, chs. i and ii. For the opposite view, see Stephens, I, ch. vi.

[2] This surrender was voluntary: it was not caused by the action of the third estate.

[3] Anderson, No. 4, and *Pennsylvania Reprints*, I, No. 5, give the decrees, as finally put in order a few days later.

319. Summary: May 5 to August 5. — Thus in three months France had been revolutionized. The third estate had asserted successfully its just claim to represent the nation, and had compelled the King and the privileged orders to acknowledge its right to recast society and government. The odious inequalities at law and the class distinctions of the Old Régime had been forever swept away. The local units of the country had already set up new popular governments, and had organized new citizen armies to protect them: and the Assembly was hard at work upon a new constitution for the nation at large.

B. THE CONSTITUENT ASSEMBLY IN PARIS, OCTOBER, 1789–OCTOBER, 1791.

320. The March of the Women, October 5. — Two years more were spent in making the constitution and in putting it into operation, piece by piece. Early in this period the scene changed from Versailles, with its danger of royal interference, to Paris, with its mob influence. Even after the new harvest of 1789, food remained scarce and riots continued. To maintain order, the King brought to Versailles one of the foreign regiments. Suspicion awoke that he was again plotting to undo the Revolution. Extravagant loyal demonstration at a military banquet emphasized the suspicion. It was reported that young officers, to win the favor of court ladies, had trampled upon the tricolor and had displayed instead the old white cockade of the Bourbon monarchy. The men of Paris tried to go to Versailles to secure the person of the King, but the National Guards turned them back. Then thousands of the women of the market place, crying that French soldiers would not fire upon women, set out in a wild, hungry, haggard rout to bring the King to Paris. In their wake, followed the riffraff of the city. Lafayette permitted the movement to go on, until there came near being a terrible massacre at Versailles; but his tardy arrival, late at night, with twenty thousand National Guards, restored order. In the early morning, however, the mob broke into the palace; and probably the Queen's life was saved only by the gallant self-sacrifice of some of her guards. The King yielded to the demands of the crowd and to the advice of Lafayette; and the same day a strange procession escorted the royal family to Paris, — the mob dancing in wild joy along the road before the royal carriage, carrying on pikes the heads of the slain soldiers, and shouting, "Now we shall have bread, for we are bringing the baker, the baker's wife, and the baker's little boy."[1] The King's brothers and great numbers of the nobles fled from France; and many of these "Emigrants" strove at foreign courts to stir up war against their country, so that the name "Emigrant" became hateful to all patriotic Frenchmen.

321. The Assembly in Paris: Parties; the Galleries; the Clubs.
— Gradually the Assembly divided into parties. On the Speaker's right, the place of honor, sat the extreme Conservatives, known from their position as the *Right*. They were reactionists, and stood for the restoration of the old order. Next to them sat the *Right-Center*. This party did not expect to restore the old conditions, but they did hope to prevent the Revolution from going any farther, and they wished to keep political power in the hands of the wealthy landowners. The *Left-Center*, the largest body, wished neither to restrict power to the very wealthy, nor to extend it to the very poor, but to intrust it to the middle class. In this group sat Mirabeau, Lafayette, and Siéyès. Both parties of the Center wished a constitutional monarchy. The *Extreme-Left*[2] comprised some thirty deputies who were disciples of Rousseau. They wished manhood suffrage, and possibly they already believed in a republic, though at the time they had no serious hope of one. In this group sat Robespierre.

---

[1] Read Carlyle's account of this March of the Women. For another picture, see Taine, *French Revolution*, I, 96–107.

[2] In the legislatures of continental Europe a like arrangement of parties is still customary. The Conservatives sit on the right, the Liberals on the left; and they are still known by the party names, the Right and the Left. In England, the supporters of the ministry sit on the right, and the opposition on the left, and the two parties change places with a change of ministry; so in that country the "Left" and the "Right" are not party names.

When the Assembly followed the King to Paris, nearly a fourth of the members withdrew, declaring that the deliberations were now controlled by the mob. Among the withdrawals were some of the earliest leaders of reform, but of course the great body of them came from the Right. The sessions were all public, and the galleries interrupted unpopular and conservative speakers with jeers or threats, and sometimes attacked them afterward on the streets. Sometimes, too, the galleries were packed by a mob paid to hiss down certain speakers and to secure the passage of particular measures.

Another important political power was found in the clubs. Of these the most important was the *Jacobins*.[1] Here some of the deputies of the Left-Center met to discuss measures that were about to come up in the Assembly. Others beside deputies were admitted, and the club became the chief organ of the radical democracy. Lafayette and Mirabeau tried to counteract the Jacobin influence by organizing a Constitutionalist Club, of more moderate sentiments; but, as with various royalist clubs, the effort came to little. The clubs, like the galleries, were best suited to add strength to the Extreme-Left.

322. Mirabeau and his Plan. — One man in the Assembly was a party in himself. Mirabeau was a marvelous orator, a statesman of profound insight, and a man of dauntless courage. He never hesitated to oppose the mob, if his convictions required it; and often he won them to his side. But he had lived a wild and dissolute life, and so could not gain influence over some of the best elements of the Assembly, while his arrogance aroused much jealousy. Both Necker and Lafayette hated him.

Mirabeau was resolutely opposed to anarchy, and he believed in a stronger executive than the Assembly was willing to create. After the events of October, he saw truly that the

---

[1] It took its name from the fact that it met in a building belonging to the Dominican friars. This order in Paris was called Jacobins, because its first home in the city had been at the church of St. Jacques.

danger to the Revolution lay not so much in the weakened King as in the mob; and thereafter, he sought to preserve the remaining royal power and to direct it. He wished the King to accept the Revolution in good faith, and to surround himself with a liberal ministry chosen from the Assembly. No doubt, Mirabeau expected to be the guiding genius of that ministry. His hopes were ruined by a decree of the Assembly that no deputy should take office under the King. Almost fatally thwarted, Mirabeau sought next to become the King's unofficial adviser; and, as the mob grew more furious, he wished the King to leave Paris and to raise the provinces against the capital in behalf of the Revolution so far accomplished.[1]

323. Attempted Flight of the King: Clash between Constitutionalist Bourgeoisie and Republican Mob. — The King hesitated, and Mirabeau died (April 2, 1791), broken down by the strain of his work. Then Louis decided upon a wild modification of Mirabeau's plan. He would flee, not to the French provinces, but to Austria, to raise war not against the Paris mob but against France and the Revolution. The plot failed, because of the King's indecision and clumsiness. The royal family did get out of Paris (June 20, 1791) and well toward the frontier, but they were recognized, arrested, and brought back as prisoners.[2]

This attempt of the King led to another popular rising, this time not to save the Assembly from the King, but to force the Assembly to dethrone the King. A petition for such action and for the establishment of a republic was drawn up, and crowds flocked out from Paris to the Champs de Mars to sign it. Some disorder occurred. The municipal authorities seized the excuse to forbid the gathering; and finally Lafayette's National Guards dispersed the jeering mob with volleys of musketry. This "Massacre of the Champs de Mars" (July 17)

---

[1] Exercise: report upon Mirabeau's sincerity. Note the excellent statement in Gardiner's *French Revolution*, 82–85.

[2] Read Carlyle's interesting account. See Anderson for documents.

took place three days after the second anniversary of the Fall of the Bastille, and indeed it was connected with the celebration of that event. It marks a sharp division between the mob and the bourgeoisie. For the time, the latter carried the day. In the next six weeks the victorious Assembly completed and revised its two-years' work; and September 14, 1791, after solemnly swearing to uphold the constitution, Louis was restored to power.

C. THE CONSTITUTION OF 1791.

324. General Characteristics. — The constitution made all Frenchmen equal before the law and equally eligible to public employment; it permitted no exemptions, no special privileges, no hereditary titles; and it established jury trial, freedom of conscience, and freedom of the press.[1] That is, socially it aimed to secure *equality* for all citizens and *uniformity* for all provinces of France, with a large amount of *personal liberty*. Politically, it provided for a *limited monarchy*, with extreme *decentralization* (*i.e.* a large amount of local self-government) and with *middle-class control*.

325. Local Government. — The historic provinces, with their troublesome traditions of peculiar privileges and customs, were wiped from the map. France was divided into eighty-three "departments," of nearly equal size. The departments were subdivided into districts (*arrondissements*); and the district was made up of communes (villages or towns, with their adjacent territory). Each department and district elected a "General Council" and an executive board, or "Directory." The forty thousand communes had each its elected Council and mayor. So much authority was left to the communes, that France under this constitution has been called "a loose alliance of forty thousand little republics."[2]

---

[1] Read the "Declaration of the Rights of Man," in the *Pennsylvania Reprints*, I, No. 5, or in Anderson, No. 5.

[2] The extreme decentralization was not to last long, but the plan of the local government in many respects survives to-day.

326. The Central Government was made to consist of the king and a Legislative Assembly of one chamber. The Assembly was to be elected anew each two years. The king could not dissolve it, and his veto upon any measure could be overridden by the action of three successive legislatures. Indeed, one serious error of the constitution was in weakening the executive unreasonably, so that it became little more than a figurehead.

327. The Franchise. — Middle-class supremacy was secured by *graded property qualifications* and by a *system of indirect elections*.[1] Citizens who did not pay taxes equal in amount to at least three days' wages for an artisan had *no* vote. These "passive citizens" made about one-fourth the adult male population. The other three-fourths were known as "active citizens." They composed the National Guards and the primary political assemblies in each commune; but to hold even the lower offices was possible only to those who paid a higher tax, such as to shut out all workmen. Out of these "more active" citizens, the primary assemblies elected municipal authorities and chose district electoral colleges. From those who paid still higher taxes, these electoral colleges elected district and departmental authorities, and chose departmental electoral colleges, which elected deputies to the National Assembly.

328. The Church under the New Constitution. — For much of its existence, the Constituent Assembly had been forced to wrestle with the problem of an empty treasury and to find means to run the government. In the disorders of 1789, people ceased to pay the old taxes, and it was many months before a new system could be devised and put into operation. Meantime the Assembly secured funds by seizing and selling the church lands, — more than a fifth of all France and over a half-billion of dollars in value.

---

[1] Both these devices to dodge democracy were employed in the American states of that day. Advanced students may search the constitutions of the thirteen states for illustrations. No state had manhood suffrage; and, of the thirteen, five allowed only owners of real estate to vote.

At first, sales were slow; and so, with these lands as security, the Assembly issued paper money (assignats), which was received again by the government in payment for the lands. This currency was issued in such vast amounts that it depreciated rapidly.[1] Serious hardships followed;[2] but in the final outcome, the lands passed in small parcels into the hands of the peasantry and the middle class, and so laid the foundation for future prosperity. A later Assembly (the Convention, §§ 338 ff.), in like manner seized and sold the land of the Emigrant nobles, when that class levied war against France. Thus France became a land of small farmers, and the peasantry rose to a higher standard of comfort than such a class in Europe had ever known.

When the government took the revenue of the church, of course it also assumed the duty of paying the clergy and maintaining the churches. This led promptly to national control and reorganization. The number of higher clergy was greatly reduced. Ecclesiastical organization was based upon the new local divisions, and only one bishop was allotted to each department. Unfortunately, the clergy of all grades were made elective, in the same way as other civil officers, and were required to take an oath of fidelity to the constitution in a form repulsive to many sincere adherents to the pope. Only four of the old bishops took the oath; and two-thirds the curés, including no doubt the most sincere and conscientious among them, were driven into opposition to the Revolution. On the other hand, the elected "Constitutional clergy" contained many men who had little interest in religion. The greatest error of the Constituent Assembly was in so arraying against each other patriotism and the old religion.

D. THE LEGISLATIVE ASSEMBLY AND FOREIGN WAR.

329. Elections. Influence of the Jacobin Organization. — France had been made over in two years, — on the whole with little violence, — and the bulk of the nation accepted the result

---

[1] Cf. our "Continental currency" of a few years earlier.
[2] In the financial difficulties all Necker's popularity vanished, and he finally retired from office, thoroughly discredited by all parties.

enthusiastically, except as to some portions of the new organization of the church. Most men believed that the Revolution was over; and moderate Liberals very largely withdrew from active politics, not even attending the polls. On the other hand, a small but vigorous minority of radical spirits was dissatisfied with the restrictions on the franchise and with the restoration of monarchy. This minority possessed undue weight, because of its superior organization in political clubs over France. These clubs took the name Jacobin. They were all closely affiliated with the mother-club in Paris, and were strictly obedient to its suggestions. No other party had any political machinery whatever. Moreover, the Jacobins had the sympathy of the "passive citizens"; and in many cases these citizens, though they had no vote, proved an important factor in the election, terrorizing the more conservative elements by mob-violence.

330. Composition and Parties. — By a nobly intended but unwise law, the Constituent Assembly had made its members ineligible to seats in the Legislative Assembly, where their political experience would have been of the utmost value. The seven hundred and forty-five members of the Legislative Assembly were all new men. On the whole, too, they were of lower ability than the preceding Assembly. They were mostly young provincial lawyers and journalists; and there was not among them all one great proprietor or practical administrator.

The old Right and Right-Center of the first Assembly had no successors in the second. The new Right corresponded to the old Left-Center. Its members were known as *Constitutionalists* (or Feuillants), because they wished to preserve the constitution as it was. Outside the House, this party was represented by Lafayette,[1] who, since the death of Mirabeau, was the most influential man in France. In the Assembly,

---

[1] Students may profitably compare the estimates of Lafayette by different historians. Carlyle is severe; Mallet, 116-118, gives a judicial summary.

the party counted about one hundred regular adherents, but, for a time, the four hundred members of the Center, or "The Plain," voted with it on most questions. The Plain, however, was gradually won over to the more radical views of the Left. This section of the Assembly consisted of about two hundred and forty delegates, many of them connected with the Jacobin clubs. The greater part were to become known as *Girondists*.[1] They wished a republic, but they were unwilling to use unconstitutional means to get one. They feared and hated the Paris mob, and they wished to intrust power to the provinces rather than to the capital. The leaders were hot-headed, eloquent young men, with ability for feeling and phrasing fine sentiments, but with no fitness for action. The members of the Extreme-Left, known from their elevated seats as the "Mountain," were the quintessence of *Jacobinism*. This party wished a democratic government by whatever means might offer, and it contained the men of action in the Assembly.

331. The War Policy. — The significant fact about the Legislative Assembly was its influence in hurrying on foreign war. The Emigrants, breathing threats of invasion and vengeance, were gathering in arms on the Rhine, under protection of German princes. They were supported by mercenary troops, and they had secret sympathizers within France. In the winter, a treacherous plot to betray to them the great fortress of Strasburg all but succeeded. The danger was certainly real; but a proper though stern decree of the Assembly, condemning to death all Emigrants who should not return to France before a certain date, fell before the royal veto.

Back of the Emigrants loomed the danger of foreign intervention. The attempted flight of Louis in June had revealed his true position as a prisoner. His brother-in-law, the Emperor Leopold, then sent to the sovereigns of Europe a circular note (the Padua Letter), calling for common action against

---

[1] From the Gironde, the name of a department from which the leaders came.

the Revolution, inasmuch as the cause of Louis was "the cause of kings"; and a few days later, Leopold and the King of Prussia united in the Declaration of Pilnitz,[1] asserting their intention to arm, in order to act in aid of their "brother" Louis. Thus war was almost inevitable. The Revolution stood for a new social order. It and the old order could not live together. Its success was a standing invitation to revolution in neighboring lands. If the cause of Louis was "the cause of kings," so was the cause of the Revolution "the cause of peoples"; and the kings felt that they must crush it before it spread.

However, both Leopold and the Constituent Assembly had wished to avoid war if possible; and after Louis accepted the constitution in September, Leopold withdrew his offensive declaration. But the reception given the Emigrants within the Empire renewed the hard feeling; and the Legislative Assembly, unlike its predecessor, welcomed the prospect of war. It demanded of Leopold that he disperse the armies of the Emigrants and that he apologize for the Declaration of Pilnitz. Leopold replied with a counter-demand for a change in the French government such as to secure Europe against the spread of Revolutionary movements. He had finally decided upon war. Just at this moment, Leopold died, but his successor, Francis II, was even more eager for war. Compromise was no longer possible, and in April, 1792, France declared war against Austria. For the next twenty-three years Europe was involved in almost constant strife, upon a greater scale than ever before in history.

332. Attitude of Parties and Leaders. — The attempts of German princes to dictate the internal policy of the French people rightly aroused a tempest of scorn and wrath; but the light-heartedness with which the Assembly rushed into a war for which France was so ill-prepared is at first a matter of wonder.

---

[1] See Anderson, Nos. 13, 14, for this and for the Padua Letter.

The explanation, however, is not hard to find. The Constitutionalists expected war to strengthen the executive (as it would have done if Louis had honestly gone with the nation), and they hoped also that it would increase their own power, since their leader, Lafayette, was now in command of the most important army of France. On the other hand, the Girondists and the bulk of the Assembly suspected Louis of being in secret league with Austria (suspicions only too well founded), and they knew that France was filled with spies and plotters in the interests of the Emigrants. The nervous strain of such a situation was tremendous, and the majority of the Assembly preferred open war to this terror of secret treason. Moreover, the Girondists hoped vaguely that the disorders of war might offer some good excuse to set up a republic.

Indeed, the only voices raised against the war were from the Mountain and its sympathizers in the Jacobin club. Strangely enough, both Constitutionalists and Girondists were to find their ruin in the war they so recklessly invited, while the three men most active in opposing it — *Robespierre, Danton,* and *Marat* — were to be called by it to virtual dictatorship.

Marat had been a physician of considerable eminence and of high scientific attainments. His nature was jealous and suspicious, and he seems to have become half-crazed under the strain of the Revolution. Early in the days of the Constituent Assembly, his paper, "The Friend of the People," began to preach the assassination of all aristocrats. Marat was moved, however, by sincere pity for the poor and oppressed; and he opposed war, because, as he said, its suffering always fell finally upon the poor.

Robespierre before the Revolution had been a precise young lawyer in a provincial town. He had risen to the position of judge, the highest he could ever expect to attain; but he had resigned his office because he had conscientious scruples against imposing a death penalty upon a criminal. He was an enthusiastic disciple of Rousseau. He was narrow, dull, pedantic, logical, envious, incorruptible, sincere. "That man is dangerous," Mirabeau had said of him; "he will go far; he believes every word he says." In the last months of the Constituent Assembly, Robespierre had advanced rapidly in popularity and power; and now, although without a seat in the Assembly, he was the most influential member of the Jacobin Club. He opposed the war, because he feared what the Constitutionalists hoped, — a strengthening of the executive.

Danton was a Parisian lawyer. He had early become prominent in the radical clubs; and next to Mirabeau he was the strongest man brought to notice in the early years of the Revolution. He was well named "the Mirabeau of the Market Place." He was a large, forceful, shaggy, nature, and a born leader of men. Above all, he was a man of action. Not without a rude eloquence himself, he had no patience with the fine speechifying of the Girondists, when deeds not words were wanted. He opposed the war, because he saw how unprepared France was and how unfit her leaders. When it came, he was to brush aside these incompetent leaders and himself to organize France.

FOR FURTHER READING. — The three best one-volume histories of the Revolution are those by Shailer Mathews, Mallet, and Mrs. Gardiner; the two latter are somewhat conservative. There are excellent brief treatments in H. Morse Stephens' *Revolutionary Europe, 1789-1815,* Rose's *Revolutionary and Napoleonic Era,* and Morris' *French Revolution.* The best of the larger works in English is H. Morse Stephens' *History of the French Revolution* (3 vols.). Taine's *French Revolution* (3 vols.) is violently anti-democratic. Carlyle's *French Revolution* remains the most powerful and vivid presentation of the forces and of many of the episodes of the Revolution, and it should certainly be read; but it can be used to best advantage after some preliminary study upon the age, and it is sometimes inaccurate; it should be used in one of the recently edited and annotated editions (cf. bibliography at the close of this volume). Among the biographies, the following are especially good: Belloc's *Danton,* Belloc's *Robespierre,* Willert's *Mirabeau,* Blind's *Madam Roland,* and Morley's "Robespierre" (in *Miscellanies,* I). For fiction, Dickens' *Tale of Two Cities* and Victor Hugo's *Ninety-Three* are notable. (The last half dozen titles pertain especially to the period treated in the next Division.) Anderson's *Constitutions and Documents* and the *Pennsylvania Reprints,* I, No. 5, contain illustrative source material.

IV. SECOND PERIOD, 1792-1795: THE FIRST FRENCH REPUBLIC UNDER REVOLUTIONARY GOVERNMENT.

A. BREAKDOWN OF THE CONSTITUTION IN WAR.

333. New Character imparted to the Revolution by War. — The internal conditions in France would have led in any case to further constitutional changes. If France had been left to herself, however, these future changes might have been brought about as quietly as the earlier ones; but in the terrible stress of foreign war, the Revolution took on a new character of bloodshed and violence.

The massacres and disorders which we are now to survey, and which have brought reproach upon the Revolution, were not a necessary part of the Revolution itself, but were incidental to the fear of foreign conquest. Not the Revolution proper, but the war, caused the "Reign of Terror" (§ 344). Even in internal policy, the Revolution was thrown by the war into the hands of extremists who were able to carry through sweeping changes under the color of "war measures."

334. June 20: the Mob invades the Tuileries. — At the declaration of war, the raw French levies at once invaded Belgium (then an Austrian province), but were rolled back in two defeats. The German Powers, however, were no more ready than France, and a few weeks more for preparation were given before the storm broke. The Assembly decreed the banishment of all non-juring priests, many of whom were spies, and the formation of a camp of twenty thousand chosen patriots to guard the capital. Louis vetoed both Acts,[1] and immediately afterward he dismissed his Liberal ministers (June 13). The populace was convinced that he was using his power treasonably, to prevent effective opposition to the enemies of France; and on June 20 there occurred an armed rising like those of July and October, 1789. An immense throng presented to the Assembly a monster petition against the King's policy, and then broke into the Tuileries, the palace of the royal family. For hours a dense throng surged through the apartments. Louis was crowded into a window, and stood there patiently, not without courageous dignity. A red cap,

---

[1] Despite the veto, a small camp was formed, under the pretense of celebrating the festival of the destruction of the Bastille. Among the forces so collected were the six hundred Marseillaise, sent in response to the call of the deputy of Marseilles for "six hundred men who knew how to die." These men were to be the chief reliance in the coming insurrection of August 10 (§ 335). They entered Paris, singing a new battle hymn, which was afterward chanted on many a Revolutionary battle field and which was to become famous as *The Marseillaise*. Special report: the Marseillaise. Cf. Felix Gras' *The Reds of the Midi*.

sign of the Revolution, was handed him, and he put it upon his head; but to all demands for a recall of his vetoes he made firm refusal. By nightfall the building was cleared. Little harm had been done, except to furniture; and indeed the mob had shown throughout a surprising good-nature.

There followed an outburst of loyalty from the Moderates. Lafayette, in command on the frontier, left his troops and hastened to Paris, to demand the punishment of the leaders of the mob and the closing of the Jacobin Club. The middle class was ready to rally about him; and, if the King had been willing to join himself to the Constitutionalists, Lafayette might have saved the government. But the royal family secretly preferred to trust to the advancing Austrians; and Lafayette was rebuffed and scorned. Even yet he might have seized a temporary dictatorship by force, and saved the King in spite of himself, but either conscience or timidity withheld him. He returned to his army, and the management of affairs passed rapidly to the Jacobins. The Moderates had lost their last chance.

335. Insurrection of August 10: Deposition of Louis. — France was girdled with foes. The Empire, Prussia, and Sardinia were in arms; Naples and Spain were soon to join the coalition; Sweden and Russia both offered to do so, if they were needed. In July a Prussian army, commanded by old officers of Frederick the Great, crossed the frontier; and two Austrian armies, one from the Netherlands and one from the upper Rhine, converged upon the same line of invasion. The French levies were outnumbered three to one. Worse still, they were utterly demoralized by the resignation of many officers in the face of the enemy and by a justifiable suspicion that many of those remaining sympathized with the invaders. Within France were royalist risings and plots of risings; and the King was in secret alliance with the enemy.[1]

---

[1] There is no doubt now that the Queen had even communicated the French plan of campaign to the Austrians.

Brunswick, the Prussian commander, counted upon a holiday march to Paris. July 25, he issued to the French people his famous proclamation, written by the Emigrants, declaring that the allies entered France to restore Louis to his place, that all men taken with arms in their hands should be hanged, and that, if Louis were injured, he would "inflict a memorable vengeance" by delivering up Paris to military execution.[1]

This insolent paper was fatal to the King. Patriotic France rose in rage and defiance, to hurl back the boastful invader. But before the new troops marched to the front, some of them insisted upon guarding against enemies in the rear. The Jacobins had decided that Louis should not be left free to paralyze national action at some critical moment by his veto. They demanded his deposition; but the Girondists were not ready for such extreme action. Then the Jacobins carried their point by insurrection. Led by Danton, they displaced the municipal council of Paris with a new government[2] representing the most radical elements, and this "Commune of Paris" publicly prepared an attack upon the Tuileries for August 10. If Louis had possessed ability or decision, his Guards might have repulsed the mob; but, as it was, after confusing them with contradictory orders, the King and his family fled to the Assembly, leaving the faithful Swiss regiment to be massacred. Bloody from this slaughter, the rebels forced their way into the hall of the Assembly to demand the King's instant deposition. Two-thirds of the deputies had fled, and the "rump" of Girondists and Jacobins decreed the deposition and imprisonment of Louis, and the immediate election, *by manhood suffrage*, of a Convention to decide upon the government of France.[3]

---

[1] Anderson, No. 23, gives the Declaration.

[2] Special report: the details of this reorganization of the government of Paris; see especially the account in Stephens' *French Revolution*.

[3] This was the first trial of manhood suffrage in any modern nation. Cf. § 327, note. The only exception in this case was the class of male domestic servants, who, it was feared, would be influenced by their employers, and who, therefore, were not permitted to vote. The decree is given by Anderson.

§ 336] BREAKDOWN OF THE CONSTITUTION IN WAR. 345

Lafayette arrested the Legislative Commissioners who brought him the news, and tried to lead his troops against Paris to restore the King. He found his army unwilling to follow him, and so he fled to the Austrians.[1] The nation at large had not desired the new revolution, but it accepted it as inevitable, and chose a Convention which was to ratify it unanimously. The nation was more concerned with repulsing foreign foes than with balancing nice questions as to praise or blame in Paris.

336. The September Massacres. — The same causes that led to the rising of August 10, led, three weeks later, to one of the most terrible events in history. The "Commune of Paris," under Danton's leadership, had packed the prisons with three thousand "suspected" aristocrats, to prevent a royalist rising. Then, on August 29 and September 2, came the news of the shameful surrender of Longwy and Verdun, — two great frontier fortresses guarding the road to Paris. Paris was thrown into a panic of fear, and the Paris volunteers hesitated to go to the front, lest the numerous prisoners recently arrested should break out and avenge themselves upon the city, stripped of its defenders. So, while Danton was pressing on enlistments and hurrying recruits to meet Brunswick, the frenzied mob attacked the prisons, organized rude lynch-courts, and on September 2, 3, and 4, massacred over a thousand of the prisoners with only the shadow of a trial.[2] These events are known as "the September massacres."

How far the Jacobin leaders were responsible for starting the atrocious executions at the prisons will probably never be known. Certainly they did not try to stop them; but neither did the Assembly, nor the Gironde leaders, nor any other body of persons in Paris.[3] The Jacobins, however, did

---

[1] Read Carlyle's account. Lafayette was cast into prison by the Austrians, to remain there until freed by the victories of Napoleon.

[2] The fairest account in English of these massacres is that by Stephens, II, 141–150.

[3] The apathy in Paris at the time of these events is amazing. Mallet, page 179, has a good brief statement. Says Carlyle: "Very desirable indeed

openly accept the massacres, when once accomplished, as a useful means of terrifying the royalist plotters and of unifying France. When the Assembly talked of punishment, Danton excused the deed, and urged action instead against the enemies of France. "It was necessary to make our enemies afraid," he cried, ". . . Blast my memory, but let France be free."

B. THE REVOLUTION MAKES CONVERTS WITH THE SWORD.

337. France at War with Kings. — After August 10, Danton became the leading member of a provisional executive committee, and at once infused new vigor into the government. "We must dare," his great voice rang out to the doubting Assembly, "and dare again, and ever dare, — and France is saved!" In this spirit he toiled, night and day, to raise and arm and organize recruits. France responded with the finest outburst of patriotic military enthusiasm the world has ever seen in a great civilized state. September 20 the advancing Prussians were checked at *Valmy;* and November 9 the victory of *Jemmapes,* the first real pitched battle of the war, opened Belgium to French conquest. Another French army had already entered Germany, and a third had occupied Nice and Savoy.

These successes of the raw but devoted French soldiery over the veterans of Europe intoxicated the nation, and called forth an orgy of democratic enthusiasm. The new National Convention (§ 338) became, in Danton's phrase, "a general committee of insurrection for all nations." Flamed out one fiery orator, — "Despots march against us with fire and sword: we will bear against them liberty!" The Convention ordained a manifesto in all languages, offering the alliance of the French nation to

---

that Paris had interfered; yet not unnatural that it stood even so, looking on in stupor. Paris is in death-panic, the enemy and gibbets at its door: whosoever in Paris hath the heart to front death, finds it more pressing to do so fighting the Prussians than fighting the killers of aristocrats." See, too, Stephens' *Revolutionary Europe,* 115.

all peoples who wished to recover their liberties; and French generals, entering a foreign country, were ordered "to abolish serfdom, nobility, and all monopolies and privileges, and to aid in setting up a new government upon principles of popular sovereignty." [1]

Starving and ragged, but welcomed by the invaded peoples, the French armies sowed over Europe the seed of civil and political liberty. The Revolution was no longer merely French. It took on the intense zeal of a proselyting religion, and its principles were spread by fire and sword.

C. The Convention: Revolutionary Government.

338. The Republic declared: Execution of the King. — The new Convention had assembled September 21, 1792. The Constitutionalists had disappeared.[2] The Girondist leaders now sat upon the Right and seemed to have the adherence of the Plain, and indeed of the whole Convention, except for a small party of the Mountain, where sat Robespierre, Danton, and Marat, with the rest of the deputies of Paris and the organizers of the Revolution of August 10. On the first afternoon,[3] the Convention declared monarchy abolished, and enthusiastically established "The French Republic, One and Indivisible."

The Mountain was bent also upon punishing Louis. They were satisfied of his guilt, and they wished to make reconciliation impossible. Said Danton: "The allied kings march against us. Let us hurl at their feet, as the gantlet of battle, the head of a king." Most of the Girondists wished to save

---

[1] The decrees are given by Anderson, No. 28.

[2] Note the progress of the Revolution: the old Royalists who made the Right of the First Assembly had no place in the Second; while the Constitutionalists who made the Left of the First Assembly and the Right of the Second had vanished in the Third.

[3] Read Carlyle for an account of this first session of the Convention. The next day, September 22, the fall equinox, was afterward named the first day of the "Year One" of the new era. The new Calendar (cf. Carlyle or Stephens) may be presented as a special report.

Louis' life, but they were intimidated by the mobs and the galleries; and finally the Convention declared him guilty of "treason to the nation," and condemned him to death. He was executed January 21, 1793.

339. The Constitution of the Year I. — Somewhat later, the new Republic secured the sanction of a written constitution, known as "the Constitution of the Year I." All adult males were declared equally sovereign and equally eligible to office. A one-chambered legislature was to be renewed annually, and its decrees were to be subject to veto by popular vote. *The constitution was ratified by the vote of the French nation*, but it never went into operation. It was suspended unconstitutionally, as soon as ratified, by a simple decree of the Convention declaring that, as France was in danger, the government must be revolutionary until the war was over.

340. New Enemies. Treason of Dumouriez. — The execution of the King was one factor in deciding England, Spain, Holland, Naples, and Portugal to join the allies against France, and it fatally offended many French patriots. Dumouriez, an able but unscrupulous general who had succeeded Lafayette as the chief military leader, tried to play traitor, in the spring of 1793, by surrendering Belgian fortresses to the Austrians and by leading his army to Paris to restore the monarchy. His troops, however, refused to follow him, and he fled to the enemy; but Belgium was lost for a time, and once more the frontier was in danger.

341. Ruin of the Girondists. — Ever since the Convention met, dissension had threatened between the Gironde majority and the Mountain (§ 338). The Girondists were men of theories and sentiment; the Mountain were men of action. The Girondists wished a mild and enlightened government; the Mountain were determined to have a strong government. Some of the Mountain, moreover, were zealous for radical social changes, — the leveling of the rich, the abolition of poverty, and the destruction of all who stood in the way of sweeping reforms. For success, they depended upon the support of the Paris mob. The Girondists abhorred such doctrines and methods. They wished to remove the Convention from Paris, and they were accused of desiring to "federate" France, — to break up the "Indivisible Republic" into a federation of provinces.

After the death of the King, the quarrel broke out fiercely, and the Girondists took the moment of foreign danger, in the spring of 1793, to press it to a head. They had been calling for the expulsion of Marat, and finally they ordered his trial, for complicity with the September massacres. Then in April they were mad enough to charge Danton with royalist conspiracy. Danton, who was straining his mighty strength to send reenforcements to the armies of France, pleaded at first for peace and union; but, when this proved vain, he turned savagely upon his assailants. "You were right," he cried to the Mountain, who had pressed before for extreme measures against the Girondists, "and I was wrong. There is no peace possible with these men. Let it be war, then. They will not save the Republic with us. It shall be saved without them, saved in spite of them." And then, while the Assembly debated and resolved, the Mountain acted. It was weak in the Convention, but it was supreme in the galleries and in the streets and above all in the Commune of Paris. The Commune, which had carried the Revolution of August 10 against the Legislative Assembly, now planned another rising. June 2, 1793, armed forces marched against the Convention and held it prisoner until it passed a decree imprisoning thirty of the leading Girondists. Others of that party fled, and the Jacobin Mountain was left in power.[1]

342. The Committee of Public Safety : a Strong Executive. — Fugitive Girondists, however, roused the provinces against the

---

[1] The fate of the Girondists has aroused much sympathy; but says John Morley (Essay on Robespierre), "The deliverance of a people beset by strong and implacable foes could not wait on mere good manners and fastidious sentiments, when those comely things were in company with the most stupendous want of foresight ever shown by a political party." Certainly the victory of the Jacobins was the only means to save the Revolution with its priceless gain for humanity.

Jacobin capital. Armies were gathered at Marseilles, Bordeaux, Caen, and Lyons. Lyons, the second city in France, even raised the white flag of the Bourbons and invited in the Austrians.[1] Elsewhere, too, royalist revolt reared its head, and in Vendée[2] the savage peasantry rose in wild rebellion for church and king. The great port of Toulon admitted an English fleet and army. For a time, it seemed as though Paris, with a score of central departments, must face the other three-fourths of France and united Europe.

Out of this terrible danger was born a new government. For the first time since the States General met, France found a strong executive. This was a great *Committee of Public Safety*, which was to rule for over a year with despotic power. So far, in matters of government, the Revolution had been tearing down; it had been decentralizing and disorganizing. Now it was beginning to build up, to centralize and organize; and never has French genius in these lines shown itself with more triumphant vigor than in the months that followed. In the language of one of its members, the Convention was forced "to establish the despotism of liberty, in order to crush the despotism of tyrants." The great Committee had been created by the Convention in April, after the treason of Dumouriez. Its twelve members, all chosen from the Mountain, were at first to hold office only for one month, but soon they came to retain their places without even the form of a reëlection. Its original purpose had been mainly to hurry enlistments; but, as perils thickened, after the Gironde revolt, the Convention put all authority into its hands. All other national committees and officers became its servants; the Convention itself became its mouthpiece; and every petty municipal functionary in France was ordered to obey its decrees. This obedience was enforced through nearly a hundred "Deputies on Mission," who were sent out by the Convention to all departments, with

---

[1] Whereupon the Girondists in Lyons refused to fight longer, preferring death to alliance with the enemies of France.

[2] A province of old Brittany.

absolute power, — subject only to the Committee, to which they were to report every ten days. They could replace civil authorities; they could seize goods or money for national use; they could imprison and condemn to death by their own tribunals.[1] To prevent further treachery and to secure energy in military operations, "Deputies on Mission" were sent out also with each army of the Republic, with power even to arrest the general at the head of his troops.

The Committee were not trained administrators, but they were men of practical business sagacity and of tremendous energy, — such men as a Revolution must finally toss to the top. In the war office, *Carnot* "organized victory"; beside him, in the treasury, labored *Cambon*, with his stern motto, "War to the manorhouse, peace to the hut"; while a group of such men as *Robespierre* and *St. Just* sought to direct the Revolution so as to refashion France according to new ideals.[2]

343. Energy and Victory abroad. — Never has a despotism been more absolute or more efficient. In October, Lyons was captured, and ordered razed to the ground. A like fate befell Toulon, despite English aid. Other centers of revolt, paralyzed with fear, yielded. Order and union were restored; and a million of men, according to report, were sent to join the armies of France. Before the year closed, French soil was free from danger of invasion, and French armies had taken the offensive on all the frontiers. Serious peril from without was past until Napoleon's overthrow, twenty years later.

"All France and whatsoever it contains of men and resources is put under requisition," said the Committee, in a stirring proclamation to the nation (August 23, 1793).[3] "The republic is one vast besieged city. . . . The young men shall go to battle; it is their task to conquer; the married men shall forge arms, transport baggage and artillery, provide

---

[1] On these great proconsuls of 1793 and 1794, read Stephens, II, 367-370, and Taine, III, 55-58.

[2] On the personnel of the Committee, read Stephens, II, 285, or *Revolutionary Europe*, 133-135; and see a dramatic account of their meetings by Morley in his "Robespierre" (*Miscellanies*, I, 67).

[3] The decree is given in full by Anderson.

subsistence; the women shall work at soldiers' clothes, make tents, serve in the hospitals; children shall scrape old linen into surgeon's lint; the old men shall have themselves carried into public places, and there, by their words, excite the courage of the young and preach hatred to kings and unity for the Republic."

"In this humor, then, since no other will serve," comments Carlyle, "will France rush against its enemies; headlong, reckoning no cost, heeding no law but the supreme law, Salvation of the People. The weapons are all the iron there is in France; the strength is that of all the men and women there are in France. . . . From all hamlets toward their departmental town, from all departmental towns toward the appointed camp, the Sons of Freedom shall march. Their banner is to bear 'The French People risen against Tyrants.'"

Only Carlyle's words do justice to the result. "These soldiers have shoes of wood and pasteboard, or go booted in hay-ropes, in dead of winter. . . . What then? 'With steel and bread,' says the Convention Representative, 'one may get to China.' The generals go fast to the guillotine, justly or unjustly. . . . Ill-success is death; in victory alone is life. . . . All Girondism, Halfness, Compromise, is swept away. . . . Forward, ye soldiers of the Republic, captain and man! Dash with your Gallic impetuosity on Austria, England, Prussia, Spain, Sardinia, Pitt, Coburg, York, and the Devil and the World!

"See accordingly on all frontiers, how the 'Sons of Night' astonished, after short triumph, do recoil; the Sons of the Republic flying after them, with temper of cat-o-mountain or demon incarnate, which no Son of Night can withstand. . . . Spain which came bursting through the Pyrenees, rustling with Bourbon banners, and went conquering here and there for a season, falters at such welcome, draws itself in again, — too happy now were the Pyrenees impassable. Dugomier invades Spain by the eastern Pyrenees. General Mueller shall invade it by the western. '*Shall*,' that is the word. Committee of Public Safety has said it, Representative Cavaignac, on mission there, must see it done. 'Impossible,' cries Mueller; 'Infallible,' answers Cavaignac. 'The Committee is deaf on that side of its head,' answers Cavaignac. 'How many want'st thou of men, of horses, of cannon? Thou shalt have them. Conquerors, conquered, or hanged, Forward we must.' Which things also, even as the Representative spake them, were done."

344. The Reign of Terror at Home. — The Committee had not hesitated to use the most terrible means to secure union and implicit obedience. Early in September it adopted "Terror" as a deliberate policy. This "Long Terror" was a very different thing from the "Short Terror" of the mob, a year before. The Paris prisons were crowded again with "Suspects"; and each day the Revolutionary tribunal, after farcical trials, sent batches of the condemned to the guillotine. Among the victims were the Queen, many aristocrats, and also many Constitutionalists and Girondists — heroes of 1791 and 1792. In some of the revolted districts, too, submission was followed by horrible executions, and at Nantes the cruelty of Carrier, the Deputy on Mission, half-crazed with blood, inflicted upon the Revolution an indelible stain.[1] In all, some fifteen thousand executions took place during the year of the Terror, — nearly three thousand of them in Paris. Over much of France, however, the Terror was only a name. The rule of most of the great Deputies on Mission was bloodless and was ardently supported by the popular will.

The temporary use of this terrible policy in parts of France had been made almost inevitable by the anarchy of the preceding years and by the danger of foreign invasion. At all events, it was the weapon nearest at hand, and the Committee did not shrink from its use. It proved effectual. By the end of October, 1793, after only two months of the Terror, Paris was tranquil and had resumed its usual life.[2] There were no more riots and almost no crime, even of the ordinary kind. France was again a mighty nation, united and orderly at home and victorious abroad.[3]

However, when all has been said in excuse and explanation, the Reign of Terror remains a blot upon the history of mankind. If it was begun to save France, it was continued for

---

[1] Special report: Carrier's "Noyades" and "Republican Marriages," which became so famous in literature.

[2] "Singular city," says Carlyle; "for overhead of all of this, there is the customary brewing and baking. Labor hammers and grinds. Frilled promenaders saunter under the trees, white-muslin promenadresses, with green parasols, leaning on your arm. . . . In this Paris, are twenty-three theaters nightly ; some count as many as sixty places of dancing." Cf. for similar ideas, Taine, II, 188, and Stephens, II, 343-345.

[3] For a general verdict, read Stephens, II, 230.

party ends; and though the leaders were personally incorruptible and were animated, most of them, by lofty motives, the subordinate agents were unspeakably cruel and sordid.

At the same time the crimes of the Terrorists do not stand by themselves. They have attracted attention because of the class of society against which they were directed. John Morley, a cultivated and liberal English scholar, calls their deeds "*almost* as horrible as the scenes an English army was to enact six years later in Ireland" (§ 551); and certainly they were less terrible than the needless vengeance inflicted by the conservative government of Paris in 1871 upon twenty thousand victims of the Commune (§ 436), — a matter of which the world hears very little.

345. Constructive Work of the Convention. — The grim, silent, tense-browed men of the great Committee, working their eighteen hours out of every twenty-four, and carrying their lives in their hands, were doing more than organizing "terror" within and victory abroad. They were solving multitudes of vexing questions, left over from the preceding Assemblies, — cutting knots they could not loosen, and laying anew the foundations of society. In the midst of war and tumult, the Convention carried through much good work. It created and organized the splendid army with which Napoleon was to win his victories. It made provision for the public debt, adopted the beginning of a simple legal code, accepted the metric system for weights and measures, abolished slavery in the French colonies, instituted the first Normal School, the Polytechnic School of France, the Conservatory of France, the famous Institute of France, and the National Library, and planned also a comprehensive system of public instruction, the improvement of the hospitals and of the prisons, and the reform of youthful criminals. As Shailer Mathews says, "No government ever worked harder for the good of the masses"; and says H. Morse Stephens (*Yale Review*, November, 1895, page 331): —

It is probable that as the centuries pass, the political strife . . . may be forgotten, while the projects of Cambacérès and Merlin toward codification, the plans of Condorcet and Lakanal for a system of national education, and Argobast's report on the new weights and measures, will be regarded as making great and important steps in the progress of the race. . . . The Convention laid the foundations upon which Napoleon afterward built. In educational as in legal reform, the most important work was done during the Reign of Terror. . . . Their work was finally appropriated by Napoleon to his own glory.

346. The Factions of the Jacobins and their Ruin. — In the spring of 1794, after some ten months' rule, the Committee of Safety began to encounter opposition.[1] In the Convention, Danton, weary of bloodshed, had been urging that the policy of Terror was no longer necessary, and his friend Desmoulins had suggested a "Committee of Mercy." On the other hand, Hébert and the Paris Commune wished more radical measures. Hébert planned an atheistical republic, and proposed to substitute a Worship of Reason[2] for that of God.

The great Committee proved strong enough to strike down both Danton and Hébert (March and April); and then for a few months, Robespierre, the best-known member of the Committee, appeared to rule, sole master of France. He reopened churches in Paris, and, to offset Hébert's Festival of Reason, he made the Convention solemnly celebrate a "Festival to the Supreme Being." He seems to have hoped to refashion society with a strong hand and to create a new France with simple and austere manners.[3] But, perhaps to clear the field of possible opponents to his ideals, perhaps merely to remove personal rivals, Robespierre used his brief preëminence bloodily. The number of executions mounted with frightful rapidity. Then,

---

[1] Marat had been murdered by Charlotte Corday. The story may be presented as a special report.

[2] In Paris, Hébert carried his point for a time. Religious exercises were forbidden, and in the ancient Cathedral of Notre Dame a service was performed to Reason personified by a beautiful but dissolute woman seated on the altar.

[3] A decree of the Convention providing for public education read: "The transition of an oppressed nation to democracy is like the effort by which nature rose out of nothingness to existence. We must entirely refashion a people whom we wish to make free, — destroy its prejudices, alter its habits,

in the last days of July (1794), the Convention rose against him and sent him and his adherents to the guillotine. The factions of the Jacobins had devoured one another.

347. The Conservative Reaction. — In December, 1794, encouraged by the reaction against the Radicals, the fugitive members of the Right once more appeared in the Assembly; and in March, 1795, even the survivors of the Girondists were admitted. The Jacobins raised the populace of Paris in a desperate attempt to undo the reaction; but the middle classes had rallied at last, and the mob was dispersed by troops and by organized bands of "gilded youth" from the bourgeoisie. The populace was disarmed, the National Guards were reorganized, and there followed over France a "White Terror," wherein the conservative classes executed or assassinated many hundreds of the Jacobin party.[1]

V. THIRD PERIOD, 1795-1799 : THE REPUBLIC UNDER THE DIRECTORY.

348. The Constitution of the Year III. — The Constitution of the Year I was too democratic and provided too weak an executive for the new conditions; and the reaction was confirmed by a new constitution, known as the Constitution of the

---

limit its necessities, root up its vices, purify its desires. The state must therefore lay hold on every human being at his birth and direct his education with powerful hand."

The most enthusiastic follower of Robespierre was St. Just; and the fragments of St. Just's *Institutes*, with which he hoped to regenerate his country, express the ardent hopes of the Terrorists. Boys of seven were to be handed over to the "school of the nation," to be trained "to endure hardship and to speak little." Neither servants nor gold or silver vessels were to be permitted. As St. Just said elsewhere, he wished "to offer the nation the happiness of virtue, of moderation, of comfort, — the happiness that springs from the enjoyment of the necessary without the superfluous. The luxury of a cabin and of a field fertilized by your own hands, a cart, a thatched roof, — such is happiness." St. Just declared that he would blow his brains out if he did not believe it possible to remodel the French people along such lines.

[1] For further reading on Division IV, see page 341. This is a good place to stop for a careful review of the years 1789-1795. Topical outlines and "catchword reviews" of the three Assemblies are suggested.

Year III (1795). The government established by this document is called "The Directory." This was the name of the executive, which consisted of *a committee of five*, chosen by the legislature. The legislature consisted of two houses. Property qualification for voting was restored, with the use of electoral colleges; and the local governments were made subordinate to agents sent out by the Directory. The liberal principles of 1791 were reasserted, — individual liberty, liberty of worship, freedom of the press, and jury trial. The constitution resembled that of 1791, except in three points: (1) the new executive was stronger than the old constitutional king of 1791; (2) the legislature had two houses, so as to check hasty legislation; and (3) the administration was centralized.[1]

349. Insurrection against the Directory. — The constitution was submitted to a popular vote, but before the vote was taken, at the last moment, the expiring Convention added a peculiar provision. There seemed danger that a new legislature might restore some form of monarchy; and, dreading this result, the Convention decreed that two-thirds of its members should hold over as members of the new Assembly. This arrangement was submitted to the people, along with the constitution, and was practically made a condition to the latter's going into effect. It was carried by a small majority, while the constitution was ratified by an overwhelming vote. Indeed, the Convention was accused of falsifying the returns,[2] to carry this special provision at all; and, in any case, the interference with a full election was extremely unpopular. In Paris, where the opposition was strongest, the secret Royalists took advantage of the dissatisfaction to stir up a revolt against the Convention. They were joined by twenty thousand National Guards, but their gallant attack was dispersed by four thousand regular troops under the firm command of Napoleon Bonaparte. This young officer in the service of the Convention mowed

---

[1] The constitution is given in Anderson's *Constitutions and Documents*.
[2] Cf. Borgeaud's *Adoption and Amendment of Constitutions*, 215, 216.

down the attacking columns with grapeshot, and the rising was crushed. This was the "affair of Vendémiaire."[1] The Directory was inaugurated quietly and remained in power over four years.

350. The Military Situation in 1795 : French Gains before the Appearance of Napoleon. — In 1795, when the government of the Convention was merged in the Directory, France had already made great gains of territory. On the northeast, Belgium had been annexed, in accordance with the vote of its people. Nice and Savoy, on the southeast, had been added, in like manner. The eastern frontier had been moved to the Rhine, by the seizure of all the territory of the Empire on the west side of the river. Holland had been conquered and converted into a dependent ally, as the "Batavian Republic," with a constitution molded on that of France. Prussia, Spain, and most of the small states had withdrawn from the war. Only England, Austria, and Sardinia kept the field.

351. Napoleon Bonaparte in Italy. — The Directory determined to attack Austria vigorously, both in Germany and Italy.[2] Two splendid armies were sent into Germany, and a small, ill-supplied force in Italy was put under the command of Napoleon Bonaparte. The wonderful genius of the young general made the Italian campaign the decisive element in the war. By rapid movements, he separated the Austrian and Sardinian forces, beat the latter in five battles in eleven days, and forced Sardinia to conclude peace. Turning upon the gallant but deliberate Austrians, he won battle after battle, and by July he seemed master of Italy. Austria, however, clung stubbornly to her Italian provinces; and, during the following year, four fresh armies, each larger than Napoleon's, were sent in succession from the Rhine to the Po, only to meet destruction. In October, 1797, Austria agreed to accept Venice from Bonaparte, in exchange for Lombardy and Belgium, which

---

[1] The name of the French month.
[2] Austria at this time held a considerable part of North Italy.

she had lost; and war on the continent closed with the *Peace of Campo Formio*.

352. Effect of the Italian Campaign upon Italy. — Bonaparte's proclamation upon taking command of the Army of Italy had been significant of much that was to come: "Soldiers, you are starving and in rags. The government owes you much, but can do nothing for you. I will lead you into the most fruitful plains of the world. Teeming provinces, flourishing cities, will be in your power. There you may reap honor and glory and wealth."

To the Italians, Bonaparte posed at first as a deliverer; and his large promises awoke the peninsula from the sleep of centuries to the hope of a new national life. This hope was to bear fruit in the next century, and something was accomplished at the time. Oligarchic Genoa became the *Ligurian Republic*, and the Po valley was made into the *Cisalpine Republic*. The French conquerors swept away feudalism and serfdom and the forms of the old Austrian despotism, and introduced civil equality and some appearance of political liberty. At the same time, however, with amazing perfidy, the independent state of Venice was goaded and tricked into war, seized by a French army, and afterward coolly bartered away to Austria.[1] Upon even the friendly states, Bonaparte levied enormous contributions, to enrich his soldiers and officers, to fill the coffers of France, and to bribe the Directory. Works of art, too, and choice manuscripts were ravished from Italian libraries and galleries, and sent to Paris in vast quantities, to gratify French vanity; and when the Italians rose against this spoliation, the revolts were stamped out with ferocious and deliberate cruelty.

353. Bonaparte's Character and Aims. — Napoleon Bonaparte was born in Corsica in 1769. His parents were Italians, poor, but of noble descent. In the year of Napoleon's birth, Corsica became a possession of France. The boy passed through a

---

[1] Special report: Napoleon and Venice; see Rose's *Napoleon I*, 130–133, 153–158.

French military school, and, when the Revolution began, he was a junior lieutenant of artillery.[1] The war gave him opportunity. He had distinguished himself at the capture of Toulon (§§ 342, 343); and, chancing to be in Paris at the time of the rising against the Directory in 1795, he had been called upon to defend the government. In reward, he was given, the next year, the command of the "Army of Italy." Then followed the brilliant campaigns which called the attention of the world to the man who was to dominate European history for the next eighteen years.

Bonaparte was one of the three or four supreme military geniuses of all history. He was also one of the greatest of civil rulers. He had profound insight, a marvelous memory, and tireless energy. He was a "terrible worker," and his success was largely due to his wonderful grasp of masses of details, — so that he could recall the smallest features of geography where a campaign was to take place, or could name the man best suited for office in any one of a multitude of obscure towns. He was not insensible to generous emotions; but he was utterly unscrupulous and selfish, and he deliberately rejected all claims of morality upon his conduct.[2] Perfidy and cruelty, when they suited

NAPOLEON AT ARCOLA, in his Italian campaign; after the painting by Gros.

---

[1] Special report: Napoleon's early dislike for France and his Corsican patriotism, illustrated by his career from 1789 to 1794.

[2] "Morality," said he, "has nothing to do with such a man as I am." To this it has been fitly rejoined, "Was he then above morality, or below it?"

his ends, he used as calmly as appeals to honor and patriotism. In early life, Bonaparte seems to have been a sincere Republican; but he hated anarchy and disorder, and, before his campaign in Italy was over, he had begun to plan to make himself ruler of France under some semi-republican form. He worked systematically and successfully to transform the army's earlier ardor for liberty into a new passion for military glory and plunder. He became the idol of the soldiery, and then used the military power to overthrow the civil authority.

Before Campo Formio he had said to a friend, " Do you suppose I conquer for the lawyers of the Directory ? . . . Do you think I mean to found a Republic ? What an idea ! . . . The nation wants a head, a chief illustrious for great exploits ; it does not care for theories of government. . . . The French want glory. As for liberty, of that they have no conception. . . . I am everything to the army. Let the Directory try to take my command from me, and they will see who is master."

354. Bonaparte in Egypt. — The war with England continued; and the next year (1798) Bonaparte persuaded the Directory to let him attack Egypt, as a step toward the conquest of England's power in India. He won a series of brilliant battles, but suddenly his fleet was annihilated by the English under *Nelson*, in the *Battle of the Nile*, and the gorgeous dreams of Oriental empire faded away.

355. Bonaparte overthrows the Directory : Revolution of Brumaire, 1799. — Then Bonaparte deserted his doomed army, and escaped to France. There his failure was not at first comprehended, and he found the nation ready to welcome him as a savior. War on the continent had been renewed. In 1798 the Directory had brought about a change in the government of Switzerland and had organized that country as the *Helvetic Republic* (§ 513). They had also driven the Pope from Rome and dispossessed other Italian rulers, to make way for new republican states. The Great Powers of Europe were alarmed at these measures. England succeeded in drawing Russia and Austria into another coalition; and so far, in the new war, the campaigns on the whole had not favored France.

At home the French people were wearied, and anxious for peace; and the Directory had proved incapable, corrupt, and despotic. According to the Constitution of 1795, one of the five Directors and one-fifth the Legislative Chambers were to be renewed each year, beginning in the spring of 1797. In the elections of that year, the Constitutional Monarchists had been so successful that the old Directors, fearing a restoration of the Bourbons, resorted to a *coup d'état*.[1] First making sure of leading generals of the army, including Bonaparte, they arrested fifty of the new members of the Legislature, and banished them without trial to Cayenne, a French penal colony in South America. The following year (1798), there was almost equal danger of a Jacobin revival, and the Directory guarded against this by another *coup d'état*, — declaring a large number of elections void, and itself filling the places with its own adherents. In 1799, for the third time in succession, the elections went against the existing government; and, though the Directory could keep control through the majority that held over, it was plain that the people were ready for its overthrow.

It was plain, too, that this overthrow was coming through the army. Siéyès had just been chosen Director, and was already planning a new constitution to oust his colleagues. He expected to accomplish his purpose through some of the victorious generals of France; but the sudden return of Napoleon, the most available general, left him, not Siéyès, master of the situation. All hostile members of the Legislature were cleared from the hall by troops; and a Rump, made up of Bonaparte's adherents, abolished the Directory and elected Bonaparte, Siéyès, and one other as *Consuls*, intrusting to them the preparation of a new constitution. This was the *Revolution of*

---

[1] Literally, a "stroke of state." This is the name given in France to infractions of the constitution by some part of the government through the use of force. Happily the thing itself has been so unknown to English history that the English language has to borrow the French name. The coming century was to see many a *coup d'état* in France; and like phenomena have been common in other European countries.

Brumaire.[1] "Now," said the peasantry, "we shall have peace, thanks to God and to Bonaparte"; and by a vote of some three million to fifteen hundred, the French people accepted the Constitution that virtually made Bonaparte dictator.

No doubt the French Republic would have become a military dictatorship for a time, even though there had been no Bonaparte. The French were not ready for free government, and could not learn it all in eight years of constant war and turmoil. For a time they needed repose and a strong hand at the helm. Moreover, many men appear to have thought that in putting Bonaparte into power they were averting, in the only way possible, the overthrow of the Republic by the Royalists. And it is quite probable that if leadership had fallen to a general of more sincere republican sentiments, — for instance to Moreau, Napoleon's chief rival, — then France might never have gone so far in reaction toward despotism as she was to go. Napoleon did reëstablish social and political institutions for France, as indeed any leader at that time must have tried to do; but, to a wholly unnecessary degree, he built them upon despotic lines: he aimed from the first at hereditary monarchy; he played upon the vainglory of his people, and, after a short period of dizzy elevation, he brought vast calamities upon his country, besides deluging all Europe in blood.

FOR FURTHER READING. — High school students will hardly get time to read upon the Directory, apart from Napoleon's career. For that, see the references on page 381.

VI. THE CONSULATE AND THE EMPIRE, 1799-1815.

A. PEACE AND THE RECONSTRUCTION OF FRANCE.

356. Marengo and Hohenlinden, 1800. Peace of Amiens, 1802. — The campaign of 1800 dissolved the hostile coalition. Bonaparte in person won the great battle of *Marengo* over the Austrians in Italy, and General Moreau crushed another Austrian army in Bavaria at *Hohenlinden*. Austria and Russia made peace; and Napoleon, anxious to impress the European rulers with a sense of his moderation, wisely allowed essentially the old terms of Campo Formio (§ 351). Then, in 1802,

---

[1] Anderson, No. 57, gives the decree. Special report: the story of Brumaire; see especially the admirable chapter in Rose's *Napoleon I*.

France and England laid aside their contest by the *Treaty of Amiens*, and, for a brief period, the world was free from war. Napoleon appeared both a conqueror, with dazzling victories, and also the restorer of the long-desired peace; and the popularity of his government was established.

357. The "Constitution of the Year VIII" (1800), which confirmed the Revolution of Brumaire, had been devised in its main outlines by Siéyès. The government was to rest on manhood suffrage, but that suffrage was to be *refined by successive filtrations*. The adult males, some five million in all, were to choose one-tenth their number; the five hundred thousand "Communal Notables," so chosen, were in turn to choose one-tenth their number; these fifty thousand "Departmental Notables" were to choose five thousand "National Notables." But all this voting was only to settle *eligibility: the executive was to appoint* communal officers at will out of the Communal Notables, departmental officers out of the Departmental Notables, and members of the legislature and other chief officers out of the National Notables.

The legislature was to be broken up into four parts: a *Council of State* to prepare bills; a *Tribunate* to discuss them, without right to vote; a *Legislative Chamber* to accept or reject them, without right to discuss or amend; and a *Senate*, with power to veto.

Siéyès had intended to break up the executive in like manner into one Consul for war, another for peace, and a "Grand Elector" who should appoint the consuls and other great officials, but should then have no part in the government. Here Napoleon intervened. He was willing to accept the system of elections that never elected anybody, and a legislature that could not legislate, but he meant to have a real executive; so he changed the shadowy "Grand Elector" into a *First Consul*, with all other parts of the constitution subject to his will. Bonaparte became First Consul. His colleagues, as he put it, were "merely counsellors whom I am expected to consult, but whose advice I need not accept." Directly or indirectly, he

EUROPE AT THE PEACE
OF AMIENS
(1802)
SCALE OF MILES
0 50 100 200 300 400
ATLANTIC OCEAN
NORTH SEA
BALTIC SEA
BLACK SEA
ADRIATIC SEA
MEDITERRANEAN SEA
Bay of Biscay
English Channel
GREAT BRITAIN
LONDON
Edinburgh
Dublin
HEBRIDES
ORKNEY IS.
Stavenger
The Naze
CHRISTIANIA
DENMARK
COPENHAGEN
Kiel
HELGOLAND (To Den.)
SWEDEN
STOCKHOLM
GOTHLAND
G. of Finland
PETERSBURG
Peipus L.
RUSSIA
Riga
Dwina R.
Vilna
Niemen R.
1772-1794
Smolensk
Moscow
Oka
Volga
Don R.
Kief
Dnieper R.
Bug R.
Dniester R.
1792
Odessa
Kherson
Crimea
Sea of Azof
Bessarabia
1793
PRUSSIA
Königsberg
Danzig
Stettin
BERLIN
Posen
Vistula R.
Warsaw
Oder R.
Breslau
1772-1794
Krakow
Hamburg
Bremen
Hanover
BATAVIAN REP.
Amsterdam
Antwerp
Cassel
Cologne
Rhine R.
Elbe R.
SAXONY
Leipzig
Dresden
Prague
Frankfort
ELECT. OF BAVARIA
Munich
WURTEMBERG
BADEN
Stuttgart
EMPIRE OF AUSTRIA
VIENNA
Budapest
Danube
Theiss R.
Drave R.
Save R.
Innsbruck
Trieste
Venice
Verona
Transylvania
Moldavia
Jassy
Pruth R.
Wallachia
Bucharest
FRANCE
PARIS
Seine R.
Loire R.
Garonne R.
Rhone R.
Brussels
Boulogne
Cherbourg
CHANNEL IS.
Quiberon
Luxemburg
Metz
Strasburg
Lyons
Bordeaux
Avignon
Marseilles
Toulon
Nice
BERN
Basle
SWITZERLAND
Geneva
Milan
1790
Turin
CISALPINE REP.
LIGURIAN REP.
Genoa
K. OF ETRURIA
Florence
STATES OF THE POPE
Ancona
ROME
KINGDOM OF THE TWO SICILIES
NAPLES
LIPARI IS.
Palermo
C. Passaro
MALTA (To Eng.)
CORSICA
Ajaccio
ELBA (To Fr.)
KINGDOM OF SARDINIA
Cagliari
SPAIN
MADRID
Valladolid
Douro R.
Ebro R.
Saragossa
Barcelona
Tagus R.
Guadiana R.
Valencia
Cadiz
Gibraltar (To Eng.)
Tarifa Pt.
C. St. Vincent
PORTUGAL
LISBON
Oporto
C. Finisterre
C. Ortegal
BALEARIC IS.
MINORCA
MAJORCA
MOROCCO
ALGERIA
Algiers
Tunis
TURKISH EMPIRE
CONSTANTINOPLE
Bosnia
Belgrade
Servia
Bulgaria
MONTENEGRO
Scutari
CORFU
IONIAN IS. (To Rus.)
Athens
MOREA
CHIOS
Smyrna
CRETE

himself filled all offices, and no law could even be proposed without his sanction.[1]

358. Local Administration[2] was again highly centralized. For each department, Napoleon appointed a Prefect, and for each subdistrict a Subprefect. These officers were intrusted with almost absolute power. They were free even from the local checks upon the Intendants of the Old Monarchy, since the Revolution had cleared away the obstructing parlements and other local institutions.[3] The despotic centralization of the Old Régime was outdone. Even the forty thousand mayors of towns and villages were appointed by the First Consul or by his agents, and held office at his will; "nor did there exist anywhere independent of him the authority to light or repair the streets of the meanest village in France."

This new administration was vigorous and fearless; and under Napoleon's energy and genius, it did confer upon France great and rapid benefits. But, in the long run, the result was to be unspeakably disastrous. The chance for Frenchmen to train themselves at their own gates in the duties and responsibilities of freemen, by sharing in the local government, was lost; and the willingness to depend upon an all-directing central power was fixed even more firmly than before in their minds. Through almost all the next century, the various national governments of France — imperial, monarchic, or republican — alike preserved this despotism in local government. Under such conditions, so far as real liberty was concerned, it mattered little whether the central government was called a monarchy or a republic. About the middle of the nineteenth century the

[1] For more precise details of the constitution, see Dickenson, *Revolution and Reaction*, 36–38, or Rose, I, 210–214. The document is given by Anderson.

[2] Rose, I, 246–249; Fyffe, I, 207, 208.

[3] In 1790, within a year of the meeting of the States General, Mirabeau had written to the king, trying to reconcile him to the Revolution: "Is it nothing for the royal power to be without parlements, without pays d'état, without a body of clergy, without a privileged class? . . . Several successive reigns of an absolute monarch would not have done so much for royal [centralized] authority, as this one year of Revolution." So Burke, in England, about the same time, foretold the coming military despotism and its centralized character: "When the dictator appears, he will find that the legislation which has crushed and leveled all orders in the state, has greatly facilitated his career. . . . He will be able to construct the most completely absolute power that has ever appeared on earth."

French patriot, Tocqueville, despairingly confessed that, owing to the vice of centralization, all attempts to set up a free government in France had resulted at best in putting "a free head on servile shoulders"; or, as the same statesman exclaimed at another time, "There is only one thing we can't create in France : that is a free government. And there is only one institution we can't destroy, and that is centralization." Even under the present Third Republic, this poison of centralization has been a serious drawback to the development of French liberty. Since about 1884, however, great advance has been made in introducing self-government in local units (§ 447); and in this reversal of Napoleon's work live the best hopes for France to-day.[1]

359. Restoration of Order and Prosperity. — For a time, Bonaparte used his vast authority to restore order, to heal strife, and to reconcile all elements to the state. Royalist and Jacobin were welcomed to public employment and to favor; and a hundred and fifty thousand exiles, of the best blood and brain of France, returned, to reënforce the citizen body.[2] In the public administration, corruption, extravagance, and inefficiency were replaced everywhere by order, precision, and symmetry. Education was organized. The church was reconciled to the state. Law was simplified; and justice was made cheap and easy to secure. The material side of society was not neglected: the depreciated paper money was restored to a sound basis, and industry of all kinds was encouraged. Paris was made the most beautiful city of Europe, and it was endowed with an excellent water supply. The narrow streets were widened into magnificent boulevards; parks and public gardens were provided; while here and there rose triumphal arches and columns [3]

---

[1] Cf. *Ancient History*, §§ 526-527.

[2] Extreme Royalists and early "Emigrants," who believed in absolute monarchy and in the Old Régime, of course did not return. Those who were now restored to France were the liberal aristocrats and the clergy and Constitutionalists who had fled during the Reign of Terror.

[3] The Vendome column (see next page) was made from Russian and Austrian cannon captured in the Austerlitz campaign. The figures on the spirals represent scenes in that campaign, and upon the summit, 142 feet high, stands a statue of Napoleon. The name Vendome comes from the name of the public square. The column was restored in 1875, from the fragments into which it had been broken by the Communards (§ 436).

to commemorate French victories.[1] Throughout the country, roads, canals, and harbors were built or improved. *Political liberty was destroyed, but equality was preserved, along with the economic gains of the Revolution.*

The Revolution had greatly improved the condition of the laborer. The peasantry were all landowners, free from their old burdens; and workmen secured two or three times the wages they had received ten years before. Under such conditions the people displayed new energies, and, with the establishment of quiet and order, they quickly built up a vast material prosperity.

360. The Concordat and the Code. — Two of the reforms of the Consulate call for special attention.[2]

a. The Concordat. Religion and patriotism were reconciled. For ten years

THE VENDOME COLUMN, PARIS.

---

[1] Read Rose, I, 292, 293.
[2] If time can be spared for other Napoleonic institutions, special reports may be assigned upon the Legion of Honor, the University of France, and Napoleon's encouragement of science throughout his career.

the condition of the church had been unsatisfactory and full of danger to religion and to France. Bonaparte at once freed the non-juring clergy from banishment and from prisons. But these priests had still neither churches nor support, while the established Constitutionalist clergy were not recognized by the Pope nor by the most devout Catholics. Bonaparte now forced the Pope to agree to a Concordat,[1] which reconstituted the church. All bishops, non-juring and Constitutionalist alike, were requested to resign or were dismissed, and new ones, appointed by Napoleon, were consecrated by the Pope. Thus the church became Roman again; but its property was not restored, and it was supported and strictly controlled by the state.

b. The Code. Under the ancient monarchy, the contradictions and complexities of the legal system had called loudly for reform; and the Revolution, with its new principles and its sweeping changes, had made the need of codification still more imperative. The work had been begun in 1793 (§ 345); and now the First Consul took up the task and carried it to completion with wonderful dispatch and success. A commission of great jurists, working under Bonaparte's inspiration and oversight, reduced the vast chaos of French legislation to a compact, simple, symmetrical code, known later as *the Code Napoleon*.[2] This code, embracing many of the most important principles of the Revolution, was introduced during the next few years, by French control or influence, into Holland, Italy, Spain, and nearly all the German states except Austria and Prussia. Even these two countries imitated it for themselves, so that it became the basis of law for practically all Europe, except England, Russia, and Turkey. Moreover, from Spain it spread to all Spanish America, and to-day it lies at the foundation of the law of the State of Louisiana.

361. Napoleon's Share in the Reconstruction of France. — In all this reconstruction of France, the controlling and designing

---

[1] The name commonly given to a treaty between a pope and a temporal state. For brief accounts, see Rose, I, 249-262; Seeley, 99.

[2] Rose, I, 262-271; Fyffe, 173-175.

mind was that of the First Consul. Functionaries worked as they had worked for no other master. Bonaparte knew how to set every man the right task; and his own matchless activity (he sometimes worked twenty hours a day) made it possible for him to oversee countless designs. His penetrating intelligence seized the essential point of every problem, and his indomitable will drove through all obstacles to a quick and

ARCH OF TRIUMPH, PARIS, commemorating Napoleon's victories.[1]

effective solution. His ardor, his ambition for France and for glory, his passion for good work, his contempt for difficulties, inspired every official, until, as one of them said, "the gigantic entered into our habits of thought."

362. Despotism veiled by "Plebiscites." "Emperor of the French," 1804. — But after all, the great benefits that Napoleon conferred upon France were the work of a beneficent despotism, not of a free government. The First Consul worked as a

---

[1] Napoleon followed Roman models. Cf. *Ancient History*, 410, 411.

Joseph II might have done (§ 280) had he possessed the ability and the opportunity. The Constitution of the Year VIII needed little change to accommodate it to avowed monarchy, and the slight forms of freedom in it were for the most part soon discarded.[1] Even the Tribunate's right to discuss proposed laws was suppressed. In 1802, Bonaparte had himself elected Consul for Life. He set up a monarchic court and began to call himself by his first name — Napoleon — after the custom of monarchs. Then, in 1804, he secured a vote of the nation declaring him "Emperor of the French," and he solemnly crowned himself at Paris, with the presence and sanction of the Pope, as the successor of Charlemagne.

Napoleon always claimed, it is true, that he ruled by the "will of the French people"; and each assumption of power was given a show of ratification by a popular vote, or *plebiscite*. But the plebiscite was merely the nation's Yes or No to a question framed by the master. The result of a negative answer could never be foreseen; and it was not hard so to shape questions that men would rather say Yes than risk the indefinite consequences of saying No. *The nation had no share at any stage in shaping the questions upon which it was to vote.* Even if the result of the vote had not been largely affected by skillful coercion, the plebiscite would have been a poor substitute for representative legislatures and free discussion. It was but a thin veil for military despotism. It was, however, a standing denial of the old doctrine of "divine right."

363. Personal Liberty vanishes. — Personal liberty was no longer safe. Napoleon maintained a vast network of secret police and spies; and he sent thousands of men to prison or into exile by his sole decree. The press was subjected to stern and searching censorship.[2] No book could be published if it contained opinions offensive to the Emperor, even in matters most

---

[1] For a detailed statement of the modifications made by the later constitutions, advanced students may consult a concise summary in Dickenson's *Revolution and Reaction*, 38–41.

[2] Read Dickenson, 46–48.

distantly related to politics.[1] Newspapers were restricted in number, and, on pain of losing their licenses, they were forbidden to print anything "contrary to the duties of subjects." They were required to omit all news "disadvantageous or disagreeable to France," and in political matters they were allowed to publish only such items as were furnished them by the government. Moreover, they were required to praise the administration. "Tell them," said Napoleon, "I shall judge them not only by the evil they say, but by the good they do not say." Even the schools were made to preach despotism, and were commanded to "take as the basis of their instruction fidelity to the Emperor." Religion, too, was pressed into service. Every village priest depended, directly or indirectly, upon Napoleon's will, and was expected to uphold his power. Indeed, a catechism was devised expressly to teach the duty of all good Christians to obey the Emperor.[2]

B. The Wars of the Empire.

364. Renewal of War. — There is no doubt that Napoleon wished peace in 1800, to enable him to consolidate his power and reorganize France. It is equally clear that soon he again desired war. In 1802 he told his Council of State that he should welcome war and that he expected it. The existing peace, he said, and any that might follow, could be only a truce. In 1804 he declared that Europe needed a single head, an Emperor, to distribute the various kingdoms among lieutenants. He felt, too, that victories and military glory were needful to prevent the French nation from murmuring against his despotism. On the other hand, the other nations felt that there could be no lasting peace with Napoleon except on terms of absolute submission. Under such conditions as these, war

---

[1] Madame de Staël was not allowed to say that the drama of Iphigenia by the German Goethe was a greater play than the work of the French Racine upon the same plot.

[2] Read extracts in Anderson, No. 65, or in Dickenson, 54-55.

soon broke out afresh. England and France renewed their strife in 1803, and between these Powers there was never again to be a truce until Napoleon's fall. During the next eleven years, Napoleon fought also three wars with Austria, two with Prussia, two with Russia, a long war with Spain, and various minor conflicts.

The European wars from 1792 to 1802 belong to the period of the French Revolution proper. Those from 1803 to 1815 are *Napoleonic wars*, due primarily to the ambition of one great military genius. In the first series, Austria was the chief opponent of the Revolution: in the second series, England was the relentless foe of Napoleon.

365. Austerlitz, Jena, Peace of Tilsit (1805-1807). — On the breaking out of war with England, Napoleon prepared a mighty flotilla and a magnificent army at Boulogne, and for over a year England was threatened with overwhelming invasion if she should lose command of the Channel even for a few hours. But all Napoleon's attempts to get together a fleet to compete with England failed; and in 1805 Austria and Russia joined England in the war. With immediate decision, Napoleon transferred his forces from the Channel to the Danube, annihilated two great armies, at *Ulm* and *Austerlitz* (October and December), and, entering Vienna as a conqueror, forced Austria to a humiliating peace. That country gave up her remaining territory in Italy, and her Illyrian provinces, and surrendered also many of her possessions in Germany.

Prussia had maintained her neutrality for eleven years; but now, with his hands free, Napoleon goaded her into war, crushed her absolutely at *Jena* (October, 1806), occupied Berlin, and soon afterward dictated a peace that reduced Prussia one-half in size and bound her to France as a vassal state.

Less decisive conflicts with Russia were followed by the *Peace of Tilsit* (July, 1807). The Russian and French Emperors met in a long interview, and Tsar Alexander was so impressed by Napoleon's genius, that, from an enemy, he became a friend and ally. France, it was understood, was to rule

Western Europe; Russia might aggrandize herself at the expense of Sweden, Turkey, and Asia; and the two Powers were to unite in ruining England by excluding her commerce from the continent (§ 366).

366. The "Continental System." — Meantime, England had proved as supreme on the seas as Napoleon on land. In 1805, at *Trafalgar*, off the coast of Spain, Nelson destroyed the last great fleet that Napoleon collected. Soon afterward, it is true, a secret article in the Treaty of Tilsit agreed that Denmark, then a considerable naval power, should be made to add her fleet to the French; but the English government struck first. It demanded the surrender of the Danish fleet into English hands until war should close, and finally it compelled the delivery by bombarding Copenhagen.

After this, Napoleon could not strike at England with his armies, and he fell back upon an attempt to ruin her by crushing her commerce. All the ports of the continent were to be closed to her goods, and no intercourse was to be allowed with the island. This "Continental System" did inflict damage upon England, but it carried greater harm to the continent, which simply could not do without the manufactures of England, at that time the workshop of Europe.[1] Smuggling became universal, and the System never worked successfully. In attempts to enforce it, Napoleon was led on from one high-handed measure to another, until Portugal and Russia rose against him (§ 367), and gave oppressed Central Europe another opportunity.[2]

---

[1] At times, even the French armies had to be clothed in smuggled English goods, and they marched into Russia in English shoes. Napoleon stirred French scientists into desperate efforts to invent substitutes for the goods now shut out of the continent. One valuable result followed. The English cruisers prevented the importation of West India cane-sugar; but it was discovered that sugar could be made from the beet, and the raising of the sugar-beet became a leading industry of France.

[2] England's retort to the Continental System was an attempt to blockade the coast of France and her dependencies to all neutral vessels. In these war measures, both France and England ignored the rights of neutral states; and

367. Military Events from Tilsit to Wagram. The Peninsular War. — Portugal refused to confiscate the English vessels in her ports. Thereupon Napoleon's armies occupied the kingdom. From this act, Napoleon passed to the seizure of Spain, placing his brother Joseph upon the throne. But the proud and patriotic Spanish people rose in a " War for Liberation," and it was soon plain that a new force had appeared. *Hitherto, Napoleon had warred against governments and regular armies, and had dictated peace when the capitals and rulers were in his power: now, first, he had to fight with a people in arms.* He found that brilliant victories merely transferred the outbreaks from one quarter to another and called for more and more of his energies. England seized her opportunity, too, and sent an army under Wellesley (afterward Duke of Wellington) to support the Peninsular revolt.

In 1809, encouraged by the Spanish rising, Austria once more entered the lists, but the defeat of Wagram forced her again to submission.[1] For the next two years, no opposition raised its head on the continent, except for the seemingly insignificant guerrilla war in Spain. This "Peninsular War," however, continued to drain Napoleon's resources until the final expulsion of the French in 1813, after the Russian campaign (§ 373). Afterward, at St. Helena, Napoleon declared that it was really the Spanish war that worked his ruin.

C. Napoleon's Reconstruction of Europe.

368. Territorial Rearrangements on the North Sea and in Italy. — At the moment, the campaigns of 1808–1809 seemed trivial. For five years after Tilsit, Napoleon was supreme in Central Europe. This period was marked by sweeping changes in territory, government, and society. Of course, many of the changes were designed in pure selfishness, merely to strengthen the supremacy of France; but almost all of them were to result beneficially to Europe. In particular, the Germany

---

the result was our War of 1812. Advanced students should read the magnificent treatment of the Continental System by Captain Mahan in *The Influence of the Sea Power upon the French Revolution* (chs. xvii and xviii).

[1] Napoleon now married a princess of Austria. He was anxious for an heir, and so divorced his former wife, Josephine, who had borne him no children, to make way for the new alliance with a grandniece of Marie Antoinette. This union of the Revolutionary Emperor with the proud Hapsburg house marks in some respects the summit of his power.

and Italy of to-day were made possible by Napoleon's vigorous clearing away of old institutions and by the impulse he gave to the new movements of political unity and of social reform. Outside of Germany, which requires special treatment (§ 369), the most important of the territorial changes may be grouped under three heads.

a. The Batavian Republic was converted into the Kingdom of Holland, with Napoleon's brother Louis for its sovereign. Later, when Louis refused to ruin his people by enforcing the Continental System rigidly, Napoleon deposed him, and Holland, along with the whole north coast of Germany as far as Denmark, was annexed to France.

b. In Italy the new republics and the old petty states were disposed of, one after another; even the Pope was deprived of his principality and, indeed, was made a French captive. When these changes were complete, Italy lay in three fairly equal divisions: in the south, Napoleon's brother, Joseph, ruled as King of Naples;[1] in the northeast was the "Kingdom of Italy," with Napoleon himself as king; and all the rest of the peninsula was a part of France, and was organized as a French department.

c. The Illyrian provinces on the eastern coast of the Adriatic were annexed directly to the French Empire.

At the time, these changes added enormously to Napoleon's power, but at his fall, they were for the most part undone. For this reason they were less important than the changes wrought in Central Europe, which in the main were to survive. But to comprehend the significance of Napoleon's work in Germany, one must first grasp the bewildering conditions there before his interference (§ 369).

369. Territorial Conditions in Germany before Napoleon. — Before Napoleon there was no Germany. The Holy Roman Empire was made up of (1) two great states, Austria and Prussia, each of them half Slavonic in blood; (2) some thirty states of the second rank, like Bavaria and Wurtemberg;

---

[1] When Joseph was promoted in 1809 to the throne of Spain, he was succeeded in Naples by Murat, one of Napoleon's generals.

(3) about two hundred and fifty petty states of the third order, many of them ecclesiastical, — ranging in size from a small duchy to a large farm, but averaging a few thousand subjects.[1] Each of these states was an absolute monarchy, with its own laws, its own tariffs, its own mimic court, its own coinage, its own army,[2] and its crowd of pedantic officials.

Besides these three hundred states already mentioned, there were also about fifteen hundred "knights of the Empire." In England this class would have been country squires; but in Germany they were virtually independent sovereigns, with an average territory of less than three square miles, ruling with power of life and death over half a million subjects, — some three hundred apiece. Each such state, too, had its tolls, its army, and its own system of taxation. And, lastly, there were some fifty "free cities," all in oligarchic decay and misrule.

One more factor must be taken into account in order to get an idea of the indescribable confusion. Few even of these petty principalities had their territory compact. Many a state of the second or third order consisted of several fragments (obtained by accidents of marriage or war), sometimes widely scattered, — some of them perhaps wholly inside a larger state to which politically they had no relation. No map can do justice to the quaint confusion of this region, about the size of Texas, thus broken into eighteen hundred governments varying from an Empire to a small estate, and scattered in fragments within fragments. The "Holy Roman Empire," as Voltaire said, "was neither Holy, nor Roman, nor yet an Empire." It is little wonder that the philosopher Lessing, the greatest German between Luther and Goethe, should have said: "Patriotism I do not understand; at best it seems an amiable weakness which I am glad to be free from."

The next seventy years were to see this "political crazy quilt" transformed into a mighty German state. The transformation was to be the work of German patriotic leaders, like Stein (§ 371) and Bismarck (§ 465), and of a new national enthusiasm in the German people, aroused by poets and statesmen; but the work of the patriots, it is well to remember, was made possible by the preliminary work of the foreign despot, Napoleon.

---

[1] Eighty of these states averaged less than twelve square miles in area.
[2] The "Sovereign Count" of Leimburg-Styrum-Wilhelmsdorf maintained a standing army of one colonel, nine lower officers, and two privates.

370. Territorial Consolidation of Germany. — At Campo Formio (§ 351), Napoleon had begun his rearrangement of Germany: at that treaty, and by subsequent arrangements, princes of the Empire were allowed to recompense themselves for the territories they had lost to France *by absorbing the ecclesiastical states and most of the free cities.* After Austerlitz, Jena, and Wagram, more radical changes followed. Austria and Prussia were weakened. The first became an inland state. The second was halved and pushed altogether beyond the Elbe, while its recent Polish acquisitions were turned into the Duchy of Warsaw. After so depressing the two great states, Napoleon proceeded to form a further check upon them by augmenting the states of the second rank. Bavaria, Saxony, and Wurtemberg were made kingdoms, with territories enlarged at the expense of Austria and of smaller neighboring states; while out of old Prussian territory and of the electorate of Hanover was formed a new "Kingdom of Westphalia," for Napoleon's brother Jerome.

At the same time the large states were encouraged or compelled *to absorb the territories of the knights and of the petty principalities within or adjoining their borders. Thus eighteen hundred states were reduced to about forty ; and this tremendous consolidation, surviving the rearrangements after Napoleon's fall, paved the way for later German unity.*

Nearly all these German states, too, except Austria and Prussia, were leagued in the "Confederation of the Rhine," under Napoleon as "Protector." Of course the formation of this League amounted to a dissolution of the Holy Roman Empire; and in 1806 Francis II laid down the venerable title. So closed a government that dated from Augustus Caesar. Two years before, Francis had assumed the title "Emperor of Austria," instead of his previous title, "Arch-Duke of Austria"; but the new Austrian Empire must not be thought of as the successor of the Holy Roman Empire.

371. Social Reform. — In the Confederacy of the Rhine and in the various kingdoms of Napoleon's brothers and generals, serfdom and feudalism were abolished, and civil equality and the *Code Napoleon* were introduced. Everywhere, too, the administration of justice was made cheap and simple, and the old clumsy and corrupt methods of government gave way to order and efficiency.

Most striking of all was the reform in Prussia. Elsewhere the new methods were introduced by French agents or under French influence. In Prussia they came from a Prussian minister, and were adopted in order to make Prussia strong enough to cast off the French yoke. Jena had proved that the old Prussian system was utterly rotten. The leading spirit in a new Prussian ministry was Stein, who labored to fit Prussia for leadership in freeing and regenerating Germany. The serfs were changed into free peasant-landowners; the caste distinctions [1] in society were broken down; some self-government was granted to the towns; and many of the best principles of the French reforms were adopted. Napoleon's insolence and the domination of French armies at last had forced part of Germany into the beginning of a new national patriotism; and that patriotism began to arm itself by borrowing weapons from the arsenal of the French Revolution.

D. Fall of Napoleon.

372. The Situation before the Russian Campaign. — In 1810, Napoleon's power had reached its widest limits. The huge bulk of France filled the space from the Ocean to the Rhine, — including not only the France which we know, but also Belgium, half of Switzerland, and large strips of German territory, while from this central body two outward-curving arms reached toward the east, — one along the North Sea to the

---

[1] In Prussia, the old law had recognized distinct classes, — peasants, burgesses and nobility, — and had practically forbidden an individual to pass from one class into another. Even the land had been bound by the caste system: no noble could sell land to the citizen of a town, or vice versa; nor could a townsman sell to a peasant. All this was now done away. Advanced students may consult Seeley's *Stein*, I, 291-294.

EUROPE
AT THE TIME OF
NAPOLEON'S GREATEST POWER
(1810)
SCALE OF MILES
0 50 100 200 300 400
French Empire
French Dependencies
Dependent Allies
ATLANTIC OCEAN
NORTH SEA
BALTIC SEA
BLACK SEA
MEDITERRANEAN SEA
ADRIATIC SEA
Bay of Biscay
English Channel
GREAT BRITAIN
LONDON
Edinburgh
Dublin
HEBRIDES
ORKNEY IS.
CHANNEL IS.
HELGOLAND (To Eng.)
DENMARK
COPENHAGEN
CHRISTIANIA
SWEDEN
STOCKHOLM
GOTHLAND
G. of Finland
PETERSBURG
RUSSIA
Moscow
Smolensk
Riga
Vilna
Kief
Odessa
Kherson
Crimea
Sea of Azof
Volga R.
Oka R.
Dwina R.
Niemen R.
Dnieper R.
Bug R.
Konigsberg
Danzig
Stettin
BERLIN
Hamburg
Kiel
Bremen
Hanover
Amsterdam
Antwerp
Brussels
Cologne
Boulogne
Cherbourg
Luxemburg
Metz
Strasburg
Basel
BERN
SWITZERLAND
Geneva
Lyons
PARIS
FRANCE
Bordeaux
Loire R.
Garonne R.
Rhone R.
Rhine R.
Marseilles
Toulon
Avignon
Nice
K. OF WESTPHALIA
G. DUCHY OF BERG
Cassel
Leipzig
K. OF SAXONY
DRESDEN
CONFEDERATION OF THE RHINE
Frankfort
WURTEM-K. OF
STUTT.
BADEN
BERG
MUNICH
BAVARIA
Innsbruck
Posen
WARSAW
GR. DUCHY OF WARSAW
Vistula
Oder R.
Breslau
Krakow
Prague
VIENNA
AUSTRIA
Budapest
Trieste
ILLYRIA
Milan
Venice
Turin
Genoa
Po R.
K. OF ITALY
Leghorn
Florence
ELBA
Rome
CORSICA
Ajaccio
KING. OF SARDINIA
NAPLES
KING. OF NAPLES
Palermo
KING. OF SICILY
CORFU
IONIAN IS. To Fr.
Bessarabia
Jassy
Moldavia
Wallachia
Bucharest
Belgrade
Servia
Bosnia
Bulgaria
TURKEY
MONTENEGRO
Scutari
CONSTANTINOPLE
Athens
Morea
CRETE
SPAIN
MADRID
Valladolid
Saragossa
Barcelona
Valencia
Seville
Cadiz
Tarifa Pt.
Gibraltar (To Eng.)
Ebro R.
Duero R.
Tagus R.
Guadiana R.
PORTUGAL
LISBON
Oporto
C. Ortegal
C. Finisterre
BALEARIC IS.
MINORCA
MAJORCA
MOROCCO
ALGERIA
Algiers
Tunis

Danish Peninsula, and the other down the coast of Italy past Rome. Besides this vast territory, all organized in French departments, the rest of Italy and half the rest of Germany were under Napoleon's protection and were ruled by his appointees or favorites. Moreover, Denmark and Switzerland were his dependent allies, and Prussia and Austria were unwilling ones. Only the extremities of the continent kept their independence. The islands of England, Sicily, and Sardinia and the rebels in the mountains of Portugal and Spain were in arms against him; while Sweden and Russia were in alliance with him. And even these allies, though nominally equals, had, in fact, become mere upholders of his policy.

373. Quarrel with Russia; the Retreat from Moscow. — Russia had been friendly since Tilsit, but was growing hostile.

NAPOLEON toward the close of his rule.

Alexander was offended by the partial restoration of Poland (in the Duchy of Warsaw), and he believed that Napoleon had intrigued against Russian gains in Finland and in Turkey. The Continental System, too, was growing more and more burdensome, and in 1811 the Tsar refused to enforce it longer. Napoleon at once declared war. In 1812 he invaded Russia and penetrated to Moscow. The Russians set fire to the city, so that it should not afford him winter quarters; but, with rare indecision, he stayed there five weeks, hoping in vain that the Tsar would offer to submit. Then, too late, in the middle of October, when the Russian winter was already upon them, the French began a terrible retreat, fighting desperately each foot of the way against cold, starvation, and clouds of Cossack cavalry. Nine weeks later, twenty thousand miserable scarecrows recrossed the Niemen. The "Grand Army," a half-million strong, had left its bones strewn among Russian snows.

374. From Leipzig to Paris. — The Russians kept up the pursuit into Germany, and the enthusiasm of the Prussian people forced the government to declare against the oppressor. The next summer, Austria also took up arms. By tremendous efforts, Napoleon raised a new army of boys and old men from exhausted France, and for a time he kept the field victoriously in Germany; but in October, 1813, he met crushing defeat at *Leipzig,* in the "Battle of the Nations." He retreated across the Rhine, and his vassal kings fled from their states. Most of the small Powers of Central Europe now joined his enemies, but as yet there was no plan to dethrone him. England, Russia, Austria, and Prussia, acting in close concert through numerous congresses, took to themselves the name "The Allies," and maintained a perfect understanding. After Leipzig, they proposed peace, offering to leave France the Rhine for her boundary. When this liberal proposal was rejected by the desperate gamester who opposed them, the Allies advanced to the Rhine, and offered peace with the French boundaries of 1792. Napoleon again refused. Then the Allies invaded France at several points, with overwhelming numbers, and, in spite of Napoleon's superb defense, they entered Paris victoriously in March, 1814.

375. The Peace of 1814. Louis XVIII. — The French Senate rejected Napoleon's offer to abdicate in favor of his young son, and decreed his immediate deposition. The Allies made him a large allowance, and granted him the island of Elba, in the Mediterranean, as an independent principality. France now had no government; but the Bourbon heir, one of the Emigrant brothers of Louis XVI, appeared, promised a constitution, and was quietly recognized by the Senate as Louis XVIII.[1] The Allies had avoided the appearance of imposing this king upon France, but they were pleased with the arrangement; and, to make it popular, they granted liberal terms of peace. France kept her territory of 1791, and received back nearly all her colonies. The Allies withdrew their armies without imposing any war indemnity, such as France had exacted repeatedly from other countries; nor did they even take back the works of art that French armies had plundered from so many famous galleries in Europe.

FOR FURTHER READING. — The best brief accounts of the Napoleonic era are given in Stephens' *Revolutionary Europe, 1789-1815*, Rose's *Revolutionary and Napoleonic Era*, and Fyffe's *Modern Europe*, 135-367. Andrews' *Modern Europe* has an excellent fifty-page treatment (I, 37-85), and Dickenson's *Revolution and Reaction* has a valuable chapter (ch. ii). The many histories of Napoleon are most of them defaced by extreme partisanship on one side or the other, or are too long for general use. Probably the best treatment is also the most recent, — Rose's *Napoleon the First*. Fournier's older but excellent *Life of Napoleon* has just been translated into English. Seeley's *Short History of Napoleon* is exceedingly readable and forceful, but it is unjust to Napoleon. Campaigns are admirably dealt with in Ropes' *The First Napoleon*, and that volume is also one of the best brief treatments of other phases of the time. Seeley's *Life and Times of Stein* gives a full and excellent account of Germany and Prussia in this age. Students who wish further details may consult works upon the separate countries. Anderson's *Constitutions and Documents* gives an admirable selection of documents. Kennan's *Folk-tales About Napoleon* is a curious and interesting volume.

---

[1] The son of Louis XVI had died in prison in Paris in 1795; according to the theory that he began to reign upon his father's death in 1793, he is known as Louis XVII.

CHAPTER II.

THE PERIOD OF REACTION, 1814-1848.

I. THE CONGRESS OF VIENNA — REARRANGEMENTS.

376. Call and Composition of the Congress. — Napoleon had wiped away the old map of Europe, and now, in turn, his territorial arrangements fell to pieces. All the districts which had been annexed to France since 1792, and all the states which had been created by Napoleon, were left without governments; and the old rulers of these and other European countries were clamoring for restoration of territories or for new acquisitions. To settle these problems, the four great Allies invited all the sovereigns of Europe to a Congress at Vienna, but by a secret treaty they reserved important questions for their own decision.

The *Congress of Vienna* assembled in November, 1814. The crowd of smaller monarchs and princes were entertained by their Austrian host in a constant round of masques and revels, while the great Allies did the work in committee. From time to time, as they reached agreements, they announced results to the Congress for public ratification. Before the work was concluded, however, Talleyrand, the French representative, forced his way into the inner circle, by taking adroit advantage of a quarrel among the Allies (§ 377 *d*). Thus the results were really the work of England, Russia, Austria, Prussia, and France; and the three men of most weight were Alexander of Russia, Talleyrand of France, and Metternich, the Austrian diplomat.

377. The Political and Territorial Rearrangements of the Congress fall under four heads.

a. The old German and Italian principalities were restored, under their former ruling families, except that no one thought of reëstablishing the ecclesiastical states (other than the Pope's) or the petty German states below the second rank (§ 369). *Italy was left in twelve states, and Germany in thirty-eight.* These German states, moreover, were organized into a loose confederacy, under the presidency of Austria, for protection against foreign attack (§ 387).

b. The states along the French frontier were strengthened. Holland was made into the Kingdom of the Netherlands, under the famous House of Orange, and to it was added Belgium, despite the fact that the Belgians wished to be independent. Switzerland received new French territory and was taken under the protection of the Powers, her neutrality being guaranteed.[1] Nice and Savoy were given back to the Kingdom of Sardinia, to which was added also the old Republic of Genoa. The old German territory west of the Rhine was given to Bavaria or Prussia. Thus aggression from France was guarded against by leaving no really weak state touching its borders.

c. Denmark, the ally of France, was weakened ; and Sweden became a purely Scandinavian power, confined to the northern peninsula. Denmark was forced to cede Norway to Sweden,[2] in compensation for that country's loss of Finland to Russia and of Pomerania to Prussia.

d. There remained the matter of *compensation to the four Allies*. England had stood out alone for years against the

---

[1] The Powers agreed, that is, that in time of war no state should send troops through Swiss territory or occupy any part of it. Switzerland was the one republic left in Europe, and its constitution was remodeled upon an oligarchic and ineffective basis, very inferior to that it had possessed as the Helvetic Republic. The ancient republics of Venice, Genoa, and Holland were none of them restored.

[2] The Norwegians resented the transfer, and tried to set up an independent government. The Powers ignored their wishes, however, and they had to be contented with a constitution approved by the King of Sweden, recognizing them in some respects as a distinct state with rights of their own (§ 523).

whole power of Napoleon, and she had incurred an enormous national debt by acting as paymaster of the various coalitions. In some small repayment, she kept Malta, the Ionian Islands, Cape Colony, Ceylon, and a few other colonial acquisitions. Alexander of Russia claimed his reward in Poland: he insisted that the Duchy of Warsaw, with the Russian parts of Poland, should be made into a Kingdom of Poland, of which he should wear the crown. Austria and Prussia had both been enlarged after the beginning of the French Revolution, by the partitions of Poland. It was understood, now, that they were to be given territory enough to make them as large as they were after those partitions, but that they would not seek other extension.

Austria was easily made content: she received back most of her provinces in Germany and Italy and on the Adriatic, and she accepted Venice in exchange for Belgium.[1] But on the matter of the Russian and Prussian indemnity, serious difficulty arose. Prussia had expected her old territories, including the Duchy of Warsaw. Alexander's plan interfered with this; and he finally won the support of the Prussian King by promising to aid Prussia in obtaining Saxony.[2] Austria dreaded the approach of either Russia or Prussia toward the heart of Germany, and opposed the plan. England and France[3] joined her, and the Allies came to the verge of war. Finally, however, it was arranged that Prussia should have half Saxony and the rest of her indemnity from German territory recovered from France west of the Rhine. Alexander secured his crown of Poland.

378. The Congress interrupted by the Return of Napoleon. — Suddenly the Congress was startled by the news that Napo-

---

[1] The Venetians bitterly resented the transfer, but their opinions were not regarded as in any way a matter of consideration.

[2] The King of Saxony had remained faithful to Napoleon, and so, Alexander urged, it would be proper to make an exception in his case to the careful respect shown by the conquerors toward all other "legitimate rulers."

[3] This was the occasion when Talleyrand made France a party to the real Powers in the Congress (§ 376).

leon had left Elba. A few months of Bourbon rule had filled France with disquiet and dread. The tricolor, under which Frenchmen had marched in triumph into nearly every capital in Europe, had been replaced by the old white flag, and many Napoleonic officers had been dismissed from the army to make way for returned Emigrants, who for twenty years had fought against France: thus the army was restless. The extreme Royalists were talking, too, of restoring the land of the church and of the Emigrants, though it had passed for a generation into other hands: and in consequence, the peasants and the middle class were rendered uneasy. Napoleon, learning how matters stood, had landed in France, almost unattended. The forces sent to capture him joined his standard, and in a few days, without firing a shot, he entered Paris in triumph. The King and the old Emigrants emigrated again. Napoleon called upon a liberal statesman to draw up a free constitution; France accepted it; and Napoleon solemnly promised to respect it. The Allies at Vienna, however, refused even to treat with Napoleon. They declared unrelenting war upon him as "the disturber of the peace of Europe," and promptly moved powerful armies to the French frontier.

379. Waterloo and the Second Treaty with France. — No time was given Napoleon for preparation. The Allies were ready, and the odds were overwhelming. After a brief rule, known as "The Hundred Days," Napoleon was crushed at *Waterloo* by the English under *Wellington* and the Prussians under *Blücher* (June 18, 1815). The Allies reëntered Paris, "bringing Louis XVIII in their baggage," as the French wits expressed it. Napoleon was imprisoned on the distant volcanic rock of St. Helena; and to France was dictated a new treaty, much more severe than that of 1814. The Powers were alarmed at the ease with which the Bourbon monarchy had again been overthrown, and they wished to punish the nation for its voluntary acceptance of Napoleon. Prussia urged that France should be dismembered, as she herself had been after

Jena;[1] but Alexander and England insisted upon a milder penalty. In the end, some small strips of territory were taken away, containing about a half-million of people, and a huge war indemnity was imposed, payable in five years. Meantime, France was required to receive and maintain a garrison from the troops of the Allies. This time, too, the works of art which Napoleon's armies had brought to France were restored to their proper homes.

380. Closing Work of the Congress. — During the Hundred Days, the Congress of Vienna finished its work. Some of its later measures were highly praiseworthy. England induced most of the Powers to unite in an earnest declaration against the slave-trade, and the navigation of all the rivers of Western Europe which flowed through or between different countries was declared free.[2] Moreover, it was worth much for Europe to recognize that it had common interests and that they could be arranged by a peaceful Congress. This was an advance from eighteenth century politics toward a better international organization. To be sure, *the Congress of Vienna represented only governments, not peoples. But democracy was to come into control of the governments, and then it would have only to utilize this machinery.* Thus even the gathering of despots at Vienna contained promise of the Hague Conference (§ 594), of international tribunals, and of Tennyson's "federation of the World."

---

[1] Moderate Prussian statesmen demanded the cession to Germany of Alsace and Lorraine, — all the conquests made by France since the time of Louis XIV. These were essentially the terms imposed by Bismarck upon France, fifty years later, after the Franco-Prussian War (§ 434). Radical Prussian papers talked of breaking France up into Neustria, Aquitaine, etc., and even of killing off the French people "like mad dogs."

[2] A country in possession of the mouth of a river had been in the habit of closing it against the trade of other nations, to the serious disadvantage of countries on its upper course and of other commercial Powers. For instance, while Spain owned the mouth of the Mississippi (1783–1801), she had wished to follow this policy, — to the wrath of our western settlers on the river and its tributaries. The principle established at Vienna was a step forward for civilization.

Of course, nothing of this was designed by the statesmen at Vienna. That "assemblage of princes and lackeys," in its desires, stood wholly for reaction. As Fyffe says, "It complacently set to work to turn back the hands of time to the historic hour at which they stood when the Bastille fell." It ignored the peoples of Europe,— their wishes, rights, and interests. It considered only princes, and applied the phrase of "legitimacy" to consecrate the claims of ruling families against all popular movements. It even dismembered peoples among princes at will, to serve its own selfish purposes. The sentiment for national unity and independence had roused the peoples against Napoleon in Spain, Russia, Germany, and Italy, and had wrought his overthrow. The Congress of Vienna, though reaping the result, ignored the cause; and its work, therefore, had to be slowly undone through the next half-century.

Still, even this selfish work contained many germs of progress. Napoleon's consolidation of Germany was not undone. Austria had lost territory in Central Europe and gained it in Italy: thus the energies of this despotic Power were drawn, even more than before, away from Germany and into Italian and Danubian questions. Meantime, renovated Prussia, from whom now a true German union might be hoped, had lost Slav territory, hard to organize, and gained German districts. With her new Saxon lands, she reached down to the heart of Germany; and with her distant isolated districts to defend, on the Rhine and the Niemen, she stood forth as the natural champion of German independence against both Slav and Gaul. In the next half-century, Prussia was to thrust Austria out of Germany and to organize the Fatherland into a grand empire under her own leadership. The possibility of this glorious result was one of the things hidden in the arrangements at Vienna.

In like manner, the addition of Genoa to the Kingdom of Sardinia began the consolidation of Italy by absorption into Sardinia,— a process which was to reach completion, together with that for German unity, in 1870.

FOR FURTHER READING. — One or more of the following works should be consulted: Andrews' *Modern Europe*, I, 90–113; Seignobos' *Europe since 1814*, 2–8; Phillips' *Modern Europe*, 1–13; Fyffe's *Modern Europe*, 368–418. Additional material will be found in Stephens' *Revolutionary Europe*, Rose's *Revolutionary and Napoleonic Era*, and Seeley's *Life and Times of Stein*. The most important documents are given in Anderson's *Constitutions and Documents*.

II. ATTEMPTS TO MAINTAIN THE SYSTEM OF 1815.

A. GENERAL CHARACTER OF THE PERIOD, 1815–1848.

381. Reactionary Sentiment among the Restored Rulers. — The immediate result of the Congress of Vienna was a victory for reaction and despotism over liberal thought and free government. In many states, especially in the pettier ones, the restoration of the old rulers was accompanied by ludicrous absurdities. The princes who had scampered away before the French eagles came back to show that they had "learned nothing and forgotten nothing." They set out to ignore the past twenty years. Even in France, a school history spoke of Austerlitz as "a victory gained by General Bonaparte, a lieutenant of the King"! The Elector of Hesse restored the ancient uniforms and the wearing of queues by the soldiers, and censured his military Commandant for "omitting quarterly reports during the preceding ten years," — in which the Elector had been a fugitive. The King of Sardinia restored serfdom. In the Papal States and in Spain, the Inquisition and other medieval institutions were restored. In some places French plants were uprooted from the botanical gardens and French material improvements were abolished, — from street-lamps to vaccination.[1]

382. Attitude of the Five "Great Powers." — The statesmen of the Great Powers must have smiled to themselves at some of these absurd extremes; but they, too, almost universally

---

[1] Andrew D. White gives an interesting account of a "Catechism of Reaction," in the American Historical Association Papers, IV, Part I, 69–92.

EUROPE AFTER THE CONGRESS OF VIENNA (1815)

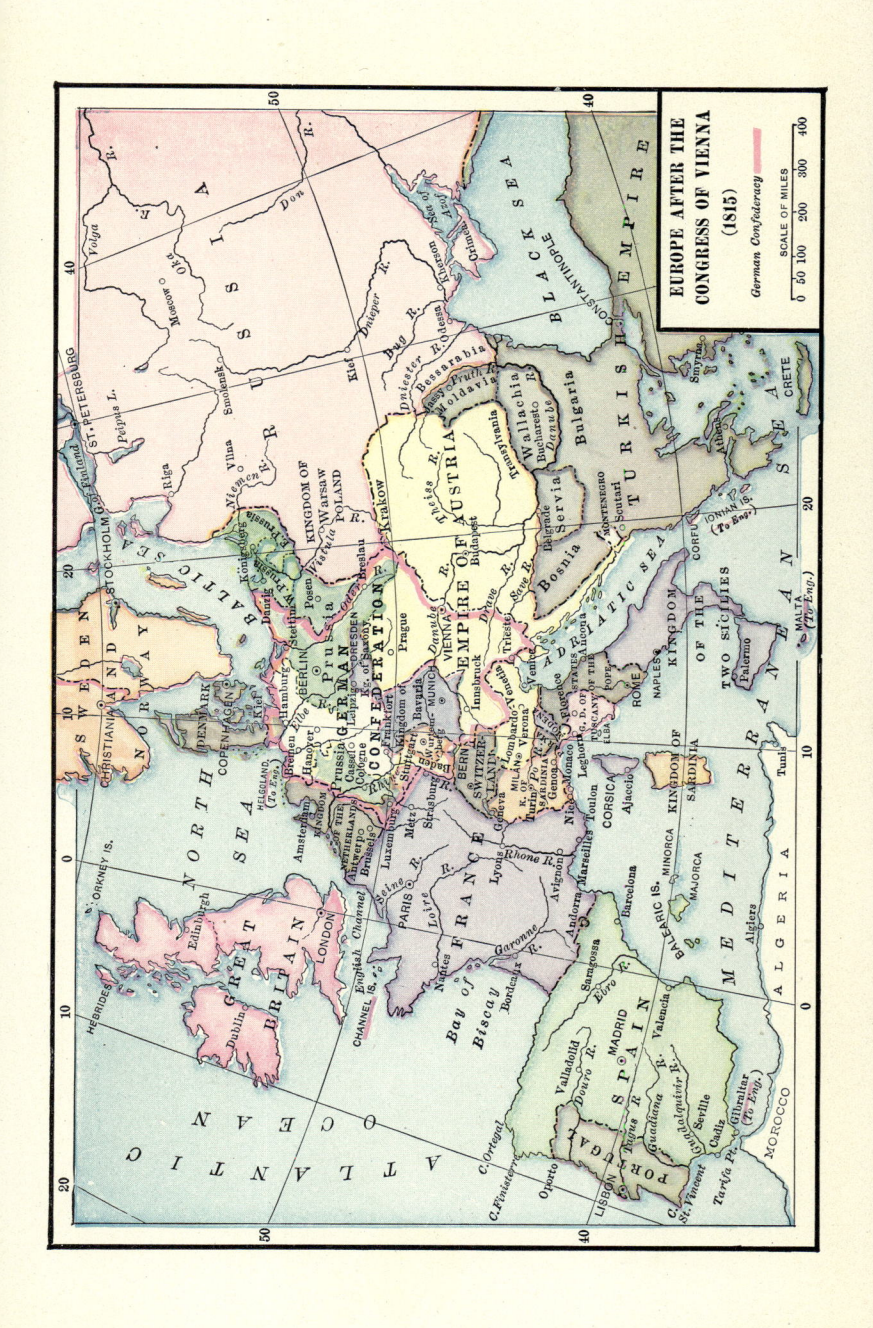

strove to suppress all progress. Five states — Russia, Austria, Prussia, France, and England — really determined the policy of Europe. The first three were "divine right" monarchies. Russia had not been modified by any phase of the French Revolution. Prussia, with all her recent reforms, was an absolute despotism, dependent upon the whim of her king. Austria in the main was still medieval. And though the Tsar Alexander and Frederick William III of Prussia both played a little at liberalism, they were easily terrified by the bogie of "Revolution," and were soon drawn to the Austrian policy. That policy from the close of the Vienna Congress was frankly reactionary. The Emperor Francis expressed it in an address to the professors of an Austrian college: "New ideas are being promulgated of which I can not and will not approve. Abide by the old. They are good; our fathers prospered under them; why should not we? . . . I do not need wise men, but brave and obedient subjects." And while the government thought so to harness thought at home, it established rigid quarantine against ideas from abroad: students might not go abroad for study; no foreign teachers were allowed to get places in Austria; and all printed matter was carefully supervised.

The western states, France and England, were at first not much better than these eastern Powers. Louis XVIII gave France a limited Charter, but the theory of divine right was carefully preserved until the Revolution of 1830 (§§ 411 ff.). That theory, of course, could have no place in England, where the monarchy rested on the Revolution of 1688; but even England for several years was to be in the hands of the Tory party, which was bitterly opposed to further progress (§ 529).

383. The "Rule of Metternich."— The central figure in the period of reaction from 1815 to 1848 was the subtle Austrian statesman, Metternich. No one has phrased the reactionary creed better than he: "Sovereigns alone are entitled to guide the destinies of their peoples, and they are responsible to none but God. . . . Government is no more a subject for debate than religion is." Metternich was too shrewd to think it possible to return altogether to the days before the French Revolution; but he did strive to arrest all change at the lines the Congress of Vienna had drawn. The "new ideas" of democracy and equality and nationality [1] ought never to have been allowed to get into Europe, he said; but, since they were in, the business of governments must be to keep them down out of sight. His policy has been aptly described as "Do nothing and let nothing be done." For over thirty years he was the evil genius of Europe. The rule of Napoleon, it is well said, was followed by the rule of Metternich.

Metternich was a polished cynic and a master of intrigue. Napoleon said of him that he "mistook intrigue for statesmanship," and, again, that he "narrowly missed being a statesman"; and Stein complained that, though he had industry and ability, he was "overfond of complications" and did not know how to do business "in the great and simple way." The one good thing to be said for his long rule is that it permitted no war between the Great Powers. The hundred years of almost incessant strife was followed, for the leading states of Europe, by forty years of almost unbroken peace.

384. Disappointment of the Liberals. — The political reaction was the more galling to the friends of liberty because the Wars of Liberation in 1812–1814 had been essentially popular uprisings. The Austrian and Prussian rulers had made repeated appeals to national patriotism, and had promised national unity and constitutional liberties. Austria and England had held out like hopes to the Italians;[2] and the Spanish rebels had adopted a free constitution for their country (§ 393). Thus the Liberals of Europe had greeted Napoleon's overthrow with

---

[1] The sentiment of nationality is the feeling among all the people of one race, speech, and country that they should make one political state, or become a "nation." This feeling tended to draw all Germans into a German state, and all Italians into an Italian state. It threatened Austrian supremacy, especially in Italy, because it made the Italian subjects of Austria wish to break away from Austria to join the rest of their fellow Italians. Thus in any conglomerate state, like Austria, the feeling of nationality was likely to be a disrupting force.

[2] Cf. § 393; and read Andrews, I, 57, 114–115, and especially 185, 186.

joyous acclaim; but they soon came to see that Leipzig and Waterloo had done nothing toward freeing Europe. These victories simply "replaced one insolent giant by a swarm of swaggering pygmies." Only a few months after Waterloo, Byron[1] lamented that "the chain of banded nations has been broke in vain by the accord of raised-up millions"; and, "standing on an Empire's Dust" at the scene of the great battle, and noting "how that red rain has made the harvest grow," he mused: —

> "Gaul may champ the bit and foam in fetters,
> But is Earth more free?
> Did nations combat to make *one* submit,
> Or league to teach *all* kings true sovereignty? . . .
> Then o'er one fallen despot boast no more."

385. Progressive Forces: Democracy and Nationality. — However, underneath all the wave of reaction, the principles of the French Revolution survived.[2] *The two positive forces in politics for the nineteenth century were to be Democracy and Nationality,* — just the two principles ignored by the Congress of Vienna and warred upon by Metternich. The league of princes for a time compelled these forces to work underground, in secret societies and plots; but before the middle of the century they emerged in three series of revolutions, — in 1820, 1830, and 1848. In 1820, almost no gain was made, except, after some delay, in Portugal and Greece. In 1830, gains were confined for the most part to France and Belgium. But after 1848, — "the Year of Revolutions," — the system of Metternich lay in ruins.

The work of the second half of the century was to reorganize Europe out of those ruins. Through the principles of Democracy and Nationality, there was created a new Germany, a new Italy, a new, stable French Republic, a new Swiss Federal Republic, a democratic England, a constitutional, federal

---

[1] An English poet of strong liberal sympathies in politics. See § 399.

[2] There is an admirable statement of the permanent results of the Revolution in Judson's *Nineteenth Century*, 64-70.

Austria-Hungary, and a group of free Slav states in the Balkan peninsula. All these and the other small states of Europe in great measure remodeled their governments upon English or American forms. Russia and Turkey remain the only two Powers in Europe not reconstructed; and the latter of these has been nearly thrust back into Asia.

386. Plan for the Treatment of the Period to 1848. — In our survey of the reactionary period to 1848 we are to note (1) Metternich's control over Germany through the Germanic Confederacy; and (2) his control over Southern Europe through the concert of Austria, Russia, and Prussia. These two topics are treated in subdivisions *B* and *C*, below. The revolutionary forces, which were to overthrow the "European system" of Metternich, emanated mainly from France, and will be referred to upon occasion; but their systematic treatment will be left until a following chapter.

B. GERMANY AND METTERNICH.

387. The Germanic Confederation. — The chief victory won by Metternich at the Congress of Vienna lay in the new organization adopted by Germany. Liberal Germany, represented by Stein, had hoped for a real union of the nation, either in the revival and strengthening of the Empire, or in a new federal state. But Metternich saw that in a true German Empire, Austria, with her Slav, Hungarian, and Italian interests, could not long keep the lead against Prussia. He preferred to leave the various states practically independent, so that Austria, the largest of all, might play them off against each other and so dominate them all. The small rulers, too, were hostile to a real union, because it would limit their sovereignties. In the settlement of the question, Metternich allied himself with these princes of the small states against Prussia and the Liberals. Stein was without official position; the Prussian King and his ministers were mild-mannered and not very acute; and the Prussian opportunity was lost.

But some sort of alliance was necessary to guard against foreign invasion; and the *Federal Act* of June 12, 1815, created the "Germanic Confederation." *This union was a loose league,*

THE
GERMANIC
CONFEDERATION
FROM
1815 to 1867
SCALE OF MILES
0 25 50 75 100 125
NORTH SEA
BALTIC SEA
DENMARK
JUTLAND
SWEDEN
RUSSIA
PRUSSIA
POLAND
POMERANIA
BRANDENBURG
POSEN
SILESIA
KINGDOM OF HANOVER
WESTPHALIA
NETHERLANDS
BELGIUM
DUCHY OF SCHLESWIG
DUCHY OF HOLSTEIN
MECKLENBURG-SCHWERIN
STRELITZ
OLDENBURG
SAXONY
THURINGIA
ELECT. OF HESSE
HELGOLAND (British)
GOTTLAND
BORNHOLM
RÜGEN
COPENHAGEN
Friedericia
Kiel
Rendsburg
Hamburg
Luneburg
Bremen
Hanover
Brunswick
Wilhelmshaven 1854 PRUSSIA
Oldenburg
Osnabrück
Münster
Düsseldorf
Cologne
Aix la Chapelle
Cassel
Göttingen
Gotha
Weimar
Halle
Leipzig
Altenburg
Dresden
Magdeburg
Dessau
Brandenburg
Potsdam
Berlin
Stettin
Stralsund
Rostock
N. Strelitz
Kolberg
Danzig
Marienburg
Königsberg
Memel
Tilsit
Thorn
Posen
Frankfort
Görlitz
Breslau
Ols
Kalisz
Warsaw
Minsk
Amsterdam
Utrecht
Zuyder Zee
LIPPE DETMOLD
R. Elbe
R. Weser
R. Ems
R. Rhein
R. Oder
R. Spree
Vistula
R. Bug
Warta
Memel R.
Eider
Maas
Prosna
1827
1865 PRUSSIA
6
8
10
12
14
16
18
20
22
56
54
52

KINGDOM OF BAVARIA
AUSTRIAN EMPIRE
HUNGARY
BOHEMIA
MORAVIA
GALICIA
STYRIA
TYROL
SALZBURG
CARINTHIA
CARNIOLA
ISTRIA
CROATIA
SLAVONIA
VENETIA
LOMBARDY
PIEDMONT
SAVOY
SWITZERLAND
LIECHTENSTEIN
BADEN
WURTEMBERG
HO.
PALATINATE
LICHTENBURG
LUXEMBURG
FRANCE
ITALY
PARMA
MODENA
EMILIA
TUSCANY
MARCHES
TURKEY
ADRIATIC SEA
MEDITERRANEAN SEA
Carlsbad
Prague
Pilsen
Königgrätz
Krakow
Troppau
Olmütz
Brünn
Nikolsburg
Budweis
Gänserndorf
Pressburg
Vienna
Passau
Salzburg
Gastein
Innsbruck
Bozen
Trent
Gratz
Klagenfurt
Laibach
Agram
Görz
Trieste
Fiume
Buda
Pest
Stuhlweissenburg
Temesvar
Belgrade
Nuremburg
Ratisbon
Augsburg
Munich
Ulm
Stuttgart
Karlsruhe
Mannheim
Darmstadt
Frankfort
Wiesbaden
Mainz
Meisenheim
Treves
Hambach
Landau
1815
Luxemburg
Metz
Nancy
Strasburg
Plombières
Mühlhausen
Basel
Constance
Zürich
Lucern
Bern
Neuenburg
Geneva
Magenta
Novara
Milan
Turin
Custoza
Solferino
Verona
Padua
Villafranca
Venice
Mantua
Ravenna
Genoa
Florence
Leghorn
R. Danube
R. Moldau
R. Elbe
R. Rhine
R. Inn
R. Etsch
R. Rhone
R. Po
R. Drave
R. Save
R. Theiss
R. March
R. Leitha
R. Main
R. Mosel
SCHUTT I.
6
8
10
12
14
16
18
20
44
46
48
50

and it was composed of sovereigns,[1] *not of peoples.* Each of the thirty-eight states controlled its own government, its own army, its own tariffs, and its own foreign diplomacy, and they even kept the right to form alliances among themselves or with foreign powers, — although they did promise not to make war upon each other. The Confederacy did not even send ambassadors to foreign countries. It had no distinct executive, judicial, and legislative departments: its one organ was the Federal Diet at Frankfort. This was merely a standing conference of ambassadors appointed by the sovereigns to speak their wills. The Austrian representative presided; but no really important action could be taken without the consent of every state.[2] Naturally, it was almost impossible to do business. Before many years the Diet was the laughingstock of Europe. As Dr. Judson says, "It was not a government at all; it was a polite and ceremonious way of doing nothing." The union amounted to little more than a possible means of securing concerted action by agreement among sovereigns; and in practice this agreement was to be secured only for the purpose of repressing liberal movements.

This Confederacy is the form in which Germany was organized from 1815 until 1866, when Prussia thrust Austria out by war and began the present German state. The fact that the Confederacy lasted so long, however, calls for no praise : it means only that for half a century there was little progress in national life.

388. The Promised Constitutions in the German States. — The chance for making a German nation had been lost at the Congress of Vienna, but the Liberals still hoped, for a time, for free political institutions in the separate states. In the "War of Liberation" the King of Prussia had twice promised his people a constitution; and at the Congress of Vienna he had

---

[1] Thirty-four of the members were sovereign princes; the other four were the governments of the surviving "free cities," Hamburg, Bremen, Lübeck, and Frankfort.

[2] Details of the Constitution are given in *Pennsylvania Reprints*, I, No. 3. Excellent analyses are given by Andrews, I, 232-238, and by Phillips, 38-44.

urged that the Federal Act should provide for setting up representative assemblies within a year in all the states and that these bodies should be given power over taxation. Metternich got this resolution softened into a vague and meaningless declaration that representative assemblies "would be" established. No time was stated, no powers enumerated; and it soon became plain that the pledge was worthless for most members of the Confederation.

Within the next four years, it is true, constitutions were granted by the liberal Grand Duke of Weimar, and by the rulers of Nassau and of the four South German states, Wurtemberg, Bavaria, Baden, and Hesse-Darmstadt.[1] These constitutions left the princes still the real rulers of their states; but they provided for equality of all classes before the law, for freedom of the press, and for representative assemblies with control over new taxes.

The King of Prussia might have put himself at the head of the movement and so rallied the liberal enthusiasm of Germany around his country. But Frederick William III was weak and vacillating, and when the first glow of patriotic sympathy was over, he began to see difficulties in the way of constitution making.[2] He did appoint a committee to prepare a constitution; but that body dawdled along for four years without result, and finally Frederick William formally repudiated his promise. This last event happened after the intensified reaction now to be described (§§ 389, 390).

---

[1] Germany south of the river Main is known as South Germany. The people in these districts had been greatly influenced by the French Revolution, and their rulers granted constitutions largely in order to secure popular support against possible attempts of Austria or Prussia upon their sovereignty.

[2] Some of these difficulties were real. Prussia was a mass of heterogeneous provinces, — Polish, German, and Germanized Prussian (Slav). The east was Protestant and intensely conservative; the new and distant western provinces were Catholic and zealously liberal. A third of the territory had just become Prussian for the first time, and large portions of the rest had been parts of other states for the preceding ten years. Moreover, the Prussian nobility railed bitterly at the thought of free institutions for the people, and the King's associations were chiefly with this nobility.

389. Liberal Indignation, Demonstrations, and Crimes: Reaction intensified. — By 1817, the Liberals[1] had become indignant and uneasy from the many delays and evasions by which in most states the promised constitutions were withheld. In October of that year, the three-hundredth anniversary of Luther's defiance of the Pope and the fourth anniversary of the Battle of Leipzig were celebrated together at the Wartburg castle in the Duchy of Weimar. The Jena University students took part in the celebration and turned it into a demonstration of liberal feeling. Patriotic and religious songs were sung; ardent speeches were made; and, in the evening, some old text-books were thrown into a bonfire, — having first been labeled with the names of reactionary works especially hated by the liberal party.[2]

This harmless and boyish ebullition threw sober statesmen into spasms of fear, and seemed to them to prelude a revolutionary "Reign of Terror." Metternich took shrewd advantage of the opportunity to wean the King of Prussia from whatever remained of his earlier liberalism and to make him a satellite in the Austrian system of reaction. Unhappily, more serious weapons than the Wartburg Festival were soon put into the hands of the Reactionists. A small section of radical agitators preached that even assassination in the cause of liberty was right; and, in 1819, a fanatical student murdered Kotzebue, a Russian representative in Germany, because he was supposed to have drawn away the Tsar from liberal sympathies. Soon after, a like attempt was made upon an absolutist minister in Hesse. These crimes shut out all prospect of political progress for many years.

390. The Carlsbad Decrees. — Austria at once called together the greater sovereigns of Germany to a conference at Carlsbad, and Metternich secured their approval for a series of resolu-

---

[1] Outside the Rhine districts the party was not large, but it comprised an influential body, — writers, journalists, students, professors, and most of the rest of the small educated middle class.

[2] Read Andrews, I, 242-243, or Phillips, 54-55.

tions, which were then hastily forced through the Diet at Frankfort. For once, that body was coerced into prompt action by the urgent unanimity of the leading monarchs. The "Carlsbad Decrees," so adopted, were especially directed against free speech in the press and in the universities. They forbade secret societies among students; they appointed a government official in every university to discharge any professor who should preach doctrines "hostile to the public order"; they set up a rigid censorship of all printed matter; and they created a standing committee to hunt out conspiracies. These regulations broke in upon the sovereignty that had been promised the rulers over their respective states, and compelled some of the rulers to infringe constitutions they had just granted. A few of the small states protested, but the resolute attitude of Austria and Prussia forced them to yield or risk conquest.

The decrees were renewed in 1824 and in 1833, and remained the law of the Confederacy, with little interruption, for nearly thirty years. During this time, thousands of enthusiastic youths were sent into exile or to prison for long terms, for singing forbidden patriotic songs, or for wearing the colors black, red, and orange, — the symbol of German unity. "Turnvater Jahn," the organizer of the patriotic Turner societies in the time of Napoleon, and the poet Arndt, whose songs had done much to arouse the people against French rule, were both persecuted. Learned professors who would not consent to be completely muzzled were driven from the universities. Men ceased to talk politics in society, and left matters of government to princes.

391. The Revolutions of 1830. — In 1830 the reaction was broken by a brief interruption. The "Second French Revolution" (§ 412) drove out the reigning "divine right" monarch in France and set up a new monarchy resting upon popular authority. The success of the sudden rising was followed by revolts all over Europe, and for a time the European system seemed crumbling. Belgium broke away from the King of

Holland, to whom the Congress of Vienna had given it. Poland rose against the Tsar, to whom the Congress had given it. The states of Italy rose (§ 394) against Austria and the Austrian satellites, to whom the Congress had given them. And in Germany there were various uprisings in all absolutist states, to demand the constitutions which the Congress had not given.

392. Reaction restored until 1848. — The final gains, however, were not so vast as at first they seemed. Belgium did become an independent monarchy with the most liberal constitution on the continent: and to that country and to France the Revolution brought permanent profit. But Tsar Nicholas crushed the Poles, took away their constitution,[1] and made them a Russian province. Austria crushed the Italian revolts. And though four new constitutions appeared in small German states, after almost bloodless risings, still the general despotic character of the Confederacy was not modified. While Austria was busied in Italy, it is true, there had seemed some hope of progress for Germany; but Metternich soon had his hands free, and at once he set about restoring "order." In 1832 an opening was given by a liberal demonstration at Hampach in Bavaria. The meeting was as harmless as the Wartburg Festival of 1817; but it answered Metternich's purpose. Troops were marched to Hampach to put down the "insurrection," and the Diet was frightened into restoring the Carlsbad Decrees in an intensified form.

Still, in the period from 1830 to 1848, reaction had lost much of its vigor and confidence, and it was being slowly undermined by a quiet but growing public opinion. Metternich's genius sufficed to keep his system standing, as long as it was not disturbed from without; but when the next year of Revolutions came (1848) that system fell forever in Western Europe. (See §§ 452–456.)

---

[1] Tsar Alexander had given a liberal constitution to his "Kingdom of Poland," but in 1825 Alexander was succeeded by Nicholas (§ 573).

C. Revolutions in Southern Europe, and "Intervention" by the Despotic Monarchs.

393. The Spanish Revolution of 1820. — The Spanish patriots who rose in 1808 against Napoleon found themselves without a government. Their king, with all their government machinery, was in the hands of the French. The insurgents set up a representative Cortes, and, in 1812, they adopted a liberal constitution. This "Constitution of 1812" was far from perfect; indeed, it was modeled largely upon the French Constitution of 1791 (§ 324); but it was the standard about which the Liberals of Southern Europe were to rally for a generation.

After the fall of Napoleon, King Ferdinand returned to the Spanish throne. He had promised to maintain the new constitution; but he soon broke his pledges, restored all the old iniquities, and cruelly persecuted the liberal heroes of the "War of Liberation."

This condition lasted until 1820. In that year came a revolution. Troops had been collected to subdue the revolted American colonies;[1] but the service was unpopular, and, instead of embarking, one of the regiments raised the standard of revolt and proclaimed the Constitution of 1812. Tumults followed in Madrid and other large towns; and the King, cowardly as he was treacherous, yielded, called a Cortes, and restored the Constitution.

394. Other Revolutions of 1820-1821. — This success in Spain became the signal for like attempts in other states. Before the year closed, Portugal and Naples both forced their kings to grant constitutions modeled upon that of Spain; and Sicily

---

[1] When Napoleon seized Spain, the Spanish American states refused to recognize his authority, and so became virtually independent under governments of their own. At first, most of these new governments were in name loyal to the Spanish crown. During the next few years, however, the Spanish Americans experienced the benefits of freedom, and began to desire to emulate the example of the United States, which had so recently been merely a group of European colonies. Accordingly, by 1815, all the Spanish states on the continent of America had declared themselves independent nations.

rose against the Neapolitan government for a constitution of its own. Early in the next year, the people and army of Piedmont [1] rebelled, to secure a constitution for the Kingdom of Sardinia and to unite Italy; Lombardy and Venetia, though held in the overpowering grasp of Austria, stirred restlessly; and the Greeks began their long and heroic struggle for independence against Turkey.

The wide-spread unanimity of action was due in part to secret revolutionary societies, already in existence. The most important of these was the *Carbonari* ("charcoal burners"). It had been formed in Italy, in the time of Napoleon, to drive out the French, and was continued there to drive out Austrian rule and to unite Italy. It was particularly strong among army officers, and it had branches or connections in other countries.

395. The Congress of Troppau and the Alliance of the Three Eastern Despots against Revolution. — We have seen how Metternich used the Germanic Confederacy, designed for protection against foreign attack, to stifle liberalism in Germany. We are now to observe how he adroitly twisted an alliance of monarchs from its original purpose in order to crush these revolutions in Southern Europe.

After Waterloo, while the four "Allies" were still in Paris (November 20, 1815), they had agreed to preserve their union and to hold meetings from time to time. The purpose was to guard against any future aggression by France. But when the revolutions of 1820 began, Metternich invited France also to a Congress of the Great Powers at Troppau. The French King had been terrified by recent radical movements in France (§ 407), and these same events, together with the Wartburg affair and the murder of Kotzebue (§ 389), had made the Tsar and the King of Prussia pliable to Metternich's molding hand.

---

[1] Piedmont ("Foot of the Mount") was the district between the Alps and the plains of Lombardy. It was the most important part of the old Duchy of Savoy and of the later Kingdom of Sardinia. The name is often used for the whole state of Sardinia.

At Troppau, the absolute sovereigns of Austria, Russia, and Prussia signed a declaration that they would intervene to put down revolution against any established government. Thus the principle of "intervention" was a proclamation that the "divine right" monarchs would support each other against the nations: it was directed against the right of a people to throw off despotic rule and to make its government for itself. England protested against this doctrine, both before and after the meeting, and formulated in opposition to it the principle of "non-intervention," or the doctrine that each nation should manage its internal affairs as it chose. On this issue, the alliance of 1815 was broken up. Undaunted by England's protests, however, the united eastern despots, known popularly from this time as "the Holy Alliance,"[1] prepared to enforce the Troppau program.[2]

396. The Congress of Laibach: Intervention in Naples and Sardinia. — A few months after Troppau, the three allied monarchs met again at Laibach. The King of Naples, another treacherous Bourbon Ferdinand, was present. That monarch had sworn solemnly to uphold the new Neapolitan constitution and had invoked the vengeance of Heaven upon his head if he should prove unfaithful; but at the moment of these protesta-

---

[1] This name belongs strictly not to this outgrowth of the political alliance of November, 1815, but to a wholly different league organized two months earlier by the Tsar, under the influence of strong religious emotion. In September, 1815, Alexander had presented to the monarchs a brief agreement whereby the signers would promise to govern their respective peoples as "branches of one Christian nation" in accordance with "the precepts of justice, charity, and peace." (The document is printed in the *Pennsylvania Reprints*, I, No. 3.) No one took very seriously this "pious verbiage," as Metternich called it, except the Tsar himself and his friend Frederick William of Prussia; but, from motives of courtesy, it was signed by every Christian ruler on the continent, except the Pope. This League called itself the Holy Alliance. Its name has come to be applied to that other league of the three eastern states, — so different in composition, origin, and purpose. No doubt the confusion was helped by the fact that the three despotic sovereigns who signed the Troppau agreement were also the first three signers of the Holy Alliance.

[2] The document is given in *Pennsylvania Reprints*, I, No. 3.

tions he was in secret correspondence with Metternich, and now he had come to Laibach for help to regain his absolutism. The Laibach meeting sent an Austrian army to Naples. The Neapolitan army was defeated; and Ferdinand returned, surrounded by Austrian bayonets, to glut his vengeance upon the Liberals, with dungeon and scaffold.

Three days after the Neapolitan defeat, came the revolt in Piedmont (March 10, 1821). If the two risings had been simultaneous, there would have been at least some show of success. As it was, the "Congress of Laibach" promptly marched eighty thousand Austrians into North Italy, while one hundred thousand Russians were held ready to support them; and the Piedmontese were easily crushed.

397. The Congress of Verona: Intervention in Spain. — Flushed with success, the Holy Alliance determined to overthrow also the Spanish constitution, from which the "contagion of liberty" had spread. In 1822 the Great Powers were summoned to a Congress at Verona. England again protested vigorously;[1] but France now joined the eastern Powers, and, with the sanction of the "crowned conspirators,"[2] a French army restored the old absolutism in Spain. Then the Bourbon Ferdinand in Spain, like his namesake in Naples, busied himself for many months in a reactionary "Reign of Terror."

398. Failure of Intervention in Spanish America. — The next wish of the Holy Alliance was to restore monarchic control in the revolted Spanish colonies. But here they failed. England's protests they had been able to disregard as long as only the continent of Europe was concerned; but on the sea

---

[1] The French representative tried to reconcile England by pleading that a constitution might be all very well in Spain, but that it should be a constitution *granted by the King*, not one *forced upon him* by rebels against his authority. Wellington, the English representative, Tory though he was, fitly answered this "divine right" plea: "Do you not know, sir, that it is not kings who make constitutions, but constitutions that make kings?"

[2] Sydney Smith, an English Liberal, called the allied Powers at the Congress "the crowned conspirators of Verona."

England was supreme. The Allies could not reach America without her consent, and she made it known that she would oppose the intended expedition with all her great might. America shares in the credit of checking the despots. Canning, the English minister, urged the United States to join England in an alliance to protect Spanish America. The United States chose to act without formal alliance, but it did act along the same lines. President Monroe's message to Congress in 1823 announced to the world that this country would oppose any attempt of the despotic Powers to extend their "political system" to America.[1] Probably the decided position of either England or the United States would have caused the Powers to abandon their project. Acting together, the two nations were certainly irresistible in the proposed field of combat, and the plan of the Holy Alliance was quietly dropped.[2]

399. Intervention in Greece, for Freedom. — Almost at once Metternich met another check, in the affairs of Greece. The rising there had been accompanied by terrible massacres of all Turks dwelling in the country, and the exasperated Turkish government was now putting down the rebellion by a war of extermination. For a time Metternich had hoped to bring about intervention by the allied Powers to restore Turkish authority quickly; but he failed from two causes.

---

[1] This is one part of the famous Monroe Doctrine.

[2] When reproached afterward, in Parliament, for not having done more to preserve constitutionalism in Spain, Canning replied with the proud boast, "I called the New World into existence to redress the balance of the Old." It is possible to argue that both America and England acted from selfish motives, rather than from love of liberty. England wanted to keep her commerce with the free Spanish states; and the United States objected to the neighborhood of a strong Power that might interfere with her leadership or with her safety. There is no doubt, however, that, along with these proper though selfish motives, both countries were actuated also by principle and by sympathy with freedom, just as the Holy Alliance was moved by contrary principle. England had refused to listen to any offer securing her commercial advantages upon condition that she should in turn leave the Holy Alliance a free hand; and the accusation against Canning and the tone of his reply are evidence of the real feeling of the English people.

a. The educated classes of western Europe had been nourished mainly on the ancient Greek literature, and now their imagination was fired by the thought that this struggle against the Turks was a contest akin to that ancient war against the Persians, which Herodotus, Xenophon, Plutarch, and Æschylus had made glorious to them. The man who did most to widen this sympathy was Byron, the English poet. He closed a career of mingled genius and generosity and wrong-doing by a noble self-devotion, giving fortune and life to the Greek cause; and his poems, invoking the magic of the old names of Marathon and Salamis, stirred Europe to passionate enthusiasm.[1] Great numbers of volunteers followed him to fight for Greek liberty, and before any government had taken action, the Turks complained, with some truth, that they had to fight all Europe.

b. The Russian people, untouched by this western passion, still felt a deep sympathy for the Greeks as their co-religionists, and a deeper hatred for the Turks as their hereditary foes; and so Metternich lost his chief ally. For though the Tsar at first discountenanced the Greek rising and even punished Russian officers who had encouraged it, still he was too much influenced by the feeling of his people to join in open intervention against the revolution.

Finally, indeed, intervention came, but *for* the Greeks, not against them. The English, French, and Russian fleets had proceeded to Greece to enforce a truce, so as to permit negotiation. The three fleets were acting together under the lead of the English admiral, who happened to be the senior officer. Almost by chance, and chiefly through the excited feelings of

---

[1] This feeling is called *Philhellenism*. No schoolboy to-day can read the sad but stirring lyric, "The Isles of Greece," without quicker pulse-beat; but the European youth of Byron's time were moved more deeply than the present generation can easily understand by the allusions in such passages as this:—

"Standing on the Persian's grave,
I could not deem myself a slave";

or this: "Ye have the letters Cadmus gave;
Think ye he meant them for a slave!"

the sailors, they came into conflict with the Turkish fleet at *Navarino* (October, 1827) and annihilated it. The English commander had exceeded his instructions, but there could be no going back; the three Powers intervened to secure Greek independence, and Russian troops soon forced Turkey to grant it.

400. The Holy Alliance and the Revolution of 1830 ; Renewal in 1833; Final Overthrow in 1848. — The French Revolution of 1830 dealt the next blow to Metternich's "European System." France — her own government now resting on revolution (§ 413) — was definitely lost to the Alliance, and joined England in protecting revolutionary Belgium against hostile intervention, so that Metternich called London and Paris "the two madhouses of Europe." Then the risings in Italy and Poland gave Austria and Russia each its hands full for many months. To be sure, these revolts were put down; but the despotic allies had not been able to hold Congresses and to act with united and overwhelming force, as in 1820.

Metternich went to work again patiently, to build up his shattered system; and for a time, to some degree, he succeeded. Soon, however, it became plain that his day was over. In 1833 a new Congress of the monarchs of Austria, Russia, and Prussia, at Münchengrätz, renewed the pledge to unite in suppressing revolution; but before there was occasion to put this agreement in force,[1] the revolutions of 1848 shattered absolutism in Prussia and weakened it beyond recovery even in Austria (§§ 452 ff.). Russia, it is true, continued to act on the promise of Münchengrätz, in assisting Austria to put down the Hungarian rebellion (§ 453), and, from that time to the present, she has shown a disposition to continue a like policy; but never

---

[1] In 1847 a civil war broke out in Switzerland (§ 517) and the Münchengrätz Allies made some preparation to interfere. The French government, too, was just then reactionary in feeling (at the moment before its overthrow) and was ready to join the intervention. But England showed great firmness and seemed to threaten war, and in a few months came the 1848 revolutions all over Europe, preventing further action.

again has there been a concert of European powers in the interests of despotism.[1]

401. Summary. — The System of Metternich and The Holy Alliance was triumphant at Troppau, Laibach, and Verona, over Sardinia, Naples, and Spain; and, upon the whole, it remained victorious in Europe until 1830. With reference to the South American continent it had been defeated by England and the United States; and in 1830 it was weakened in Europe by the withdrawal of France. France and England then checked its plan to restore Belgium to the King of Holland. Metternich rebuilt the Alliance, in form, at Münchengrätz; but the Revolution of 1848 swept it away forever.

Since that date, demands for intervention have usually come from the Liberals, in behalf of oppressed peoples.

FOR FURTHER READING. — A number of valuable documents (referred to in footnotes above) are given in the *Pennsylvania Reprints*, I, No. 3. Good recent accounts of the rule of Metternich are given by Andrews, *Modern Europe*, 113-133; Seignobos, *Europe Since 1814*, 374-389, 326, 335, and especially 719-746; Phillips, *Modern Europe*, 37-134; and Fyffe, *Modern Europe*, 419-645. Special works upon Germany, Italy, and Spain may also be consulted.

---

[1] The nearest approach was the Congress of Berlin in 1878 (§ 547), when the Powers, led by the Tory government of England, gave back to Turkey some provinces which Russia had taken away. But plainly this was a political attempt to maintain Turkey as a balance to Russia: it was not despotic in purpose, and it would not have occurred if men had believed that the surrendered provinces could have maintained a real independence of their own.

CHAPTER III.

FRANCE SINCE 1815.

I. THE "DIVINE RIGHT" MONARCHY, 1815–1830.[1]

A. THE CHARTER.

402. Theory and General Character. — Before the French Senate proclaimed Louis XVIII (§ 375), it had drawn up a hasty constitution. Louis refused to accept it. Still, he recognized that France must have some written form of government,[2] and in June, 1814, he promulgated a *Charter*. In form this was a free grant from the King, not a restriction forced upon him. Thus the theory of "Divine Right" was not sacrificed.[3] In other respects, however, the Charter closely resembled the rejected constitution, and for its day it was a liberal document. It gave to the French people more self-government than they had ever exercised in a regular way for any length of time, and more, too, than was to be found until 1830 in any other continental state.

403. Provisions. — There were *two houses* in the legislature. The *House of Peers* was to be appointed by the king, either for

---

[1] The student will observe that events in France during this period have been referred to in §§ 387–399.

[2] The experiences of the past twenty years and the uncertainty of the people as to the intention of the new government, made this particularly necessary in France. The people had shown that they would not necessarily object to a political master, but they were by no means ready for the restoration of the old privileged orders, and they wished to be sure of the titles to the old church lands.

[3] Read the preamble to the charter, in *Pennsylvania Reprints*, I, No. 3, or in Anderson's *Constitutions and Documents*, where the document is given entire.

life or with hereditary seats. The lower house (*Chamber of Deputies*) was to be elected and was to have full control over taxation. It was chosen, however, upon a high property qualification. To vote for a deputy, one must pay a direct tax of sixty dollars a year. This confined the franchise to less than one hundred thousand voters, in a population of nearly thirty millions. In other words, only one man out of about seventy could vote. Moreover, no one could be elected as deputy unless he paid a direct tax of about two hundred dollars.[1] The members were to hold office for five years, and one fifth of them were to be renewed each year. *The king* retained an absolute veto, and also the sole right to introduce legislation. *For civil liberty*, the provisions were fairly satisfactory. The purchasers of the lands confiscated during the Revolution were guaranteed titles. The principles of religious liberty, equality before the law, admission of all to public employment, free speech, and freedom of the press[2] were confirmed. *On local government* the Charter was silent; but in practice the centralized system of Napoleon was retained: all prefects, subprefects, mayors, district and municipal councils, and bishops were appointed by the crown.

B. First Period, 1815–1820.

The Monarchy tries Constitutional Government.

404. The Rage of the Ultra-royalists. — The Charter did not really go into effect until after the Hundred Days (§ 379); and the second restoration, after Waterloo, was followed by a bloody proscription of the Bonapartists and of the old Revolutionists, — in the "White Terror" of 1815. In the midst of this fury of the returned Emigrants, the elections took place for the first Chamber of Deputies. The Reactionists, taking

---

[1] This amount was so high that some districts hardly had enough eligible men to fill the places ; and so, of course, in such districts, the right of choice was practically annihilated.

[2] "Within the limits necessary to public tranquillity." This limitation was to be taken advantage of by the government in 1830 (§ 410).

advantage of the panic into which the moderate and liberal parties were thrown, secured a large majority of the representatives, and they at once showed a determination to nullify the Charter. These "Ultra-royalists" were headed by the King's brother, the Count of Artois, the heir to the throne. They wished to restore the church lands and the lands of the Emigrants, to hand education over to the church, and to wreak vengeance upon their old enemies.

405. Louis sides with the Constitutionalists. — A new civil strife was averted only by the moderation of the King. Louis was wise enough, in a cynical way, to see the folly of his friends. He perceived that the Ultra majority was accidental and that it did not truly represent even the narrow body of electors; and in 1816 he dissolved the Chamber. The new election justified him, by giving a legislature of a more moderate character. For the next four years, the King continued to support the Liberals against the Ultras. France enjoyed order and tranquillity, and was prosperous and happy.

406. Parties in the Assembly. — There were four groups in the Assembly. During the years 1816–1821, the Extreme-Right (the Ultras) and the Extreme-Left (Radical Republicans) both desired revolution, though in opposite directions; but they were both small in numbers. The bulk of the Assembly was divided between the Right-Center and the Left-Center. Both these parties were upholders of the Charter; but while the first regarded it as a finality and were opposed to all further change, the second regarded it as a basis for future development. The King chose his ministers from one or the other of the two Center parties, usually from the Right-Center; but the ministry governed by keeping up an alliance between the two moderate parties against the extremes in the two wings.[1]

---

[1] This principle of government has held good through so much of the subsequent history of France that it is worth while for the student to try to grasp it. It differs radically, of course, from party government in England and America. Government in France has been carried on mainly by the Center, and when the Moderates there have failed to get on together, the government has commonly broken down before a joint attack from the two opposing extremes.

407. Louis frightened into the Arms of the Ultras. — By 1820 the King was breaking in health and will, and the Ultras finally captured him by playing upon his fear of Revolution. The annual renewal of a fifth of the Chamber had increased the number of the Liberals. In 1818 Lafayette had appeared in the legislature; and in 1819 more than half the new members were men who had served Napoleon or who had been active in the earlier Revolutionary movements. The King, terrified by such conditions, began to seek support from the Ultras. Then the Radicals, discouraged or terrified, fell back upon secret plots. In 1820 the Duke of Berry, the most promising nephew of Louis and the hope of the Royalists, was assassinated. This crime drove the King wholly into the arms of the Ultras.[1]

C. Second Period, 1820–1830.

The Monarchy tries Reaction.

408. Reactionary Measures. — In 1824 Louis XVIII was succeeded by his brother, the Count of Artois, with the title of Charles X; and, for the whole period from 1820 to 1830, reaction held unbroken sway. The representative Chamber had become Ultra, partly through the natural popular reaction against the Radicals, partly through force and fraud at the polls on the part of the government. There followed a long series of reactionary measures. Liberty of the press was curtailed; the historical lectures of Guizot (§ 415) were closed; the government joined the Holy Alliance at Verona (§ 397) in conspiring against constitutional liberty in Spain; the "Emigrants" were given two hundred million dollars from the treasury, to compensate them for their losses in the Revolution; a law against sacrilege was enacted, with medieval features;[2] a double vote in elections was given to the greater

---

[1] Cf. events in Germany (§ 389). The assassination strengthened the hands of Metternich at Troppau and Verona. Between 1821 and 1824 there were eight conspiracies of Revolutionists in France, followed by a number of executions.

[2] Read Andrews, I, 162.

landowners, and electoral colleges were introduced to strengthen still further the influence of the higher aristocracy; prefects and subprefects were dismissed in great numbers to make way for new appointees more in harmony with absolute rule; and finally the sitting legislature lengthened its own life from five years to seven, abolishing, too, the annual renewal of a part of its number.

409. Defeats of the Ultras at the Polls. — The few Liberals in the Chamber annoyed Charles by their vigorous protests against these measures; and in 1827 he dissolved the legislature, expecting under the new laws to secure a still more submissive body. The issue was drawn clearly. Thiers, then a brilliant young journalist,[1] preached the liberal constitutional theory in the words, "The king *reigns*, but does not *govern*," and he made repeated and significant references in his paper to the English Revolution of 1688; while Charles announced that he regarded the legislature only as an advisory council, and that in case of a conflict of views his decision must control.

The elections showed that the nation, and even the narrow body of voters, were earnestly opposed to the King's doctrine. The intellect of France and the influential part of the press were with the liberal party; and, despite all court influence, the Liberals received a decisive majority at the polls.

In a half-hearted way, Charles tried a more liberal government for a few months; but he was not willing to go far enough to win the confidence of the legislature. Then, as clashes continued, he felt justified in falling back upon his older policy, and he called together a ministry of the Ultras. The Assembly answered his challenge by a bold address (March 2, 1830), calling for the dismissal of the ministry, which it called "a menace to public safety." The address was carried by a vote of 221 to 182. Charles at once dissolved the Chamber.

---

[1] Afterward a prominent statesman and later still a president of France (§§ 415, note, and 434 ff.).

Public interest was intense,[1] and the aged Lafayette journeyed through France to organize the Liberals for the contest. The new elections in June effaced the Ultra party in the Chamber: every deputy who had voted against the ministry was returned, and the Liberals gained also fifty of the remaining seats.

D. The Revolution of 1830.

410. The "July Ordinances." — No whit daunted by the unanimity of the nation, the stubborn monarch prepared a *coup d'état*.[2] He looked upon the Charter merely as "a declaration of policy" on the part of the royal power, and he believed that he had the right to modify or abolish it whenever such action might seem to him advisable.[3] Accordingly, he now suspended the Constitution by a series of edicts, known in history as the "July Ordinances."

These ordinances forbade the publication of newspapers without royal approval (a measure designed to prevent agitation against the rest of the changes), dissolved the new legislature (which had not yet met), promulgated a new law for elections (designed to make the court supreme at the polls), and called for new elections under this rule.

411. The Protests of the Journalists and the Barricades of the Revolutionists. — The Ordinances were published July 26, 1830. Forty-one leading journalists of Paris at once signed and printed a protest, declaring the ordinances illegal, announcing their

---

[1] Tocqueville's *Memoirs* (I, 18) gives an interesting picture. Anderson gives the King's speeches to the Chamber and its Address.

[2] Shrewd observers had foreseen it and its probable result. Even Metternich, while lamenting the free press and the representative system in France, had warned the French ambassador that an attempt now to do away with these "plague spots" would ruin the dynasty: "The men of lead," said he, "are on the side of the Constitution; Charles X should remember 1789."

[3] The preamble to the Ordinances (Anderson, No. 114) expresses this conviction, which was no doubt sincere. Some additional color for the King's action was found in Article 14 of the Charter, which declared that the King might issue ordinances "necessary for the execution of the laws and for the safety of the state."

intention to resist, and calling upon France to do so. Copies of this paper were read eagerly by the disaffected classes of the city, and added to the public excitement. The journalists, however, seem to have had in mind only legal resistance, not violence; but there were in Paris a few obscure Radicals who were ready to go further, and they were powerful in a crisis, because of their organization in secret societies. The same evening they decided upon armed revolt, and appointed "Committees of Insurrection" for the various districts of the city. The next morning saw the streets thronged with angry crowds who threw up barricades out of paving stones, but who for the most part were still unarmed and were easily dispersed at any given point when troops arrived. That night, however, Lafayette reached Paris, to take charge of the revolt, and on the following morning the fighting began.

412. The "July Days." — The 28th, 29th, and 30th are the "Three Days of July." On the 28th the crowd cried "Down with the ministry!" but, as their blood became heated with fighting, they came under the influence of the old Revolutionists, and began to shout "Down with the Bourbons!" About four thousand men were slain in the three days. Out at the palace at St. Cloud, in the suburbs, the King hunted as usual; and, on each evening, messengers from the sorely beset troops were kept waiting overnight, so as not to disturb the royal game of whist, while the scepter was slipping forever from the old line of French kings. *Outside Paris, there was no fighting, but the nation gladly accepted the Revolution when it had been accomplished.*

While the fighting was still going on, some thirty liberal Deputies of the legislature assembled at the Hotel de Ville and appointed a Provisional Government. The leaders at the barricades would have liked a republic, but they knew they had little support in the country. The Deputies and the Provisional Government wished, not a republic, but a change of dynasty. They decided to pass over the direct heir of Charles X, and give the crown to *Louis Philippe*, Duke of Orleans, a distant cousin of the King.[1] Lafayette threw his influence for this policy, and his popularity won the crowd to it. Philippe was made Lieutenant General, with the understanding that the office should be a step to the throne.

FOR FURTHER READING. — Excellent accounts are given in Andrews, I, 134–189; Seignobos, 103–132; Fyffe, 427–446, 469–475, 603–619; and Dickenson, *Revolution and Reaction*, 63–103.

II. THE CONSTITUTIONAL MONARCHY, 1830–1848.

413. Changes in the Charter. Election of Louis Philippe. — As soon as possible after the "July Days," the legislature[2] assembled to regulate the government. It restored the tricolor as the national flag, modified the Charter in the direction of constitutional freedom, and then offered the crown to Louis Philippe, upon condition that he should first accept the amended Charter. The Revolution was then completed during 1831 by the passage of a number of further reforms.[3]

The changes in the Charter and these supplementary laws may be grouped together. The divine-right preamble to the Charter was cut out, as was also the king's power of issuing ordinances and the clause suggesting the possible need of limiting the freedom of the press (§ 403, note). The right to introduce bills was given to the legislature. The reactionary measures of the years 1820–1830 were repealed, including the "double vote" and the electoral colleges; and a new electoral law extended the franchise to all who paid forty dollars in taxes. This doubled the voters, raising the number to nearly two hundred thousand. At the same time the number of those

---

[1] As a youth, Louis Philippe had taken the side of the First Revolution, and had fought gallantly in French armies until the excesses of the Revolution drove him into exile. Then, by a happy chance, instead of joining the royalist Emigrants in their attempts against France, he had fled to England and the United States.

[2] This was the body which had been elected in June (§ 409) and which had been declared dissolved by the July Ordinances.

[3] See Anderson, for documents.

eligible to seats in the legislature was increased by reducing the property qualification one-half.

More significant than any of these details, however, was the new relation between the crown and the nation. The doctrine of divine right was still to find support from time to time in a small body in the legislature, but it was never again to control the government. *Louis XVIII had ruled by hereditary title, and had given a charter to France. Louis Philippe, " King of the Barricades," ruled by election, and a constitution was imposed upon him.*[1]

414. Character of the "Orleans Monarchy." — The Orleans Monarchy, or the "July Monarchy," as it is sometimes called, lasted from 1830 to 1848. It rose out of a Revolution, and it fell before a more serious one. While it stood, it represented the bourgeoisie, and was sustained by their favor.[2] This was the class to which the King himself belonged in habits and character. Louis Philippe earned fairly his title of "a bourgeois king"; he walked the streets with a green cotton umbrella under his arm, and he sent his children to the public schools; but he offended the taste of the aristocratic elements by his small economies and hoarding, and he was always offensive to the Radicals.

415. The Conservative Ministry of Guizot. — The first ten years of the new reign (1830–1840) were disturbed by insurrections and plots, and by incessant changes of ministry. During the remaining eight years, the government was administered by *Guizot*. This statesman belonged to the new Right-Center, or the "party of resistance."[3] The period was one of rapid growth, and France needed peace and internal reform. The first need Guizot met: his ministry was the most stable government France had enjoyed since Napoleon's days; but

---

[1] The effect of the Revolution outside France has been referred to in § 391.

[2] The National Guards had been reorganized and were made up altogether of this class.

[3] Guizot was an eminent historian and had written a philosophic treatise upon the history of civilization. His leading opponent, *Thiers* (§ 409), was famous

in his anxiety to secure tranquillity, he opposed all change and all reform.

Thus, after a few years, the intellect of France was driven into opposition, and even the selfish interests of the bourgeoisie suffered from the inaction of the government. Proposals were made in the legislature to reduce the salt tax, to extend education, to reform the postal system, to improve the prisons, to care for youthful criminals; but all these ideas came from the liberal opposition and were quietly suppressed by the ministry.[1] Said Lamartine in 1842, in an attack upon Guizot in the Chamber: "According to you, political genius consists in taking your stand on a position which chance has won for you, and remaining there immovable, inert, implacable to every reform. If this were true . . . there would be no need of statesmen; a post would suffice."

416. Narrow Electorate; "Placemen"; Corrupt Use of Patronage. — Under such conditions the nation soon became indifferent or hostile to Guizot; but he intrenched himself so skillfully that he could hardly be overthrown by constitutional methods. Personally he was incorruptible, and even austere, but he ruled by corrupting others. He used the vast patronage of the government to control the elections, and afterward to control the legislature.

Two evil conditions made this possible: (1) the narrowness of the franchise; and (2) the fact that members of the legislature could become "placemen," or receive appointment to salaried offices.[2] These evils were both increased by the fact that

---

for brilliant works dealing with the French Revolution and with the Napoleonic era. Thiers represented the Left-Center, or the "party of action." Other prominent Liberals who joined the opposition were Tocqueville, the author of *Democracy in America* and of various treatises upon French history, and Lamartine, a poet and the historian of the Girondists.

[1] Guizot merits some praise, however, for beginning a system of primary schools for France. Cf. § 449.

[2] As though in America the President could appoint Congressmen to lucrative positions as custom-house collectors or postmasters, — a proceeding which our constitution prohibits.

the government appointed all local officers,[1] and therefore had a vast patronage at its disposal. Guizot organized this influence for purposes of corruption. Less than two hundred thousand men had the right to vote, and large numbers of these were bought up by some of the three hundred thousand offices in the gift of the government. Then, when the elections were over, the ministry strengthened its majority by appointing members of the legislature to important offices or by giving them profitable state contracts. At one time, it is said, half the members held lucrative positions at Guizot's will, and so gave their votes at his nod.[2]

417. Agitation for Political Reform. — The Liberals finally began to demand political reforms: (1) the extension of the franchise,[3] and (2) the doing away with placemen. In the legislature, Guizot successfully opposed both proposals. A new election took place in 1847, and the Liberals had high hopes of success; but Guizot's tactics again secured his usual majority. Then the Liberals began to appeal to the thirty-nine fortieths of the nation who had no vote. They planned a series of mass meetings and demonstrations, to bring public opinion to bear upon the legislature. According to English or American ideas, the proceeding was perfectly proper; but the French government believed it dangerous, and tried to prevent it. This action of the government brought on the Revolution of 1848; but to understand the Revolution it is necessary to know something of another force which had been growing up almost unnoticed by political leaders (§ 418).

418. Rise of Socialism. — The chief cause of the coming Revolution was the growth of Socialism in Paris among the workingmen. Through the preceding third of a century, wealth

---

[1] As though in America the President appointed state and county officers and mayors and chiefs of police.

[2] Tocqueville's *Recollections*, 38, 39, or *Correspondence*, I, 78. Read Andrews, I, 329.

[3] They asked only to double the number of voters. At the time not more than one adult male out of thirty-five or forty had the franchise.

had been increasing rapidly, but workingmen felt that they had not been getting their share. Certainly the distinction between capitalist and wage-earner had been growing sharper, and it was becoming more and more difficult to rise from the one class into the other. A number of remarkable writers had been so impressed by these facts that they attacked the whole existing organization of society. In general these "Socialists" taught that the state, not individuals, ought to own all capital, and to direct all labor, and to divide the product in some way that would give the working classes a larger share than they had been receiving. The writers and thinkers who led in these speculations were moved by sincere and passionate pity for the masses, and were themselves high-minded, unselfish idealists.[1] Among their followers there were many crack-brained enthusiasts, some criminal fanatics, and a large number of ignorant men easily inclined to violence. Large masses of Parisian workingmen had adopted phrases about the "right to labor" and the "crime of private property" as their creed. In the coming Revolution, Socialism was to be revealed for the first time as a political force.

FOR FURTHER READING. — See the works named on page 413. Tocqueville's *Recollections*, too, is a most interesting volume for this period.

EXERCISE. — Review §§ 381–399 and 402–418, so as to get a view of the period for France and the rest of Europe together.

III. THE REVOLUTION OF 1848 AND THE SECOND REPUBLIC: 1848–1852.

419. The "February Days": Overthrow of the Orleans Monarchy. — The Liberals had set February 22[2] for a monster

---

[1] Among the French Socialists of the period were St. Simon, Fourier, and *Louis Blanc*. The last of these three was to play a prominent part in the coming Revolution. Various secret societies, like "The Society of the Friends of the People" and "The Society of the Rights of Man," were organized to propagate socialistic doctrines. For an example of criminal fanaticism, read Dickenson's *Revolution and Reaction*, 127.

[2] The date is said to have been chosen in honor of the American celebration.

political demonstration in Paris (§ 417). At the last moment the government forbade the meeting. The leaders obeyed, but the streets were filled all day with angry crowds shouting for the dismissal of the ministry. The National Guards, when called out to disperse the mob, themselves took up the cry. The next day, Guizot resigned. Peace seemed restored; but that night a collision occurred between some regular troops and the mob; and the Socialists and Radicals seized the chance to rouse the masses against the monarchy. By the morning of the 24th, the streets bristled with barricades and the mob was marching on the Tuileries. Louis Philippe abdicated, and, like Charles X, fled to England. His government had lost the support of the middle classes, and it simply collapsed.[1] It remained to be seen what was to come from the victory of the Radicals.

420. The Provisional Government: Composition. — The Chamber of Deputies was about to proclaim the infant grandson of Louis Philippe as king, under a regency, when the room was invaded by a howling mob, flourishing muskets and butcher-knives and calling for a republic. In the midst of this tumult the few deputies who kept their seats hastily appointed a committee as a "Provisional Government." This body was at once escorted to the Hotel de Ville, where it found another provisional government already set up by the Radicals and Socialists. By a compromise, some of this latter body were incorporated in the first. The Provisional Government was now made up of three conflicting elements: Lamartine, the poet historian (§ 415 and note), represented the Moderate Republicans; Ledru-Rollin was the representative of the Radical Republicans ("the Reds"), who wished to return to the "Terror" of 1793; and Louis Blanc and the workingman Albert represented the Socialists. On the whole, the Provisional Government followed Lamartine and stood for order and property, but it was forced to concede much to the radical forces within and without.

---

[1] Read Tocqueville's *Recollections*, 114.

421. The Difficulties before the Government were tremendous. For sixty hours it was in the presence of an infuriated and drunken mob. This crowd of one hundred thousand armed men was packed into the streets about the Hotel de Ville, and self-appointed delegations from it repeatedly forced their way into the building to make wild demands upon the "government." That government must at once disperse this seething multitude, avert plunder and massacre, clear away barricades, bury the dead and care for the wounded, and supply food for the great city wherein all ordinary business had ceased. All this, too, had to be accomplished without any military or police assistance.

Time after time, during the first long session, was Lamartine called from the room to check an invasion by some new band of Revolutionists. Said the spokesman of one of the bands: —

We demand the extermination of property and of capitalists, the instant establishment of community of goods, the proscription of the rich, the merchants, the bourgeoisie of every condition above that of wage-earners, ... and finally the acceptance of the red flag, to signify to society its defeat, to the people its victory, to all foreign governments invasion.

Lamartine grew faint with exhaustion and want of food, but his fine courage and wit and persuasive eloquence still won the victory over every danger.[1] To help appease the mob, however, the government hastily adopted a number of radical decrees, declaring a Republic, abolishing the House of Peers, establishing manhood suffrage, and *affirming the duty of the state to give every man a chance to work.*[2]

422. "National Workshops." — A few days later, the decree recognizing the "right to work" was given more specific meaning by the establishment of "national workshops"[3] for the

---

[1] Lord Normanby, the English Ambassador, says that in one of these encounters Lamartine's face was scratched by a bayonet that was thrust at him.

[2] A number of these decrees are given by Anderson.

[3] The plan was in accordance with the teaching of Louis Blanc, and the unwilling majority of the government were coerced into joining in it by the mob. The government put the management, however, into the hands of a personal

unemployed. In the panic that followed the Revolution, great numbers of men had been thrown out of work. The government now organized these men in Paris, as they applied, into a "workshop army," in brigades, companies, and squads, — paying full wages to all it could employ and a three-fourths wage to those obliged to remain idle.

Over one hundred thousand men were finally enrolled in this way; but, except for a little work on the streets, the government had no employment ready for such a number. The experiment, of course, was not in any sense a fair trial of the socialistic idea. It was more of a police provision and a temporary poor-law. For the moment, it did preserve order and distribute alms; but it also gave a formidable organization to a terrible force with which the new Republic would soon have to reckon.

423. The Constituent Assembly : Conflicts with the Socialists. — Twice in its ten weeks' rule, after the first disorders, the Provisional Government was attacked by the mob; but the middle class rallied to its support and enabled it to maintain order until it was replaced by a *Constituent Assembly*. The Assembly, elected by manhood suffrage, met May 4. The Revolution, like that of 1830, had been confined to Paris. The rest of France had not cared to interfere in behalf of Louis Philippe, but it felt no enthusiasm for a republic and it abhorred the "Reds" and the Socialists. This, too, was the temper of the Assembly. It accepted the republic as inevitable, for the time at least; but it was bent upon putting down the Radicals. As soon as this fact became evident, the mob rose once more (May 15), and burst into the legislative hall, holding possession for three turbulent hours.[1] At last, however, some middle-class battalions of the National Guard arrived, under Lamar-

---

enemy of Blanc's, and it seems to have been their intention that the experiment should fail, so as to discredit Blanc with the populace. Cf. Ely's *French and German Socialism*, 113. Special report : Louis Blanc, life and character.

[1] Read Tocqueville's account in his *Recollections*, 156 ff., or Lamartine's in his *Revolution of 1848*, and Andrews, I, 354, 355.

tine's leadership, to sweep away the rabble and save the Assembly.

The rescued Assembly promptly followed up its victory. After making military preparations, it issued a series of decrees, virtually abolishing the workshop army.[1] Then the men of the national workshops rose. This time the Revolutionists were not a mere rabble: they comprised the great body of the workingmen of Paris, and they were aided by the semi-military organization of the "workshop army." The Assembly made General Cavaignac dictator, and the conflict raged for four days, — the most terrible struggle that even turbulent Paris had ever witnessed. Probably not less than twenty thousand men perished; but in the outcome, the superior discipline and equipment of the troops and of the bourgeoisie National Guards crushed the Socialists for another generation.[2]

424. The Constitution of the "Second Republic": Louis Napoleon President. — The Assembly now turned to its work of making a constitution. The document was promulgated in November.[3] It provided for a legislature of one house, and for a four-year president, both to be chosen by manhood franchise. A month later (December 10) *Louis Napoleon*, a nephew of Napoleon Bonaparte, was elected the first president by an overwhelming majority.

Napoleon's political capital was his name. A group of brilliant writers had created a "Napoleonic legend," representing the rule of the First Napoleon as a period of glory and prosperity for France, broken only by wars forced upon Napoleon by the jealousy of other rulers. These ideas had become a blind faith for great masses in France. Louis Philippe, curiously enough, had added to their fervor by bringing home Napoleon's ashes from St. Helena for triumphant interment in Paris.

---

[1] A conservative French statesman has styled this legislation "a brutal, unjust, blundering end to a foolish experiment."

[2] Tocqueville's *Recollections* is especially good for the story of these "June Days"; see, in particular, pages 187, 193, 212.

[3] It was not submitted to a popular vote. The document is given in Anderson's *Constitutions and Documents*.

Louis Napoleon had long believed that he was destined to revive the rule of his family. Twice in the early years of Louis Philippe's reign he had tried to stir up a Napoleonic revolution.[1] After the last of these fiascoes he had been imprisoned for some time, but he finally escaped to England and lived there quietly until the Revolution of 1848 called him back to France. To the peasantry and the bourgeoisie, alarmed as they were by the specter of "Red Republicanism" and Socialism, Napoleon's name seemed the symbol of order and peace. He received over five and a half million votes, to about one and a half million for Cavaignac, the stern Republican, and only eight thousand for Lamartine, shortly before the idol of French Liberalism. Rollin received three hundred and seventy thousand.

IV. THE SECOND EMPIRE, 1852-1870.

425. Preparation: Napoleon and the Assembly at Loggerheads. — Louis Napoleon had repeatedly pledged his faith to the Constitution, but he seems to have plotted from the first to overthrow it. The Assembly gave him opportunity. In 1849, there was a rising of the "Reds," led by Ledru-Rollin. This event, together with rapid radical gains in Paris, terrified the Assembly into passing a reactionary suffrage law which virtually disfranchised a large part of the population.[2]

After the law had been passed, Napoleon criticised it vehemently, and so appeared to the artisan class as the champion of their constitutional rights, in opposition to a reactionary Assembly. At the same time, the discontent of the artisans made the bourgeoisie fear a revolution, and that class turned to Napoleon as the sole hope for order and stable government. Thus the chief elements in the state viewed with dread the approaching close of Napoleon's presidency. The constitution forbade a reëlection; and an attempt to amend it in this matter was defeated in the Assembly. Thus that body had now seri-

---

[1] Special report: the story of these efforts of Louis Napoleon, especially of the curious attempt at Boulogne.

[2] Tocqueville says it took the franchise from about three men out of ten. (*Correspondence*, I, 100, 259). Read the statement in Fyffe, 811, 812, or in Andrews, II, 22.

ously offended both the artisan class and the bourgeoisie, and Napoleon could overthrow it with impunity.

426. The Coup d'État. — In semi-royal progresses through France,[1] Napoleon had been preparing the nation for his blow. He found fault with the Assembly freely, and his speeches were filled with references to the "glory" of the former French Empire, and to the benefits conferred upon France by "my great uncle." Meantime the important offices in the army and in the government were put into the hands of his tools and his trusted friends, and on December 2, 1851, he carried out the most striking *coup d'état* in all French history.

During the preceding night nearly eighty men whose opposition was especially feared — journalists, generals, and leaders in the Assembly — were privately arrested and imprisoned; and all the printing offices in the city were seized by Napoleon's troops. In the morning the amazed people found the city posted with startling placards announcing the dissolution of the Assembly, proposing a new government with Napoleon at its head, and promising an appeal to the nation for ratification.[2] The Assembly tried to declare Napoleon deposed, but it was dispersed by soldiers, and most of the members were imprisoned. During the next few days a few Radicals began to raise barricades here and there in the streets, but these were carried by the soldiers with pitiless slaughter, and the conflict was made an excuse for a "reign of terror." Batches of prisoners, taken at the barricades, were shot down after surrender; the most dangerous districts of France were put under martial law; and thousands of men were transported to penal settlements, virtually without trial.[3]

Under these conditions, a few days later, the country was invited to vote Yes or No upon a new constitution making Napoleon President for Ten Years with dictatorial power. France "ratified" this proposal by a vote of seven and a half

---

[1] Read Andrews, II, 23, 24.
[2] See Anderson, for the proclamation.
[3] See Seignobos, 171, for precise figures; or Andrews, II, 36, 37.

million out of eight million.[1] In November of the next year, a still more unanimous vote sanctioned a second step in the usurpation, and made the daring adventurer *Emperor of the French*, under the title Napoleon III.[2]

427. The Constitution. Character of the Empire and the Periods of its History. — The Second Empire was modeled closely upon that of Napoleon I. The people elected a Legislative Chamber (a greater popular power than existed under the First Empire); but the Emperor appointed a Senate and a Council of State (with powers like those of the corresponding bodies under Napoleon I), while he kept in his hands the sole right to introduce laws. Moreover, of his own will, he filled all offices, made treaties, and declared war.[3]

NAPOLEON III.

---

[1] This unanimity was due in large measure to the government's shameless interference at the polls: the army was voted first, for an example; and in many places the rural population was marched to the polls, virtually under military authority. Such measures, however, were not necessary to secure a large majority. Apart from them, France threw itself into Napoleon's arms, with only a small body of Liberals and of Socialists in Paris to oppose him. There can be no doubt that the vast majority of the people were content to give to a master a power almost equal to that of a Tsar. Tocqueville gives a valuable contemporary account of the *coup d'état* in a Letter to the *London Times*, reprinted in his *Remains*, II, 173-189. Victor Hugo, who fought at the barricades, tells the story in his *History of a Crime*.

[2] The Bonapartists counted the son of Napoleon I as Napoleon II, although he never reigned.

[3] Seignobos, 171-173; Dickenson's *Revolution and Reaction*, 228-229; and Andrews, II, 151-153. The Constitution is given by Anderson.

Napoleon's methods had been those of a conspirator, and his rule ignored real political liberty; but he was not a mere selfish adventurer. He desired to benefit France, and he honestly regarded himself as "a democratic chief." His government, he insisted, rested upon manhood suffrage, in elections and plebiscites. The Restoration (1815–1830), he said, was the government of the great landowners; the Orleans Monarchy was the government of the bourgeoisie; the Empire was the government of the people. He seems really to have wished to introduce liberal features into the workings of the Constitution, as fast as he could safely do so.[1] Unfortunately, he could find tools only among second-rate men, often more despotic in temper than their master; and the actual administration was exceedingly tyrannical.

The Empire lasted from 1852 to 1870, just about as long as the Orleans Monarchy. This period falls into two divisions. During the first eight years (1852–1860) the government was successful abroad and despotic at home. During the next ten years (1860–1870) it encountered a series of humiliations abroad and it grew more and more liberal at home. Then, in 1870, it was overthrown in the Franco-Prussian War, and replaced by the Third Republic (§§ 433 ff.).

428. The Despotic Period, 1852–1860. — During the first years of the Empire, political life was suspended. The elections, at best, could not have greatly affected the government; but the government did effectually control elections. It presented for every elective position an "official candidate," for whom the way was made easy. Opposing candidates could not hold public meetings, nor hire the distribution of circulars, while they were seriously hampered even in the use of the mails, and their placards were torn down by the police or industriously covered by the official bill-poster for the government candidate. Moreover, the ballot boxes were supervised by

---

[1] Advanced students will find a good summary of Napoleon's ideas in Andrews, II, 146–151, or in Dickenson's *Revolution and Reaction*, 223–228. For the liberal modifications of the constitution after 1860, see Dickenson, 230–231.

the police, and, no doubt, were sometimes "stuffed." The government subsidized a large number of newspapers, and it suppressed, on slightest pretext, all that were unfavorable to it.[1]

In private life, prominent men lived in an atmosphere of espionage and corruption. Their servants were likely to be the paid spies of the police. Personal liberty was wholly at the mercy of the government. Under the "Law of Public Security" (1858), the government could legally send "suspects," without trial, to linger through a slow death in tropical penal colonies,[2] as it had been doing illegally before; and many thousands are said to have perished in this way.

Upon the passage of this law, an order was sent to each prefect to arrest a fixed number of men in his department, using his own choice in selecting them. The number varied from twenty to forty, according to the character of the department. That is, the total arrests under this order must have exceeded two thousand. The purpose seems to have been merely to intimidate the nation.

"FRANCE IS TRANQUIL." — A cartoon from *Harper's Magazine*, representing France under Napoleon III.

In partial recompense for this loss of liberty, the Empire gave to France great material and economic progress. Industry was encouraged; Paris and other leading cities were rebuilt upon a more magnificent scale; asylums and hospitals

---

[1] For anecdotes, read Seignobos, 174–175.
[2] See Tocqueville's *Correspondence*, II, 195–197. A striking story illustrating the administration of the law is given by Dickenson, 234, 235, and others are given in Senior's *Conversations*, I, 90 and 160–161. See also, for the tyranny of this period, Tocqueville's *Remains*, II, 186.

were founded; schools were encouraged, and school libraries were established; while a system of vast public works throughout the Empire afforded employment to the working classes. France secured her full share of the increase of wealth and comfort that came to the world so rapidly during these years.[1]

429. Foreign Wars to 1860. — In 1852 Napoleon had declared "The Empire is Peace"; but he found himself irresistibly impelled to war, in order to keep the favor of the army and of the populace by reviving the glories of the First Empire. Thus his foreign policy soon became aggressive, and the first period of his reign saw a series of military and diplomatic victories that dazzled France. The two most important wars of the period were the *Crimean* (1854–1856) and the *Italian* (1859).

a. France had a trivial quarrel with Russia over the guardianship of Christian pilgrims at Jerusalem. England was hostile to Russia, fearing lest that Power should force itself to the Mediterranean and endanger England's route to India. Russia and Turkey were at war in the Black Sea. Through Napoleon's intrigues, in 1854, France and England joined Turkey, by declaring war upon Russia. The struggle was waged mainly in Crimea, and took its name from that peninsula. It became essentially a war for the defense of Turkey against Russia. Russia was defeated, but no permanent results of importance were achieved. However, at the close of the contest, Napoleon gathered representatives of all the leading Powers to the *Congress of Paris*, to make peace, and France seemed again to have become the leader in European politics.[2]

b. In 1859 Napoleon joined the kingdom of Sardinia in a war against Austria (§ 460). His ostensible purpose was to free Italy. He won great victories at Magenta and Solferino,[3] near the scene of the early triumphs of the First Napoleon over the same foe; and then he made unexpected

---

[1] Review §§ 419–428 and 400–401, to get a view of France together with the rest of Europe for this period. Such a review should be repeated at § 456.

[2] Europe had enjoyed freedom from great wars for forty years, — since the fall of the First Napoleon. The important achievement of the Congress of Paris was the abolition of privateering by the great European Powers. Unfortunately the United States refused to accede to this policy, and so suffered soon afterward in the American Civil War from European sympathy for Southern privateering.

[3] Some military critics call these victories accidental.

peace, to the dismay and wrath of the half-freed Italians. For his pay, Napoleon received from Italy the provinces of Nice and Savoy, and so restored some of the territory which his uncle had lost.

430. Foreign Policy, 1860-1870. — The second period of Napoleon's rule was a long series of humiliations and blunders in foreign affairs.

a. In aiding Italy against Austria in 1859, Napoleon had offended the Pope and also the clerical party in France. Napoleon, however, wished to keep the Pope a temporal prince, and so he stepped in to prevent the new Kingdom of Italy from seizing Rome for its capital. This act lost him the friendship of the Italians also.

b. He favored the Southern Confederacy in the American Civil War, and repeatedly urged England to unite with him in acknowledging it as an independent state. Thus he incurred the hostility of the United States. Then, in 1863 he entered upon a disastrous attempt in Mexico. That country had repudiated its debts. Several European governments had sent fleets to its ports to enforce payment; but soon it became evident that Napoleon meant much more than the mere collection of debts. Thereupon, the other governments withdrew from the enterprise. Napoleon then sent a large army to overthrow the Mexican Republic and to set up as "Emperor" his protégé, Maximilian, an Austrian prince. Napoleon's motives were to secure a larger share of the Mexican trade for France, to increase the prestige of France as arbiter in the destinies of nations, and to forward his plan of a union of the Latin peoples of Europe and America, under French leadership, against the Teutonic states. His act was a striking defiance of the Monroe Doctrine of the United States; but his purpose seemed triumphant until the close of the American Civil War. Then the government of the United States, in unmistakable terms, demanded the withdrawal of the French troops from Mexico. Napoleon was obliged to comply. Soon afterward Maximilian was overthrown by the Mexicans, and captured and shot.

c. Most serious of all Napoleon's checks were his disappointments regarding the Rhine frontier. He wished to restore the old boundaries there, and he made fruitless attempts to do so by diplomacy and by taking advantage of wars in Germany. All these efforts failed; and Bismarck, the Prussian statesman, turned them to such advantage that the small German states came to look upon Napoleon as an unscrupulous and dangerous neighbor (§ 469). Thus the way was paved for their warm alliance with Prussia against France, when war broke out, soon after, between the two countries.

431. Second Period: Internal Policy. — Napoleon intended to keep his pledges and to give to France, from time to time, a larger measure of self-government. A beginning was made in 1860, when the Legislative Chamber was permitted to discuss fully the policy of the government and to express its judgment in an address to the throne. From this time the party of constitutional opposition increased rapidly. In the election of 1857 only five opposition candidates had secured seats; in the next election (1863) the numbers of the opposition rose to forty-three; and in 1869 the Chamber was almost equally divided.

When the government's corrupt control over elections is taken into account, this result indicates that France was ready to repudiate Napoleon. That ruler, feeling his weakness, tried vainly to win back popular favor by concession after concession, until at his fall he had nearly restored parliamentary government.[1]

432. The Franco-Prussian War and the Fall of the Empire. — In 1870, as a last resort, Napoleon tried to win back the favor of the nation by war with Prussia. The opening of the con-

[1] In 1870 Napoleon appealed to the nation in a plebiscite for a vote of confidence, and the vote stood in his favor by about seven million to one and a half million. But this meant only that France would rather endure his rule than meet the certain revolution that would follow if he were to be overthrown by violence. Even so, the cities showed a surprisingly large vote against him. Advanced students will find a good passage in Von Sybel's *German Empire*, VII, 268-270, upon this matter.

flict showed that the government was honeycombed with corruption and inefficiency. Regiments lacked men and discipline; arsenals were empty; supplies of all kinds were wanting or were of poor quality. Prussia had been preparing diligently for the long-foreseen conflict, and every step in the opening of her campaign was carefully planned. The Prussians won victory after victory. In a few weeks, one French army of one hundred and seventy-three thousand was securely besieged at Metz, and another of over one hundred and thirty thousand, with Napoleon in person, was defeated and captured at Sedan.[1]

For Further Reading. — As before. Note especially the references in the footnotes. Advanced students will find an admirable treatment of the diplomatic history of the period in Von Sybel's *German Empire*, VII.

V. THE THIRD REPUBLIC.

A. Through Foreign and Civil War: September, 1870, to May, 1871.

433. The Government of National Defense. — The news of Sedan reached Paris, September 3, 1870. The city had been kept in ignorance, as far as possible, of the previous reverses of the French armies; and now it went mad with excitement and dismay. The next day a mob invaded the hall where the legislature was already debating Napoleon's deposition, and, with this reënforcement, a few radical deputies tumultuously proclaimed the Third Republic and set up a provisional *Government of National Defense*.

The armies of France were already destroyed, except the one besieged at Metz, and this one was soon to surrender, through the treachery or faint-heartedness of its general. France seemed utterly incapable of further resistance to the invader, and the new government tried at first to secure an

---

[1] Napoleon remained for a few months a prisoner of war, and died in England a few years later (1873).

honorable peace. But when Prussia made it plain that she intended to punish France by taking large slices of her territory, the conflict entered upon a new stage and became a heroic struggle for defense.

For this second stage of the Franco-Prussian War, there are two main features: the gallant resistance of Paris through a four-months' siege, and a magnificent, patriotic uprising in the provinces. *Gambetta*, a leading member of the Government of Defense, escaped from Paris, in a balloon, to organize the movement in the provinces, and ruled there with dictatorial power. For a time success seemed possible. Exhausted France raised army after army, and amazed the world by her tremendous exertions. But in the end it became apparent that the iron grasp of the German armies, with their perfect organization, could not be broken. The great population of Paris began to suffer the horrors of famine; and on January 28 the city surrendered. Plainly France must accept the terms of the conqueror.

434. The National Assembly, and the Terms of Peace. — There was no government with any real authority to make peace; and so an armistice was arranged, to permit the election of a National Assembly. The Assembly was chosen by manhood suffrage. It met toward the close of February, 1871, and created a provisional government by electing Thiers "Head of the Executive Power of the French Republic."

The terms of peace were hard. The Prussians demanded that France should cede Alsace and part of Lorraine, with the great fortresses of Metz and Strasburg, and pay a huge war indemnity of one and a fifth billion dollars. Day after day the aged Thiers wrestled in pleading argument with Bismarck, the grim German Chancellor, to secure better terms. He did finally secure a slight reduction in the indemnity, to one billion, and the retention by France of Belfort, one of the cities of Alsace. In return for these concessions, Bismarck humiliated Paris by marching German troops in triumphal progress into the capital.

435. The Paris Commune of 1871. — The National Assembly had hardly arranged peace with the foreign foe, before it had to meet a terrible rebellion at home. During the siege of Paris, all the adult males of the city had been organized and armed as National Guards. Twice during the siege (in October and in January) the Radicals had tried by violent rebellion to supplant the Government of Defense with a more radical committee, but in both cases they had been quickly put down. When the siege was over, however, nearly every one who could get away from the distressed city did temporarily remove, including one hundred and fifty thousand of the wealthier National Guards, and so Paris was left in control of the radical element. This element, too, kept its arms and its military organization, and it now set up a kind of government by choosing a large "Central Committee."

The National Assembly had established itself, not at Paris, but at Versailles. The Republicans of Paris suspected it of wishing to restore the monarchy. In fact, a large majority of the members were Monarchists, as events were soon to prove (§ 437). The Assembly, too, had put in command of the army a man who had assisted in Napoleon's *coup d'état* and who might not unreasonably be suspected of trying another such move in favor of some of the royalist pretenders. Moreover, it had aggrieved the poorer classes of Paris by some of its decrees: it had insisted upon the immediate payment of rents and other debts incurred during the siege; and it did away in large measure with the pay of the National Guard, which since the surrender had been a kind of poor-relief. In addition to all this, the Reds and Socialists were always ready for any rising that promised success.

For two weeks Paris and Versailles faced each other with ill-concealed hostility. The National Guards collected a large number of cannon in one of the strongest forts of Paris. March 18 the Assembly sent a detachment of troops to secure these guns. A mob gathered to resist them; and the troops refused to fire, and looked on while two of their officers were seized and shot by the rebels. This was the opening of the insurrection.

For a time, however, there was still hope that a conflict might be averted. Paris decided to hold an election for a "General Council," and it was possible that the moderate element might win. Two hundred thousand votes were cast, and the Radicals and Revolutionists elected sixty-four[1] members, to about twenty Moderates. This hopeless minority refused to take their seats. Then the Radical Council, acting with the "Central Committee" of the Guards, *set up the Commune and adopted the red flag.*

In 1848 the Paris Radicals had learned that the country districts of France were overwhelmingly opposed to Socialism and to "Red Republicanism"; and these elements had now become advocates of extreme local self-government. If each city and village could become an almost independent state, then the Radicals hoped to carry out their policy in Paris and in the other large cities. The supporters of this program wished the central government of France to be merely a loose federation of independent "communes";[2] and so they called themselves "Federals." They are properly described also as "Communards"; but the name "Communist," which is often applied to them, is likely to give a false impression. That latter name is generally used only for those who oppose private property. Many of the Communards were also Communists, but probably the majority of them hardly went to such an extreme.

The supporters of the Paris Commune certainly included the greater part of the citizens remaining in Paris; but France, still bleeding from invasion, very properly refused to be dismembered by internal revolt. The excited bourgeoisie felt, moreover, that the institution of property itself was at stake, and they confounded all Communards together as criminals seeking to overthrow society. Little chance was given to show what the Commune would have done, if left to itself; but its government was made up of visionary enthusiasts and unpractical or criminal revolutionists, and certainly, in actual operation, it tended toward anarchy. Like attempts to set up Communes took place at Marseilles, Toulouse, Narbonne, and Lyons; but they came to little, and civil war was confined to Paris.

---

[1] About twenty of these were workingmen.

[2] As Hanotaux, a prominent French statesman and historian puts it, "The men of the Commune wished to make a Switzerland of France, — a socialized Switzerland."

436. The Civil War. — April 2 the Versailles Assembly attacked Paris with the regular troops that had now returned from captivity in Germany. The struggle lasted two months and was utterly ferocious. Both sides were guilty of horrible atrocities. The Assembly refused to treat the Communards as regular combatants, and shot down all prisoners taken in sorties. In retaliation, the Commune seized several hundred hostages from the better classes left in Paris, declaring that it would execute three of them for each of its soldiers shot after surrender. In fact, however, it did not carry out this threat; and the hostages were not harmed until the Commune had been overthrown, when, in the final disorder, an unauthorized mob did put sixty-three of them to death, — the venerable Archbishop of Paris among them.

The bombardment of Paris by the Versailles government was far more destructive than that by the Germans had been. Finally the troops forced their way into the city, which was already in flames in many sections. For eight days more, desperate fighting went on in the streets, before the rebellion was suppressed.[1] Court-martial executions of large batches of prisoners continued for many months afterward; and, besides the slaughtered, some thirteen thousand survivors were condemned to transportation, before the rage of the victorious bourgeoisie was sated. There are few darker stains on the page of history than the cruelty and brutality of this middle-class vengeance.[2]

---

[1] The Commune had arranged mines in the sewers to blow up certain portions of the streets where the invaders were expected to enter; and, during its brief rule, it had cast down the triumphal column of Napoleon I, commemorating his victories, on the ground that such glorification of wars of conquest was unworthy a civilized people. These facts, together with some destruction by the mob after the Commune had ceased to control the city, gave rise to the report that the Commune tried to destroy Paris when it could no longer retain possession. No such intention is needed to explain an enormous destruction under the conditions of the war. The world has never ceased to lament the loss to the art collections of the city.

[2] Cf. § 344, close; and, for details, see Hanotaux, *Contemporary France*, I, 221-228.

B. From the Suppression of the Commune to the Secure Establishment of the Republic, 1871–1879.

437. Nature and Powers of the Assembly. — The Assembly had been elected simply with a view to making peace. In choosing it, men had thought of nothing else.[1] It was limited by no constitution and it had no definite term of office. Certainly it had not been commissioned to make a constitution or to continue to rule indefinitely; but it did both these things.

At the election, people had chosen conservative candidates, because they wanted men who could be counted upon not to renew the war rashly. It turned out that the majority of the members were Monarchists; and they failed to set up a king, only because they were divided into three rival groups, — Imperialists (Bonapartists), Orleanists (supporters of the Count of Paris, grandson of Louis Philippe), and Legitimists (adherents of the Count of Chambord, grandson of Charles X). The three factions agreed in believing that a new election would increase the strength of the Republicans; and so for five years they resisted all demands of the republican members for dissolution. The Republicans also were divided into three groups, — the Moderates, the Left, and the Extreme-Left, or the Radicals.

438. Presidency of Thiers, 1871–1873. — Peace had been made, and the rebellion crushed. Now the Assembly felt compelled to replace the Provisional Government by some form that would *seem* more regular. Accordingly Thiers was made "President of the Republic." In truth, however, the government remained "provisional." The majority of the Assembly hoped to change to a monarchy at some favorable moment, and they gave Thiers no fixed term of office. Still, this presidency lasted more than two years longer, — the most glorious years of the old statesman's life, — and it was marked by three important features.[2]

---

[1] Read Hanotaux, I, 30–33 and 70.
[2] For Thiers' character and work, see Hanotaux, I, 43–62.

a. France took up gallantly the huge work of reorganization. Schools, army, and church were reconstructed (§§ 446, 449, 483).

b. France was freed from foreign occupation, and Thiers won the proud title of "Liberator of the Territory." It had been intended that the vast war indemnity should be paid in installments through three years, and German garrisons were to remain in France until payment was complete. But France astonished all beholders by her rapid recovery of prosperity; and, in eighteen months, the indemnity was paid in coin, and the last German soldier had left French soil. The government loans (§ 308, note) were taken up enthusiastically by all classes of Frenchmen, and in great measure by the industrious and prosperous peasantry, so that it appeared that the government would not have been forced to borrow at all from foreign capitalists, had it not chosen to do so.

c. Republicanism was strengthened. Thiers was an old Orleanist; but he saw that to set up a king was to risk civil war. Accordingly, he allied himself with the Moderate Republicans in the Assembly, and baffled triumphantly the efforts of the Monarchists. Meantime Republicanism grew stronger daily in the country.

439. Monarchists in Control.—In 1873, a momentary coalition of Monarchists and Radicals in the Assembly forced Thiers to resign. In his place the Monarchists elected Marshal MacMahon, an ardent Orleanist. For some months a monarchic restoration seemed almost certain. Legitimists and Orleanists had at last united in support of the Count of Chambord, who had agreed to adopt the Count of Paris as his heir. The Monarchists had the machinery of the government in their hands, and all arrangements were complete for declaring the Bourbon heir the King of France, when the two factions split once more on the question of a symbol. The Orleanists wished to keep the tricolor, the flag of the 1830 Revolution, and certainly the only flag the army would have followed. But the Count of Chambord denounced the tricolor as the "symbol of revolution," and declared that he would not give up the white lilies of the old Bourbon monarchy, the symbol of divine right. On this scruple the chance of the Monarchists came to shipwreck.

440. The Constitution. — Then in 1875, despairing of an immediate restoration, the Assembly adopted a series of laws fixing more precisely the frame of government. As modified slightly by later amendments, these "constitutional laws" make the present constitution of the French Republic. They have never been submitted to the people.

The Constitution is very brief, because the Monarchist majority preferred to leave the details to be settled by later legislation, hoping to adapt them to a kingly government. The word "republic" did not appear in the original draft, but it was introduced indirectly by amendment: the first draft spoke of a "Chief Executive"; an amendment changed this title to "President of the Republic." The change was adopted by a majority of one in a vote of seven hundred and five. Later, in 1884, a new amendment declared the republican form of government to be "not subject to repeal."

The legislature consists of two houses. The Senate contains three hundred members, holding office for nine years, one-third going out each third year. At first, seventy-five of the members were to hold office for life, but in 1884 an amendment declared that no more life members should be chosen. Senators are elected by the departments of France, in electoral colleges, and the number from the different departments varies with the population. The Deputies (lower house) are chosen by manhood suffrage for a term of four years. When the Senate and the House of Deputies agree that it is desirable to amend the constitution, or when it is necessary to choose a President, the two houses meet together at Versailles, away from possible disturbances in Paris. In this joint form, they take the name *National Assembly.* A majority vote of the National Assembly suffices to change the constitution.

The executive consists of a *President,* elected for seven years by the National Assembly, and of *the ministry* he appoints. The President has much less power than the President of the

United States. He is more nearly in the position of a short-term, elective, English king. That is, he is little more than a figurehead. He can act only through his ministers. The ministers, as in England, are the real executive, and they wield enormous power, directing all legislation, appointing a vast multitude of officers, and carrying on the government. Nominally, the President appoints the ministers; but, in practice, he must always name those who will be acceptable to the chambers, and the ministry is obliged to resign when it ceases to have a majority of Deputies to support its measures. The Deputies maintain a control over the ministers, by the right of *interpellation*. That is, any Deputy may address to the ministers a formal question, calling upon them to explain their action in any matter. Such a question must be answered fully, and it always affords a chance to censure and overthrow the ministry.[1]

441. The Republicans gain Possession of the Government, 1876-1879. — Even after the adoption of the constitution, the Assembly did not give way at once to a new legislature. But almost every bye-election[2] resulted in a victory for the Republicans, and by 1876 that party had gained a bare majority of the seats. It at once dissolved the Assembly, and the new elections created a House of Deputies two-thirds Republican.

The Senate with its seventy-five life members was still monarchic; and, with its support, MacMahon tried to keep a Monarchist ministry, but after a short contest he was forced to yield. During this contest the President and Senate dissolved the House of Deputies (as the constitution gives them power to do when they act together), and the ministry changed prefects and local officers all over France, in order to control the election; but the Republicans rallied under the leadership of the fiery Gambetta (§ 433), and the new House of Deputies was even more strongly Republican than the preceding one.

---

[1] Advanced students should consult Lowell, *Governments and Parties*, I, 120-122, and compare with English ministerial government.

[2] To fill a vacancy, upon death or resignation.

This body then withheld all votes of supply, until MacMahon appointed a ministry acceptable to it.[1]

In 1879 the renewal of one-third the Senate gave the Republicans a majority in that House also, and, soon after, MacMahon resigned. Then the National Assembly elected to the presidency *Grévy*, an ardent Republican; and all branches of the government had at last come under Republican control.

For the first time in the history of France, republican government was established by the calm will of the nation. Four times between 1792 and 1871 had the Republicans seized Paris; three times they had set up a republic; but never before had they truly represented the deliberate determination of the nation. In 1879 they came into power, not by violence, but by an eight-years' constitutional struggle against the political tricks of an accidental Monarchist majority. This time it was the Republicans whom the conservative, peace-loving peasantry supported.

442. Constitutional Relations of President and Deputies. — Grévy served out the full seven years of his presidency; and in 1886 he was reelected. Then a curious constitutional question came up for settlement. Grévy's son-in-law had been guilty of shameful corruption in office, and the President, though personally incorruptible, had tried to shield him from punishment. When this became known, the Deputies demanded that Grévy should resign, and they overthrew ministry after ministry, making it clear that they would not support any administration appointed by him. Finally the President resigned; and the Deputies had established a valuable precedent as to their control over the executive.[2]

---

[1] Cf. Lowell, *Governments and Parties*, I, 22–24, and, for later developments, 97–99.

[2] Not until 1906 had any other president of France served a full term. The subsequent presidents, with their terms of office, have been as follows: —

F. Sadi-Carnot, grandson of the great Carnot who " organized victory " (§ 342), 1887–1894: assassinated by an Italian anarchist before the close of his term.

Casimir Perier, June, 1894–January, 1895; resigned because of trouble with the legislature.

Felix Faure, 1895–1899: died in office, after two attempts upon his life by anarchists.

Emile Loubet, 1899–1906.

Armand Fallières (Radical), 1906–.

C. Crises since 1879.

Since 1879, as we can see now, France has not been in serious danger of revolution. There have been, however, several brief political crises, during which revolution seemed possible to men of the time. Two of these crises deserve attention,[1] — the kulturkampf and Boulangism.

443. The Kulturkampf. — In 1875, the Catholic clergy of France were mainly Monarchists, distrusting and fearing the Republic. Moreover, the extreme clerical party looked to the Pope for direction in political affairs, and acknowledged an allegiance to him superior to that they felt for the national government. Because of this devotion to a power "beyond the mountains," they were called "Ultramontanists."

The Republican leaders turned this passive attitude into open political war. They adopted Gambetta's famous phrase in the elections of 1876 and 1881, — "Our foe is Clericalism," — and the first Republican ministries (especially in the years 1880–1884) entered upon a struggle to take from the church its control over the family and the child. This conflict between the church and the state over education is called the kulturkampf.[2] France is mainly Catholic in religion; but the majority of French Catholics were not Ultramontanists, and the state was victorious. The Jesuits were expelled from the country. All other religious orders were forbidden to keep private schools or to teach in the public schools. Marriage was made a civil contract,[3] not a religious sacrament; and divorce was made legal, despite the doctrines of the church.

This policy of the Republicans aroused a fierce opposition; and in the elections of 1885 the Monarchists and Clericals made decided gains. They did not secure a majority, however, and soon afterward the conflict was moderated by the statesmanship of Pope Leo XIII. Before the elections of 1893, Leo made clear his desire that French Catholics should rally to

---

[1] Two minor crises, suitable for special reports, were connected with the *Panama Scandals* (1893) and the *Dreyfus Trials* (1898 and 1905).

[2] For like contests in other Catholic countries, see §§ 482, 490, 508.

[3] It is performed by a civil officer. The religious ceremony may follow.

the support of the Republic and try to get such privileges as they needed by influencing legislation, not by trying to change the government.[1] The order was generally obeyed. The irreconcilable withdrew from public life, and the rest of the old Ultramontanists took the name of "Rallied Republicans." On its side, the Republican government quietly ceased for a time to enforce most of the new legislation against church schools.

444. Boulanger. — While this Ultramontane dissatisfaction was at its height, danger threatened for a time from another quarter. From 1885 to 1888, Boulanger, a popular general and an advocate of a war of revenge against Germany, seems to have hoped to make himself master of France, after the fashion of the Napoleons; but the movement, if ever serious, came quickly to utter collapse. When the government ordered a trial, Boulanger fled, and soon afterward took his own life.

D. FRANCE TO-DAY.

445. Stability and Progress. — For nearly a century France passed from revolution to revolution so incessantly that the world came to doubt whether any French government could be stable.[2] But the present Republic has lasted twice as long as any other government in France since 1789, and to-day (1907) it seems as secure as most European monarchies. Even the ministries change less frequently than formerly, and when a political crisis comes it is met more and more with moderation, much as in English-speaking countries. Since 1893, the Monarchists have had little weight in the Assembly; while the Socialists, at the other extreme, have become a true political party, working for their ends by constitutional means. *The age of Revolution in France seems to have ended; the age of a parliamentary republic has fairly begun.* Other progress has not been neglected. In literature and science, France once more (after long eclipse) shines forth as a leader of European

---

[1] McCarthy's *Leo XIII*, 182–201.

[2] The French felt in the same way toward England for some time after the English revolutions of the seventeenth century.

thought, and in material wealth her people as a whole are the richest in Europe.

Aside from the practice of self-government the chief lines of *political* interest in recent years have been two: (1) *radical legislation to improve the condition of the laboring class*, — such as an eight-hour law for miners (1902), — and (2) *legislation regarding church and state* (§ 446).

446. The Kulturkampf again: New Relations between Church and State. — Seventy-eight per cent of the people of France are Catholics. Other religions comprise about two per cent. Twenty per cent have no religious connection. In the reorganization of France under Thiers' presidency, the principles of Napoleon's Concordat (§ 360 a) were extended to all religions. No church was "established," in the sense in which the Episcopal Church is the established church in England. That is, no church was given political power or special privileges. But the state assumed the support and the control of four religions, — Catholic, Protestant (Lutheran and Reformed), Jewish, and Mohammedan (in Algeria); and it agreed to treat in like manner any other sect which could show one hundred thousand members. For all these organizations, until 1905, the state provided buildings and paid the clergy, *and likewise supervised the appointment of the clergy.*

The agitation connected with the Dreyfus trial (§ 443, note) made it clear that monarchic sympathies were still strong, at the end of the century, among both the army officers and the aristocratic classes in general. French statesmen concluded that this was due largely to the remaining clerical influence in the schools; and, in 1901, drastic legislation shut out the churches from all share in education, public or private. These laws, unlike those of twenty years earlier, were enforced rigorously. During the next two years many thousands of church schools were closed by the police, sometimes amid riot and bloodshed.

This new kulturkampf led to a mightier issue. The Pope protested against the anti-clerical laws and deposed two bishops who had acquiesced in them (1904). The government declared this act a breach of the Concordat (§ 360 *a*). It recalled its ambassador from the Papal Court and prepared a plan which it called "Separation of Church and State," but which zealous Catholics denounce as robbery inspired by anti-religious feeling. In 1905 this plan became law, and in the elections of 1906, the nation gave an overwhelming endorsement to the whole anti-clerical policy.

According to the law of 1905, the state is no longer to control the appointment of the clergy, though it continues to exercise a jealous oversight to keep them from interfering in politics or schools. The state also ceases to pay the clergy (this withdrawal of support to be gradual, over a period of years), and it assumes possession of all churches and church property. Each religious congregation, however, was to be permitted the permanent use of its former church property, if within a year it organized as a "cultural association." The Protestants universally complied with this provision; but, despite the advice of the French bishops, the Pope declared that such control of church matters by "associations" was incompatible with the Catholic organization. He forbade Catholics to recognize the law. "Compromises" offered by the government were rejected. When the "year of grace" expired, in December, 1906, the government shrewdly declined to close the churches, but it evicted great numbers of clergy from their homes, and banished some from the country, for disregard of the law. Other measures of coercion are under consideration (January, 1907). Meanwhile the extreme Catholic party hope that the "martyrdom" of the faithful and beloved clergy will rouse the nation to repudiate the government's policy.

447. Local Government. — France is divided into eighty-six departments; the departments are subdivided into arrondissements; these are divided again into cantons; and the cantons are made up of communes. This arrangement dates from the First Revolution (§ 325), but the communes, of course, are ancient units. The two important divisions of these four are the two extremes — the department and the commune.[1] Each of these has its own "budget": that is, it levies taxes for local purposes and expends them in its own way. Each is a corporation, and can own property and sue and be sued at law. Each has a large amount of self-government, with machinery for managing affairs. The department has an executive officer, called a prefect, and a General Council. The prefect is appointed by the Minister of the Interior, and he may be removed by the same authority. He appoints police, postmen, and other local officers. The General Council is elected by universal suffrage. It exercises control over local taxation and expenditures, especially for roads, asylums, and, to some degree, for schools; but its decisions are subject to the supervision of the central government, which may even dissolve it.

The thirty-six thousand communes vary in size from great cities like Marseilles, to rural villages with only two or three hundred people. For all of them there is one system of government. Each has a mayor and a council. Until 1884, the mayor was appointed by the Minister of the Interior; since 1884, he has been elected by the municipal council, but he is still regarded as the officer of the central government, which may revise his acts or even remove him from office. The municipal council varies in number, according to the size of the commune. It is elected by manhood suffrage. All its acts are subject to the approval of the perfect or the central government, and the latter may dissolve the council. Paris and Lyons are each organized as a department, with even less self-government than the other departments of the country.

Such conditions do not seem very encouraging at first to an American student; but the situation, as compared with the past in France, is full of promise. Political interest in the

---

[1] The two middle divisions are less important than counties in our Northern states. The canton is the unit for the administration of justice. The arrondissement is the unit for the election of a deputy to the national legislature, like our congressional district. It has an elective council of its own, however, and some powers resembling in slight measure those of our counties.

communes is steadily growing, and Frenchmen are learning more and more to use the field of self-government open to them.[1]

448. The Judicial System and Political Liberty. Administrative Courts.[2] — The French system of law seems to an American or an Englishman to be wanting in safeguards for personal liberty. Unlike the previous French constitutions, the present constitution has no "bill of rights." That is, there are no provisions in the fundamental law regarding jury trial, habeas corpus privileges, or the right of free speech. Moreover, even if there were, the courts could not protect the individual from arbitrary acts of the government by appealing to such provisions, because, in case of conflict between a citizen and the government, the case is tried, not in ordinary civil courts, but in *administrative courts* made up of government officials. This does not mean that in ordinary times an individual is likely to be treated unjustly. As a rule, the administrative courts mete out excellent justice. But in case of any supposed danger to the government, they are liable to become careless of the rights of an individual.

449. Education. — The plans of the early Revolutionists for educating the people (§ 345) came to little; and for a long time after the Restoration, nothing was done. In 1827, over a third of the communes of France had no primary school whatever, and nearly a third of the population could neither read nor write. In the latter part of the reign of Louis Philippe, a fair beginning was made in a system of primary schools, but the real growth of popular education dates from the Third Republic. Almost as soon as the war with Germany was over, France adopted in large measure the German plan for schools and for her army. To-day, in every commune there is a primary school or group of schools. Education is free and compulsory and strictly regulated by the state. That is, the central government appoints teachers and regulates the courses of

---

[1] Cf. § 358, and read Boutmy, *Constitutional Studies*, 145.

[2] For an excellent statement of the growth of such courts, see Lowell's *Governments and Parties*, I, 50-55.

study. Each department has an excellent system of secondary schools, called *lycées*. When its recent birth is considered, the educational system seems marvelously efficient.

450. The Land and Peasantry. — The peculiar thing about French society is the large number of small landowners and the prosperity of this landed peasantry. Half the entire population live on the soil, and three-fourths the soil is under crops. The subdivision of the soil is carried so far that it is difficult to introduce the best machinery (though neighborhood associations are being founded to own machinery in common); but the peasant is industrious, thrifty, prosperous, happy, and conservative.

The peasant wishes to educate his son, and he has a high standard of living, compared with other European peasantry. With five or six children, a farmer owning five or ten acres would almost necessarily find it impossible to keep up this high standard, and to leave his children as well off as he himself had been. Therefore the peasantry do not wish large families, and population is almost stationary. At present it is a little under forty millions.

451. Colonies and Foreign Relations. — About 1750 France bade fair to be the great colonial power of the world. The century-long duel with England was then half over. "New France" was written on the map across the valley of the St. Lawrence and the Mississippi, and the richest lands of the Orient seemed within the French grasp. Fifty years later saw France stripped of all possessions outside Europe, except a few unimportant islands in the Indian Ocean and in the Antilles and some small ports in India (§§ 275, 277, 282-283).

But in the nineteenth century France became again a colonial power. In 1830, the government of Charles X took advantage of an insult by the Dey of Algiers to a French consul to seize territory in North Africa. In the middle of the century this foothold had grown, through savage and bloody wars, into complete military occupancy of Algeria; and in the early years of the Third Republic civil rule was introduced. Since

1880 Algeria has been not so much a foreign possession, or a colony, as a part of France separated from the rest by a strip of sea. The French make only a small part of the population, it is true, but the country is orderly and civilized.[1] It is divided into three departments, which are ruled essentially like the departments in European France; and it has representatives in the French legislature. French rule has restored to the long-desolate Barbary coast the fertility and bloom which belonged to that region when it was the garden of the Roman world.

In 1881 France seized upon Tunis as a "protectorate." That is, France controls its relations with foreign governments, but leaves it to manage its own internal matters — except that the French enjoy special traveling privileges in the country. In 1904, France began to reduce Morocco to a like condition; but this process was checked temporarily, by German opposition, and Morocco is (1907) only a semi-protectorate (§ 587 *b*).

The rest of the vast colonial empire, apart from these possessions in North Africa, has been acquired since the Franco-Prussian War, except for some slight beginnings made by Napoleon III. The seizure of territory has very commonly been based upon ancient claims connected with the period before the French Revolution, and it has been carried on in some cases with high-handed disregard of the rights of weaker peoples.[2]

In Asia, France has chief possession of the great peninsula of Indo-China.[3] In Africa, France kept a hold upon Senegal from her ancient colonial empire, and since 1884 she has acquired huge possessions on both the east and west coasts, besides the great island of Madagascar (map, facing page 611). In America, France holds Guiana, or Cayenne, with a few islands in the Antilles. In Oceania, between 1884 and 1887, she secured New Caledonia and several smaller islands.

---

[1] All these statements apply to the settled portions under civil rule. The vast districts farther inland are still barbarous.

[2] As in Siam and Madagascar.

[3] The order in which the different provinces in Asia have been acquired is as follows: Cambodia (1862), Cochin China (1863), Tonking (1884), Annam (1886), Siam, to the Mekong River (1893–1896).

Though France has these immense possessions, she is not a colonizing nation. Large parts of these regions are almost unpeopled, or are inhabited by savage tribes and are under military government. Even in the settled portions the European population is small. The total area of the colonial possessions is about four million square miles, of which about three and a half million are in Africa. All the settled and orderly regions have a share in self-government, and most of them have representatives in the legislature at Paris.

For a generation after the Franco-Prussian War, France had little weight in European politics. For a long time she hoped to recover her lost provinces by another war; and, to that end, she sought feverishly for alliance with Russia (§ 558). This alliance may have helped to give France a freer hand in her colonial expansion, but on the whole it proved of little value to her. Happily, French statesmen have now given up thought of a "war of revenge." They have shown a tendency to ally their country with England; and a good understanding between these two powers will do much to prevent European war. *The Democratic Republic is Peace.*

FOR FURTHER READING. — The works mentioned on page 413 continue to be valuable well into the Third Republic. Fyffe closes in 1878. Coubertin, *France under the Third Republic*, or Hanotaux, *Contemporary France*, may be used by advanced students for further details. Lebon and Pelet's *France as It Is* (1890) was an excellent treatment of institutions and conditions at its publication. Wilson's *The State*, 215-244, outlines the government. Advanced students can use Lowell's *Governments and Parties*. All the important and constitutional documents are given in Anderson's *Constitutions and Documents*.

For recent history, every high school should have one or more good Reviews accessible or in the reading rooms, besides an *International Year Book* or *The Statesman's Year Book*, at least for every second or third year, and *The World Almanac*.

SPECIAL REPORTS. — 1. Great strikes in France since 1880. 2. The anarchistic plots since 1893. 3. The French army law of to-day, and the strength of the organization. 4. Church and state since 1906.

CHAPTER IV.

CENTRAL EUROPE SINCE 1848.[1]

I. THE REVOLUTIONS OF 1848 AND THE RESTORATIONS.

452. The Year of Revolutions: Threefold Character in Central Europe. — The system of Metternich lasted in Europe until 1848 (§ 401); but for some years before that date the forces of revolution had been gathering strength for a general explosion. Metternich himself saw this. "The world is very sick," he wrote to a friend in January, 1848; "the one thing certain is that there will be tremendous changes." A few weeks later, the February Revolution in Paris (§ 419) gave the signal for March risings in other lands; and that month saw Metternich a fugitive, escaping from Vienna in a laundry cart, while thrones were tottering everywhere in Europe, between Russia and Turkey on the one side and England on the other. The kings of Spain, Holland, Denmark, and Sweden made concessions to popular demands. Even England trembled with a Chartist movement (§ 533) and the threat of an Irish rebellion; but the chief interest of the period, outside France, centers in Germany and Italy. In these countries the movement was threefold: (1) for constitutional liberty and social reform within the several states; (2) for the union of the fragments of the German race into a new nation; (3) for the independence of the other nations held in subjection by Austria. The three forces were interlaced, working sometimes in unison, sometimes

---

[1] This chapter continues the story from where chapter ii left it. Chapter iii was a necessary interlude, inserted because of the influence of France on Central Europe in 1848 and 1870.

in opposition: and thus the period is one of indescribable confusion. The March risings resulted in new constitutions, radical reforms, and liberal ministries, in every German state, — including Prussia and Austria, — and also in Sardinia, Tuscany, Rome, and Naples. The remains of feudal privilege in these lands, too, were swept away. The movement for German nationality brought together representatives of all the German peoples in a National Assembly at Frankfort. The sentiment of nationality in the conglomerate Austrian Empire brought on wars for independence by the Italians, Hungarians, and Bohemians.

453. In Detail: Austria and the Revolution. — Of course Austria was the storm center. On March 13 came the rising in Vienna, to the cry, "Down with Metternich!" Metternich fled, and the Emperor proclaimed a series of reforms, promised a constitution, and named a liberal ministry. Bohemia and Hungary, where revolt was imminent, were pacified with promises of constitutional governments of their own, and all efforts were concentrated on putting down the Italian rising.

On the news of Metternich's overthrow, the people of Milan and Venice had driven out the Austrian troops; and all Italy had been swept with a storm of feeling for the permanent expulsion of Austria. Charles Albert, King of Sardinia, put himself at the head of the movement. The Pope, the Grand Duke of Tuscany, and even the King of Naples promised him loyal aid; and Venice, Modena, and other small states in northern Italy voted for incorporation into the Kingdom of Sardinia. But soon the dukes and the King of Naples began to be jealous of Sardinia; the Pope was unwilling to break finally with Austria; and, on the eve of the struggle, Charles Albert found himself deserted by all Italy south of Lombardy, save for a few thousand patriotic volunteers. July 25, he was defeated at *Custozza*, and was forced to withdraw into his own dominions and to sign a truce.

Then the movement in Italy passed into the hands of the Radicals. Venice set up a republic. Florence drove out her

[§ 453] THE AUSTRIAN EMPIRE.

Grand Duke, and did the same. At Rome, the minister whom the Pope had appointed to carry out reform in the Papal States was assassinated; the Pope was driven from the city; and in February, 1849, the "Roman Republic" was proclaimed, under the leadership of Mazzini (§ 458).

While this second series of events was going on in Italy, Austria was reëstablishing her authority elsewhere. Her great ally was race jealousy. The Germans in Bohemia dreaded the rule of the Czechs,[1] and the disturbances between the two races gave an excuse for military intervention. The Austrian army was now ready; and in July the newly granted self-government for Bohemia was suddenly replaced by military rule. Soon afterward the Radicals in Vienna, alarmed at the signs of reaction, rose again and gained brief possession of the city; but in October they were reduced to submission by the victorious army recalled from Bohemia. Then the incapable Emperor Ferdinand was induced to abdicate in favor of his nephew, the shrewd *Francis Joseph*, who could plead lack of consent to all the recent concessions; and a reactionary ministry was appointed under the vigorous *Schwarzenberg*.

Austrian reaction was now well under way. The next victory was won in Hungary. In that country, as in Bohemia, race dissensions favored Austria. The Hungarians were the dominant race; but the various Slav peoples,— Croats, Serbs, Slavonians, etc.,— who made the majority in the border districts of the country, preferred German rule from Vienna to Magyar rule from the nearer Budapest. Just before the reactionary victory in Vienna, the Croats had risen against the new Hungarian government. The Hungarians were victorious; but after the accession of Francis Joseph, the struggle was renewed, with the Emperor plainly in alliance with the Slav rebels. Accordingly, Hungary refused to recognize Francis Joseph. It declared itself a republic, and, under the presi-

---

[1] The Czechs are the Slav natives of Bohemia, and they make the majority of the inhabitants.

dency of the heroic Kossuth, waged a gallant war for independence. But now the Russian Tsar took a hand in the reactionary movement. In accordance with the Münchengrätz compact between the monarchs (§ 400), he sent a large army to assist Austria; and the Hungarians were crushed (April–August, 1849). A bloody vengeance followed, and Hungarian liberty seemed annihilated.

By this time, too, the old order had been restored in Italy. Sardinia had renewed the war in March, 1849, but had met decisive defeat from the Austrians at *Novara,* after only a five-days' campaign. Venice held out gallantly through a siege until August;[1] but after her fall the only gain that remained to the peninsula from 1848 was the Sardinian constitution. Louis Napoleon had sent French troops to escort the Pope back to Rome, where he remained under French protection until 1870.

454. The Failure to unite Germany: the Frankfort Assembly and the Prussian King. — It remained only for Austria to reëstablish her authority in Germany. For a time this seemed improbable enough. While she had been busied in her non-German provinces, Germany had been left to Prussia and to the National Assembly at Frankfort; and if either of these forces had been prompt to act, German unity might have been achieved. As it was, little had been done.

In Berlin, the people thronged the streets from March 13 to March 18, in excited crowds, but with no serious revolutionary purpose. But on the 18th, in some way, a sharp conflict was brought on, and the troops inflicted terrible slaughter on the mob. Frederick William IV,[2] however, lacked either the reso-

---

[1] This siege of Venice and the history of the Roman Republic are good topics for special reports. The best treatment probably is given in Bolton King's *Italian Unity*. Advanced students may make an excellent study by presenting the Italian movements of these years as they are reflected in the poems of Mrs. Browning.

[2] In 1840 Frederick William III had been succeeded by his son, Frederick William IV, a man even weaker and more vacillating than his father.

luteness or cold-heartedness to follow up the victory. To pacify the people, he not only sent into temporary exile his brother William (who was commander of the troops and was regarded by the mob as responsible for the conflict), but he also took part in a procession in honor of the dead, wearing the red, gold, and black colors of the German patriots, and he summoned a Prussian Parliament to draw up a constitution. He put himself at the head, too, of the nationalist movement, and declared in a public address, "From this time, Prussian interests will be absorbed in those of Germany." Still, what would come of all this was to depend largely on the success of the people's movement for German unity in the National Assembly.

May 18, 1848, the National Assembly met at Frankfort. It had been chosen by manhood suffrage,[1] and it now took the place of the Diet of the Confederation, which quietly slipped away. For nearly two years the unsatisfactory Confederation of 1815 seemed defunct. In its place was a new national union, with its government vested in the Frankfort Assembly.

The Assembly had two tasks: (1) to provide a provisional government; (2) to adopt a plan for permanent union, or a constitution, and to put it into operation. Unhappily the meeting was led by theorists, and talkers, and scholars, not by statesmen or men of action, and it showed over again the weakness of the Assemblies of the First French Revolution. The leaders could not understand the virtue of compromise or the necessity of prompt action, and they spent precious months in wordy contests over abstract principles. May and June did see an ineffectual provisional government organized; but meanwhile Austria had crushed Bohemia, and the "June Days"

---

[1] A previous Parliament of Liberals at Heidelberg (March 5) had arranged the basis for representation for the different German states, and the plan had been sanctioned by the Diet of the Confederacy. The Assembly contained nearly six hundred members and was the first representative body in history that could claim to speak for all Germany.

(§ 423) had dealt a death-blow to Radicalism in France. The next four months went to debating a bill of rights, while all chance of securing any rights was being lost; for during this time Italy was defeated at Custozza, and Vienna was captured by the Reactionists, while the commercial class all over Germany was becoming alienated by the long-continued business panic. Moreover, the Prussian Parliament at Berlin, which was to have drawn up a liberal constitution, had provoked King Frederick William into dissolving it. To be sure, the King himself then gave a constitution to Prussia; but it was of a very conservative character, and Frederick William was fast becoming hostile to what he had shortly before called the "glorious German Revolution." In other German states, too, the liberal ministries which were set up after the March Days were being replaced with startling rapidity.

These were the conditions when in October the Frankfort Assembly at last took up the making of a constitution. Two questions then divided the Assembly: (1) should the new government be monarchic or republican; and (2) should the new nation include the German part of Austria, or exclude that dangerous state altogether. Over these problems[1] the wrangling went on through the winter of 1849, until Austria finally got her hands free in Italy and had elsewhere so far regained her old power that she announced that she would permit no German union into which she did not enter with all her provinces.

Then the Radicals gave up the impossible republic, and the Assembly took the step it should have taken months before: it decided for a union *without Austria,* under the name of the German Empire, and it offered the proposed imperial crown to Frederick William of Prussia. But it was at least six months too late. The public sentiment which at that earlier time would have forced the Prussian King to accept, had spent itself.

---

[1] The Republicans had no chance whatever to succeed, but they helped to delay action on the other and more practical question.

Frederick William personally was disinclined: he was timid; he was influenced by a sense of honor among kings, so that he hesitated to take advantage of Austria's embarrassments with her revolted subjects; and he felt a growing aversion to the Revolution. After some hesitation, he declined the crown. Then the German Radicals, in despair, resorted to arms to set up a republic. Of course they were promptly crushed,[1] and the National Assembly vanished in the spring of 1849.

455. Failure of the Princes under Prussian Leadership. — The people's attempt to make a German nation closed with the dissolution of the Frankfort Assembly. But when Frederick William declined the crown "bespattered by the blood and mire of revolution," he expressed his willingness to assume the leadership of a league of princes; and accordingly, in the summer of 1849, despite the protests of Austria and Bavaria, twenty-eight states of northern Germany did organize a Prussian League.

Several of the princes composing it, however, were half-hearted or treacherous, joining only through fear of popular risings if they did not. Austria, with Hungary now at her feet and with Russia for her ally, organized the South German states into a counter-league and proposed the restoration of the old Confederation. Schwarzenberg announced bluntly his policy, — "First humiliate Prussia, then destroy her." Plainly Austria would intervene, at the first opportunity, to put down the Prussian League. The opportunity came at once, through a quarrel in Hesse between the ruler and his people. Hesse was a state of the Prussian League, and the people appealed to the Council of the League and to Prussia. The Elector of Hesse appealed to Austria. Austria and Prussia both moved troops,[2] which met on the borders of Bavaria. Shots were exchanged: but the Prussian army was not ready; Russia

---

[1] This was the period when so many German Liberals, like Carl Schurz and General Siegel, fled to America.

[2] The Austrian forces were really the army of Bavaria, which was moved under Austrian influence, in the name of the old Diet.

showed strong Austrian sympathies; and finally Frederick William made ignominious submission in a conference with Schwarzenberg at *Olmütz* (November 28, 1850). *Then Austria restored the old Diet, and the German Confederation upon the basis of* 1815.

456. Summary : the Apparent Restoration of the Old System of 1815 and the Real Gains. — Thus the restoration seemed complete. The Revolution had closed in Italy with Novara (March, 1849), in Hungary with the downfall of the Republic (July, 1849), and in Germany with the "humiliation of Olmütz" (December, 1850). A year later it was to close in France with Napoleon's *coup d'état*.

Still, there had been some gains.[1] European feudalism was finally gone, — even from the Austrian realms. In Italy, Sardinia kept her new constitution; and her King, Victor Emmanuel, recognized his proper mission to be to free and unite Italy (§ 459). Prussia, shamed at Olmütz, had statesmen who would see that another time she should not be caught unprepared.[2] Out of these conditions were to be born a new Kingdom of Italy and a new German Empire.

These new births were to be the work of the next twenty years (1850–1870). The period was to be one of "blood and iron." The making of Germany and Italy was accompanied by a series of great wars,[3] and ushered in a new period in European history.

FOR FURTHER READING. — Seignobos, Andrews, Fyffe, and Phillips, as before. Murdock's *Reconstruction of Europe* has a clear account. Headlam's *Germany, 1815–1819;* Henderson's *Short History of Germany* and Bolton King's *Italian Unity* are excellent for their respective fields.

EXERCISE. — Review §§ 414–428 and 452–456, to get a view of the 1848 movements in France and the rest of Europe.

---

[1] Read especially Andrews' *Modern Europe*, I, 444–448.

[2] The years just following Olmütz, it is true, were among the least promising in all Prussian history. But the humiliation had done its work, and the results were to show ten years later (§§ 464 ff.).

[3] Some of these wars have been touched upon in the chapter on France.

II. THE UNIFICATION OF ITALY.

457. Historical Review to 1815. — Through the Middle Ages, enthusiastic Italians like Dante and Savonarola had dreamed of national unity, and some of the great popes had adopted the union of the peninsula under papal leadership as a political program. No progress was made, however, until about 1800. The proclamations of Napoleon I in his Italian campaigns (§ 352), promising liberty and independence, again awoke hope in Italian hearts. Some consolidation, too, was accomplished; and, though the various "republics," set up under the Directory, were short-lived, some advance was made in civil liberty (§§ 352, 360 *b*). Then, when the final coalition was struggling with Napoleon, in 1813 and 1814, the generals of the Allies appealed to the Italian populations with glowing promises. An English force landed at Genoa, with its flag inscribed "Italian Liberty and Independence"; and Austrian proclamations announced: —

> We come to you as liberators. Long have you groaned beneath oppression. You shall be an independent nation. . . . Do not fear that under new masters you will be forced back into the old conditions. No, Italians, this is not the purpose of the Allies. Your independence is among the causes of the war, — that you may become a single nation . . . free from the dominance of foreigners.

These pledges were shamefully ignored at the Congress of Vienna in 1815. Even the Napoleonic improvements were undone, and medieval conditions were restored. Lombardy and Venetia became Austrian provinces, and most of the rest of the peninsula was handed over to Austrian influence. Bourbon rule was restored in the south over the Kingdom of the Two Sicilies, where the King pledged himself to allow no institutions more liberal than those permitted by Austria in her districts. Dukes, dependent upon Austria, were set up in Tuscany, Modena, and Parma. Between these duchies and Naples lay the old Papal States, now restored to clerical rule and in close sympathy with Austria. In the northwest the Kingdom of

Sardinia (Piedmont, Savoy, Genoa, and Sardinia) was given back to its native line of monarchs, to whom the people were loyally attached; but even in this state — the hope of Italy — the government until 1848 was a mere military despotism. No Italian state had a constitution. From Rome south, the country was infested with brigands. Such political life as existed was to be found only in secret societies. "Italy," said Metternich, "is a mere geographical expression."

458. Three Periods of Revolution: 1820, 1830, 1848. — The story of the Italian revolutions of 1820 and of the intervention of the Holy Alliance has already been told (§§ 394-396). In 1830, after the success of Greece and of the July Revolution in Paris, new revolutions broke out in the Papal States and in the small duchies, but these movements also were soon suppressed by Austria.

The next ten years are famous for the organization of *"Young Italy"* by *Mazzini*. Mazzini was a Genoese lawyer and a revolutionary enthusiast, who was to play in freeing Italy a part corresponding somewhat to that taken by Garrison and Phillips in preparing for our American Civil War. His mission was to create a great moral enthusiasm. His words and writings worked wonderfully upon the younger Italians of the educated classes, and his Society of Young Italy replaced the older Carbonari (§ 394). Young Italy had for its program a united Italian Republic. The ideals were noble and lofty, but the methods of the Society were stained by various plots for assassination.

MAZZINI.

Still, the idea of a free and united Italy constantly gained strength, until even some of the rulers became imbued with it. In 1846, at the election of a new pope, the Austrian candidate was rejected and the Italian cardinals chose Pius IX, a liberal Italian. Many Italians hoped that this potentate would realize ancient dreams and put himself at the head of a federation of Italy; and, for a time, Pius did seem ready to take up this work. In 1846 and 1847 he granted many reforms in the Papal States; and when the revolutions of 1848 broke out in Italy, beginning in Naples in January, he refused to permit Austrian troops to pass through his territory, — the only land route to Naples. But it soon became apparent that he was unwilling to quarrel decisively with Austria; and leadership in the critical struggle passed to Piedmont. The story of Italy in 1848 has been told (§§ 452 ff.). In 1820-1821, the extremities of the peninsula had been convulsed; in 1830, the middle states; in 1848, there was no foot of Italian ground not shaken. The movement failed; but it revealed the fact that "United Italy," once a dream of scattered enthusiasts, was at last a passionate faith in the hearts of a whole people, and it showed one state willing to risk annihilation to carry on the work. From this time, the making of Italy is the history of Piedmont.

459. Victor Emmanuel and Cavour. — The night after the defeat of Novara (§ 453), Charles Albert abdicated, and *Victor Emmanuel II* became King of Sardinia. The young prince was an intense Italian patriot, and a popular story tells how, as he rallied his shattered regiment at the close of the fatal day of Novara and withdrew sullenly from the field, he shook his clenched fist at the Austrian ranks with the vow, "By the Almighty, my Italy yet shall be!"

The new King was at once called upon to stand a sharp test. Sardinia had been completely crushed; and victorious Austria insisted that Victor Emmanuel should abolish the constitution recently given to his country (§ 452). In that event, Austria offered easy terms, and promised military support against any revolt. At the same time the obstinate and inexperienced Sardinian Parliament was embarrassing the King by foolish opposition. But Victor Emmanuel refused the Austrian bribe, declaring indeed that he would rather lose his crown. In consequence, he had to submit to severe terms; but a frank appeal to his people gave him a new loyal Parliament, which ratified the peace, and his conduct won him the title of "the Honest King."

Then, for several years, the King and his great minister, *Cavour*, bent all energies to strengthening Sardinia for another struggle and to securing allies outside Italy. Victor Emmanuel was essentially a soldier. Cavour was the statesman whose brain was to guide the making of Italy. The King's part was loyally and steadily to support him. Exiles and fugitive Liberals from other Italian states were welcomed at the Sardinian court and were often given high office there, so that the government seemed to belong to the whole peninsula; and between 1851 and 1859 Cavour carried through the Parliament many economic, military, and social reforms.[1] Closer trade relations with England and France were adopted, chiefly in order to awaken the interest of those countries; and in 1854 Cavour sent a small but excellent Sardinian army to assist the allies against Russia in the Crimean War (§ 439).

VICTOR EMMANUEL II.

---

[1] In this last work, the government came into conflict with the church. Great numbers of the superabundant monasteries were closed, and the ecclesiastical courts, with their medieval jurisdiction, were abolished; but the church was left to manage its own affairs in its own way. Cavour's motto was, "A free church in a free state."

Mazzini called this action a monstrous moral degradation; and many Liberals, unable to understand Cavour's policy, condemned it bitterly as a political blunder and a crime. The policy had two justifications.

a. The Crimean War, unnecessary as it was, was, after all, in a way a defiance of despotic Russia by more liberal France and England.[1] Italy had special reason to join in this hostile feeling toward Russia: the Tsar had been strongly opposed to the liberal movements of 1848; he had helped to crush Hungary, virtually an ally of Sardinia in the war of that period; and he had even declined to recognize the accession of Victor Emmanuel.

b. Cavour wished to show Europe that Sardinia was a military power, and to secure for her a place in the councils of Europe, so as to obtain foreign intervention for Italy against Austria.

This second reason, of course, was the real motive. The first argument was at best only an excuse. It is interesting to know that the army felt the motive and its importance, though liberal statesmen did not. Said an Italian officer to the soldiers digging in the trenches before Sebastopol, "Of this mud our Italy is to be made."

Possibly the action of Cavour in joining in such a war may lack full justification to the strict moralist; but at all events, it was infinitely less wrong than the policy by which Bismarck was soon to make a new Germany, and it was to be triumphant over greater difficulties even than beset that statesman.

At the Congress of Paris in 1856, Cavour's policy bore fruit. Cavour sat there on full equality with the

CAVOUR.

representatives of the Great Powers, and, despite Austria's protests, he secured attention for a strong statement of the needs of Italy and of her claim upon Europe. Upon all minds it was forcefully impressed *that Italian unrest could never cease so long as Austria remained in the peninsula.*

460. First Step in the Growth of Sardinia into Italy: Annexation of Lombardy. — Three years later, this patient diplomatic

---

[1] This is the explanation in part of the tone of Tennyson's *Maud*, in the passages where this war is mentioned.

game was won. Cavour drew Louis Napoleon into a secret alliance. The exact terms are not known; but, probably in return for a pledge of Nice and Savoy (§ 429) and for a marriage alliance,[1] Napoleon promised to come to the aid of Sardinia if that Power could provoke Austria into beginning a war. Austria was easily inveigled into the attack. Then Napoleon entered Italy, declaring his purpose to free it from the Alps to the Adriatic; and the victories of Magenta and Solferino (§ 429) drove Austria forever out of Lombardy, which was promptly incorporated into Sardinia. *This was the first step in the expansion of Sardinia into Italy.* The population of the growing state had risen at a stroke from five millions to eight.

Venetia remained in Austria's hands, but Napoleon suddenly made peace. Possibly he had reason to fear Prussian interference if the war continued. But the Italians felt that they had been betrayed, and probably they were right. Napoleon had intended a federation of Italy, perhaps in four states, under the Pope's presidency; but the movement for annexation of all Italy to Sardinia was gaining ground fast, and he had no wish to see Italy one strong, consolidated nation.

461. The Second Step: Annexation of the Duchies by Plebiscites. — Despite the bitter disappointment of Italy at the peace, it soon became apparent that more had been accomplished than the mere freeing of Lombardy. At the beginning of the war, the peoples of the duchies had driven out their dukes[2] and set up provisional governments, in order to join Sardinia. At the peace, Napoleon had promised Austria that the dukes should be restored. He had stipulated, however, that Austria should not use force against the duchies; and the people now refused to receive back their old rulers, insisting instead upon incorporation with Sardinia. For eight months this situation continued, while Cavour played a second delicate diplomatic game with Napoleon. Finally it became

---

[1] Victor Emmanuel was persuaded to sacrifice his young daughter by giving her in marriage to the dissolute Prince Napoleon, a relative of Louis Napoleon.

[2] Dependents of Austria; see § 457.

evident that only a foreign army could again place the dukes upon their thrones, and Napoleon was persuaded to leave the matter to a plebiscite, his favorite device in France. Then in March, 1860, the three duchies (Parma, Modena, and Tuscany) by almost unanimous votes [1] declared again for annexation. *This was the second step in expansion.* Sardinia was enlarged once more by one-third, and had now become a state of eleven million people.

462. The Third Step: Garibaldi's Expedition and the Annexation of the Two Sicilies and of Part of the Papal States. — The new state now comprised all Italy north of the Papal districts, except Venetia; but the impulse to annexation was not yet exhausted. The next advance was due in its beginnings to *Garibaldi*, a famous Republican soldier, who had now given his allegiance loyally to Victor Emmanuel. In May, 1860, Garibaldi sailed from Genoa with a thousand fellow-adventurers, to arouse rebellion in Sicily. Cavour secretly favored the expedition, though he thought it needful to make a show of trying to stop it.[2] Garibaldi landed safely in Sicily and won the island almost without bloodshed. Crossing to the mainland he easily occupied Naples also, while the Bourbon King fled.

GARIBALDI.

Obeying a popular demand, Garibaldi proclaimed Victor Emmanuel "King of Italy," and then he planned to seize

---

[1] In Tuscany the vote stood 366,571 to 14,925; and this was the largest adverse vote.

[2] It is said that Cavour secretly furnished guns and money. When the expedition was under way, Cavour issued a diplomatic note expressing his regret; but the admiral of the Sardinian fleet says that he received instructions, which, while ambiguous, really meant that he should protect Garibaldi from the Neapolitan navy.

Rome. Such a move would have brought on intervention from both Austria and France, and would have put at hazard all that had been gained. Cavour was forced to hurried action. An understanding was reached with Napoleon; and Victor Emmanuel with the Sardinian army moved south, occupying Naples and checking Garibaldi's mad march. Rome and the surrounding territory was left to the Pope; but the Marches and Umbria (the eastern part of the Papal States) were allowed, with the Kingdom of Naples, to vote on the question of annexation to Sardinia. The vote was even more unanimous than that in the duchies had been.

These additions made the third step in the expansion of Sardinia into Italy. The new state now comprised all the peninsula except Rome and Venetia; and it reached continuously from the Alps to Sicily. This time the population was raised from eleven to twenty-two millions. In February, 1861, the first Italian Parliament met at Turin and enthusiastically confirmed the establishment of the "Kingdom of Italy." Cavour's statesmanship was triumphant. The Italy he had labored for was made, and in this first Parliament of the new nation an opposition party to the great minister hardly raised its head. Five months later, Cavour was dead. His achievements rank as perhaps the most marvelous in all modern statesmanship.

463. Fourth and Fifth Steps: Venetia and Rome (1866 and 1870). — The acquisition of the two remaining provinces was to be intertwined with the making of Germany (§§ 467 ff.). Here we need only note that Italy joined Prussia in war against Austria in 1866, and received Venetia as her reward. Then in 1870, when the Franco-Prussian war began, Napoleon recalled the French troops from Rome, and, despite the vehement protest of the Pope, Italy quietly took possession of her ancient capital (§ 490).

For Further Reading. — Bolton King's *Italian Unity* is the best single work. Good accounts will be found in Probyn's *Italy*, Bolton King's *Mazzini*, Dicey's *Victor Emmanuel*, or Cesaresco's *Cavour*. Andrews, Seignobos, Phillips, Fyffe, and Murdock all contain brief treatments.

Special Report. — Garibaldi's life.

GROWTH OF ITALIAN UNITY, 1859-1860.

III. THE UNIFICATION OF GERMANY.

464. William I of Prussia, and the Army. — In Germany the years from 1850 to 1861 were barren of political results. It had become plain that the only nucleus for a German nation was Prussia, but from Prussia nothing could be expected as long as Frederick William IV reigned. In 1861 that prince was succeeded by his brother, *William I.*[1] The preceding eleven years had seen the making of Italy: the next ten were to see the making of Germany, — and incidentally the rounding out of Italy.

William I, destined to become the most revered of German kings, was the prince who had been banished for a time in 1848 to satisfy the Liberals (§ 454). That party hated him for his open opposition to political reform, and they had nicknamed him "Prince Cartridge." He was a Conservative of the old school, and he had bitterly opposed the mild constitutional concessions of his brother; but he was also a patriot to the core. He tingled with indignation at the humiliation of Olmütz; and he was determined that Prussia should never again have to suffer such disgrace. He hoped, too, with all his heart, for German unity; and he believed that this unity could be made only by force, and only after the expulsion of Austria from Germany. He had been known mainly as a brave soldier and an Ultra-conservative, but he was to prove a strong, sagacious, practical, statesmanlike sovereign, and a larger factor in uniting Germany than Victor Emmanuel had been in making Italy.

The Prussian army differed from all others in Europe. Elsewhere the armies were of the old class, — standing bodies of mercenaries and professional soldiers, reënforced at need by raw, undisciplined levies from the population. The Napoleonic wars had resulted in a different system for Prussia.

---

[1] William had already been regent for two years. Frederick William had become hopelessly insane in 1859.

In 1807, after Jena, in order to keep Prussia helpless, Napoleon had required her to reduce her army to forty-two thousand men. The Prussian government, however, had evaded Napoleon's purpose, by passing fresh bodies of Prussians through the regiments at short intervals, — dismissing a part of each regiment after two years' service and filling the places with new levies, who in turn took on regular military discipline, while those who had passed out were held as a reserve. After the Napoleonic wars were over, Prussia retained this system. The design was to make the entire male population a trained army; but until the time of William I the plan had not been fully followed up. Since 1815, population had doubled, but the army had been left upon the basis of that period. No arrangements had been made for organizing new regiments; and so twenty-five thousand men each year reached military age without being summoned into the ranks. King William's first efforts were directed to correct this condition by increasing the number of regiments and by rearranging the term of service.

To do these things required a large increase in taxes. But the Prussian Parliament was jealous of military power in the hands of a sovereign so hostile to constitutional liberty, and it resolutely refused the needed grants of money. Then William found a minister to carry out his will, Parliament or no. This man, who was to be the German Cavour, was *Otto von Bismarck*.

465. Bismarck and the Parliament. — Thirteen years earlier, Count Bismarck had been known as a grim and violent leader of the "Junkers," the extreme conservative party, made up of young landed aristocrats. He held at that time, in words at least, to the doctrine of the divine right of kings; and now, after the conflict between the King and Parliament, when Bismarck was announced as the head of a new ministry, the Liberals prophesied a *coup d'état*. Something like a *coup d'état* did take place. The Prussian constitution declared that the ministers must be "responsible" to the Landtag or

Parliament; but this did not mean responsible in the modern English sense: that is, it did not mean that they must resign if outvoted, but only that they might be held to account for their actions. The Prussian Parliament consisted of a chamber of representatives and an upper house of nobles. Bismarck now invented the novel theory, that, if the two houses did not agree, the King and the upper house could govern and even raise taxes, without the consent of the representative chamber; and for four years he ruled and collected taxes without a legal budget.

Over and over again, the Landtag demanded Bismarck's dismissal, and many violent scenes took place. The Liberals threatened to hang him, — as very probably they would have done if power had fallen to them by another revolution,[1] — and, unable to do that, they challenged him repeatedly to duels. Bismarck in turn railed at the Liberals contemptuously as "mere pedants," and told them bluntly that the making of Germany was to be "a matter not of speechifying and parliamentary majorities, but of blood and iron"; and he grimly went on, muzzling the press, bullying or dissolving Parliaments, and overriding the national will roughshod. Meantime, the army was greatly augmented and many times multiplied in efficiency. First of any large army, it was supplied with the new invention of breech-loading, repeating rifles, instead of the old-fashioned muzzle-loaders, and it was made the most perfectly organized military machine in Europe.

From the first, Bismarck had intended that this reconstructed army should expel Austria from Germany and force the princes of the rest of Germany into a true national union. Of course it had not been possible for him to avow his purpose; but time was growing precious, and he began to look anxiously for a chance to use his new tool. By a series of master-strokes of unscrupulous and daring diplomacy, he

---

[1] The Liberals were fond of comparing the King and Bismarck to Charles I of England and Strafford (§ 243).

brought on three wars in the next seven years, — the Danish War (1864), the Six Weeks' War with Austria (1866), and the Franco-Prussian War (1870–1871). Out of these war-clouds emerged a new Germany.

466. The Schleswig-Holstein Question and the Danish War. — The southern part of the Danish peninsula was not included in the Kingdom of Denmark, but was known as the Duchy of Schleswig. Adjoining it, at the base of the peninsula, lay the Duchy of Holstein. Schleswig was partly Danish, partly German in character; Holstein was almost wholly German. For centuries the duchies had experienced varying political fortunes, — sometimes Danish possessions, sometimes German, sometimes divided between the two countries, — but the Congress of Vienna had left them both attached to the Danish crown. They were not, however, made part of Denmark; the union was purely "personal"; that is, the King of Denmark was also Duke in Schleswig-Holstein. Holstein, indeed, was one of the states of the Germanic Confederation.

The Danes, of course, tried to consolidate the duchies with Denmark and to introduce the Danish law and language. The German population resisted, and rose gallantly in attempt after attempt at independence. Naturally, the sympathies of the German race went out to them in their aspirations for nationality; and for many years the Schleswig-Holstein Question had been the danger-point in European politics.[1] In 1863, the crisis became acute. The King of Denmark died without direct male heirs. The new Danish King inherited the crown through a woman, but the law of the duchies did not recognize succession through females. The Danes, of course, claimed that their new King was the ruler of the duchies also; but those states called to their ducal throne a petty German prince who was the heir under their law. The Diet of the German Confederacy sanctioned this position; but the Congress of Vienna had certainly intended the union with Denmark to be permanent, and, after this coming complication had been clearly foreseen, the Danish claim had been again confirmed, in 1853, by a Congress of the Powers at London.

The new Danish king complicated matters still further by publishing a new constitution for Schleswig, incorporating it in Denmark. Then, Bismarck stepped in, ignoring all the conflicting claims, to secure the

---

[1] Lord Palmerston, the great English Prime Minister, had called it "the match that would yet set Europe on fire," and Metternich had styled it "the bone on which the Germans whet their teeth." The subject has become proverbial for obscurity. Good brief accounts are to be found in Headlam's *Bismarck* and in Munro Smith's *Bismarck*.

duchies for Prussia, who had no claim at all. The scheme would have been impossible to a scrupulous statesman, and hopeless to a less dauntless one. Bismarck, however, felt no moral hesitation, and he had skillfully guarded against interference by the Powers. Russia he had conciliated by aiding her a few months before to put down a Polish rebellion, so that, in gratitude, the Tsar was willing to give him a free hand; Napoleon III would not interfere because, as Bismarck afterward said, he "had been allowed to deceive himself" into thinking that France would be permitted to annex Rhine territory to "indemnify" her for Prussia's proposed gain; England would not fight unsupported; and Austria, the natural ally of Denmark,[1] Bismarck had made his accomplice. In 1864, the Prussian and Austrian armies entered the duchies. Despite the gallant resistance of the Danes, the war was quickly concluded, and the fate of the two duchies was left to be fixed by the conquerors.

467. The Six Weeks' War with Austria. — Bismarck intended next to force Austria into war over the division of the spoils, and so attain his great end of excluding her from German affairs. He virtually claimed both duchies for Prussia, and, though at Austria's indignant protest a system of joint protection was temporarily arranged, it was plain that the Prussian minister meant to secure all the booty for his country.

King William, however, had scruples. He was quite willing to fight Austria, but he wanted a just cause. Bismarck was driven to new wiles in order to gain William's approval. Strangely enough, Austria was now trying the experiment of constitutional government (§ 491), and her administration in Holstein was liberal, while Prussia's military rule in Schleswig was despotic. The Holsteiners held public meetings to express sympathy for their oppressed fellow-subjects, and so gave Bismarck a chance to arouse William's prejudices against Austria, by representing her as a source of revolutionary danger. The feeling between the two states became bitter. Bismarck drew Italy into an alliance by which that country promised to join in an attack upon Austria, in order

---

[1] Of course, it was to Austria's interest to keep Denmark as strong as possible, in order to check Prussian aggression.

to secure Venetia. Negotiations dragged on, however, and the Austrian government showed itself so conciliatory, that it won the sympathy of the other German rulers. Bismarck continued to make demands which he knew could not be granted; and when summoned by the Diet to refer the matters in dispute to that body (as indeed the constitution of the Confederation required), he replied by a proposal for a wholly new confederation which should exclude Austria. The Diet rejected the proposition, and prepared for war against Prussia as "the wanton disturber of the national peace." Then, June 14, 1866, war was declared between Austria and Prussia.

There followed a marvelous display of military energy. Except for a few small states north of the Main, all Germany adhered to Austria; but in three days, Prussia had occupied Hanover, Hesse, and Saxony; and July 4, Austria was overthrown at *Sadowa*,[1] in Bohemia, and lay at the mercy of the conqueror.

468. The Peace of Prague: Prussian Preponderance in Germany; the North German Confederation. — Out of the Six Weeks' War came a real German State such as had never before been seen, except faintly in the twelfth century. This result was embodied in the *Peace of Prague* and the other treaties which closed the war. These treaties gave Venetia to Italy (§ 463) and required the payment of war indemnities by Austria and her South German allies;[2] but the really significant provisions lay (1) *in the augmentation of Prussia* and (2) *in the reorganization of Germany*.

a. Prussia annexed Hesse, Hanover, Nassau, and the former free city of Frankfort, besides the Schleswig-Holstein duchies with the magnificent harbor of Kiel. These acquisitions

---

[1] Sadowa, or Königgrätz, is one of the greatest battles in history, both from its significance and from the size of the armies engaged. Nearly a half-million men stood in the opposing lines.

[2] The South German states were let off easily, however, because Bismarck wished to draw them soon into friendly relations with Prussia. Cf. § 469.

enlarged Prussia by one half, making a state of thirty millions of people, with overwhelming preponderance in Germany.[1]

b. Austria definitely withdrew from German affairs, and the other German states were reorganized. The Confederation of 1815 was replaced by two federations. The first is known as *The North German Federation.* This union was placed under Prussian presidency. It was not a loose league like the old Confederacy, but a true federal state, with essentially the same constitution as the present German Empire, which replaced it four years later (§ 471). The second federation was to include the four South German states, — Bavaria, Wurtemberg, Hesse-Darmstadt, and Baden. This union was intended to be similar to the old Confederacy of 1815 (of which, indeed, it was a temporary survival), but no organization was really effected (§ 470).

469. Steps toward Further Union. — As soon as Bismarck's determination to fight Austria had become plain, the liberal opposition in Prussia had been hushed; and after Sadowa he found himself the idol of the Prussian people, while the Landtag enthusiastically passed the act of indemnity he requested for his previous illegal acts. This hearty support made it easier for him to complete his work. The South German states were yet to be brought into the more complete North German union; and this consummation was secured by Bismarck through the third of his wars, — the contest with France in 1870–1871.

Before the war, however, two important steps toward union were taken. (1) In 1868, a *Customs Parliament,* representing all Germany, north and south alike, organized a national

---

[1] When Prussia became a kingdom, in 1701, her population was about one and a half millions. Frederick II received the state with a population of two and a half millions, and it was doubled during his reign. By 1815, it had been doubled once more. In the next fifty years, 1815–1866, without territorial growth, the population had risen from ten to twenty millions. The Six Weeks' War added a half more. Compare the map opposite with that on page 297.

GROWTH OF
PRUSSIA
1815-1871
SCALE OF MILES
0 20 40 60 80 100
Prussia 1807-1813
Territory recovered in 1815
New Acquisitions 1815
Acquisitions of William I
NORTH SEA
BALTIC SEA
DENMARK
SWEDEN
NETHERLANDS
BELGIUM
FRANCE
POLAND
RUSSIA
AUSTRIA-HUNGARY
BOHEMIA
MORAVIA
GALICIA
SAXONY
BAVARIA
HANOVER
SCHLESWIG-HOLSTEIN 1866
GRAND DUCHY OF MECKLENBURG
SCHWERIN
STRELITZ
POMERANIA
PROVINCE OF WEST PRUSSIA
PROVINCE OF EAST PRUSSIA
POSEN
SILESIA
BRANDENBURG
WESTPHALIA 1815
RHENISH PROVINCES 1815
ELECTORATE OF HESSE CASSEL
THURINGIAN STATES
UPPER LAUSITZ
LOWER LAUSITZ
From SAXONY 1815
LIPPE
BRUNSWICK
OLDENBURG
PALATINATE
GR. DUCHY OF BADEN
HELGOLAND
BORNHOLM (Den.)
RÜGEN
Berlin
Königsberg
Danzig
Stettin
Breslau
Warsaw
Copenhagen
Hamburg
Lübeck
Hannover
Frankfort
Leipzig
Dresden
Prague
Cologne
Vistula R.

Customs Union, and so joined all Germans into one nation commercially.[1] (2) Secret treaties bound the South German states to Prussia in a military league against France.

This last arrangement was a diplomatic victory for Bismarck over Napoleon III. Napoleon had been outwitted in both the preceding wars. After the Danish war, he had failed to get Belgium or Luxemburg, one of which he had expected Prussia to help him secure; but when the Six Weeks' War drew on, he thought his chance had come. France would remain neutral at first, but would be ready to strike, and at the critical moment she would step in and save the vanquished. Napoleon did not doubt that the vanquished would be Prussia; and, as the price of his protection, he expected to compel Prussia to help him to the coveted Rhine territory. But the war was over, and over the other way, before the French armies were ready to act. Napoleon had lost his chance; but he then weakly tried negotiation. He suggested secretly to Bismarck, that, to offset Prussia's annexations, France be allowed to annex part of Bavaria (one of Prussia's opponents in the war), in which case France would allow Bismarck to remodel Germany at will. Bismarck did not need the consent of France. Indeed, war with France was the next move decided on in his game,[2] and this proposal simply delivered Napoleon into his hands: he revealed it to the South German states, and so terrified them into secret but hearty alliance with Prussia.

470. The Franco-Prussian War: the German Empire. — The French people looked with rage upon the growth of a German nation upon their frontier, and were clamoring for war in order to undo it. Bismarck saw that a successful war with France

---

[1] This was the outgrowth of a Prussian Customs Union, which had been growing among the North German states for over forty years. "All Germany," of course, no longer included Austria. This Customs Parliament was chosen by manhood suffrage, and indeed consisted of the regular Reichsrath of the North German Confederation, in special session, with delegates from the South German states added to it.

[2] Bismarck wrote afterwards, "That a war with France would succeed that with Austria lay in the logic of history."

would fuse the two German federations; and this war he hurried on with characteristic craft, for which the envy and military vanity of France and the desperation of Napoleon's government gave him only too much opportunity.

The immediate occasion grew out of a proposal of the Spaniards to place upon their throne Leopold of Hohenzollern, a German prince and a distant relative of King William of Prussia. Napoleon called upon William to prevent this, urging that such augmentation of Hohenzollern power would be dangerous to the peace of Europe. Officially William declined to interfere; but privately he did induce his relative to decline the offered crown. Napoleon, however, was bent upon humiliating William; and the French ambassador insisted that William should give a definite pledge that the offer, if renewed, would not be accepted. King William very properly declined to do this; but his refusal, though firm, was so courteous that there was no cause for offense. That

BISMARCK.

night, however, Bismarck sent out reports of the interview so colored as to represent that the King had insulted the French envoy.[1] As Bismarck hoped, France took fire, and war was promptly declared.

Twelve days after the declaration of war, Germany had put one and a quarter million of trained troops into the field and had massed most of them on the Rhine. The world had never seen such marvelous perfection of military preparation. As Carlyle wrote, "It took away the breath of Europe." August 2 the Emperor took command at Mainz. September 2

---

[1] Anderson's *Constitutions and Documents* gives in parallel columns the King's original "Ems Dispatch" and Bismarck's version of it.

The Proclamation of the German Empire at Versailles, January 18, 1871.

the only important French army in the field was defeated and captured at Sedan, and Napoleon was a prisoner.

The story of the later course of the war has already been told (§ 433). What we care to note here is the effect upon Germany. The popular enthusiasm of the South Germans for the war, and for Prussia as the champion for Germany, led rapidly to a series of treaties by which the South German states[1] entered the North German Federation. Then the King of Bavaria and other German rulers invited William I to take the title of German Emperor; and, on January 18, while the siege of Paris was still in progress, in the ancient palace of the French kings at Versailles, William formally assumed that name. A few months later, a Parliament of all Germany ratified a constitution for the new *German Empire*.

471. The Moral Question. — The story of the making of Germany shows plainly enough that the process was one not only of "blood and iron," but also of fraud and falsehood. It is hard to tell the story of such gigantic and successful audacity and craft without seeming to glorify it. It is to be remembered, of course, that Bismarck did not work for personal or low ends, nor for merely Prussian ends, but that he was inspired by a true and broad patriotism. Only through

WILLIAM I OF PRUSSIA.

---

[1] Those states secured some slight concessions not enjoyed by most of the states in the union.

such a national union as he accomplished could the German people reach to the better elements in modern life. At the same time, Bismarck's success has tended, too probably, to lower the tone of international morality; and his policy of fraud and violence has left to Germany a legacy of burning questions which will grieve it long. The rule of the drill-sergeant and of the police officer in modern Germany, the hostility to the Empire felt by the Danes of Schleswig and the French of Alsace-Lorraine, the bitter jealousy between Prussia and Bavaria, and the immense armies of all Europe are among the results of his policy. It is too early yet to say that that policy is truly victorious. (Cf. §§ 479–481, 483, 487.)

FOR FURTHER READING. — Seignobos, Phillips, Andrews, Fyffe, Henderson, as before. Murdock's *Reconstruction* gives a readable account of this period. Headlam's *Bismarck*, and his *Germany, 1815–1889*, and Munroe-Smith's *Bismarck*, are excellent and scholarly.

IV. GERMANY SINCE 1871.

A. THE CONSTITUTION.

472. A Federal State made up of Monarchic Units. — The Germanic Confederation (1815–1867) was a confederacy of sovereign states, a union even weaker than that of our American states under our Articles of Confederation. The present German Empire is a true federal state, like our present union. It has this peculiarity, however: it is the only strong federal state in history made up of monarchies. Of the twenty-five states composing the Empire, four are kingdoms (Prussia, Bavaria, Saxony, Wurtemberg); eighteen more are duchies, grand duchies, or principalities; and only three are republican in character, — the city-republics, Bremen, Hamburg, and Lübeck.

473. The Emperor is not in theory a ruler, but rather a *president* of the federation.[1] The presidency is hereditary, however, in the kings of Prussia.[2]

---

[1] His title was carefully guarded: he is not called "Emperor of Germany," but "German Emperor."

[2] Somewhat as if the governor of New York were ex-officio president of the United States.

The Emperor cannot be impeached. He has extensive power of patronage, and almost absolute control over foreign relations. He has no veto upon imperial legislation, though his overwhelming influence in the Federal Council almost amounts to that power (§ 474). His chief authority in the Empire comes from the fact that he is master of Prussia. That state is larger and more powerful than all the rest of the union put together, and its constitution leaves its king almost an absolute monarch within its territory.

474. The Bundesrath. — *The sovereignty* of the Empire is vested in a *Federal Council,* or *Bundesrath.* This body consists of fifty-six delegates *appointed by the sovereigns* of the different states in fixed proportions. Prussia has seventeen; seventeen small states have one each; and the other seven states have from two to six each.

The Bundesrath is not a mere upper house of a legislature, like our Senate, though it has great control over legislation.[1] Its powers are executive rather than legislative, and it does not go through legislative forms. It looks after the administration, prepares most of the measures for the law-making body (the Reichstag, § 475), and it has a veto upon all laws passed by that body. It has been called the "Diet of the old Confederacy, with powers enlarged."

475. The National Legislature is the *Reichstag.* It consists of one house. The members are elected by manhood suffrage, in single districts, like our congressmen, for a term of five years. There are three hundred and ninety-seven delegates, of which Prussia has two hundred and thirty-six.

The constitution calls for a periodic reapportionment of representatives, to suit changes in population: but so far (to 1904) there has been none. (The United States, of course, has had three reapportionments of congressmen within this period.) The following table shows the distribution of representatives in the Reichstag. The eleven states not named have one representative each.

---

[1] The Bundesrath can be said to be part of the legislature only in the sense in which Elizabeth or Henry VIII of England might have been called part of the English legislature, or an American president (for his veto power) part of the American legislature.

Prussia	236	Hesse	9	Saxe-Weimar	3
Bavaria	48	Mecklenburg-Schwerin	6	Saxe-Meiningen	2
Saxony	23	Oldenburg	3	Saxe-Coburg	2
Wurtemberg	17	Brunswick	3	Anhalt	2
Baden	14	Hamburg	3	Alsace-Lorraine[1]	15

The power of the Reichstag is much less than the American student would at first expect in a national legislature. It can introduce bills, but they are not likely to receive the approval of the Bundesrath unless they were originally submitted from that body. Thus, practically, the Reichstag is limited to accepting or rejecting Bundesrath measures. Even its control over taxation is incomplete, because most revenue measures, instead of being annual appropriations, are standing laws: that is, once passed, they remain in force until changed; and they can be changed only with the consent of the Bundesrath. At the same time, debates in the Reichstag are highly important as expressions of national desires, and they have a special value in a country like Germany, where all other methods of expression of opinion are subject to rigid police control (§ 481).

476. The Imperial Ministry is appointed by the Emperor. Its most important member is the *Chancellor*. Ministers are declared responsible; but this is in the Prussian, not in the English sense. They are not obliged to resign if outvoted in the Reichstag.

477. Amendments to the constitution are made just as ordinary laws are passed, except that fourteen negative votes in the Bundesrath are enough to veto a proposal. Thus the king of Prussia alone, or the small states alone, or the South German states alone, can prevent change.

478. The Constitutions of Prussia and of the Other States. — The important elements in the imperial constitution are the Emperor and the Bundesrath; and these depend for their character on the constitutions of the different states. Of these states Prussia is the most important. Her population is three-fifths

---

[1] Alsace is not a state and has no vote in the Bundesrath; it is an "imperial territory," but it was given representation in the Reichstag in 1874.

THE GERMAN EMPIRE
since 1871

1. *Schwarzburg-Sondershausen*
2. *Saxe-Coburg-Gotha*
3. *Saxe-Weimar*
4. *Saxe-Altenburg*
5. *Saxe-Meiningen*

that of the whole Empire; her king is Emperor; her representative in the ministry is usually Chancellor; and in general her military and political system is extended as far as possible throughout the Empire.

The Prussian constitution to-day is the one granted by Frederick William IV in 1850. In the view of many German writers, it maintains the doctrine of divine right, and the royal authority is limited only by its own consent. The legislature (Landtag) consists of a House of Lords and a House of Representatives. All males have a vote in the election of the lower house; but they vote in three orders, in such a way as to give two-thirds of the representation to the wealthiest one-sixth of the voters.[1]

The authority of the legislature is limited. The king may adjourn or dissolve it, and he keeps an absolute veto. In practice he has the initiative in legislation, and the ministry is not compelled to resign if outvoted. Prussia and England are both constitutional monarchies, but the student must not be misled by the likeness of name. They stand at the two extremes of such government: England is almost or quite a democracy; Prussia is almost as autocratic as Russia.

The constitutions of the other states vary in considerable degree, but few of them give the representative legislature any real control over the administration, as in England or in France. Usually, too, the franchise rests upon property qualifications, and everywhere the officials come from the aristocratic classes. In general, however, South Germany is less military and more democratic than Prussia and North Germany.

B. The Government in Operation.

479. Paternal Despotism, Police Rule, Militarism. — The German government is honest and frugal, and it is paternal in the

---

[1] The threefold division is based upon wealth, and the wealthiest class (153,808 voters) elect as many representatives as the poorer class (2,591,950 voters). In the city of Berlin, a rich man's vote counts for that of fifty poor men. This applies, of course, to Prussian elections only. In imperial elections, manhood suffrage exists.

extreme. Justice between man and man is easy to obtain; land-transfer is cheap; food-adulteration is carefully guarded against; the public health is zealously protected. But at the same time, alongside this kindly and watchful paternalism, there are grievous faults. Germany has been made by violence, and the result still shows in the spirit of militarism and in the predominance of the methods of the drill-sergeant and the policeman. No other state with so high a civilization is so infected with these evils.[1] A policeman's evidence in a court is equal to that of five independent witnesses and his rule is all-pervading. Says a somewhat hostile English critic (in the *Contemporary Review* for February, 1896): —

> The policeman strolls into your house or garden when he likes, much as a master enters the class-room to see that all is going on properly. He will count the caterpillars in your garden and summon you if he finds too many of them. If you go for a bath, he will forbid you to get out of your depth, swim you never so strongly. In fine, half schoolmaster, half nurse, he will supervise your every action, from the cradle to the grave, with a military sternness and inflexibility which robs you of all independence and reduces you to the level of a mere plastic item. To live in Germany always seems to me like a return to the nursery.

Even worse is the contemptuous and oftentimes brutal treatment of civilians by army officers. For years the papers have abounded with reports of gross and unprovoked insults, and sometimes of violent assaults by officers upon unoffending citizens, for which the courts afford no redress.

480. The Emperors, and their Attitude toward Constitutionalism. — At his coronation, *William I* took the crown from the communion table, declaring, "The crown comes only from God, and I have received it from His hands." William never modified this conception of kingship, although he allowed Bismarck to coquette with liberalism at times, when that policy suited the Chancellor's ends. In an election manifesto of 1882, the

---

[1] Some writers claim that these features of German society are due to the position of Germany, without natural frontiers, between great military states. To some extent, this geographical condition may explain the devotion of the Germans to their army.

Emperor reminded all officials that "the duty which you have sworn to perform [in the oath of office] extends to supporting the policy of the government at the elections."

In 1888, William was succeeded by his son, *Frederick III.* Frederick was an admirer of parliamentary government upon the English [1] pattern, and he had long been hostile to Bismarck; but he was suffering from a fatal disease at the time of his accession, and his three months' reign brought no change in the government.

William II, the son of Frederick, returned to the principles of his grandfather. As a youth, he had been a great admirer of Bismarck; but it soon became plain that the two men were each too masterful to work together, and in 1890 the Emperor curtly dismissed the Chancellor from office. Since that time, William II has himself directed the policy of the Empire, and he has been a greater force in European politics than any other sovereign in Europe. He believes thoroughly in the "divine right" theory, and he has repeatedly stated it [2] in as striking a

---

[1] Frederick's wife was Victoria, daughter of the great English Queen.

[2] Perhaps the Emperor's most concise statement is the sentence he wrote in the Visitors' Book in the Town Hall of Munich, "The will of the king is the supreme law." In 1890, in an address to a body of instructors upon the proper teaching of history, he told his hearers that they should teach that the French Revolution was "an unmitigated crime against God and man." In 1891, in an address to a body of military recruits, he said: "You are now my soldiers. You have given yourselves to me, body and soul. There is now but one enemy for you, and that is *my* enemy. In these times of socialistic intrigue, it may happen that I shall order you to fire upon your brothers or fathers. God save us from it! But in such a case you are bound to obey me without a murmur!" In 1897, the Emperor, in a prepared address, set forth at length his office as a "vice-regent of God"; and the same year, his brother Henry, when about to set sail for China, in command of a German expedition, used the following words in a public address to the Emperor: "Of one thing I can assure Your Majesty. Neither fame nor laurels have charm for me. One thing is the aim that draws me on: it is to declare in foreign lands the *evangel of Your Majesty's hallowed person,* — to preach it to every one who will hear it, and also to those who will not hear it. . . . This gospel I have inscribed on my banner, and I will inscribe it whithersoever I go." Other illustrations of this character can be found in a curious and authentic volume, *The Kaiser's Speeches,* published by Harpers in 1903.

form as it was ever put by James I of England or Louis XIV of France.

481. Insecurity of Personal Rights. — The imperial constitution contains a *bill of rights*, but the courts have no power to declare void an unconstitutional law. The administration, too, can appeal cases in which it is interested to *administrative courts without juries*.[1] As a result, trial by jury, freedom of the press, freedom of public meetings, and free speech exist only in a limited degree.[2] To criticise the Emperor in the press, ever so lightly, is likely to land the offender in jail for a considerable term, through prosecution for *lèse-majesté*. In January, 1898, it was reported on good authority that seventy German editors were in jail for that offense.

C. Recent Movements.

Since the formation of the Empire, the chief features in German development have been the kulturkampf, the determination of the government to enlarge the army and navy, the rapid increase in commercial activity, an aggressive colonial policy, and the growth of Socialism. The only one of these movements which has come to an end is the kulturkampf; and possibly in that one the peace is only a truce.

482. The Kulturkampf. — The new Empire had brought together Catholic and Protestant states; and this contact resulted in a serious conflict between church and state. The immediate outbreak came in connection with a famous decree of the Vatican Council of 1870, affirming the Pope to be infallible in

---

[1] Read Lowell, *Governments and Parties*, I, 282-285 and 294-297. Russell's *Social Democracy*, 48-50, gives an interesting account of a famous trial of Lassalle (§ 485).

[2] The following anecdote illustrates how limited is the right of public meeting. In 1897, a landed proprietor gave a harvest festival for his workmen. Some fifty in all, they marched to a wood and had a picnic. A few days later the proprietor and several of the men were arrested on the charge of having held a public meeting without notifying the police. No other fault was alleged, but the offenders were sentenced to fines or short terms in jail. The treatment of Socialists and others, who systematically oppose the government's policy, will be noted in § 485.

matters of faith and morals. The German bishops at the Council refused to assent to the new statement of the doctrine, and withdrew in a body, but within a year they had for the most part fallen into line. Some of the German Catholics, however, maintained their position and took the name of *Old Catholics*. This sect was soon attacked vigorously by the orthodox bishops. Instructors in the clerical schools who did not teach the dogma of infallibility were suspended from their offices and excommunicated; teachers in the primary schools were dismissed; and the orthodox clergy refused to perform the marriage ceremony for Old Catholics.

Then Bismarck stepped in for the defense of the Old Catholics; and apparently he was not altogether sorry for so good an occasion to assert the supremacy of the state over the church. For some months the conflict raged bitterly; and, to wage it better, Bismarck allied himself with the Liberals in Parliament. In May, 1873, a series of laws was passed, known later as the "May Laws": marriage and all education, private and public, were taken from the church and placed under the control of the state; the Jesuits were expelled; the state assumed control over the education of priests; and the church was forbidden to exclude its own members except with government permission.

The bishops and orthodox clergy formally refused to obey these laws. Then Bismarck fell back upon a series of violent measures. Priests were deprived of office and were refused their salaries, and were even punished by long terms of imprisonment or by exile. The Pope protested, and in 1875 he declared that the May Laws ought not to be obeyed. The Empire had already withdrawn its ambassador from the papal court, and Bismarck had appealed confidently to German national feeling in his boast, "We shall not go to Canossa" (§ 74). The government now confiscated ecclesiastical salaries and took into its own hands all the property and revenues of the church, at the same time expelling from Prussia all Catholic religious orders.

These measures have been described as having a military character, — "designed to cut off the enemy from his commissariat and to deprive him of his most active troops." Certainly there is a reminder of the "blood and iron" policy in all the story; but such a policy was not suited to internal problems. From 1875 to 1879, it is true, the government held its position. One-fifth the parishes in Prussia had no clergy; schools and seminaries were closed; chairs of theology in the German universities were vacant; houses of the clergy were raided by the police; and numbers of men of devoted Christian lives and broad scholarship languished in prison or in exile. But this persecution was ineffective against the heroic resistance of the clergy, and it steadily lost favor among the people. A strong and growing party in the Reichstag, "*the Center*," hampered all Bismarck's projects; and finally he was forced to make terms with it, in order to secure the legislation he desired against the Socialists and for tariffs. In 1880, the government began its retreat; and, if it did not "go to Canossa," it abandoned step by step every position it had assumed in the quarrel. The chief result of the contest to-day is the large, watchful Conservative party, "the Center."

483. The Prussian Army System (§ 464) has been extended all over Germany. The fundamental principle is *the universal obligation* of all adult males to serve. The army is the armed nation. At twenty, each man is supposed to enter the ranks for two years' *active service*. For four years more he serves in the *active reserves*, with two months each year in camp. This takes the soldier to his twenty-seventh year. For twelve years more he forms part of the *territorial reserve*, or army of defense (Landwehr). The army on a peace footing comprises those who are undergoing the two years' service. In case of war, this body and the active reserves are ready for offensive operations, while the territorial reserves form garrisons and guard lines of communication. In case of actual invasion, all other males between seventeen and forty-five, or the *army of emergency* (Landsturm), are called out. In 1901 the German army on a peace footing counted 580,023 men under arms. In case of war, Germany could put nearly four million veterans into the field.

This system constitutes an enormous burden; but the Prussian victories in 1866 and in 1870 convinced all Europe of its military utility, and since 1870 every state in Europe has adopted it, with slight modifications as to the number of years' service. Thus Europe is a group of armed camps. The tax involved in giving so large a part of each man's best years to camp life weighs heavily upon the civilized world. England, relying on her navy, and the United States, trusting to her position, are the only great countries that are now free from it. No doubt, certain good results come from the military discipline; but, on the whole, the present European army system is the most woeful and immense waste of energy that the world ever saw, and the great problem of the future is to get rid of it (§ 594).

As a matter of fact, it is not possible to bring every man into the ranks. Exemption is allowed in Germany to the only son of a widow, to theological students, to those weakened by physical defects, and in some other cases. Moreover, young men who have passed through the higher educational institutions are allowed to get off with only one year's service in the ranks. As population grows, new legislation is called for, from time to time, to create and support new regiments, into which to draft the increased number of recruits. In default of such legislation, considerable numbers liable to service must escape. The contests over the successive "army bills" have been among the liveliest features of the Reichstag history, but so far (1904) the government has always had its way.

484. Trade and Colonies. — The sudden emergence in Central Europe of a powerful nation of fifty-six millions of people, with the most powerful army in the world, out of fragmentary and helpless states, compelled, of course, the recasting of all old political alliances (§ 583); but it soon appeared that the new Germany was to be hardly less a factor in revolutionizing trade relations. The old Germany had been essentially an agricultural country, and its foreign trade had been of little consequence. After 1880, German manufactures, encouraged by the government, mounted by great leaps, and the label "Made in Germany" began to appear on all sorts of articles in all parts of the globe. Before 1900 Germany had passed all other nations except England and America in manufactures and trade, and the economic contest between these three peoples is growing increasingly close.

German population increases rapidly. In 1815, the states in the present German Empire had a population of twenty-five millions. In 1900, the number was over fifty-six millions. This increase has resulted in a large German emigration, which has gone mainly to the United States and to South America. Partly to secure commercial advantages for her citizens abroad, and partly in hopes of keeping future German emigrants under the German flag, the government has recently adopted the policy of acquiring colonies.

Bismarck announced this plan in 1884. At that time, Germany had no possessions outside of Europe; but, though she was late in entering the nineteenth century scramble for foreign possessions, she has made rapid progress. In Africa, she has vast possessions, nearly a million square miles in all, mainly on the Guinea coast and in the southwest and southeast. In the western Pacific, she owns several groups of valuable islands.[1] Shortly after 1890, she began acquiring concessions in Asia Minor from the Turkish government; and this rich region, so long abandoned to barbarism, is perhaps to be the most important field for German enterprise in the near future.[2] But in 1897, another field opened, probably even more attractive. Two missionaries of German birth were murdered in China, and the German government made that event an excuse to seize a valuable Chinese port, Kiau-Chau, with a

---

[1] See maps facing page 608 and following page 612.

[2] Germany does not own territory in Asia Minor, but she has obtained by treaties valuable rights of trade and railroad-building; and in case of a break-up of Turkey's power, she would probably convert these rights into full occupancy of territory. Largely in order to secure these concessions, the Emperor has courted the Sultan's favor on all occasions. Cf. § 582.

large adjacent territory. From this center, Germany has acquired a "sphere of influence" in eastern China, in which German capitalists are developing mines and building railroads, as Russians are doing to the north, and Englishmen and Frenchmen to the south. In case of a break-up of China, Germany is in a position to secure a rich share of the plunder; and, in any event, her "sphere of influence" is for practical economic purposes a foreign dependency.

As a colonizing nation, however, Germany so far is not a success. Capitalists go in small numbers to Asia Minor and to China, but they do not go to Africa; and the mass of emigrants still sail to America, giving up German citizenship. The government is believed to be anxious to obtain possessions in South or Central America, where these emigrants might make their homes; and but for the Monroe Doctrine of the United States, some attempts in these lines would undoubtedly be made.

485. Social Democracy. — Socialism, which was so important a factor in France in the first half of the century, did not appear prominently in Germany until after 1848. German Socialism was founded by *Karl Marx*, a profound philosophic thinker,[1] and its doctrines were thrown among the masses by his disciple *Lassalle*, a brilliant writer and speaker; its more recent leaders have been *Liebknecht* and *Bebel*.

There was of course no opening for Socialism in politics until manhood suffrage was introduced in the elections for the Reichstag of the North German Confederation (1867). The first Reichstag contained eight Socialists. These men bitterly opposed the war with France, especially after it became a war for conquest, and criticised the seizure of Alsace-Lorraine against the will of the inhabitants.[2] This "unpatriotic" atti-

---

[1] Marx teaches that "Collectivism" is a natural stage in historical evolution. "In savagery each one produces separately for himself; in our recent civilization, the many produce mainly for the few; in a more perfect state, all will produce collectively for all."

[2] The party in Germany and elsewhere is opposed to all wars of conquest. It calls upon the workingmen of all countries to combine against the capitalist

tude resulted in a check. The leaders were tried for treason and condemned to a few years' imprisonment, and in the first imperial Reichstag (1871) the party had only two representatives. In 1874, the number had risen to nine, and in 1877, to twelve. Bismarck then began to feel it needful to put down Socialism. His first effort to secure repressive legislation from the Reichstag failed, but it called out two attempts by Socialist fanatics to assassinate the Emperor (1877, 1878). The criminals had no sanction from the Social Democratic party;[1] but they played into Bismarck's hands. The Reichstag was dissolved, and the new election gave a legislature ready to go all lengths against the "Red Specter." New laws gave to the government the authority to dissolve associations, break up meetings, confiscate publications, suspend habeas corpus privileges and jury trial, and banish suspects by decree, without any trial at all.[2]

But here again the Iron Chancellor failed. The Socialists met his ruthless severity with as much fortitude and heroism[3] as the Catholic clergy had shown in their conflict, and all that he could do was to make Socialism for a time an underground current. In 1881, just after the beginning of the repressive legislation, the Socialist vote fell off somewhat; but after that it again gained steadily. In the election of 1884 the popular vote had risen to over half a million — much more than ever before — and in 1887 it was over three-fourths of a million. Then the repressive laws were allowed to expire; and in 1890 the vote was doubled. Since 1898 the Socialists have been much the largest German party, and they have captured the wage-earners of the great cities almost in a body. The following table shows their progress: —

---

classes, and it teaches that the burdens and losses of wars between nations fall in the end on the working classes, who ought to be brothers.

[1] The Social Democratic party is not a party of violence, but of political methods. Cf. Russell, *Social Democracy*, 98, 99.

[2] Not content with these extraordinary powers, Bismarck made them retroactive, and at once banished from Berlin sixty or seventy men who had formerly been connected with the Socialists.

[3] For an account, see Russell, 103–114.

Election.	Votes Cast.	Percentage of Total Vote.	Members in Reichstag.
1871	124,000	4	2
1874	351,000	7	9
1877	493,000	8.5	12
1878	437,000	8	9
1881	312,000	6.3	12
1884	549,000	6	24
1887	763,000	7.6	11
1890	1,427,000	20	36
1893	1,786,000	23	44
1898	2,107,000	28	56
1903	3,025,000	32.3	81
1907	3,259,000	31.6	43

The total vote in 1907 was 10,273,528, divided among twelve parties. The Socialists lost nearly half their seats, and — a more serious fact — a small percentage in the popular vote. But they are still fifty per cent stronger than the next largest party (the Center, or Catholic, with 2,183,000 votes), and no other party is more than half their size. The number of Socialist representatives is small in proportion to the popular vote, because of the unjust apportionment. The Socialist vote is strongest in the cities. The cities have grown rapidly in population (Berlin has tripled since 1860); but, from fear of Socialist gains, the distribution of representatives has not been changed since the establishment of the Empire (§ 475). If a fair apportionment, such as the constitution calls for, were to be made, the Social Democrats would have, not forty-three delegates, but one hundred and twenty-five. The Center, with two-thirds the votes of the Socialists, has two and a half times as many delegates; but a fair apportionment would reduce its one hundred and five to eighty-three. So absurd an electoral system cannot last indefinitely.

William II, for a time, seemed disposed to use gentler methods than those that Bismarck had followed; but he, too, soon became alarmed at the growth of the Socialist vote, and in 1894–1895 and again in 1897–1898 he tried vehemently to secure another "exceptional law," even more sweeping than Bismarck's legislation. The proposed bill of 1894 provided two years' imprisonment for "publicly attacking religion, the monarchy, marriage, the family, or property, by insulting utterances." Under such a law, to suggest a change in the government to a republican form, or, indeed, to urge much milder changes, might constitute a crime; and all Liberals very properly joined with the Socialists in voting down the proposal.[1] Even the Catholics did not dare to vote for it, lest their opposition to civil marriage should be treated as a crime.

In 1897, a like attempt was made in the more conservative Prussian Parliament; but even there the bill was rejected by a decisive vote. These are the most serious checks that Emperor William has met (1904).

The above account suggests some of the causes of strength in Social Democracy. That party has for its adherents, not only Collectivists, or Socialists proper, but also great numbers of political Radicals, or Democrats and believers in Republican government. Indeed, a large part of the vague discontent with the arbitrary nature of the government finds expression in votes for Socialist candidates. It is unfortunate that the two great forces in Germany, Autocracy and Socialism, should be so far apart.[2] But perhaps the remedy will come in modification of the Socialist program. At recent congresses of that party, it has placed first in its platform a number of practical political and economic measures which the average American or Englishman would not regard as dangerous, — such as universal suffrage without discrimination against woman, equal electoral districts, payment of members of the Reichstag, responsibility of the government to the Reichstag, popular local government, securities for free speech, a militia system in place of the present army system, an eight-hour labor day, freedom to organize labor unions, and progressive income taxes. If the party leaves "collectivism" in the background for the present, and selects wisely from such a list for its working program, it may yet fill the place of a true liberal party and play a great part in gradually regenerating Germany in politics and industry.

---

[1] A few days before this defeat, William had suffered another repulse from the same quarter. At the opening of the Reichstag in December, 1894, when cheers for the Emperor were called for, the Socialists kept their seats. The government, at the Emperor's desire, introduced a request for permission to bring the offenders to trial for lèse-majesté, but the request was refused by a vote of 168 to 88. Of course members of the Reichstag cannot be prosecuted for anything that they say or do in that body, except by its consent.

[2] The various "Liberal" parties have been shrinking, upon the whole, in recent years, and so the contest between the Ultra-radicals and Ultra-conservatives has seemed to threaten more ominously.

486. State Socialism. — Early in the contest with the Social Democrats, Bismarck tried to cut the ground from under their feet by adopting part of their program of social betterment.

In 1883, a public address of the Emperor declared, "That the state should care for its poorer members in a higher degree than in the past is not only a duty demanded by humanity and Christianity, but is also a measure *necessary to preserve the state.*" In 1884, Bismarck said, "Give the workingman a right to work while he is in health, and assure him care when he is sick and maintenance when he is old, and the Social Democrats will get no hold upon him." In accordance with these principles, Bismarck favored the introduction of great public works to afford employment, and he created a state fund to help insure the injured and the aged. The state compels the laborers to insure against sickness; it insures them against accident, taking the premium from the employer, and it pays old-age pensions to men over seventy years of age, out of a fund created partly by payments from the insured, partly by payments from the employers, and partly by a payment from the state treasury. Many excellent results have come from this legislation, but it is too early to pass judgment finally upon it. Certainly it has not weakened Social Democracy, whose adherents rail at it as fear-inspired, poor-law legislation.

To Bismarck and William II, it is the duty of the divine-right government to care for the laborer. To the Social Democrats, it is the right of the laborers themselves to control the government and to care for themselves through it. State Socialism in a democratic country like America would be the same thing as Social Democracy: in Germany at present it is old-fashioned paternalism.[1]

---

[1] Said Emperor William II in 1894, "The noblest task of the state is to protect the weaker classes of society and to aid them to higher economic and moral development; and the duty of the state is to smooth away the difficulties and to preserve an increased content and solidarity, *but this must be done by the state and not by the people.*"

487. Political Parties. — Of the ten parties in the German Reichstag besides the Socialist and the Catholic Center, four stand for different shades of liberalism, three are conservative, one is anti-Semitic, and the rest represent race feeling. The Polish representatives from the eastern provinces of Prussia, the one Danish representative from Schleswig, and most of the representatives from Alsace-Lorraine are standing protests against the attempts to crush their respective nationalities by the compulsory introduction of the German law and language. Besides these there are two or three distinct South German parties; and indeed the great "Center" is to a large extent a sectional South German delegation. South Germany (Bavaria and Wurtemberg in particular) has opposed bitterly all attempts to increase the army and navy; and the feeling of the vivacious people in these districts toward the severe, stern Prussian is one of the most serious factors of present German politics[1] (§ 471).

For Further Reading. — See references on page 478. Dawson's *Bismarck and Socialism* and Russell's *German Social Democracy* give good statements of the topic suggested by the names. Wilson's *The State* gives a clear treatment of the constitution; and advanced students may use Lowell's *Governments and Parties*. For recent events and special topics, the student must consult recent Reviews, Year Books, and Annual Encyclopedias.

Special Report. — Prussia's schools and their history.

V. ITALY SINCE 1870.

488. Internal Conditions, Political, Educational, and Economic. — The constitution of Italy is essentially that given to Sardinia in 1848. It provides for a limited monarchy, somewhat of the Prussian type, but more liberal. By custom, as in France and England, the ministries resign when they no longer have a parliamentary majority. Local government and admin-

---

[1] For political parties and tendencies at the close of the nineteenth century, see table in Lowell, II, 42, or in Russell, 149.

istrative courts are patterned upon the French model. Until 1882, a high property qualification was required for voters. At that date, after two years' agitation, the franchise was given to all who could read and write, or who paid certain rents or four dollars in direct taxes. This raised the electorate from about six hundred thousand to over two millions, but it still excluded half the adult males. Since that time, however, with the progress of education, the proportion of voters has been increasing.

In 1861, Italy had no schools except those taught by religious orders. In the next twenty years, a fair system of public education was built up. Primary education is gratuitous, compulsory, and regulated by the state, but attendance is not well enforced. In 1861, seventy-four per cent of the population over six years of age could not read or write. In 1881, this percentage of illiterates had fallen to sixty-two. The decrease since that time has been rapid, but the exact figures cannot be given. The higher educational institutions are excellent, and in many fields Italian scholars hold a foremost place.

The Kingdom of Italy at its birth was far behind the other great states of Europe. Its proper tasks were to provide for public education, to repress brigandage, to build railroads, to foster useful industries, to drain malarial swamps and reclaim abandoned lands. In all this, much progress has been made; but the government has been hampered by its poverty and by the tremendous expenditure for military purposes. Taxation is crushing; and yet, much of the time, the government can hardly meet expenses. Half the revenue goes to pay the interest on the national debt, and two-thirds the rest is for military purposes, leaving only a small part for the normal and helpful purposes of government.[1] To make ends meet, the

---

[1] Italy was freed by force of arms, in 1859-1861; and the same power completed her union between 1861 and 1870. The new-born state, for many years more, feared that the work might be undone by France or Austria; and to the present time she has maintained the usual European military system (§ 483), with longer terms of active service than are required in Germany or France. From her position, too, Italy has had some reason to wish to be

government has been driven to desperate financial expedients. Salt and tobacco are government monopolies; the state runs a lottery; and taxation upon houses, land, and incomes is so exorbitant as seriously to hamper industry. The financial and military problem is the great question before Italy at present (1904).

The economic distress has led to political and socialistic agitation. The government in general has met this by stern repressive legislation. Socialists and Republicans have been imprisoned by hundreds, often on the charge of being Anarchists; and for years at a time large parts of Italy have been in "state of siege," or under martial law. The Radicals and Socialists, however, have gained slowly in the Parliament.

489. Colonial and Territorial Questions. — A large emigration leaves Italy each year, mainly for Brazil and the Argentine Republic. Partly in hope to retain these emigrants as Italian citizens, the government took up a policy of securing colonial dependencies. Attention was first turned to Tunis, but when France supplanted Italian influence there, Italy acquired valuable territory on the Abyssinian coast in Northeast Africa (1885). From 1889 to 1896, indeed, Italy held a protectorate over all Abyssinia; but in the latter year, an Italian army was destroyed in the interior, and Italian control was reduced again to the coast district, Eritrea. Up to the present time, however, emigration has not been directed in any considerable degree to this possession.

One other territorial difficulty annoys Italy. Austria still keeps the district of Trentino on the southern slope of the Alps, with its three hundred thousand people. The population is Italian in race and language, and the district geographically is part of Italy. Italians look forward to the ultimate acquisi-

---

strong in the Mediterranean, and at an immense cost she has kept up a navy, among the most powerful in the world, after England's. Italy, however, is much less able to endure this tremendous burden than are rich countries like France and Germany, and she is one of those states in which the present military system is likely soonest to break down.

§ 490] THE PAPAL QUESTION. 497

tion of this region. The party that most zealously demands this is known as *Italia Irredenta*.

490. The Papal Question. — Italy has also a serious problem in the relations of state and church. Almost all Italians are Roman Catholics, in name at least; but the government and the popes have been hostile to each other ever since the Kingdom of Italy was established. The clergy, of course, in the main adhere to the pope, while the great mass of the people earnestly support the government.

In 1870, when Italy took forceful possession of Rome, Pope Pius IX protested against the act as a deed of brigandage.[1] The government has left to the papacy every power consistent with the territorial unity of Italy. The pope is not an Italian subject, but, in all matters of form, is an independent sovereign, though his territory has been reduced to a single palace (the Vatican) and some small estates. Within this domain he keeps his own court, maintains his own diplomatic service, and carries on the machinery of a state. A generous annual income is also set aside for him by the government of Italy, but this has never been claimed. The clergy and church throughout Italy are left by the government to manage their own affairs as completely as in the United States, except that the state pays the salaries in compensation for the church lands it has seized.

In common with many zealous Catholics, however, Pope Pius IX felt that to exercise his proper influence as head of the church, he must be also an independent temporal prince. He refused to recognize the Italian state or to have anything to do with it: he styled himself a prisoner and called upon all loyal Catholics to take no part in elections or in public affairs. For some time, no doubt, it was possible that in case of a general European war, France or Austria might restore the papacy as a temporal principality, but that possibility has

---

[1] In spite of this, the citizens of Rome ratified the act by a vote of 130,000 to 1500, or ninety to one.

become very faint indeed; and though the popes have not yet announced a change of attitude[1] toward the Italian state, it is probable that the present unhappy condition will not long continue. Certainly, so far, the papacy has not suffered from the arrangement of 1870-1871. Never before have the popes been so independent of foreign interference; nor, since Gregory VII and Innocent III, have they been more powerful in spiritual and temporal concerns than in the recent period since they ceased to rule a petty principality.

FOR FURTHER READING. — See references on page **464**, with Wilson's *The State*, and, of course, Reviews, Year Books, and Annual Encyclopedias.

VI. AUSTRIA-HUNGARY — A DUAL MONARCHY.

491. Historical Sketch from 1848 to the Establishment of the Dual Monarchy in 1867. — The medieval system lasted in the Austrian realms until 1848. The revolutions of that year abolished the feudal burdens of the peasantry and the feudal privileges of the nobles; and even the counter-revolution under Schwarzenberg (§ 453) did not undo these social reforms. It did restore absolutism, however, and from 1850 to 1860 strenuous efforts were made to centralize and Germanize the various districts that had risen for national independence in 1848. The former rights of local government in Bohemia and Hungary[2] were trampled under foot, and only the German language was allowed in the schools, the press, the courts, and the administration. For a Bohemian to publish a paper in his native language was a penal offense.

The defeat of Austria in 1859 by France and Italy (§ 460) was hailed with delight by Bohemia and Hungary; and the

---

[1] This is still true in 1907, though the election of Pope Pius X (1903) was thought by some observers to herald a change in papal policy.

[2] The movement in Hungary for self-government and reform, from 1815 to 1849, is an excellent subject for a brief special report by an advanced student. Another report may be made upon the life of Deak, the greatest Hungarian statesman.

Emperor awoke to the absolute necessity of conciliating these provinces. Liberal reforms were begun, and a parliamentary system was introduced, both for the Empire as a whole and for its chief divisions. Representation in the central Parliament was so arranged, however, as to allow the Germans still to swamp all the other nationalities; and the plan for such a body failed, because Hungarians, Bohemians, and Croats refused to elect delegates. Then, in 1862, the Emperor made still greater concessions, granting a kind of federal constitution. But Hungary was not content with this; and, after the overthrow of Austria at Sadowa (1866), it became necessary at any cost to satisfy Hungary. The Emperor and Francis Deak (the Hungarian leader) arranged a compact, which was then ratified separately by the Hungarian and Austrian parliaments; and this compact is the present constitution of Austria-Hungary.

492. The Dual Monarchy: Central Government. — Austria-Hungary is now *a dual monarchy,* a confederation of two states. Each state has its own constitution, its own parliament, its own system of local government and law. The connection between the two is threefold: they have (1) the same monarch, (2) common ministers for war, finance, and foreign affairs, and (3) a curious kind of a common council (*the Delegations*).

The monarch is crowned separately, with different titles, in Vienna and in Budapest, and his powers differ in the two states. The Delegations are two committees of sixty each, the one chosen by the Austrian Parliament, the other by the Hungarian. They meet one year at Vienna, the next at Budapest; and they carry on their work, one in German, the other in the Magyar language. If the two bodies disagree on any measure, they hold a joint session [1] and vote without debate.

---

[1] If members are absent from one Delegation, then at such a joint session, the same number must be excluded by lot from the other, so as to keep the two bodies equal.

Strictly, the Delegations do not compose a real legislature, and their functions are very limited, but they make the dual monarchy something more than a mere "personal union."

Financial arrangements between the two parts of the Empire rest upon agreements, or treaties, between the legislature (Reichsrath) of Austria and that of Hungary. These arrangements are passed for periods of ten years, and their renewals are each time an occasion for bitter contests, especially in Austria, where the Bohemians are strongly opposed to the dual arrangement. In 1897, the conflict was particularly sharp, and for weeks the Reichsrath was the scene of disgraceful confusion and uproar, with several cases of personal violence.

Hungary holds a favorable position in the Empire. Her people are aggressive and politically gifted, and the Magyars are more supreme in the Hungarian state than any one party is in the Austrian, and so they act with greater unanimity. Hungary pays only thirty-two per cent of the imperial expense, though her wealth and population are much larger in proportion and though she has half the imperial power. In practice, she has more than half: she has controlled the foreign policy of the government most of the time since 1867.

493. The Race Question and the Future of the Empire. — Austria has been and still is "a tangle of races and a Babel of tongues." Until 1868, the full official title of the Emperor ran: "Apostolic King of Hungary, King of Bohemia, King of Croatia, King of Slavonia, King of Galicia, Archduke of the Austrias, Grand Duke of Transylvania, Duke of Styria, Carinthia, and Carniola, and Princely Count of Hapsburg and Tyrol." The inhabitants of this conglomerate state speak eleven distinct languages,[1] besides numerous dialects. Half the population are Slavs, broken up, however, into many sub-races, Czechs, Croats, Serbs, Slavonians, Poles, Ruthenians; a fourth are Germans; a fifth are Magyars; and the rest are Italians, Jews, or Illyrians.

If we regard the Slav sub-races as separate peoples, the Germans are more numerous than any other people. They number eight and a half millions. The Magyars come next, with seven and a half millions. Of the Slavs, the Czechs lead with nearly six millions. The Poles count three

---

[1] At the opening of the Austrian Reichsrath the official oath is administered in eight languages.

MAP TO ILLUSTRATE IN PART
THE DISTRIBUTION OF RACES IN
AUSTRIA-HUNGARY
SCALE OF MILES
0 50 100 150 200
REFERENCE
Germans
Czechs
Slovaks
Ruthenians
Poles
Magyars-Hungary
Slovenes
Serbo-Croats
Italians
Roumanians
GERMANY
SAXONY
BAVARIA
RUSSIA
BOHEMIA
(Czechs)
MORAVIA
SILESIA
GALICIA
(Poles)
(Ruthenians)
BUKOWINA
LOWER
UPPER
AUSTRIA
(Germans)
SALZBURG
STYRIA
CARINTHIA
TYROL
TRENTINO
(Italians)
(Slovaks)
HUNGARY
(Magyars)
(Roumanians)
TRANSYLVANIA
(Slovenes)
CARNIOLA
KUSTENLAND
CROATIA
SLAVONIA
(Serbs)
DALMATIA
VENETIA
ITALY
ADRIATIC SEA
BOSNIA
HERZEGOVINA
MONTENEGRO
SERVIA
ROUMANIA
BELGRADE
VIENNA
BUDAPEST
Prague
Pilsen
Iglau
Budweis
Olmutz
Brünn
Troppau
Krakow
Kashau
Czernowitz
Tokay
Erlau
Komorn
Gran
Raab
Neustadt
Salzburg
Innsbruck
Graz
Trent
Laibach
Agram
Karlstadt
Trieste
Venice
Istria
Zara
Ragusa
Elorence
Klausenburg
Kronstadt
Versecz
Pancsova
Elbe R.
Oder R.
Vistula
San R.
Bug R.
Dniester R.
Sered R.
Pruth R.
Theiss R.
Danube
Inn R.
Rhine R.
Drave R.
Save R.
W. Koros R.
Maros R.
Temes R.
Po R.
10
15
20
25
45
50

and three-fourths millions; the Ruthenians, three millions; the Slavonians, about a million. Then there are over a half-million Croats and Serbs, and about two hundred thousand Roumanians. There are also seven hundred thousand Italians, and about half a million of other peoples.

The arrangements of 1867 sacrificed the Slavs of the Empire to satisfy the demands of Hungary. Hungary and Austria, however, each has a race question. Until recently, the Germans have been the dominant people in the Austrian half, and the Magyars still are in their half; but in the latter part of the nineteenth century, with the growth of education and prosperity, the other races pushed forward toward an equality of culture, and, in those provinces where they are most numerous, they began to demand not only equal political rights, but even national independence. This fact gives the key to all the recent history of the Empire.

In Hungary, Croatia has been allowed some privileges of its own; but elsewhere, despite violent protests, the Magyars are slowly but successfully imposing their language and nationality upon the scattered Slav fragments.

In Austria the case is much worse. Bohemia in particular demands, if not independence, at least that she be admitted into the imperial federation as a separate state upon an equality with Hungary. In the last decade of the nineteenth century, the struggle was particularly vehement. The Czechs make about two-thirds of the population of Bohemia, but the other third are mainly German, and the Austrian Germans elsewhere are unwilling to abandon these fellow-citizens to Czech rule. On two or three occasions Bohemia was under martial law for months at a time; but, upon the whole, the Czechs have been steadily winning ground, until the Germans in that country begin to long for annexation to the German Empire. Says Lowell (*Governments and Parties*, 121): —

In Austria, everybody is irreconcilable. Almost the only party who admit the legality of the existing constitution . . . are the German Liberals, and [for many years] they have been opposed to the government [the ministry]. The task of the ministers, therefore, has been hard. It has resembled that of an Esquimaux trying to drive a team of dogs, all of which want to break loose from the sledge, except the strongest, which pulls the wrong way.

Thus Austria-Hungary is the uncertain factor in European politics. Her German population is drawn toward the German Empire: her Italians want to be annexed to Italy; her Poles look to the revival of the Polish kingdom; the Roumanians in eastern Hungary wish to be joined to neighboring Roumania, and her many Slav elements desire independence or annexation to neighboring Slav states. The condition of the Empire is one of unstable equilibrium, and it offers the most probable field for future rearrangements in Europe. However, despite all these weaknesses and the jealousy between the two great halves, the dual state has lasted nearly half a century and may endure for long to come.

"If France has been a laboratory for political experiments, Austria-Hungary is a museum of political curiosities, but it contains nothing so extraordinary as the relations between Austria and Hungary themselves. The explanation for the strange connection is to be found in the fact that the two countries are not held together from within by any affection or loyalty for a common fatherland, *but are forced together by a pressure from the outside* which makes the union an international and military necessity. Austria, on the one hand, would not be large enough alone to be a really valuable ally to Germany and Italy, and, if not an ally, she would be likely to become a prey, for she contains districts which they would be glad to absorb. Moreover, there would be imminent danger of some of her different races breaking into open revolt, if the Emperor had not the Hungarian troops at his command. On the other hand, the Magyars without Austria *would not be sufficiently strong to block the ambition of Russia, or resist the tide of Panslavism.* They would not only have little interest outside their own dominions, but they would run a grave risk of foreign interference in favor of the Slavs in Hungary. A union is therefore unavoidable and it is very little closer than is absolutely necessary to carry out the purposes for which it exists. . . . One would naturally suppose that a mechanism so intricate and so unwieldy would be continually getting out of order, and in constant danger of breaking down. But political necessity is stronger than perfection of organization, and . . . the forces which have made the dual system work smoothly in the past are likely to produce the same result in the future." — LOWELL. *Governments and Parties*, II, 177-179.

In foreign policy, Austria has abandoned Italy, and has been excluded from German affairs. She turns naturally, therefore, to the Black Sea and the Ægean, and in 1878, after the war between Turkey and Russia (§ 577), she received from Turkey the provinces of Bosnia and Herzegovina, which are administered as an imperial territory, without being joined to either of the separate states. The Hungarians, however, do not look with favor upon the acquisition of more Slav population, and so Austria-Hungary is not in position to take advantage of the weakness of her neighbors to the southeast.

For Further Reading.— Andrews or Seignobos for the narrative, and Wilson or Lowell for the constitutions.

CHAPTER V.

THE SMALL STATES OF WESTERN EUROPE.[1]

494. Enumeration. — Besides the great states (of which Great Britain and Russia are still to be treated for the nineteenth century), the usual map of Europe shows thirteen[2] small states. All of these except Switzerland are constitutional monarchies. Five — the Slav and Greek states — are in the southeast of Europe in the Balkan region. The other eight belong to Western Europe and claim treatment at this point.

Of these small states of Western Europe, two are in the south, in the Iberian peninsula; three are in the north, in the Scandinavian peninsulas; two lie at the mouth of the Rhine, and the remaining one at its source. Four of the eight — Spain, Sweden, Denmark, and Holland — have at some time ranked as Great Powers.

I. THE IBERIAN PENINSULA.

A. SPAIN.

495. From 1800 to 1833: Revolution and Absolutism. — Before 1800 the ideas of the French Revolutionists began to filter into Spain, but for a long time their welcome was confined to the small educated class. Napoleon's attack broke down the old monarchy and gave these Liberals a chance. They took the lead in the War for Independence (1809–1813), and, in the midst of that struggle, a national Cortes drew up the famous Constitution of 1812. Then followed the return of the cruel

---

[1] It is suggested that this chapter be read and talked over without much attempt to fix details.

[2] There are also four or five others, like the little Republic of San Marino in the Italian Alps, so small that few maps take notice of them. A student may be asked to look them up in a Year Book for a special report.

and suspicious *Ferdinand VII*, his treacherous overthrow of the constitution, its restoration by the Revolution of 1820, and the armed intervention of the Holy Alliance in 1823 (§§ 393, 397).

For the next ten years no constitutionalism could raise its head, and the old Liberals were vigorously persecuted. To own a foreign book was a crime. In 1831 a young man was hanged in Madrid for shouting "Hurrah for Liberty!" and a widow met the same fate, for embroidering on a flag the words, "Law, Liberty, Equality."

496. From 1833 to 1873: Paper Constitutions and "Government by Revolt." — In 1833 Ferdinand died, leaving the crown to his infant daughter *Isabella*, under the regency of his wife Christina. Ferdinand's brother, *Carlos*, also claimed the throne; and since Carlos was the acknowledged leader of the Ultra-reactionists, Christina necessarily threw herself upon the support of the Liberals and restored the constitution, — a movement the more natural since she was the sister-in-law of Louis Philippe, who had just been crowned in France by a revolution against absolute monarchy. There followed seven years of ferocious warfare between Constitutionalists and Carlists. England and France gave sympathy and aid to the former, while Metternich and the reorganized Holy Alliance sent secret aid to the latter.

Finally, in 1840, Carlos was driven from the country; but meantime the Constitutionalists had split into two factions. In 1834 Christina had replaced the old constitution with one of a less radical character. The adherents of the new constitution were known as Moderates; those who supported the old were called Progressionists. The two parties had already come to blows while both were fighting the Carlists; and in 1840, when Christina showed that she was bent upon still further usurpation, *Espartero*, a Progressionist general, compelled her to abdicate the regency in his own favor.

Espartero was an honest gentleman and a gallant soldier, but in politics he was an idealist, without executive ability.

Two years later he was replaced by a military rising of a Moderate general, *Narvaez*, a merciless ruler, who was described by his enemies as "a brigand of considerable intelligence."

Both Espartero and Narvaez had more than one lease of power in the years that followed, and there were occasional intervals when smaller men controlled the government; but political methods remained essentially unchanged until 1876. During this middle half of the century, the government is well described as "government by revolt." The successive military revolutions, however, were marked by surprisingly little bloodshed. It has been wittily said, that during this period, "revolution in Spain became a fine art." When an administration had grown sufficiently unpopular, some officer, with docile battalions and a grievance, would issue a "pronunciamento," declaring the existing government dissolved and naming the members of a new one. If the Revolutionist had counted his strength advisedly, the old government would accommodatingly vanish; if it stayed, the revolt usually disappeared. It was part of the political game to know, without fighting, when one was beaten; and, as some one has said, Spaniards developed a delicate tact in working revolutions, as English-speaking people work elections, with the least possible disturbance to the affairs of everyday life.[1]

In the first third of the nineteenth century, Spain had no constitution, even in name, except for two brief periods, 1812–1814 and 1820–1823; and indeed constitutionalism was only a vague aspiration in the minds of a few. After 1833 there was always some paper constitution; but in practice, until 1876, there was absolutely no constitutional government. During this second period of the century, revolutions, new paper constitutions, regencies, dictatorships, and ministries which were dictatorships in all but name, succeeded each other in bewildering confusion, — each change effected by a *coup d'état*, never by a constitutional election.

To be sure, after each of the meaningless commotions of these forty

---

[1] It is difficult to avoid an appearance of levity in an honest description of this peculiarity of politics both in Spain and in many of the Spanish American states through most of the nineteenth century. With our clumsier northern races, in such a play some one would be likely to get hurt.

years, the victorious faction would "appeal to the nation" for sanction; but it used all the machinery of the government, including the police, to carry its candidates; and members of an opposing party, if active, were liable to be mobbed by the government party (which was always the "party of the club"), or, if they resisted, to be locked up "to prevent a disturbance." Elections always showed a gratifying unanimity in favor of the existing government, whatever it was.

As the young Isabella approached womanhood she developed despotic principles and profligate morals, and her reign was one of the most shameful episodes in modern history. Wasteful taxation and miserable misgovernment alienated faction after faction; and, though the prisons were crowded with political prisoners, the country was seething with discontent. The later part of the reign, too, was diversified by new Carlist risings in favor of the son of the first Carlos.

In 1868, the various disturbances culminated in a successful Liberal rising, led by *Serrano* and *Prim*, exiled military adventurers. The Queen fled to France and abdicated in favor of her son Alphonso; but the Progressionist cry had become "Down with the Bourbons!" and a Provisional Government was set up, with Prim as dictator. A group of Republicans now appeared, led by *Castelar*, demanding an immediate Republic, and new Carlist insurrections broke out in favor of the grandson of the first Carlos, — Cuba meantime blazing with rebellion. The Provisional Government fashioned a new constitution of a liberal monarchic type, and then for two years the crown went begging. It was offered in succession to Espartero, to a Prince of Portugal, to Pedro I, who had already abdicated the crown of Brazil (§ 502), to two Italian princes, and to Leopold of Hohenzollern (§ 471). Finally, in 1871, *Amadeo*, a younger son of Victor Emmanuel of Italy, accepted the throne, and made an honorable attempt to rule as a constitutional king; but after two years he gave up the task in despair and left the country.

497. The Republic of 1873-1874: Castelar's Dictatorship. — Then, in 1873, the Republicans were allowed to have their turn. The majority of the republican Cortes, however, wished a strong, centralized republic, like France, while a minority wished a federal republic, with the ancient provinces, Castile, Aragon, etc., for the separate states. After months of wrangling, the Federalists carried their point by a *coup d'état*, and Castelar became president of the new republic. The constitution, said to have been drawn up in twenty-four hours, was never more than a form. The leaders had made absurd promises which could not be kept: to reduce taxes, though the treasury was bankrupt; to do away with conscription, though the army was demoralized and revolt flourished; to abolish capital punishment, though crime was rampant. But Castelar could learn; and six months of anarchy changed his views. The Carlists were making rapid progress in the northern provinces; the seaboard cities of the south had declared themselves independent communes, after the plan of Paris two years before; taxes ceased to come in; the remnants of the army were in mutiny; the towns were at the mercy of ruffians, and the country districts in the hands of bandits. Then, in a fortunate recess of the Cortes, Castelar turned his vague legal authority into a beneficent dictatorship. The choice, he saw, lay between bayonet-rule in the hands of disciplined troops controlled by good men, and pike-rule in the hands of a vicious rabble led by escaped galley-slaves. He candidly abandoned his old theories, broke his foolish pledges, and with wise energy brought order out of chaos. He centralized the federal state; he crushed the communes with an army recruited by a strict conscription; and he checked crime and anarchy by military executions after swift drumhead courtmartials.

It was natural that he should be assailed as a tyrant and suspected of selfish motives. When the Cortes reassembled, his old friends passed a vote of lack of confidence. The commander of the troops asked for permission to disperse the Cortes, but, by promptly resigning, Castelar showed that he had no wish to prolong his personal authority. To-day no one doubts his good faith or good judgment, and the name of this republican statesman-author-dictator stands out as the chief glory of Spain in the nineteenth century.[1]

498. Restoration of the Monarchy. — Castelar's resignation was followed by brief anarchy; but two more revolutions brought the nation to the restoration of the old Bourbon line, at the close of 1874, in the person of the young *Alphonso XII*,[2] son of Isabella. This restoration was accomplished in the usual way, by a military pronunciamento by a general; but it was welcomed with delight by the exhausted nation, and it seems to have closed the period of revolution. The new government proved vigorous and prudent. In two years the Carlists were driven out, and the constitution of 1876 introduced Spain to a more hopeful period.

499. The Constitution of 1876 and its Workings. — The government in theory rests mainly in the Cortes. This body consists of a Senate and a Congress. Half the senators are elected, by complex arrangements; while the rest are appointed for life, or hold the position by virtue of other office or of relationship to the king. The congressmen are elected by manhood suffrage (since 1890). Local government has been organized wisely on the basis of historic provinces, with a larger amount of local self-control than is found in either France or Italy.

The ministry is expected to resign if outvoted in the Cortes, but in practice parliamentary majorities do not yet really make ministries: instead, ministries make parliamentary majorities. A ministry is formed by coalition between factions, and then it supplies itself with a good working majority by a new election. The ministry controls the elections pretty thoroughly; but such things are managed more decorously than formerly, and since 1876 no party has "called in the infantry" to change the government. Pronunciamentos seem to be outgrown, and, in the near future, Spain may be expected to secure the spirit,

---

[1] Castelar had been professor of philosophy in the University of Madrid before he entered politics, and he ranks among the great orators of modern times.

[2] In 1885 Alphonso's death left the crown to his son, *Alphonso XIII*.

as well as the form, of Parliamentary government. There is still a Carlist faction, however, which now and then threatens to rise, and of late years the Socialists have made some disturbances.

500. Reform Legislation, 1881-1890. — Until 1881, the energies of the government went mainly to restoring order. Then, for ten years, reform crowded upon reform. Jury trial was introduced; civil marriage was permitted; popular education was encouraged; the franchise was extended; the slaves in the colonies were freed; honest but vain attempts were made to improve the government of the colonies; and above all, so far as Spain's welfare is concerned, the system of taxation was reformed. In 1876, taxes were still levied in the wasteful, demoralizing way characteristic of France before the First Revolution, and both foreign trade and home industries were strangled by them. Conditions are still far from ideal, but the heaviest shackles have been struck off. As a result, trade has mounted by bounds, manufactures have developed, railroads and telegraphs have been tripled. Population has almost doubled in the last century, rising from ten millions to over eighteen, and the growth has been especially rapid in the last decades. The number of peasant landowners is rapidly increasing. To be sure, the shiftless, excitable, bigoted character of the mass of the people has not yet become perceptibly altered. Still, Spain is far from being a dying nation, as she is sometimes called. She is a reviving nation: and the increase in population and in material wealth is a chief reason for the greater political stability of the last forty years. Under the new conditions, *constant revolution would be too costly*.

Castelar and the more moderate of the old Republicans gave their allegiance to the liberal monarchy; but Castelar, though taking a prominent part in politics, always refused to accept office, feeling that in that case he might be suspected of selling his old convictions. The leading statesman in this long course of reform, from 1880 to 1898, was *Sagasta*, whose name stands next to Castelar's in honor in modern Spanish history.

501. Religion ; Illiteracy ; Poverty ; Loss of the Colonies ; Outlook. — Catholicism is the state religion; and though the constitution promises freedom of worship to other sects, no other religious services are permitted *in public*. In this respect, Spain is the most backward of European lands. The schools are poorly attended (despite a compulsory education law) and poorly taught. These conditions are improving, but it will be several years at least before even half the adults can read and write.

Castelar and Sagasta wished to change all this radically, (1) by the complete *separation of church and state,* and (2) by the *exclusion of clerical control* from the schools. But the introduction of manhood suffrage strengthened the Clericals and Conservatives in the Cortes after 1890 (because of the blind obedience paid at elections by the ignorant peasants to their priests), and for many years no serious attempt at change in these lines was possible. In 1906, however, *wide-spread and earnest agitation* began for both reforms.

Until 1898, the great drag upon Spanish progress was the surviving colonial empire. After 1876 a series of efforts was made to give good government and some measure of self-control to Cuba, which had been in incessant and wasting rebellion. But the problem was probably too difficult to be worked out under the most favorable conditions by a country politically so backward at home. Corrupt officials oftentimes ruined the designs of the government; and in any case, the colonies were already so alienated by long misgovernment as to make the task hopeless. In 1894, Cuba rose again for independence. Spain made tremendous efforts to hold her colony, and for some years, at an immense cost, maintained an army of two hundred thousand men at a distance of two thousand miles from home. The warfare, however, was reducing Cuba to a desert; and finally, in 1898, the United States interfered. The Spanish-American War resulted in the surrender of all the Spanish colonies, except some districts in northwest Africa.

It may be hoped that this loss will prove a gain. The poverty of the government has been a serious hindrance to economic and educational development. The national debt is almost two billions of dollars. The interest charge is a crushing burden, and until 1900 the debt was constantly growing. Now that Spain no longer has the task of holding distant colonial possessions, she may conclude to reduce her absurd army system and to use the money for the development of the intellect of the people and of the resources of the land. When she does so, a rapid prosperity is assured, and the national debt will no longer be alarming.

The Spaniards, however, are still unwilling to give up their army. They hope, in case of a European war, to recover Gibraltar from England and perhaps to incorporate Portugal, and they feel also that they must be prepared for Carlist and Socialist rebellions. Spain still has ambitions, moreover, to extend her colonial possessions in Africa, and she looks with hungry eyes at Morocco across the straits.

Just before the loss of the Spanish colonies, Castelar expressed the hopes of thoughtful Spaniards in effective words: "When we turn our eyes to the sad past and compare it with the present, we see what may be accomplished without trying to fulfill Utopian dreams. . . . Men who have seen an absolute monarchy, see to-day a democratic monarchy. Men who once scarcely dared express their thoughts, can write to-day anything that they wish. Men who were once dismissed from the universities for proclaiming free thought and scientific truth have the right to-day to teach what they believe. . . . We may well be content with the work of the last forty years."

B. PORTUGAL.

502. Historical Survey. — When Napoleon I seized Portugal (1807), the royal family of the Braganzas fled to Brazil, the most important of Portugal's dependencies; and after the expulsion of the French, *King John* preferred to rule the home country from the colony. The Portuguese were deeply dissatisfied with this arrangement, and, after the Spanish Revolution of 1820, they rose for a constitution. To save his European crown, the King left his son Pedro to rule Brazil, and returned to Portugal, accepting the radical constitution which the Revolutionists had drawn up (1821).[1] The Queen and her younger son Miguel plotted to restore absolutism, and, for years, Portugal was distracted by revolutions and civil wars. King John died in 1826; and *Pedro,* the heir, preferring to keep his Brazilian crown,[2] abdicated the throne of Portugal in favor of his infant daughter *Maria,* having first granted a charter less radical than the constitution of 1821, but more workable. *Miguel* seized the crown, and held it for six years[3] (1829–1835). Finally he was driven out, but not until Pedro had come to Portugal to act as regent for his daughter, resigning the throne of Brazil to his son Pedro II.[4] Turmoil and civil strife, mixed up with the Carlist wars in Spain, continued until 1851. Since the middle of the nineteenth century, however, Portugal has been at peace, and has made some progress in constitutional government. English influence is dominant in foreign relations, so that Portugal is, in practice, almost an English protectorate.

503. Conditions: Political, Religious, Educational. — The Cortes consists of two houses. The Peers contain a hundred members appointed for life by the king, and fifty elected on a high property basis. The lower house is elected, and the franchise (since 1885 and 1901) is given to all adult males who can read or write or who pay a trifling tax, and to all heads of families, even if they have no other qualification. The king has a slight veto, called the "moderating power": if the Cortes passes a bill he dislikes, he can *suspend* it until the next Cortes meets; but if it is then passed again, it becomes law.

---

[1] This document was modeled upon the Spanish Constitution of 1812.

[2] In 1823 a secret treaty between Brazil and Portugal had agreed that the crowns should never again be united.

[3] In these six years, according to the claims of the Liberals, seventeen thousand men were put to death and more than twice that number were transported or imprisoned for political opinions.

[4] The wise rule of this prince was the last remnant of monarchy in America, outside the shadowy survivals in the English colonies. It lasted until 1890. Then the people of Brazil demanded a Republic, and Pedro resigned the throne, winning the admiration of the world by his dignified moderation.

Catholicism is the state religion (indeed, there are only a few hundred Protestants in the country), but all religions are tolerated. Portugal, too, has had its kulturkampf, and education has been taken away from the church. On paper, education is universal and gratuitous, but in practice the children of the poorer classes do not attend school. The schools themselves are still very poor, and Portugal is as illiterate as Spain.

504. Problems: Economic, Colonial, Military. — Despite these backward conditions, Portugal is making some progress toward better things. The population, including that of the Azores and Madeira, which are in all respects part of the kingdom, is about five and a half millions (census of 1890), and it is rapidly increasing. The country is naturally rich, but the mines and other natural resources are poorly developed, owing to ignorance, poverty, and lack of enterprise.

Portugal's foreign possessions are still extensive (in the Verde islands, in Africa, and in India), but they do not pay expenses financially, and it is doubtful if so poor a country can afford to keep them. Their administration, too, is very bad.

Finances are in a deplorable condition. In 1893 Portugal was obliged to suspend payment of two-thirds the interest on her national debt.[1] The government has had an annual deficit for several years, and European Powers are liable to intervene to secure payment of the debts due their citizens.[2] Portugal, it would seem, must abandon her army, and perhaps sell her colonies.

Probably the chief reason for not giving up the army is fear lest Spain might seize the country, so closely allied to herself in race and language. A federation between the two states would be a natural solution of the problem, and would make possible a stronger and cheaper government for both; but the Portuguese dread any kind of union, fearing to be swallowed up in the larger state. The government wishes a considerable

---

[1] Of course the balance is added each year to the debt.

[2] In 1894 France withdrew her representative from Portugal because of dissatisfaction at the treatment of French creditors.

armed force, also, to suppress anarchistic plots, of which there have been many in recent years.

For Further Reading. — Seignobos, *Europe since 1814*, 286–324; Phillips, *Modern Europe*, 21, 22, 84–90, 122–129; recent Year Books and Annual Encyclopedias. Longer and very readable accounts are given in Hume's *Modern Spain*, Curry's *Constitutional History of Spain*, Hannay's *Castelar*, and Stroebel's *Spanish Revolution of 1868–1874*.

Special Report. — Important events since 1900 in Spain and Portugal.

II. HOLLAND AND BELGIUM.
A. The Union of 1815.[1]

505. Unfortunate Nature of the Union. — In 1815, the various provinces of the ancient Netherlands were once more united, by the Congress of Vienna; and the Kingdom of the Netherlands, so formed, received a constitution similar to the French Charter of 1814. The union proved ill-advised. The northern provinces (Holland, or the United Provinces) were Dutch in race and language, and Protestant in religion. The southern provinces (Belgium) were French in blood and tongue, and Catholic in religion. In industries, also, the two regions had different interests.

Moreover, Belgium was more democratic than Holland, and, though the richer and more populous half, it had been forced to receive a Dutch king and was ruled largely by Dutch officials.[2] Dutch was the language of the court and of the government, and representation in Parliament was so arranged that Belgium had the smaller influence.

506. The Separation in 1830. — In 1830, after the French Revolution, Belgium revolted against Dutch rule. The "Three Days of July" in Paris were followed by the "Four Days of September" in Brussels. Dutch officials and the Dutch army

---

[1] For the earlier division of the two countries, see § 222.
[2] In 1830, only 11 out of 117 officials in the Department of the Interior were Belgian, and only 288 out of 1967 army officers.

were driven out, and a Provisional Government called together a National Assembly. In 1831 this body drew up a constitution, — at the time, the most liberal in Europe, — and called to the throne Leopold of Coburg, a wise and able prince. With the support of England and France (§ 400), these arrangements were confirmed, despite the bitter hostility of Holland; and Belgium became an independent kingdom.

B. Belgium.

507. The Constitution is that of 1831, with a few amendments which will be noted. It contains an admirable bill of rights. The king acts only through ministers; and by custom the ministers are "responsible," and must resign if outvoted in Parliament.[1] The Parliament contains two houses. Both are elective; but part of the Peers are chosen indirectly (by local councils), and the rest must own a large amount of property. The franchise has been subject to three amendments, and in late years it has been connected with the other important question in Belgian politics, — the kulturkampf.

508. Franchise, the Kulturkampf, and Parties. — In 1831 the franchise rested upon the payment of a considerable tax. When the revolutions of 1848 were upsetting so many governments, Belgium made only a slight reduction in this qualification for voting. For nearly fifty years there was no further change; but meanwhile great city populations were growing up, with masses of artisans who had no votes. Indeed, in the eighties, only one man in ten had the right of suffrage, and agitation began for further extension of the franchise. The proposal secured little support in Parliament, however, and bill after bill was voted down. In the early nineties the discontent of the Radicals became violent. In 1893 the Labor party declared a general strike, in order to exert political pressure, and the

---

[1] The firm establishment of parliamentary government was due in great measure to the liberal disposition and wisdom of Leopold, whose long reign was a model for all constitutional kings. Leopold was succeeded in 1865 by his son, Leopold II.

crowds of unemployed men in Brussels about the parliament house threatened serious riots. The militia was called out, but it showed a dangerous disposition to side with the rioters. Under such conditions the Parliament yielded and passed the present franchise law, providing for *manhood suffrage, with plural votes for wealth and education.* Each man has one vote; two votes are given to each man over thirty-five years of age, if he possesses certain wealth, or if he is the head of a family with children; and three votes are given to men of high educational qualification and to those who have held important public office.

The new franchise produced unexpected results. From 1850 to 1884 the leading question in politics had been whether state or church should control education. The Liberals were in power the greater part of the time, and, by one bill after another, they took the schools wholly away from clerical influence. This resulted, however, in the growth of a large Clerical party; the Liberals became badly divided over the proposed extension of the franchise; and, in 1884, the Clericals came into power and began to restore church control over education. Just before the franchise law of 1893, the Chamber of Representatives stood ninety-two Clericals and fifty Liberals. The election of 1894 returned one hundred and four Clericals, fifteen Liberals and thirty-three Socialists. Of the two million votes cast, over a third were "plural votes," and these very largely reënforced the Clericals. That party at once carried its policy to complete victory. A new education bill (1895) placed the public schools under the supervision of the church, and provided state support for the church schools.

In 1899, a further electoral reform introduced *proportional representation*, — a method which attempts to secure a fair share of representatives for minorities, instead of shutting them out altogether;[1] and in the next elections (1900) the

---

[1] This device is admirably explained in the *International Year Book* for 1900, page 119.

Socialists made still further gains. The old Liberals have practically disappeared, and the field is left to the two extremes, — the Clerical Conservatives and the Socialists. This is not a condition favorable to orderly progress, and for some years Belgian politics have been marked by unrest and tumult.

509. Relations to France. — Belgium is among the leading industrial countries. The population is about six and a half millions, and it has nearly doubled since 1815. A considerable party looks forward to annexation to France; and, in case of a general European war, with consequent territorial rearrangements, this might be brought to pass. Germany and England would be strongly opposed to such action.[1]

C. HOLLAND.

THE KINGDOM OF THE NETHERLANDS.

510. Constitution and Politics. — Since 1830, Holland has experienced no violent change. In 1848 a new constitution replaced the one of 1814, and in 1896 the electorate was extended. The royal family belongs to the great House of Orange, and the nation is loyally devoted to it.[2] The Parliament keeps the ancient name of the States General. The upper house is chosen by the local legislatures of the various provinces for nine years, one-third going out each third year.[3] Its powers are very slight. The House of Representatives is elected directly by the people; and since 1896 practically all men of twenty-five years have the franchise, except vagabonds and paupers and sometimes unmarried sons in the poorer families. The kings have kept some control over the ministries, but under the recent regency and the reign of a girl, ministers are becoming truly "responsible" to the Representatives.

---

[1] For Belgium and the Congo State, see § 586.

[2] The present sovereign (1907) is Wilhelmina, who succeeded to the throne in 1890, at ten years of age. In 1900 she married.

[3] This arrangement of partial renewals of a branch of the legislature, which has been adopted in many countries, as in our Senate, seems to have originated in Holland under her ancient constitution.

The leading question in politics in the second half of the nineteenth century was the kulturkampf. About one-third the population are Catholics, and they and the Protestant Conservatives show some disposition to unite against the Liberals, who desire to exclude religious control from the schools.

511. Conditions and Problems. — Holland is rich and prosperous. The population is a little over five millions, and it has grown in the last century even faster than that of Belgium. The colonial empire, despite the great losses in the wars of the French Revolution, is still vast and produces large revenues.

From time to time there has been talk of a desire on the part of Germany to annex Holland. The House of Orange will die out with the childless Queen, and a German Prince will probably claim the throne as the lawful heir. But the Dutch, though allied to the Germans in speech and blood, are proud of their separate nationality and their free institutions, and would fight vehemently against absorption by the larger Power. On a recent occasion, when annexation talk was prevalent, a Dutch paper published a significant cartoon showing the dikes cut and the land flooded, with the tops of the helmets of the German army just visible beneath the waves. Germany would have to reckon also with France and England.

FOR FURTHER READING. — Seignobos, 229–255; Phillips, 187–199; 454.

SPECIAL REPORTS. — 1. Elections and parties in each state since 1900. 2. Recent political questions and happenings.

III. THE SWISS REPUBLIC.

A. HISTORY FROM 1789 TO 1848.[1]

512. Conditions before the French Revolution. — The Peace of Westphalia (1648) had recognized the independence of the thirteen Swiss cantons. They had already been independent in fact for two centuries and a half, and they remained without further change a hundred and fifty years more. During most of this

---

[1] For a review of earlier Swiss history, see § 161.

time the history of these isolated districts was far from happy. The sovereign cantons were divided into hostile groups by conflicting democratic and aristocratic preferences,[1] and, after the Reformation, by bitter religious differences, while within many of the single cantons — the wealthier and more aristocratic ones — there were incessant class struggles.

513. The Helvetic Republic and the Act of Mediation, 1798-1815. — After the beginning of the French Revolution, the democratic revolts grew more general, and in 1798 the French Directory took advantage of the dissensions to occupy the country and to consolidate the squabbling communities into a centralized democratic state, under the name of the Helvetic Republic (§ 355). The constitution, however, ignored altogether the ancient self-government of the separate cantons, and so proved unpopular. Civil war broke out between the Federalists, or the upholders of the old arrangement, and the Centralists, or adherents of the new government; and in 1803, after conferring with the different leaders, Napoleon imposed upon the nation a wise compromise. His *Act of Mediation* gave to each canton a separate constitution, — modifying the old aristocratic ones, however, in the interests of liberty, — and it provided for a central Diet with authority to compel obedience to its laws. At the same time, six new cantons were added, by raising subject or allied territories to the same rank as the old thirteen states.

514. The Federal Pact of 1815. — Napoleon's fall carried with it the fall of the Act of Mediation. The aristocratic cantons wished to recover their old subject territories, and the conservative elements wished to do away with all French reforms; while the new cantons, of course, were willing to fight for the

---

[1] The original "Forest Cantons" were pure democracies and governed themselves by folkmoots, or primary assemblies of all the people. In Bern, Luzern, and some other cantons, a few families had obtained exclusive possession of the government, so that the rule was an hereditary oligarchy. In other states the city inhabitants controlled the government, while the rural inhabitants had no political rights.

existing constitution. Finally a compromise was effected through the influence of the Congress of Vienna, and the *Federal Pact* was adopted. This constitution resembled in general character the old Articles of Confederation of the American States. The union was a loose confederacy, with emphasis upon state sovereignty and with less strength in the central government than there had been under Napoleon's constitution. The Congress of Vienna added to the union three new cantons, taken from French and Italian territory, and so raised the number of states to twenty-two, as at present.

515. Reform of the Constitutions of the Cantons in 1830. — Under the Federal Pact, each state was free to make its own constitution, and several of the more aristocratic ones returned to the ancient governments of the eighteenth century. Disorders, of course, began again, similar to those preceding the French Revolution; but in 1830, after the second revolution in France, popular risings compelled the aristocratic cantons to adopt liberal constitutions. For the next three years the Radicals (as the democratic party was called) attempted also to compel a change in the national government; but for the time the effort failed, and the Federal Pact remained the constitution of the union until 1848.

516. Religious Strife, 1830-1847. — The next change grew out of religious strife. The reorganized cantons of 1830 were Protestant, and now they became radical in politics. The old democratic cantons were Catholic, and were coming to be controlled by a new Clerical party. Hostility between the Catholics on the one side and the Protestants and Free Thinkers on the other, threatened to split in twain not only the Confederacy, but also some of the cantons themselves. Many armed conflicts took place, transferring authority in a given canton from one party to another, and Switzerland was soon organized in two camps.

The final struggle began in Aargau. In this canton, in the election of 1840, the Radicals won. The Clericals rose in revolt; and, in punishment, after suppressing the rising, the

Radicals dissolved the eight monasteries of the canton. This act was contrary to the Federal Pact; and the seven Catholic cantons[1] in alarm formed a separate league, — *the Sonderbund*, — and declared that they would protect the Clericals in their rights in any canton where they might be attacked.

517. The Sonderbund War. — For the Sonderbund to exist at all was practically to dissolve the union; for it to take this tone was to threaten war between two distinct governments. In 1847, the Federal Diet, now controlled by the Radicals, replied to the challenge by calling on the Sonderbund to dissolve and by ordering the expulsion of the Jesuits from Switzerland. The Sonderbund withdrew its deputies from the Diet, and war was begun (1847).[2] The despotic Powers were preparing to interfere in behalf of the Sonderbund (§ 400), and did furnish it with arms and money, but the Unionists (warned and encouraged by the English government) acted with remarkable celerity and crushed the Secessionists in a three weeks' campaign, before foreign intervention had seriously begun. Metternich still intended to interfere, but the revolutions of 1848 rendered him harmless. Then the Radicals expelled the Jesuits, remodeled the constitutions of the conquered cantons, so as to put power into the hand of the Radicals there, and adopted a new national constitution.

The constitution was submitted to a popular vote, and received a large majority. It needed a majority of the cantons as well as of the people, and it was announced to have been adopted by fifteen cantons. In one of the fifteen, however, the vote was given only by a government installed by force of arms, and in four of the others the majority was made by

---

[1] Including the original "Forest Cantons."

[2] There are many interesting points of likeness and also of contrast between the party strife and civil war in Switzerland and that a little later in the United States. In both countries there was a conflict between a national and a states' sovereignty party. In both, as a result of war, the more progressive part of the nation forced a stronger union upon the more backward portion: in both, too, the states which tried to secede did so in behalf of rights guaranteed them in the old constitution, which they believed to be endangered by their opponents. Students may be led to see other likenesses.

counting *Yes* all those voters who failed to vote. The change in the government, like the adoption of our fourteenth amendment, was in considerable degree a war measure.

B. Switzerland To-day.

518. The Constitution of 1848. — By the new constitution, which with slight amendments is that of to-day, the union became a true Federal Republic.

The Federal Assembly, or national legislature, has two houses, — *the Council of the States* and *the National Council.* The first consists of two delegates from each canton. The delegates are chosen by the cantonal legislatures, by whom also their term of office is fixed and their salaries are paid. This Council *represents the states' rights principle,* and in form it is a survival of the old Diet. The other parts of the constitution, however, are new and tend toward nationalism. The second house of the legislature, the National Council, *represents the people of the union;* and the members are elected in single districts, like our Representatives, for a term of three years. The franchise is given to all adult males, and elections take place on Sundays, so that all may vote.

The Federal Executive is not a single president, but a committee of seven[1] (*the Federal Council*), whose members are chosen by the Federal Assembly. One of the seven, especially named for the purpose, is *the President of the Council;* but he possesses little more authority than the other members. The Federal Council acts somewhat as an English ministry, except that its powers are much more limited. Besides attending to the usual duties of an executive, it helps frame bills and it takes part in legislative debates; but it cannot dissolve the legislature, and it need not resign if its measures are rejected.

There is also *a Federal Judiciary,* chosen by the Federal Assembly; but it lacks the power of our American Supreme

---

[1] This is in accordance with the ancient practice of the separate cantons.

Court to declare laws void: it is bound to accept as valid all acts of the legislature.

Each Canton has its own constitution and government. In a few cantons, the old folkmoot, or primary Assembly, is still preserved; in the others, the legislature consists of *one chamber*,[1] chosen by manhood suffrage. In all there are *executive councils*. The subdivisions of the cantons enjoy a large amount of democratic self-government.

519. Direct Legislation. — As a rule, even in modern democratic countries, the people govern themselves only indirectly: they choose representatives (legislatures and governors), and these few delegated individuals attend directly to all matters of government. Radical democratic thinkers, however, demand that some way be found for the people themselves to take a direct part in law-making; and so far, Switzerland, more than any other country, has shown how this may be done. The two Swiss devices for this end are known as *the referendum* and *the popular initiative*.

Historically the referendum is the older. It consists merely in referring laws that have been passed by the legislature to a popular vote. This practice really originated in America. The State of Massachusetts submitted its first constitution to a popular vote in 1778 and in 1780, and there were a few other applications of the principle in America at about the same time. A little later, the French Revolutionists adopted the practice for their constitutions, and the plebiscites of the Napoleons extended the principle to some other questions besides constitutions.[2] In America since about 1820 nearly all our states have used the referendum on the adoption of new constitutions and of constitutional amendments, and there has been a growing tendency to submit other important measures

---

[1] A two-chambered legislature is contrary to Swiss practice, and the plan was adopted in the national constitution, from the United States, to reconcile the claims of the adherents of states' rights and of the Nationalists.

[2] The French Constitution of the Year I provided for a referendum on ordinary laws; but this constitution never went into effect. Cf. § 339.

SWITZERLAND — DIRECT LEGISLATION.

to popular decision, both in state and city governments. But in Switzerland the practice goes farther. By the Constitution of 1848, all constitutional amendments, cantonal or national, must be submitted to popular vote, and in some cantons *this compulsory referendum is extended to all laws;* while, by an amendment of 1874, a certain number of voters *by petition may require the submission of any national law.* This last provision is known as the *optional referendum,* and it has been in use in the separate cantons for most of the nineteenth century.

The popular initiative is a purely Swiss development. It consists in the right of a certain number of voters by petition to frame a new bill and to compel its submission to the people. A little before 1848, this device began to be regarded as the natural complement of the referendum. Four cantons had already made some use of it, and the new Constitution of 1848 required all cantons to permit it in constitutional amendments, if a majority of voters took part in a petition. The cantons rapidly adopted more generous measures than this, however, and, by 1870, in nearly all of them a small number of voters could introduce any law they desired. In 1891, by amendment, this liberal principle was adopted for the national government: *a petition of fifty thousand voters may frame a law, which must then be submitted to a national vote.*

Thus the people can act directly, without the intervention of the legislature: they can frame bills by the initiative, and pass on them by the referendum.[1] These devices for direct legislation are the most important advances made in late years by democracy. The referendum has worked well, both in federal and cantonal governments, and the voters have shown themselves rather more conservative than the legislature. It must be remembered, too, that since the Swiss executives have no veto, it is especially fit that the people should have one: **and**

---

[1] A good account of the referendum and initiative in Switzerland is given in Seignobos, *Europe since 1814,* 271-279 and 283-284. A very full account, including analysis of bills passed and rejected, is given by Lowell, *Governments and Parties,* II, 238-300.

this is particularly the case in cantons where the legislature has only one chamber. The initiative also has been successful in the cantons, but on the national scale it has been on trial too short a time to permit a safe judgment upon its value.

520. Social and Political Prosperity. — Switzerland fills a far larger place in political history than her territory does on the map. Since 1848 the Swiss have been one nation. The defeated party quickly accepted the result of the Sonderbund war in good faith, and now all Swiss look upon each other as fellow-countrymen. In the last half-century Switzerland has made amazing advances, and to-day it is one of the most progressive countries in the world. The schools are among the best in Europe, and no other country has so little illiteracy. Comfort is well diffused. The population increases rapidly, and in 1896 it numbered three and a third millions. The army system is a universal militia service, lighter than is known anywhere else in Europe.

Two-thirds of the people are Germans; but French and Italian, as well as German, are "official" languages, and the debates in the Federal Assembly are carried on in all three tongues. Race feeling, which is so disintegrating a force in Austria, works no harm in Switzerland. The universal patriotism of the people is a high testimonial to the strength of free institutions and of the flexible federal principle, in binding together diverse elements.

"The Swiss Confederation, on the whole, is the most successful democracy in the world. Unlike almost every other state in Europe, it has no irreconcilables, — the only persons in its territory who could in any sense be classed under this name being a mere handful of anarchists, and these, as in our land, are foreigners. The people are contented. The government is farsighted, efficient, economical, and steady in its policy. . . . Corruption in public life is almost unknown, and appointments to office are not made for political purposes. Officials are selected on their merits, and are retained as long as they can do their work; and yet the evils of a bureaucracy scarcely exist. . . . The Swiss statesmen deserve the highest praise for their labors, and the greatest admiration for their success; but we must beware of thinking that their methods would produce the same results under different conditions. The problem they have had to solve is that of self-government among a small, stable, and frugal people; and this is far simpler than self-government in a great, rich, and ambitious nation." — LOWELL, *Governments and Parties*, II, 334-336.

"Is Switzerland not already in her way a miniature parliament of man? . . . It is the will of the Swiss people and their fixed determination which keep them united. Consider the mixture of races and religions which they represent. Of the twenty-two cantons, thirteen are German-speaking; four are French; in three, German and French both are spoken; in one, Italian; and in another, Romansch. The population of German Switzerland is almost purely Teutonic; that of French Switzerland, about half and half Teutonic and Celto-Roman; while Italian and Romansch Switzerland can boast of Celto-Roman, Ostro-Gothic and even Etruscan elements. Some of these cantons are Protestant, others Roman Catholic, and others, again, have a mixed population of both faiths. If these incongruous, often antagonistic, cantons can meet upon some common plane and conform to some common standard, can live side by side in peace and prosperity, surely the task of some day uniting the nations of the world upon a similar basis is not altogether hopeless and chimerical." — McCRACKAN, *The Rise of the Swiss Republic*, 363.

FOR FURTHER READING. — Seignobos, *Europe since 1814*, 255-284; Lowell, *Governments and Parties*, 180-336; Wilson, *The State*; recent Year Books, Annual Encyclopedias, and Reviews. Fuller accounts may be found in McCrackan, *Rise of the Swiss Republic*; Adams and Cunningham, *Swiss Confederation*; Winchester, *Swiss Republic*; and Vincent, *State and Federal Government in Switzerland*.

IV. THE SCANDINAVIAN KINGDOMS.

A. DENMARK.

521. Survey to 1866. — In the later Middle Ages, Denmark was an elective monarchy distracted by feudal anarchy. In 1660, after a shameful defeat by Sweden, Frederick III called a Diet, to which he invited representatives of the towns and the clergy, and with the aid of these elements he took away much of the power of the nobles. The Diet authorized him to establish a charter, and he set up an hereditary absolutism.

There was no further change, except in matters of territory, until well into the nineteenth century. After 1831, the four provinces of the kingdom were given "provincial estates" to advise with the monarch; and in 1848, the king felt obliged to grant a modern constitution. For many years, all energies were turned toward retaining the Schleswig-Holstein territory (§ 466); and not until after the defeat[1] of 1864 did Denmark begin to have any real constitutional development. When the matter of the duchies was settled, a Democratic party ("Friends of the Peasants") at once began to demand reform, and, after two years of clamor, a constitution was established.

522. Constitution and Politics. — The constitution of 1866 promises freedom of speech and of the press, and creates a Diet (Rigsdag) of two houses. The Landthing, or upper house, is composed partly of members appointed by the king, partly of members elected on a very high property basis. The Folkthing, or lower house, is elected by manhood suffrage.[2]

Since 1873 there has been a long contest over the question of ministerial responsibility. The lower house, controlled by the Democratic parties, passed a resolution, declaring it to be "a necessary condition of constitutional monarchy" that the king choose a ministry "in harmony with the people's representatives." This was the English practice, which had now become established in several other countries. The King replied that he was entitled to keep a ministry which was supported by either house of the legislature, and he virtually took up Bismarck's theory of the right of the king and the upper house to rule without the consent of the lower chamber (§ 465). From 1877 to 1891 the government raised taxes and passed laws without regarding the lower house, ruling much of the time by martial law. Then the Democratic party split into factions, and the King's party secured control in the lower house also (1894). The conflict, however, will undoubtedly be reopened.

Iceland, the only important Danish colony, received a constitution in 1874 and a larger measure of "home rule" in 1893. Since the latter date it has had its own Diet, and it no longer pays taxes into the Danish treasury.

B. Sweden and Norway.

523. The Establishment of the Dual State (1815). — For some centuries before 1814, Norway had been a dependency of Denmark. The Congress of Vienna gave it to Sweden, to reward

---

[1] Compare with the case of Austria after 1866, and France after 1870.
[2] All self-supporting men, thirty years of age, can vote.

that country for services against Napoleon. But between 1810 and 1814 a national feeling had been growing up in Norway, and the people declined to be bartered from one ruler to another without their own consent. A Diet assembled at *Eidvold*, declared Norway a sovereign state, adopted a liberal constitution, and elected a king (*May 17, 1814*). Sweden, backed by the Powers, made ready to enforce its claims, and finally a compromise was arranged. The recently elected king abdicated, and the Diet elected the Swedish king as King of Norway, on condition that he should recognize the new Norwegian constitution.

Thus Norway and Sweden became a dual monarchy. The union was looser, however, than that of Austria-Hungary. The two countries had the same king, but they had no shadow of a common ministry and nothing to correspond to the Austrian Delegations (§ 492). Each kingdom kept its own constitution and its own legislature. The arrangement lasted almost a century.

524. Swedish Politics in the Nineteenth Century. — Until after 1850 the Diet in Sweden was composed of four estates, — nobles, clergy, citizens, and peasants, — so that the king could easily play off one class against another. Such a legislature could not check royal power. But in 1866 this arrangement was replaced by a modern parliament of two houses. The upper house is elected by district councils, and only men of large property are eligible. The lower house is elected by all men who pay taxes on an annual income of about $225. This franchise excludes a large part of the adult males from voting. In 1895 there began a vehement agitation in Sweden for a reduction of the tax qualification by one-half, while Socialist and Radical parties appeared, calling for universal suffrage. Recently (January, 1907) this demand has promised success; but Sweden is still much more aristocratic, both in politics and in society, than Norway.

525. Norway: Struggle for Self-government; Separation from Sweden. — In 1814 the Norwegian legislature (Storthing) was chosen on the basis of a low property qualification; and since

1884 it has been elected by manhood suffrage. It assembles as one house, but divides itself for most purposes into two chambers. The king of the dual state could not dissolve it, and a bill became law in spite of his veto, if passed in three successive annual sessions.

The chief interest in Norwegian politics in the nineteenth century lay in the agitation for a greater amount of self-government. Except for one period of about thirty years in the middle of the century, the contest was incessant, and after 1872 it grew increasingly bitter. In the early part of the century the Storthing succeeded in abolishing nobility in Norway, after two vetoes by the King. In the latter part, the two chief points of dispute were (1) the Storthing's control of the ministry and (2) a separate consular service.

In 1872–1874 the Storthing passed a bill three times, ordering the ministers to attend the debates and requiring them to resign if outvoted. King Oscar II[1] declared truly that this was an amendment to the constitution, and therefore a change in the compact between the two countries: in such a case, he urged, the rule limiting his veto could not apply. He offered, however, to yield the point if the Storthing would give the ministry the power of dissolution, — which elsewhere goes with "ministerial responsibility," — so that the government might appeal to the voters when it wished. The Storthing refused all compromise. The King declined to recognize the law. The Storthing impeached the ministers, and civil war seemed at hand; but a new election in 1884 showed that the Norwegians were almost unanimous in the demand, and the King yielded, after a twelve years' struggle.

---

[1] Oscar II came to the throne in 1872, just before the Norwegian national movement became violent, and his wise moderation and his fairness had much to do with preventing an armed conflict, which impetuous men on either side were ready to precipitate. He is one of the greatest men who have sat upon European thrones in the last century. Foreign nations have paid a deserved tribute to his ability and fairness, by requesting him frequently to act as arbitrator in international disputes. The United States has been interested in some of these arbitrations.

By this success the Storthing transferred the real executive power for all internal affairs into the hands of its own committees. It passed on at once to a demand for power to appoint Norwegian consuls, separate from the Swedish service, so as to secure partial control over trade relations. This demand also seemed to the King to involve a change in the constitution, — which put the regulation of foreign affairs into his hands, — and the Swedish party claimed that the proposed arrangement would virtually ruin the slight union that remained between the two countries.

The struggle waxed vehement. In the course of the contest, the Norwegians removed the symbol of union from their flag (1886–1888), after passing the bill to that effect each year for three sessions, and both countries at times made preparations for war. Indeed, Norway erected a great and costly line of fortifications on the frontier toward Sweden.

Suggestions began to be heard for Norwegian independence. Before the close of the century a strong political party avowed that end, and the nation soon came to unite in that policy. In May, 1905, when once more a long negotiation for separate consular service had failed, the Storthing, by unanimous vote, decided to provide by its own act for Norwegian consuls. This was virtual secession, and the King refused to recognize it. The Storthing then declared the union dissolved, and set up a provisional government. The aristocratic elements in Sweden called for war; but King Oscar was nobly resolute that his two peoples should not imbrue their hands in each other's blood, and the Swedish labor-unions threatened a universal strike to prevent a violent coercion of their Norwegian brethren. Therefore when, in July, the Norwegians declared in favor of independence in a great national referendum, by a vote of 368,000 to 184, Sweden bowed to the decision; and in September, 1905, to the eternal honor of both peoples, *a peaceful separation* was fully arranged upon friendly terms.

Thus Norway became an independent nation. A small party wished the new nation to become a republic; but, in a second referendum, a large majority chose for king a Danish prince, who was crowned in June, 1906, as Haakon VII.

When Norwegian independence was mooted in the nineteenth century, many friends of Scandinavia feared lest Sweden, if so weakened, might fall a prey to Russia, which had already swallowed up so much Swedish territory. But Russia's collapse in the war with Japan (§ 591) had removed this peril for the time; and further safeguards are now being sought (1907) either in the "neutralization" (cf. § 377 *b*, note) of the Scandinavian states by the European Powers, or in a new and true federation between the three Scandinavian kingdoms.

526. Internal Conditions. — Norway has two and a quarter millions of people; Sweden, more than twice as many.[1] Sweden is also the richer country. The Norwegians, however, have the larger merchant navy, — more than four times as large as Sweden's, and the fourth in size in all Europe. This was one reason why Norway felt it had a special interest in controlling the consular service. Norwegian authors, like the novelist-statesman Björnson and the poet Ibsen, stand in the front ranks of European literature, and such facts, no doubt, helped to make the people more discontented with their recent political inferiority.

There has appeared a small Republican party in Norway and also a Socialist party; but this fact so far has aided the Conservatives. In all three Scandinavian kingdoms, until recently, the Democratic strength has been in the peasants, while the towns have been centers of Conservative power. But while the new Radicals in all three countries have gained some supporters in the towns, the peasants are alarmed at the idea of Socialism, and are passing over to some extent to the Conservative party.

---

[1] Each of the three Scandinavian kingdoms at least doubled in population in the nineteenth century. This rapid growth of population is one of the striking phenomena of modern times. It has been made possible, of course, by the improved economic conditions and the growth of great cities with new kinds of employment for men.

CHAPTER VI.

ENGLAND IN THE NINETEENTH CENTURY.

Reconstruction without Revolution. — JUDSON.
England in the nineteenth century has served as a political model for Europe. The English developed the political mechanism of constitutional monarchy, parliamentary government, and safeguards for personal liberty. Other nations have only imitated them. — SEIGNOBOS.

I. CONDITIONS IN 1815.

527. Absence of Progress in the Eighteenth Century: Parliament becomes the Organ of an Oligarchy. — Except for the romantic acquisition of a vast world-empire (§§ 283-284), the eighteenth century was singularly uninteresting in English history. In the study of England to 1689, attention has been called to the preëminence of that country in social and political progress. The nineteenth century was to witness a further glorious advance; but in order to appreciate its story, we must understand that the period between was one of retrogression. From 1689 to 1815, England did not simply stand still: she went backward, in both political and social conditions.

There was some slow gain for ministerial government (§ 252) in place of royal government, — though that principle was by no means carried to perfection,[1] — but in all other political matters there was a positive loss. Parliament had never been democratic, of course; but after 1689 it shriveled up more and more into the selfish organ of a small oligarchy of landlords.

---

[1] Professor Seeley says very truly of the great Pitt that he was not made minister because he had a majority, but he had his majority because he had been made minister. This suggests the condition of Spain in 1900 (§ 499).

Each of the forty counties of England, large or small, sent two representatives to Parliament, as did also nearly two hundred and fifty parliamentary boroughs.[1] There were also one hundred members from Ireland and forty-five from Scotland. The older kings had summoned representatives from whatever boroughs they chose, but gradually a borough which had been sending delegates secured the right, by custom, to continue to send them; and this held good, even if, in the change of centuries, the place had utterly decayed.

The case was the worse, because the Tudor Kings, in order better to manage the Parliaments, had summoned representatives from a great number of little hamlets which never had just claim to representation, but which from the first were "pocket boroughs," — owned and controlled by some lord of the court party. Then, too, in earlier English history, the south of the island with its fertile soil and its Channel ports had been the populous district; but in the eighteenth century, with the growth of manufactures, population had shifted to the coal and iron regions of the north and west. Before 1800, great cities had grown up there; but they could get no representation in Parliament, because, after 1660, the kings had lost their old right to make parliamentary boroughs, just when that power might have been exercised to public advantage.

Thus the conditions had become unspeakably unfair and corrupt. *Dunwich* was under the waves of the North Sea, which had gradually encroached upon the land, but a descendant of an ancient owner of the soil still possessed the right to row out with the sheriff on election day and choose himself as representative to Parliament. *Old Sarum* was once a cathedral city on the summit of a lofty hill; but new Sarum, or Salisbury, a few miles away on the plain, drew the population and the cathedral to itself until not a vestige of the old town remained. Then the grandfather of William Pitt bought the soil where Old Sarum had stood, and it was for this "pocket borough" that the great Pitt entered Parliament.[2] So, *Gatton*

---

[1] A few of the boroughs had come to have only one representative, and this was true also of the twelve counties of Wales.

[2] It was wittily said at the time, that the Pitt family had "an hereditary seat in the House of Commons."

was a park, and *Corfe Castle* a ruin; and the list might be considerably extended.

Then there were a great number of "rotten boroughs" — petty villages or little towns, with six, or a dozen, or fifty, voters.[1] Some of these, too, were "pocket boroughs," where the voters were dependent upon a neighboring landlord,[2] and always returned his nominee without the form of a contest. Often these borough owners sold the parliamentary seat as a regular part of their revenue, — usually, of course, to a member of a particular political party.

The condition was as bad or worse when these small boroughs were independent of a landlord. The right to vote in them was determined by varying and quaintly fantastic rules and by historical accidents (which even in the larger towns shut out all but a fraction of the inhabitants[3]), and the few privileged voters usually sold the seat in Parliament for their own benefit, with less conscience than the single proprietors

---

[1] A petition for reform in 1793 stated that seventy members were chosen for thirty-four places "in which it would be trifling with patience to mention any electors whatever, the election being notoriously a matter of form"; ninety more came from places of less than fifty voters each. The *Annual Register* for 1793, pp. 83–103, gives the document.

[2] In 1828 at Newark the Duke of Newcastle drove out five hundred and eighty-seven tenants who had ventured to vote against his candidate. Complaint was made in Parliament, but the Duke answered calmly, "Have I not a right to do what I like with my own?"

[3] It was not living in a town any length of time that gave a man the right to vote, but some one of about a dozen complex qualifications. Molesworth (*Reform Bill*, 107, note) counts fifteen of these peculiar qualifications; Medley, 197–199, has a good classification of them. In Weymouth, in 1826, the right to vote went with the right to share in the rents of certain ancient village property; and so twenty persons, some of them paupers, voted because of their title each to one-twentieth of a sixpence. Portsmouth, with forty-six thousand people, had only one hundred and three voters. Lord John Russell, who framed the great Reform Bill of 1832, says in his *Recollections* that there were regular dealers in borough seats (borough mongers), who bought up the borough tenures whenever possible, so as to reduce the number of "freemen" to be dealt with; and he adds that if a man refused to sell, "it was not an uncommon practice to blow up his house with gunpowder, and so disfranchise a political opponent."

used. In 1766 the corporation of Sudbury advertised in the public press that the parliamentary seat was for sale to the highest bidder.

Then, it must be remembered that until 1832 by far the greater number of large cities sent no representatives at all. This was true for Manchester, Leeds, Birmingham, Sheffield, and indeed for nearly all the manufacturing centers of the west and north of England, though some of them had come to have one hundred thousand inhabitants.

These were the conditions that Lord Russell referred to in 1832 in a speech introducing the Reform Bill (§ 531), when he asked the House to consider the amazement of a stranger who had come to observe the boasted representative institutions of England, and who was taken to a ruined mound and was told that that mound sent two representatives to Parliament, and then taken to a stone wall with three niches in it, and told that those niches sent two representatives to Parliament, and then taken to a green park with many signs of flourishing vegetable life but none of human habitation, and told that that park sent two representatives to Parliament, while he would see populous towns full of enterprise, industry, and intelligence, which, he would be told, sent no representatives to Parliament.

The case was not quite so bad in the counties; but here, only the freeholders[1] could vote, and the smaller freeholders usually feared to offend a powerful neighbor. Moreover, when there were two candidates, and a real contest, the voting was *viva voce*, and the polls were kept open two weeks, so that there was every chance for the sale and purchase of votes. In many counties there were very few voters, and in Scotland, in the county of Bute, with fourteen thousand people, it is said that at one time, aside from the absentee landlords, there was only one voter. A humorous account tells how this one man went to the polling place, made a nominating speech for himself, voted for himself, and then declared himself unanimously elected. All Scotland, with two million people, had not over three thousand

---

[1] The freeholders, too, comprised only a small part of those who correspond to landowners with us.

voters, and the Irish members of Parliament were nearly all nominated by landlords.

Thus the boasted representative system of England had become, in Macaulay's words, "a monstrous system of represented ruins and unrepresented cities." In 1800, one hundred and ninety-seven patrons controlled a majority of the whole house. The Duke of Norfolk could fill eleven seats. An estimate, generally accepted, says that four hundred and eighty-seven of the six hundred and fifty-eight members were really nominees of single individuals. The House of Commons was hardly more representative than the House of Lords.

528. Retrogression in the Condition of the Workers. — The sufferings of the working class from 1450 to 1600 have been noted (§§ 234, 235). The seventeenth century was a period of prosperity; and the middle class, both merchants and country gentry, continued to grow rich through the eighteenth century; but after 1760 there began another deplorable falling off of prosperity for working men, both in country and in town.

a. Rural Conditions. Personal serfdom and servile land tenure had disappeared from England at a time when they still flourished vigorously on the continent; but it is not certain that the English workman of to-day is better off in consequence. The recently freed peasantry of the continent now hold the land their fathers tilled as serfs, and legislation and custom tend to keep them in possession. In England the peasantry became landowners four centuries ago, but their descendants have lost all hold upon the soil. This evil tendency had begun in Tudor times (§ 234); but the government of that age at least tried to check it, and, before 1600, new economic conditions had practically put a stop to it. After 1700, however, and especially after 1760, the movement began again, and it was intensified by the selfish class-legislation of the landlord Parliaments. Law after law "inclosed" the old "common lands," essentially for the benefit of landlords, depriving small landowners of a place to graze their cattle. This made it harder for the peasants to maintain themselves, and forced them to sell out, while the wealthy merchants and gentry were anxious to buy, because political power and social position both rested upon the possession of large estates. Moreover, the improved methods and costly machinery of the new landlords could not be adopted or competed with by the small holders, who were therefore under constant economic pressure to sell.[1]

In 1700, despite previous inclosures, there were still one hundred and eighty thousand small freeholders in England, who with their families comprised a million people, or nearly a fifth of the whole population at that time; and there were a still larger number of other small proprietors known as "copyholders" (§ 234). By 1800, these classes had almost disappeared. They drifted to the towns, to swell there the unhappy class that is yet to be described, or they remained to till the landlord's land, living on his estate as cottagers, subject to removal at his order. On the other hand, another class of laws (providing for "entail" and "right of Primogeniture") prevented the breaking up of the great estates even if the owners wished to sell. So the large estates grew larger, and could not grow smaller, while the small ones were eaten up, and England became, even more than before, the country of large landlords.

Since this change, the classes connected with the land are three, — landlords, tenant-farmers, and laborers. The first class comprise a few thousand gentry and nobles. Each such proprietor divides his estate into "farms," of from a hundred to three hundred acres, and leases them

---

[1] Read Goldsmith's *Deserted Village*. It was the accepted policy of landlords to buy out these poorer neighbors. An eighteenth century treatise on *The Duty of a Steward* contains the injunction, "He should not forget to make the best inquiry into the disposition of the freeholders, within or near any of his lord's manors, to sell their lands." A popular rhyme of the period expresses the feeling of the poorer classes: —

> "The law locks up the man or woman
> Who steals the goose from off the common;
> But leaves the greater villain loose
> Who steals the common from the goose."

out to men with a little capital, who are known as "farmers." This second class work the land directly, with the aid of the third class, who have no land of their own, but who labor for day-wages.

The landlords as a rule pride themselves upon keeping up their estates. They introduce costly machinery and improved methods of agriculture more rapidly than small proprietors could, and they furnish some of the money necessary to put farms and buildings into good condition; while their own stately homes, encompassed by rare old parks, give a beauty to rural England such as no other country knows. The farmers, as compared with the farm-laborers, are an aristocracy, and, by any standard, they are a prosperous class; but, of course, they have always been largely influenced by their landlords.

b. The Artisan Class. During nearly the same period (1760–1830), while the freeholders were disappearing, there took place also a change in manufacturing so marked that it is known as *the Industrial Revolution.* Until 1760 almost all manufactures were practically hand-made, as the name signifies. In the first half of the eighteenth century, each farmhouse eked out its income by hand-weaving and spinning and by other simple home manufactures; while even in the towns the making of cloth was carried on by great numbers of masters, each with two or three journeymen and apprentices working under his personal supervision and perhaps living in his household. But about 1760 English inventors began to replace the single hand-wheel with great machines driven by water power. The new machinery was costly and called for a large, organized force of workmen. Thus the gap between employer and workman was widened immensely. Manufactures were centralized and came under the direction of large capitalists, while great smoke-hung factories sprang up, with perhaps thousands of artisans packed in one of them, to work amid the incessant whirl of steam-driven spindles and looms. A like change followed rapidly in other manufactures, and the old "domestic system" (§ 235) was suddenly replaced by the "factory system."[1]

---

[1] Cheyney's *Industrial and Social History,* 188, describes the domestic system, and, 203–213, the new inventions and the factory system.

The change of course has been of supreme benefit to the world and to the working classes as a whole. It has made possible more life and better life. In England alone there are tens of millions of men and women more than could subsist there but for these mechanical inventions; and the wages of this vast population have risen greatly in purchasing power. But it is also true that, from time to time, new inventions with their new processes have worked great loss to whole classes of laborers, whose only capital was their skill in the old processes, and who through no fault of their own have been reduced from honorable independence to misery. And never has that loss been so general as in the great change just before 1800. The old hand-weavers could not understand the drift of the times. Great numbers of them maintained a losing fight, under harder and harder conditions;[1] and at intervals, for many years, laborers rose in riots, to smash machinery and burn factories.

But the more serious evils of this period were felt, not by the old operators, but by the new factory workers, and in a degree that has never since been paralleled. The rapid growth of city populations created problems which at first received no attention. Water supply, drainage, and cleanliness were all ignored, and proper housing did not exist. The masses of workmen and their families dwelt in denlike garrets and cellars, bordering upon crowded pestilential alleys, in perpetual filth, misery, and disease. Moreover, while the old society by slow growth had fitted itself in some measure to the needs of the working man, the old customs were wholly unsuited to these new conditions. The English courts for a long time treated all labor unions as conspiracies and sent the members promptly to prison. Thus the artisan class was kept in unorganized hordes, almost wholly at the mercy of employers who had no close touch with them and who were engaged in a new and mad race for wealth.

---

[1] George Eliot's *Silas Marner* is founded in part upon this fact.

Until after 1700, England was still essentially the old rural England. In 1700 Bristol was the second city of the kingdom, and it had only twenty-nine thousand inhabitants, while almost no other city except London contained more than five or six thousand people. After 1800, England almost at once became a land of cities. A like change, of course, was to take place in all civilized lands, but even yet it has nowhere else occurred so suddenly or on so large a scale. England led the way and had to face the first and the greatest transformation. In 1700 the population of England and Wales was between four and five millions. During the eighteenth century it doubled, rising to 8,893,000 in the census of 1801 (the first reliable census), and most of this growth was in the last thirty years of the century. In the next fifty years, the population doubled again, amounting in 1851 to 17,928,000 and in the second half of the century it very nearly doubled once more, amounting in 1901 to 32,526,000. No other country but the United States has experienced such an increase, and in no other did the rapid growth begin until England had done much to solve the new problems. The figures given above are for England and Wales. The "United Kingdom," including Ireland and Scotland, contained about 41,605,000 people in 1901.

FOR FURTHER READING. — On industrial conditions an excellent concise treatment, especially designed for high school students, is to be found in Cheyney's *Industrial and Social History of England*, 203–223. Fuller discussions are given in Toynbee's *Industrial Revolution*, Gibbins' *Industrial History of England*, and Cunningham and McArthur's *Outlines of English Industrial History*. Advanced students may consult Lecky's *England in the Eighteenth Century*, Walpole's *England since 1815*, and Cunningham's *Growth of English Industry and Commerce*, II.

On the political conditions, the treatments are usually interwoven with the account of the Reform Bill (§§ 539 ff.), and the references are given on page 554. The student at this point may read with profit Seignobos, 10–17, or McCarthy, *Epoch of Reform*, 25–29.

EXERCISE. — Note the transitions in rural labor in England : (1) serf and villein labor to about 1350, and then a decay of that system until it disappears, about 1450 ; (2) inclosures (for sheep farming), driving a large part of the peasantry from the soil, 1450–1600, — overlapping (3) another period of "inclosures" which changed the old common holdings into individual holdings, 1550–1640 ; then, after a prosperous period, (4) the new period of inclosures for large farming, 1760–1830. (The recent attempts to restore the peasantry to the soil will be noted in § 554.)

Note also the transitions in manufacturing (which hold good also for other countries besides England): (1) the gild system to about 1550; (2) the domestic system to about 1760; (3) the factory system.

Review the industrial history of modern Europe as a whole.

II. POLITICAL REFORM.

The sixteenth century had seen a new absolutism rise upon the ruins of the old feudalism and the old church. The struggle of the seventeenth century had resulted in replacing this absolutism with representative government highly aristocratic in character. Then, by natural decay, without any special design, this had hardened into the narrow oligarchy of the eighteenth century. The nineteenth century was to see the rebellion and victory of democracy.

A. THE CENTRAL GOVERNMENT.

529. Beginnings before 1815. — The failure of Parliament to represent the nation had long been recognized by progressive men as an evil; and the only reason why reform had not been accomplished was that all energies were given to the long French wars, which filled most of the period from 1689 to 1815. At each important interval in the conflict, efforts at reform were begun. In the twelve years in the middle of the century, between the French war and the American Revolution, and again in the seven years between that and the French Revolution, the Whig leaders seemed determined upon wise and temperate changes. But with the mutterings of the French Revolution, reaction set in. The excesses of the Revolutionists turned the English middle class vehemently against all change; and reform slumbered for forty years more (1790–1830).

In 1766 the elder Pitt declared that Parliament must reform itself from within, or it would soon be reformed "with a vengeance from without," and during the next few years many mass meetings were held to induce Parliament to act. Indeed, the war with America was connected with the determination of George III not to allow this claim in England. George felt that his two indolent and gross predecessors had allowed kingly power to slip from their hands, and he designed to regain it and to be a king in fact as well as in name. Of course, the corrupt nature of Parliament favored him: it would be much easier to control such a Parliament than one representing the whole nation. Therefore, when just at this time the Americans began to cry "No taxation without representation," King George felt it necessary to put them down. If their claim were allowed, then certainly so must that of Manchester and all new towns in England be granted; but if the demand could be made to seem a treasonable one on the part of a distant group of rebels, then the King could check the movement in England also and perhaps become the master of Parliament. This consideration explains why King George took such an active part against America. When the American war was over, however, in 1783, the younger Pitt took up the work for reform. "Parliament," he vehemently asserted, "is not representative of the people of Great Britain. It is representative of nominal boroughs and exterminated towns, of noble families, of wealthy individuals, of foreign potentates"; and he declared that this composition of Parliament alone had made it possible for the government to wage against America "this unjust, cruel, wicked, and diabolical war." In the years that followed, he introduced three bills for reform, until the French Revolution shelved all prospect of success.[1]

This check was particularly unfortunate because it came just when the evils of the Industrial Revolution were becoming serious. The sudden and enormous growth of population in the factory towns, together with the piling up of taxation [2] to support the wars against Napoleon, called imperatively for new adjustments. But the Tory party, which had stubbornly carried England to victory through the great war with the continent of Europe, was utterly unfit to cope with internal questions. Its leaders looked upon every privilege and every time-sanctioned abuse as sacred. Even after the fall of Napoleon, they angrily or sullenly refused to listen to projects for reform, and

---

[1] After this, only a few Radicals without influence kept up the struggle. In 1780, the Whig Duke of Richmond, an ardent sympathizer with America in the war, introduced a bill for annual elections, equal electoral districts, and manhood suffrage; but such proposals never received serious consideration. In 1790, on the occasion of a very moderate proposal for reform, the keynote of the opposition was struck by a speaker who exclaimed, "Would a wise man select a hurricane season to repair his house, however dilapidated?"

[2] National taxes in the first years of the nineteenth century are reported to have absorbed a fifth of the whole national income. In recent years they take less than one-twentieth, and they produce many returns, such as public education, not then afforded.

except for the admission of Catholics to political rights (1829), and for some reform of the atrocious penal code,[1] nothing was accomplished until 1830.

530. From 1815 to 1830. — The peace of 1815 was followed by a general business depression, accompanied by many labor riots and disorders, and by radical political agitation. The Tory government met these conditions with stern repressive laws, forbidding public meetings without the consent of the magistrates, under penalty of death, suspending habeas corpus, and suppressing debating societies.[2] In 1819, at a great public meeting at Manchester, the people were charged by the yeomanry,[3] through a stupid blunder of an officer, and several score of unarmed men and women were trampled under foot or sabered. This was the "Peterloo Massacre." The government thanked the yeomanry, and ordered the orator of the meeting to trial for conspiracy.

531. 1830-1832: the First Reform Bill. — In 1830, King George IV was succeeded by his brother William IV. William

---

[1] The English penal code of the eighteenth century has been fitly called a "sanguinary chaos." Its worst faults, like the abuses of the rotten borough era in politics, were due to the English dislike for change. Whenever in the course of centuries a crime had become especially troublesome, some Parliament had fixed a death penalty for it, and then no later Parliament had ever revised the code. In 1660, the number of "capital crimes" was fifty (three and a half times as many as there were in New England at the same time under the much slandered "blue laws"), and by 1800, the number had risen to over two hundred. To steal a sheep, to snatch a handkerchief out of a woman's hand, to cut down trees in an orchard, were all punishable by death. In 1823, Sir Robert Peel, the Tory leader, began the reform of this atrocious system, by removing the death penalty from a hundred offences. The reform was due to a long agitation carried on by *Romilly*. Lecky, *English History in the Eighteenth Century*, VI, 247 ff., gives an admirable account of conditions.

[2] In 1812, two editors were condemned to a year's imprisonment for saying that a rival paper had been guilty of exaggeration in calling the Prince of Wales an Adonis; and between 1808 and 1821, ninety-four journalists were punished for libel or seditious utterances, twelve of them being condemned to transportation to penal colonies. An interesting account of government prosecutions of men who signed petitions for parliamentary reform is given in Rosebery's *Pitt*, 163.

[3] A name now given to cavalry militia, organized on an aristocratic basis.

was supposed to be more liberal in his opinions than the preceding king, and the reform party was greatly encouraged. During the parliamentary elections, too, came the French Revolution of 1830, and its success and moderation probably aided the Whig candidates.

When the new Parliament met, the Whigs at once introduced a motion for a reform of the representation. The prime minister, Wellington, declared in reply that the existing legislature answered "all purposes of good legislation to a greater degree than any other legislature in any other country, at any time." He had never read or heard anything, he said, which could in any way satisfy him that the representation "could be improved."

This speech cost the hero of Waterloo his popularity. In a few days the Tory ministry resigned, and the Whigs came into power, with Earl Grey [1] as prime minister, pledged to Parliamentary reform. Lord John Russell [2] drew the bill and managed it in the House of Commons. It aimed (1) to distribute representation more fairly, and (2) to extend the franchise.[3]

a. The absurd apportionment was remedied (1) by taking away representation from fifty-six "rotten boroughs" (with **less than two thousand people** each) and by taking one member from each of thirty more small boroughs (under four thousand people), and then by creating forty-three new boroughs to include the new cities. London was made to consist

---

[1] Earl Grey was a stately English lord, whose eloquence in the trial of Warren Hastings, over forty years earlier, has been celebrated by Macaulay.

[2] Lord Russell was not yet a peer. He was the son of a duke, and the title Lord was a title of courtesy. But "Lord" Russell at this time was a commoner and sat in the House of Commons. Later in his life, he was a great prime minister. During the American Civil War he was the member of the English ministry most directly responsible for carelessly letting the *Alabama* escape, to prey upon the commerce of the Union, — a fact which he afterward admitted and apologized for.

[3] The manner of voting was not changed, except by providing separate polling places for subdivisions of the counties and by limiting the time to two days. The ballot was not introduced, because of Grey's objections.

of four boroughs with eight representatives. The larger counties received new members, according to their population, and the representation of Scotland was increased.

b. The suffrage in the boroughs was given to all "£10 householders,"[1] and, in the counties, to the farmers, who rented lands. Thus the artisan class in the towns, and the ordinary laborer in both town and country, were still left out.

Such a measure seems mild[2] enough to-day, but to the Tories it then seemed to threaten the foundations of society. The debates were unrivaled in fierceness, and lasted month after month. In March, 1831, the ministry carried the second reading[3] of the bill by a majority of one vote; but it was plain that they could not save it from hostile amendment, and they decided to dissolve Parliament and appeal to the country for better support. The King was extremely opposed to a new election so soon, and a passionate scene took place between him and his ministers; but he was forced to give way, and so, incidentally, it was settled that the ministry, not the king, really dissolves Parliament.

The dissolution was hailed by the radical elements with wild rejoicings, because it showed that the ministry meant to stand or fall on the issue of reform. Illumination was general, and a mob smashed the windows of the residence of the Duke of Wellington because they were not lighted. The Liberals went into the elections with the program, "The Bill, the whole Bill, and nothing but the Bill"; and, despite the unrepresentative nature of Parliament, they secured an overwhelming majority. In June, Lord Russell introduced the bill again.

---

[1] All who owned or rented a house worth ten pounds rental a year. Lodgers and men living in tenements were still excluded.

[2] Lord Russell in his *Recollections* rather apologizes for its timid nature. "I had," he says, "like many others, somewhat of a superstitious reverence for a system which seemed entwined with our liberties." Indeed the English people have had and still have a "superstitious" regard for old institutions and an instinctive aversion to change.

[3] A bill must pass three readings. Amendments are usually considered after the second.

In despair, the Tories used all tactics of delay, but in September the bill passed the Commons by a vote of 345 to 239. Then the Lords voted it down.

One session of the second Parliament was gone. There was passionate outcry against the Lords, with vehement demands for the abolition of that house. There was much violence, too; and England seemed on the brink of a violent revolution.

The same Parliament met for a new session in December, and Lord Russell again introduced the bill. It passed the Commons with an increased majority; and this time the Lords passed its "second reading," but immediately afterward they tacked on some unfriendly amendments. Already, sixteen new peers had been made to strengthen the Whigs; and now Lord Grey demanded authority to create enough more to save the bill. The King refused, and Grey resigned. There followed eleven days of peril and no-government. The Tories tried to form a ministry, but could not get one able to secure a majority or with any hopes of securing a majority by a new election. There were mobs and tumults even about the King's carriage. It was feared that William and Wellington might try a *coup d'état*, and it seems certain that the Whigs went so far as secretly to prepare for civil war. Finally, however, the King recalled the Whig ministry.

William still urged, however, that he be allowed other measures than the creation of new lords, and he offered to use his personal influence with the peers to secure the bill. Happily, Earl Grey was resolute to show where the real sovereignty lay; and finally the King signed the scrap of paper (still exhibited in the British Museum) on which the Earl had written, "*The King grants permission to Earl Grey . . . to create such a number of new peers as will insure the passage of the Reform Bill.*" This ended the struggle. The Tory lords withdrew from the sessions, and the bill passed, June 4, 1832.

532. Constitutional Settlements: the Lords; the Ministry. — Incidentally the long contest over the Reform Bill had settled two other points in the constitution.

a. It had shown how the Lords could be controlled,[1] and it made clear the subordinate nature of that house in the constitution. When the Commons have passed a bill, the Lords may throw it out once; but if the Commons pass it again, after an appeal to the country, the Lords must give way.[2]

b. It finally settled the relation of the monarch to the ministry, and showed that the ministers are not *his* ministry, except in name, but that they are really the ministry, or servants, of the House of Commons. This principle has never since been threatened. The king acts only through the ministers. Even the speech he reads at the opening of Parliament is written for him, and without consulting him; and he cannot change a phrase in it.

The way in which a change in ministry is brought about should be clearly understood. If the ministry is outvoted on any matter of importance, it must resign. If it does not do so, and claims to be in doubt whether it has really lost its majority, its opponents will test the matter by moving a vote of "lack of confidence," and if this carries, the ministry takes it as a mandate to resign. There is only one alternative: if the ministry believes that the country will support it, it may dissolve Parliament, and "appeal to the country." If the new Parliament gives it a majority, it may go on; if not, it must at once give way to a new ministry.

In form, the new ministry is chosen by the king, *but in reality, he simply names those whom the will of the majority in the Commons has plainly pointed out.* Indeed, he names only one man, whom he asks to "form a government." This man becomes *prime minister* (Premier), and he selects the other ministers. Usually, in a parliamentary election, Englishmen really vote also for the next prime minister, just

---

[1] Gladstone (§ 546) used the same method once afterward.

[2] This has been the invariable practice since, except on Gladstone's "Home Rule" bill just before his retirement from public life in 1894; and this bill, on its second appearance, was so altered as to afford the Lords an excuse to claim that the nation had not really been consulted (§ 552).

as truly, and about as directly, as we in this country vote for a President.[1]

A curious feature to the American student is that all this complex procedure rests only upon custom, nowhere upon a written constitution. The group of ministers who meet to determine the policy of the government are commonly called the Cabinet. Neither this body nor its functions are ever referred to in any written law; but, in reality, the Cabinet is the "Government," and is often referred to by that title.

The dissolution, it should be remembered, is a sort of referendum (§ 517), and it affords the people a better chance to express their will upon particular issues than we usually get in America.

533. Absence of Agitation for Further Parliamentary Reform until the Sixties, except for the Chartist Movement. — The "First Reform Bill," gave votes to six hundred and fifty thousand citizens, or to about one man out of six.[2] It enfranchised the middle class, and shifted political power from a narrow and selfish oligarchy to a liberal aristocracy. It was the most important of the three great reform bills (§§ 534, 535), because it insured the success of the others, with many more reforms. England has not been in the remotest danger of violent revolution during the revolutionary nineteenth century, except for a few months during this first struggle in 1831–1832; and Parliament, which had previously been so contemptuous of public opinion, now became quickly responsive to that force.

For thirty-five years, however, there was no further change in the franchise. The Tories at once accepted the result of 1832 (as the Conservative party in England always does, when

---

[1] If the king asks any one else to form a ministry but the man whom the Commons have accepted as their leader, probably the man asked will respectfully decline to act. If he tries, he will fail to get other strong men to join him, and his ministry will at once fail. If there were any real uncertainty as to which one of several men were leader, the matter would be settled by conference among the leaders, and the ministry would, of course, include all of them. In 1902, Balfour was chosen by the Conservatives in such a conference.

[2] France, after the Revolution of 1830, with over twice as large a population, had less than a third as many voters (§§ 413, 414); and, until shortly before, few American states had had much more liberal provisions.

a new reform has once been forced upon them), but planted themselves upon it as a finality; and even the Whigs, who were by no means democrats and who were absorbed in using their new power to carry out social reforms, agreed in this "finality" view regarding Parliamentary reform.[1] A few eager Radicals in Parliament for a time kept up a cry for a more liberal franchise, but soon they gave up the contest, to take part in the great social legislation of the period (§§ 542–545).

But outside Parliament, and outside the sovereign middle class, lay the masses of workingmen, who knew that the victory of 1832 had been won largely by their sympathy and public demonstrations, and who felt that they had been cheated of the fruits.[2] This class continued restless and discontented; but they lacked leadership, and, in ordinary times, their claims secured little attention. Two marked periods of agitation there were, however, at intervals of nearly twenty years, — just before 1848 and again before 1867. The first was futile; the second led to the Second Reform Bill.

The earlier of the two agitations is the famous *Chartist* movement. Even before the First Reform Bill, there had been an extensive agitation for a more radical change, and the extremists had fixed upon six points to struggle for: (1) manhood suffrage, (2) equal electoral districts, (3) abolition of all property qualification for membership in Parliament, (4) payment of members, (5) the ballot, and (6) annual elections.[3] In 1837 the Radicals renewed their agitation, and the "Six Points" were embodied in a *Charter*. The excitement grew for ten years,[4] and in the forties, many of these *Chartists* looked forward to

---

[1] In the Parliament of 1837 a Radical moved a resolution in favor of a further extension of the franchise; but Lord Russell, speaking for the ministry, condemned it savagely, and only twenty-two votes supported it.

[2] Read an admirable treatment in Rose's *Rise of Democracy*, ch. ii.

[3] To the average British "Liberal" of 1832, such demands seemed revolutionary, but the first, third, and fifth, and practically the second, have been adopted (§§ 535–537), while the fourth probably will be. The sixth is no longer demanded.

[4] Charles Kingsley's *Alton Locke* is a powerful story of this period.

an armed rebellion. Men drilled and armed; and the government was terrified into taking stringent precautions. Forty-eight was the critical year: the Chartists adopted a resolution, "All labor shall cease till the people's Charter becomes the law of the land";[1] but the plan for monster demonstrations, with great petitions and processions, fizzled out, and the "Year of Revolutions" saw no disturbance in England that called for more than a few extra policemen. The Chartist movement never revived from the disappointment.

534. The "Second Reform Bill," 1867. — The next agitation took its rise from the suffering of the unemployed while the American Civil War cut off the supply of cotton and so closed the English factories.[2] The progress of the intervening years appears in the fact that this time no one dreamed of force: the agitators could count safely on winning, through the rivalry of the two great political parties.

In 1865 a new Parliament was elected. The "Liberals" (as the old Whig party was now called) were "in office," and they were pledged to extend the franchise; but the bill the leaders introduced was trifling and inadequate, and was finally smothered by amendments. The ministry was discredited, and it resigned. Then *Lord Derby* (in the Peers) and *Disraeli* (in the Commons) "took office."[3] The new ministry was Conserva-

---

[1] Cf. the strike in Belgium in 1893 to secure suffrage extension (§ 508).

[2] So, too, the distress after 1815 had assisted the First Reform Bill, and the intensity of the Chartist agitation in 1847-1848 rested mainly on economic distress (§ 544).

[3] Lord Derby was prime minister, but, as he sat in the Lords, it was necessary to intrust some Commoner with special leadership in the lower house. This task fell upon Disraeli, who became (as is usually the case under such conditions) the real genius of the administration. By birth Disraeli was a Jew. He was an author, and a man of remarkable genius. He was "a Conservative with Radical opinions," as some critics said, while others insisted that he had no principles in politics. Carlyle, who was no friend to Parliamentary reform, expressed the general amazement at Disraeli's attitude and at his success in drawing his party with him — "a superlative Hebrew conjurer, spell-binding all the great lords, great parties, great interests, and leading them by the nose, like helpless, mesmerized, somnambulant cattle."

tive (or Tory), and really had no majority behind it. Of course, it could remain in power only by Liberal support. The ministers surrendered the old position of their party, and introduced a hastily drawn bill, which, by the addition of sweeping amendments from the Liberals,[1] was made a measure of far-reaching reform.

The bill abolished a few remaining rotten boroughs, and reapportioned the seats so as to do justice to the large towns; but its important feature lay in the extension of the franchise. Votes were now given in the towns to *all householders*[2] (owners or renters) and to *all lodgers who paid ten pounds a year for their rooms.* In the counties the franchise was lowered so as to include some small leaseholders, before excluded; but the chief effect was felt in the towns. Thus the bill gave the franchise to *the artisan class*, raising the number of voters to over three million, or to something over half the adult male population of that time.

535. The " Third Reform Bill," 1884. — The unskilled laborers in town and country, and the male house-servants, still had no votes; but England had taken a tremendous step toward democracy; and this victory of 1867, like that of 1832, was followed by a period of sweeping legislation for social reforms, — mainly in Gladstone's Liberal ministry, 1868–1874 (§ 546). Then, after a Conservative ministry, led by Disraeli and chiefly concerned with foreign matters (§ 547), Gladstone took office again, and the "Third Reform Bill" (1884) enfranchised the self-supporting but unskilled laborer and the servant class. Under this bill, all householders and all £10 lodgers, in town and country, have votes, — servants being regarded as "lodgers."

This raised the electorate to over six millions, and (except for unmarried sons, without property, living in the father's

---

[1] Gladstone proffered ten amendments, all but one of which were accepted by the Conservatives.

[2] All who were listed for rates, or local taxes.

family) it enfranchised practically all self-supporting men. Since 1884, England has been a democracy.[1]

536. The Reapportionment of 1885. — The two previous Reform Bills had dealt both with the franchise and with reapportionment. It had been designed that the Third also should do so; but finally Gladstone separated the two measures, and the Third Reform Bill dealt only with the suffrage. Then Gladstone and the Liberals lost office; but the Conservatives took up and passed the other part of the reform measure (1885), redistributing the seats. Towns with less than fifteen thousand people lost their separate representation as boroughs, and were merged in the counties in which they lay; and the larger towns and counties were divided into districts, like our congressional districts, each containing, as nearly as might be, fifty thousand people.[2]

537. Minor Reforms Concerning Elections. — The great Parliamentary Reform Bills have been completed by four minor measures, which have made English politics clean and honest to a remarkable degree.

a. In 1870, the secret ballot was introduced.[3] The form adopted was the one known as the Australian ballot, from its use in Victoria. Many of the States of our Union have since then adopted the same model.

b. Between 1855 and 1870, the civil service was thoroughly reformed. In earlier years, public offices had been given to reward political partisans, in as disgraceful a degree as ever marked our own politics. But since 1870, appointments have always been made after competitive examina-

---

[1] It is well to fix clearly the nature of the three Reform Bills. The First (1832) enfranchised the middle class (merchants, shopkeepers, professional men, etc., besides the gentry, freeholders, and members of borough corporations, who had the franchise before). The Second (1867) enfranchised the artisans in the towns. The Third (1884) enfranchised the unskilled laborers. In 1901, the number of registered electors was 6,822,585, or over one-sixth the population. In the United States the proportion is a little under one-fifth.

[2] To be absolutely accurate, the arrangement is not quite as simple or so fair as this. Towns of over fifteen thousand people but under fifty thousand, have one representative; towns between fifty thousand and one hundred and sixty-five thousand have two members; and towns over one hundred and sixty-five thousand have one more for each added fifty thousand people.

[3] The delay in adopting the ballot was due largely to a feeling among many Liberals that a man should not fear to announce publicly his choice.

tions, and now no official is removed for party reasons. England had completed this great reform, so essential to good democratic government, just when the United States began it.

c. In 1868, Parliament turned over to the courts the trial of contested elections. In earlier times, when the kings sometimes attempted to control the composition of Parliament (§ 238), it was needful for the Commons themselves to have the right of deciding between two men who claimed the same seat. Since the royal power had ceased to be dangerous, that need had passed away; and the decision of contested elections in Parliament, as in our legislatures still, was often marked by disgraceful abuses, — the decision generally being made by a strict "party vote," without any regard to the value of the opposing claims. In transferring these cases to the courts for more impartial consideration, England has led the way in a reform which other free countries will in time adopt.

d. Bribery in elections, direct and also indirect, was effectively checked by the "Corrupt Practices Prevention Act" of 1883.[1]

FOR FURTHER READING. — On the First Reform Bill, the most brilliant brief account is Justin McCarthy's *Epoch of Reform*, 25–83, or perhaps the treatment in the same author's *England in the Nineteenth Century*. A clear statement is given in Seignobos, 23–37; and, of course, all the constitutional histories of England that deal with the nineteenth century are very full upon this topic. Lee's *Source Book* gives several pages of excellently selected extracts regarding the bill, including one of Russell's speeches and a letter from Macaulay.

On the Second and Third Bills, a concise account is given by Seignobos, 50–54, 64–66, and 82–84. More interesting treatments are to be found in McCarthy's *History of Our Own Times* and in the younger McCarthy's *England under Gladstone*. There is an excellent treatment covering the whole period in Rose's *Rise of Democracy*, and in Walpole's *Electorate and Legislature*. Walpole's *England since 1815* (6 vols.) contains the most detailed account available. The present electoral laws are discussed clearly in Porritt's *Englishman at Home*.

B. LOCAL GOVERNMENT.

538. Conditions in 1832: Aristocratic, not Democratic. — The extensions of the franchise in 1832, 1867, and 1884 applied only to parliamentary elections, not to local government. In earlier centuries, local government in England had been *popu-*

---

[1] Special report, for an advanced student.

lar self-government ; but between 1600 and 1800 this had ceased to be true. Local government had not been centralized, as in France, but it had utterly ceased to be democratic. Each local unit was still in local hands, but in the hands of the *local aristocracy, not of the people.*

a. The two rural units, the counties and the parishes, were altogether controlled by the country gentry of the locality concerned, without even the form of a popular election anywhere. *Boards of Justices of the Peace,* appointed for life by the crown from the most important gentlemen of a county, managed all matters of county government, acting both as judges and as county commissioners; while each parish was ruled by a *vestry* of twelve gentlemen who formed a *close corporation,* holding office for life and themselves filling vacancies on occasion. Both justices and vestrymen served at their own expense; and this gentry rule was honest, public spirited, and generally popular. It proved unequal, however, to the new demands of the nineteenth century, and it deprived the mass of the people of all political training.

b. In the towns, the government was usually vested in *a mayor and a council,* who were virtually self-elected for life. This rule by privileged bodies had long been indescribably corrupt. The "corporation," as the government was called, never represented any large part of the inhabitants. The members spent public funds as they pleased, — largely in salaries to themselves, and in entertainments and state dinners, — and they rented public property to each other at nominal prices, while all the pressing needs of the great and growing city populations were ignored.

539. Municipal Reform. — The corrupt city government was the first to be reformed. Earl Grey's ministry in 1833 appointed "a commission of inquiry"; and, after the report of the commission in 1835, Lord Russell introduced a Municipal Reform Bill. The measure provided that a hundred and eighty-three boroughs (indicated by name) should each have a municipal council *elected by all who paid local taxes.* The Lords went wild with dismay at this "gigantic innovation," and by votes of one hundred and sixty or one hundred and seventy to twenty or thirty, they amended nearly every clause in the bill so as to make it worthless. The Commons refused the amendments; and after a four months' struggle [1] the Lords yielded. From time to time, through the century, new towns were added to the list, as need arose, and finally, in 1882, it was provided that any town might adopt this form of government for itself.

The municipal reform of 1835 was immediate and successful. English town government ever since has been honest, efficient, and enlightened, — a model to all other democratic countries. The best citizens serve in the town councils; the appointed officials, like the city engineer, city health officer, etc., are men of high professional standing, who serve virtually for life and are never appointed or removed for political purposes; the government costs less and gives more than in American cities; and the scandals that disgrace our city governments are unknown. The form of government is that known as the "Council Plan": the mayor is hardly more than a presiding officer; he is elected by the council, and he has no veto. The cities own their own water and lighting and street car systems to a much greater degree than in America.[2]

540. Reform in the Rural Units, in 1888 and 1894. — In the counties and parishes, the old system of local administration broke down in the nineteenth century, under the burden of new duties. For a long time, however, the only reform attempted was to add a multitude of new appointive "Boards," such as sanitary commissioners and poor-law commissioners. These changes left the administration as aristocratic as be-

---

[1] At this time, O'Connell, the Irish agitator, started a movement to abolish the House of Lords. "It is impossible," said he, "that it should last, — that such a set of stupid, ignorant, half-mad fops and coxcombs should continue so to lord it." Like later agitation of this kind, however, despite some rapturous applause from the streets, the suggestion was soon dropped.

[2] There is much good matter upon English municipal government in the leading periodicals from about 1880. Especially worthy of mention is an article in the *Forum* (14 : 267) by Joseph Chamberlain, entitled "Municipal Institutions in America and England." The best account in book form is Shaw's *Municipal Government in Great Britain*. The student may read especially the account of Glasgow in that work.

fore, and they created a chaos of overlapping areas and conflicting jurisdictions, so that they failed to give satisfactory results.

Finally, in 1888, the Conservative ministry of Lord Salisbury passed the *County Council Bill, providing for the popular election of a Council for each county by all local tax payers.*[1] A new interest in local affairs followed, and the popular Councils began to change the face of England by their energetic government. Six years later, the last ministry of Gladstone extended this movement by the still more important *Parish Councils Bill.*[2] These two laws have made local government in the rural units thoroughly democratic. The elements are four: (1) the parish has a primary assembly (*parish meeting*); (2) the parishes with more than three hundred people have also an elective *Parish Council;* (3) larger subdivisions of the county, known as districts, have elective *District Councils;* and (4) at the top is the elective *County Council.*

The powers of all these local bodies are very great (§ 554). England is not only a democracy in fact in her central government, but she is now also a democracy in her local administration, ruling herself through several thousand of these freely chosen Councils. Women have the franchise in electing local Councils on the same terms as men, and they are eligible to serve in any but the County Councils.

---

[1] London had not been included in the previous municipal reform acts, but it was now made an "administrative county," and so obtained liberal self-government. Since 1888 the County Council of London, ruling six million people, has been one of the most interesting governing bodies in the world. Advanced students will find a striking account of its workings in an article in the January *Contemporary Review* for 1895, by Sidney Webb, a Radical member of the Council at that time.

[2] The Lords twice sent back the bill to the Commons, the second time with numerous amendments. Gladstone's last speech in Parliament was in defense of the bill against the attempts of the Lords to weaken it; but, as he was about to resign on account of his health, the ministry accepted some relatively unimportant measures from the Lords, rather than appeal to the country.

III. LEGISLATION FOR SOCIAL REFORM, TO 1884.[1]

541. Reference Table of Administrations.

	Liberals.	Conservatives.		Liberals.	Conservatives.
1830–34	Grey		1868–74	Gladstone	
1834–35		Peel	1874–80		Disraeli (Beaconsfield)
1835–41	Melbourne				
1841–46		Peel	1880–85	Gladstone	
1846–52	Russell		1885–86		Salisbury
1852		Derby	1886	Gladstone	
1852–58	(1) Aberdeen (2) Palmerston		1886–92		Salisbury
			1892–95	(1) Gladstone (2) Rosebery	
1858–59		Derby			
1859–66	(1) Palmerston (2) Russell		1895–1906		(1) Salisbury (2) Balfour
1866–68		Derby	1906	Campbell-Bannerman	

542. Social Reform by the Grey Ministry, 1832–1834.—The thirties were a period of humanitarian agitation in English society. Charles Dickens wrote his moving stories of the abuses in the courts, the schools, the factories, the shops. Carlyle thundered denunciation against injustice, in *Chartism* and in *Past and Present;* Mrs. Browning pleaded for the abused children in touching poems (§ 543). Public men, like Wilberforce, Romilly, and Shaftesbury, had long been urging reform upon Parliament. The old Parliament had been indifferent; the new Parliament felt a new responsibility to public opinion, and the reformers secured a ready hearing.

After carrying the Reform Bill of 1832, Earl Grey dissolved Parliament, and the new Parliament contained a large majority for the Liberals. (Indeed, for the next thirty-five years, down to the Second Reform Bill, the Liberals were in power two-thirds of the time). Earl Grey's ministry remained in office for three years more,— years packed with social reforms. It freed the negro slaves in the West India colonies, paying the colonists for their loss.[2] It began to free the hardly less

---

[1] In 1884, reform at home was interrupted by the Irish Question (§ 548).
[2] Special report: Wilberforce, and his work for emancipation.

miserable "white slaves" of the English factory towns, by a new era of factory legislation (§ 543). It freed the English small farmer and the honest rural laborer from the worst abuses of the poor-law system, which had been tempting them to improvidence and crushing them if they tried to remain independent.[1] And it freed the Irish peasants in some measure from the obligation of paying tithes to support the Episcopalian clergy, whom they hated. Moreover, it swept away some more excesses of the absurd and bloody criminal code (§ 529), abolishing the pillory and the whipping post, and purifying the prisons. It made a first step toward public education, by a national grant of £100,000 a year to schools. And it began the reform of city government (§ 539), by an act scarcely less important than the parliamentary reform itself.[2]

543. Excursus: Factory Reform and Labor Legislation through the Century. — The most important legislation of the century was the labor and factory legislation. The new factory system (§ 528) had proved fatally cruel to women and children, who for a long time made up the greater portion of the employees. Parish authorities had the power to take children from pauper families, in order to apprentice them to employers; and destitute or dissolute parents sold their offspring into such service by written contracts. In the early years of the century, gangs of helpless little ones from six and seven years upward,

---

[1] The English poor-law had been for over half a century in the "pig-stye" era. Relief was given recklessly, and in such a way as to put a premium on improvidence and a tax on self-respect. The laborers were coming to regard public alms *as a right* at all times; they were being educated into depending upon charity instead of upon themselves. Employers expected the laborers to receive alms, and they paid lower wages in consequence, so that the workmen who did not apply for aid were at an unfair disadvantage. The nation was becoming utterly demoralized. In 1815 one person out of seven in all England received relief from the parish authorities, and in some parishes the paupers outnumbered the independent citizens. In 1830 England paid in poor rates almost as much as she did in 1900, when population had tripled. The legislation of 1834 did not make things ideal, but it cut the cost in half and helped to save the nation from being educated into pauperism.

[2] The best brief treatment of this period of reform is in McCarthy's *Epoch of Reform*, chs. vii-ix.

secured in this way, were auctioned off, thousands at a time, to great faqtories, where their life was a ghastly slavery. They received no wages; they were clothed in rags; their food was insufficient and of the coarsest kind, and often they had to eat standing at their work, while the machinery was in motion. They were driven to work from twelve to sixteen hours a day, often by inhuman torture; they had no holidays; and the few hours for sleep were spent in filthy beds, from which some other relay of little workers had just been roused. Schooling or recreation there was none; and the poor little waifs — girls as well as boys — grew up, if they lived at all, amid shocking and brutal immorality. When one batch of such labor had been used up, another was always ready, at practically no cost; and the employers showed a disregard for even the mere physical well-being of their "white slaves," such as no negro-driver could ever afford toward his costly black chattels.

In 1800, a terrible epidemic among children in certain factory districts aroused attention; and in 1802, a law "reduced" the hours of labor for child-apprentices to *twelve* a day. Then the apprentice system was soon given up, and its place was taken by the labor of children who were supposed to live under their parents' care, — to whom, therefore, the law did not apply. In 1819 and 1831, mild attempts were made to shorten the hours of labor for these children also to twelve hours a day; but the laws were not enforced, and, even on paper, they applied to only a part of the factory system. Thus the old conditions in the factory continued with little change.

Lord Ashley (Earl of Shaftesbury), whose championship helped finally to remedy such evils, spoke with great emotion forty years later (1873) of how he used to stand at the factory gates and watch the children come out, — "sad, dejected, cadaverous creatures," among whom "the crippled and distorted forms might be counted by hundreds"; and the poet Southey in 1833 declared of the factory system that the "slave trade is mercy compared with it." Indeed, the piteous story defies language, but it found its best expression in a passionate protest from the great heart of England's chief woman poet against this hideous phase of English civilization (Mrs. Browning's *Cry of the Children*): —

> " 'For oh,' say the children, 'we are weary,
>   And we can not run or leap.
> If we cared for any meadows, it were merely
>   To drop down in them and sleep. . . .'
> They look up, with pale and sunken faces,
>   And their look is dread to see,
> For they 'mind you of their angels in high places,
>   With eyes turned on Deity.
> 'How long,' they say, 'how long, O cruel nation,
> Will you stand to move the world on a child's heart —
> Stifle down with a nailed heel its palpitation,
> And tread onward to your throne amid the mart!
> Our blood splashes upward, O gold heaper,
>   And your purple shows your path.
> But the child's sob in the silence curses deeper
>   Than the strong man in his wrath.' "

These evils were the first fruits of a new economic theory which dominated English thought at the time, — the "let-alone-theory" (*laissez faire* theory). Briefly stated, this doctrine held that "demand" and "supply" should be left to regulate themselves in all economic matters, and that the best results would be obtained for all concerned by "free competition." Any interference by legislation, it was urged, would work only harm, and labor, like any other commodity, should be bought in the cheapest market.

This doctrine became known as "the Manchester doctrine," because it was held so universally by the English manufacturers. It had much excuse in the fact that the paternal and protective legislation in past centuries had usually worked harm; but it was also reënforced by the selfish interests of this capitalist class. The same doctrine and the same men who were to help free England from the Corn Laws (§ 544) strove to ward off interference with these terrible factory conditions.[1]

---

[1] England, of course, was no worse than other countries, except that the factory system was more rapidly developed there. Even in America, according to Professor Ely (*Labor Movement in America*, 49), New England mills in 1830 worked employees from twelve to fifteen hours a day, the year round,

Gradually, however, Englishmen awakened to the ugly fact that the factory system was ruining, not only the souls, but also the bodies of hundreds of thousands of women and children, so as to threaten national degeneracy. In 1833, among the first acts of the "Reformed Parliament," Lord Ashley secured a factory law limiting the work of children (under thirteen years) to forty-eight hours a week, and that of "young people" (from thirteen to eighteen years) to sixty-nine hours a week (or twelve hours on five days and nine hours on Saturdays). Some provision was made also for educating children and for a few holidays, and the employment of children under nine was strictly forbidden.

The bill was fought bitterly by most of the manufacturers, who urged (1) that it would oblige them to reduce wages and raise prices, (2) that it took from the workingman his "freedom of contract," or right to sell his labor as he chose, and (3) that it would cost England her industrial leadership in competition among nations. But public opinion had at last been aroused, and the bill became law. Fortunately, it provided for salaried "factory inspectors"; and these officers, after many prosecutions, compelled the employers to obey it.

In 1847 a still greater factory law limited the labor of women and young persons to ten hours a day, with only half-time for children and with provision for schooling in the vacant half of the day. Indirectly, this law fixed a limit upon the hours of men also, because, after the women and children had all left a factory, it was not profitable to keep the machinery going. Thus ten hours became the factory working-day.

---

with a large proportion of child-labor. One mill at Griswold, Connecticut, ran fifteen hours, ten minutes. In many places, women and children were driven at the work by the rawhide; and in Patterson, New Jersey, women and children were required to be at work by 4.30 A.M. See also McMaster, *History of the People of the United States*, III, 112-115, and V, 121, 122. In Illinois, in 1895, when after sharp agitation a law had been passed forbidding the employment of women in factories over ten hours a day, the supreme court of that state declared it unconstitutional, on the ground that it interfered with the personal liberty of the women to contract their labor as they pleased To the England of 1895 this seemed shocking enough.

This legislation of 1833 and 1847 applied only to factories for weaving goods. But in 1840, a parliamentary commission made public the horrible condition of women and children in the coal mines, — stunted, crippled, misshapen wretches, living in brutal indecency;[1] and a law at once forbade underground labor by women and children. Then the principles of factory legislation were soon extended to almost all other lines of manufactures. Of the long series of later acts, the most important is *Asquith's Factory Act of 1895*, which, along with other wholesome provisions, prohibits the employment of any child under eleven years of age.[2]

These acts have been accompanied by many provisions to secure good lighting and ventilation in factories and workshops, and to prevent accidents from machinery, by compelling the employer to fence it in with every possible care. In 1880 an *Employers' Liability Act* made it easy for a workman to secure compensation for any injury for which he was not himself to blame; and in 1897 a still more generous *Workman's Compensation Act* secured such compensation for the workmen by a simple process without lawsuits.[3]

544. Repeal of the Corn Laws and Adoption of Free Trade. — Lord Grey retired in 1834, but, except for a few weeks' interval, his party remained in power, under Lord Melbourne, until 1841. The Melbourne ministry contented itself, for the most part, with pointing to the record of its past, but it did introduce

---

[1] Children began work underground at five or six years of age, and rarely saw daylight. Girls and women worked almost naked among the men. The working hours were from twelve to fourteen a day; and in the wet underground passages, two or three feet high, women were compelled to crawl back and forth on hands and knees, hauling great carts of coal by chains fastened to their waists.

[2] For an excellent summary of recent legislation along these lines, see Cheyney's *Industrial and Social History*, 258-260.

[3] For Further Reading: Gibbin's *Industrial History of England*, 175-176, and Cheyney's *Industrial and Social History*, 224-262. Vivid statements are given also in Justin McCarthy's *Epoch of Reform*, *History of Our Own Times*, and *England in the Nineteenth Century*, and in Lecky's *History of England*, VI, 219-225.

penny postage[1] in 1840, and it also began the modern liberal policy toward the colonies by a new Government Act for Canada in 1839 (§ 561).

Then the Conservative ministry of Peel (1841-1846) was marked by *the abolition of the Corn Laws*. These laws put an excessively high tariff on imported grain. The aim, of course, was to encourage the raising of food-stuffs in England, so as to make sure of a home supply; and during the great wars this policy perhaps had been justifiable. The money profits, however, had always gone mainly to the landlords, who enacted the laws in Parliament and who raised rents enough to confiscate the benefits which the high prices might have brought to the farmer. After the rapid growth in population had made it impossible for England to produce enough food anyway, the landlords' practical monopoly of breadstuffs had become an intolerable burden upon the starving multitudes.

FIRST ADHESIVE PENNY POSTAGE STAMP. The design was used without change for thirty years, from 1840 to 1870.

The needless increase of misery among this class finally aroused a great moral indignation. In 1838 the Anti-Corn-Law League was organized by *Richard Cobden* and *John Bright*, and for years it carried on a wonderful campaign of education through the press and by means of great public meetings. The manufacturing capitalists were made to see that the Corn Laws taxed them, indirectly,[2] for the benefit of the landlords; and so the selfish interests of this influential manufacturing class were thrown to the side of reform. Finally, in 1846, a huge calamity was added to the same side of the scales. This

---

[1] Previous to this, the charge on letters had been very high, sometimes several shillings, and had been collected in cash by the carriers. When the change was suggested, the postal authorities protested earnestly, declaring that under the proposed plan the carriers would never be able to handle the letters, or that it would cost ruinous sums to do so.

[2] To enable their workmen to live, they had to pay higher wages than would otherwise have been necessary.

was *the Irish Famine*. The population of Ireland had been increasing rapidly, until it amounted to over eight millions. The greater part were poor peasants, living in misery, with the potato for almost their sole food. Suddenly, in 1846, in a night, came a blight that ruined the crop for the year; and, despite generous gifts of food from all the world, two millions of people died before even the old conditions could be restored.[1] The government in England had already been considering a reform of the Corn Laws, and this terrible event in Ireland forced it to act. As John Bright afterward said, "Famine itself, against whom we fought, took up arms in our behalf." Peel decided to sweep away the tax and to let food in free; and, despite some bitter opposition from his own party, the reform was adopted.

Sir Robert Peel.

Peel was at once overthrown by a revolt among his old followers; but the Liberals took up the work and carried it farther. They abolished one protective tariff after another, until, by 1852, England had become a "free trade" country, as she has ever since remained.

This policy was never afterward seriously questioned in England (whose manufactures and commerce have prospered so marvelously under it) until 1903. For some years preceding this date, to be sure, some of

---

[1] A million more emigrated to America in the next four years (1847-1850). This was the first large immigration of Catholic Irish to this country.

the Conservative party talked of a policy of "fair trade," or a system of retaliatory tariffs against countries whose tariffs shut out British manufactures; and finally, in 1903, Joseph Chamberlain, a member of the cabinet, declared that the time had come for England to adopt a policy of that kind and at the same time to secure closer trade relations with her colonies.[1] The tumult that followed, in and out of Parliament, indicates that "protection" may again become an issue in English politics.

545. Minor Reforms, 1846-1870. — Lord Russell's ministry of 1846-1852, which carried the free-trade policy to completion, adopted also further sweeping factory reforms (§ 543), extended the state grants to schools, abolished the press gang,[2] gave property rights to married women, and extended the generous policy already adopted for Canada to the Australian colonies (§ 561). The fourteen years from 1852 to 1866 were largely a period of inaction or of foreign interests. The Crimean War (§ 430), the Danish troubles (§ 466), and the Civil War in America, with the consequent distress of the English manufacturing districts, absorbed public attention; but even in this period the window tax and an old stamp tax on newspapers ("taxes on light and intelligence") were abolished, and the system of taxation was reformed in the interest of justice to the small householders, who until this time had paid almost as high taxes on petty shops as great dukes paid on princely castles.

546. The Gladstone Administration of 1868-1874. — Then, after the enfranchisement of the artisan class (by the Reform Bill of 1867), came Gladstone's great reform administration (1868-1874), which rivals in importance that of Earl Grey itself. In 1870, it established alongside the old private and parochial schools a new system of public schools, or, as the English call them, Board Schools.[3] It abolished purchase of office in the army, and completed the civil service reform (§ 537). It

---

[1] Special report: the cabinet crisis and the elections that followed.

[2] To kidnap poor men by force, carry them on board a war vessel, and compel them to act as sailors, had been for many generations a recognized method of keeping up the British navy; and the importance of the navy was so great that even enlightened English opinion had offered little protest, until the middle of the century. The impressment of American sailors, in the years preceding the war of 1812, was, of course, connected with this practice.

[3] So called because they are managed by elected boards. The term "public school" in England had been appropriated by the great secondary schools, like Rugby and Eton, though there is, of course, no public control over them.

introduced the ballot (§ 537). It opened English universities to others than the members of the Church of England. It passed further factory laws; it definitely repealed the old conspiracy laws, under which labor-unions had been persecuted; and it gave legal rights to such unions, permitting them to incorporate and secure the rights at law of an individual. It also arranged honorably the Alabama Arbitration Treaty with the United States; and, finally, it "disendowed" and "disestablished" the English Church in Ireland,[1] and carried through important land reforms for Ireland (§ 552).

But Gladstone would not go far enough to satisfy the Irish; and, despite the trade-union law, he offended the labor party by a law regarding strikes.[2] The ministry lost more and more of its support, and finally Gladstone "dissolved." In the election, the labor-unions voted for the Conservatives; and that party secured a large majority, for the first time since 1832.[3]

547. Disraeli's Dazzling Foreign Policy Administration, 1874–1880. — Gladstone's ministry had been exceedingly peaceful and honorable in dealing with foreign nations. Disraeli, leader of the new ministry, characterized this attitude as weak, and said that it had "compromised the honor" of England. He adopted an aggressive foreign policy, and tried to excite

---

[1] After this time, the Episcopal Church in Ireland was separated from political power, and was upon an equal footing legally with any other church. The "disendowment" was only partial. The church lost all income from taxes (tithes), and much of its property was taken from it to create funds for the Catholics and Presbyterians in the island; but it kept its buildings and enough other property to leave it still very rich. All this, which to one party seemed only a partial remedying of a huge ancient injustice toward a whole people, seemed to another party an unpardonable injustice; and many good churchmen never forgave Gladstone for this "act of robbery."

[2] This law recognized the right of a union to strike, but made criminal any show of intimidation. It forbade strikers to revile those who remained at work; and it is reported that under the law seven women were sent to prison for crying "Bah!" at a workman who had deserted the strikers.

[3] All the preceding conservative ministries, except Peel's in 1841–1846, had been mere makeshifts without a steady majority, or at best they had had a bare working majority.

English patriotism by "jingo"[1] utterances and conduct. By act of Parliament, Queen Victoria[2] was declared "Empress of India"; the Boers of the Transvaal were forced into war; and in 1878, when Russia conquered Turkey (§ 577) and seemed about to exclude the Turks from Europe, Disraeli interfered. He got together a Congress of the Powers at Berlin, and preserved to Turkey a considerable part of her European empire, so as to shut Russia off from the Mediterranean. In home affairs, the only reform was to repeal the law of 1871 regarding strikes.

548. Gladstone and Ireland. — Gladstone had carried on a great campaign against the policy of supporting the Turk in his mastery over the Christian populations of Southeastern Europe, and in the election of 1880 the Liberals secured an overwhelming majority. Gladstone's new ministry passed the Third Reform Bill and it also completed the purification of English politics, by adopting the law against "Corrupt Practices" (§ 537); but it soon found itself occupied with Irish questions, about which English politics were to revolve for the next fifteen years. Some explanation of Irish affairs must precede further survey of English matters.

GLADSTONE.

---

[1] For this use of "jingo," see McCarthy's *Our Own Times*, II, 382, 383.

[2] Victoria ascended the throne as a young girl in 1837, and ruled until 1901. She never took an active part in politics, but her influence for pure morals and her natural kindliness and good sense helped on a reform of English society in a marked degree. Few sovereigns have ever experienced a more devoted loyalty.

FOR FURTHER READING ON DIVISIONS II AND III. — Details on particular topics, as on the repeal of the Corn Laws, can be found in McCarthy's *Epoch of Reform* (for the years 1830 to 1850), *History of Our Own Times* (1837–1880), and in the younger McCarthy's *England under Gladstone*; and briefer accounts are given in McCarthy's *England in the Nineteenth Century* and in Rose's *Rise of Democracy*. The most comprehensive general treatment is in Walpole's *England since 1815*. The various histories of England previously referred to are good. References for labor and factory legislation have been given on page 563.

IV. THE IRISH QUESTION.

In the history of Ireland . . . we may trace with singular clearness the perverting and degrading influences of great legislative injustices. — LECKY.

549. Ireland to 1700. — Like so many other European countries, England has a race question. The English people proper are Saxon-Norman mixed with Celtic blood: the Welsh, Highland Scots, and Irish are pure Celts. In the larger of the British Isles, the English, Welsh, and Scots live at peace; but for centuries the Irish of the smaller island have been restless under British rule.

Ireland has been an unfortunate and misgoverned land. In the seventh and eighth centuries, she had begun to show brilliant promise (§ 178, note); but this early civilization vanished in the wars of the Danish invasions, which, for three hundred years, inflicted upon Ireland all the woes suffered by England for the generation before Alfred the Great.

Thus Henry II of England found the island sunk in misery and barbarism and torn by incessant tribal strife. Unhappily for both English and Irish, Henry's conquest was left incomplete; and war, anarchy, and misgovernment filled three centuries more, down to the time of Henry VIII, so that Sir John Davis, a poet-historian and statesman of Elizabeth's time, wrote, "If it had been practised in Hell as it has been in Ireland, it had long since destroyed the very kingdom of Beëlzebub." Henry VIII and Elizabeth completed the subjugation of the island; but now the English and Irish civilizations had grown far apart, and the two people could not easily mingle. Moreover, the English had become Protestant, and the difference in religion added a tremendous difficulty. There was real danger that Catholic Ireland might join Spain against Protestant England; and so the mutual hate and fear between Irish and English grew more and more intense. About 1600, the government began to try to make Ireland English by crushing out the native language and customs and religion, and by reducing the native population to mere tillers of the soil for their conquerors. On trumped-up charges, with every imaginable form of force and fraud, the lands of even the loyal Irish gentry were confiscated to furnish estates for English adventurers; and a war of extermination was waged against all who remained in arms.

Under Charles I, the "pacification" of the island was apparently completed by Wentworth (§ 243); but just before the Civil War in England, the goaded Irish rose in fierce rebellion and massacre. A little later the merciless hand of Cromwell restored order with a cruelty which makes his name a by-word in Ireland to-day. Toward the close of the century, the Irish sided with James II against William III (§ 250), but were defeated at the *Battle of the Boyne* (1690). The Treaty of Limerick (1691), however, promised them the enjoyment of their own religion and certain other privileges; but these promises were treacherously broken by the English settlers, who controlled the Parliament of the island.[1]

550. Ireland in the Eighteenth Century. — For the next century the fate of Ireland was wretched beyond description. Six-sevenths of the land belonged to English landlords, most of whom lived in England and spent their rents there. Those who stayed in Ireland made up the ruling class of the island. Six-sevenths of the people were Catholic Irish.[2] A few of these, especially in the west, were country gentlemen, but they lived under vexing legal restraints;[3] a considerable number more were tenant farmers; but the great bulk were a starving peasantry, working the land for Saxon landlords and living in mud hovels, — each with an acre or two of ground about it. Farmers and laborers alike were "tenants at will." That is, they could be evicted at the landlord's word.[4] The landlord, therefore, could raise the rent at his own will; and if the tenant improved the buildings or drained the land, he commonly found at once that he had to pay more rent, so that he

---

[1] So that Limerick is known as "the City of the Broken Treaty."

[2] This was not true in Ulster, the northern province of the island; but there the population was mainly English.

[3] Special report. (If accessible, consult Lecky's *England in the Eighteenth Century*.)

[4] Population was so crowded that there was always sharp competition to get farms and cottages, and so the landlord could make his own terms.

himself got no profit from his extra labor. Naturally, this system of "rack rent" made the peasantry reckless, improvident, and lazy. At the same time, the fact that the law of their masters was used only to trick and oppress them, trained them to hate and break the law.

551. The "Union" with England, 1800. — In 1798 a rebellion took place; but the expected aid from the French Directory did not come in time, and the rising was put down with horrible cruelty. A change in the government followed. For several centuries, there had been a separate Parliament for Ireland. This Dublin legislature had been controlled wholly by the English settlers, and, except for a brief time, it had been strictly subordinate to the government at London. Shortly before the rebellion, it is true, in 1783, the "Irish Parliament" had possessed extensive powers; but after 1798 England consolidated the government of the two islands. The *Act of Union* (1800) abolished the Irish legislature, and gave Ireland one hundred representatives in the English Parliament. Ireland became subject directly to English rule and English officials.

These were the conditions at the opening of the nineteenth century. In 1803 a brilliant young Irishman, *Robert Emmet*, tried to organize a rebellion for Irish independence; but the effort failed miserably, and Emmet died on the scaffold. There was no further movement in Irish politics until 1830.

552. Irish History since 1830 has two main features: (1) an almost constant effort to repeal the Union of 1800, in favor of greater self-government; and (2) an effort to secure better conditions for the peasantry. The first movement has been mixed up with rebellions for complete independence; and the second has been complicated by innumerable crimes of the peasantry against the persons and the property of the landlords.

The struggle for the repeal of the Union began in 1830, in the first Parliament in which Catholics were allowed to sit.[1] Forty of the Irish delegation were pledged to work for repeal,

---

[1] After the Catholic Emancipation Act of 1829 (§ 529).

and they were led by the dauntless and powerful Daniel O'Connell. This was the first "Home-Rule" movement. In 1837 it had assumed formidable proportions; but the Irish famine of 1846 checked the agitation, and just afterward O'Connell died. Then a band of hot-headed young men tried conspiracy, and the fruitless and rather farcical rebellion of *Young Ireland* marked the year 1848.

The next twenty years saw no progress. In 1866 came another rebellion, — *the Fenian Conspiracy*, organized by Irish officers who had served in the American Civil War. The danger did not become serious, but it seems to have convinced the more liberal Englishmen that something must be done for Ireland, and Gladstone's reform ministry of 1868–1874 took up the task.

Then there opened a new period in Irish history. The Episcopalian church in Ireland (§ 546) was disestablished, and this act was followed in 1870 by the first of a long series of important reforms of the land laws. Two things were attempted: (1) in case of eviction, it was ordered that the landlord must pay for any improvements the tenant had made; and (2) the government arranged to loan money on long time to the tenants, so that they might buy their little patches of land. Neither of these measures was very effective at first; but in 1881 and 1885 Gladstone's ministries extended and improved them until the peasants began to be true landowners. It is hoped that under the new conditions they will develop new habits of thrift and industry.

Meantime, in 1870, a group of Irish members of Parliament had begun a new agitation for "Home Rule," and soon afterward the same leaders organized the "Land League," to try to fix rents, as labor unions sometimes try to fix wages. For the time, the liberal ministries frowned on both these movements, and sternly prosecuted the Land League on the ground that it encouraged crime against landlords. At the same time, indeed, that the government was passing beneficent land laws, it was also passing "Coercion Acts" to establish martial law in Ireland in order to repress disorder. The Coercion Acts were resisted by the Irish members with a violence never before seen in an English Parliament, and Irish conspirators outside made various attempts to wreck the English government buildings with dynamite and to assassinate English officials.

But suddenly Gladstone made a change of front. In the new Parliament of 1884, eighty-six of Ireland's hundred and five members were "Home Rulers." They were determined to block all legislation; and Gladstone could go on only by securing their alliance. Moreover, he had become convinced that the only way to govern Ireland was to govern it in coöperation with the Irish, not in opposition to them. So in 1886 he adopted the "Home-Rule" plan and introduced a bill to restore a separate legislature to Ireland. The Conservatives declared that this policy meant disunion and ruin to the Empire, and in this belief they were joined by many of the old Liberals (led by *Joseph Chamberlain*), who took the name of *Liberal Unionists*. The Home Rule Bill was defeated; but it made the issue in the next election a few years later, and in 1893 Gladstone tried to carry another such measure. This time, the Commons passed the bill, but the Lords threw it out.[1] Then Gladstone's age compelled him to retire from parliamentary life, and his party, left without a fit leader, soon went out of power.

The Conservatives and Unionists are apparently fixed in their determination not to grant Ireland a separate Parliament; but since 1895, they have made liberal concessions in all other respects. In particular, they have carried the provision for government loans to the peasantry farther even than the Liberals did,[2] though formerly they had railed at such acts as robbery and socialism; and they have granted a kind of *local*

---

[1] The bill differed in important particulars from the one before considered (cf. § 532, note). Moreover, the majority for it in Parliament was narrow and plainly due only to the Irish vote.

[2] The Land Bill of 1903 is the most comprehensive measure of this kind ever passed, and it seems to give perfect satisfaction to the Irish.

"home rule," by establishing elective County Councils like those in England. To some extent these measures seem to have cut the ground from under the feet of the "Home Rulers." A large part of the Irish representatives in Parliament strive to keep up the agitation, but the English Liberals have lost enthusiasm in the matter and the Irish peasantry themselves care less about it as their material condition improves. Meantime, English political energies, which for twenty years (1880–1900) went almost wholly to Irish matters, may now turn again to reform in England itself.

V. ENGLISH POLITICS IN THE TWENTIETH CENTURY.

553. Problems left over from the Nineteenth Century: Church and State; Church and Education; the Lords. — For Western Europe the nineteenth century was an age of democratic reform in politics. The great need of the twentieth century is democratic reform in industrial and economic matters, so as to improve further the condition of the workers. But even in progressive European countries this supreme question (§ 554) is partially obscured by other unfinished business left over from the nineteenth century, — especially by the struggle to *separate church and state* and *to free education from church control*. Though a Protestant country, England has an established church and is hampered by both these questions; and in the political conflict they have become involved with a third question, — how *"to mend or end"* the *House of Lords*.

The last months of Gladstone's public life saw a sharp conflict between the two houses of Parliament over the Irish question (§ 552 and note) and the Parish Councils Bill (§ 540 and note 2); and, had the "grand old man" been able to keep up the fight in person, some remodeling of the Upper House would soon have become a practical issue. Before his retirement, in 1894, Gladstone also declared himself in favor of disestablishing the English Church *in Wales*, where nine-tenths of the population belong to other sects. The Liberal party, indeed, had been committed to this policy in its platform for some years, and, in 1895, just before it went out of power, it carried through the Commons a resolution for disestablishment in Wales.[1]

The victory of the Conservatives in the elections of 1895 and 1902 postponed both questions; and, when the Liberals returned to power (1906), they found themselves confronted first with a more pressing but related question, the problem of church and school. During the long lease of power by the Conservatives, that party had placed the Board Schools (§ 546 and note 3) under the control of the English Church. These schools are still mainly the schools of the laboring classes, who for the most part are dissenters; and the injustice of this educational policy aroused intense indignation. When the Liberals came back to power in 1906, the first important measure passed by the Commons was a radical "Education Bill" removing church control from the Board Schools.[2] The Lords ruined the Bill by "amendments" such that one of the ministry in the House of Commons likened the process to amending the Ten Commandments by striking out in each the *not*. Thus the contest stands at this juncture (January, 1907). The Lords insist that the Commons should dissolve, inasmuch as this particular Bill has not been before the country (cf. § 532 *a*, and note). The Liberals call this an inexcusable demand for costly delay, since the *principle* of the Bill was an issue in the elections; and they insist that the Lords must give way. *Otherwise some reconstruction of that body is threatened.* The Liberals have chosen their ground well, and they have a heartier support from the voters in England itself ("the predominate partner") than earlier ministries had in the conflicts over Irish or Welsh questions.

554. Non-partisan Progress. — Toward 1890 the Conservative party began to show itself as zealous for the welfare of the laboring man as ever the Liberals had been; and whichever

---

[1] Cf. the disestablishment in Ireland (§ 546 and note).
[2] The church has still its own schools, and these are even aided largely from the public treasury.

party is in power, rapid progress is now to be expected in labor legislation.

The most notable advance in recent years has been in the matter of the peasantry. In 1890 twelve hundred men out of thirty-two millions of people owned over a fourth of all the land in England; while twenty-four twenty-fifths of the families in the island, including almost all farm-laborers, had no land at all. But a long series of Allotment Acts (1883, 1887, 1892, 1894) has tried to remedy this state of affairs. Since 1894 the democratic "Parish Councils" have authority to buy land, or even to condemn it and take it at a forced sale, and then to turn it over in small holdings to the peasantry, either on long leases or for purchase on easy terms. This policy ought in time to restore the peasantry to the land.

In the cities, the artisan class has certain well-defined demands, such as an eight-hour working day, old-age pensions, state insurance, better sanitary regulation of tenement houses, and tax reforms in favor of the poor man;[1] and some attention must soon be given to these questions.

555. English Socialism: the Independent Labor Party. — There are various groups of Socialists in England, under different names, and in 1903 there was organized an *Independent Labor Party*. Despite the apparent willingness of both Liberals and Conservatives to yield to the demands of labor, this new party pledges its members to abstain from connection with any other political party. So far it has been especially hostile to the old Liberals, because it expects by their overthrow to become one of the two leading parties. Its program is distinctly socialistic. Up to the present time, its representatives in Parliament have been very few, but they have been able and excellent men.

---

[1] The abolition of tariffs on coffee and sugar and other food-stuffs which the poor man uses almost as freely as the rich man does, is one thing demanded. These taxes are spoken of as the "breakfast table duties." It is proposed also to tax large incomes at a much higher rate than small ones; and England already has a "progressive" tax of this kind on inheritances, — the rate increasing with the value of the estate.

VI. COLONIES AND DEPENDENCIES.

After many years of wandering I have come to the conclusion that the mightiest factor in the civilization of the world is the imperial policy of England. — ADMIRAL GEORGE DEWEY (1899).

556. Excellence of the English Colonial System. — Of all peoples the English are the most successful in colonizing new lands and in ruling semi-barbarous races. The British Empire covers eleven million square miles, or over three times the area of the United States, and its population numbers four hundred millions, or about one-fourth of the whole human race. Forty millions of this number dwell in the British Islands, and about ten million more of English descent live in self-governing colonies, — mainly in Canada and Australia. The other seven-eighths of the vast population of the Empire are of non-European blood, and for the most part they are subject peoples.

557. Colonies classified as to Importance. — The outlying possessions are of two kinds: (1) those of continental importance in themselves, such as Canada, India, Egypt, Australia, South Africa, and the West Indian and South American colonies; and (2) coaling stations and naval posts commanding the routes to these possessions, such as Gibraltar, Malta, Cyprus, Ceylon, St. Helena, Trinidad, and scores more.

558. Political Classes. — Some of these colonies are completely self-governing, with no dependence upon England except in form. This is true of Canada and Australia, and, not quite so completely, of Cape Colony. These colonies are said to have "*responsible governments.*" The English ministry appoints a *Governor General,* a nominal executive, whose powers resemble those of the figure-head monarch in England; *but the people of the colony elect the local legislature, and the real executive is the local ministry, " responsible " to the legislature,* as the ministry in England is to Parliament.

In another group of colonies, the governors and officials sent out from England really control the whole government. This class of *"crown colonies"* comprise most of the naval posts, like Gibraltar, and also those colonies lying in the torrid zone, where the population, of course, is mainly non-European.

Between the "responsible governments" and the "crown colonies" there is a third class of colonies with representative legislatures, but without responsible ministries. Some colonies of this class have as large a degree of self-government as Massachusetts or Virginia did in 1700, while in others the colonial legislature is only partly representative and is allowed very little power. Thus the colonies of this group merge by imperceptible degrees into those of the other two groups.

Only a few of the foreign dependencies can be studied in detail; but India, Egypt, and the three responsible governments are worthy of particular attention.

559. India is a huge crown colony. Until 1857 it remained under the control of the East India Company,[1] but in that year came the *Sepoy mutiny*,[2] — a rising of part of the native soldiers, — and when order had been restored, India was annexed to the British crown. The English ministry appoints a Viceroy and a Council, and these authorities name the subordinate officials for the subdivisions of the vast country. In the smaller districts, the English officials are assisted by native officers, and to some extent, by elected councils of natives.[3]

The English are making a notable attempt to introduce self-government and to get the natives to care for it. Towns are invited to elect municipal councils and to take charge of their streets and drainage and other matters of local welfare; but the Hindoo seems practically unable to take any interest in self-government. He wants these things done for him.

The officers of the old East India Company were sometimes rapacious robbers, oppressing the natives to fill their own and the Company's coffers; but since India became a crown colony, English rule, for the most part, has been wise, firm, and just, and has aimed unselfishly at the good of the natives.[4] The petty, constant wars, which formerly were always wasting the land, have been wholly done away with, and the terrible famines, which from time immemorial have desolated it at intervals, have become fewer, and on the whole, less serious. As a result, population

---

[1] Supervised more or less by Parliament.   [2] Special report.

[3] Outside the territory ruled directly by England there are also nearly a thousand native principalities, large and small, where the governments are really directed by resident English "agents."

[4] India pays no taxes into the English treasury; indeed, she is a drain on that treasury, but her trade is a chief source of British wealth.

has increased rapidly, — over fifty per cent in a century, — and to-day nearly three hundred million people dwell in India.[1] Except as to numbers, however, and except that the people have been forced to stop burning widows alive, the condition of India is little better than before, and there seems to be no attachment among the natives for English rule. The Hindoos cannot understand western civilization, and they do not like it. Whether England can leaven this vast mass and lift it to a higher life is one of the great problems of the future.

560. Egypt in name is one of the tributary states of Turkey. In fact, however, it had been independent for the greater part of the nineteenth century, until, in 1881, a new master stepped in. The government had borrowed recklessly and spent wastefully, and the land was misgoverned and oppressed by crushing taxation. Then, in 1879, England and France jointly intervened to secure payment of debts due from the Egyptian government to English and French capitalists. In 1881 came a native Egyptian rising against the government and the foreigners. France withdrew. England stayed,[2] restored order, and "occupied" the country.

Since that time, Egypt has really been an English protectorate. The Khedive and all the machinery of the old government remain unchanged; but an English agent is always present at the court "to offer advice," and the Khedive understands that this advice must be followed. Many Englishmen have entered the service of the Egyptian government, too, and all such officers look to the English agent as their real head.

When England put down anarchy in 1881, the ministry declared that the occupancy would be only temporary. This statement of Gladstone's ministry was made in good faith, and was in keeping with other parts of Gladstone's modest foreign policy. None the less, it is certain now that no English government will willingly give up Egypt. The possession of that country, together with the mastery of the Suez Canal, insures the route to India; and Egypt has been made a base of operation, also, from which English rule has been extended far toward Central Africa.

To Egypt, English rule has been an unmixed good. The system of taxation has been reformed, so that it is less burdensome and more productive. The irrigation works have been revived and improved, so that Egypt is a richer land than ever before. The population is increasing rapidly and the peasantry are vastly better off than a generation ago.

---

[1] Read Kipling's *William the Conqueror*.

[2] England had a special motive for staying. The Suez Canal was opened in 1869. In 1875 the English government bought from the Egyptian government its share of the Canal stock, and the English intervention in Egypt was largely to protect this property.

561. Development of "Responsible" Colonial Governments. — One of the most important features of the nineteenth century progress was the development of self-government in the Anglo-Saxon colonies of England. No doubt the loss of the American colonies had taught a serious lesson, and the next colony to show violent dissatisfaction had all its wishes granted.

This event took place in Canada in 1837. The two provinces of Upper and Lower Canada had been governed for many years much as Massachusetts or Virginia were governed before 1776. There had been a growing dissatisfaction because the legislatures did not have a more complete control over the finances and over the executive; and the accession of the girl-queen in England in 1837 was the signal for a rising. The rebellion was stamped out quickly; but an English commissioner, sent over to investigate, recommended that the demands of the conquered rebels should be granted. Parliament adopted this recommendation. In 1839 the two provinces were united and were granted "responsible" ministries. England, in name, retains a veto upon Canadian legislation; but it has never been used. In 1850, a like plan for self-government was granted to the Australian colonies, and, in 1872, to Cape Colony.

562. Federation of Groups of Colonies. — In 1867 another great advance was made by the organization of the Dominion of Canada. This is *a federal state*, similar to the United States, composed now of eight members. The union has a two-house legislature, with a responsible ministry; and each of the eight states has its own local legislature and ministry. A similar union of the various Australian colonies into one federal state was agitated for many years, and, after two federal conventions and a popular vote, it was finally established on the first day of the twentieth century.

Thus two new English nations were formed, — each large enough to command respect among the nations of the world (each nearly double the size of the United States when its independence was achieved). A similar federation will no doubt sometime unite the English and Dutch colonies in South Africa.

563. South Africa is not an altogether satisfactory part of the Empire for Englishmen to contemplate. England seized Cape Colony from the Dutch during the Napoleonic wars, and it was one of the few parts of Holland's possessions which were not restored at the peace. English settlers came in rapidly, but in 1834 a portion of the old Dutch colonists "trekked" (moved with families, ox-wagons, herds, and flocks) north into the wilderness, and set up an independent government in Natal. A few years later the British annexed Natal, and the Dutch again trekked into what is known as the Orange Free State, and, in 1848, once more into the country beyond the Vaal river. These "Transvaal" settlers became involved in serious difficulties with the native blacks, and a native rising threatened to exterminate Europeans in South Africa. England interposed, put down the Zulus, and extended her authority once more over the Boer states.

In 1880, the Boers rebelled, and, with their magnificent marksmanship, destroyed a British force at the *battle of Majuba Hill*. Gladstone adopted the view that the Boers had been wrongfully deprived of their independence, and, without attempting to avenge Majuba Hill, he magnanimously withdrew the British claims and left to the Boers of the Transvaal a virtual independence, under British "protection." The exact relations between the two countries, however, were not well defined, and much ground was left for future disputes.

Soon afterward, gold was discovered in the Transvaal, and English and other foreigners rushed in, so as to outnumber the Boer citizens. The Boers, who were simple farmers, unable themselves to develop the country, had at first invited immigrants, but soon became jealous of their growing numbers and refused them all political rights. England attempted to secure better treatment for her citizens among these new settlers, and was bent upon reasserting her authority in general. The Boers saw that England had determined to force them to a policy which would put the government of the little land into the hands of these foreign immigrants ("Outlanders"), and they declared war (1899). The Orange Free State joined the Transvaal, and the little republics carried on a marvelous and heroic struggle. They were finally beaten, of course; and England adopted a generous policy toward the conquered, making large gifts of money to restock their ruined farms, and granting liberal self-government, without any discrimination against her recent foes. The Boers accepted the situation in good faith; and South Africa, it is to be hoped, has seen its last race quarrel between European peoples.

564. Imperial Federation. — The Boer War showed that there was a strong tie between England and her self-governing colonies; for Australia, New Zealand, and Canada all made liberal gifts of troops and money to assist the mother country. The tie which holds together the Anglo-Saxon parts of the Empire is, however, almost wholly one of sentiment. Certainly, if either Canada or Australia wished to set up as an independent nation, England would not dream of trying to hold it. At present the colonists in these lands have no cause to complain, except in one respect: namely, they have no voice in deciding the policy of the Empire toward foreign nations, and therefore they may possibly become involved in serious wars without their own consent. Probably this evil is largely or wholly offset by the fact that the English navy affords protection to the Canadian and Australian trade, so that these great and wealthy countries are practically freed from all burden of military and naval defense. Still, the situation is not altogether satisfactory. A Canadian may properly wish a voice in the policy of the Empire; that is, he may wish to be a citizen in as full a degree as if he lived in England: and England may properly think that Canada ought to contribute something to imperial defense. It has been proposed to meet both these wants by some form of *Imperial Federation*. This means that the different parts of the Empire would be left their present parliaments for local matters, but that the management of matters that concern the Empire as a whole would be turned over to a new parliament made up of representatives in fit proportion from England and her colonies. As Canada and Australia grow larger and wealthier, it is probable that some such plan will be tried or that the bonds between the different parts of the Empire will grow weaker and weaker. If such a federation can be carried out successfully, it will be the greatest triumph ever yet achieved by federal government and a new boon to civilization, equal perhaps to any political device yet developed by the great English-speaking race.

CHAPTER VII.

SLAV EUROPE.

I. RUSSIA.

565. Russia a Factor in Western Politics since 1800. — The growth of Russia upon the edge of Western Europe has created new problems in European politics. The appearance of this vast, aggressive, semi-Oriental state as a factor in western politics dates, of course, from Peter the Great (about 1700). During the next century, Russia tore away half of Sweden's power, annihilated Poland, and began to absorb Turkey; but, except for some part in the wars of Frederick the Great, she did not greatly affect the countries that we think of as "western," until the Napoleonic wars. Her destruction of Napoleon's Grand Army revolutionized Europe and revealed her tremendous power. Since that time, it has always been necessary for western statesmen to keep in mind her military force and her political sympathies.

The important phases of Russian development in the nineteenth century may be classed under the following heads: (1) growth in territory and power; (2) persistence of absolutism; (3) emancipation of the serfs; (4) introduction of the germs of representative institutions in local government; (5) the rise and fall of the Nihilists; (6) the turning away of the mass of the upper classes from western civilization toward a native Slavic culture; and (7) the consequent tendency to Russianize the western provinces of the empire, where German or Latin culture had had some part. These movements, of course, became interlaced, and were greatly affected by the characters of the different tsars (§ 574), and they are now all overshadowed by the twentieth century movement for constitutional government (§ 575).

566. Area and Population. — Including her Asiatic territory, Russia covers over eight and a half million square miles (between two and three times the area of the United States), or about one-seventh the area of the habitable earth. She has a population of one hundred and thirty millions,[1] of which all but about twenty millions live in European Russia. The population is made up of some seventy different nationalities, but the great central core, comprising over two-thirds the whole, is composed of Russian Slavs. The subject races form only a fringe about the center, and are rapidly being Russianized (§ 574). The largest of the subject nationalities are the Poles (nearly ten millions) and the Finns (something over two and a half millions). There are also about four million Jews[2] dispersed throughout the larger cities of the empire, especially at the seaports, and nearly twelve million Tartars; but both these peoples are widely scattered and have never formed governments of their own as the Finns and Poles each have done.

567. Territorial Expansion. — In the fifteenth century, when the Russians threw off the Tartar yoke (§ 170), they held only a part of what is now South Central Russia, nowhere touching a navigable sea. Territorial expansion has come about through two distinct agencies, — colonization and war.

a. Until the time of Peter the Great, the chief advance was made by a ceaseless movement of real settlers into the savage wilderness, especially to the north and northeast. Like swarming hives, the Russian villages along the frontier sent out bands of people, each band to advance a little way and form a new

---

[1] This population is just about equal to the whole group of English-speaking peoples in the United States and the British Empire.

[2] In 1815 nearly one-half all the Jews in the world were in Russia. During the Middle Ages they had been persecuted in Christian lands in Europe and had fled to Turkey, settling in provinces about the Black Sea which afterward passed under Russian control. In the last century and in recent years (1903) they have been subjected to persecuting laws and to massacres, much as they were in England and France six hundred years ago. As a result, great numbers of them have been coming to the United States. This treatment of the Jews in Russia is a good subject for a special report.

village, driving out or absorbing the Tartar barbarians. On the south and southeast, and to some extent in Siberia, the advance was made by another kind of frontiersmen, called Cossacks. The Cossacks lived partly by agriculture, partly by grazing. At times they were almost independent of the central government, with a military organization of their own. They were admirably fitted to extend Russian authority over new lands at the expense of weaker peoples, and often they waged war on their own account against Turks and Tartars, somewhat as our early American frontiersmen won Kentucky from the Indians and Texas from Mexico. Indeed, as early as the time of Ivan the Terrible (§ 170) a Cossack horde seized part of Siberia.

b. Besides this advance, due to the unauthorized action of the people themselves, the tsars have added great stretches of territory by war. The most important of such additions come under five heads: —

(1) The Baltic Provinces from Sweden, by Peter the Great, about 1700 (§ 269).
(2) Poland, by Catherine II, 1772–1793 (§§ 269, 278).
(3) Finland from Sweden, in 1743 and 1807 (§§ 269, 365).
(4) The provinces along the Black Sea from Azof to the Danube, in a century of war against the Turks, — from 1772 to 1878.
(5) In Asia: (*a*) the occupation of Siberia at the expense of savage Tartar tribes (completed to the Pacific in the seventeenth century), and of Kamchatka in 1707; (*b*) a district of Asia Minor from the Caucasus to the Caspian, and the Trans-Caspian region — between the Caspian Sea and Persia — at the expense of Mohammedan principalities and of Turkey; and (*c*) recently, northwestern China, until checked by Japan.

Naturally Russia has sought outlets to the sea. She reached the frozen ocean of the north early. Peter the Great reached the Baltic. In war, however, the narrow outlets from that sea are easily closed by a hostile power, and hence Russia has been suspected of looking covetously towards the Atlantic ports of Sweden and Norway (§ 525, close). Peter began a struggle also for the Black Sea, and Catherine II won those waters; but Constantinople closes the exit from them to the outer world. Russian ambition therefore has aimed, for over half a century, at that ancient city, the former capital of the Greek faith; but it has been the settled policy of England to oppose Russian advance in this direction,

In Asia, until recently, Russian advance has been steady and terrifying. In that continent Russia aimed at the Pacific ports on the east, and at the Persian Gulf and the Indian seas on the south (besides the rich realms of central Asia and India). Shortly after the middle of the nineteenth century she came into conflict with China on the extreme northwest (5 c, above). In 1858 she advanced to the Amur (seizing northern Manchuria). Two years later she secured Vladivostock, and so obtained a Pacific port ice-free for most of the year. In 1895 the great Trans-Siberian Railway was begun, and in 1902 the vast undertaking was completed to Vladivostock.[1] Meanwhile Russia had compelled China to cede the magnificent harbor of Port Arthur (§ 591) and the right to extend the Trans-Siberian Railroad through Chinese Manchuria to that port (1898).

On the south (5 b, above), more resistance had been encountered, but Russian advance had never turned back. Just after the opening of the nineteenth century, Russia secured the passes of the Caucasus. By the middle of the century she had advanced into Turkestan. From that lofty vantage ground she contested with England the diplomatic control of Persia, and planned a further advance toward India. In swift succession, heedless of England's threats, she secured Bokhara (1868), Khiva (1873), and Merv (1884, despite explicit pledges to England three years before).[2] In 1893 she reached the "roof of the world," the great Pamir plateau, and soon extended her military railroad to within seventy-five miles of Herat, the "key to India." It was believed that Great Britain would resist further advance by war; but the clash in Central Asia has now been postponed by Japan's victory in the extreme east (below).

In the last years of the nineteenth century, Russia was busied with vast internal improvements, — not only the great railroads mentioned above, from Moscow to the Pacific and to the frontiers of India, but also a stupendous system of canals to connect her internal waterways. She

---

[1] This road is more than 5000 miles long, — nearly double the length of the great American transcontinental roads. Eventually it must prove one of the great steps in the advance of civilization; and it has been fitly compared in importance to the finding of the passage around the Cape of Good Hope or the building of the Suez or Panama canals.

[2] These Trans-Caspian districts are in the main rich and fertile, with valuable mines, and with a teeming, industrious population.

is still in a primitive stage industrially, and these useful projects have been carried on largely by foreign workmen and foreign capital. Under such conditions at home, Russia had every reason to desire peace abroad; but in 1904 the arrogant folly of her military classes plunged her into a war with Japan as unjust as it proved ruinous.

The story of this struggle is told briefly in another place. Here a few words will suffice. In 1900, during the Boxer disorders in China (§ 591), Russia seized Chinese Manchuria; and, though she promised solemnly that the occupation should be temporary only, it soon became plain that she was determined to remain there. To Japan, this near approach of an all-devouring, hostile power seemed to threaten not only her prosperity but also her independence, and in 1904 she resorted to war. To the amazement of the world, Russia's huge power collapsed utterly on land and sea. She was thrust back from Port Arthur and Manchuria; and, apparently, her aggressive expansion has ceased for a long time to come.

568. The Government to the year 1907 has been an absolute despotism. The will of the tsar is limited only by the necessity of using a multitude of agents to manage his vast realm. The leading body of advisers and helpers about the tsar are four, all dependent upon his will: (1) *a body of ministers* at the heads of various departments of government, with complex hierarchies of officials below them; (2) *a Council of State*, which advises the tsar in the matter of new laws and which puts into definite form those he decides to issue; (3) *the Senate*, which has now become little more than a court of appeals; and (4) *the Holy Synod*, which oversees religious matters. (For *the Duma*, see § 575.)

The police agents of the central government have tremendous power and use it tyrannically. The government, of course, desires to be just, but it is often at the mercy of its agents. In the case of political offenses, the government itself is usually merciless: often it imprisons men for indefinite periods in secret dungeons, or sends them to exile in Siberia, all merely by decree, without judicial trial.

Russia surpasses all other countries, ancient or modern, in centralization and absolutism. The government is not only supreme: it meddles with everything. Not a scholarship in a school can be founded, not a bed in a hospital can be estab lished, without the solemn approval of the tsar. Until 1855, no village church or school could be built until the plan had been sent to St. Petersburg for approval. Under Nicholas I (1825-1855), even a private house with as many as five windows required a special royal permit.[1]

569. Emancipation of the Serfs, 1861. — The greatest event in Russian history between the reforms of Peter the Great and the present constitutional movement, is the emancipation of the serfs by Alexander II. The serfs numbered over forty-seven millions of people (nearly twelve times as many as the slaves who were freed in the United States at nearly the same time), and they comprised over four-fifths the population of European Russia in that day.

Not only were the peasants freed from the jurisdiction of the nobles and from obligation to serve them: they were also assigned land for themselves. They had always dwelt in little village-communities; and now each village, or *mir*, was left to manage its own local matters [2] and was given land for its support. The land, like the serf labor, was taken away from the noble, but it was not confiscated: each mir was to pay an annual rent (fixed by the tsar's commissioners) or to buy the land outright, as it chose. If the mir wished to buy, the tsar paid the noble landlord, and the mir undertook to repay the tsar in small installments spread over forty-nine years. Most mirs adopted the purchase plan and own their own land.

570. The Peasantry: Misery; Recent Agrarian Reforms; Outlook. — Alexander and other Liberals hoped that marvelous

---

[1] Read Leroy-Beaulieu's *Tsars and Russians*, especially II, 60 and 112-116.

[2] This may seem to contradict what was said above about Russian centralization, but both statements are true. Russia is a strange compound of autocracy and democracy, — autocracy at the top in the government of the tsar, reaching down through all Russian society to the peasantry, and democracy at the bottom in these peasant villages. Indeed, the Slavophil Russian party, who believe in the destiny of their country as the future regenerator of Europe, have for their motto, "A free people under an omnipotent tsar." Advanced students may be called upon to report upon the mir, its government and its system of land cultivation. Cf. especially Wallace's *Russia* or Leroy-Beaulieu.

improvement would follow the emancipation; but such hopes have hardly been realized in the two generations that have elapsed. The great body of the peasantry remain constantly near the starving point. This unfortunate condition has been due in great measure to the fact that the peasantry did not get land enough for their support. The tsar intended each village to receive at least as much land as its inhabitants had cultivated for their own support while they had been serfs; but the nobles, who carried out the details of the arrangement, managed to cut down the amount, desiring, indeed, that the peasants should be forced to eke out their income by tilling the land of the larger proprietors about them. Moreover, Russia is a poor country and the taxes are excessive, so that much more than half the peasant's labor goes to the tax collector. To pay even then the peasant has been forced often to borrow money at extortionate interest, *as high as ten per cent a month*. Nearly one-third the entire peasant body, indeed, have been so reduced that they have pledged their labor for one or more years in advance to neighboring landlords, and so have been forced back into a kind of temporary serfdom.

In addition, the government, until 1907, held the mir responsible *as a unit* for the annual rent or annual installment of the purchase price of the land, and for other taxes.[1] In consequence, methods of cultivation are poor, and labor brings small returns. The artisan has not been allowed to leave his village to seek opportunity in the cities, except under hampering restrictions; and, as a rule, agriculture has been carried on carelessly and uneconomically, by a communal system. The mir assembly, each year or two, has redistributed its land in strips among its families, and the cultivation has been by the primitive three-field arrangement (§ 36).

A recent attempt has been made to remedy these evil conditions. In October, 1906, after a year of terrible disorder and anarchy (§ 575) the tsar by edict declared the communal system

---

[1] Cf. the French *taille* before 1789 (§ 296).

no longer binding. Freedom of movement was promised; some taxes were abolished, and vast amounts of state land were offered to the peasantry, to be paid for on low terms in fifty annual payments.[1]

It is too early, as yet, to see how far these reforms may improve the material situation of the rural workers. The peasantry, up to the present time, are unaffected by western civilization, and live in a world wholly different from that of the small class of educated Russians. Nowhere else in the civilized world is the gap between the upper and lower classes so complete (§ 268). The peasants can hardly be said to be civilized. They are filthy, stolid, ignorant, and wretched, and they have been trained into habits of improvidence and lawlessness. Disease is prevalent and terribly fatal. The death rate is a half higher than in the countries of Western Europe, and higher in the country than in the cities. One-half of all children die before they reach the age of five, and every year large districts are desolated by famine, as in France before the Revolution (§ 290), while vast districts of fertile land lie uncultivated.

On the other hand, the peasants have sometimes shown themselves capable of sublime self-sacrifice and of lofty religious enthusiasm, and like the new Slavophil party among the nobles, the whole peasantry have a blind faith in future Slav supremacy (§ 571).

571. The Higher Classes: Slavophil Sentiment. — Besides the peasants, the rural population comprises a numerous nobility and other landed proprietors. These elements, with the educated professional and mercantile classes of the few cities, make up Russian "society," and their opinions are the only "public opinion" that can be referred to in this vast empire.

For the last two hundred years (since Peter the Great), the upper classes have had a veneer of western civilization. At

---

[1] Enormous amounts of private lands, formerly owned by the nobles, passed into the hands of the peasants in the year of riot and anarchy, 1906; cf. § 575.

the opening of the nineteenth century, their conversation was carried on, not in Russian, but in French; and their books, customs, fashions, and ideas were imported from Paris. A little before the middle of the century, however, a reaction began in favor of native ideas and customs. This is the *Slavophil movement*, which for a while dominated Russian society and politics.

Notwithstanding their recent humiliation, the Russians believe zealously in themselves as the future leaders of civilization. They look forward to a Pan-Slavic Empire which shall include the Slav states of Bohemia and of Southeastern Europe, and which shall, both in power and in the character of its culture, surpass the western civilization which now sways the world.

572. Local Government and the Germs of Representative Assemblies. — Russia is divided into *vice-royalties;* these in turn into *provinces;* these into *districts.* The districts are subdivided into *volosts*, and each volost is made up of several *mirs.* The tsar appoints governors and advisory councils for the higher divisions, and his agents and police officers now exercise very complete control in the volost and in the mir. The mir, however, has its primary assembly (§§ 569, 570); and the provinces, districts, and volosts have representative assemblies. These assemblies (*zemstvos*) are gatherings of "estates" — representatives of the nobles, of other individual proprietors, and of the mirs. The functions of the zemstvos are very limited; they have some supervision over the expenditure of local funds for roads and schools; but they cannot take up the consideration of any matter until it has been laid before them by the royal governor of the district or province, and that officer has an absolute veto upon all their resolutions. Indeed, their powers are hardly more than advisory, even upon matters laid before them.

573. Russianizing the Favored Provinces. — The western provinces of Russia — Finland and the Baltic provinces — had drawn their civilization from Sweden and Germany; indeed, in the Baltic provinces, the upper classes are still mainly German in blood. In both regions until recently the leading religion has been Lutheran. The Poles, too, have been marked off from the Russian Slavs mainly by the greater German influence in their customs and by their adherence to the Catholic church. These three countries all excel Russia proper in civilization; and each at its acquisition was solemnly promised the perpetual enjoyment of its own language, religion, customs, and laws.

Despite such pledges, the Slavophils determined to Russianize the provinces.[1] Such a policy is a blessing to the barbarous regions on the east, but it has been bitterly hard upon the more progressive western districts. Since 1881 the German language has been forbidden in schools and churches in the Baltic provinces; in Poland a like policy had been begun as regards the Polish language, after the insurrection of 1863. Finland, however, was connected with Russia only through a "personal union": the tsar was also grand duke of Finland, but the duchy had its own constitution, its own representative Diet, and its free institutions, all guaranteed in the most solemn manner by each grand duke at his accession. Moreover, the Finns were industrious, peaceful, and prosperous, and gave no handle for interference. Still, the Slavophils finally got their way. In 1900 the process of making Finland a mere province of despotic and Slav Russia began, and, de-

---

[1] The desire is natural enough, if it can be honorably secured. At the bottom, it is the same sense of nationality which has helped to make Germany, Italy, and Belgium, and which leads the German Empire now to try to Germanize its Polish and Danish subjects, or which makes us desire to Americanize the foreigners who come to live among us. The difference, however, between the American position, on the one hand, and that of Germany or Russia, on the other, is easily appreciated.

The determination to Russianize all Russia is one element in the religious persecution in that country. Just as it leads to attempts to convert all Mohammedans in the eastern districts, and as it is crushing out Catholicism in Poland and Lutheranism in the Baltic lands, so it inclines the government to look calmly at the persecutions inflicted upon the Jews and upon the heretic sects that have fallen away from the Russian (Greek) church.

spite the sympathies of the western world for Finland, it was carried on rapidly, until in 1902 the last vestiges of the ancient liberties of this little northern land had been swept away. The revolutionary disorders of 1905–1906 (§ 575), however, afforded the Finns an opportunity which they were quick to seize. In the helplessness of the Russian state, the tsar was forced to restore their ancient privileges. A Constituent Assembly, elected by manhood suffrage, adopted a new constitution for Finland, which received the tsar's approval in September, 1906.[1] The Poles, too, seem in a fair way to recover some of their former privileges.

574. The Tsars. — The government, of course, has varied in character with the tsars. *Alexander I* (1801–1825) has been mentioned several times in connection with the period of Napoleon and Metternich. He had been educated by a liberal French tutor, and, in a weak and indecisive way, he favored a liberal policy in the management of Russia and Poland. His brother, *Nicholas I* (1825–1855), was wholly Russian in feeling. This had not been true of any tsar before for over a century, and accordingly this reign marks the beginning of the Slavophil movement. Nicholas despised western ideas and western civilization, and he believed in Russia with all his heart. He abandoned all his brother's attempted reforms and returned openly to the policy of despotic autocracy.

In the last years of Nicholas' reign, however, the humiliation of the Crimean War (§ 429) seemed to reveal a weakness in the despotic bureaucratic system when pitted against western civilization; and *Alexander II* (1855–1881), the son of Nicholas, returned again to a liberal policy. He emancipated the serfs, against the almost unanimous opposition of the nobles, and he introduced the zemstvos, though the people cared so little for such institutions that many times the mirs and towns petitioned to be relieved from the burden of sending

---

[1] This constitution replaced the old clumsy assembly of four estates (cf. Sweden, 524) by a single-chambered legislature to be elected by universal suffrage, — women to vote as well as men.

representatives. Jury trial was introduced; the press was left more unshackled; the universities were allowed a freedom never before permitted; and attempts were made to secure just treatment for the Jews.

But Alexander soon found himself threatened with a movement by liberal agitators altogether too radical for his taste. In the years 1860–1870 many educated Russians, especially the younger men and women, were carried away by vague but enthusiastic speculations regarding some regeneration of society, and in the years 1870–1878 the ardent disciples of these new theories began to spread socialistic doctrines among the peasantry. To Alexander this seemed full of danger; and in 1877–1878 the police put down the movement sternly, and indeed with barbarous cruelty. Then the Radicals fell back upon a policy of terrorism. They organized a secret society of *Nihilists,* and, by assassination after assassination, tried to avenge the persecution of their friends and to terrify the tsar into granting a constitution and full representative government.[1]

Alexander finally decided to grant part of these demands. He had prepared a draft of a constitution which was to set up a national Zemstvo, to be made up of deputies from the provincial representative Assemblies. Unhappily, the day before the project was to be published, the Nihilists succeeded in murdering the tsar with a dynamite bomb.

Alexander III (1881–1894) returned to the policy of his grandfather Nicholas, and the Slavophil party became dominant in society and at the court. Many of the liberal reforms of Alexander II were undone. In nearly half of European Russia the zemstvos were abolished. The press was again subjected to stern censorship. The teachers in the universities were muzzled, and the royal officers and police were given great authority to interfere in the self-government of the mirs. This policy, both as to despotism and to Slavophilism, was con-

---

[1] The demands of the Terrorists at a little later time are published by Stepniak in a note appended to his *Underground Russia.*

tinued by *Nicholas II*, who became tsar in 1894; and the police seemed to have stamped out the Nihilists, as well as all constitutional agitation, until the system of absolutism collapsed disgracefully in the war with Japan in 1904-1905 (§ 591).

575. The Constitutional Movement of 1905-1906. — The Japanese War showed that the bureaucratic despotism was dangerously inefficient and shamefully corrupt. The intelligent classes were exasperated by the humiliating defeat, and the peasantry were direfully oppressed by war taxes. These facts revived revolutionary movements, and gave them new importance. Early in 1905, European Russia was convulsed, as never before, by peasant uprisings, by industrial strikes, and by mutiny in army and navy. The educated classes spoke out forcefully for a constitutional government; and, for a time, the tsar and his advisers felt constrained to yield. In March a *representative assembly* was vaguely promised; and soon after the close of the war, in October, an imperial decree guaranteed complete *freedom of conscience* and *freedom of speech*, private and public.

Amid growing anarchy and ruin, the promised *Duma* was finally brought together, after many delays, in May, 1906, — the first Representative Assembly of the Russian nation. The tsar had arranged the elections so as to leave most weight in the hands of the wealthy classes, but the revolutionary movement had swept everything before it. A great majority of the members were liberals and called themselves *Constitutional Democrats*. Among them were many leaders of wise and moderate statesmanship, and the world was amazed at the show of political ability in this first, inexperienced Russian Assembly.

By unanimous vote the Duma asked for four great political reforms, — universal suffrage, a "responsible" ministry, the abolition of martial law, and amnesty for all political offenders then in prison or in exile, — and for a long programme of social reform, including the turning over of state lands to the suffering peasantry. All these demands were refused. After proper persistence, the Duma wisely withdrew all but the agrarian demand. Reactionary councils, however, were gaining ground with the tsar, and on July 21 he dissolved the Duma, announcing that the autocracy must itself care for the needed reforms. Accordingly, in October, 1906, an imperial edict decreed the agrarian reforms mentioned in § 570, and also abolished the special privileges of the nobles, making all Russians equal before the law and equally eligible to public employment. Another Assembly was promised, also, for March, 1907; but plainly the government meant to control it.

The dissolution has been followed by months of anarchy. The government fell back upon stern repression and intimidation, to suppress not only disorder, but also political agitation. The extreme revolutionists resorted to a campaign of systematic political assassination. Meantime the unhappy land was again distracted by peasant risings and by strikes, which were put down brutally by Cossack "punitive expeditions" in which thousands of unoffending people perished; while a new famine desolated many provinces. In January, 1907, a population of thirty millions is said to be in terrible want of food.

Fifty officials were assassinated in one week in August, just after the dissolution of the Duma, the victims ranging from ministers of state to petty police officers, and many others were wounded. During the following four months, according to the best figures obtainable, 1629 riots occurred and 244 bombs were thrown at officials. On the other hand, more than a thousand political offenders were executed, and fifty thousand were sent to Siberia or to prison, while the Revolutionists count up 24,239 others slain by the soldiery in putting down or punishing riots.

The extremists who engage in the desperate policy of assassinating government agents manifest a reckless disregard of their own lives, and expect death on the scaffold or by torture in prison. But the worst feature of the whole terrible history is that the government has virtually proscribed the Constitutional Democratic party, to prevent its further political activity. In November, of the leaders of that party in the dissolved Duma, one (a learned professor) had been murdered; two had been cruelly beaten in prison, and another had been driven insane by treatment there; ten were in hiding; five had been exiled; twenty-four

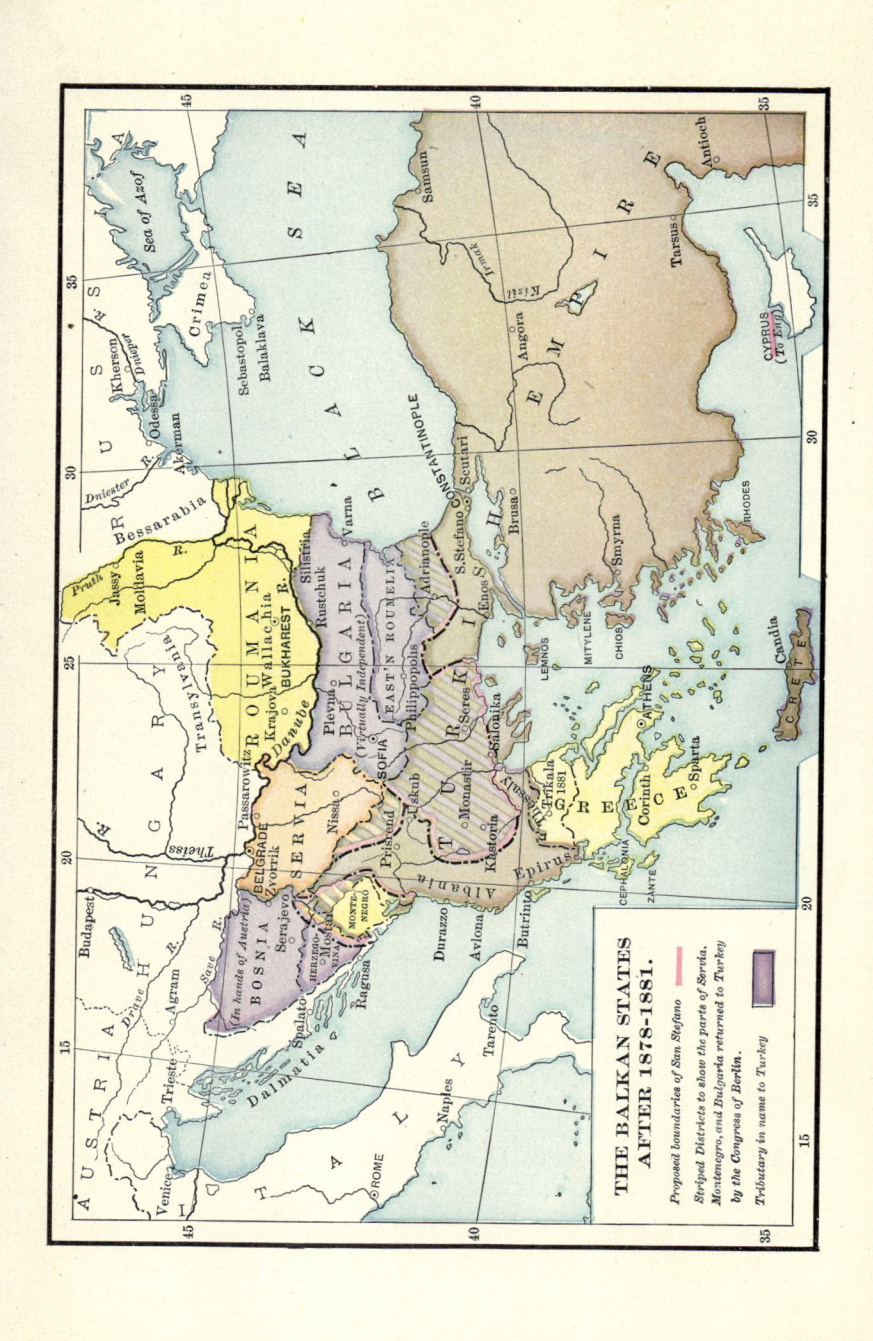

THE BALKAN STATES
AFTER 1878-1881.

Proposed boundaries of San Stefano

Striped Districts to show the parts of Servia, Montenegro, and Bulgaria returned to Turkey by the Congress of Berlin.

Tributary in name to Turkey

were imprisoned; and 182 others, including the president and the vice-president of the Duma, were under indictment for treason. Apparently the tottering despotism is endeavoring to wage war upon Russian intelligence.

None the less, it seems impossible that Russia should settle back permanently into its former autocracy. The revolution, by bloody or peaceful means, must lead ere long to some form of constitutional government. Despite all this terrorism and the prosecution of nearly seven hundred editors in 1906, the Russian press teems (January, 1907) as never before, with outspoken demands for reform. The Duma of 1907 will be watched with intense interest by the civilized world.

II. THE BALKAN STATES.

A. GENERAL SURVEY TO 1878.

576. The Subject Races and the Turks in 1815. — In 1815 all Southeastern Europe beyond Austria-Hungary and Russia was part of Turkey. The Turk, however, was merely an invader, and had no part in European civilization; and the history of Southeastern Europe began only as the native races regained their freedom.[1] The Turks made a small part of the population, and the bulk of the people had kept their Christian (Greek) Faith. In the old Hellenic peninsula dwelt the *Greeks*. North of the Danube, in the provinces of Wallachia and Moldavia, dwelt the Latin *Roumanians*, claiming descent from Trajan's colonists in Dacia.[2] Between the Greek and Latin peoples lay two great Slav nations, — the *Bulgarians* in the east, from the Aegean to the Danube, and the *Servians* on the west. On the Adriatic were the *Albanians*, who had abandoned Christianity for Mohammedanism.

The boundaries between these subject peoples were sadly mixed, and the line between them and their kinsmen in Austria

---

[1] Reread § 2. For the earlier history of the region, see § 169.
[2] *Ancient History*, § 474.

and in southern Russia had been drawn merely by the accidents of war. A fourth of the Roumanian race were in the Russian province of Bessarabia, which had been seized from the Turks in 1812, and another fourth were in Transylvania, which the Hungarians had reconquered from Turkey in the eighteenth century. The Croats and Serbs in southern Hungary, too, were merely part of the old Servian race living in the lands Hungary had reconquered from Turkey; while in the mountain fastnesses of Montenegro dwelt a few thousand Servians who had never yielded to the Turks.

577. The Subject Races win Freedom, 1821-1878. — The Roumanians, beyond the Danube, and the Servians, in their rugged country, had risen in various rebellions early in the nineteenth century; but the first successful revolt of a subject people was the Greek rising of 1821-1828 (§ 399). European aid resulted in Greek independence; and, in connection with the final settlement (1829), the two Roumanian provinces and Servia were granted a large measure of internal self-government: they were to have rulers chosen by themselves and confirmed by the Sultan; they remained tributary, however, to the Turkish Empire.

The next advance came in 1848. In that "year of revolutions," the Roumanians rose once more and appealed to Russia for aid. Russia and Turkey both took up arms, but a convention between the two Powers provided for the nominal restoration of Turkish authority, subject, however, to Russian supervision. These events soon afterward led the Tsar Nicholas to suggest to England that it was time to decide what was to be done with the possessions of the Turks as Turkish rule decayed. This was a formal statement of the "Eastern Question," as that question was long to be understood.[1]

Nicholas was disappointed at the cool reception given his

---

[1] "We have on our hands a sick man, a very sick man," said Nicholas to the English ambassador; "it would be a great misfortune if one of these days he should slip away before the proper arrangements have been made." This is the origin of the phrase, "the Sick Man of Europe."

suggestion for the partition of Turkey. England preferred to bolster up the Ottoman power as a barrier to Russian advance. England and France and Russia had acted in concert twenty-five years before, in freeing the Greeks; but in 1854 the two western states fought Russia to prevent any further breaking up of Turkey (§ 429), and the Congress of Paris (1856) guaranteed the "integrity" of that state.

In return, the Sultan promised reforms for his Christian subjects; but the next twenty years saw no serious attempt to carry out the pledge, and in 1875–1876 the Serbs in Herzegovina and the Bulgarians rose for independence. The Herzegovinian herdsmen in their distant mountains were able to carry on a kind of warfare for some time without extreme suffering; but the Bulgarians in their easily accessible country felt the full force of Turkish vengeance. There followed the horrible events known as the "Bulgarian Atrocities." Turkish soldiers destroyed a hundred villages, with every form of torture and cruelty, and massacred thirty thousand people, carrying off also thousands of Christian women into terrible slavery. The Servians then sprang to arms; and in 1877 Alexander II of Russia, in sympathy with the unanimous demands of his people, declared war. The universal horror in Western Europe at the crimes of the Turks prevented for a time any interference with Russia, and in ten months her armies held the Turks at their mercy.[1] The *Peace of San Stefano* arranged for the withdrawal of the Turk from Europe, except for the city of Constantinople itself, with a little adjacent territory, and for the Mohammedan district of Albania. Roumania, Servia, and Montenegro were to be wholly independent, and the two latter were enlarged in territory; while Bulgaria, from the Danube to the Aegean, was to become a self-governing state, tributary in name to the Sultan.

But now Europe interfered. The Congress of Berlin, at the

---

[1] The Turks fought with their ancient gallantry, and made a stouter resistance than had been thought possible. Special report: the defense of Plevna.

suggestion of Disraeli (§ 547), cut down the size of Servia and Montenegro, to keep the southern districts under Turkish rule, and divided Bulgaria into three parts. The southern third (Macedonia) was left as a part of the Turkish empire; the middle third ("Eastern Roumelia") was partly returned to the Sultan, who was, however, to rule it through a Christian governor responsible to the Powers; and only the northern division (between the Balkans and the Danube) was left the practical independence Russia had won for it, with liberty to choose its own prince.

This shameful surrender of the half-freed Christian populations left ancient Thrace and the southern part of old Macedonia still in Turkish hands, and postponed indefinitely the final settlement of the "Eastern Question." It has also made much more difficult the progress of the parts of the peninsula that have been freed, since they must give their energies to preparation for war with the Turks, in order to protect themselves and to complete the emancipation of their southern brothers (cf. § 582 and note).

During the past year (1903) there has been a state of anarchy in Macedonia. Insurrectionary committees, operating from Bulgaria, have fomented armed risings and the Turks have put them down with outrages scarcely less horrible than those of 1876. The jealousies between the Powers have prevented any intervention; but Austria and Russia, the two Powers most concerned, have finally agreed upon a plan, which, if adopted, will virtually put these districts under their joint administration.

B. The Separate States.

578. Roumania. — After 1848 the districts of Wallachia and Moldavia clamored for union. The Congress of Paris (§ 429) took the two provinces under the protection of the Powers and permitted each of them to choose an assembly and a prince. The demand for union was not heeded; but in 1859 the two provinces chose the same prince, Alexander I, and three years later the two provincial Assemblies merged into one.

The Powers objected, but they did not interfere by force, and the new state took the name of *the Principality of Roumania*, remaining, of course, tributary to Turkey.

Up to this time, the political activity of the country had come wholly from the nobles, or country landlords: the great mass of the population had been serfs. In 1864, while Russia and the United States were carrying out their great acts of emancipation, Roumania took a like step. The serfs were freed and were given one-third the land of the country, — the state paying the nobles, the former landlords, and receiving repayment from the peasants in annual installments. In 1884 it was enacted that the new peasant landowners should not sell or mortgage their lands until thirty years had elapsed, — a measure designed to protect the new and ignorant peasantry from the greed of money-lenders.

In 1866 there occurred a political revolution. Alexander was forced to abdicate, and a National Assembly adopted a liberal constitution and elected *Charles of Hohenzollern* as Prince of Roumania. Prince Charles gave special attention to the army. When the Russo-Turkish war began, *Roumania declared itself independent*, and the new army proved a gallant and efficient force, rendering material aid to Russia in the struggle. In 1881 Roumania took the style of *Kingdom of Roumania*. Since that time, the nation has been peaceful, and has made steady progress in political and industrial development. Nine-tenths of the population are still illiterate, but this condition will soon begin to improve. All tax-paying adult males have the franchise. The legislature consists of two houses, chosen by electoral colleges. King Charles has maintained the attitude of a constitutional sovereign and has governed through "responsible" ministries.

The country has a population of nearly six millions, and it is ardently desirous to annex the two and a half million fellow Roumanians who are subject to Hungary, just across the Carpathian mountains (§ 499). Roumania and Hungary, however, are both sadly out of place, lying as they do between the great

Slav Empire of the north and the new Slav kingdoms of the south; and Roumania's greatest danger is, that she may be absorbed in some future movement to unite the separated Slav peoples. As long as she can maintain herself, she forms an important barrier to Russian advance.

579. Montenegro. — After the overthrow of the ancient Servian empire by the Turks in 1389 (§ 169), some bands of Servians, who preferred exile to submission, retired into the fastnesses of *Montenegro*, or the Black Mountain. Here, for five hundred years, these "Swiss of the Balkans" maintained their independence. The story has been called one of "ferocious heroism." The incessant struggle trained the people into a semi-savage race with some traits of barbarous cruelty. Since 1878, however, the little state has begun to make some progress in civilization.

The people number a little over two hundred thousand, and the country is not much larger than a good-sized county. The prince is virtually absolute, though he is assisted by a council of eight members. One half of the council are elected by all who bear arms; the other half the prince appoints.

580. Servia is a land of warlike herdsmen, the ancient nobles having been destroyed in the Turkish wars. The people began the nineteenth century struggle for independence as early as 1804, under *Kara George* (Black George), a swineherd and a national hero; but the self-government of 1829 (§ 577) was finally secured under another leader, *Milosh Obrenovitch*, who became Prince of Servia. Members of the Kara George and the Milosh family followed each other in swift succession on the princely throne, through revolution or assassination, until 1859. From that time until 1903 the Milosh dynasty kept the crown.

Servia became an independent kingdom in 1878 (§ 577). In 1863 and 1888 liberal democratic constitutions were introduced, modeled upon those of Western Europe, but so far the country has shown itself little fitted for constitutional government. *King Milan*, whose arbitrary temper had made him excessively unpopular, abdicated in 1889 in favor of his son, the boy *Alexander*. Four years later, Alexander, still only seventeen years of age, arrested the regents while they were dining at his table, and, by a simple decree, suspended the constitution and modified it at will, against the desires of nine-tenths of the population and of the National Assembly. Then in 1903 the civilized world was shocked by the murder of King Alexander, together with his Queen and a few friends, in the palace, by a midnight attack of some army officers. Apparently, however, the nation approved the deed, and *Peter Karageorgevitch* was at once summoned to the throne. The whole story resembles the army revolutions that characterize Oriental states, and, along with all her recent history, it shows how far Servia is from having really adopted European civilization.

The nation is distracted by vehement quarrels of political factions who differ from each other mainly in their pro-Russian and pro-Austrian sympathies. The peasantry are well-to-do, but Servia contains almost no men of any considerable wealth. The people are ambitious of adding Slav territory on the south now held by Turkey; but the Servian army in 1878, and again in 1888 in a conflict with Bulgaria, proved a poor fighting machine.

In 1900, the population was about two and a half millions. The Servian peasant villages are groups of family-communities, each containing thirty or forty members, living in one group of buildings with a common hall, and forming a self-governing unit. This *Zadruga*, or family-community, seems to be an ancient Slav institution.

581. Bulgaria has never been reconciled to the way it was treated by the Congress of Berlin, though part of the wrong done it at that time was redressed a few years later. In 1885, Eastern Roumelia (southern Bulgaria) drove out its governor and called for union with self-governing Bulgaria. The people in the northern province were enthusiastic in their sympathy, and a Bulgarian army at once occupied Roumelia, to prevent the restoration of Turkish authority. The two provinces have not been actually incorporated into one state in form, but they have the same prince, and they enjoy similar institutions. Since this merging of the two provinces, the Bulgarians have carried on an active agitation for a similar occupation of Macedonia, and more than once Europe has seemed on the verge of war in consequence.[1]

In 1885, when Bulgaria and Roumelia were joined, Servia declared war, — jealously opposed to this enlargement of a neighboring state. By quick and decisive victories, the Bulgarians not only confirmed their hold upon Roumelia, but established themselves as the leaders of the Southeastern Slavs.

After the settlement of 1878, the Bulgarians adopted a constitution and chose for their ruler a German noble, *Prince Alexander of Battenberg*. The legislature (*Sobranje*) consists of one chamber, elected by manhood suffrage. It goes through the forms of western parliamentary government; but in truth the peasantry, the mass of the nation, take no interest in politics at ordinary times, and the government controls elections almost at will.

The real political question is, whether Bulgaria shall have a policy of her own or whether she shall be a mere satellite of Russia. Prince Alexander proved honorably unwilling to submit to Russian dictation, but in 1886 he was kidnapped and dethroned. The President of the Sobranje, *Stambuloff*, then became for a time the head of a national government, and continued the independent Bulgarian policy, with the enthusiastic support of the mass of the nation. In 1887, *Prince Ferdinand of Coburg* was elected to the vacant throne, but until 1894 Stambuloff continued to control the government. Stambuloff was a patriotic Bulgarian and a powerful statesman, a "Balkan Bismarck"; but his harsh treatment of political enemies and his arrogance created many enemies and made him hateful to the court. In 1894, Prince Ferdinand succeeded in getting him out of office. To keep him out, however, was not easy; but his political enemies seized the moment's advantage to plot against his life. Stambuloff took all possible precautions; but in broad daylight, in a public street, with the police looking

---

[1] Especially in 1903. See § 577, close.

on, his carriage was stopped and he was hacked to pieces by a band of brutal assassins, whom the government made no effort to punish. The court was probably not a party to the crime, but it had exposed Stambuloff to the vengeance of private enemies, and his death was certainly grateful to the Prince. This dastardly action made it evident that Bulgaria, like Servia, is far from the standard of western civilization. Since the removal of Stambuloff, the government has made strenuous efforts to regain Russian favor.

The people are mostly a prosperous peasantry, living in rude comfort: indeed, Bulgaria is sometimes called the "Peasant State." The Zadruga is found in parts of Bulgaria, as well as in Servia. The population is about three and three-quarter millions.

582. Greece. — While Greece was winning its freedom in 1828, a National Assembly elected as president *Capodistrias*, a Russian Greek. This provisional government, however, proved both tyrannical and ineffective. In 1830, at the suggestion of the Western Powers, the Assembly voted for a monarchic government and offered the crown to Leopold of Coburg. Leopold, afterward to win honorable fame as king of Belgium, declined the throne, because the territory of Greece had been so limited, in the settlement with Turkey, that he saw inevitable trouble before the new state. In 1831, Capodistrias was assassinated; and the Assembly, with the approval of the Powers, placed a young Bavarian prince upon the throne as *Otto I.*

Otto surrounded himself with Germans, and soon became exceedingly unpopular. In 1843 a national rising forced him to grant a liberal constitution, and in 1862 a second revolution drove him from Greece. The next year, the Assembly elected a new king in the person of *Prince George of Denmark*, and in 1864 the present constitution was adopted. The legislature consists of one chamber of deputies, chosen by manhood suffrage; and the ministers are "responsible."

The enthusiastic hopes of the Philhellenes of 1821–1828

(§ 399) have not been realized. Greece has abounded in brigandage and crime, and the public order is still far from satisfactory. The population increased rapidly after 1830, but in 1900 it still amounted only to two and a half millions. Schools are better and more universal than in the other Balkan states, but over a third of the adults are still illiterate. The most serious problems since 1864 have been (1) territorial and (2) financial.

a. Like the other Balkan states, Greece has been bitterly dissatisfied with its boundaries, and eager to bring under its government the several millions of Greeks still in bondage in Macedonia, in Constantinople, and in Crete. The boundary of 1828–1830 left even Thessaly and Epirus to Turkey. Most of these districts were added to Greece in 1881, as a result of the wars of 1877–1878.[1] Then, in 1896, Crete rebelled against Turkey; but the Powers interfered to prevent her union with Greece, and confusions and massacres followed for many months. The next spring, in spite of the opposition of the Powers, Greece declared war upon Turkey, with the intention of increasing her territory on the north. The Greeks hoped that the Bulgarians would rise at the same time and that the European Powers would then feel compelled to intervene. In fact, however, Bulgaria remained quiet, and the Powers left Greece to her fate. The German Emperor, indeed, had sent the Sultan German officers to organize and command the Turkish army, and that force showed a military excellence wholly unexpected. Greece was quickly defeated, and forced to pay a war indemnity, while Turkey took small strips of territory all along her northern frontier, so as to command all the passes into Greece in case of another struggle.[2]

---

[1] Greece, at a staggering cost, had built up an army, and in 1877 she wished to join in the attack upon Turkey. The Western Powers forbade such action, promising Greece that she should get as much by peace as by war; and, after some delay, the promises were partially kept.

[2] With Bulgaria, Servia, and Greece all asking for extension into Macedonia, and each jealous of the others, the Eastern Question is still far from settled.

b. Greece was "born in debt." By the settlement of 1830, she was obliged to pay Turkey a large sum in return for her independence. Her army expenditure plunged the little country deeper in debt; and before the last war the interest on her foreign debt took half the revenue, while taxation had become crushing. In 1894 the government announced that it could pay only a third of the interest on the national debt. Talk of European intervention followed; and after the Turkish war the Powers did assume joint control of the finances, to guarantee payment of the new debt to Turkey and of that to the old bondholders in Western Europe. Like Spain and Portugal, and, in some degree, like Italy, Greece seems sunk in hopeless bankruptcy, unless she will give up her military expenditures and turn zealously to the development of her internal resources.

FOR FURTHER READING. — Of the general histories of modern times, Seignobos (587–637) gives the best treatment of the Balkan states, and as much, probably, as students can take time for. The following special treatments are good: Beaman, *Stambuloff;* Dicey, *The Peasant State* (Bulgaria); Miller, *The Balkans;* Minchin, *Rise of Freedom in the Balkan Peninsula;* Samuelson, *Roumania;* Sergeant, *New Greece;* Beckford-Smith, *Greece under King George.* Laveleye's *Balkan Peninsula* (1887) is an older work, but valuable. Freeman's *Ottoman Power in Europe* is a powerful indictment of Turkish rule down to 1878, and Freeman's *Essays* contain several valuable papers on Southeastern Europe. The Reviews, Year Books, and Annual Encyclopedias will be consulted, of course, by students particularly interested.

EXERCISE. — Review of certain general topics for the Europe of to-day: (1) Education and illiteracy; (2) the kulturkampf; (3) the army system; (4) financial conditions of the governments in the small states; (5) the state of the franchise, with dates for progress toward democracy.

CHAPTER VIII.

THE NEW AGE.

I. INTERNATIONAL RELATIONS, 1871-1900.

583. Rearrangement of Political Relations after 1881: the Triple and Dual Alliances. — The years 1866–1871 saw a new "Great Power" added to the small European circle. The emergence of Germany as a strong united nation, in place of the former petty jealous states of Central Europe, of itself would have compelled a recasting of political alliances; and about the same time other causes contributed to a like result.

(1) France was bent upon revenge for the Franco-Prussian War, and she longed to recover her severed provinces. For twenty years after 1870 the Alsace-Lorraine matter was the burning question in European politics; and, to strengthen herself for the expected conflict, France cultivated cordial relations with Russia. (2) Meantime, Bismarck offended Russia by supporting Austria's claims in the Balkans, where lay the other chief storm-center of Europe. (3) In 1880, Italy was angered by the French seizure of Tunis (§ 451), — the first important conflict of interest in recent times outside Europe.

Thus, in curious fashion old enemies were drawn together and old associates divided. In 1881, Germany, Austria, and Italy leagued themselves in a union known as the *Triple Alliance,* and a few years later Russia and France formally adopted a dual alliance. The continent was thrown into two great hostile camps, jealously watching each other's slightest movement.

584. Some Results of this Rearrangement. — Three results of this rearrangement particularly impress the observer, — the "armed peace" of the generation since 1871, the loss of importance by France in international matters, and the isolation of England.

a. Each of the two alliances professed that its aim was to maintain peace; and, in a sense, the maintenance of peace has been one of the results. A conflict between such enormous forces, under the new conditions of army organization, quick transportation, and destructive explosives, would be so frightful that the most reckless government must hesitate to enter upon it; and, though Europe has repeatedly been on the verge of war, no great conflict has actually taken place there since the Franco-German struggle. Europe rests under a costly "armed peace," based upon fear.

b. Russia proved to be the chief gainer from the Franco-Russian alliance. Russian loans were taken up freely by French capital, and so Russia secured the funds necessary for her vast internal improvements (§ 567). French support, too, made it easy for Russia to carry her point many times in the East against the policy of England. But France herself, in European matters, reaped little apparent benefit. She was in no danger of attack, and she was not able to make an attack herself. Critics described her position as that of the "tail to the Russian kite." Russian backing, however, did enable her to act firmly at times in African matters (§ 451).

c. In the eighties, England looked with natural jealousy upon the French advance in North Africa, and so drew near the Triple Alliance. Especially did she cultivate friendly relations with Italy, whose powerful fleet in the Mediterranean would have insured control of that sea in case of war. The relation, however, did not ripen into an alliance. Bismarck wanted England formally to join the Triple Alliance; but she feared entanglement in continental wars in which she might have no interest, and so maintained a position which some of her statesmen liked to call one of "splendid isolation."

All these relations have begun to undergo sweeping changes in connection with new problems (§§ 585 ff.).

II. THE EXPANSION OF EUROPE INTO AFRICA AND ASIA.

585. European Politics merge into World Politics. — Toward the year 1900, another mighty change took place in international politics, vaster and swifter than any other in history. European politics were suddenly merged in world politics.

This means that for the future we have to consider a new stage, new actors, and new problems. Within the last few years the questions at issue between the Great Powers have ceased to be mainly Rhenish or Danubian, and have become African or Asiatic. The possession of petty counties on a little European river, though perhaps still in dispute, has ceased to interest statesmen and peoples who have fixed their eyes instead on vast continents.

When this new greed for territory seized upon Europe, the only important lands left to appropriate consisted of Africa and parts of Asia, with some islands in the Pacific. Australia was English. North America was held by the United States or England; and the rest of the American continent was protected beneath the shield of the Monroe Doctrine. Africa, however, was largely unappropriated, and in Asia the stationary and apparently helpless empires of China, Turkey, and Persia invited attack.

586. The Partition of Africa. — There followed a swift and peaceful division of the vast African continent. In 1880, only a few patches here and there on the coast were European: in 1891, the continent was mapped out between European claimants.[1]

For half a century, France had been extending her sway over Algeria on the north, and for nearly double that time England had held Cape Colony on the south. The events of 1881 (§ 560) put Egypt and the Nile valley into English control, and a little earlier the explorations of Livingstone and Stanley

---

[1] Caldecott's *English Colonization*, 112, has a good map illustrating the transformation of this decade of years. Note also the dates on the map in this volume, facing page 611.

AFRICA
1903

§ 586]   EXPANSION OF EUROPE INTO AFRICA.   611

had awakened interest in the heart of the "Dark Continent." In the early seventies Stanley had proved that the upper portions of the Congo extended far into the interior, and that the immense region in the center of the continent was a rich and accessible country. In 1876, at the suggestion of Leopold of Belgium, the *Congo International Association* was organized to explore Central Africa and to stop the horrible slave trade carried on by the Arabs; and in 1879, Stanley, now in the service of Leopold and the Association, returned to the upper Congo and made the beginnings of a European state there.

Some disputes arose at once between the new Congo state and the Portuguese, regarding territory bordering the lower Congo; and in 1884, to prevent conflict, Bismarck called an international Congress at Berlin.[1] This conference recognized the Congo State and the sovereignty of the International Association. In return, the Association was pledged to permit free trade to all nations. The next year, Leopold became head of the "Congo Free State." The union with Belgium was declared to be merely personal; but in his will (1889) Leopold made Belgium heir to his rights of sovereignty in the new state. Belgium has also advanced money for internal improvements; and in return, by treaty with the Congo State, has acquired the right fully to annex the territory, if she chooses to do so. The administration is Belgian; and in 1903, of the European population (some twenty-five hundred), about half was Belgian. The territory covers about one million square miles, and the natives number some thirty millions. In 1903 it came to light that the Belgian officials, in their efforts to secure large amounts of ivory, were treating the natives with horrible cruelty; and for the past three years (1907) many attempts have been made to secure European or American intervention in the interest of humanity.

The establishment of the Congo State and the Berlin Conference were followed by the raising of the German flag in

---

[1] This was the first European Congress at which the United States was represented.

Africa (§ 484); and then began a wild scramble for territory, which at the end of six years (1891) left all the continent European, except Abyssinia, Tripoli, and Liberia. The possessions of Italy and Spain, however, are little more than footholds and are not likely to be materially extended, while the Portuguese territories are not new acquisitions, but the remains of a fading empire. The three leading European Powers in Africa, and the only ones that need to be considered seriously, are England, France, and Germany. Of these, England is far in the lead. Aside from small territories at other parts on the coast, her sway extends over the whole Nile valley, the richest part of the continent, and over extensive territories in the south. Her ambition has been to unite her possessions north and south; but the Congo State and German East Africa were thrust between too soon. However, in the near future, an English railway (through the neutral Congo State) will undoubtedly join Cairo and Cape Town, and open Africa to English civilization.

France comes second in importance. She would have liked to join her realms on the east and on the west of the continent; but she found English territory thrust in between. German ambition was thwarted in like manner. Thus these three Powers seem to have mutually stalemated one another's efforts to completely dominate Africa.

587. Threatened Conflicts. — So far, only twice has the rivalry between the Great Powers in Africa threatened war. *a.* About 1895, the English and French "spheres of influence" met at Lake Tchad. Then, in 1898, while the upper Nile valley and the Soudan were temporarily in revolt against Egypt and England, an enterprising French explorer, Marchand, advanced from Lake Tchad far into the disputed districts and raised the French flag at Fashoda on the Nile. A victorious English force soon appeared, and, for a time, conflict in Africa and Europe seemed imminent; but the French government finally withdrew its explorer, and the following year a convention between the two Powers arranged the dispute peacefully.

b. In 1904, Germany encouraged Morocco to resist French encroachment (§ 451). War seemed probable; but a compromise was effected through an international conference at Algeciras (1906). French influence was sanctioned; but the process of turning Morocco completely into a protectorate was checked.

588. The Situation in Asia before 1894. — The occupation of Asia by European states has proceeded more slowly than that of Africa, but it has moved with increasing rapidity in recent years. England, Russia, and France are the three European countries concerned. Central and Northern Asia is Russian. The great, densely populated peninsula of Hindostan, with adjoining Burma, is English. The southeastern peninsula, since the plundering of Siam in 1896, is mainly French. The only independent states left in this greatest of the continents are Asia Minor (Turkey), Persia, Afghanistan, Siam, and China. Of these Afghanistan and Siam are mere remnants of "buffer states," separating England from Russia on one side and from France on the other. Apparently they are doomed to absorption by these powerful neighbors, though it has been the purpose of English policy in recent years to preserve them as barriers to her rivals. Persia, too, is virtually a dependency either of England or Russia, according to the varying fortune of the diplomacy of those countries; and in the closing years of the nineteenth century it seemed that even the ancient Chinese Empire had begun to go to pieces.

589. Appearance of Two New World Powers. — In the nineties two new actors appeared upon the stage of world politics. A war between Japan and China and the Spanish-American War added the United States and Japan to the circle of Powers interested in international politics.

Until the year 1900 the United States found scope for its energies in peopling its great territories and in developing resources at home; and, content with primacy on the American continents, it resolutely abstained from European complications. But the Spanish-American War left it in possession of the Philippines; and during the war, Hawaii was annexed. Thus it held the mastery of the Pacific and was brought to the door of Asia; and men saw at once that, under the modern conditions of trade and intercourse, the United States must henceforth be reckoned with as one of the leading Powers interested in world politics.

In particular, the United States is desirous of securing a fair show for its trade in China, which has become one of its important customers. The similarity of English and American views regarding China and the likeness of the English and Americans in politics and culture incline the two peoples to act together in the East, in opposition to Russia, France, and Germany. Germany, too, seems to look with jealousy upon the American Monroe Doctrine as applied to South America. These conditions inclined to new combinations among the five "World Powers"— the United States, England, Russia, Germany, and France. Germany and Russia, too, treat their dependencies as estates to be managed for the benefit of the peoples possessing them. This low standard has long since been rejected by the English-speaking nations. Thus a broad humanitarian interest was given to the question as to which group of powers should impose its civilization upon the industrious but passive millions of China. But the victory of Japan over Russia (§ 590) has introduced still another factor into the problem.

Until the middle of the nineteenth century Japan had kept herself sealed to the outer world. For more than two centuries, indeed, to hold communication with foreigners had been a capital crime. But in 1853, Commodore Perry, under orders from the United States Government, by a show of force secured the admission of American trade to certain Japanese ports; and then, after a short interval, Japan began to exchange her Oriental civilization for western culture. Before the close of the century this transformation had been carried to a marvelous completeness. Army and navy, schools and industry, took on modern character; and in 1889 the liberal

THE WORLD POWERS

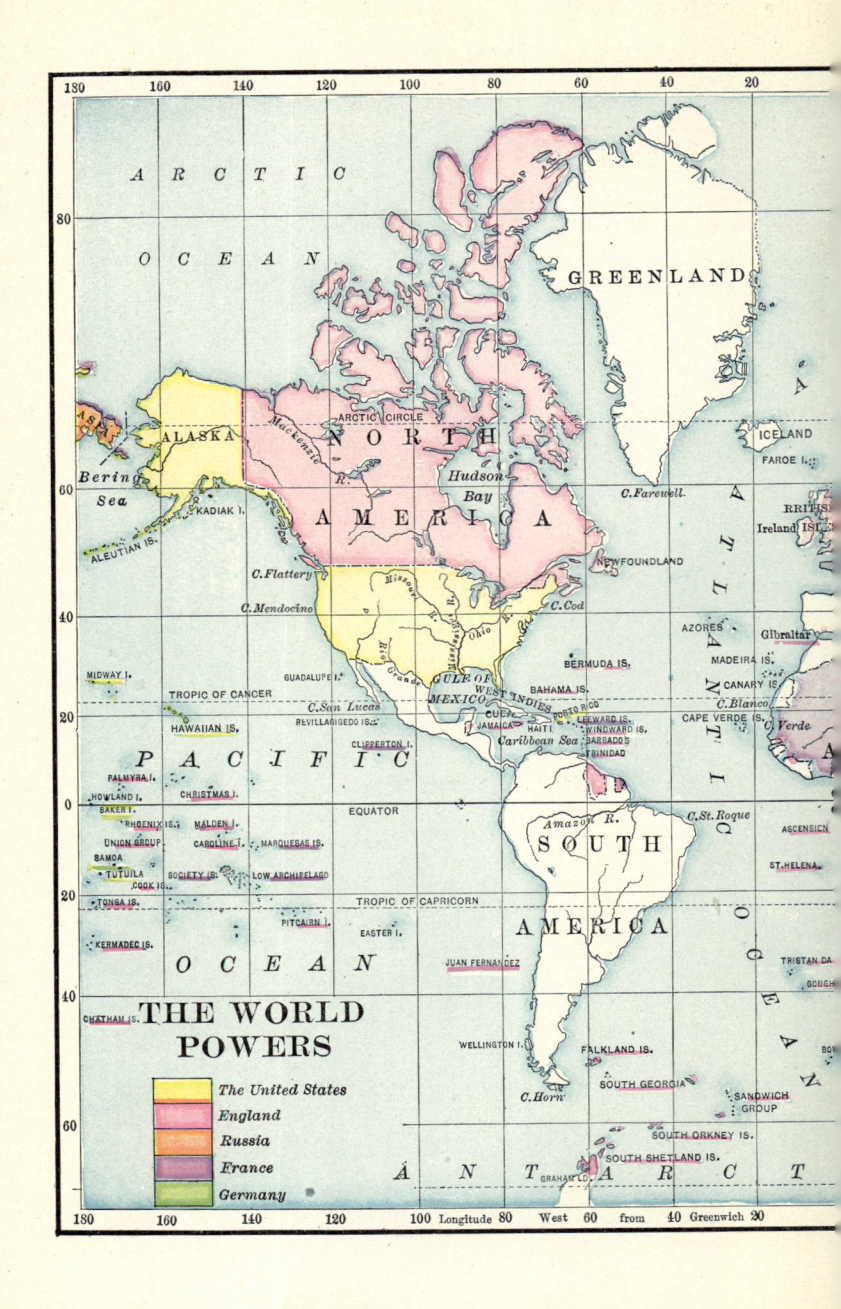

- The United States
- England
- Russia
- France
- Germany

FRANZ JOSEPH LAND
SPITZBERGEN
C. Chelyuskin
NEW SIBERIA IS.
NOVA
ZEMBLA
Kara Sea
North C.
ARCTIC CIRCLE
Ob R.
Yenisei R.
Lena R.
Baltic Sea
Sea of Okhotsk
EUROPE
ASIA
Volga R.
Danube R.
Black Sea
Caspian Sea
Aral Sea
TURKISH EMPIRE
MALTA
CYPRUS
Manchuria
CHINESE EMPIRE
Port Arthur
Wei-hai-wei
Kiao-chau
KOREA
Japan Sea
JAPAN
PERSIA
AFGHANISTAN
Yangtze R.
Nile R.
Red Sea
Arabian Sea
KURIA MURIA
SOKOTRA I.
C. Guardafui
LACCADIVE IS.
C. Comorin
MALDIVE IS.
CEYLON
Bay of Bengal
ANDAMAN IS.
NICOBAR IS.
Hongkong
FORMOSA
China Sea
PHILIPPINE IS.
TROPIC OF CANCER
MARIANA OR LADRONE IS.
GUAM
WAKE IS.
MARSHALL IS.
CAROLINE IS.
PELEW IS.
PACIFIC OCEAN
BORNEO
CELEBES
SUMATRA
JAVA
SUNDA IS.
NEW GUINEA
SOLOMON IS.
EQUATOR
SEYCHELLES IS.
CHAGOS IS.
Congo R.
INDIAN OCEAN
MADAGASCAR
Mozambique Channel
MAURITIUS
REUNION
KEELING IS.
CHRISTMAS I.
LOUISIADE ARCH.
Coral Sea
LOYALTY IS.
FIJI IS.
TROPIC OF CAPRICORN
NEW CALEDONIA
AUSTRALIA
NORFOLK I.
C. of Good Hope
C. Leeuwin
Gt. Australian Bight
ST. PAUL I.
TASMANIA
NEW ZEALAND
PR. EDWARD IS.
CROZET IS.
KERGUELEN I.
ANTIPODES I.
MACQUARIE I.
CAMPBELL I.
OCEAN
ANTARCTIC CIRCLE
ENDERBY LAND
WILKES LAND
20 Longitude 40 East 60 from 80 Greenwich 100 120 140 160 180

Mikado (emperor) proclaimed a constitution which created a limited monarchy, with a Diet of two houses and a responsible ministry.

Then, in 1894–1895, Japan and China engaged in war over Korea. With amazing rapidity little Japan overcame her huge antagonist on land and sea. The victory was complete. China ceded not only the island of Formosa, but also Port Arthur and sovereignty over the kingdom of Korea. Russia, however, was already longing for these districts, and, backed by France, she forced Japan to renounce her gains upon the mainland. Japan was unprepared for war with these powers, and was wise enough to yield, but she began at once to make ready, patiently and skillfully, for the struggle with Russia which was to come ten years later (§ 591).

590. The Opening of China. — In return for her interference against Japan (§ 589) Russia secured from China the right to extend her Trans-Siberian railroad through Manchuria (§ 567), with provisions regarding the stationing of troops there which went far to make that great province a Russian possession. Then in 1898 Russia also secured Port Arthur, on the Gulf of Pechili, — the strongest naval fortress that China possessed. Roused by this advance of her rival, England at once demanded and obtained Wai-hei-wai, on the opposite shore of the Gulf, to enable her to check Russian movements. Somewhat earlier too (§ 484), on a curious pretext, Germany had seized Kiau Chau, with the surrounding district; and now France seized the port of Kwang-Chau-Wau. Still earlier, it is true, France had begun to occupy the far southeast (§ 451), and England had held the island of Hong Kong ever since 1842; but the recent seizures commanded Pekin itself and the heart of the Empire, and it began to look as if China were doomed to partition among the Powers of the west.

In 1900, the Chinese resentment against the "western barbarians" culminated in popular patriotic and fanatical uprisings which sought to exterminate the Occidentals. The movement was organized by a secret society known as the *Boxers*. Missionaries and scattered Europeans were massacred and the foreign embassies themselves were besieged at Pekin. The Powers (the United States and Japan included) sent joint forces to relieve their beleaguered representatives. After horrible and almost incredible barbarities by the invading armies, especially by the Russians, Pekin was taken and sacked and the European residents were rescued.

591. The Russian-Japanese War. — Largely through the insistance of the United States, no territorial indemnities were demanded from China at the suppression of the Boxer troubles. During the campaign, however, Russia occupied Manchuria with troops, claiming that such action was necessary to protect her railroad there, and promising to withdraw at the return of peace. In 1902, this pledge was solemnly repeated to the Powers; but, before 1904, it was clear that such promises had been made cynically, only to be broken, and that Russia was determined not to loosen her grasp upon the coveted province. Moreover, she began to encroach upon Korea. To Japan this treacherous Russian approach seemed to imperil not only her commercial prosperity (in Korea), but her independence as a nation; and after months of futile negotiations, and a pressing ultimatum for Russian withdrawal, she resorted to war.

Diplomacy had at least assured Japan that she would have only Russia to fight. England and Japan, in 1902, in a treaty designed to preserve the integrity of China, had agreed to aid each other in war if either were attacked by more than one power. France and Russia, with just the opposite policy in China, were allied by an old and similar treaty. Thus the two alliances neutralized each other, and France and England kept out of the struggle. The United States gave its sympathy frankly to Japan, but to take part in the war would have been contrary to its fixed policy. Moreover, just before the outbreak of the war, England and France had drawn so close to each other in diplomacy, both in their African policy and in their arbitration treaty of 1903 (§ 594), that French support for Russia was by no means certain even if England were drawn into the war. Under such conditions Germany was not likely to enter the contest, despite the sympathy of her ruling classes for Russia.

Still the case for Japan looked dark. To most of the world, Russian advance in Asia seemed irresistible, and the little island-state was thought doomed to defeat. But Russia fought at long range. She had to transport troops and supplies across Asia by a *single-track* railroad. Her railway service was of a low order (like all her forms of engineering), and her rolling stock was inferior and insufficient. Congestion of traffic and long delays at critical moments were the inevitable results. To be sure, it was supposed that immense supplies had already been accumulated at Port Arthur and in Manchuria, in expectation of war; but it proved that high officials had made way with the larger part of the money and that neither army nor navy was properly equipped. Inefficiency, corruption, lack of organization, were matched only by boastful overconfidence and silly contempt for the foe. These drawbacks could not be counterbalanced by Russia's immense but unavailable resources nor by the desperate bravery and heroic endurance of her poorly led soldiery.

Japan, on the other hand, had the most perfectly organized army, hospital service, and commissariat the world has ever seen. Her leaders, whether or not they had great military genius, were at least patriotic, honest, faithful, and always equal to the occasion; and the whole nation was animated by a spirit of ardent self-sacrifice. By her admirable organization, Japan was able, at all critical moments, to confront the Russians with equal or superior numbers, even after a year of war, when the line of battle had rolled back several hundred miles toward the Russian base.

At the outset, Japan could hope for success only by securing naval control of Asiatic waters. Russia had gathered at Port Arthur a fleet supposedly much stronger than Japan's whole navy; but (*February 8, 1904*) Japan struck the first blow, torpedoing several mighty battleships and cruisers. The rest of the Russian fleet was blockaded in the harbor; and, to the end of the war, Japan transported troops and supplies by water almost without interference.

Korea was swiftly overrun, and, on February 23, its government recognized a Japanese protectorate. The Russians were driven back from the *Yalu* in a great battle, and *Port Arthur* was invested (May 28) by land as well as by sea. Seven months later (January, 1905), that fortress, which had been boastfully declared invulnerable, capitulated, after terrible suffering and reckless sacrifice of life on both sides. Meantime, in September, the Japanese army won a remarkable victory at *Liaou Yang*, and, soon afterward, repulsed a desperate attack, driving the Russians back on Mukden. The severe northern winter interrupted the campaign; but in March, 1905, the Japanese resumed their advance. The *Battle of Mukden* is the most tremendous military struggle in history. It lasted fifteen days. The battle front extended a hundred miles, and a million men were engaged, with all the terrible, destructive agencies of modern science at their command. The Russians were completely routed. They lost more than a hundred thousand men, and were driven back on Harbin in disorder. It seemed that Russia would be unable, for that summer at least, to gather another army in the East able to take the field.

Russia's only chance was to regain command of the sea. During the winter of 1905, after a year of delays, an attempt had been begun. A huge fleet, far exceeding the Japanese navy in number and in size, but poorly equipped and miserably officered, set out on the long voyage from the Baltic. By a breach of strict neutrality on the part of France, it was allowed to rest and refit at Madagascar, and again at the French stations near Southern China; and in May it reached the Sea of Japan. There it was annihilated by the splendidly handled Japanese fleet, under Admiral Togo, in the greatest of the world's naval battles.

Theodore Roosevelt, President of the United States, now

"offered his good offices" to secure peace; and a meeting of envoys was arranged (August, 1905, at Portsmouth, N.H.), at which the *Treaty of Portsmouth* was signed. Japan's demands were exceedingly moderate, and she yielded even a part of these at President Roosevelt's urgent appeal for peace. Russia agreed (1) to withdraw from Chinese Manchuria, (2) to cede the Port Arthur branch of her railroad to China, (3) to recognize the Japanese protectorate in Korea, and (4) to cede to Japan the southern half of Sakhalin, — an island formerly belonging to Japan but occupied by Russia in 1875.

The most important results of the war were indirect results. Russia was checked in her career of aggression in Europe and toward India, as well as in the Far East, and the collapse of her despotic government gave opportunity for the beginning of a great revolution in society and politics (§ 575). Japan, on the other hand, won recognition as one of the foremost "world powers," and, apparently, will take over, from the western nations, the mighty task of regenerating China. This last consideration, alone, makes the victory of incalculable significance.

III. MORAL AND SCIENTIFIC MOVEMENTS — THE OUTLOOK.

592. Increasing Rate of Progress. — The world of 1900 is further removed from the world of 1800 than the world of 1800 was from the world of 800. That is, the last century has counted more for human progress than the preceding thousand years, and Napoleon's day is really closer to Charlemagne's than to ours. The three mighty agents in this recent transformation have been *democracy* in politics and industry, *humane sentiment* in morals, and *scientific invention* in the intellectual field. The growth of democracy has been the chief theme of the latter half of this volume: since 1789 practically all the civilized peoples of the western world, except the Russians, have wrested constitutions from their rulers and now control their own political destinies, with such machinery as manhood suffrage and compulsory universal education to assist them. The gentler spirit of recent times has abolished slavery and serfdom, ameliorated the laws, and brought about zealous, organized, and intelligent efforts to lessen suffering and misery all over the globe. But perhaps the most marvelous phase of the "Wonderful Century" is the scientific advance.

593. Science and Human Life. — The nineteenth century at different times has been called the age of steam, the iron age, the steel age, the age of electricity. Each name has been deserved. Since the inventions of making fire, of the bow, of domesticating animals, of smelting iron, and of the alphabet, all the inventions of man up to the year 1800 probably count

THE FIRST RAILWAY PASSENGER TRAIN, from Liverpool to Manchester, September 1, 1830, drawn by Stephenson's improved engine, *Rocket*. (The first locomotive had been built about fifteen years earlier, but it had been used only to haul coal from the mines.)

for less than those since that year.[1] Anciently, science was rather the plaything of philosophers. Now it has become the servant of mankind. In civilized countries, during the nineteenth century, human life was lengthened over a fourth, and the population of the civilized world was nearly trebled. This larger amount of life, too, has been lifted to a higher plane. There is more life and better life. Wealth is more abundant; and the laboring masses, though still getting far too little of it, get a larger proportion than formerly. A day's

---

[1] A. R. Wallace, in *The Wonderful Century* (Dodd, Mead and Co.), enumerates fifteen epoch-making inventions from the preceding ages up to the year 1800, and then counts up twenty-four of essentially equal rank for the nineteenth century.

work buys more comfort than in 1800 or in 1850. Owing to this increased wealth and to the new conveniences of modern life, the people of the world have undergone a marvelous change in their daily habits. It is probably true that the life of an industrious, healthy artisan of to-day is more enjoyable than was that of a great noble a century ago.

As we have seen, this larger and better life has been spreading over the globe; but steam and electricity bind the most scattered portions together more closely than adjacent villages were joined in the near past. The world is more and more compact. The ox-cart and the pack-horse of 1800 are replaced as carriers by long trains of cars, swiftly carrying their hundreds of tons of all kinds of freight across continents. New methods of banking make it possible to transfer credit and to do business with magical quickness between distant portions of the earth. To say nothing of the telegraph, lines of communication are so organized that it costs no more to send a letter around the globe than to send it around the corner. The Minnesota farmer's market is not Minneapolis, or Chicago, or London, but the world. The sheep-raiser in Australia, the Kansas farmer, the New York merchant, the London banker, are parts of one industrial organism, and whatever touches one of them, affects all the rest. There is a new social unity, or solidarity, among men.

And this new unity is not merely one of material interests: it has its intellectual and its moral side. Any happening of consequence is known within an hour in London, St. Petersburg, Pekin, New York, and San Francisco, and, within a day or two, in almost every hamlet where civilized men live. News spreads over the entire surface of the globe as fast as gossip used to run down a village street. Hence a closer human interest, and a greater unity of sympathy and opinion. A "world opinion" now takes form and makes itself felt in important human concerns almost as promptly as village opinion could be brought to bear upon an individual citizen's conduct a century ago.

594. The Hague Conference and the International Tribunal. — The picture of course has its darker side. The crowded populations of the modern world still live and work under conditions of misery and disease and oftentimes of want. Great cities are breeding-places of crime. Sometimes the civilized nations show callous disregard of humane principles, when weaker or barbarous peoples are concerned. And over the civilized peoples themselves broods the danger of annihilating war, more terrible because of the new inventions of this scientific age.

Happily, a great movement to lessen this last peril is in progress. The nations have begun to adopt permanent arbitration treaties with one another, and to establish standing international tribunals for the settlement of disputes.

In earlier times an impending war was sometimes averted by diplomacy or by the mediation of a powerful neighbor; but arbitration, in the modern sense, means neither diplomatic negotiation nor mediation. It means adjudication of disputed points by an impartial body of experts resembling a low court, following the forms of a court of justice, hearing evidence and argument in public, and basing its decision on the merits of the case. The first arbitration of this kind in modern times was arranged by one clause [1] of the Jay Treaty of 1794 between England and the United States. For nearly a hundred years this sensible device continued to be used mainly by the two English-speaking nations, but before the close of the nineteenth century it had begun to spread rapidly to other lands. During that century several hundred disputes between nations were settled honorably, peacefully, and justly, by this process, — many of them critical disputes, which might easily have led to war.[2]

But all these cases of arbitration concerned some individual dispute, regarding which a special treaty had to be negotiated

---

[1] Regarding the disputed boundary between Maine and Nova Scotia.

[2] The student of American history will recall the arbitrations with England regarding the Alabama damages, the Behring Sea Seal Fisheries, the Venezuela territory, the Alaskan boundary, and several other disputes concerning our northern boundary at the eastern and western extremities.

before arbitration could begin. This left much to be desired; and the closing years of the nineteenth century saw agitation for something better — in the form of "general arbitration treaties" by which nations might agree *in advance* to submit disputes to a certain court of arbitrators. In 1897 a treaty of this kind between England and the United States failed of adoption because of opposition in the United States Senate, though it had been recommended vigorously first by President Cleveland and afterward by President McKinley. Then leadership in this great movement passed for the time away from the English-speaking peoples, but progress grew even more rapid.

On August 24, 1898, by order of the Tsar, the Russian Minister of Foreign Affairs handed to the representatives of the different nations in St. Petersburg a written suggestion for a world conference to consider some means for arresting the danger of war and for lessening the burden of the armed peace. Out of this suggestion there grew the *Hague Conference* of 1899. Twenty-six nations were represented, including Mexico, Siam, Japan, and Persia, — practically all the independent states of the world except the South American republics. Never before has any gathering so nearly approached a "parliament of man," and never has a great international congress accomplished so great a work. It was not found possible to provide for any limitation upon the armament of different nations; but certain agreements were reached to regulate the methods of war in the interests of greater humanity, and the Congress did provide a permanent International Tribunal for arbitration between nations.

No nation, of course, is compelled to submit its quarrels to this court; but it is of supreme consequence that machinery is ready so that nations can escape war, without loss of dignity, if they desire. No doubt the battle flags will yet be unfurled more than once; but the Hague Conference, with the establishment of the Hague Tribunal, is the longest single step ever taken toward the "federation of the world."

The next step was for groups of nations to pledge themselves to make use of this machinery, or of similar machinery. This pledge is the essence of a "general arbitration treaty." The first such treaty was adopted by two South American countries. While the Hague Conference was sitting, Chili and Argentina (which had not been invited to the Conference) were on the verge of war over a boundary dispute in the Andes. For the next two years both governments made vigorous preparations, — piling up war taxes, increasing armaments, building and buying ships of war. But at the last moment a popular movement, led by bishops of the Catholic Church in the two countries, brought about arbitration; and soon after, the boundary was adjusted rationally by a commission of geographers and legal experts. So well pleased were the two nations with this individual case of arbitration that they proceeded to adopt a "general treaty" by which they bound themselves, for a period of five years, to submit *all* disputes which might arise between them to a specific tribunal.

This was the first "general arbitration treaty" ever actually adopted (June, 1903). But others were already in preparation in Europe; and, four months later (October, 1903), France and England adopted one, agreeing (with certain reservations) to submit future disputes to the Hague Tribunal. Since that time some thirty such treaties have gone into operation. Today (January, 1907) every European state[1] west of Russia is a party to at least one general arbitration treaty, and some of them are parties to seven or eight; while in several cases traditional enemies, like France and Italy, and Italy and Austria, are joined by these peaceful compacts.

---

[1] The United States as yet has no standing arbitration treaty with another nation. In the spring of 1906 the Senate slaughtered a bunch of ten treaties of this character which had been negotiated with the leading nations of the world by John Hay, our Secretary of State, and which were strenuously recommended by President Roosevelt.

APPENDIX.

A CLASSIFIED BIBLIOGRAPHY.

The following works are classified, first by period, and then under each period in two groups. In the judgment of the writer, all high school libraries should contain Group I, or an equivalent, under each division, and large high schools may with advantage possess Group II also. A reduction of from twenty to thirty per cent from the list price can usually be secured.

When a book belongs to a series, the name of the series, in quotation marks, is usually given in parenthesis. Works marked with a * should be present in more than one copy.

THE MEDIEVAL PERIOD (800–1520 A.D.).

Group I.

SOURCE MATERIAL.

Anglo-Saxon Chronicle (Bohn edition). $1.50.
Colby, *Selections from the Sources of English History.* $1.50. Longmans.
Chronicles of the Crusades (Bohn Library). $1.50.
English History from Contemporary Writers, edited by F. York Powell. A series of ten small volumes, 40 cents each, published from 1886 to 1894 by Putnams, as follows: Archer, *Crusade of Richard I*; Ashley, *Edward III and His Wars*; Barnard, *Strongbow's Conquest of Ireland*; Hutton, *Misrule of Henry III*; Simon of Montfort; St. Thomas of Canterbury; Jacobs, *The Jews of Angevin England*; Powell, *Alfred and the Danes*; Smith, *Troublous Days of Richard II*; Taylor, *England under Charles II.*

APPENDIX.

The Boy's Froissart, edited by Lanier. $2.50. **Scribners.**
* HENDERSON, *Select Historical Documents.* $1.50. Macmillan.
* HILL (MABEL), *Liberty Documents.* $2.00. Longmans . . 1901.
JOINVILLE, *Memoir of St. Louis.* (Various editions.)
JONES, *Source Extracts for Medieval Civilization.* $0.50. Ainsworth . . . . 1899.
MANDEVILLE (SIR JOHN), *Travels.* $1.50. Macmillan.
Marco Polo, The Story of. $0.20. Cassell.
Pennsylvania Translations and Reprints from Original Sources.
7 vols. $1.50 each. University of Pennsylvania . . 1892–1900.

MODERN ACCOUNTS.

* ADAMS (G. B.), *Growth of the French Nation.* $1.25. Macmillan 1897.
* ——— *Civilization during the Middle Ages.* $2.50. Scribners . 1894.
* ANDREWS (C. M.), *History of England.* $1.50. Allyn & Bacon . . . . 1903.
* ARCHER AND KINGSFORD, *The Crusades* ("Nations"). $1.50. Putnams . . . . 1895.
BALZANI, *The Popes and the Hohenstaufen.* $0.80. Longmans . 1888.
BOYESEN (H. H.), *Norway* ("Nations"). $1.50. Putnams . 1886.
BROWN (HORATIO), *The Venetian Republic* ("Temple Primer"). $0.40. Macmillan . . . . 1902.
* BRYCE, *Holy Roman Empire.* $1.85. Macmillan . . 1887.
* CHEYNEY (E. P.), *Industrial and Social History of England.* $1.40. Macmillan . . . . 1901.
CHURCH, *Beginnings of the Middle Ages.* $0.75. Longmans . 1877.
CLARKE, *The Cid Campeador* ("Heroes"). $1.50. Putnams . 1897.
CORNISH, *Chivalry.* $1.75. Macmillan . . . . 1901.
CUNNINGHAM, *Western Civilization* (Vol. II, Medieval and Modern). $1.25. Macmillan . . . . . . 1900.
* EMERTON, *Medieval Europe.* $1.65. Ginn . . . 1896.
——— *Desiderius Erasmus* ("Heroes"). $1.50. Putnams . 1901.
FISHER (G. P.), *History of the Christian Church.* $3.00. Hodder 1888.
FREEMAN, *William the Conqueror.* $0.75. Macmillan . . 1894.
GARDINER, *A Student's History of England to 1885.* $3.00. Longmans . . . . 1898.
GIBBINS, *Industrial History of England.* $1.00. Methuen, London 1891.
GRAY, *The Children's Crusade.* (New ed.) $1.50. Houghton . 1900.
* GREEN, *Short History of the English People.* $1.20. Harpers 1879.
GREEN (MRS.), *Henry II.* $0.75. Macmillan . . . 1889.
HUGHES (T.), *Alfred the Great.* $1.50. Macmillan . . 1878.

A CLASSIFIED BIBLIOGRAPHY.

HUNT, *English Church in the Middle Ages* ("Epochs of Church History"). $0.80. New York . . . . . 1898.
JENKS, *Edward Plantagenet* ("Heroes"). $1.50. Putnams . 1900.
JESSOPP, *The Coming of the Friars.* $1.25. Putnams . . 1888.
JIRICZEK, *Northern Hero Legends.* $0.40. Macmillan . 1902.
JOHNSON (A. H.), *Normans in Europe.* $1.00. Longmans . 1893.
KINGSFORD, *Henry V* ("Heroes"). $1.50. Putnams . . 1903.
LANE-POOLE, *Saladin* ("Heroes"). $1.50. Putnams . . 1898.
LAURIE, *Rise and Constitution of Universities.* $1.50. Appleton 1886.
LODGE, *Close of the Middle Ages* ("Periods"). $1.40. Macmillan 1890.
MABIE (H. W.), *Norse Stories Retold.* $1.00. Dodd, Mead, & Co. 1882.
*MONTAGUE, *Elements of English Constitutional History.* $1.25. Longmans . . . . 1897.
*MUNRO AND WHITCOMB, *Medieval and Modern Europe.* $1.50. Appleton . . . . 1903.
NORGATE (KATE), *John Lackland.* $1.50. Macmillan . 1901.
OLIPHANT (MRS.), *Jeanne d'Arc* ("Heroes"). $1.50. Putnams 1894.
OMAN, *The Dark Ages* ("Periods"). $1.40. Macmillan . 1893.
—— *The Byzantine Empire* ("Nations"). $1.50. Putnams . 1898.
PEARS (E.), *Fall of Constantinople.* $2.00. Harpers . . 1885.
PERRY (F.), *St. Louis* ("Heroes"). $1.50. Putnams . . 1901.
PLUMMER, *Alfred the Great.* $1.50. Oxford . . . . 1902.
POOLE, *Wycliffe and Movements for Reform* ("Epochs of Church History"). $0.80. Longmans . . . . . 1889.
POOLE, *Turkey* ("Nations"). $1.50. Putnams . . . 1889.
POWELL (EDGAR), *The Peasant Rising in East Anglia in 1381.* $1.50. New York . . . . 1899.
*ROBINSON, *Western Europe.* $1.50. Ginn . . . 1902.
SAINTSBURY, *Flourishing of Romance.* $1.50. Scribners . 1897.
SEIGNOBOS, *The Feudal Regime.* $0.50. Holt . . . 1902.
SERGEANT, *John Wyclif* ("Heroes"). $1.50. Putnams . 1892.
STEPHENS (W. R. W.), *Hildebrand and his Times* ("Epochs of Church History"). $0.80. Longmans . . . 1889.
Story of the Burnt Njal (The). (Dasent, translator.) $1.50. New York . . . . 1891.
*STUBBS, *Early Plantagenets* ("Epochs"). $1.00. Longmans 1887.
TERRY, *History of England to 1901.* $2.00. Scott, Foresman, & Co. 1901.
TOUT (T. F.), *Edward I.* $0.60. Macmillan . . . 1893.
—— *The Empire and the Papacy* ("Periods"). $1.40. Macmillan 1898.
WIEL, *Venice* ("Nations"). $1.50. Putnams . . . 1894.
YORK-POWELL, *Alfred the Truth Teller.* $1.50. Putnams . 1894.
ZIMMERN (H.), *The Hansa* ("Nations"). $1.50. Putnams . 1890.

GROUP II.

SOURCE MATERIAL.

ADAMS AND STEPHENS, *Select Documents of English Constitutional History.* $2.50. Macmillan . . . . 1902.
FROISSART, *Chronicles of England, France, and Spain* (Johnes' translation). $5.25.
LEE, *A Source Book of English History.* $2.00. Holt.
MARCO POLO (The Story of, by Noah Brooks). $1.00. Century Co.
Paston Letters (The). (Gairdner's edition). 3 vols. $5.25.

MODERN ACCOUNTS.

ALZOG, *A Manual of Universal Church History.* 3 vols. (A strong work by a conservative Roman Catholic.) $8.00. Robert Clark & Co. . . . . 1874.
AMEER ALI, *A Short History of the Saracens.* $3.00. Macmillan 1899.
ASHLEY, *Introduction to English Economic History.* Vol. I, Part I, $1.25; Part II, $2.60. Longmans . . . 1892–1896.
BÉMONT AND MONOD, *Medieval Europe.* $1.60. Holt . . 1902.
BOWKER (AND OTHERS), Alfred the Great. $1.75. Macmillan . 1899.
BRODERICK, *The University of Oxford.* $0.60. Longmans . 1887.
Cambridge Modern History (The). Vol. I. $3.75. Macmillan . 1902.
COX, *The Crusades* ("Epochs"). $1.00. Longmans . . 1874.
CREIGHTON, *History of the Papacy.* 6 vols. $12.00. Longmans 1882.
CUNNINGHAM, *English Industry and Commerce.* 2 vols. $8.50. Macmillan . . . . 1901.
CUNNINGHAM AND MCARTHUR, *Outlines of English Industrial History.* $1.50. Macmillan . . . . 1895.
CUTTS, *Scenes and Characters of the Middle Ages.* $3.75. New York 1872.
—— *Parish Priests and Their People.* $3.00. London . . 1898.
DU CHAILLU, *The Viking Age.* 2 vols. $5.75. Murray . . 1889.
DUFFY, *Tuscan Republics* ("Nations"). $1.50. Putnams . 1892.
DURUY, *History of the Middle Ages.* $2.00. Holt . . 1891.
FARNELL (IDA), *Lives of the Troubadours.* $3.00. London . 1896.
FISHER (HERBERT), *The Medieval Empire.* 2 vols. $6.30. Macmillan . . . . 1898.
FREEMAN, *Ottoman Power in Europe.* $1.50. Macmillan . . 1879.
GAIRDNER, *Houses of Lancaster and York* ("Epochs"). $1.00. Longmans . . . . 1886.
GILMAN, *The Saracens* ("Nations"). $1.50. Putnams . . 1887.
GREEN (J. R.), *The Conquest of England.* $4.50. Macmillan . 1883.

A CLASSIFIED BIBLIOGRAPHY. 631

GREEN (MRS. J. R.), *Town Life in the Fifteenth Century.* 2 vols.
   $6.40. Macmillan . . . . 1894.
HAZLITT, *Venetian Republic.* 2 vols. $8.50. London . . 1900.
HENDERSON, *Short History of Germany.* 2 vols. $4.00. Macmillan 1902.
JAMES (G. P. R.), *History of Chivalry.* $2.00. Harpers . . 1845.
JUSSERAND, *English Wayfaring Life in the Middle Ages.* $3.00.
   London . . . . 1891.
KEARY, *The Vikings in Western Christendom.* $2.50. Putnams 1891.
LAVISSE, *General View of the Political History of Europe.* $1.25.
   Longmans . . . . 1891.
LEA, *Sacerdotal Celibacy.* (2d edition.) Boston . . . 1884.
LÜBKE, *History of Art.* 2 vols. $7.50. Dodd, Mead & Co. . 1875.
MIJATOVICH, *Constantine, the Last Emperor of the Greeks.* $1.85.
   Low . . . . 1892.
MILMAN, *Latin Christianity.* 9 vols. $11.00. London . . 1867.
MOORE (C. H.), *Gothic Architecture.* $4.50. Macmillan . . 1890.
MORISON, *Life and Times of St. Bernard.* $1.85. Macmillan . 1861.
MULLINGER, *University of Cambridge.* $1.00. Longmans . . 1888.
OLIPHANT (MRS.), *Makers of Venice.* $2.65. Macmillan . . 1881.
—— *Makers of Florence.* $2.65. Macmillan . . . 1882.
OMAN, *History of the Art of War.* $4.50. Putnams . . 1898.
PASTOR, *History of the Popes from the Close of the Middle
   Ages.* 6 vols. (A scholarly Roman Catholic work.) $18.00.
   Herder . . . . 1891.
POOLE, *Illustrations of the History of Medieval Thought.* $2.75.
   London . . . . 1884.
RASHDALL, *Universities of Europe in the Middle Ages.* 3 vols.
   $14.00. Clarendon Press . . . . . . 1895.
SABATIER, *St. Francis of Assisi.* $2.50. Scribners . . . 1894.
SEEBOHM, *The Oxford Reformers of 1498.* $3.50. Longmans . 1867.
SMITH (J. H.), *The Troubadours at Home.* $2.00. Putnams . 1890.
STILLÉ, *Studies in Medieval History.* $1.50. Lippincott . . 1882.
STORRS, *Bernard of Clairvaux.* $2.50. Scribners . . . 1892.
STUBBS, *Constitutional History of England.* 3 vols. $9.00.
   Clarendon Press . . . . 1883.
SYMONDS, *Short History of the Renaissance in Italy.* (Edited by
   Pearson.) $1.25. Scribners . . . . . . 1893.
TASWELL-LANGMEAD, *English Constitutional History.* $6.00.
   Houghton . . . . 1886.
TREVELYAN, *England in the Age of Wycliffe.* $4.00. Longmans 1899.
VILLARI, *The Two First Centuries of Florentine History.* 2 vols.
   $7.50. Scribners . . . . 1901.

VINCENT, *The Age of Hildebrand.* $2.00. Scribners . . . 1896.
WALKER (THOS.), *The End of Villeinage in England.* $1.25.
London . . . . 1900.

FROM THE REFORMATION TO THE FRENCH REVOLUTION
(1520–1789).

GROUP I.

BEESLY, *Elizabeth* ("English Statesmen"). $0.60. Macmillan. 1892.
BRADLEY, *Wolfe.* $0.75. Macmillan . . . . . . 1895.
—— *Fight with France for North America.* $5.00. New York. 1900.
CREIGHTON, *Age of Elizabeth* ("Epochs"). $1.00. Longmans. 1889.
FIRTH, *Cromwell* ("Heroes"). $1.50. Putnams . . . 1902.
GARDINER, *Thirty Years' War* ("Epochs"). $1.00. Longmans 1874.
* —— *The First Two Stuarts and the Puritan Revolution*
("Epochs"). $1.00. Longmans . . . . 1890.
HALE, *Fall of the Stuarts, 1678–1697* ("Epochs"). $1.00.
Longmans . . . . 1889.
HASSALL, *Louis XIV* ("Heroes"). $1.50. Putnams . . 1895.
HÄUSSER, *The Period of the Reformation.* $2.00. Edinburgh. 1868.
* JOHNSON, *Europe in the Sixteenth Century* ("Periods"). $1.40.
Macmillan . . . . 1897.
* WAKEMAN, *Europe, 1589–1715* ("Periods"). $1.40. Macmillan 1898.
* WALKER, *The Reformation* ("Ten Epochs"). $2.00. Scribners 1900.
WARD, *The Counter-Reformation.* $0.80. Longmans . . 1889.
WILLERT, *Henry of Navarre* ("Heroes"). $1.50. Putnams . 1893.
WILSON, *Lord Clive.* $0.75. Macmillan . . . . . 1890.
WOODWARD, *Expansion of the British Empire.* $1.00. Macmillan 1899.

GROUP II.

BEARD, *Martin Luther.* $2.50. London . . . . . 1889.
BEAZLEY, *Prince Henry the Navigator* ("Heroes"). $1.50. Putnams . . . . 1898.
CHURCH, *Anselm.* $1.25. Macmillan . . . . . . 1870.
COMPAYRÉ, *Abelard.* $1.00. Scribners . . . . . 1893.
CREIGHTON, *Queen Elizabeth.* $2.00. Longmans . . . 1899.
DODGE, *Gustavus Adolphus* ("Great Captains"). $5.00. Houghton . . . . 1895.
FISHER, *The Reformation.* $2.50. Scribners . . . 1894.
FLETCHER, *Gustavus Adolphus* ("Heroes"). $1.50. Putnams. 1890.

A CLASSIFIED BIBLIOGRAPHY. 633

Fox-Bourne, *Sir Philip Sidney* ("Heroes"). $1.50. Putnams. 1891.
Froude, *Erasmus.* $2.50. Scribners . . . . . 1894.
Gardiner, *Cromwell's Place in History.* $1.00. Longmans . 1900.
Jenks, *Constitutional Experiments of the Commonwealth.* $0.65.
    Macmillan . . . . 1890.
Köstlin, *Life of Luther.* $2.00. Scribners . . . . 1883.
Lea, *History of the Inquisition.* 3 vols. $6.00. Harpers . . 1887.
Malleson, *Dupleix.* $0.60. Macmillan . . . . . 1890.
—— *Lord Clive.* $0.60. Macmillan . . . . . . 1893.
Motley, *The Student's Motley.* (Edited by W. E. Griffis.)
    $1.50. Harpers . . . . 1898.
Perkins, *Richelieu* ("Heroes"). $1.50. Putnams . . . 1901.
Perry, *The Reformation in England.* $0.80. Longmans . 1886.
Putnam (Ruth), *William the Silent* ("Heroes"). 2 vols.
    $3.75. Putnams . . . . 1901.
Robinson and Rolfe, *Petrarch.* $1.50. Putnams . . . 1898.
Seebohm, *The Protestant Reformation.* $0.65. Longmans . 1874.
Seeley, *Expansion of England.* $1.10. Macmillan . . . 1885.
—— *Growth of British Policy.* 2 vols. $2.75. Cambridge University Press . . . . 1895.

THE FRENCH REVOLUTION AND THE NAPOLEONIC ERA
(1789–1815).

Group I.

SOURCE MATERIAL.

* Anderson (F. M.), *Constitutions and other Documents illustrative of the History of France, 1789–1900.* $2.00. The
    H. W. Wilson Co., Minneapolis 1904

MODERN ACCOUNTS.

* Andrews, *Historical Development of Modern Europe* (in the
    single volume edition). $2.75. Putnams . . . . 1896.
* Carlyle, *The French Revolution.* (3 vols. Rose, editor.
    $9.00. Macmillan. 1902) *or* (3 vols. Fletcher, editor.
    $4.50. Putnams. 1902.) . . . .
* Dickenson, *Revolution and Reaction in France.* $1.25. London . . . . 1892.
Fyffe, *Modern Europe to 1878.* 3 vols. in one. $2.75. Holt . 1884.

APPENDIX.

*GARDINER (MRS.), *French Revolution* ("Epochs"). $0.60.
Longmans . . . . 1901.
LOWELL, *Eve of the French Revolution.* $2.00. Houghton,
Mifflin & Co. . . . . 1892.
MALLET, *French Revolution.* $1.00. Scribners . . . . 1893.
*MATHEWS (SHAILER), *French Revolution.* $1.25. Longmans . 1901.
ROSE, *Life of Napoleon I.* 2 vols. $4.00. Macmillan . . 1901.
STEPHENS (H. MORSE), *The French Revolution.* 3 vols. $3.50
each. Scribners . . . . 1886.
—— *Revolutionary Europe, 1789–1815* ("Periods"). $1.75.
Macmillan . . . . 1893.
WILLERT, *Mirabeau.* $0.75. Macmillan . . . . . 1898.

GROUP II.

BELLOC, *Danton.* $2.50. Scribners . . . . . . 1899.
—— *Robespierre.* $2.00. Scribners . . . . . . 1902.
BLIND, *Madame Roland.* $1.00. Roberts Bros. . . . . 1886.
DABNEY, *Causes of the French Revolution.* $1.25. Holt . . 1888.
FOURNIER, *Life of Napoleon.* (Translated and edited by E. G.
Bourne.) $2.50. Holt . . . . 1904.
JOHNSTON (R. M.), *Napoleon, a Brief Biography.* $1.00. Barnes
& Co. . . . . 1904.
MORRIS, *The French Revolution and the First Empire.* $1.85.
Scribners . . . . 1874.
ROPES, *The First Napoleon.* $2.00. Houghton . . . . 1890.
SEELEY, *Life and Times of Stein.* 3 vols. $7.50. Macmillan . 1878.
—— *Short History of Napoleon.* $1.00. Little . . . . 1888.
TAINE, *Ancient Régime.* $2.50. Holt . . . . . . 1876.
—— *French Revolution.* 3 vols. $7.50. Holt . . . . 1878.
TOCQUEVILLE (ALEXIS DE), *France before the Revolution of 1789.*
$3.00. London . . . . 1856.
—— *Remains.* 2 vols. $1.00. Ticknor . . . . . 1862.

EUROPE SINCE 1814.

GROUP I.

Annual publications: *The Statesman's Year Book.* $3.00. Macmillan.
The International Year Book. $3.00. Dodd, Mead, & Co. *The Annual
Encyclopædia*, $5.00 a volume. Appleton.

HANNAY, *Castelar.* $0.75. New York . . . . . . 1896.
HEADLAM, *Bismarck* ("Heroes"). $1.50. Putnams . . . 1901.

A CLASSIFIED BIBLIOGRAPHY.

McCarthy (Justin), *Leo XIII.* $1.25. Warne . . . 1894.
—— *Epoch of Reform, 1830–1850* ("Epochs"). $1.00. Longmans 1881.
—— *History of Our Own Times, 1837–1881.* 2 vols. $4.00. Harpers . . . . 1882.
Minchin, *Growth of Freedom in the Balkan Peninsula.* $4.20. Scribners . . . . 1887.
Phillips, *Modern Europe, 1814–1899* ("Periods"). $1.40. Macmillan . . . . 1902.
* Seignobos, *Europe since 1814.* $3.00. Holt . . . . 1899.
* Wilson (Woodrow), *The State.* $1.50. Heath. (Revised.) . 1898.

Group II.

Adams and Cunningham, *Swiss Confederation.* $3.50. Macmillan 1889.
Bagehot, *English Constitution.* $2.00. Appleton . . . 1885.
Beaman, *Stambuloff.* $1.00. Warne . . . . . 1895.
Beaulieu (Leroy), *The Empire of the Tsars and Russians.* 3 vols. $9.00. Putnams . . . . 1893.
Blauvelt, *Development of Cabinet Government in England.* $1.50. Macmillan . . . . 1902.
Borgeaud, *Rise of Modern Democracy in Old and New England.* $1.00. Scribners . . . . 1894.
—— *Adoption and Amendment of Constitutions in Europe and America.* $2.00. Macmillan . . . . . 1892.
Bourinot, *Canada under British Rule, 1760–1900.* $1.75. Macmillan . . . . 1902.
Boutmy, *Studies in Constitutional Law.* $1.75. Macmillan . 1885.
Caldecott, *English Colonization and Empire.* $1.00. Scribners 1891.
Cesaresco, *Cavour.* $0.75. Macmillan . . . . . 1898.
Cotton and Payne, *Colonies and Dependencies.* $1.00. Macmillan 1883.
Coubertin, *The Evolution of France under the Third Republic.* $2.50. New York . . . . 1897.
Curry, *Constitutional Government in Spain.* $1.00. Harpers . 1889.
Dicey, *Victor Emmanuel.* $0.75. Putnams . . . . 1886.
—— *The Peasant State* (Bulgaria). $2.75. London . . . 1894.
Fonblanque, *How We Are Governed.* $0.50. Warne . . 1889.
Griffis, *Brave Little Holland.* $1.00. Houghton . . . 1894.
Hanotaux, *Contemporary France.* 4 vols. 1870–1900. Vol. I (1870–1873), published in 1903. Putnams . . . 1903.
Hume, *Modern Spain* ("Nations"). $1.50. Putnams . . 1900.
Jenks, *Australasian Colonies to 1893.* $1.75. Macmillan . 1899.
Keltie, *Partition of Africa.* $4.00. London . . . . 1893.

KING (BOLTON), *History of Italian Unity, 1814–1871.* $5.75.
Scribners . . . . 1899.
—— *Mazzini* ("Temple Biographies"). London . . . 1903.
LEBON AND PELET, *France As It Is.* $1.85. Cassell . . . 1889.
*LOWELL (A. L.), *Governments and Parties in Continental Europe.*
2 vols. $5.00. Houghton . . . . 1897.
MCCARTHY (JUSTIN), *England in the Nineteenth Century.*
Putnams . . . . 1902.
MCCARTHY (J. H.), *England under Gladstone.* $1.50. London 1886.
MCCRACKAN, *The Rise of the Swiss Republic.* $2.50. Arena
Publishing Co., Boston . . . . 1892.
MORAN, *Theory and Practise of English Government.* $1.20.
Longmans . . . . 1903.
MORLEY, *Life of Gladstone.* 3 vols. Macmillan . . . . 1903.
—— *Life of Voltaire.* $1.50. Macmillan . . . . 1886.
—— *Life of Rousseau.* 2 vols. $3.00. Macmillan . . 1873.
—— *Miscellanies.* 3 vols. $1.50 each. Macmillan.
MORRIS, *History of Colonization.* 2 vols. $3.00. Macmillan . 1900.
MURDOCK, *Reconstruction of Europe.* $2.00. Houghton . . 1889.
PARKIN, *Imperial Federation.* $1.25. Macmillan . . . 1892.
PORRITT, *The Englishman at Home.* $1.50. Crowell . . 1893.
ROSE, *Rise of Democracy in Great Britain.* $1.25. Chicago &
New York . . . . 1898.
ROSEBERY, *Pitt* ("English Statesmen"). $0.75. Macmillan . 1891.
RUSSELL, *German Social Democracy.* $1.00. Longmans . . 1896.
SAMUELSON, *Roumania, Past and Present.* $1.50. London . 1882.
SERGEANT, *New Greece.* $5.25. Cassell . . . . . 1879.
SMITH (BECKFORD), *Greece under King George.* $3.00. London 1893.
SMITH (MUNROE), *Bismarck and German Unity.* $1.00. Macmillan 1898.
STEPNIAK, *The Russian Peasantry.* 2 vols. $6.25. Sonnenschein 1888.
STILLMAN, *Union of Italy, 1815–1895* (Cambridge Series).
$1.75. Cambridge . . . . 1899.
STROEBEL, *Spanish Revolution of 1868–1874.* $1.50. Boston . 1898.
TOCQUEVILLE (ALEXIS DE), *Recollections.* $3.50. Macmillan . 1896.
TOYNBEE, *The Industrial Revolution of the Eighteenth Century
in England.* $2.00. Rivington . . . . . . 1887.
VINCENT, *State and Federal Government in Switzerland.* $1.50.
Johns Hopkins University Press . . . . . 1891.
WALPOLE, *History of England since 1815.* 6 vols. $12.00.
Macmillan . . . . 1878.
—— *Electorate and Legislature.* $0.85. Macmillan . . 1881.
WINCHESTER, *The Swiss Republic.* $2.00. Lippincott . . 1891.

INDEX.

The references are to sections, unless otherwise indicated.

Pronunciation, except for familiar names and terms, is shown by division into syllables and accentuation. When diacritical marks for English names are needed, the common marks of Webster's Dictionaries are used. German and French pronunciation can be indicated only imperfectly to those who are not familiar with the languages; but attention is called to the following marks: the soft aspirated guttural *g* of the German is marked G; the corresponding *ch* (as in *Ich*) is marked *čh*; the nasal French *n* is marked *ň*; the sound of *n* like *ny* in *canyon* is marked *ñ*; for the German *ä* and *äu* the equivalents are indicated, to prevent confusion with English *ä*; *ö* is always the German letter; and *ü* is the German diphthong or the equivalent French *u*. In French words with an accent on the final syllable, that accent only is marked; but it should be understood that in such words the syllables as a rule receive nearly equal stress.

Aachen (äčh'en), 14.
Ab'e-lard, 180 *c*, 183.
Absolute Monarchy, 256; in Austria, 491; in Denmark, 521; in England, 237, 249; in France, 149, 200; in Germany, 369; in Russia, 568, 573; in Spain, 156, 397, 495.
Act of Settlement (in England), 253.
Adelheid (äd'el-hīt), 53.
A'dri-an, Pope, p. 84 note.
Africa, England in, 547, 558, 560, 563; France in, 451; Germany in, 484; Italy in, 489; Portuguese in, 197; Spain in, 501; partition of, 586.
Agincourt (aj'in-kōrt, Fr. ä-zhäň-koor'), battle of, 139.
Agriculture, feudal, 26, 34, 36; Mohammedan, 89; gives place to other industries, 107; in Holland, 225; ruined in Germany, 231; in England, 234, 528 *a*; in France, 290, 292–294, 450; in Prussia, 273; in Russia, 570.
Aix-la-Chapelle (āks-lä-shä-pĕl'), Peace of, 274.
Al-bi-gen'sēṣ, 82, 83, 150, 152 *a*, 214.
Alexander I, of Russia, 365, 373, 376, 377, 382, p. 400 note, 573.
Alexander II, 569, 570, 572, 573, 577.
Alexander III, 573.

Alfred the Great, of England, 16, 178.
Al-ge'ri-a, 446, 451, 586.
Alliances of European powers, in religious wars, 223, 229, 230, 232; for balance of power, 255, 259, 261, 263, 276–278; against Napoleon, 351, 355, 356, 367, 372–375; in Congress of Vienna, 376–381, 457, 466, 505, 523; the "Holy Alliance," 395–401; in Europe to-day, 583–584.
Al-säce', 232 *b*, 292, 379 note, 434, 583.
Äl'vä, Duke of, 221.
Amadeo (ä-mä-dā'ō), 496.
America, discovered, 172 note, 197; Spain in, 220, 380 note, 393 note, 398; immigration of persecuted Protestants, 232 note, p. 257 note 3, 236, 243 note, 260 *b*; England in, 261, 275, 277, 281 *c*, 283; France in, 255, 258, 261, 282, 308, 315, 451; wars in, 261, 275, 277, 283; American Revolution, 284, 285, 303 note 3, 529. See Monroe Doctrine, United States, Canada.
Amiens (ä-mē-äň'), Peace of, 356.
Anabaptists, 208 note.
Anarchists, in France, 442 note; in Italy, 488. See Nihilists.

637

INDEX.

References are to sections.

An'dre-a del Sar'to, 193.
Anglo-Saxon Chronicle, 187, 188.
Anjou (än'joo; Fr. pron., ŏṅ-zhōō'), 41, 127, 151.
Anne, Queen of England, 204 d, 253, 281 a.
Anne Boleyn (bōōl'in), 218.
An'selm, p. 83 note 2, 183.
Aquitaine (ăk-wē-tān'), 41, 127, 139, p. 164 note.
Arabs, in Italy, 180 a, 184; slave trade, 586. See Mohammedans.
Arbitration (international), 594.
Archbishops, feudal position, 38; duties and powers of, 72.
Architecture, feudal, 37; Mohammedan, 89; medieval, 192; of Renaissance, 193.
A-ri-os'to, 189.
A'ris-tot-le, 182, 184, 189.
Är-mä'dä, 201, 218, 223.
Army, feudal, 28; in England, 245, 246, 249, 251; in France, 42 c, 345; in Germany, 48, 272, 274, 369, 464, 465, 483; in Italy, 488.
Arnulf, of Germany, 47.
Arrondissement (är-roṅ-dēs-moṅ'), 325, 447.
Art, medieval, 192; of Renaissance, 193, 194.
Artois (är-twä'), Count of. See Charles X of France.
Asia, early progress in, 1; Crusades, 92–105; Tartars in, 91, 168; England in, 275, 277, 588; France in, 451, 588; Russia in, 266, 365, 588, 589; Turkey in, 385; the Powers in, 588, 589. See India.
Asia Minor, Turks in, 91; Germany in, 484.
Augsburg (âgz'bėrg, Ger. owgs'-boorG), and Hungarians, 49; Confession of, 210; Peace of, 211, 219, 232.
Aus'ter-litz, battle of, 365, 370, 381.
Australia, 545, 556–558, 562, 564.
Austria, beginning, 50 note; seized from Bohemia, 158; basis of power of the later Emperors, 160; threatened by Mohammedans, 170; table of rulers, 202; in Grand Alliance, 259; War of Spanish Succession, 261; Danubian policy, 262; wars of Austrian Succession, 274; Seven Years' War, 276; war with France, 331, 335, 340, 342, 350, 351, 355, 356; with Napoleon, 364, 365, 367, 370, 372, 374, 375; "Austrian Empire," 370; Congress of Vienna, 376, 377, 380, 381, 457; President of German Confederacy, 377 a; attitude toward Reaction, 382; rule of Metternich, 383–385, 387–392, 395, 400, 452; Austria-Hungary, 385, 491–493; Italian War, 429 b, 430 a; in 1848, 452–456; in Italy, 457–461; Schleswig-Holstein affair, 466; Six Weeks' War, 467; Peace of Prague, 468; alliance after 1871, 583–584.
Austrian Succession, wars of the, 274, 275.
Avignon (ä-vēn-yŏṅ'), 165; Great Schism, 166.

Babylonian Captivity of the church, 87, 165.
Bacon, Francis, 182, 199, 234.
Bacon, Roger, p. 156 note, 186, 195 note, 197.
Balance of Power, origin of theory, 255.
Balkan Peninsula, invaded by Turks, 168; free states in, 385; to 1878, 576–577; since 1878, 578–582. See Bulgaria, Greece, Montenegro, Roumania, Servia.
Ball, John, 141.
Ballot development in England, 537 a, 546.
Bannockburn, battle of, 139 note 2.
Barbarian Invasions, 11; Hungarian, 12; Norse, 13–16; results of, in 9th century, 17; Tartars, 168; Turks, 169.
Barbarossa, see Frederick I, Emperor.
Bastille (băs-tēl'), fall of, 316, 317, 334 note.
Bavaria, 45, 369; wars of French Revolution, 356; made a kingdom, 370; after Congress of Vienna, 377 b; Constitution, 388; in 1848, 455; Peace of Prague, 468.

INDEX.

References are to sections.

Beaumont (bō'mont), 199.
Bebel (bä'bel), 485.
Belgium (part of Netherlands), 162, 172 note; separated from the independent United Provinces and reconquered by Spain (*Spanish Netherlands*), 222 note; seized by Louis XIV, 259; becomes *Austrian Netherlands*, 261; invaded by French, 334, 337, 340; annexed by France, 350, 357, 372; annexed to Holland, 377 b, 385; independent after revolution of 1873, 391, 392, 400, 401, 506; socialism in, 445 note; in the 19th century, 505-509; and Congo Free State, 586.
Bellini (bel-lē'nē), the, 193.
Benedictine Rule, the, 58; restored, 59.
Beneficium, 24.
"Benefit of Clergy," 69.
Benevolences, 241.
"Benevolent despots," 280.
Berlin, March Rising of 1848, 454; Congress of, 1878, p. 405 note, 547, 577; 1884, 586.
Bernard of Clairvaux (klār-vō'), 72 note; preaches second Crusade, 96.
Bible, the, Wyclif's, p. 156 note, 188; translated by Laurentius Valla, 195; by Erasmus, 195; by Luther, 207; use of English, in churches, 218.
Bills, in Parliament, origin, 143.
Bishop, feudal position, 32, 38; duties of, 72; in English shire, 119.
Bismarck, 74 note, 369, 379 note, 430 c, 434, 459 b, 464; and Landtag, 465; Schleswig-Holstein War, 466; Six Weeks' War, 467; popularity, 469; Franco-Prussian War, 469, 470; effect of his policy, 471; dismissed, 480; kulturkampf, 482; colonial policy, 484; and socialism, 485, 486.
Black Death, the, 138, 140.
Black Hole of Calcutta, the, 277.
Blanc (blŏṅ), **Louis,** 418 note, 420, 422 note.
Blenheim (blĕn'im), battle of, 261.
Blois (blwä), 41.
Blücher, 379.
Boccaccio (bōk-kät'chō), 189.

Boer War, the, 563.
Bohemia, 50, 64 c; fief of Empire, 65; and Rudolph of Hapsburg, 158; an electorate, 159; Hussites in, 166, p. 183 note 1; added to Hapsburg realms, 202; Protestantism in, 230; Revolution of 1848, 452-454; and Austria, 491-493.
Bologna (bō-lōn'yä), 180.
Boniface VIII, Pope, 163, 164.
Bordeaux (bōr-dō'), 14, 342.
Boroughs, 121; basis of representation, 135; parliamentary, 527, 529, 531 a, 534, 536.
Boulanger (bōō-lŏṅ-zhä'), 444.
Bourbons, in France, 203, 226-228, 375; in Italy, 396, 457, 462; in Spain, 201, 261, 393, 397, 495. See France, Spain, Italy.
Bourgeoisie (bōōr-zhwä-zē'), in France, 291, taxation, 295; local organization, 317; clash with mob, 323. See Towns.
Boxer Rising, 591.
Boyne, battle of, 549.
Braddock, 276 note, 282.
Brahe, Tycho (brä'ĕ), 198.
Brandenburg, 159, 270; Grand Alliance, 259; becomes kingdom of Prussia, 261 note, 273; accession of Hohenzollerns, 271; expansion into kingdom of Prussia, 272, 273. See Prussia, Germany.
Brézé (brä-zā'), Marquis de, 315.
Bruges (Fr. pron. brüzh), 116 b.
Bru-maire', Revolution of, 355, 357.
Brunswick, House of, 204 e, 253.
Bulgaria, 576, 577, 581.
Bundesrath (bun'des-rät), 474.
Bunyan, John, 249 note.
Burgundy, Treaty of Verdun, 8; rise, 41; added to Empire, 64 b; seized by France, 150, 152 b; in 1500, 170.
Byzant (bĭz'ănt), 90.
Byzantine Empire, 53, 90; map, 90; appearance of Turks, 91; calls for Western aid, 91, 92; and crusades, 95, 98; Turks, 169; in 1500, 170.

Caen (kŏṅ), 342.
Cahiers (kä-yā'), p. 325 note 3.

INDEX.

References are to sections.

Calais (kä-lā'), 139.
Căl'mär, Union of, 157.
Calonne (kä-lŏn'), 309, 310.
Calvin, John, 199 note, 217.
Calvinism, 216, 217; in England, 218; in France, 226. See Presbyterians, Huguenots.
Cambon (kŏn-bōn'), 342.
Campo Formio, Peace of, 351, 356, 370.
Canada, 277; France in, 282; England in, 544, 556–558, 561–564.
Canon Law, in the Age of Hildebrand, 69.
Canton, in France, 447; in Switzerland, 161, 512, 520.
Cape Colony, 558, 563, 586.
Capetians, early, 42–44; to 1547, 148.
Cap-o-dis'tri-as, 582.
Cär-bō-nä'ri, 394, 458.
Carlists, adherents of Carlos, claimant for the Spanish throne, 496.
Carlos, claims Spanish throne, 496.
Cärls'bäd Decrees, 390, 392.
Carnot (kär-nō'), 342.
Carnot, F. Sadi, 442 note.
Carolingians, 7, 8, 9; later, 10, 11, 41; in Germany, 45, 47.
Carrier (cä-re-ā'), 344.
Castelar (käs-tä-lär'), 496; President, 497; in liberal monarchy, 500, 501.
Castles, medieval, 20, 37; of robber knights, 111 note.
Catherine II of Russia, 269, 278, 280, 567 b.
Catherine of Aragon, 218.
Catherine of Medici (mā'dē-chē), 203, 226, 227.
Cavaignac (kä-vän-yäk'), 423, 424.
Cavalier Parliament, 249.
Cavaliers, 245.
Cavour (kä-vōōr'), 459–462.
Center (party in German Reichstag), the, 482, 487.
Chamberlain, Joseph, 541, 552.
Chambord (shŏn-bōr'), Count of, 437, 439.
Châmpagne (sham-pān', Fr. pron. shŏn-päñ'), 41, 300.
Champs de Mars (shŏn-de-mär'), "Massacre" of, 323.

Charlemagne, 1, 4, 6, 7 note, 13, 14, p. 52 note 2, 46, 55, 60, 72, 155, 178.
Charles IV, Emperor, 159.
Charles V, Emperor (Charles I of Spain), p. 127 note 2, 162, 172, 201, 202; in Italy, 173; Diet of Worms, 207; Reformation, 209–212; in Netherlands, 221, 225.
Charles VI, Emperor, 261, 274.
Charles I of England, 204 b, 237, 239; early Parliaments of, 240; benevolences and forced loans, 241; "No Parliament," 243; Civil War, 245; executed, 247.
Charles II of England, 204 b, 247–249, 263.
Charles V of France, 148, 149, 151.
Charles VI of France, 149, 151.
Charles VIII of France, 171.
Charles IX of France, 203; Huguenots, 226; St. Bartholomew, 227.
Charles X of France, 404, 408, 409–412; July Ordinances, 410; in England, 419.
Charles I of Spain, see Charles V, Emperor.
Charles II of Spain, 201, 261.
Charles III of Spain, 201, 280.
Charles XII of Sweden, 269.
Charles Albert, of Sardinia, 453, 459.
Charles of Anjou in Sicily, 86.
Charles of Roumania, 578.
Charles the Bald, 41.
Charles the Bold, Duke of Burgundy, 152 b, 161, 162, 170.
Charles the Fat, 41, 47.
Charles the Simple, 15, 41, 47.
Charter of 1814 (France), 402, 403; workings of, 404–409; suspended, 410; modified, 413.
Charters, of towns, 111; of Henry I, 125; Magna Carta, 132; of Universities, 180.
Chartists, in England, 452, 533, 542.
Chaucer, p. 46 note, 98 note, 188; and the church, 141, 205.
China, invaded by Tartars, 168, 197; Germany in, 484; Russia in, 567 b; United States and, 590; partition of, 585, 588, 589; Boxers, 591.
Chivalry, 37.

INDEX. 641

References are to sections.

Christendom, 4; and feudalism, 18; a political state, 57; supremacy of Popes, 87; gives way to "Europe," 117; in 1500, 170.

Christianity, 1; condition at time of Empire, 57; conversion of Poles and Hungarians, 164 c; Renaissance study of early, 195.

Christina, Queen Regent of Spain, 496.

Church, the, 3, 4, 18; feudalized, 32, 73; in feudal France, 43 b; in Germany, 49; and empire, 54, 55; bond of union for Europe, 57; decline in 9th and 10th centuries, 58; influence of Cluny, 59; reforms of Henry III of Germany, 65 b; democracy, 66 note; power, 68; organization, 69–72; courts, 69; weapons, 70; revenues, 71; in England, 123 note, 141, 218; character at close of Middle Ages, 167; and Renaissance, 176, 195; and scholasticism, 183; Counter-Reformation, 213–215; in France, 289, 311, 328, 360 a; Kulturkampf, 443, 482, 501, 503, 505, 508, 516, 517. See Clergy, Holy Roman Empire, Kulturkampf, Monasteries, Papacy, Protestantism, Reformation.

Church and State in France, Civil Constitution of the Clergy, 328; Concordat of Napoleon, 360 a; to-day, 446.

Church of England, 204 a, 218, 236, 242, 243, 249; disestablished in Ireland, 546 and note; attempt at disestablishment in Wales, 553.

Cinque Ports (sĭnk pōrts), 108, 113.

Cis-al'pine Republic, 352.

Civil Service (English), 537 b, 546.

Civil War in England, 245.

Clarendon, Constitutions of, 128, 163 note.

Classicism, 174.

Clergy, privilege of trial, 69; revenues, 71; in English Parliament, 136; and taxes, 163, 164; in France, 288, 289; in States General, 313, 314; in National Assembly, 315; Civil Constitution of the Clergy, 328; Concordat of Napoleon, 360 a. See Church and State in France, Kulturkampf, Papacy.

Clermont, Council of, 93.

Cluny, 59–61; Henry III of Germany and, 65 b; Gregory VII and, 66.

Code Napoleon, 360 b, 371.

Colbert (kōl-bēr'), 258.

Col'et, John, 195, 205.

Coligny (kō-lēn-yē'), 227.

College of Cardinals, 67 note 2.

Cologne (kō-lōn'), 14, 112, 159.

Colonial System, of England, 200, 251, 261, 275, 277, 282–284, 544, 545, 556–564, 586–590; of France, 258, 282, 586–589; of Germany, 484, 586, 589; of Holland, 225, 511; of Italy, 489; of Portugal, 197, 504; of Spain, 197, 275, 380 note, 393 note, 398, 500, 501.

Columbus, 155, 172 note 3, 197.

Combat, trial by, 130.

Commendation, 24.

Commerce, 3, 197; in Dark Ages, 23; of Mohammedans, 89; of Byzantine Empire, 90; growth as result of Crusades, 103; Hanseatic League, 116 b; in England, 139, 234, 235, 263, 284, 366; in Netherlands, 162; internal, of France, 288; of Germany, 232 b, 484; of Spain, 500; of Sweden and Norway, 232 b, 526.

Committee of Public Safety, in French Revolution, 342–346.

Common Law (in England), 128.

Commons, House of, see Parliament.

Commonwealth in England, 204 b, 247.

Communards, 435, 436.

Commune of 1871, 435–436.

Commune of Paris, 335, 336, 341, 346.

Communes, 325, 447.

Compass, invention of, 186, 196 d.

Concordat of Napoleon, 360 a, 446.

Concordat of Worms, 75.

Confederacy of the Rhine, in the Middle Ages, 108, 116 a.

Confederation of the Rhine, 370; social reforms in, 371.

Congo Free State, 586.

References are to sections.

Congress of Berlin, 1878, p. 405 note, 547, 577; 1884, 586. See **Hague Conference**.
Congress of Laibach, 396.
Congress of London, 1853, 466.
Congress of Münchengrätz, 400.
Congress of Paris, 429 a, 577, 578.
Congress of Troppau, 395.
Congress of Verona, 397.
Congress of Vienna, 376-380, 381, 457, 466, 505, 523.
Conrad the Franconian, of Germany, 47, 62.
Conrad II, 62 c, 64, 129.
Conrad III, 62 e, 77; and Second Crusade, 96.
Conrad IV, 62 e, 86.
Conservative Party (English), 541; and political reform, 534-536; and social reform, 544; and Irish question, 552; and progress, 554.
Constance, Council of, p. 156 note, 167; Peace of, 80.
Constantine Pal-æ-ol'o-gus, 169.
Constantine the African, 180 a.
Constantinople, 90, 91; Latin Kingdom, 98; surrender to Turks, 169, 197; introduces Greek learning, 179; and Russia, 269, 567, 577.
Constituent Assembly, 315, 328, 423.
Constitution, American States, 519; Belgium, 507; Bulgaria, 581; Denmark, 521, 522; France, 1791, 324-328, 333-336; of Year I, 339; of Year III, 348; of Year VIII, 357, 362; of Second Republic, 424; of Third Republic, 440; Finland, 573; German States, 388, 454; German Empire, 472-478; Greece, 582; Holland, 510; Italy, 488; Japan, 589; Netherlands, 505; Norway, 525; Portugal, 502, 503; Roumania, 578; Spain, 1812, 393, 495, 496; paper constitutions of Spain, 496; of Spanish Republic, 497; Spain, 1876, 499; Sweden, 524; Switzerland, 513-519.
Consulate, French, 355-363.
"Continental System," 366, 373.
Coote, Sir Eyre, in India, 284.

Co-per'ni-cus, 198.
Copyholders in England, 234, 528 a. See **Freeholders, Land tenure**.
Cor-day', Charlotte, 346 note.
Cor'dō-va, University of, 179.
Corneille (kōr-nāy'), 265.
Corn Laws, repeal, 544.
Correggio (kōr-ĕd'jō), 193.
Cortes, of Portugal, 503; of Spain, 156, 393, 495, 497, 499, 501.
Corvée (kōr-vā'), 296 b, 307.
Council of Blood, 221.
Council of Constance, p. 156 note, 167.
Council of Pisa, 167.
Council of Trent, 205 note, 215.
Councils of Church, 67 c, 72; of Clermont, 93; demand for general councils, 167; Vatican, of 1870, 482.
Counter-Reformation, 213-215.
Counties, of England, local government, 538 a, 540. See **Shire**.
Courts, feudal, 29; King's Court, 42 a; ecclesiastical, 68, 69; of gilds, 69 note; town, in England, 113; shire, 119; hundred, 120; Saxon feudal, 122; itinerant, 128; Royal, of Middle Ages, 129; papal and local, 165; of the Stuarts in England, 243, 244; in England, after revolution of 1688, 251; of Louis XIV, 260; in France to-day, 448; ecclesiastical, abolished in France, 459 note; in Germany, 479.
Covenanters, 243, 244.
Crécy (krĕs'si ; Fr. krā-sēe'), 139, 234.
Crimean War, 429 a, 459 a, 545, 573.
Croats (krō'ats), 453, 492, 493, 576.
Cromwell, Oliver, 244-248.
Crusades, 4 a, 44, 92-105; place in history, 92; causes, 93; First, 94, 95; Second, 79, 96; Third, 97; Fourth, 98, 169; later, 99; why they ceased, 100; results of, 101-105, 150.
Customs Parliament, 469.
Cus-toz'za, battle of, 453, 454.
Czechs (chĕks), 453, 493.

Danelagh, 16, 119 note.
Danes, 13; in Normandy, 15; in England, 16. See **Denmark**.

INDEX.

References are to sections.

Danish War, 465, 466. See Schleswig-Holstein Question.
Dante (dăn'te; It. pron. dăn'tä), 54, 85, 189, 457.
Danton (dŏṅ-tōṅ'), 332, 335, 338, 341, 346.
"Dark Ages," 4; studies in, 178.
Declaration of Independence of United States, 303 note.
Declaration of Rights, English, 250.
Democracy, growth of, 303, 385.
Denmark, 16, 18, 50; dissolution of Empire, 64; Union of Calmar, 157; in 1500, 170; and Protestant cause in Germany, 230; Napoleonic wars, 366, 372; after Congress of Vienna, 377c; Revolution of 1848, 452; Schleswig-Holstein affair, 466; to 1866, 521; Constitution and politics, 522.
Derby (där'by), Lord, 534, 541.
Desmoulins (dā-mōō-lăṅ'), Camille, 316, 346.
Despotism, reforms by, 200, 279, 280; in Europe, 400; in England, 200, 237; in France, 301, 307, 358, 362, 367, 427, 428; in Germany, 382, 479; in Italy, 457; in Russia, 568, 573. See Absolute Monarchy.
Diaz (dē'äs), **Bartholomew,** 197.
Diderot (dē-drō'), 302.
Diet, of Empire, in 1347, 159; of Worms, 207, 209; of Speier, 210; of Augsburg, 210; of Switzerland, 513, 517, 518; of Denmark, 521; of Sweden, 524. See Rigsdag.
Directory, French, 348–355.
Disestablishment of English Church, in Ireland, 546 and note; proposed in Wales, 553.
Disraeli (diz-rā'li), 535, 541, 547.
Döff'ing-en, battle of, 116 *a*.
Domain, feudal, 26; in France, 292–294, 318.
Domesday Book, 125 note 130.
Dō-min'ĭ-cans, 84, p. 332 note.
Dreyfus (drī'fus; Fr. pron. drā-füs'), 443 note ; 446.
"Duchy of Athens," 98.
Dukes of Francia, 41, 42, 43.
Duma (dōōma), 575.
Dumouriez (dü-mōō-rē-ā'), 340, 342.

Dupleix (dü-plā'), 275, 277.
Dürer, Albert, 193.
Dū-shan', Stephen, 169.
Dutch Republic, see Netherlands.

Ealdorman (ēl'der-man), 119.
East, the, in history, 1, 2. See Oriental Civilization, China, Asia.
Eastern Empire, see Byzantine.
"Eastern Question," 577.
East Indies, 220.
Economic Conditions, in feudal times, 23; in Belgium, 509; in England, 234, 235, 239 note, 528, 530, 533, 534, 543; in France, 260 *b*, 264, 428, 450; in Germany, 231, 279, 484; in Holland, 511; in Italy, 488; in Norway, 526; in Portugal, 504; in Spain, 501; in Sweden, 526; in Switzerland, 520.
Education, 3, 4; in Alfred's England, 16; of Mohammedans, 89; in Dark Ages, 178; Universities, 178–181; affected by Renaissance, 191; in Belgium, 508; in England, 542, 545, 546; "benevolent despots" and, 280; in France, 345, 346 note 3, 359, 415 note, 428, 443, 449; in Germany, 482; in Holland, 510; in Italy, 488; in Portugal, 503; in Spain, 500, 501; in Switzerland, 520. See Kulturkampf.
Edward I of England, 135, 137, 164.
Edward II of England, 137.
Edward III of England, 138, 139, 140; Parliament, 143; and French crown, 148 note; and Papacy, 165.
Edward IV of England, 146, 233 note, 235.
Edward V of England, 146.
Edward VI of England, 204 *a*, 218, 234.
Edward VII of England, 204 *e*.
Edward the Confessor, 16.
Egbert, King of Wessex, 16.
Egypt, Crusades in, 99; Napoleon in, 354; England in, 557, 560.
Eleanor, Queen of England, 127, p. 164 note.
Electoral College (Holy Roman Empire), 62 note, 159, 270.

644 INDEX.

References are to sections.

Eliot, Sir John, 240, 242.
Elizabeth of England, 199, 204 a, 233, 281; ecclesiastical system, 218; aids Netherlands, 223; Puritans, 236; Parliament, 237; Ireland, 549.
Elizabeth of Russia, 269.
Emigrants, French, 320, 328, 331, 335, 359 note, 378, 404, 408.
Emmet, Robert, 551.
Empire, French, First, 362-375; Second, 427-432.
Empire of Charlemagne, 6, 7, 41; attempts to revive, 46, 51; more universal than Holy Roman Empire, 55 b. See Holy Roman Empire.
Enclosures, see Inclosures.
England, Danish invasions, 16; beginning of nation, 18, 55 b, 64 a; and Roman Church, 82, 87, 163-166; growth of towns, 108, 110, 111, 113, 163, 166; to 1500, 118-147, 170; Saxon institutions, 118-122; Norman period, 123-125; effect of Conquest, 123; early Plantagenets, 126-137; territories of Plantagenets, 127; Magna Carta, 132; Parliament, 134-136, 143, 144; Hundred Years' War, 139; Black Death, 140; social discontent, 141, 234, 528 a, 533; Peasant Rising, 142; alliance with Netherlands, 162; learning in Dark Ages, 178; early literature, 188; Renaissance, 199; Stuarts and Parliament, 200, 240-244; struggle with France for world-empire, 200, 261, 274-277, 282; table of Kings, 204; Protestantism in, 218; development of political liberty, 219, 233-254; aids Netherlands, 223; in 17th century, 233-254; Yorkist and Tudor periods, 233-235; condition under early Stuarts, 236-244; Civil War and the Commonwealth, 245-248; Restoration and the Revolution, 249, 250; foreign expansion and growth of Parliament, 251-254; ministerial government, 252; war with Louis XIV, 259, 261; expansion, 281-284; wars of French Revolution, 340, 343, 350, 354-356; wars with Napoleon, 364-366, 372, 374, 375, 379, 457, 529; Congress of Vienna, 376, 377, 380, 457; reaction in, 382; Congress of Troppau, 395; Congress of Verona, 397; and Holy Alliance, 398-400; aids Greece, 399; Crimean War, 429 a, 459 a; American Civil War, 430 b; Chartists, 452, 533, 542; in China, 484; in 19th century, 527-564; in 1815, 527-528; political reform, 529-540; in central government, 529-537; in local government, 538, 540; social reform to 1884, 541-548; Irish Question, 549-552; politics, in the 20th century, 553-555; colonies and dependencies, 556-564, 585-590; and the alliances of the new age, 584.
E-räs'mus, 195, 205, 215 note.
Espartero (es-par-tā'ro), 496.
Estates General, French, 154; and Papacy, 164. See States General.
Eth'ĕl-red the Rēde'less, 16.
Eves'ham, battle of, 133.
Excommunication, 68, 70; used by Gregory VII, 74; of Henry IV of Germany, 74; of Frederick II, 86; in England, p. 137 note.

Factory Legislation, in England, 542, 543, 545, 546.
Factory System, 528 b, 543.
Fa-shō'da Incident, 587.
Faure (fōr), Felix, 442 note.
February Days in Paris, 419, 452.
Federal Act of 1815, Germany, 387.
Federal Assembly of Switzerland, 518.
Federal Pact of 1815, in Switzerland, 514.
Fenians, 552.
Ferdinand I, Emperor, 202, 212, 230 note.
Ferdinand of Aragon, king of Spain, 155, 156; in Sicily, 171; power of Spain, 172.
Ferdinand VII of Spain, 393, 397, 495, 496.
Ferdinand I of Austria, 453.
Ferdinand of Bulgaria, 581.
Ferdinand of Naples, 280.

INDEX.

References are to sections.

Festival of Reason, 346.
Feudalism, 3, 18–40; origin, 19; classes, 21, 26, 34; privileges, 21, 22; causes, 23, 24; theory and practice, 25; feudal contract, 27; lord and vassal, 28–31; aids, 30; in the church, 32, 73; violence, 33; society, 34–37; economic effects, 36; and chivalry, 37; in France, 42; in Germany, 48; organization under Otto the Great, 49; undermined by the Crusades, 105; and civilization, 106; undermined by cities, 108; Anglo-Saxon, 122; in England, 124, 125; in France, 153, 292–294, 302, 318; in Spain, 156; in Scandinavia, 157; in Confederacy of the Rhine, 371; in Italy and Germany, 452, 456; in Austria, 491; in Denmark, 521.
Fiefs, 21, 26.
Fine Arts, medieval, 192; in Renaissance, 193–194.
Finland, seized by Russia, 269, 567 *b*, 574; Napoleon, 373; after Congress of Vienna, 377 *c*; loss of liberties, 573; recovery, 573, close.
"Fist-law" in Germany, 88.
Flanders, 41, 139, 152 *b*, 162, 235.
Florence, 114, 171; and Renaissance, 193; in 1848, 453.
Forest Cantons, 161, 512 note, 516 note. See Switzerland.
For′tes-cue, Sir John, 144, 234.
Fourth of August Decrees, 318.
France, beginnings, 8, 18; from Verdun to the 12th century, 41–44; not part of Empire, 55; and Innocent III, 82; rebels against papal domination, 87, 163–165; population, p. 106 note 1; towns, 108–111, 115; and Henry II of England, 127; royal justice, 129; regains Normandy, 131; Hundred Years' War, 138–139; to 1547, 148–154; in 1500, 170; early literature, 188; predominance, 200; kings, 203; Protestantism, 211, 212; religious wars, 219, 226–229; Thirty Years' War, 230; Treaty of Westphalia, 232 *b*, 255; disturbs balance of power, 255; Age of Louis XIV, 258–265; war in America, 275, 277; War of Austrian Succession, 274; Seven Years' War, 276; Revolution, 285–375; conditions in 1789, 288–312; 1st period of Revolution, 313–332; 2d period of Revolution, 333–347; 3d period of Revolution, 348–355; Consulate and Empire, 356–375; return of Napoleon, 378, 379; after Congress of Vienna, 380; Reaction, 381, 382, 408; Revolution of 1830, 385, 391, 392, 410–412; Congress of Troppau, 395; in Greece, 399; since 1815, 402–451; Divine Right Monarchy, 402–409; Constitutional Monarchy, 413–418; Revolution of 1848, 417, 419–423, 452; Second Republic, 424–426; Second Empire, 427–432; Franco-Prussian War, 432–434, 465, 469, 470; Third Republic, 433–451; Foreign and Civil War, 433–436; Republic established, 437–442; Kulturkampf, 443; Boulanger, 444; to-day, 445–451; in Italy, 459; China, 484; Belgium, 509; alliances of new age, 583–584; Africa, 586, 587; Asia, 588, 589.
Franchise, in Belgium, 507–508; in Denmark, 522; in England, 527, 529, 531 *b*, 533–535; in France, 357, 409, 413, 416, 417, 421, 424, 434, 440; in Germany, 454, 475, 485; in Greece, 582; in Holland, 510; in Italy, 488; in Norway, 525; in Portugal, 503; in Roumania, 578; in Spain, 500, 501; in Sweden, 524.
Francia, 41, 42, 43.
Franciscans, the, 84.
Francis I, Emperor, 202, 274.
Francis II, Emperor, 331.
Francis I of France, 172, 203; in Italy, 173, 209; patron of art, 193; Huguenots, 226.
Francis II of France, 203, 226.
Francis Joseph I, of Austria, 453.
Francis of Assisi, 84.
Franconia, 45, 47, 62, 77.
Franco-Prussian War, 427, 432–434, 465, 469–470.
Frankfort, 107, 387; and Prussia, 468 *a*; National Assembly, 452, 454, 455.

References are to sections.

Frederick I (Barbarossa), Emperor, 62, 75 note; Lombard League, 79–81, 108; character and policy, 79; place in history, 81; Third Crusade, 97; University of Bologna, 180 b.

Frederick II, Emperor, 62, 82; character, 85–86; recovers Jerusalem, 99; and Swiss League, 161 note; and Popes, 163; and Tartars, 168; University of Naples, 180 a.

Frederick III, Emperor, 160.

Frederick I of Prussia, 273.

Frederick II of Prussia (the Great), 200, 256, 274–276, 278–280; greatness of, 279, 280.

Frederick III of Prussia, 480.

Frederick of Hohenzollern, 271.

Frederick William, "Great Elector" of Brandenburg, 273, 279.

Frederick William I, Prussia, 274.

Frederick William III, 382, 388, 395 note.

Frederick William IV, 454, 455, 464.

Freeholders in England, 234, 528 a.

Free Trade in England, 544, 545.

French and Indian War, 277.

French Revolution of 1789, 4 b, 203, 285–376; character, 285–287; causes, 288–304; feudal burdens, 292–294; taxation, 295–297; government, 298–301; men of letters, 302–304; attempted reforms, Louis XVI, 305–310; 1st period, 313–332; Constituent Assembly, at Versailles, 313–319; at Paris, 320–323; March of the Women, 320; Constitution of 1791, 324–328; Legislative Assembly and foreign war, 329–332; 2d period, 333–347; breakdown of constitution, 333–336; converts with sword, 337; Convention and revolutionary government, 338–347; 3d period, 348–355; results, 385.

French Revolution, Second, 391, 400, 410–412.

French Revolution, Third, 417, 419–423, 452; Commune of 1871, 435–436. See Napoleon, Consulate, Empire.

Friars, 82, 84.

Froissart (froiss'ärt), 141.

Fronde, 258.

Ga-belle', 297, 302.

Gal-i-lē'o, 198.

Găm-bett'a (Fr. pron. gŏṅ-bĕh-tä'), 433, 441, 443.

Game Laws, feudal, 21; in France, 294; abolished, 318.

Găr-i-băl'di (It. gä-rē-bäl'dē), 462.

Genghis Khan (jĕn'ġis kän), 168.

Genoa, and commerce, 103; Ligurian Republic, 352; after Congress of Vienna, 377 b, 380, 457; Garibaldi sails from, 462.

Geoffrey Plantagenet, 126.

George I of England, 204 e, 252.

George II, 204 e, 252.

George III, 204 e, 529.

George IV, 204 e, 531.

George of Greece, 582.

Gerbert, Pope, 63.

Germanic Confederation of 1815, 387.

Germany, beginning, 8, 18; from Verdun to restoration of the Empire, 45–51; and Holy Roman Empire, 52–88; kings, 62; under Otto II and III, 63; restored strength, 64; small scattered units, 64; reaches highest point under Henry III, 65; Henry IV, 74; feudal anarchy, 76; peace and order under Frederick I, 79; separation from Italy, 86; effects of struggle between Empire and Papacy on, 88; towns, 108, 110, 111, 116; royal justice, 129; from Great Interregnum to Charles V, 158–160; and Papacy, 165; in 1500, 170; early literature, 188; Reformation in, 205–212, 215, 219; Thirty Years' War in, 230–232; wars of French Revolution, 337, 351; Napoleon, 368–371, 374, 380; after Congress of Vienna, 377 a; New Germany, 385; Metternich in, 386, 387–392; Revolution of 1830, 391; and Napoleon III, 430 c; Socialists in, 445 note, 481 note, 482, 485, 486; in 1848, 452, 454–456; unification of, 464–471; since 1871, 472–487; Constitution, 472–478; operation of, 479–481; kulturkampf, 482; militarism, 483; trade and colonies, 484; and Sweden and Nor-

INDEX.

References are to sections.

way, 525 and note; a world power, 583; in Africa, 586; in Asia, 589. See Holy Roman Empire, Prussia.
Ghibelline (gĭb′el-lēn), 77, 82, 86.
Gibraltar, 261, 284, 501, 557, 558.
Gilds, 69 note, 108, 112; and university organizations, 179 note 3; breaking down, 235; in France, 290, 307.
Giotto (jŏt′tō), 193.
Girondists, 330, 332, 335; in convention, 338; fall, 341; fugitive, 342, 347; Lamartine and, 415 note.
Gladstone, p. 548 notes, 534–536, 540, 541, 546–548, 552, 553, 560, 563.
Golden Bull, the, 159.
Golden Horde, the, 168.
Good Parliament, the, 143.
Grä-nä′dä, 155, 197.
Grand Remonstrance, of Long Parliament, 244.
Great Council, of Norman kings, 134.
Great Privilege, Netherlands, 162.
Greece, 385, 394, 399, 458, 576, 577, 582.
Greek Church, in Russia, 266.
Greek Civilization, 1, 3; among the Mohammedans, 89; influence on literature, 189–191.
Gregory V, Pope, 63.
Gregory VII, youth, 66; work as counsellor, 67; policy, 68; legates, 72; investitures, 74; and Henry IV of Germany, 74, 75, 93; and William the Conqueror, 123.
Gregory XI, 166.
Grévy (grā-vē′), 441, 442.
Guelf, 77, 82. See Welfs.
Guiana (gē-ä′nä), 451.
Guise (güēz), House of, 226–228.
Guizot (gē-zō′), 408, 415–417, 419.
Gunpowder, invention of, 186, 196 *a*.
Gustavus Adolphus, 230.
Gustavus Vasa (vä′sä), 157.
Gutenberg (gōōt′en-bĕrG), 196 *b*.

Habeas Corpus Act, 249.
Hague (hāg) Conference, 380, 594.
Hăm′burg (Ger. pron. häm′bōōrG), 14, 116 *b*.
Hampden, John, 241, 243, 244, p. 247 note.

Han-ō-vēr′i-ans, 204 *e*, 253.
Han′se-at′ic League, 108, 116 *b*, 162.
Hapsburgs (häps′bōōrGs), 158, 160; Counts in Switzerland, 161; Charles V, 172; last of Spanish, 201, 261; and Protestantism, 230; wars, 259, 261, 262; and France, 264.
Harold Blue-Tooth, 50.
Harold the Saxon, 16.
Harvey, William, 199.
Hastings, battle of, 16 *d*.
Hawaii (hä-wī′ē), 590.
Hébert (ā-bĕr′), 346.
Heidelberg (hī′del-bĕrG), 454 note.
Heimskringla (hīms′kring-la), 188.
Henry I of England, 75 note, 125, 183.
Henry II of England, 126; territories, 127, 151; and courts, 128; jury, 130; Great Council, 134; Constitutions of Clarendon, 163 note; and Ireland, 549.
Henry III of England, 133, 139.
Henry IV of England, 138; Lollards, 141 note; Parliament, 143.
Henry V of England, 138, 139; Lollards, 141 note; Parliament, 143; France, 151 and note.
Henry VI of England, 138, 139, 145, 151.
Henry VII of England, 146, 147, 197.
Henry VIII of England, 147, 172, 204 *a*; the Church, 218, p. 257 note 2; popular risings, 234; and Parliament, 237, and Ireland, 549.
Henry II of France, 203, 212, 229; Huguenots, 226.
Henry III of France, 203, 226, 228.
Henry IV of France (of Navarre), 227, 228, 237.
Henry I of Germany, 47, 48, 49, 62, 110; repulse of Hungarians, 48.
Henry II of Germany, 62, 64.
Henry III of Germany, 62; reformation of church and state, 65.
Henry IV of Germany, 62; opponent of Gregory VII, 74, 75.
Henry V of Germany, 62; and investitures, 73 note 4, 75.
Henry VI of Germany, 62, 82.
Henry the Navigator, 197.

References are to sections.

Herzegovina (hert-se-gō-vē'nä), 577.
Hesse, 455, 468 *a*.
Hesse-Darmstadt (hĕs-därm'stät), 468 *b*.
Hierarchy, in the church, 68, 72.
Hildebrand, see Gregory VII.
Hohenlinden (hō-en-lin'den), battle of, 356.
Hohenstaufen (hō-eñ-stauf'en), 62, 77–88; origin, 77; fall, 86, 158.
Hohenzollerns (hō-en-tsōl'lerns), 271–273.
Holbein (hōl'bīn), 193.
Holland, 162; in 1500, 170; art in, 193; independence, 224, 232 *b*; prosperity, 225; wars with Louis XIV, 259, 261; decline of commerce in, 263; wars of French Revolution in, 340; conquered by France, 350, 368 *a*; after Congress of Vienna, 377 *b*; Revolution of 1830, 391; Revolution of 1848, 452; in 19th century, 505, 506, 510, 511. See Netherlands.
Holles (hŏl'lĕs), 244.
Holstein (hōl'stīn), 466.
Holy Alliance, the, 395–398, 400, 408, 458, 495.
Holy Roman Empire, 52–88; restoration, 53; results of restoration, 54; nature, 55; coronation of Emperor, 56; relations with Popes, 61; restored strength, 63; addition of Burgundy, 64 *b*; eastern kingdoms, 64 *c*; Hungary, Poland, and Bohemia, 65 *a*; conflict with Popes over investitures, 73–76; compromise, 75; the Hohenstaufen, 77–88; Italian policy, 78; conflict over Italy, 78–88; Interregnum, 86; results of struggle, 87; growth of towns, 108, 116; from Interregnum to Charles V, 158–160; position in 1500, 170; table of Emperors, 202; Austrian House, 262; composition before Napoleon, 369; close, 370.
Holy Vehme (vām), 129 note.
Home Rule in Ireland, 552.
Hos'pĭ-tal-lers, see Knights of St. John.
Hugh Capet (kä-pā'), 41, 42, 148.

Huguenots (hū'ge-nŏts), 226–229; condition in France, 226; St. Bartholomew, 227; Edict of Nantes, 203, 228; edict revoked, 260 *b*; political power crushed, 229; in England, 235; in Brandenburg, 273; immigration to America, 282.
Humanism, 189–191, 196 *b*; in the Reformation, 205 note.
Hundred, the, in Saxon England, 118–121.
Hundred Days, in French Revolution, 379.
Hundred Years' War, 139; effect on France, 150, 151; and Netherlands, 162; and Papacy, 163.
Hundred Years' War, Second, 261, 275–279, 283, 284.
Hungarians, 11, 12; repulse by Henry I of Germany, 48; conquered, by Otto I, 49; organized state, 64 *c*. See Hungary.
Hungary, 55; fief of Empire, 65 *a*; ravaged by Tartars, 168, 170; won back from Turks by Austria, 262; war of 1848, 452, 453, 455, 456, 459 *a*; Austria-Hungary, 491–493. See Austria.
Huss, John, 166, 167, 181 note 4.

Inclosures in England, 234, 528 *a*.
India, invaded by Tartars, 168; attempts to reach from the West, 197; Dupleix in, 275; Coote in, 284; England, 547, 557, 559, 588.
Indulgences, 205, 206.
Industrial Revolution in England, 528 *b*.
Industry, of Mohammedans, 89; in English towns, 113, 235; of France, 228, 260 *b*, 264; destroyed in Germany by Thirty Years' War, 231; in Prussia, 273, 279; encouraged in France, 359, 428; in Germany, 484; in Italy, 488; in Spain, 500; in England, 528; of 20th century, 593.
Innocent II, Pope, 75 note.
Innocent III, 72 note, 82; and Albigenses, 83; and friars, 84; death, 86; and John of England, 131.
Innocent IV, 86.

INDEX.

References are to sections.

Inquisition, 213, 214; in Netherlands, 221; restored in Papal States, 381.
Intendants, 298, 300.
Interdict, 68, 70.
Interregnum, the Great, in Germany, 88, 158.
Inventions, 4, 196; in England, 528 b; in new age, 592, 593.
Investitures, 27, 73; cause of conflict, 74.
Ireland, 127; Strafford in, 243, 549; massacre in, 244; Cromwell in, 248, 549; conquest by England, 281, 344; threat of rebellion, 452; in Parliament, 527; reform, 542, 546–548; famine, 544; Ireland to 1700, 549; in the 18th century, 550; "union" with England, 551; since 1830, 552.
Irish Famine, 544.
Ir-nē'ri-us, 180 b.
Ironsides, Cromwell's, 234, 245.
Isabella of Castile, 155, 197.
Isabella of Spain, 496.
Isle of France, 149.
Italy, at Treaty of Verdun, 8, 18; German conquest, 51; disintegration, 53; Holy Roman Empire, 53–88; effect on Italy, 54; conflict of policies, 78; Peace of Constance, 80; union of South, with Empire, 82; in 1500, 170; Frederick II, 86; separation from Germany, 86; results on, of struggles between Empire and Papacy, 87; growth of towns, 108, 109, 114; anarchy, 165; movement toward unity, 171; Renaissance in, 174, 176, 179, 189, 193, 209 note; inquisition in, 214; Napoleon in, 351, 352, 356, 368 b, 372, 380; after Congress of Vienna, 377 a; Revolution of 1830, 391, 392, 400; War of Napoleon III for, 429 b, 430 a; Socialism in, 445, note; Revolution of 1848, 452–456; unification of, 457–463; since 1870, 488–490; alliances of the new age, 583–584. See Holy Roman Empire, Sardinia.
Ivan (ē-vän') the Great, 170.
Ivan the Terrible, 170, 567 a.

Jăc'ō-bĭns, 321, 329, 330, 332, 334–336, 341, 346, 347.
Jacquerie (zhäk-rē'), 142, p. 166 note 1.
James I of England, 204 b, 236, 237, 281 a.
James II of England, 204 b, 237, 249.
Jăn'is-sā-ries, 169.
Japan, 197, 584 b, 589–591.
Jăx-är'tēṣ, 89, 91, 169.
Jemmapes (zhā-mäp'), 337.
Jena (yā'nä), battle of, 365, 370, 371, 379, 464; University of, 389.
Jerome of Prague, 167.
Jerusalem, captured by Turks, 93, 99; in the Crusades, 94, 97, 99; Crimean War, 429 a.
Jesuits, 84, 215, 443, 482, 517.
Jews, 104 note; persecution, 214; in France, 446; in Russia, 566, 573.
Jingoism, 547.
Joanna of Spain, 162.
Jō-ăn' of Arc, 151.
John of England, 82, 131, 134, 139, 151.
John of Portugal, 502.
John So-bi-es'ki, of Poland, 257.
John XII, Pope, 60.
Joinville (zhwăn-vēl'), extracts from Memoir of St. Louis, 22 note, 40, 100, 129.
Joseph II, Emperor, 202, 280.
Josephine, Empress, 367, note.
July Days (in Paris), 412, 458.
July Ordinances, 410, 411.
June Days (in Paris), 423, 454.
Jury, 130, 144; established in France, 324; in Germany, 481; in Spain, 500; in Russia, 573.
Justice, in feudal courts, 25, 29, 33; in feudal France, 42 a; royal justice, in the Middle Ages, 129; in France, 299, 359, 448; in Confederation of the Rhine, 371; in German Empire, 479; in England, 128, 529, 542; in Russia, 568, 573.

Kas-sō'va, battle of, 169.
Kepler, 198.
Kett's Rising, p. 257 note 2.
Kief (kē-ĕf'), 108.

650 INDEX.

References are to sections.

Kingdom of Jerusalem, 95.
King William's War, 261.
Knights, 20, 37; Chaucer's, p. 46 note; of the shire, 128 note 2, 136; robber knights, p. 123 note, 158.
Knights of St. John, 95, 99, 224.
Knox, John, 236.
Knut the Great, 16, 64, 157.
Königgrätz (kö'nĕG-rĕts), Sadowa.
Korea, 589, 591.
Kos-çi-us'kō,•278.
Kossuth (kosh'ōōt), 453.
Kot'ze-bue, 389, 395.
Kulturkampf, Belgium, 508; France, 443, 446; Germany, 482; Holland, 510; Spain, 501; Portugal, 503.
Kyffhäuser (kĭf'hoi-zer) Mountain, 81.

Labor, feudal, 34; change in character, 107; social discontent in England, 140-142, 234, 528, 530, 533, 534, 543, 554; in France, 290, 359, 418; beginnings of socialism, 418; troubles in Belgium, 508. See Factory legislation, Factory system, Industrial Revolution, Industry, Serfs.
Labor Unions, 528 b, 546.
Lafayette (lä-fā-yĕt'), in America, 308 note; in Assembly of Notables, 310; National Guards, 317, 320; in Assembly, 321, 322; foreign war, 330, 332, 334, 335; succeeded by Dumouriez, 340; in legislature of the restored Monarchy, 407; Revolution of 1830, 411, 412.
Laibach (lī'bächl), Congress of, 396.
Lamartine (lä-mär-tēn'), 415 and note, 420, 421, 423, 424.
Lancastrians, 138, 143; Wars, 145, 147, 233; and Lollards, 166.
Landtag (länt'täG), 454, 464, 465, 469, 478.
Land Tenure, feudal, 26, 34; in France, 292, 293, 328, 359, 450; in Prussia, 371; in England, 234, 528 a, 554; in Russia, 569. See Copyholders, Freeholders, Serfs.
Languedoc (läng'gwĕ-dŏk), 83, 188, 300.

La Rochelle (lä rō-shĕl'), 229.
La Salle (lä säl), 282.
Lassalle (lä-säl'), 485.
Lateran Council, 130.
Latimer, execution of, 218.
Latin States of Syria, established, 95, 96; effect on European commerce, 103.
Laud, William, 243, 244.
Lechfeld (lĕćh'felt), battle of, 49.
Legates, Papal, 72.
Legnano (län-yä'nō), battle of, 80, 81.
Leipzig (līp'tsĭG), battle of, 374, 384, 389.
Leo IX, Pope, 65 c.
Leo X, 206, 207.
Leo XIII, 443.
Leonardo da Vinci (lā-ō-när'dō dä vĭn'chē), 193.
Leopold of Coburg, King of Belgium, 506, 582.
Leopold II, 507, 586.
Leopold II, Emperor, 202, 331.
Leopold of Tuscany, 280.
Lē-păn'tō, battle of, 224.
Letters of the Seal (*Lettres de Cachet*, Fr. pron. lĕt'r-de-kä-shä), 299, 302.
Leuthen (loi'ten), battle of, 276.
Lewes (lū'es), battle of, 133, 134.
Lewis the Child, 47.
Leyden (lī'den), relief of, 222; University of, 222 note 2; Puritans at, 236.
Liberal party (English), the, political reform, 534, 535; table of administrations, 541; social reform, 542-544; and Ireland, 552; and progress, 554.
Liebknecht (lēp'knĕćht), 485.
Liege (lēġe), see Suzerain.
Ligurian Republic, 352.
Limerick, treaty of, 549.
Literature, medieval, 187-188; renaissance, 189-191; in England, 187, 199, 249, 265 note; in France, 265, 302-304; in Prussia, 279.
Lollards, 141, 166.
Lombard League, 80, 108, 114.
Long Parliament, 243; and Civil War, 245.

INDEX.

References are to sections.

Longwy (lŏṅ-vē), 336.
Lorraine (lor-rān'), 292, 379 note, 434, 583.
Lothair I, 8.
Lothair II, 62, p. 84 note.
Lotharingia, 8, 9, 45; added to Germany, 48. See Lorraine.
Loubet (loo-bā'), Émile, 442 note.
Louis the Pious, 7.
Louis the Stammerer, p. 51 note.
Louis III, p. 51 note.
Louis VI, 148, 149.
Louis VII, 96, 127, 148.
Louis VIII, 148, 153.
Louis IX (St. Louis), 22 note, 40, 99, 100, 129, 149, 153, 197.
Louis XI, 148, 149, 152 b, 153, 162.
Louis XIII, 203, 229.
Louis XIV, 200, 203, 249, 251, 256, 273, 282, 301; age of, 258–265; early years, 258; first wars, 259; "reunions" and the Edict of Nantes, 260; second series of wars, 261; estimate of, 264; court of, 265; taxes, 295.
Louis XV, 203, 295, 300 b, 301, 305.
Louis XVI, 301; character, 305; attempted reforms, 306–310; states general, 310, 313, 314; royal session of June 23, 315; attempts flight, 323; war, 331, 334; deposed, 335; executed, 338.
Louis XVIII, 375, 378, 379, 382; charter of, 402, 403; moderation, 405.
Louis Napoleon, see Napoleon III.
Louis Philippe, 412, 413; bourgeois king, 414–418.
Lō-yō'lä, Ignatius, 215.
Lü'beck, 116 b.
Luther, p. 156 note, 173, p. 199 note 4, 195, 205–208; and indulgences, 205; posts theses, 206; papal bull burned, 207; at Worms, 207; death, 211.
Lutherans, in Germany, 211, 216.
Lutzen (lŏŏt'sen), battle of, 230.
Lu-zern', 161, 512 note.

Machiavelli (mäk-ē-ä-věl'lē), 189.
MacMahon (mäk-mä-ôṅ'), Marshal, 439, 441.

Mad-a-gas'car, p. 447 note 1.
Magdeburg (mäg'de-boorG), 108, note 2.
Ma-gĕn'ta, battle of, 429 b, 460.
Magna Carta, 131, 132, 144, 242.
Magyars (mŏd'yŏrz'), see Hungarians.
Mahomet I, 169.
Mahomet the Conqueror, 169.
Mainz (mīnts), 159, 196 b.
Majuba Hill, battle of, 563.
Malplaquet (mäl-plä-kā'), battle of, 261.
Malta, siege of, 224; England and, 377 d, 557.
Manchuria, 589, 591.
Mandeville, Sir John, p. 219 note 4.
Mansfeld (mäns'fĕlt), 230.
Manufactures, domestic system of, 235; factory system, 528 b.
Marat (mä-rä'), 332, 338, 341, 346 note 1.
Mä-rĕng'ō, battle of, 356.
Margaret of Denmark, 157.
Maria (mä-rē'ä), of Portugal, 502.
Maria Theresa (tĕ-rĕs'a), of Hungary, 160 note, 202, 274, 276, 305.
Marie Antoinette (mär-ē' ŏṅ-twä-nĕt'), 305, 307, 320, p. 343 note; executed, 344.
Market, grant of, 110.
Marlborough (mawl'bro), 261.
Marseillaise (mär-se-lyāz'), the, 334 note.
Marseilles (mär-sāl'), 342, 435, 447.
Marston Moor, battle of, 245.
Martin V, Pope, 167.
Marx, Karl, 485.
Mary, Queen of England, 204 a, 218.
Mary of Burgundy, 162.
Matilda of England, 125, 126.
Maximilian I, Emperor, 160–162, 172.
Maximilian, "Emperor" of Mexico, 430 b.
May Laws (of the German Empire), 482.
Mazarin (măz-a-rēn'), 258.
Mazzini (mät-sē'nē), 453, 458, 459.

INDEX

References are to sections.

Medici (mä'dē-chē), 114, 226, 227.
Mediterranean, decay of trade on, 197; ravaged by Turks, p. 232 note 1; power of England in, 261, 429 *a*; Italy in, 488 note; Turkey and Russia in, 547.
Melbourne, Lord, 541, 544.
Met'ter-nich, Congress of Vienna, 376; Rule of, 383, 385–392, 395, 396, 399, 400, 410 note; overthrow, 452, 453; Italy, 457; Spain, 496; Switzerland, 517.
Michael Angelo (mī'ka-el än'jā-lō; It. pron. mĕ-kĕl-än'jā-lō), 193.
Middle Ages, characteristics, 175; learning, 178; literature, 187, 188; arts, 192.
Mi-lan', 80, 171, 173, 261; rising of 1848, 453.
Military Orders, 95.
Milton, John, 249 note 1.
Ministerial government, in Austria-Hungary, 492; in Belgium, 507; in Denmark, 522; in England, 252, 527, 531 *b*, 532 *b*, 534, 541; in France, 440, 443; in Germany, 465, 470; in Greece, 582; in Holland, 510; in Italy, 488; in Norway, 525; in Roumania, 578; in Spain, 499.
Min'ne-sing-ers, 188.
Mirabeau (mē-rä-bō'), in National Assembly, 315, 316, 318, 321; his plans, 322, 332, p. 365 note 3; death, 323.
Modern history, 2, 200.
Mohammedans, 1, 2, 11; civilization and government, 89; fall of empire, 91; crusades, 92, 94, 96; attitude toward pilgrims, 93; in Egypt, 99; in 1500, 170; in France, 446.
Molière (mō-lyĕr'), 265.
Monarchic government, 4; growth of idea in France, 43 *d*; weakness in Germany, 46; in Germany under Henry I and Otto I, 48–51; rise of monarchic states, 117; period of, 200; in France, 154; in Spain, 156; in France under Louis XVIII, 402–409; Orleans Monarchy, 413–418. See **Absolute monarchy, Despotism,**

Ministerial government, "New Monarchy."
Monasteries, 3, 38, 58; reform, 59; growth, p. 79 note 2; characteristic of the Middle Ages, 175; and literature in the Dark Ages, 187; destruction of, in England, 218, 234; in Italy, 459 note.
Mongol Empire, 168.
Monroe Doctrine, 398, 430 *b*, 484, 585, 590.
Montcalm (mŏnt-käm'), 277.
Montenegro (mŏn-te-nā'grō), 576, 577, 579.
Moors, 11, 99, 155, 214.
Morality, of society in feudal age, 37, 40; low in Germany after Thirty Years' War, 231; corruption of Restoration in England, 249; international, selfish, 255; effect of Bismarck's policy on international, 471; of laboring class in England, 543.
More, Sir Thomas, p. 238 note 2, 234.
Moreau (mō-rō'), 355, 356.
Morgarten, battle of, 161.
Moriscoes, expulsion of, 201, 224.
Moscow (mŏs'kō), 108; burned by Tartars, 168; in 1500, 170; retreat of Napoleon, 373.
Mountain, the, in French Assemblies, 330, 332, 338, 341, 342.
Münchengrätz (mün'chēn-grĕts), Congress of, 400, 453.
Municipal Reform in England, 539, 542.
Murillo (mōō-rē'lyō), 193.
Mutiny Act, 251.

Nantes (nănts; Fr. pron. nŏṅt), 14; Edict of, 203, 228; revoked, 260 *b*, 273; cruelty of Carrier, 344.
Na'pi-er, 199.
Naples, 171; University, 180 *a*; ceded to Austria, 261; Ferdinand of, 280; wars of French Revolution, 335, 340; Kingdom of Naples, 368 *b*; Revolution of 1820, 394, 396; Revolution of 1848, 452, 453, 458; in 1815, 457; annexed to Sardinia, 462.

References are to sections.

INDEX. 653

Napoleon I, 343, 345, 502, 513; puts down insurrection, 349; in Italy, 351, 352, 457; character and aims, 353; in Egypt, 354; overthrows Directory, 355; victories, 356; First Consul, 357–361; Emperor of the French, 362, 363; wars, 364–367; reconstruction of Europe, 368–372; fall, 372–375, 565; return from Elba, 378; Waterloo, 379.
Napoleon III, 424–426, Emperor, 427, 428; war, 429–431, 469, 470; international policy, 432; deposed, 433; Cavour, 460, 461; Bismarck, 466.
När-bŏnne', 435.
När'vă, battle of, 269.
Narvaez (när-vä'ĕth), 496.
Nāse'by, battle of, 245.
Nationality, growth of, 385.
National Workshops (in Paris), 422, 423.
Nation-States, 4; growth in France, 43, 149–154; slow growth in Germany, 46; rise of, 117; beginnings in England, 123; rivalries, 171; growth of idea, 383 note.
Navarino (nä-vä-rē'nō), 399.
Navigation Acts, 263.
Navy, of England, 218, 223, 545; of Germany, 484, 487; of Netherlands, 225; of Norway, 526; of Spain, 220, 223; of Sweden, 526.
Neck'er, 308, 310, 314 note, 316, 322, p. 336 note 2.
Nelson, at battle of the Nile, 354; at Trafalgar, 366.
Netherlands, 162; under Charles V, 172; revolt, 201, 219; separation into United Provinces and Spanish Netherlands, 221–223; Austria gains Spanish Netherlands, 261; Union of 1815, 505–506. See Belgium, Holland.
New Model Army, 245, 246, 248.
"New Monarchy," 105, 117; in England, 147.
Newton, Sir Isaac, 198.
Nibelungĕn Lied (nē-be-lung'-en lēt), 188.
Nice (nēs), 337, 350; after Congress of Vienna, 377 *b*; Napoleon III, 429 *b*, 460.

Nicholas I, of Russia, 392, 568, 573, 577.
Nicholas II, 573.
Nicholas V, Pope, 195.
Nihilists, 573.
Nile, battle of, 354.
Nobility, French, 288, 293, 294, 304; in States General, 313, 314, 315. See French Revolution.
Nobility, abolished in Norway, 525.
Norman Conquest, 16, 44, 118; effects, 123.
Normandy, 15, 125, 127, 131, 151.
Normans, 15; in England, 16; in Apulia, 67; in Sicily, 67.
Norsemen, raids, 13, 14; in Normandy, 15; in Neustria, 41; mercenaries of Byzantine Empire, 90; in Western Europe, 157.
North German Confederation, 468 *b*.
Norway, 18, 157; after Congress of Vienna, 377 *c*, 523; and Sweden in 19th century, 523–526; independence, 525.
Notables, Assembly of, 309, 310.
Notre Dame (nō'tr däm), 180 *c*, 346 note 2.
Nō-vä'rä, battle of, 453, 456, 459.
Nŏv'gō-rŏd, 108, 116 *b*.

Oath of Strasburg, 8 note.
"Old Catholics," 482.
Olmütz, 455, 456, 464.
Orange, House of, 204 *c*, 377 *b*; William of, 222.
Ordeal, trial by, 130.
Oriental Civilization, 1, 3; influence on Mohammedans, 89; Europe, 102; in Russia, 268.
Orleans Monarchy, 413–418, 419.
Oscar II, of Sweden, 525.
Otto I, Emperor (the Great), 49–54; and reform of Papacy, 60.
Otto II, 62, 63.
Otto III, 62, 63.
Otto I of Greece, 582.
Ottoman Turks, 169. See Turks.
Ou-den-är'de, battle of, 261.
Oxford, University of, p. 197 note 2; Colet at, 195.

654 INDEX.

References are to sections.

Padua, University of, p. 197 note 2.
Padua Letter, the, 331.
Palatinate, 159, 261.
Pă-nä-mä′, scandal of 1893, 444 exercise.
Papacy, organizing force in Christendom, 1, 3, 4 *a*; beginning of Holy Roman Empire, 52, 53, 55 *a*; power in Middle Ages, 57; decline of, 58; reform, 59, 61, 63, 65 *c*; Empire and, 66–88; Gregory VII, 68, 72; revenue, 71; investitures, 73–76; conflict over Italy, 78, 80; at its height, 82–84; and Frederick II, 86; results to, of strife, 87; Crusades, 93; and rise of New Monarchies, 117; and England, p. 137 note 1, 163–165, 218; in 14th and 15th centuries, 163–167; and France, 163–166, 328, 360 *a*, 443; Babylonian captivity, 165; Great Schism, 166; unity restored, 167; position in 1500, 170; indulgences, 205, 206; and Reformation, 206, 207; Inquisition, 214; Counter-reformation, 215; Turkish pirates, 224; Directory, 355; Napoleon's Europe, 368 *b*; Napoleon III, 430 *a*; in 1848, 453, 458; and Kingdom of Italy, 463, 490.
Papal States, 86; anarchy and revolution, 165; in 1500, 171; Inquisition, 381; in 1848, 453; 1815, 457; 1830, 458; Kingdom of Italy, 462, 463, 490.
Paris, 14, 41; secured by Henry of Navarre, 228; famine, 314; saves the Assembly, 316, 317; Assembly at, 320–323; Convention at, 333–347; Reign of Terror, 344; improvements, 359, 428; Napoleon, 362; entered by Allies, 374; Revolution of 1830, 411, 412, 458; socialism, 418; February Days, 419, 452; June Days, 423; siege of, 433, 434; Commune of 1871, 435–436; to-day, 447.
Paris, Congress of, 429 *a*, 459, 578.
Parish (English), local government in, 538 *a*, 540.
Parlement of Paris, 310.
Parliament, English, 113; growth, 134–136; Model Parliament, 135; Lords and Commons, 136; deposition of kings, 137, **138**, **143**; elects Henry IV, 138, 143; land-laws, 140; Peasant rising and, 142; growth, 143; Good Parliament, 143; Liberties of Englishmen, 144; decline, 147; struggle with Stuarts, 200, 237–244; "No Parliament" period, 243; Long Parliament, 244–246; Pride's Purge, 246; Cavalier Parliament, 249; after the Revolution of 1688, 250, 251; annual meetings, 251; ministerial government, 252; organ of oligarchy, 527; inclosures, 528; First Reform Bill, 529, 531, 533; Second Reform Bill, 534; Third Reform Bill, 535; reapportionment of 1885, 536; relation of Houses, 532 *a*; the ministry, 532 *b*; minor reforms, 537; social reform by, 542–545; and Ireland, 551, 552.
Paschal II, Pope, 73 note 4.
Pataria, 67 *a*.
Pauperism in England, 234, 528.
Pavia (pä-vē′ä), battle of, p. 232 note 1.
Pays d'Etat (pā-ē′ dā-tā′), 300 *a*.
Peace Conference of Hague, 594.
Peace Convention at Venice, 80.
Peace of Aix-la-Chapelle, 274.
Peace of Amiens, 356.
Peace of Augsburg, 211, 219, 232.
Peace of Campo Formio, 351, 356, 370.
Peace of Constance, 80.
Peace of Prague, 468.
Peace of San Stefano, 577.
Peace of Tilsit, 365–366.
Peace of Utrecht, 261, 265.
Peace of Westphalia, 4, 232, 255, 273, 512.
Peace of 1814, 375.
Peace of the Land, 65 *b*.
Peasant Revolt of 1381, 138, 142.
Peasantry, 105 note; of Bulgaria, 581; of Egypt, 560; of England, 124, 140–142, 528, 554; in France, 288, 290, 292–297, 328, 342, 359, 450; in Germany, 208, 231, 279, 371; of Ireland, 281 *b*, 544, 550, 552; of Roumania, 578; of Russia, 569, 570; of Servia, 580; of Spain, 500, 501.
Peasant War in Germany, 208.

INDEX.

References are to sections.

Pedro I, of Brazil, 496, 502.
Pedro II, 502.
Peel, Sir Robert, p. 544 note 1, 541, 544.
Peninsular War, 367.
Perier (pā-rē-ā'), Casimir, 442 note.
Persecutions, religious, of Inquisition, 214; in Geneva, 217; in England, 218, 236, 249; in France, 227, 260 *b*; in Germany, 232 note, 243.
Persia, civilization of, among the Mohammedans, 89; invaded by Tartars, 168; Europe in, 585, 588.
Perugino (pā-roō-jē'nō), 193.
Peter the Great of Russia, 200, 256, 266; character and aims, 267, 269, 565, 567 *b*.
Peter the Hermit, 94.
Peter Karageorgevitch, 580.
Peter's Pence, 71.
Petition of Right, 242, 243.
Petrarch, 189, 195 note.
Philip I, Emperor, 162, 172.
Philip I of France, 43.
Philip II of France (Augustus), 82, 97, 148, 149, 151, 153.
Philip IV of France (the Fair), 148 note, 149, 153, 154, 164, 165.
Philip VI of France (of Valois), 148 note.
Philip II of Spain, 162, 201, 212, 218; power, 220; Netherlands, 221–223.
Philip III of Spain, 201, 224.
Philip IV of Spain, 201, 259.
Philip V of Spain, 201, 261.
Philippines, 590.
Piedmont (pēd'mŏnt), 394, 396, 457, 458.
Pil'nitz, Declaration of, 331.
Pirates, French, 139; Turkish, 209 note, 224.
Pisa (pē'zä), Council of, 167.
Pitt, William, 277, 527, 529.
Pitt, William, the younger, 529.
Pius IX, Pope, 453, 458, 490.
Pius X, 490.
Placemen, 416, 417.
Plăn-tă'ge-nĕts, 126–143; French domains of, lost to France, 151.
Plassey, battle of, 277.
Pocket Boroughs, 527, 529.

Poitiers (pwä-tĭ-ā'), battle of, 139, 234.
Poitou (pwä-toō'), 41, 127, 139, 151.
Poland, 50, 55, 64 *c*, 272 note; ravaged by Tartars, 168, 170; decline, 200, 257; partition of, 269, 278, 565, 567 *b*; Duchy of Warsaw, 370, 373, 377; Revolution of 1830, 391, 392; Russianized, 574.
Polo, Marco, 197.
Pŏm-e-rā'nĭ-ä, 232 *b*, 273; after Congress of Vienna, 377 *c*.
Poor-law in England, 542.
Pope, Alexander, 265 note.
Portugal, 82, 155; discoveries, 197; Inquisition in, 214; seized by Spain, 220; wars of French Revolution, 340; war with Napoleon, 366, 367, 372; Revolution of 1820, 394; in the 19th century, 502–504.
Poussin (poō-săn'), 193.
Praemunire, Statute of, 165.
Pragmatic Sanction, 274.
Prague (präg), 166; Peace of, 468.
Presbyterians, in France, 211; in Geneva, 217; in England, 236; in Long Parliament, 244, 246.
Pride's Purge, 246.
Prim, 496.
Printing, 196 *b*; in Holland, 225.
Protectorate in England, 204 *b*, 248.
Protestantism, rise, 205–218; in Germany, 209–212, 219, 230–232; origin of name, 210; in South of Europe, 213; sects, 216–218; in Netherlands, 221; in France, 226–229, 446. See Calvinism, Huguenots, Lutherans, Puritans, Presbyterians, Reformation.
Provence (prŏ-vŏns'), 152 *b*.
Provisors, Statute of, 165.
Prussia, beginning, 50 note 1, 99, 200, 257; rise of, 261 note, 270–274, 276, 278–280; and wars of French Revolution, 335, 337, 350; and Napoleon, 364, 365, 370, 372, 374, 375, 379; part of Holy Roman Empire, 369; reforms of Stein, 371; Congress of Vienna, 376, 377, 379, 380; reaction in, 382; and Metternich, 387–392; Congress of Troppau, 395; Holy Alliance,

INDEX.

References are to sections.

395–400; Franco-Prussian War, 430 c, 432–434, 469, 470; risings in 1848, 452, 454–456, 464; William I, 464, 465; Schleswig-Holstein, 466; Six Weeks' War, 467; North German Confederation, 468; place of, in German Empire, 473–475, 478.
Ptolemy (tŏl'e-my), geographer, 198.
Pultava (pūl-tä'vä), battle of, 269.
Puritans, 218, 236, 240; in Ireland, 244; in Civil War in England, 245.
Pym, 244, 246 note 2.

Quad-riv'i-um, 178.
Queen Anne's War, 261.

Racine (rä-sēn'), 265.
Raleigh (rä'li), 233.
Ramillies (rä-mē-yē'), 261.
Raphael (răf'ā-ĕl), 193.
"Reds," the, 420, 423–425, 435, 436.
Referendum, the, 519.
Reformation, the Protestant, 4, 173, 176, 200, 201, 285; Age of, 205–232; in Germany, 205–212, 216, 217; in England, 218, 233; Wars of, 208, 211, 219, 220–232. See Protestantism.
Reform Bill, of 1832, 531, 533, p. 535 note 1; of 1867, 534; of 1884, 535.
Reichstag (rīchs'täG) of German Empire, 475, 482; socialists in, 485; parties in, 487.
Reign of Terror, 333, 344–346.
Religious Wars, in Germany, 211; a century of, 219–232; Spain and the Netherlands, 220–225; French Huguenots, 226–229; Thirty Years' War, 230–232.
Rĕm'brandt, 193.
Renaissance, 4, 102, 114, 174–199, p. 231 note 1, 285; in England, 199, 233.
Representation in England, 527, 529, 531 a, 533–536; local, 539, 540.
Representative Assemblies of Freemen, 3.
Representative government, beginnings of, in Austria, 491; Bulgaria, 581; Denmark, 521; England, 136; France, 154, 313, 404–409; Germany, 159 note; Greece, 582; Italy, 488; Netherlands, 162, 222 note 1; Roumania, 578; Russia, 572, 575; Servia, 580; Spain, 156, 393; Switzerland, 161. See Constituent Assembly, Cortes, Diet, Duma, Estates General, Federal Assembly, Landtag, Parlement, Parliament, Reichstag, Rigsdag, Sobranje, Storthing, Zemstvo.
Republic, French, First, 338–362; Second, 421–426; Third, 433–451; Spanish, of 1873–1874, 497.
Restoration of the Stuarts, 249.
"Reunions," under Louis XIV, 260 a.
Revolution, French, of 1789, 285–376.
Revolutions, in England, 204 b, 285; in America, 284, 285; of Brumaire, 355, 357; of 1820, 385, 393, 394, 458; of 1830, 382, 385, 391, 400, 410–412, 458; of 1848, 385, 417, 419–423, 452–456; in Spain, 495, 496, 498; in Portugal, 502; in Balkan States, 576–582. See French Revolution.
Richard I of England, the Lion-Hearted, 97, 131.
Richard II of England, 138, 143, 151, 166.
Richard III of England, 146.
Richelieu (rĕsh-le-uh'), 203, 229, 230.
Ridley, execution of, 218.
Rienzi (rē-ĕn'zē), 165 note.
Rigsdag, 522.
Robber Knights, p. 123 note, **158**.
Robert Guiscard (gës-kär'), **67 b**, 180 a.
Robert the Strong, 41.
Robespierre (rō-bes-pyĕr'), **317** note, 321, 322, 338, 342, 346.
Rolf the Dane, 15.
Rollin (rŏl'in; Fr. pron. rō-lăṅ'), Ledru, 425.
Romance, language, 9 note 2; lands remain Catholic, 213.
Roman civilization, 1, 3; influence on feudalism, 24; influence of Roman idea of government in France, 43 c; on the Saxons, 45; on Towns, 119; on gilds, 112; law, 180 a, b.
Romanesque Architecture, 192.

INDEX. 657

Rome, Rienzi, 165 note; Great Schism, 166; sacked by Charles V, p. 232 note 1; Pope driven from, 355; rising of 1848, 452, 453; Italy, 462, 463, 490.
Romilly (rŏm′il-i), p. 544 note 1, 542.
Root and Branch, the (party in Long Parliament), 244.
Röss′bäċh, battle of, 276.
Rotten Boroughs, 527, 529, 531 a, 534.
Rotterdam, 162 note.
Rouen (rōō-ŏṅ), 14.
Roumania, 576, 577, 578.
Round Heads, 245 note 3.
Rousseau (rōō-sō′), 302, 303, 321, 332.
Rubens, 193.
Rubruquis (rü-brü-kē), 197.
Rudolph of Hapsburg (bōōrɢ), 88; Emperor, 158–161.
Rump Parliament, 246–248.
Russell, Lord John, p. 535 note 3, 531, 531 b, p. 550 note 1, 539, 541, 545.
Russia, growth of towns, 108; Tartar province, 168; in 1500, 170; rise, 200, 257, 262, 266–269; Seven Years' War, 276; partition of Poland, 269, 278; wars of French Revolution, 335, 355, 356; war with Napoleon, 364–366, 372–375, 380; Congress of Vienna, 376, 377; Reaction, 382, 385; Congress of Troppau, 395; and Greece, 399 b; Crimean War, 429 a, 459 a; in 1848, 453, 455; in China, 484; and Sweden and Norway, 525; and Turkey, 547, 577; in the 19th century, 565–575; revolution, 575; and Balkan Peninsula, 577–578; alliances, 583, 584; in Asia, 588, 589–591.
Russian Japanese War, 567, 574, 591.

Sadowa (sä′dō-vä), battle of, 467, 469, 491.
Sä-gäs′tä, 500, 501.
St. Benedict, see Benedictine rule.
St. Bernard, see Bernard of Clairvaux.
St. Dominic, 84.
St. Helena, 379, 557.
St. Just (säṅ-ghüst), 342, 346 note 3.

St. Louis, see Louis IX of France.
Săl′a-din, 97.
Sä-ler′nō, 180.
Salisbury (sawlz′bŭ-rĭ), Lord, 540, 541.
Sän Stĕph′ä-nō, Peace of, 577.
Saracens, in Italy, 53. See Mohammedans.
Sardinia, 261, 335, 350, 351, 372; after Congress of Vienna, 377 b, 380, 381, 394; war of Napoleon III for, 429 b; risings of 1848, 452, 453, 456, 459; grows into Kingdom of Italy, 460–463.
Sä-vō-nä-rō′lä, p. 183 note 3, 457.
Savoy, 261, 337, 350; after Congress of Vienna, 377 b, 457; Napoleon III, 429 b, 460.
Saxons, 16; local institutions, 118; feudalism, 122.
Saxony, 65, 271; electorate, 159: kingdom, 370; after Congress of Vienna, 377.
Scandinavia, Knut's empire, 13, 16, 55, 157; early literature, 188; Lutheranism in, 211; kingdoms in 19th century, 521–528. See Denmark, Norway, Sweden.
Schleswig (viɢ) - **Holstein Question**, 466, 521. See Danish War.
Scholasticism, 182–186; in Universities, 182–186.
Schools, in Dark Ages, 178; rise of Universities, 179–181. See Education, Scholasticism, Universities, Kulturkampf.
Schwarzenberg (shwärt′sen-bĕrɢ), 453, 455, 491.
Schwyz (shwīts), 161.
Scotland, 127, 139; Presbyterians, 236; Laud, 243: Charles II, King of the Scots, 247; joined to England, 281 a; in Parliament, 527.
Scrooby, 236.
Scutage, origin, 128 note 2; in Magna Carta, p. 148 note 3.
Sebastopol, 459 b.
Sedan (se-dŏṅ′), 432, 433, 470.
Sel′juk Turks, see Turks.
Sem′paċh, battle of, 161.
Sen-e-gäl′, 451.
Senlac, battle of, 16 d.

658   INDEX.
References are to sections.

Separatists, 236.
Sepoy Mutiny, 559.
September Massacres (Paris), 336;
Serfs, 3; origin, 21; land tenure, 26, 34; better side of serfdom, 35; relation to feudalism, 39; abolition in England, 140; in Poland, 278; benevolent despots and, 280; in France, 292; abolished in Confederation of the Rhine, 371; in Prussia, 371; restored in Sardinia, 381; emancipation in Russia, 569, 573; in Roumania, 578.
Ser-rä′nō, 496.
Ser-vē′tus, p. 223 note 2, 217.
Servia, 169, 576, 577, 580.
Seven Years' War, 276.
Shakspere, p. 110 note 1, 199, 233.
Sheriffs, 119, 124.
Ship-money, 243, 244.
Shire, the, in Saxon England, 118, 119.
Siam, p. 447 note 2, 588.
Siberia, 266, 567 *a*.
Sicily, 67, 372; union with Empire, 82; Charles of Anjou in, 86; to 1500, 171; ceded to Austria, 261; Revolution of 1820, 394; annexed to Italy, 462.
Sidney, Sir Philip, 223 note.
Siéyès (sē-yäs′), 304, 314, 321, 355, 357.
Si-lē′si-a, 274.
Simon of Montfort, 133; and Parliament, 134.
Simony, 58; reform, 59, 65 *b*; connection with investitures, 73, 74.
Six Weeks' War, 465, 467.
Slavery, abolished in Spanish colonies, 500; in English colonies, 542.
Slāvs, in Europe, 1, 2, 11; forced back by Germans, 50, 54, 64 *c*; and Innocent III, 82; in Greek Empire, 169, 170; in Holy Roman Empire, 369, p. 394 note 2; in Balkan Peninsula, 385, 576; in Bohemia and Hungary, 453, 493; in Russia, 566, 570, 571,574.
Smalkald (smäl′kält), League of, 210, 211, 219.
So-bi-es′ki. See John Sobieski.
Sobranje, 581.
Social classes, feudal, 26, 34; results of crusades on, 105; changes owing to rise of towns, 105, 107, 108; affected by rise of new monarchies, 117; in France, 286–291; privileged classes in France, 295; distinctions abolished, by Assembly, 318; caste broken down in Prussia, 371; in England, 528; in Russia, 571.
Socialism, in France, 418–424, 435, 436, 445; in Germany, 481 note 2, 482, 485, 486; in Italy, 488; in Spain, 499, 501; in Belgium, 508; in Sweden, 524; in Norway, 526; in England, 555; in Russia, 573.
Solferino (sŏl-fe-rē′nō), battle of, 429 *b*, 460.
Solyman the Magnificent, p. 189 note 2; alliance with France, p. 232 note 1; attacks Germany, 210.
Sonderbund (zŏn′der-boont), the, 516, 517, 520.
Sou-dan′, 587.
South Africa, 547, 557, 558, 563.
Spain, 55, 99; growth of towns, 108, 209; to 1492, 155; growth of monarchy, 156; in 1500, 170, 171; and Netherlands, 162, 229-223; early literature, 188; art of, 193; discoveries, 197; table of Kings, 201; Inquisition in, 214, 381; decay, 224; war with England, 239; in Grand Alliance, 259; War of the Spanish Succession, 261; war in America, 275, 277, 380 note, 393 note, 398; War of Austrian Succession, 274; wars of French Revolution, 335, 340, 350; war with Napoleon, 364, 367, 372, 380; Revolution of 1820, 393, 397, 495; Revolution of 1848, 452; in 19th century, 495–501.
Spanish-American War, 501, 589, 590.
Spanish March, 150.
Spanish Succession, War of, 261.
Speier (spīr), Diet of, 210.
Stadtholder (stät′hŏl-der), 222 note.
States General, of France, 307, 310, 313. See Estates General.
States General, of Holland, 222 note, 510.
Steelyard, 116, note.
Stein (stīn), 369, 371, 387.

INDEX.

References are to sections.

Stem Duchies, 45; and Henry I, 48; and Otto I, 49.
Stephen of England, 125.
Storthing (stor'ting), 523, 525.
Sträl'sund, Peace of, 116 *b*.
Suez Canal, 560.
Suffrage, Manhood, see Franchise.
Sul'ly, Duke of, 228.
Supremacy, Act of, 218.
Suzerains (sūz'er-ānṣ), origin, 19; privileges, 21, 22; classes, 26; contract, 27; aids, 28–30; obligations, 31; in the Church, 32; relations to serfs and villeins, 34; life in the castle, 37; duties, 40; in France, 42, 292–294.
Sweden, 13, 18; independent, 157; in 1500, 170; decline, 200, 257; and Protestant cause in Germany, 230; results to, of Treaty of Westphalia, 232 *b*; war with Louis XIV, 259; and Russia, 269, 365, 565, 567 *b*; Seven Years' War, 276; reform by benevolent ministers in, 280; wars of French Revolution, 335; of Napoleon, 372; after Congress of Vienna, 377 *c*, 523; Revolution of 1848, 452; and Denmark, 521; and Norway in 19th century, 523–526.
Swegn (swän), 16.
Switzerland, growth, 161; in 1500, 170; independence recognized, 232 *b*; Helvetic Republic, 355, 372, 513; after Congress of Vienna, 377 *b*, 514; civil war, p. 404 note; from 1789–1848, 512–517; to-day, 518–520.

Tables of Rulers, in Empire and Austria, 62, 202; in England, 125, 138, 146, 204, 541; in France, p. 52 note 1, 148, 203, 442 note; in Germany, p. 56 note, 62; in Spain, 201.
Taille (tāl), 296 *a*.
Talleyrand, 376, p. 384 note 3.
Tăm-er-lāne', 168 note 3, 169.
Tartars, 91; invasions of the 13th century, 168; effect on discoveries, 197; in Russia, 566, 567. See Turks.
Taxes, in feudal France, 42 *b*; effect of introduction of money, 105; in England, 134, 143, 144, 163, 164, 239, 241–243, 249–251, 529, 545; in France, 153, 163, 164, 264, 288, 289, 295–297, 298, 307–310, 324, 327, 328, 403, 447; in Germany, 464, 465, 475; in Italy, 488; in Russia, 570; in Spain, 496, 497, 500.
Telescope, invention of, 196 *c*.
Tell, William, 161 note 3.
Templars, 95.
Tennis Court Oath, 315.
Teutonic Order, 95, 99, 170, 269, 272 note.
Teutons, 1, 2; influence on feudalism, 24; on Saxons, 45; on customs in Switzerland, 161.
Thiers (te-êr'), 409, 415 note, 434, 438.
Thirty-nine Articles, the, 218.
Thirty Years' War, the, 219, 224, 230–232, 239, p. 272 note 2, 255.
Thomas of A-qui'nō, 185.
Tilsit, Peace of, 365, 366.
Tĭn-tō-rĕt'tō, 193.
Titian (tĭsh'an), 193.
Tocqueville (tŏk'vĭl), 358, 415 note.
Tories, the (Party in England), 252, 382, 529, 530, 533. See Conservative Party.
Toulon (tōō-lŏṅ'), 342, 343, 353.
Toulouse (tōō-lōōz'), 41, 83, 152, 435.
Tours (tōōr), battle of, 14.
Towns, 3, 84; origin of, 105; rise of, 106–116; in England, 108, 113, 121, 145, 147, 233, 235, 528 *b*, 539; in France, 108, 115, 228, 229; in Germany, 74, 76, 108, 116, 369, 371; in Italy, 76, 80, 82, 87, 108, 114; in Netherlands, 162; in Russia, 108; in Spain, 108, 156, 209.
Townships, in Saxon England, 121.
Trăf-äl-gär', battle of, 366.
Transvaal, 547, 563.
Trent, Council of, p. 229 note 1, 215.
Trentino (trĕn-tē'nō), 489.
Triennial Bill, 251.
Trier (trēr), 159.
Trivium, 178.
Troppau (trŏp'pow), Congress of 395, 407 note.
Troubadours (trōō'bä-dōōrs), 188.
Trouveurs (trōō-vẽrs), 188.
Truce of God, 33, 65 *b*.

INDEX.

References are to sections.

Tudors, 146, 147, 204 *a*; survey of period, 233–235; and Parliament, 237, 240.
Tuileries (twē'le-rēz), 334, 335, 419.
Tunis, 451, 489, 583.
Turgot (tür-gō'), 307, 308.
Turkey, Russia and, 365, 373, 545, 565, 567 *b*, 577; unprogressive, 385; rebellion in Greece, 399, 577; Crimean War, 429 *a*; and Germany in Asia Minor, 484; and subject races in Balkan Peninsula, 576, 577; and Roumania, 577, 578, 585.
Turks, appearance, 91; Crusades, 92; capture Jerusalem, 93; in Syria, 99; Venice, 114; invasion of Ottoman Turks, 169; effect on discoveries, 197; wars of Charles V, 209; Lepanto, 224; driven back from Vienna, 237; Austria and, 262; Russia and, 263, 267, 269; massacre in Greece, 399.
Tuscany, 280; risings of 1848, 452, 453; in 1815, 457; annexed to Sardinia, 461.

Ulm (o͞olm), 107; battle of, 365.
Ul'tra-mon'ta-nism, 443. See Kulturkampf.
United Provinces, see Netherlands.
United States of America, 284, 398; Civil War, 430 *b*, 534, 545; Spanish-American War, 501; referendum in, 519; franchise in states, p. 553 note 1; civil service in, 537 *b*; world power, 589–591.
Universities, 178–181, 389, 390.
Unterwalden (o͞on-ter-väl'den), 161.
Urban, Pope, 93.
Urban II, 74.
Uri (o͞o'ri), 161.
Utrecht (ū'trekt, D. pron. o͞o'trĕcht), Peace of, 261, 265.

Väl'lä, Laurentius, 195.
Valmy (väl-mē'), battle of, 337.
Valois (väl-wä'), House of, 148 note.
Van Dyck (van dīk'), 193.
Vane, Sir Harry, 244, 246 note 2.
Van Eyck (vän īk'), 193.

Väs'co dä Gä'mä, 197.
Vassals, 21, 26; relations with lords 27; services, 28–30; not serfs, 39; in France, 42; towns held as vassals, p. 126 note 2.
Velasquez (vā-läs'kĕth), 193.
Vendee (vŏṅ-dā'), 342.
Vendome (vŏṅ-dōm') Column, p. 366 note 3.
Venice, 80, 98, 103, 114, 171, 179, 193, 224, 351, 352, 377, 453.
Verdun (vĕr-düṅ'), Treaty of, 8, 9, 41, 152 *b*; surrender of, 336.
Vergil, 189.
Verona (vā-rō'nä), Congress of, 397, 407 note.
Versailles (ver-sālz'; Fr. pron. vêr-säy'), 314, 435, 436; Assembly at, 314–319, 320.
Victor Emmanuel II, 456, 459, 460, 462.
Victoria of England, 204 *e*, 547.
Vienna, saved from Turks, 257, 262; conquered by Napoleon, 365; Congress of, 376–380, 381; rising of 1848, 453, 454.
Vikings, see Norsemen.
Villages, feudal, 36; Saxon, 121; in France, 296. See Towns.
Villeinage, 21; land tenure, 26, 34; relation to feudal system, 39; in England, 124; disappearance, 142, 234.
Vläd'i-mir, 108.
Voltaire (vŏl-têr'), 302.

Wagram (vä'gräm), 367, 370.
Waiblingen (vīb'lĭng-en), 77.
Wäl'dē-mär of Denmark, 116 *b*.
Wales, 127, 553.
Wallenstein (vŏl'en-stīn), 230.
Walpole, Robert, 252.
Walter the Penniless, 94.
Warsaw, Duchy of, 370, 373, 377.
Wars of the Roses, 138, 145, 147, 233, 241.
Wartburg (värt'bo͞orG), Luther at, 207; celebration at, 389, 395.
Waterloo, battle of, 379, 384, 395, 404.
Watling Street, 16.

References are to sections.

Wat the Tyler, 142.
Wedmore, Treaty of, 16 *a*.
Weimar (vī'mar), 388, 389.
Welfs, 77, 204 *e*.
Wellington, Duke of, 367, 379, 531.
Wentworth, Thomas, 243, 244, 549.
Wessex, 16, 119.
West Indies, 542, 557.
Westphalia, Brandenburg in, 273; Kingdom of, 370; Switzerland in, 512.
Westphalia, Peace of, 4 *b*, 232; effect on France and Spain, 255.
Whigs (English), the, 252, 531, 533. See Liberal Party.
White Terror, the, 347.
Wilhelmina (vĭl-hel-mēn'a), of Holland, 510.
William I of England (the Conqueror), 16 *d*; and Church, 123; and feudalism, 124; reign, 125, 151.
William II of England (Rufus), 125, 183.
William III of England (of Orange), 204 *c*, 249-251; and parties, 252; wars with Louis XIV, 259, 261
William IV of England, 204 *e*, 531.
William the Silent (of Orange), 222.
William I of Prussia, 464, 467; German Emperor, 470, 480.
William II of Prussia, 480, 485, 486.
Winkelried (wink'el-rēd), Arnold, p. 174 note 3.
Winthrop, John, p. 257 note 3.
Wĭt'an, 119, 122, 134, 137 note 2.
Wittenberg (vĭt'ten-bĕrG), University of, 205.
Wolfe, 277.
Women, effect of Chivalry on position of, 37; voting of, in English rural units, 540; woman suffrage in platform of German socialists, 485.
Worcester (wŏos'ter), 247.
Worms (vōrms), Concordat of, 75; Diet at, 207, 209.
Würtemberg (vürt'tem-bĕrG), 369; after Thirty Years' War, 231; made a kingdom, 370; constitution, 388; Peace of Prague, 468 *b*.
Wyc'lif, 141, 166, p. 199 note 4, 188.

Yorkists, 138, 145-147; review of period, 233-235.
Young Italy, 458.
Ypres (ē'pr), 162.

Zadruga (zä-drōō'gä), 580, 581.
Zemstvo (zĕmst'vō), 572, 573.
Zola (zō-lä'), 444 exercise.
Zurich (tsü'rĭċh), 161.

History of the United States

> By the late CHARLES K. ADAMS, and Professor W. P. TRENT, of Columbia University. 12mo, half leather, 630 pages. Price, $1.50.

THE authors have laid the stress on the two crises of American history — the Revolutionary War and the Civil War. They have treated both these periods very fully, and have endeavored in the case of the first to present the side of Great Britain with fairness, while, at the same time, bringing out the necessity of the struggle, and the bravery and wisdom of the American patriots. In dealing with the period of the Civil War they have aimed to give the Southern side with sympathy and, while upholding the cause of the Union, have sought to avoid recrimination, and to give each side credit for its sincerity and bravery. The other periods of our history have not been unduly subordinated to the great crises, but have been so treated as to lead up to them. The process of the making of the Constitution and the various developments in its interpretation have been fully studied. While emphasis has necessarily been laid on the political and military features of our history, the social, industrial, scientific, and literary development of the country has been given due space.

The following are some of the special features of the book:

Thirty-five maps, of which eighteen are colored.

Two hundred and three illustrations, reproduced from authentic sources. Especial care has been taken to include the best possible portraits of eminent men. Some of these were taken from private collections and have not been published before.

A full chronological table.

Foot-notes which describe the lives of persons mentioned in the text, in order that the narrative shall not be interrupted at the appearance of each new name.

The great development of the United States during the past decade makes it imperative that an adequate history be kept up to date. The present edition covers the period to January, 1909, and contains a full account of the chief events of President Roosevelt's administrations.